RAINBOWS FROM REVELATION

Other Tribune Books

Charles R. Solomon
Handbook For Christ-Centered Counseling

Jim Combs
Mysteries of the Book of Daniel

RAINBOWS FROM REVELATION

Jim Combs

Tribune Publishers

Cover and Book Design: Lee Fredrickson

Library of Congress Cataloging-in Publication Data

   Jim Combs
   Rainbows From Revelation / by Jim Combs
   p. cm.
   includes bibliographical references
   1. Theology 2. Prophecy I. Title

ISBN 1-884764-02-9

Printed in the United States of America

Dedication

This book, the product of many years of study and teaching,
is lovingly dedicated to my wife

Jeri Marquis Combs

Whose encouragement and assistance has contributed
immeasurably to the completion of this work.

Blessed is he that readeth, and they that hear the words of this prophecy, and keep those things which are written therein: for the time is at hand.

— *Revelation 1:3*

Seal not the sayings of the prophecy of this book: for the time is at hand.

— *Revelation 22:10*

CONTENTS

VIII

INTRODUCTION

By Tim LaHaye

The Book of Revelation is the most thrilling book in the Bible to me. I know the Gospel of John is the popular favorite; it was mine too, for many years, but now it has dropped to number two on my list. The reason is, Revelation glorifies our Lord Jesus Christ as no other book in the Bible. All the Gospels, including John, present the Lord as our suffering savior. Although He proved His deity in the Gospels by His incredible miracles, which have never been duplicated by mortal man, He gave masterful teachings which have never been equaled, and He is the only person in human history who ever rose from the dead, He was never presented in the Gospels in His true power and great glory.

Revelation is different! It always presents our Lord as He really is, and as He always shall be, with all the attributes of God. He is seen as the Light-bearer walking among the Churches (His lampstands to the world). He alone holds the "Key of David" and "the Keys of Death and Hell." He has power over all the events of the future personalities that will soon come on this earth, and He ultimately triumphs over all. Then, after bringing His Church back to this earth with Him in His glorious Second Coming, He takes us with Him into the millennial kingdom and then into the eternal order we call "Heaven." The marvelous plan of God for man's future will be fulfilled by Jesus Christ in this book.

No other book in the Bible challenges the Christian to live every day in the light of His soon coming. That is why every Christian should read and understand this book, and why I am glad Dr. Jim Combs has written this easy-to-understand commentary making it so clear. Many false prophets, even in our day, have devalued the book of Revelation by their unscriptural distortions of the prophecies in it. Admittedly, there are some parts of it that are difficult to understand on first reading. That's why *Rainbows From Revelation* is so helpful. Dr. Combs uses his gift of simplifying difficult passages to make them clear to the earnest student of prophecy. He has combined the best of Revelation scholarship with quotes, and has rightly divided the Word of Truth in his commentary and his exegesis of key passages.

We are living at a time in history, when it is imperative for Christians to study this book, and preachers and Bible teachers to teach it. For we have more reason to believe that Christ could come in our lifetime than any generation, since Jesus ascended to Heaven accompanied by the angelic promise, "… this same Jesus, which is taken up from you into heaven, shall so come in like manner as ye have seen him go into heaven." Unfortunately, many pastors were not taught Revelation in seminary. It was considered "controversial." That is why this excellent commentary is so necessary, for if preachers and teachers are inspired to teach it freely, the people of God will be inspired to lift up their eyes and look on the fields of this world in preparation for His coming.

Many believe the world government's current alignments, the increase in violent natural phenomena — like earthquakes, hurricanes, etc. — the Revelation-like plagues and incurable diseases and many other things, never before occurring in history, indicate we may see the prophecies of Revelation fulfilled in ours or our children's lifetime.

The time to understand Revelation is now. This commentary will help you understand it. It is my prayer, and that of the author, that studying this book will have the same effect on you that a good understanding of Bible prophecy has always had on the church. That it will motivate you to holy living in an unholy age, to soul-winning and evangelism because the time is short, and to world-wide missions through "going" to the uttermost part of the earth, or in giving more of your treasure to reach the world with the gospel in this generation. If it does, I guarantee you will not regret it, when you stand before our Lord who is coming soon.

Tim LaHaye, a successful pastor for over 25 years, founder of Christian Heritage College in California, president of Family Life Seminars is the author of dozens of books and booklets with over 9,000,000 copies in print. Among his bestsellers are *How to Study the Bible for Yourself, Revelation-Illustrated And Made Plain,* and *The Coming Peace in the Middle East.* He holds a D.Min. from Western Conservative Baptist Seminary in Portland, Oregon.

PREFACE
Jim Combs, D.Min.,Litt.D.

How To Use This Book

As a fourteen–year–old new Christian, converted through the radio ministry of Charles E. Fuller and the Old Fashioned Revival Hour at the age of twelve, I first began enjoying its riches, listening to Dr. Fuller each Sunday, as he went through the book, chapter by chapter. That was in 1942.

After turning sixteen I began teaching a Sunday School class of young people in a San Antonio, Texas church, where verse by verse studies were the norm. Securing several commentaries and studying diligently for each lesson, I shared prophetic truth with my high school age peers.

Through college and seminary days, prophetic truths continued to be an important focus both in research and preaching, a pattern continuing unto this day.

Designed as a study guide, a commentary and a resource for lesson and sermon preparation, *Rainbows from Revelation* is arranged in a unique format. Any serious student or learner can gain much knowledge and understanding by simply going through the seven separate sections for each chapter.

1. Step One: Begin by reading carefully the actual text of the Scripture which introduces the material on each chapter. "Give attendance to reading," even reading out loud if possible. Depending on the amount of time available, you might want to look up the references on the side margins in addition to comparing the verses from other Bible books, often printed beneath the chapter of Revelation under consideration. If you are teaching, I recommend you read the chapter every day for a week, prior to your presentation. You may also desire to hear your own regular study Bible open for your whole study session.

2. Step Two: Read the Summary of the Chapter, which appears on the next page, noting the overall content of the whole passage. Some material may appear here, not emphasized further in the study.

3. Step Three: Carefully go through the Outline of the Chapter, making notes in your own Bible or in your own study notebook.

4. Step Four: With the text of the chapter also before you (using your own Bible for convenience), meditate briefly on the practical spiritual lessons from the Observations columns, devotional and inspirational thoughts suggested or derived from the ideas in each verse.

5. Step Five: Now that the contents of the chapter, the general outline of its truths and the spiritual applications are sown in your hart and mind, read carefully, with your Bible open, the Quotations from Other Expositors. These have been meticulously selected from some thirty prophetic scholars and writers, mostly older classical authors, but also several contemporary prominent communicators of prophetic truth. Their insights will deepen your grasp of each section of the chapter being studied.

6. Step Six: Read the Expository Sermon, condensations of this writer's message on Revelation, preached in hundreds of churches. You will notice that different outlines are often used within the studies for personal use, Bible class lessons or sermons.

7. Step Seven: A verse by verse commentary with Anglicized Greek words in parenthesis for further edification and examination from original biblical language concludes the seven step study plan for each chapter. Information here is more advanced and technical, but devotional practical truth, not previously suggested, is amply spread through the commentary. Read through it. By this point, you will be very familiar with the text.

A fast reader, conversant with the Word of God, can move through these seven steps in a couple of hours or less, but a slower paced, thoughtful perusal of each chapter will be more beneficial and a better learning experience.

One method is to take a week and spend a half hour each day, doing one section at a time, prayerfully asking the Holy Spirit for more insights and fresh aspects of truth beyond what is set forth. He is the Guide into truth. This approach would be suitable for the teacher, who will be sharing these truths each week with a class on a chapter by chapter basis.

Permission is here granted to make a limited number of copies of the Scripture page, the summary, the outlines and spiritual observations for distribution to a small Bible class. You may prefer to use the quotations, sermons and exegetical commentary personally. You might want to advise all of your students to purchase *Rainbows from Revelation*, if you are a teacher.

On the basis of God's Word I promise you a special blessing as you study: "Blessed is he that readeth......"

RAINBOWS FROM REVELATION
The Revelation of Jesus Christ

A chapter by chapter, verse by verse study

"There was a rainbow round about the throne like unto an emerald" (4:3)

CHAPTER ONE: The Cosmic Christ of the Ages

References

John 3:32

1 Cor. 1:6
1 John 1:1

Luke 11:28
James 5:8

Ex. 3:14
John 1:1

John 8:14
Col. 1:18
John 13:34

1 Pet. 2: 5, 9
1 Tim. 6:16

Mat. 24:30
Zech. 12:10-14

Isa. 41:4
Isa. 9:6

Phil. 1:7
2 Tim. 2:12

Acts 10:10
John 20:26
2 Cor. 12:2

1. The Revelation of Jesus Christ, which God gave unto him, to show unto his servants things which must shortly come to pass; and he sent and signified it by his angel unto his servant John:

2. Who bare record of the word of God, and of the testimony of Jesus Christ, and of all things that he saw.

3. Blessed is he that readeth, and they that hear the words of this prophecy, and keep those things which are written therein: for the time is at hand.

4. John to the seven churches which are in Asia: Grace be unto you, and peace, from him which is, and which was, and which is to come; and from the seven Spirits which are before his throne;

5. And from Jesus Christ, who is the faithful witness, and the first begotten of the dead, and the prince of the kings of the earth. Unto him that loved us, and washed us from our sins in his own blood.

6. And hath made us kings and priests unto God and his Father; to him be glory and dominion for ever and ever. A-men.

7. Behold, he cometh with clouds; and every eye shall see him, and they also which pierced him: and all kindreds of the earth shall wail because of him. Even so, A-men.

8. I am Alpha and Omega, the beginning and the ending, saith the Lord, which is, and which was, and which is to come, the Almighty.

9. I John, who also am your brother, and companion in tribulation, and in the kingdom and patience of Jesus Christ, was in the isle that is called Patmos, for the word of God, and for the testimony of Jesus Christ.

10. I was in the Spirit on the Lord's day, and heard behind me a great voice, as of a trumpet,

11. Saying, I am Alpha and Omega, the first and the last: and, What thou seest, write in a book, and send it unto the seven churches which are in Asia; unto Ephesus, and unto Smyrna, and unto Pergamos, and unto Thyatira, and unto Sardis, and unto Philadelphia, and unto Laodicea.

12. And I turned to see the voice that spake with me. And being turned, I saw seven golden candlesticks;

13. And in the midst of the seven candlesticks one like unto the Son of man, clothed with a garment down to the foot, and girt about the paps with a golden girdle.

14. His head and his hairs were white like wool, as white as snow; and his eyes were as a flame of fire;

15. And his feet like unto fine brass, as if they burned in a furnace; and his voice as the sound of many waters.

16. And he had in his right hand seven stars: and out of his mouth went a sharp two-edged sword: and his countenance was as the sun shineth in his strength.

17. And when I saw him, I fell at his feet as dead. And he laid his right hand upon me, saying unto me, Fear not; I am the first and the last:

18. I am he that liveth, and was dead; and, behold, I am alive for evermore, A-men; and have the keys of hell and of death.

19. Write the things which thou hast seen, and the things which are, and the things which shall be hereafter;

20. The mystery of the seven stars which thou sawest in my right hand, and the seven golden candlesticks. The seven stars are the angels of the seven churches: and the seven candlesticks which thou sawest are the seven churches.

References

Rev. 22:16

Ex. 25:37

Ezek. 1:26
Dan. 7:9
Dan. 10:5, 6

Dan. 7:9, 10

Ezek. 1:7

Heb. 4:12
Matt. 17:2

Ezek. 1:28
Dan. 8:18;
10:10,12

Rom. 6:9
Rev. 4:9
Ps. 68:10

Rev. 1:9-18
Rev. 2:1
Rev. 4:1

Ex. 37:23
Zech. 4:2
Mat. 5:15

Scriptures for Comparison

Daniel 7:13,14

I saw in the night visions, and, behold, one like the Son of man came with the clouds of heaven, and came to the Ancient of days, and they brought him near before him.

And there was given him dominion, and glory, and a kingdom, that all people, nations, and languages, should serve him: his dominion is an everlasting dominion, which shall not pass away, and his kingdom that which shall not be destroyed."

Summary of Chapter One

The Things John Had Seen

I. The Prologue to the Revelation (1-3)

In keeping with John's style in John 1:1-14 and I John 1:1-3, the inspired writer prefaces his work with this introductory paragraph setting forth the divine title, "THE REVELATION OF JESUS CHRIST," and stating the purpose of the book. This book is to "show," not to conceal. We are to study this book to understand it and to learn what lies ahead from its careful perusal.

A threefold blessing is vouchsafed in this prologue. In Bible times, the readers were often the leaders of the churches who read orally to a largely illiterate crowd. We are to be hearers who do what God's Word tells us (James 1:22).

II. The Presentation of the Revelation (4-8)

Penned by John and addressed to the divinely-selected seven churches, the Book contains the customary apostolic greeting. Grace (unmerited favor) was a Greek means of expressing greetings. Peace was a Hebrew term of salutation. Out of the grace of God in salvation proceeds the peace with God that is our present spiritual possession in Christ.

The true source of the book is the divine Trinity, here expressed. The theme of the book appears in verse 7. All events in Revelation lead up to the personal appearance of Christ at His second advent and the chain of reactions that will follow.

III. The Person of the Revelation (9-18)

Three times in the first chapter, the writer stresses his identity. With gracious humility he introduces himself as "a brother and companion" in the general tribulations from which all believers suffer. "If we suffer, we shall also reign with him." We must in patience wait for the coming of the Lord. James 5:7.

Patmos was a bleak and cheerless isle in the Aegean Sea, about five miles wide and 10 miles long, a barren, secluded place for the exile of criminals.

Notice that John was "in the Spirit," that is, in spiritual ecstatic communion with Him who is invisible — the "Lord's Day" indicates the first day of the week, rather than the "day of the Lord."

John is commanded to write a book and send copies to seven select churches. Turning to see the voice, the eyes of the apostle view the inexpressible grandeur of the Son of Man standing in the midst of His churches. THAT IS WHERE HE WANTS TO BE SEEN TODAY!

Nine great truths are set forth about His appearance as the present, ruling Prophet, Priest and King. This is the way He appears today at the right hand of the Majesty on High. While this is to be interpreted as a literal presentation of His holy stature, each facet of His glory has a symbolic significance, stressing some phase of His glory.

So overwhelmed is the apostle that he falls in utter submission "as dead." Compare Exodus 33:20.

IV. The Preview of the Revelation (19, 20)

The threefold division of the book is set forth in this key verse. Master this verse and its meaning, and you will understand the Revelation.

The book contains, of course, what John had just seen. That is past. The present church age is described in Chapters 2 and 3. The things that are yet future, after the church age, are depicted in Chapters 4-22.

Since the Word of God explains its own symbols, Christ interprets the vision in chapter one, verse 20.

Seven Churches of Asia

Outline of Chapter One

The Cosmic Christ of the Ages

The Revelation of Jesus Christ crowns like a golden diadem the entire inspired Book of God. All truths introduced in Genesis and developed through the Bible are climaxed and concluded in the Book of Revelation.

OBJECTIVE: To reveal Christ as the All-Conquering and Almighty Lord, the Prophet, Priest, and King.

OUTLINE:

I. The Prologue to the Revelation (1-3)
- A. The Title of the Book (1)—"The Revelation of Jesus Christ"
  1. He is the Source of the Revelation.
  2. He is the Subject of the Revelation.
  3. He is the Shewer of the Revelation.
- B. The Testimony of the Writer (Verses 1, 2, 3).
  1. The Bestower of the Book (1) God— Christ—Angel
  2. The Bearer of the Book (2) John the Apostle—He says Revelation is:
     a. The Word of God.
     b. The Testimony of Christ.
     c. The Record of all things he saw.
  3. The Blessings on the Book (3)
     a. Its readers blessed—both public and private readers.
     b. Its hearers blessed.
     c. Its heeders blessed.
- C. The Time for the Book (3). Now is the time.

II. The Presentation of the Revelation (4-8)
- A. By John the Apostle. (4)
- B. To Seven Churches of Asia. (4)
- C. From the Divine Trinity. (4)
  1. From the Eternal (Father). (4)
  2. From the Sevenfold Spirit. (4) See Is. 11:2.
  3. From Jesus Christ (Son). (5-7)
     a. The Reliable One, "faithful witness"
     b. The Resurrected One, "first begotten of the dead."
     c. The Ruling One, "prince of kings."
     d. The Revering One, "him that loved us."
     e. The Redeeming One, "washed us ... in his own blood."
     f. The Royalizing One, "made us kings and priests."
     g. The Returning One, "he cometh with clouds."
- D. Authorized by the Almighty. (8)

III. The Person of the Revelation (9-18)
- A. The Vessel. (9)
  1. His Equality. (9)
     a. Just John – no title.
     b. A Brother.
     c. A Companion in Tribulation, Kingdom – and Patience.
  2. His Exile. (9)
     a. For the Word of God.
     b. For the Testimony of Christ.
  3. His Experience. (10)
     a. In the Spirit.
     b. On the Lord's Day.
- B. The Voice. (10-12a)
  1. Summons as a trumpet.
  2. Speaks with authority.
  3. Selects seven churches to receive copies of this work.
- C. The Vision. (12b-16) Christ in the midst of His churches – lampstands, lit with the oil of the Spirit).
  1. The Designation: The Son of Man. (13)
  2. The Description:
     a. His Robe – Judgeship – see Is. 63:1-4.
     b. His Golden Girdle–Deity–Compare Is. 9:6.
     c. His White Hair – Eternality – See Daniel 7:6.
     d. His Fiery Eyes – Omniscience – Compare 2 Cor. 5:10 and 1 Cor. 3:12:15 for "fire."
     e. His Brassy Feet – Vengeance – See Is. 63:3.
     f. His Sounding Voice – Majesty – See Psalm 29:3-11.
     g. His Right Hand – Protection – See vs 20.
     h. His Powerful Mouth – Word – Sword of God – See Hebrews 4:12.
     i. His Radiant Countenance–Glory Mt. 17:2.
- D. The Victor. (17,18) His glory reveals our sinfulness, overwhelms John. Compare Job 21:1-6; Isaiah 6:1-5.
  1. Christ the Creator "the first."
  2. Christ the Consummator "the last."
  3. Christ the Life "he that liveth."
  4. Christ the Atoner "was dead" (for us).
  5. Christ the Conqueror "alive forever more" over hell and death!

IV. The Preview of the Revelation (19-20)
- A. The Extent of the Book. Verse 19.
  1. THE PAST – Things John had just seen. Chapter 1.
  2. THE PRESENT – Things which are. Chapters 2, 3, The church age.
  3. THE PROSPECT – things which shall be hereafter. Chapters 4-22. The future tribulation. See Revelation 4:1.
- B. The Explanation of Symbols (20)
  1. The Seven Stars are "Messengers," Evidently the pastors.
  2. The Seven Candlesticks Are the Churches.

Observations:
Spiritual lessons and applications from each verse
Chapter One

1. God is ever giving, for it is more blessed to give than to receive. He gave his Son. He would give eternal life. John 3:16; Romans 6:23.

God wants us to be informed, not ignorant, of His objective analysis of the present and His mysterious future predictions. Let's study prophecy with interest.

2. Let us be as ready to testify of what God had done for us, as John was to set these things forth, of which we are eyewitnesses.

3. Let us keep the principles of righteousness expressed in this book. The nearness of time for the fulfillment of some of these prophecies is stressed in verse 3.

4. The eternally existent God has all power, and we may trust in Him with confidence.

5. Since the Christ is the "faithful witness," we may rely upon what He says. Believe His promises.

If Christ is the "first begotten of the dead," then we may look forward to joining Him in resurrected glory. Look for Him.

If Christ is "prince of the kings of the earth," then we may know that all earthly powers are subject to His dominion. Man may rule, but Christ overrules.

If Christ has loved us, revered us, we ought then to love one another.

If Christ has redeemed us by His blood, then we ought to experience continual cleansing. 1 John 1:7.

6. If Christ has royalized us, making us kings and priests, then we ought to walk worthy of this vocation. See 1 Peter 2:9, 10.

7. If Christ is coming again, then his coming will be visible; seen by Israel; when a nation will be born in a day (Romans 11:26; Zechariah 13:6); He will strike terror into the hearts of the world's wicked and sinful men.

8. The Almighty can surely bring all of this to pass. Expect it!

9. We would do well to imitate John's humility, patience, faith and courage as He suffered for Christ's sake.

10. All believers should be "in the Spirit" on the "Lord's Day."

11. Since He is the Alpha and Omega (the A and Z), we can trust all that we are and have to Him.

12. How often we must turn to see "Him who is invisible," for we so frequently face the wrong way!

13. Since Christ wears a robe of white (see Mark 9:3), we should ever be aware that we are clad in a garment of salvation, a robe of righteousness, making us acceptable to God. (See Isaiah 61:10).

14. His eyes, like a flame of fire, penetrate in all-seeing analysis the very depths of our souls. See Psalm 11:4. At the judgment seat of Christ, His fiery gaze will scrutinize our works and consume the dross. 1 Corinthians 3:10-12.

15. Brass in the Bible is the symbol of judgment. He will trample under His feet all opposition at His coming. See 2 Thessalonians 1:7-9.

Like the waves, ceaseless and irresistible, his voice speaks with majestic power. Let us listen!

16. Christ protects His pastor-angel-star in His right hand. None can harm him there; He can chastise him there.

The Word of God is a two-edged sword, condemning with cutting power, converting by cutting away sins. Ephesians 6:17. He is the Sun of righteousness. Malachi 4:2.

17. His word is "Fear not." Study the *fear nots* in the Bible. Let us fear not, but trust Him and obey Him.

18. The crucified, buried and risen Christ has all power and the keys of hell and death and is worthy of our worship and loyalty.

19. Memorize verse 19 and repeat it every time you read or teach this book. Let us be as obedient to the commands of Christ as was John.

20. When a symbol is used in Scripture, it is often defined.

Stars and Candlesticks

"Those stars and candlesticks have not been useless. Some hearts, communities and kingdoms have been attracted by the light, and have learned to appreciate its transforming beauty, and are found, to a greater or less degree, walking and rejoicing in it. But still the world in the main is a dark and wicked world. The light sent of God is 'a light that shineth in a dark place,' and will so continue 'until the day dawn,' for the great consummation."

—*J. A. Seiss*

Quotations
From Other Expositors
Chapter One

Title and Source (1-3)

"We note, in verse one, that the Revelation of Jesus Christ was given by the Father to the Son, as David revealed to Solomon all his plans in connection with the building of the future temple. God is represented as being in counsel with our Lord Jesus Christ concerning 'things which must shortly come to pass,' and which it is the joy of His heart to communicate to His servants. An angel becomes the medium to make all known to the beloved apostle John, who, in this sense, is to tarry in the Church till the coming of the Lord — that is, his line of ministry carries us on to that blessed event. Note then the order through which the revelation came down to us. God gave it to Jesus Christ, who sent it by His angel to His servant John to show unto His servants the coming things.

"He is said to have signified it; that is, He made it known by signs or symbols. It is important to bear this in mind. This book is a book of symbols. But the careful student of the Word need not exercise his own ingenuity in order to think out the meanings of the symbols. It may be laid down as a principle of first importance that every symbol used in Revelation is explained or alluded to somewhere else in the Bible. Therefore, he who would get God's mind as to this portion of His Word must study with earnest and prayerful attention every other part of Holy Scripture. Undoubtedly this is why so great a blessing is in store for those who read and hear the words of this prophecy, and keep the things written therein (ver. 3)."

– H.A. Ironside

Grace and Peace (4-7)

"John here announces himself simply by name. There is no assertion of his apostleship, and no flourish of trumpets in calling attention to these sublime prophecies. There is a quiet dignity befitting the introduction and disclosure of subjects which have bowed, tens of thousands, in heartfelt adoration.

Then the Godhead, each in His own Person, unites in a message of grace and peace, and that, moreover, before the mutterings of the coming storm are heard. Not a Seal can be broken, not a Trumpet blown, nor a Vial poured out til the saints are divinely assured that the strength and blessing of God are for them. God for us in blessing, and in the maintenance of His own glory at all times and under all circumstances, is our mighty stronghold."

– Walter Scott

The Second Coming (7,8)

"The King, returned at last, is none other than 'the King eternal, immortal, invisible, the only wise God' (1 Tim. 1:17). His triumph will be complete and everlasting. Hitler vowed that his infamous Third Reich would last for a thousand years. It was born on January 30, 1933, and lasted for the grand total of 148 months! Jesus is to set up a kingdom which will last for a thousand years, and then when that golden millennium has run its course, the kingdom will be dissolved, not decline or decay, not by surrender to the force of superior arms, but because He wills it so and because the time has come to set up an everlasting kingdom which will never pass away.

"This everlasting triumph of Jesus is based on the three great attributes of deity. First, He is omniscient. He says: 'I am Alpha and Omega.' Alpha and omega are the first and last letters of the Greek alphabet. The Lord Jesus is God's alphabet. The alphabet is an ingenious way of storing the accumulated wisdom of the race.

Second, He is omnipresent. He says: 'I am ... the beginning and the ending'. His omnipresence is stated here in terms of time, but it is just as true in terms of space (see Mt. 18:20). The Lord can presence Himself in the midst of any company of His people in any part of the world at any given moment of time. 'Lo, I am with you alway,' He says, 'even unto the end of the world' (Mt. 28:20).

"Third, He is omnipotent. He says: 'I am ... the Lord which is, and which was, and which is to come, the Almighty.' The first part of this expression has already been used to describe the Father (1:4); it is now used to describe the Son. He is God in every sense of the word. He is 'the Almighty,' an expression which occurs only ten times in the New Testament, nine of them in the Apocalypse itself."

– John Phillips

John's Tribulation (9)

"John writes The Revelation not as an apostle exercising authority, but as a Seer, unfolding that unveiling of the future which Christ gave him. How humble and loving is his attitude. There is absolutely no 'ecclesiastical dignity' here! Note the order: trouble and trial—tribulation—first; then the kingdom assured to us, and then the patient waiting for that kingdom's manifestation. Compare Acts 14:22: 'through many tribulations we must enter into the kingdom of God;' 2 Thess. 1:4,5: 'your persecutions and in the afflictions which ye endure … to the end that ye may be counted worthy of the kingdom of God, for which ye also suffer.' (Note here it is not The Great Tribulation, but the ordinary trials of Christians.)"

— William R. Newell

Christ amid Candlesticks (10-12)

"The apostle turned toward the voice and there burst upon his vision such a sight that he was immediately stricken to the earth. It was Jesus, his beloved Lord, but O, what a change! Once before John had seen Him in a transfigured state, but that was not like this. This was Jesus in all His glory, even the glory which He had with the Father before the world was. He appeared in the glorious apparel of the Great High Priest and around and about Him were seven golden lampstands representing the churches. It is an apt symbol, for the churches are in the world to shine as lights, holding forth the word of life. There is undoubted reference here to the golden lampstand in the Tabernacle."

— William L. Pettingill

Christ's Glory (13-18)

"The Churches are lamps; the ministers are stars; but Christ is the sun. He is to the moral world what the sun is to the natural. Such, then, is the full-drawn picture of our glorious Lord, as he walks among his Churches, and proceeds to pass his solemn judgment upon them. There have not been wanting some to pronounce it grotesque and intolerable, but I cannot so regard it. If a sublimer conception of Divine and glorified humanity, so true to the Savior's offices and work, ever entered into the imagination of man, I have never seen it, and never heard of it. And when I recall the magnificent portraiture, the human form, walking majestically amid golden furniture, clothed with the garment of royalty, girded with gold, crowned with flowing locks that reflect the light and purity of heaven, having a glance of electric power, feet glowing with the liquid splendour of melted brass, a voice of majesty at which the earth and the heavens shake, the right hand lit with starry jewels, a mouth whose words carry their own execution in them, and a countenance as glorious as the noonday sun; — when I survey such majestic lineaments, and such mighty powers, and hear the possessor of them say: 'I am the First and the Last, and The Living One; and I was dead, and behold, I am living forever and ever: and I have the keys of death and of hades;' —I say, when I bring all this before me, and try to realize it in my imagination, I am almost overwhelmed with the sublimity of the picture, and with the goodness, and grace, and power, and might with which the eternal Father hath invested the person of Jesus Christ."

— J. A. Seiss

Christ Alive (17, 18)

"This opening scene is dominated by 'the glory of our great God and Saviour Jesus Christ' (Tit. 2:13)—we know from verse 18 that it can be none other—and the sight is literally breath-taking (verse 17). John certainly sees him as God; he gives him the attributes of deity by using the same kind of language that Ezekiel and Daniel use to describe God, and recalls Christ's own claim in John 14:9, 'He who has seen me has seen the Father.' From this point onwards, the centrality of Christ is the ruling theme of Revelation. All things depend on their relation to him."

— Michael Wilcock

Past, Present, and Future (19)

"We have found that 'things which thou hast seen' refer to the vision John saw of the Son of Man in His resurrection glory, standing in the midst of the candlesticks; that 'the things which are' have to do with the present church age, as outlined in chapters 2 and 3; and that the 'things which shall be hereafter' are yet future events which will begin after the translation of the church, presented to us in chapters 4-22. Unless we grasp this outline, we shall miss the key."

— Louis T. Talbot

New Dispensation (20)

"In the tabernacle there was one lampstand with seven lamps; here, in Revelation, we have seven lampstands. Reason: during the old dispensation there was a visible unity, the Jewish church-state. The churches of the new dispensation find their spiritual unity in Christ who is present and active among them in and through his Spirit. Hence, they need not fear. 'For where two or three are gathered together in my name, there am I in the midst of them.' Matt. 18:20"

— William Hendriksen

The Cosmic Christ of the Ages
An Expository Sermon

Chapter One

Introduction

All the great ideas begun in the book of Genesis, traceable all through the Bible, find their climactic conclusions in this grand finale of the Word of God.

In Genesis we have the beginning of the Universe.

In Revelation, the final destiny of the Universe.

In Genesis we see the beginning of the human race.

In Revelation, the final destiny of the human race.

In Genesis, we find the beginning of the nations.

In Revelation, the final history of the nations.

In Genesis is the origin of the nation of Israel.

In Revelation, the final destiny of Israel.

In Genesis, access to the tree of life is lost.

In Revelation, access to the tree of life is regained.

While there are at least 35 great strains of truth introduced in Genesis that are concluded in Revelation, in summary we can say, in Genesis, paradise is lost; in Revelation, paradise is regained.

Without this final capstone of truth, dozens of loose ends would be dangling. But the Holy Spirit has crowned the canon of Sacred Scripture with this glowing and glorious account of the final triumph of Christ and righteousness both on earth and in heaven forever.

I. The Foreview (1-8)

In the first verse of this chapter is the foreview of the great truth magnified in the book; the Second Coming of Jesus Christ. "Behold he cometh with clouds" (verse 7).

Of course, this is a "revelation," an unveiling of that which was previously concealed, the apocalypse. It is to be studied, practiced, understood in its broad outline of the future. God conveyed it to Christ, who gave it to the Apostle John, who "bare record of the Word of God"—this is God's message—"and of the testimony of Jesus Christ"—who always brings the truth—"and of all things that he saw"—as an eyewitness.

John was to be transported across ages into the final judgment times already forecast in the Old Testament prophets. In fact, there are over 278 allusions or quotations to the Old Testament in the entire 22 chapters.

Here from the first three verses is the divinely-inspired title, the introduction by the writer, and the promise of blessings upon the *readers, hearers* and *keepers* of the things written therein. "Blessed" means "happy," being spiritually and personally enriched by the touch of God through His Word. To be "blessed" is to be filled with His grace, His joy, His peace, His presence. Oh, the effulgent ecstasy of being truly "blessed of God!" These three verses are an exciting introduction to what lies ahead. No wonder the Apostle observed, "for the time is at hand." That is the end time, the time of which Daniel spoke, "the time of the end."

John's personal salutation appears in verse 4:

"John to the seven churches which are in Asia" These seven local congregations, where John had personally ministered, in all probability. They were especially selected to receive a direct message from the Head of the Church and to have written copies of the Book of Revelation. Not only were these actual local assemblies with the real conditions described by Christ within them, but these churches give us, as we shall see, a prophetic foreview of the entire church age.

"Grace" and "peace"—those apostolic words—appear in the salutation, reminding us that God is the source of all grace—all unmerited favor—all undeserved mercy bestowed upon us. No person can enjoy real "peace" apart from having "peace with God through our Lord Jesus Christ."

These prime blessings come from the whole Trinity.

The FATHER is in view as the one "which is"—present tense—He is the God of the Now; "and which was"—He always has been; "and which is to come"—He continues forever and ever.

He is Jehovah, the self-existent, eternal, all-powerful ONE, maker of heaven and earth!

The HOLY SPIRIT is meant by the "seven spirits of God" (verse 4).

From Isaiah 11:2, we learn that the Holy Spirit, who would anoint the Messiah, is:

The Spirit of the Lord.

The Spirit of Wisdom

The Spirit of Understanding.

The Spirit of Counsel.

The Spirit of Might.

The Spirit of Knowledge.

The Spirit of the Fear of the Lord.

It is the Holy Ghost in His sevenfold completion

19

and perfection, described later in a figure as "the seven lamps of fire."

It is not that there are seven Holy Ghosts, but rather ONE SPIRIT with seven magnificent titles, reflecting the full range of His ministry.

This grace and peace proceed from JESUS CHRIST (verses 5, 6).

He is the Reliable Witness ... Therefore believe Him!

He is the Resurrected Lord ... Therefore receive Him!

He is the Ruling Prince ... Therefore serve Him!

He is the Revering, Loving Saviour ... Therefore love Him back!

He is the Redeeming Sacrifice ... Therefore give yourself a living sacrifice to Him!

He is the Royalizing Monarch ... Therefore praise Him!

Yes, we have been saved, elevated, royalized, made to be heaven's nobility ... "that we should show forth the praises of him who hath called us out of darkness into his marvelous light" (1Peter 2:9).

He is the Returning King ... Therefore expect Him!

"Behold he cometh with clouds" ... this is the glorious appearing, depicted in chapter 19.

"And every eye shall see him, and they also which pierced him" (verse 7). Gentiles and the living Israelis ... Jews, will look upon Him whom they have pierced (Zechariah 12:10 and 13:6). They shall then understand that He was, and He is the Messiah.

"And all the kindreds of the earth shall wail because of Him. Even so, Amen" (verse 7).

Then the voice of God thunders forth from verse 8. He is the Alpha—the first letter of the Greek alphabet, signifying the Creator; He is the Omega—the last letter, signifying the Consummator of All Things ... He is the ALMIGHTY.

II. The Interview (9-18)

In verses 9-18, we have the interview between Jesus Christ and John.

The aged John, last survivor of the original twelve apostles, brother, fellow sufferer in persecutions, but a citizen of the kingdom which cannot be moved, tells the experience of the Patmos vision. He, on this island of exile, near what is now Turkey, the grand old patriarch, perhaps confined to a cell, reaches the highest pinnacle of his 60-year ministry. Tradition says that John had refused to acknowledge the Emperor Domitian as a god, a crime punishable by imprisonment. He would never do it. He would die first.

But God can take a prison cell and make it a gateway into vistas of glory.

While in high communion with God "in the Spirit" on the first day of the week, he hears a voice he has not heard for six decades. It is Christ, the Alpha and the Omega ...

John is to behold the unfolding panorama of the future; he is to write it down, to send it to seven selected churches.

When John turns to behold the voice speaking to him, he sees the glorified God-man, the Anointed One, the Prophet, the Priest and Prince, and Cosmic Christ of the Ages, the Exalted and Sublime Sovereign of the Universe, the Head of the Church, the same Jesus who walked as the lowly Galilean on this earth ...

But now He is the King of glory (Psalm 24).

He is the King of Kings and Lord of Lords!

But John sees Him in the midst of seven golden candlesticks, the seven churches (verse 10) ... Christ is always in the midst of His churches; there He can, with the eye of faith, be seen.

Nine wonderful truths are set forth in this vivid and sole description in all the Bible of the Son of Man. Not only does this title suggest His glorified humanity, but it also harks back to Daniel 7:13 where "the Son of Man" is seen with "the Ancient of Days ..." the everlasting Father.

Christ's garment down to the foot speaks of His DIGNITY as Prophet, Priest and King.

His golden girdle or belt suggests His DEITY, for He is GOD manifest in the flesh. In biblical typology, gold represents divinity.

His white head indicates His PURITY.

His fiery eyes tell of His SCRUTINY, for He can penetrate into the depths of every human heart and read all motives, thoughts and feelings. At the judgment seat of Christ, our works will be tried by fire (1 Corinthians 3) ... the all-seeing eyes of Christ.

His brazen feet remind us of JUDGMENT, for He will trample beneath His feet all of His enemies.

His sonorous voice, like roaring waves, exalts His MAJESTY.

His right hand is full of the seven stars that typify His pastors, speaking of His MINISTERS.

They are in his hand for direction, correction, and protection.

His sword, issuing from His mouth, is indicative of the all powerful WORD OF GOD.

His face, shining like the sun, illustrates His GLORY.

Some day, as the Sun of Righteousness, He will rise with healing in His wings (Malachi 4:2).

Oh, gentle reader, this is our Lord, our Master, our Leader, our Saviour, our King. As much as words are able to describe under divine inspiration, this is the appearance of Him who is Jesus Christ, the same, yesterday and today and forever.

Pledge anew and afresh your allegiance and dedication to Him!

Overwhelmed by the sublime effulgence of His glory, John falls before Him in submission, worship, adoration and total dedication.

Then come the sweet words of the Saviour, "Fear not, I am the first and last." It is said that there are 365 "fear nots" and "be not afraids" in the Bible ... one for every day of the year.

"I am he that liveth and was dead; and, behold, I am alive for evermore. Amen; and have the keys of hell and death" (verse 18). Here is the gospel. We serve a risen Christ. No one need fear hell for Jesus has the keys. He is the mighty conqueror!

The ancient and wise prophet Daniel likewise beheld Him as the Mighty Conqueror more than a half a millenium earlier.

"I beheld till the thrones were cast down and the Ancient of Days did sit, whose garment was white as snow, and the hair of his head like the pure wool: his throne was like the burning flame and his wheels as burning fire.

"A fiery stream issued and came forth from before him: thousand thousands ministered unto him, and ten thousand times ten thousand stood before him...

"I saw in the night visions, and behold, one like the Son of man came with the clouds of heaven, and came to the Ancient of days, and they brought him near before him.

"And there was given him dominion, and glory, and a kingdom, that all people, nations and languages should serve him: his dominion is an ever lasting dominion, which shall not pass away, and his kingdom that which shall not be destroyed" (Daniel 7:9,10; 13,14).

This same Son of Man, victorious over hell and death, is the more resplendently described throughout this Book of Revelation with a full description of the process through which He emerges as the triumphant King of Kings and Lord of Lords.

Daniel saw Him before the everlasting Father, the Ancient of days, whose theophanic manifestation resembles so much the appearance of the Son in the vision.

John saw Him on the Isle of Patmos as He is now and shall be.

At the sound of the Seventh Trumpet, the glorious proclamation reverberates through heaven, "The kingdoms of this world are become the kingdoms of our Lord, and of his Christ, and he shall reign forever and ever!" (11:15).

III. The Preview (19-20)

Then, in verse 19, comes the prime command of Christ and the triple division of the book.

"Write the things which thou hast seen ..."—Chapter One, of course.

"And the things which are ..."—Chapter Two and Three, speaking of the churches and the church age. We are still in that era, the Dispensation of the Church.

"And the things which shall be hereafter"—Chapter Four through the book.

This is obvious from Chapter 4:1, where John is "raptured" into heaven with these words, "Come up hither, and I WILL SHOW THEE THINGS WHICH MUST BE HEREAFTER."

For the most part, this is still future, as we shall see.

Memorize, master this verse, and the divisions of the book will be obvious. It is a preview of all that the book contains.

Conclusion

John is told what the seven golden candlesticks mean ... the seven churches.

The "angels of the churches" are the "messengers" ... that is what the word *angel* means. God has heavenly angels; God has human angels ... His faithful messengers of truth who lead His churches, His ministers.

These, now, are some of the awesome wonders to which I invite you. Come with me through the strange visions, mysterious realities, grand facts of this book.

It is a book of stupendous facts about Christ, heaven, hell, Israel, the church, Satan, Antichrist, judgments, saints ...

It is a book of mysterious symbols ... seals, trumpets, thunders, persons, vials, dooms ...

It is a book of future events ...

It is a book for "overcomers."

It is a book of great blessing.

It is the story of the end times, figuratively and literally of the consummation of this age and of all time.

I invite you to take a time journey into the future, into eternity to behold finally that glory world, where God makes all things new.

Go with us through the Book, with Bible open, heart warm, soul uplifted!

"Blessed is he that readeth ..."

IF YOU ARE NOT A CHRISTIAN, you cannot understand this book. But you can become a Christian. You can be saved. You can be on the winning side forever. Come to Christ. Accept Him as your Savior and become an "overcomer" forever!

"He that believeth on the Son hath life everlasting: and he that believeth not the Son shall not see life; but the wrath of God abidenth on him" (Jn. 3:36).

A Commentary on the Revelation
Expository, Exegetical, Devotional and Practical
Greek words from the Textus Receptus

Chapter One

The Introductory Verses, Title, Source and Purpose of the Book (1-3)

1. **The Revelation** *(apokalupsis)* — The alternate title is **The Apocalypse of Jesus Christ;** the key word here meaning an unveiling, a disclosure, a revealing of those things previously concealed, an uncovering of truth coming from God. Burton gives a good outline of the NT usage of *apokalupsis:* "(1) An appearance or manifestation of a person, a coming, a coming to view; used of the coming of Christ. (2) A disclosure of a person or thing such that its true character can be perceived. (3) A divine revelation or disclosure of a person in his true character, of truth, or of the divine will, made to a particular individual, and as such necessarily involving the perception of that which is to be revealed ..." **to show** *(deksai)* — The word occurs again in 22:6, thus encompassing the whole book and indicating the complete picture that appears between the two uses ... **his servants** — not just the Apostle John, but all of God's servants in all times and all places ... **shortly** *(en tachei)* — meaning in or with speed, very quickly, suddenly. Not that as man counts time they would all immediately occur, but that they would commence occuring and happen speedily and suddenly, when they occur ... **by his angel** — the angel does not obviously appear until 17:1; 19:9, 10. Jesus opens the Revelation, in verse 10, 11; ch. 4. Then one of the four living creatures acts as agent in 6:1, etc.; in 7:13 it is one of the elders; in ch. 10:8, 9 the Lord and his Angel. Compare Daniel 8:16; 9:21; Zechariah 1:19.

2. **Testimony of Jesus** *(marturian Iesou Christou)* — The words witness and testimony are in the Greek, *martyr.* So many witnesses died in the first centuries that the term came to mean someone who gives his life for a cause. That is real dedication. 3. **Blessed is he that readeth** *(makarios ho anagin-oskon)* — Spiritually happy and prosperous is the one who reads, either publicly or privately. The word *makarios* is used here and in the beatitudes and a total of 28 times in the New Testament. Another word, *eulogia,* is used 40 times in the New Testament and means to speak well of or to praise or to bless.

Salutation to the Seven Churches (4-8)

4. **The seven churches** *(hepta ekklesias)* — seven local congregations, especially selected as illustrative of conditions in contemporary churches of those times ... **grace** *(charis)* — the NT word encompasses much more than the definition "unmerited favor." It does mean a gracious favor or benefit bestowed and "the gratitude appropriate to the grace received" (L. O. Richards). Here, as an apostolic greeting, it speaks of the manifold blessings, undeserved, which God freely bestows upon His people. In Romans, its deep doctrinal significance is explored and explained by Paul, as also in Galatians and Ephesians. **From him which is** *(apo ho on)* — "from, originating and emanating from the One who exists" (Garner), the self-existing, Almighty God, the eternal God, revealed in the express image of His Son (Heb. 1:1, 2). 5. **And the first begotten of the dead** *(ho prototokos ton nekron)* — The firstborn (the prototype) of the dead bodies or corpses, showing that the resurrected saints shall be like the first begotten out from among the dead and the dead bodies. 6. **And priests unto God** *(hiereis to theo)* — hence the English word *hierarchy.* All believers are priests and in God's hierarchy under the High Priest, Christ. 7. **And every eye shall see him** *(kai opsetai auton pas ophthalmos)* — hence opthalmology, the study of sight and vision in English. John emphasizes that at the glorious appearing, all eyes will see him (2 Thes. 1:7-9), including the Jews, who pierced him (Zech. 12:10), who will mourn or wail (Zech. 12:11-13; 14:1) as they receive Him as the Messiah and "a nation shall be born in a day." 8. Again, the eternal God, past, present and future is mentioned, using the Greek alphabet's first and last letter to describe His completeness. **The Almighty** *(ho pantokrator)* — The Father is in view here, the one supreme, all powerful Sovereign of the universe. Great and glorious, omnipotent, omniscient, omnipresent, infinite and unlimited, the supreme and sole Creator is the ultimate source of all things and of this Revelation.

John's Identity (9,10)

9. **I John who also am your brother** *(ego Ioannes ho kai adelphos humon)* — John here resembles Daniel, the Old Testament seer who said, "I Daniel" (Daniel 7:28, 9:2, 10:2). Only these two

prophets use such an expression. Some ancient writers questioned that the writer was John the Apostle, author of the gospel and the epistles, but ascribe the work to some other "John" of whom nothing else is known. Apostolic authorship was questioned by Dionysius, Eusebius of Ceasarea, the Council of Laodicea (about 360 A.D.), but early second and third century writers attest to its being the work of the son of Zebedee, including Justin Martyr, Irenaeus, Clement, Origen, Tertullian and Hippolytus. Guthrie says, "There are few books in the New Testament with stronger attestation." Although the style differs in some respects from the gospel, the themes, concepts and doctrinal ideas are similar. "It should be noted," says Guthrie, "that in spite of linguistic and grammatical differences the Apocalypse has a closer affinity to the Greek of the other Johannine books than to any other New Testament books." Besides that, there is no evidence that another "John the Elder" ever existed. Only the Apostle would have the prestige, authority and influence to pen so widely accepted a book among early Christians … **companion** (*sunkoinonos*) — the word indicates a fellow-partaker, a co-sharer in tribulation. Most likely this was during the heavy persecution perpetrated by the Emperor Domition in the mid A.D. 90's … **Patmos** — this Greek island, still inhabited and visited by tourists, has a circumference of about thirty miles, is irregularly shaped with an isthmus connecting two sections. It seems to have been a barren place in 96 A.D., where exiles were sent. Domition banished John there, but the Emperor Nerva later released him … **testimony** (*marturian*) — again the origin of the word martyr in English. **10. I was in the Spirit on the Lord's day** (*egenomen en pneumati en te kuriake hemera*). The Lord's day or "imperial day," honoring the emperor, was on the first day of the week in some Roman circles. But Christ is the true royal King, who arose the first day of the week and introduced the true "Lord's Day" (*kuriake hemera*). First and second century Christians so understood it … **A great voice** (*phonen megalen*) — a great, loud, blaring voice, like a megaphone, distinctly clear and understandable. Thus, John in solitude and in spiritual and ecstatic communion with God by the Holy Spirit's ministry — he was walking in the Spirit (Gal. 5:16) and was filled with the Spirit (Eph. 5:18) — enters a spiritual and visionary realm he had never before experienced; like Daniel of old, he hears a voice he had not heard, insofar as can be known, for sixty years. It comes from behind him. See Isaiah 30:21 … **As a trumpet** (*hos salpiggos*) — as a loud and blaring trumpet that calls to battle, to

a great convocation or a celebration (Garner). It is not an uncertain sound, but clear, summoning attention and accompanying God's revelation of Himself. See 1 Corinthians 14:8.

The Glorified Christ (11-17)
11. The first (*protos*) **and last** (*eschatos*) — hence He is before all things, the "proto-person" and He is the subject of eschatology, the doctrine of last things. He forever will be … **The Alpha** (*A*) **and the Omega** — In the Greek alphabet the Omega is the last letter, an O. There is also another "o" in Greek, **omicron. 12. I saw seven golden candlesticks** (*eidon hepta luchnias chrusas*) — the Greek word *luchnos* translated candle in Mt. 5:15 means an oil burning lamp. *Luchnias* is a candlestick with one or more candles or lamps. We are told that the seven branched candlestick or lampstand of the Old Testament was fed by olive oil (Zech. 4:2,3,12). Jesus explains that they signify or symbolize the seven churches (vs. 20). **13. Son of man** (*homioion huion anthropou*) — a term Jesus used of Himself in the gospels 20 times, identifying with the prophetic ministry of Ezekiel, who is called "son of man" about 89 times. As a title this is used only of Jesus and the great prophet Ezekiel. With reference to Jesus it is more than an indication of His humanity, although that is evident, but most importantly, He is the one described in Daniel 7:13: "Behold one like the Son of man came with the clouds of heaven, and came to the Ancient of Days … and there was given unto him dominion and glory and a kingdom, that all people, nations and languages should serve Him …" **Clothed with a garment down to the foot** — A mark of high rank, reminiscent of the High Priest's garments in Exodus 28:2,4,31. Aaron's robe and girdle were for glory and beauty, and combined an insignia of royalty with priesthood, the antitype of which is Christ's priesthood after the order of Melchizadek (Heb. 6:20, etc. and Ps. 110:4; Gen. 14:18-23) … **golden girdle** (*zonen chrusan*) — gold was the ornament of kings, used in Scripture to speak of Deity in Tabernacle typology. The girdle was a belt or sash, bespeaking high rank and authority, about the upper chest and over the heart. **14. As white as snow** (*leukon hos chion*) — a symbol of purity, innocence, cleanliness, holiness. See Isaiah 1:18; Mt. 28:3; Acts 1:10. Also His white head and hair suggest His eternality, the Ancient of days. **15. fine brass** (*chalkolibano*) — the word seems to indicate burnished, flashing, glowing brass, as heated in a furnace. As the feet of the priests were bare in the Tabernacle, so are the feet of our High Priest … **voice as many waters** — Ezekiel 42:2

says, "his voice was like the noise of many waters and the earth shined with his glory." See also the sound of the wings of the cherubim in Ezek. 1:24 …

16. seven stars — "He holds them as a star-studded crown of glory or royal diadem, in His hand" (See Isaiah 62:3: "Thou shalt be a crown of glory in the hand of the Lord, and a royal diadem in hand of thy God," which refers there to Israel in the millenium). **sword** (*hromphaia*) — the Thracian warrior's long and broad sword (not a slim sabre). Six times this word appears in Revelation; only once elsewhere in the New Testament, in Luke 2:35 "a sword shall pierce through thine own heart" … **His countenance as the sun** — Jesus is the Morning Star and the Sun of Righteousness (Mal. 4:2). This majestic and magnificent Prophet, Priest and King is the supreme object of our affections, worthy of our worship and praise.

Christ's Words of Strength and Triumph (17, 18)

17. laid his right hand — Daniel was also overwhelmed with the magnitude and marvel of his visions and was touched by a hand and raised up (Dan. 10:10) … **Saying unto me, Fear not** (*legon moi me phobou*) — or "Do not be afraid, do not let yourself be fearful, "consumed with obstructing fear as also to Abraham (Gen. 15:1; to Joseph Mt. 1:20; to the believers Luke 12:32; to Paul Acts 27:24). Our Lord in his love expects our reverence, but an overwhelming fear and sense of fright is but temporary, even in the presence of His glory. "Perfect love casteth out fear" (1 John 4:18). **18. I am he that liveth** (*kai ho zon*) "I exist as the ever living one." See also John 14:6, 19 … **and was dead** (*kai egenomen nekros*) — He once became dead, but now "death hath no more dominion over him" (Rom. 6:9) … **And behold I am alive for evermore** (*Kai idou zon eimi eis tous aionas ton anionon*) — "Alive I am unto and into the ages of the ages." To Him belongs "absolute being, as contrasted to the relative being of creatures; He only hath immortality; being in essence, not by mere participation, immortal" (*Theodoret as quoted by Trench*) … **And have the keys of hell and death** (*kai echo tas kleis tou hadou kai tou thanatou*) "Keys denote authority of control, jurisdiction or administration to the places of entrance" — our Lord with all authority committed to Him by the Father, holds the keys of **Hades** (*Hebrew Sheol*). He conquered death and therefore is not locked in; He has the keys and can raise the dead at His return and at the proper times.

Christ's Direction and Explanation (19, 20)

19. Write (*graphon*) — John is to record his vision up to that time, then **the things which are** (*kai ha eisen*) — the little word **ha** (*things*) is one letter, an **alpha** or **a** with a tiny mark for "ha" sound. It appears three times but includes past, present and future and all that is in this book. He is the ALPHA who operates through history … **And the things which shall be hereafter** (*kai ha mellei genesthai meta tauta*) — the things which are about to occur or take place or shall come, after these first two things (*ha*). The three-fold division is the key to the book. See 4:1 for future events … **20. mystery** (*musterion*) "It occurs twenty-seven times in the New Testament; twenty of them in Paul's writings (Rom. 11:25; 16:25; 1 Cor. 2:7; 4:1; 13:2; 14:2; 15:51; Eph. 1:9; 3:3,4,9; 5:32; 6:19; Col. 1:26,27; 2:2, 4:3; 2 Thess. 2:7; 1 Tim. 3:9,16). Its other seven uses (Matt. 13:11; Mk 4:11; Luke 8:10; Rev. 1:20; 10:7; 17:5,7) are found in connection with parables about God's kingdom or truths disclosed in the Book of Revelation. The word is always associated with a verb of revelation of proclamation (as in "I show you a mystery" — 1 Cor. 15:51). A mystery is an insight into some present day Christian experience or future expectation not unveiled as clearly in the Old Testament" (L. O. Richards). It is a mystery or sometimes a symbol with a covert meaning, but interpreted, as in this verse … **stars** (*asteres*), hence the English word astronomy, the study of stars. Some expositors have imagined that a specific angel, a heavenly being, is actually in charge of each church, but this has no basis anywhere else in the Scriptures. What is meant is that he is the angel-messenger minister, the pastor-bishop-elder of each church. It is to them that Christ addresses his commendations and corrections. See Mal. 2:7, where the priest is called the messenger (angel) of the Lord; also 3:1, where the prophet is meant … **seven** (*hepta*) — seven is indicative of perfection divine completion, total adequacy, sufficiency, meaning here that the pastor-messenger-angel-stars and the New Testament churches are ideally God's channels for His work in this Dispensation. They are to fulfill God's mission, shining as lights in a dark world.

Mentioned in this book are: (1) seven Spirits; (2) seven churches, which are (3) seven candlesticks; (4) seven stars, which are (5) the seven angels of the churches; (6) seven horns of the Lamb, and (7) seven eyes, which are the seven Spirits; (8) seven seals; (9) seven angels with seven trumpets; (10) seven thunders; (11) seven heads of the beast; (12) sevens vials with seven plagues; (13) seven kings. In addition, other sets of seven may be found by careful search.

RAINBOWS FROM REVELATION
The Revelation of Jesus Christ
A chapter by chapter, verse by verse study
"There was a rainbow round about the throne like unto an emerald" (4:3)

CHAPTER TWO: He That Hath An Ear, Let Him Hear I

References

Rev. 1:16;
13:13

Ps. 1:6
1 John 4:1
2 Cor. 11:13

Gal. 6:9
Heb. 12:3,5

John 14:15

Mark 12:9

Rev. 2:15

Mat. 11:15
Rev. 22:2, 14
Gen. 2:9; 3:22

Rev. 1:8, 17, 18

Luke 12:21
Rom. 2:17

Mat. 10:22
John 16:33

Rev. 13:9
Rev. 20:14

Rev. 1:16
Josh. 5:13
Heb. 4:12

Lev. 17:7
Deut. 32:16, 17

Num. 24:14
Num. 25
Acts 15:29

1. UNTO the angel of the church of Ephesus write; These things saith he that holdeth the seven stars in his right hand, who walketh in the midst of the seven golden candlesticks;

2. I know thy works, and thy labor, and thy patience, and how thou canst not bear them which are evil: and thou hast tried them which say they are apostles, and are not, and hast found them liars:

3. And hast borne, and hast patience, and for my name's sake hast labored, and hast not fainted.

4. Nevertheless I have somewhat against thee, because thou hast left thy first love.

5. Remember therefore from whence thou art fallen, and repent, and do the first works; or else I will come unto thee quickly, and will remove thy candlestick out of his place, except thou repent.

6. But this thou hast, that thou hatest the deeds of the Nicolaitans, which I also hate.

7. He that hath an ear, let him hear what the Spirit saith unto the churches; To him that overcometh will I give to eat of the tree of life, which is in the midst of the paradise of God.

8. And unto the angel of the church in Smyrna write; These things saith the first and the last, which was dead, and is alive;

9. I know thy works, and tribulation, and poverty, (but thou art rich) and I know the blasphemy of them which say they are Jews, and are not, but are the synagogue of Satan.

10. Fear none of those things which thou shalt suffer: behold, the devil shall cast some of you into prison, that ye may be tried; and ye shall have tribulation ten days: be thou faithful unto death, and I will give thee a crown of life.

11. He that hath an ear, let him hear what the Spirit saith unto the churches; He that overcometh shall not be hurt of the second death.

12. And to the angel of the church in Pergamos write; These things saith he which hath the sharp sword with two edges;

13. I know thy works, and where thou dwellest, even where Satan's seat is: and thou holdest fast my name, and hast not denied my faith, even in those days wherein Antipas was my faithful martyr, who was slain among you, where Satan dwelleth.

14. But I have a few things against thee, because thou hast there them that hold the doctrine of Balaam, who taught Balak to cast a stumbling block before the children of Israel, to eat things sacrificed unto idols, and to commit fornication.

15. So hast thou also them that hold the doctrine of the Nicolatanes, which thing I hate.

16. Repent; or else I will come unto thee quickly, and will fight against them with the sword of my mouth.

17. He that hath an ear, let him hear what the Spirit saith unto the churches; To him that overcometh will I give to eat of the hidden manna, and will give him a white stone, and in the stone a new name written, which no man knoweth saving he that receiveth it.

18. And unto the angel of the church in Thyatira write; These things saith the Son of God, who hath his eyes like unto a flame of fire, and his feet are like fine brass;

19. I know thy works, and charity, and service, and faith, and thy patience, and thy works; and the last to be more than the first.

20. Notwithstanding I have a few things against thee, because thou sufferest that woman Jezebel, which calleth herself a prophetess, to teach and to seduce my servants to commit fornication, and to eat things sacrificed unto idols.

21. And I gave her space to repent of her fornication; and she repented not.

22. Behold, I will cast her into a bed, and them that commit adultery with her into great tribulation, except they repent of their deeds.

23. And I will kill her children with death; and all the churches shall know that I am he which searcheth the reins and hearts: and I will give unto every one of you according to his works.

24. But unto you I say, and unto the rest in Thyatira, as many as have not this doctrine, and which have not known the depths of Satan, as they speak; I will put upon you none other burden.

25. But that which ye have already hold fast till I come.

26. And he that overcometh, and keepeth my works unto the end, to him will I give power over the nations:

27. And he shall rule them with a rod of iron; as the vessels of a potter shall they be broken to shivers: even as I received of my Father.

28. And I will give him the morning star.

29. He that hath an ear, let him hear what the Spirit saith unto the churches.

References

1 Cor. 10:20

Rev. 2:6

Isa. 11:
Rev. 19:15

Ex. 16:33
John 6:49-51
Isa. 56:5
Isa. 62:2
Isa. 65:15

Rev. 1:14,15

1 Thes. 1:3

1 Kings 16:31
1 Kings 21:25
2 Kings 9:7,
22,30
Ex. 34:15

Rom. 2:5

Ex. 20:14

Ps. 7:9;26:2
Jer. 11:20

2 Tim. 3:1-9

Rev. 3:11

John 6:29
Mat. 19:28

Ps. 2:8,9
Rev. 19:15

2 Peter 1:19
Rev. 22:16

Summary of Chapter Two

The Things Which Are (Part 1)

I. Ephesus: The Lacking Church (2:1-7)
"The Fundamental Church that Failed"

Each time Christ, the Administrator and Judge-Advocate of the churches, speaks to the spiritually-appointed leader of the local congregation, the angel-messenger-minister. He holds these ministers in His right hand for *protection, correction* and *direction*. Note that Christ walks, moves in the midst of His "churches."

In His all-seeing omniscience, He knows all things about each church, each individual, about YOU. He commends for being, faithful, unfainting, but notice the all-important NEVERTHELESS.

He does not charge them with "losing" their first love, but "leaving" it. The possibility of the loss of their "candlestick," their place as a true witness for Christ, is mentioned,

However, our Lord commends them for "hating" the deeds of the Nicolaitans, those who would "conquer the people" by operating a vast priestly hierarchy.

Finally, in the promise to the "overcomer," the true tree of life in the midst of the heavenly paradise of God brings Genesis to our minds, where the account of man's loss of access to the Edenic tree and earthly paradise is given.

II. Smyrna: The Loyal Church (2:8-11)
"The Persecuted Church that Persevered"

In this second letter, Christ emphasizes that he is the "first and the last," who had been "dead" but is "alive," a very appropriate encouragement to these persecuted Christians.

He refers to false sects that were rising to oppose true apostolic Christianity, not necessarily literal Jews, although some radical Israelites joined in attacks on Christian believers.

"Fear none of these things ... ye shall have tribulation ten days ... be thou faithful unto death." The Smyrnans literally were under great duress, exactly as here indicated, but there is a prophetic suggestion of the 10 terrible periods of persecution in the Roman Empire from about 64 to 316 A.D.

The crown of life, one of five crowns specifically promised for faithful obedience, will be worn by martyrs for Christ AND (James 1:12) by those who love Christ enough to live or die for Him, overcoming temptation.

III. Pergamos: The Lax Church (2:12-17)
"The Compromising Church that was Corrupted"

Christ stresses the right use of the Word-Sword as He exposes doctrinal errors that crept into this local assembly.

Two doctrinal aberrations are condemned. The "doctrine of Balaam" refers to the teaching, and advice of Balaam to Balak (Numbers 24:14), the Moabite king, to encourage his idolatrous people to intermingle and intermarry with the Israelites, resulting in God's judgment. This *doctrine of Balaam* means no separation between the godly and the ungodly, free intermingling with no standards of righteousness, always a sad condition in any church.

The other doctrinal error is that of the Nicolaitans, or what the reformers called "priestcraft."

Finally, in the promise to the overcomer, three blessings are assured: the hidden manna (Christ, the Bread of Life, in whom are hid all the treasures of wisdom and knowledge. See Colossians 2:3); second, the white stone, meaning approval or "not guilty" by virtue of Christ's atonement in contrast to a "black stone" which signified guilt. In some early courts of law, such stones were used as votes by juries to indicate "guilty or not guilty"—the white stone; third, engraved on the white stone for the believer in heaven is his own new and eternal name.

IV. Thyatira: The Loose Church (2:18-29)
"The Decadent Church that Drifted into Darkness"

Christ scrutinizes all hearts with his penetrating, fiery eyes, and can tread down with brazen feet the winepress of the judgment of God.

Almost all of this letter deals with that woman "Jezebel," perhaps named after that Old Testament queen who brought vile Baal worship into the Kingdom of Israel. Probably there was a woman in the Thyatiran church, whom the Lord here calls "Jezebel," who introduced idolatry and immorality into the congregation, departing from the teachings of Paul and the other apostles. But the principle of bringing in idolatry and immorality into the local church or into Christianity is also taught here, soundly condemned by Christ. Image veneration is idol worship. Immorality, both open and concealed, is evil. In these decadent days, as then, toleration of homosexuality, moral looseness and sexual sins is common.

In the promise to the "overcomers," there is an addition unique to this case. It is he that "overcometh and keepeth my work unto the end" that is to receive rulership in the kingdom age. While all true believers are "overcomers," only those faithful, loyal and dedicated share gloriously in the reign of Christ on this earth in the Millennium.

Outline of Chapter Two

Christ in the Midst of His Churches

OBJECTIVE: To reveal Christ appraising, judging and correcting conditions existent in His churches.
OUTLINE:

I. EPHESUS: The Lacking Church (2:1-7)
  A. The Address of the Administrator (1)
   1. An Epistle to the Messenger-minister
   2. An Epistle to the Ephesians (means *desirable)* (2)
   3. An Epistle from Jesus Christ (1)
     a. He holds the ministers
     b. He walks in the churches
  B. The Analysis of the Assembly (vs. 2-6)
   1. Appraisal (2-4)
     a. Full of works (2)
     b. Fundamental in doctrine (2)
     c. Faithful in labor (3)
     d. Failing in love (4). They "left their first love," thus were lacking
   2. Appeal (5)
     a. Remember ... previous ardor
     b. Repent ... of failing
     c. Renew ... first works OR ELSE there will be
     d. Removal of spiritual place and power.
   3. Approval (6) Fearless against Nicolaitans
  C. The Admonition by the Advocate (7)
   1. Open ears!
   2. Overcome! Promise of tree of life in paradise

II. SMYRNA: The Loyal Church (2:8-11)
  A. The Address of the Administrator
   1. An Epistle to the Messenger-minister (8)
   2. An Epistle to the Smyrnans (means *crushed)*
   3. An Epistle from Christ
     a. His eternality (first and last)
     b. His death and resurrection (in Time)
  B. The Analysis of the Assembly (9, 10)
  He says nothing negative about this church.
   1. Commendation (9)
     a. Knowledge about them: their works, tribulation, poverty, true riches
     b. Knowledge of their enemies: false Jews— synagogue of Satan
   2. Counsel (10)
     a. Fearlessness
     b. Foes to oppose
     c. Future: 10 days of tribulation
     d. Faithfulness—crown of life for martyrdom
  C. The Admonition by the Advocate
   1. Open ears!
   2. Overcome! Promise of no second death.

III. PERGAMOS: The Lax Church (2:12-17)
  A. The Address of the Administrator (12)
   1. An Epistle to the Messenger-minister (12)
   2. An Epistle to the Pergamosians (means *elevated or married)* (12)

   3. An Epistle from Christ. His sharp Word-Sword condemns or converts
  B. The Analysis of the Assembly (13-16)
   1. Their Dedicated Attitude (13)
     a. Their Dwelling at "Satan's seat"—place of idolatrous wickedness
     b. Their Determination —held Christ's Name
     c. Their Deaths—Antipas the martyr exemplifies
   2. Their Doctrinal Apostasy (14, 15)
     a. The Doctrine of Balaam
       The Teaching that separation from unbelievers is not a part of true religion (Study Numbers 22, 23, 24 and 25:1-5 with 2 Pet. 2:15,16 ; Jude 11.)
     b. The Teaching is the concept that the laity (Laitans) were to be ruled or conquered by the priestly hierarchy. Nicolaitanes: from "nikao," "to conquer," and "laos," people.
     c. The Directive of Christ: Repentance or Punishment—by the Word-Sword (see Hebrews 4:12)
  C. The Admonition by the Advocate (17)
   1. Open ears!
   2. Overcome! Promise of hidden manna, white stone, new name.

IV. THYATIRA: The Loose Church (2:18-29)
  A. The Address by the Administrator (18)
   1. An Epistle to the Messenger-minister (18)
   2. An Epistle to the Thyatirans (oppression)
   3. An Epistle from Christ
     a. He is the Son of God
     b. He has the flaming eyes, seeing all
     c. He has the brazen feet of judgment
  B. The Analysis of the Assembly (19-25)
   1. The Works (19) love, service, faith, patience, works increasing
   2. The Woman (20-23)
     a. Who she was: Jezebel—typified idolatrous teaching (see I Kings 16:30-33)
     b. What she did: taught error, seduced servants into sin, defiled through images
     c. How God dealt with her: allowed time for repentance
     d. What was in store for her: personal judgment, prospective tribulation, possible repentance, purging by death, punishment by the Lord
     e. What God says to the rest: those not following her doctrines are to hold to truth
  C. The Admonition by the Advocate (26-29)
   1. Overcome!
   2. Keep works and be rewarded. The only time rulership is promised in these seven admonitions is in association with faithfulness.
     a. Rulership promised
     b. Morning Star (Christ) promised
   3. Open ears!

Observations:
Spiritual lessons and applications from each verse
Chapter Two

1. Since Christ is walking in the midst of His churches, He is present at services, beholding all and upholding all who will recognize His presence.

2. Should we not repudiate evil and false teaching wherever it arises?

3. No Christian should "faint" and cease working because of hardship.

4. A church or Christian, who has "left" his first love, *lacks* that ardent love of Christ which is to be our primary motivation.

5. Churches and individuals sometimes need to *remember, repent* and *redo* their first works. What about your church and you?

6. Hatred of doctrinal error must never carry over into hatred of misguided individuals. In being controversial for Christ, we must not stoop to personal attacks in a hateful spirit.

7. To be a true Christian is to be an "overcomer," potentially. Compare 1 John 5:4, 5; Revelation 12:11. Christians are on the winning side. We should live like it.

8. How wonderful to know the LIVING CHRIST, indwelling your very being. History substantiates His literal resurrection. Our experience confirms it.

9. Earthly riches cannot be compared with heavenly rewards (see Romans 8:18).

10. It is not easy to suffer without fear, but Christ urges us to do it. Imprisonment for the cause of Christ has been the experience of millions of Christians through the centuries. Consider John on Patmos; John Bunyan at Bedford, writing *Pilgrim's Progress*; John Clarke in Boston in 1651; multitudes in dozens of countries in the 20th century. The ten days of persecution were literal in Smyrna, but foreshadow the ten great persecutions under Emperors Nero, Domitian, Trajan, Marcus Aurelius, Severus, Maximus, Decius, Valerian, Aurelian and Diocletian from 64 A.D. to 313 A.D.

11. In this promise to the "overcomers" is the positive guarantee that no believer can be hurt by the "second death," eternal separation from God (see 20:14, 15). Though physical death by martyrdom can occur, the second death will never affect the true believer. There is a reminder here that in Genesis is the account of the "first death," when man sinned, bringing upon the human race that just penalty (see Genesis 3; Romans 6:23).

12. Let us learn to wield the Sword of the Spirit.

13. The darker the night of iniquity, the brighter the light of our testimony should shine.

14. Many professing Christian churches today tolerate Balaamism (no separation) and Nicolaitanism (excessive separation of clergy from laity). All doctrinal errors should be opposed.

15. The weapon to be used against error is the Word-Sword, the Bible.

16. Many churches, even professing conservative churches, need to repent in view of divine displeasure. How about your church? You?

17. The "new name," individualized for every glorified overcomer, will doubtless be the name by which each will be known in eternity. No doubt each of us will greatly enjoy it.

18. Let us always be aware of the all-seeing gaze of Christ into our hearts.

19. Even in the worst conditions, Christ looks for something to commend.

20. Idolatry in any form and immorality of every kind is never endorsed by Christ, but rather condemned, as in the case of Jezebel (2 Kings 9:30-37).

21. God is ever longsuffering, ready to forgive the repentant.

22. Idolatry and evil with no repentance brings tribulation and misfortune.

23. Christ searches the deepest motives of the heart.

24. How often some, who suppose they have found some deep but heretical views, have really discovered the depths of Satan in a false cult.

25. Holding fast to truth is the duty of all.

26. The believers who are faithful not only enjoy the blessings of eternal life but the joy of ruling with Christ in the future.

27. The reward for faithfulness is rulership.

28. True overcomers always have Christ, the Morning Star, now and eternally, suggesting that we have Him who is the True light, the herald of the eternal day, for there is no light there.

29. Christ's words are also the Spirit's words. Heed them!

Quotations
From Other Expositors
Chapter Two

Letter to the Church at Ephesus (1-7)

"With five out of the seven, Christ finds serious fault; and in one of these five, He finds nothing whatever to commend. Two alone pass the solemn inspection, and they in contact with elements, which He quite condemns.

"The first and most distinguished was that of Ephesus. This Church was characterized by strong impulse toward God, earnestness, and zeal, and yet with a giving way in these qualities from what they were at first. He who holds the seven stars and walks in the midst of the candlesticks, found in Ephesus works, labor, endurance, steadfast opposition to evil, faithfulness and firmness in discipline, cheerfulness in bearing any burden for Christ's sake, and a just hatred of deeds and practices which Christ also hates. But He found there also this defect, which called for repentance and return to first works, if they would not be unchurched entirely: namely, that they had left their first love. There is such a thing as having and exercising a sharp penetration into the true and the false, a correctness of judgment in sacred things, a zealous and self-sacrificing devotion to the right and true, and an earnest-minded severance from false apostles and all evildoers, and yet being without that warmth and purity of love which is the first impulse in the breast of young disciples, and without which, well cherished and kept in vigorous life, there is unfitness to meet the judgment or to stand in it. And this was the sorry fault of the Church of Ephesus. Of course, it was not the estate of every particular member that is thus described."

–J.A. Seiss

"The Lord, even while reproving, has a further commendation to make. 'This thou hast, that thou hatest the deeds of the Nicolaitans, which I also hate.' Love must be a positive emotion; theirs was a negative emotion at best. Their love for the Lord, such as it was, manifested itself in a hatred of evil. All too often those who have forgotten how to love specialize in hating error. Error must be hated, of course, but there is something wrong when the Lord has to endorse the negative because he cannot find the positive. Even the endorsement He does give comes almost as an afterthought.

"The Lord saw the corporate Ephesian church in a fallen condition. He appeals to the individual, 'He that hath an ear, let him hear what the Spirit saith unto the churches; To him that overcometh will I give to eat of the tree of life, which is in the midst of the paradise of God.' Love is a personal matter. We are saved one by one; we must be restored one by one. No hint is given that the entire Ephesian church would respond to this letter, but the hope is that individuals would. When Adam fell, he lost Paradise, and he lost access to the tree of life. Here is a fallen church. It too has lost the paradise of bliss which comes from walking back to the daily quiet time with Himself. There is no other way to restore a lost love and a lost life. It is tragically possible to have a saved soul and a lost life."

–John Phillips

Letter to the Church at Smyrna (8-11)

"What the suffering Church was to the Lord is imaged in the meaning of Smyrna, myrrh — a well-known fragrant perfume, a sacred one moreover (Exod. 30.23), also one of the love perfumes of the spouse in the Canticles. The consolation that suited the Seer (Rev. 1.17,18) became the consolation of the Church. We have here the same combination of divine and human predicates, which characterized Christ in the glorious vision of His Person, as beheld by John. 'The First and the Last' is one of the grandest of divine titles, a Rock against which the utmost power of the enemy is futile. As 'the First,' He is before all in time, and above all as supreme. As 'the Last' He is after all, closing all up, for to Him all tend. He is eternal in His Being. But he stooped to die. Death had no claim on Him. He, 'the first and the last' — Jehovah's special title (Isa. chaps. 41-48) — became dead. He crested the waves of death. He rose out of it, and lives to die no more."

–Walter Scott

"As Ephesus characterizes the apostolic age of the first century, so Smyrna characterizes the period beginning about A.D. 64 and continuing to the persecution under Diocletian about A.D. 312. Again we might say it is doubtful that John knew the details of the prophetic era that was to continue for some 250 years beyond the time of writing.

"Do the Lord's words, 'ye shall have tribulation ten days' refer to the ten separate attempts to wipe out Christianity, prompted by the edicts of ten different Roman rulers? Or it is possible that the 'ten days' may allude to the tenth persecution under Diocletian, which lasted exactly ten years? Whatever the precise meaning of the 'tens days,' it suggests at least that the persecution would be for a

29

limited time.

"Dr. Walter L. Wilson sees in the number ten typically that which represents human failure. The ten spies failed to see God's power and provision, so they brought back an evil report (Num. 13:32). The ten tribes failed to walk with God and do His will, thus they established a separate kingdom given to idolatry (1 Kgs 11:31)."

–Lehman Strauss

Letter to the Church at Pergamos (12-17)

"If Ephesus was the New York of Asia, Pergamum was its Washington, for there the Roman imperial power had its seat of government. There also was built the earliest temple for the state-sponsored worship of the Emperor. Whether or not this was what Christ meant by 'the throne of Satan,' it emphasizes the kind of difficulties the Pergamene Christians had to face. For them Satan is not merely, as at Smyrna, a slanderer working through a group of ill-disposed Jews. He appears as the 'ruler of this world,' to take a phrase from John's Gospel (Jn. 14:30); and what John's first Letter would call 'the world' (1 Jn. 2:15) is in fact the great enemy of the church at Pergamum.

"In brief, Satan is working here through the pressures of non-Christian society. He persecutes; the suffering which will come to Smyrna has already come to Pergamum, and one at least has died a martyr's death (verse 13b). He seduces; the Nicolaitans we met at Ephesus are here also, and their teaching is apparently of the same kind as that of Balaam, who had led God's people into sin long before (Nu. 31:16; 25:1-3). Both the sins mentioned in verse 14 may be taken literally. Both appeared in the time of Balaam, both reappeared in the New Testament church (1 Cor. 5 and 8), and the pathway to them is the kind of temptation which is typical of worldliness in any age: 'Where is the harm in it? Everyone else does it; why shouldn't you?' "

–Michael Wilcock

"The Church of the Pergamum period showed in its early stages the purifying effects of the Smyrna sufferings. Dwelling where Satan's throne was, the whole world lying in the Wicked One, the Church held fast the name and the faith of Jesus. But just then Emperor Constantine's professed conversion occurred and the Church yielded to the temptation her Lord had overcome and allied herself with the world and settled down at ease. Church and State were united and the Church became the world's mistress. Whole legions of soldiers were marched to the rivers and baptized — not into Christ indeed, but 'into favor.' Heathen temples became 'Christian churches' and heathen priests became 'Christian priests.' This alliance with the world is the doctrine of Balaam so strongly condemned and the deeds of the Nicolaitans are now based upon a recognized doctrine, which thing the Lord hates. Judgment is again threatened for the corrupt Church and deliverance for the overcomer."

–William Pettingill

Letter to the Church at Thyatira (18-29)

"Thyatira symbolizes the longest of the church periods — about 1,000 years. Beginning with the sixth century, it lasts through till the seventeenth century. B. Holzhauser, a Roman Catholic writer, says, 'Thyatira is the middle church of the seven, and consequently stands as the symbol of the church of the Middle Ages' (*The Apocalypse,* page 158).

"A change came at the end of the Thyatiran period when the great Reformation arose. Such men as Luther, Knox, Calvin, Zwingli, and scores of others came to lead the people back to God."

–Roy Allan Anderson

"To understand this well, we need to go back to Israel's history in the days of King Ahab. Jezebel was adept in the art of mixing. She undertook to unite in one the religion of Israel and the religion of Phoenicia. That is just what Romanism is — a mixture of Heathenism and Christianity and Judaism. It is not Christianity — yet there is in it quite a little that is Christian. Where did its superstition and image worship come from? It was all taken bodily over from heathenism, under the plea that it would help to convert the pagans. The church became very accommodating.

"Romanism is Christianity, Judaism, and Heathenism joined together; and the Lord abhors the vile combination. Note two things that He holds against Rome — spiritual fornication and idolatry. The first is the union of the church and the world: and 'the friendship of the world is enmity against God.' Idolatry is the worship of images, strictly forbidden in the second commandment (Ex. 20:4, 5). God gave her space to repent and she repented not. Go back to the days of Savonarola in Italy, Wickliffe and Crammer of England, John Knox in Scotland, Martin Luther in Germany, Zwingle in Switzerland, Calvin in France — all those mighty reformers whom God raised up throughout the world to call Rome to repent of her iniquity, but 'she repented not.' "

–H. A. Ironside

Christ Forecasts the History of Christianity
An Expository Sermon

Chapter Two

The Things Which Are (Part 1)
Listen to the Spirit!

Introduction

In the second and third chapters of Revelation are Christ's seven special messages to these selected first-century churches. Outside of the gospels, only here are to be found the direct instructions of the Head of the church, Jesus Christ.

At least four purposes are involved:

First, there is the PRACTICAL PURPOSE. These were real historical churches in which the actual conditions described existed. Christ speaks to commend, condemn and correct each church, dealing directly with problems and giving His prescribed solutions. Even as Christ dealt with issues specifically in A.D. 95, when this was most likely written, so does He now. These congregations were historical entities. Christ appraises and discusses their state.

Second, there is a PLUMB LINE PURPOSE. Each church, as measured and evaluated by Christ, gives us an example as to how the Administrator of the Church may deal with similar situations in churches today. As He drops His "plumb line" beside your church, how does it measure up? Most any professing true church can be compared to one of these seven. They are therefore seven typical examples, each one applicable to local church conditions.

Third, there is a PROMISSORY PURPOSE. Christ's seven promises to overcomers are applicable, not only to the believers in these historical congregations, but to any believer in any age. (See I John 5:4, 5).

"Who is he that overcometh the world, but he that believeth ..."

Fourth, there is a PROPHETICAL PURPOSE. It is no coincidental happenstance that there is a fascinating general parallel between these seven churches, successively considered, and seven obvious eras or periods in the history of Christendom in the world. This is a divinely inspired foreview of the overall history of Christianity from the Apostolic Age until the Advent of Christ. Only in the last few centuries could this meaning be more fully comprehended, as the historic events unfolded in accordance with the divinely foreseen panorama of church history.

Each message contains a commendation, most of them a condemnation, a correction, and a call to overcome. But here we shall view each one of them as containing (1) an address by the Administrator; (2) an analysis of the assembly; and (3) an admonition from the Advocate.

In this message, we are focusing attention on the prophetic aspects of Christ's messages to his seven churches. Each letter contains suggestions, foreseen by the Head of the Church, of conditions that prevailed in seven successive eras in the history of Christianity, covering the entire church age. This in no wise nullifies the historical, practical or personal applications of truths here to Christians of every age. In chapter two, four of the churches are described, also indicating four periods in church history bringing us from about 95 A.D. to approximately 1500 A.D. The periods overlap, and dates are general.

I. Ephesus, the Lacking Church (70-100 A.D.)
The Age of Apostles (1-7)

Founded by Paul the Apostle, the Ephesian church prospered under the shadow of Diana worship (Acts 19). To this congregation Paul sent his marvelous Ephesian epistle with its emphasis on spiritual riches, the spiritual walk and the spiritual warfare. It symbolizes the Apostolic Age, of which John was the last survivor.

Even in these formative times, fledgling Christianity in general had already "left" their first love.

Being "fundamental" is not enough. A fervent first love for Christ must be maintained. This kind of ardent devotion was waning; therefore, the church was lacking in love, indicative of late first century Christianity everywhere.

II. Smyrna, the Loyal Church (90-316 A.D.)
The Age of Persecutions (8-11)

Even the word *smyrna* means "myrrh," that aromatic substance, which was crushed to enhance its fragrance.

John's disciple, Polycarp, even at the time of writing, may have been the "angel" of the church. He died a martyr's death in 155 A.D. at a very advanced age, testifying that he had known and served the Lord for 86 years.

For over two centuries, from Nero, who had

Paul executed, until Diocletian in the early 4th century, Christians were intermittently persecuted. Multiplied millions died martyr's deaths, some crucified or burned at the stake, others thrown to the lions or exiled. Ten great periods of persecution, catalogued by the historian Gibbon, are indicated in Christ's prediction of having persecution "ten days."

"The blood of the martyrs was the seed of the church." By the end of the 200's, millions of Christians were scattered all over the Roman Empire from England to India. The new aspirant to the imperial throne, Constantine succeeded the cruel Diocletian, whose vigorous persecutions lasted from 303 to about 313, about 10 years. Constantine claimed to have seen a cross in the sky, and chose it as his symbol, professing to become a Christian.

III. Pergamos, the Lax Church (316-600 A.D.)
The Age of Compromise (12-17)

Conditions described here closely resemble the historical developments of these three centuries after the Edict of Toleration issued by the Emperor Constantine, who also held the title Pontifex Maximus and was a "bishop" of the church.

During this period, as Christianity succeeded paganism, much of the old order of heathen worship was preserved. Temples to idols became church edifices. In 431 at the Council of Ephesus, the title "Mother of God" was applied to the Virgin Mary, an act which ended Diana worship, but instituted a new female figure for adoration. Doctrinal declension (the doctrine of Balaam ... no separation and the doctrine of the Nicolaitans ... a clergical hierarchy above laity) took place.

But, as always, there were still true believers, both in and out of the professing church. By 538, the Emperor Justinian appointed the Bishop of Rome (the Pope) to be "Corrector of Heretics," giving him temporal and ecclesiastical authority over all the churches of Christendom.

Anabaptists and others resisted, to their own hurt.

Christianity became a powerful political force. Many people professed to become Christians and church members to be a part of the power structure and the prevailing society. "Christianity began to wear the garments of heathenism."

During this period the Pope of Rome and the Patriarch of Constantinople became the two hierarchical leaders of the Western (Roman) and Eastern (Greek Orthodox) wings of organized Christianity.

IV. Thyatira, the Loose Church (600-1500 A.D.)
The Age of Darkness (18-29)

"The Dark Ages" is what the long period is sometimes called. During this time, Charlemagne and later German emperors established the Holy Roman Empire in western and central Europe. In 1054, the Pope of Rome excommunicated the Patriarch of Constantinople, religious leader of the Eastern Catholics in the Eastern Roman Empire (Byzantine Empire, named after Byzantium, ancient name of Constantinople). The patriarch retaliated in kind; each condemned the other and their successors to hell. Monasticism arose. European civilization entered the age of feudalism. Cities waned. But groups like the Waldenses tried to restore biblical truth, suffering persecution from Roman religionists. "Jezebel," the heathen queen who introduced idolatrous Baal worship into ancient Israel (800 B.C.) typically and prophetically indicates the rise of image worship, veneration of saints, relics and other heathen practices that prevailed during the Middle Ages in the professing church.

But there were always true believers, true born again people; God is never without witness.

"The last works" were better than the first. Toward the end of this period, great men like John Wycliffe in England, Savonorola in Italy and John Huss who preceded the Reformation, sought to bring revival and restoration to heathenized Christianity, closing the age of moral and spiritual looseness and darkness.

While Christ is the Morning Star, of course, John Wycliffe is sometimes called "the morning star of the Reformation."

And finally, always in every age, the promise of his coming looms in the future as a beacon of hope.

"But that which ye have already, hold fast till I come" (v. 25).

In spite of all the dark years of history and the trends of today as well, Christ will come in glorious power in due time to reign in sublime splendor.

A Commentary on the Revelation
Expository, Exegetical, Devotional and Practical
Greek words from the Textus Receptus

Chapter Two

The Letter to the Church at Ephesus (1-7)

1. Ephesus, a major seaport, where Paul labored for three years (Acts 19), famous for the Temple of Diana, one of the Seven Wonders of the Ancient World. Evidently, John made it the headquarters of his ministry in his latter years ... **who walketh in the midst of the seven golden candlesticks** (*ho peripaton en meso ton hepta luchion ton chruson*) — walketh about continually, thus expressing "His unwearied activity in the churches, guarding from internal and external evils, as the High Priest moved to and fro in the ancient sanctuary" (J.F.B.). **2. works** (*erga*) — indicating industrious and earnest activity. **labor** (*kopon*) — labor unto weariness, toil ... **patience** (*hupomonen*) — showing perservering endurance ... **canst not bear them which are evil** — not tolerating immorality, doctrinal aberrations, divisiveness ... **which say they are apostles** — possibly Judaizers; those who claim apostleship or divine authorization are to be tried and tested by the Word of God (See Isaiah 8:20) ... **liars** (*pseudeis*) — hence psuedo-Christians, fake and false ... **3. hast not fainted** (*kekopiakas*) — they did not grow fainthearted, weary and exhausted, but kept on in their loyalty to Christ. **4. Nevertheless** (*alla*) — The Lord sees defects and shortcomings and must in honesty correct them. ... **hast left** (*aphekas*) — "deserted, abandoned or drifted away from thy first love" (Garner). (See John 13:34; 14:21). **5. Remember** (*mnemoneue*) — hence mnemonics, the study and cultivation of the memory ... **thou art fallen** — (*peptokas*) — **remove** (*kineso*) — exercising effort and energy to do it ... taking from them, as a local congregation the empowering of administration of His work. Some churches have had their "candlestick" removed, no longer valiantly serving God in love and effectiveness. **6. Nicolaitans** — Some church fathers thought these were erring followers of Nicolas, one of the seven men appointed to care for the widows in the early church (Acts 6:5). More likely, they were, as the name means, "conquerors of the people," prophetically forecasting the rise of priestcraft over the laity. J.F.B. says, they were "professing Christians who, like Balaam of old, tried to introduce into the church a false freedom, i.e. licentiousness, as in Jude 4, "turning the grace of our God into lasciviousness." **7. paradise of God** (*paradeiso tou theou*) — Eden, the garden of God, was the original paradise. See Genesis 2:15; Luke 23:43, where the abode of the righteous is meant; and 2 Cor. 12:4, where Paul was caught up into paradise, into God's presence. It is now synonymous with heaven. See Ezekiel 28:23.

The Letter to the Church at Smyrna (8-11)

8. Smyrna, north of Ephesus, a congregation pastored by Polycarp for decades and who died as a martyr in 155 A.D. in his 90s. Only the city of Smyrna remains to this day, now called Izmir ... all other cities in the seven are in ruins. **9. poverty** (*ptocheian*) — they endured much suffering and confiscation of worldly goods, but they were spiritually **rich** (*plousios*) — as in plutocratic, meaning rule by the rich. See 2 Cor. 8:9 and 1 Tim. 6:18: "rich in good works ..." **blasphemy** (*blasphemian*) of **them which say they are Jews and are not** — some claimed to be Jews, but were without Christ and had a form of godliness. Some people today claim to be God's special people, but are not, but members of false cults. The Jewish people of course have a special destiny (see Romans 11:25-28). Any center of false worship may be a "synagogue of Satan," regardless of its name. **10. Fear none** (*me phobou*) — do not fear any of the things you are about to suffer as a church or as individuals ... **behold the devil** — "The Captain of our salvation never keeps back what those who faithfully witness for Him may have to suffer for His name's sake: never entices recruits by the promise they shall find all things pleasant and easy there" (Trench), but opposition from Satan is to be expected. See John 15:18,19 ... **devil** (*diabolos*) — means accuser ... **tribulation ten days** — a forecast of the ten major persecutions, but that does not nullify the literal meaning of ten actual days of terrible persecution the historical church at Smyrna suffered ... **crown of life** (*stephanon tes zoes*) — a crown is promised to the martyrs and those victorious over temptation, as in James 1:12 ... **11. second death** (*thanatous tou deuterou*) — a term found only in Revelation (See 20:15).

The Letter to the Church at Pergamos (12-17)

12. Pergamos — about 100 miles north of Ephesus, it was the capital of the kingdom of Pergamum, bequeathed by Attalus II to the Romans in about 133 B.C. Here was a center of education, where Babylonian wisdom, culture and cultism were maintained after the decline of that city. A temple to Aesculapius, a serpent-god, was erected here, the reconstruction of which is now in Germany and is a museum. Christians would regard this evil idolatry as Satanic in origin, spawned by that old serpent, the devil; hence it was "Satan's throne." **13.** Much persecution was directed against Christians in this citadel of idolatry and Babylonian cultic teaching. Attalus was "Pontifex Maximus," a title adopted by Roman emperors and used by popes today! **Antipas was my faithful martyr** (*ho martus mou ho pistos*) — the name Antipas means "against all," which indicates his opposition to evil by divine design; thus he was martyred for the faith. It is said he was shut up in a red hot brazen bull and ended his life in praise and prayer. **14. doctrine of Balaam** — his teaching to Balak (Numbers 31:15,16; 22:5; 23:8) was how to corrupt the Israelites who could not be cursed, by teaching them to marry Gentile women of Moab, defying their separation as a holy people and adopting heathen practices and customs ... **stumblingblock** (*skandalon*) — it was a scandalous tripping block, which caused the children of Israel much grief. They, and the Pergamosian Christians, both fell into idolatry and false worship and into immorality ... **and to commit fornication** (*kai porneusai*) — hence pornography in English and meaning immoral and promiscuous behavior. **15. doctrine of the Nicolaitans** — what was "deeds" at Ephesus became a "doctrine" at Pergamos. **16. sword of my mouth** reminds us also of the Angel of the Lord threatening (invisibly) Balaam in Numbers 22:31. The spiritual Balaamites would be smitten with the Lord"s spiritual sword ... **17. hidden manna** (*manna tou kerummenou*) — an allusion to the hidden pot of manna in the Ark, symbolical of Christ, the Bread of Life (Ex. 16:33; Heb. 9:4; John 6:51,58), suggesting eternal provision. **white stone** (*psephon leuken*) — a symbol of acceptance, approval, not a "blackball," but acquital and removal of charges, not guilty.

The Letter to the Church at Thyatira (18-29)

18. Thyatira — Lydia, the seller of purple (Acts 16:14,15) was from this smaller city, famous for manufacturing. **19. works** (*erga*) ... **charity** (*agapen*-love of the highest sort) ... **service** (*diakonian*-from which the word deacon is derived) ... **faith** (*pistis*-usual word for faith) ... **patience** (*hupomonen*), also indicating endurance and perseverance. **20. Notwithstanding** (*alla*), the same word is translated "nevertheless" in 2:4, meaning "but" in the strongest sense ... **Jezebel** — that there was an

historical "Jezebel" at the Thyatiran church is certain, but she can be compared to the wife of Israel's King Ahab (circa 800 B.C.), who brought in Baal worship, idolatry and much evil into the culture of Israel. Elijah stood against all of this. Study 1 Kings 16:31,32; 11 Kings 9:22,30. "Her spiritual counterpart at Thyatira lured God's 'servants' to the same libertinism, fornications and eating of idol meats, as did the Baalamites (vs. 6,14,15). By a false spiritualism these seducers led their victims into grossest carnality, as though things done in the flesh were outside the true man and were therefore indifferent" (J.F.B.) **22. cast into a bed** — implying a bed of sickness or pain and anguish. Idolatry, sin, immorality always carry a price and exact a toll. **23. kill with death** — the wages of sin (Romans 6:23). Jezebel was not saved, neither the Old Testament queen or this wicked woman at Thyatira. **23. all churches shall know** — other congregations would learn from the judgment of God upon the Thyatiran church and the false teacher Jezebel. **24. depths of Satan** — these false prophets claimed they knew more than others of the mysteries of God, but their teachings were of the devil. The original sin of Adam was a desire to know evil as well as good. **25. Hold fast till I come** — until the Rapture, cling to true doctrine, love, service, faith, patience as in vs. 19. **26. keepeth my works unto the end** — the only one of the seven promises to overcomers with an additional condition. **27. rule them with a rod of iron** — compare Psalm 2:8,9; Dan. 7:22; Heb. 1:8-12 and Isaiah 30:14. **28. morning star** (*astera ton proinon*) — Christ is the Star as in 22:16; See also 2 Peter 1:19.

RAINBOWS FROM REVELATION
The Revelation of Jesus Christ
A chapter by chapter, verse by verse study
"There was a rainbow round about the throne like unto an emerald" (4:3)

CHAPTER THREE: He That Hath An Ear, Let Him Hear II

References

Rev. 1:4,16

Matt. 5:48

1 Tim. 6:20
Rev. 3:19
Matt. 24:42,43
1 Thess. 5:2
2 Pet. 3:10

Acts 1:15
Jude 23
Eph. 4:1

Rev. 19:8
Ex. 32:32
Luke 12:8

Rev. 2:7, etc.

Acts 3:14
1 John 5:20
Isa. 22:22
Matt. 16:19

1 Cor. 16:9
2 Cor. 2:12

Isa. 49:23

2 Pet. 2:9
Matt. 24:21
Dan. 12:1
Mark 13:19

Phil. 4:5
2 John 8
1 Cor. 9:25-27

1. AND unto the angel of the church in Sar-dis write; These things saith he that hath the seven Spirits of God, and the seven stars; I know thy works, that thou hast a name that thou livest, and art dead.

2. Be watchful, and strengthen the things which remain, that are ready to die: for I have not found thy works perfect before God.

3. Remember therefore how thou hast received and heard, and hold fast, and repent. If therefore thou shalt not watch, I will come on thee as a thief, and thou shalt not know what hour I will come upon thee.

4. Thou hast a few names even in Sardis which have not defiled their garments; and they shall walk with me in white: for they are worthy.

5. He that overcometh, the same shall be clothed in white raiment; and I will not blot out his name out of the book of life, but I will confess his name before my Father, and before his angels.

6. He that hath an ear, let him hear what the Spirit saith unto the churches.

7. And to the angel of the church in Philadelphia write; These things saith he that is holy, he that is true, he that hath the key of David, he that openeth, and no man shutteth, and no man openeth;

8. I know thy works: behold, I have set before thee an open door, and no man can shut it: for thou hast a little strength, and hast kept my word, and hast not denied my name.

9. Behold I will make them of the synagogue of Satan, which say they are Jews, and are not, but do lie; behold, I will make them to come and worship before thy feet, and to know that I have loved thee.

10. Because thou hast kept the word of my patience, I also will keep thee from the hour of temptation, which shall come upon all the world, to try them that dwell upon the earth.

11. Behold, I come quickly: hold that fast which thou hast, that no man take thy crown.

12. Him that overcometh will I make a pillar in the temple of my God, and he shall go no more out: and I will write upon him the name of my God, and the name of the city of my God, and the name of the city of my God, which is new Jerusalem, which cometh down out of heaven from my God: and I will write upon him my new name.

13. He that hath an ear, let him hear what the Spirit saith unto the churches.

14. And unto the angel of the church of the Laodiceans write; These things saith the A-men, the faithful and true witness, the beginning of the creation of God;

15. I know thy works, that thou art neither cold nor hot: I would thou wert cold or hot.

16. So then because thou art lukewarm, and neither cold nor hot, I will spue thee out of my mouth.

17. Because thou sayest, I am rich, and increased with goods, and have need of nothing; and knowest not that thou art wretched, and miserable, and poor, and blind, and naked:

18. I counsel thee to buy of me gold tried in the fire, that thou mayest be rich; and white raiment, that thou mayest be clothed, and that the shame of thy nakedness do not appear; and anoint thine eyes with eyesalve, that thou mayest see.

19. As many as I love, I rebuke and chasten: be zealous therefore, and repent.

20. Behold, I stand at the door, and knock: if any man hear my voice, and open the door, I will come in to him, and will sup with him, and he with me.

21. To him that overcometh will I grant to sit with me in my throne, even as I also overcame, and am set down with my Father in his throne.

22. He that hath an ear, let him hear what the Spirit saith unto the churches.

References

1 Kings 7:21
Ps. 23:6
Heb. 12:22
Rev. 21:2
Rev. 22:4

Rev. 2:7, etc.

2 Cor. 1:20
Col 1:15

Rev. 3:1,8

Heb. 12:8

Isa. 55:1
2 Cor. 5:3

Job 5:17
Heb. 12:6
Titus 2:14

S. of Sol. 5:2
Luke 12:37
John 14:23

Mat. 19:28
John 16:33

Rev. 2:7, etc.

Scriptures for Comparison

Matthew 16:18
"And I say also unto thee, That thou art Peter, and upon this rock I will build my church; and the gates of hell shall not prevail against it."

Summary of Chapter Three

The Things Which Are (Part 2)

I. Sardis: The Lifeless Church (1-6)
"The Dead Church That Still Had Lights"

Since Christ has the Spirit's power (see Isaiah 11:12) and holds the ministers of the church, He will remedy any situation, if he is so allowed, but He does not coerce His people. Their name, or reputation, was that of life, but their true condition was deadness.

Yet all is not quite dead ... some things are about ready to die, like their devotion, dedication and zeal. Their external appearance, which seemed acceptable, covered up an internal dying condition and imperfect works before God. How like many believers and churches today!

When Christ indicated that the church was "dead," we may surmise that there was little lacking in the outward appearance of the church. They may have been a beehive of organized activity. They may even have had a reputation for being a forward-looking and progressive church, for they "had a name that they lived." But "man looketh on the outward appearance, but God looketh on the heart" (1 Sam. 16:7); therefore Christ with his eyes as a flame of fire pierced through the facade, diagnosing the real nature of their spiritual malady.

He did not find their works "perfect" before God, which means literally "finished" or "complete." The Great Physician felt their spiritual pulse and pronounced them "dead."

The "few names even in Sardis" historically and originally were the faithful and spiritual believers; prophetically, the passage speaks of the early leaders of the Reformation and emerging "anabaptists" of 500 years ago.

Notice that the promise of Christ assures that no true believer will be "blotted out," a promise of eternal security for overcomers, not a suggestion of being "blotted out." The verse says precisely that this will not happen.

II. Philadelphia: The Loving Church (17-13)
"The Church with the Open Door"

Here is the only church in which Christ finds no blemishes; to which he gives no warnings. Be sure to compare Isaiah 22:22: "And the key of the house of David will I lay upon his shoulder; so he shall open, and none shall shut; and he shall shut, and none shall open." This congregation had a great opportunity to evangelize, as has Christendom in the last several centuries.

Even the erring peoples called here "the synagogue of Satan," will acknowledge the true and beloved people of God. This may refer to those who claimed to be God's people in New Testament times, but were not really Jews. In a larger sense, it applies to all who claim to be God's people, but are not.

To be kept from the hour of temptation, most premillennialists believe, means that true believers are to be raptured before the Tribulation. "Hour of temptation" is thought to be synonymous with "the Great Tribulation." This is evident from the following verse, which says, "Behold, I come quickly."

While the promise of being kept from "the hour of temptation" may have had its partial fulfillment in the deliverance of the church at Philadelphia from the terrible persecutions under Domitian, from which John also suffered, the prophetic fulfillment will be realized by the born-again overcomers: the true regenerated believers, who will be caught up into the air, prior to the coming of that awful "great tribulation," which will "try them that dwell upon the earth"; a "time of trouble such as never was since there was a nation even to that time" (Dan. 12:1); an "affliction, such as was not from the beginning of creation, which God created unto this time, neither shall be" (Mark 13:19).

"That no man take thy crown" is a cautionary observation, for Christ wants each of us to receive a full reward. To fail to hold fast, and backslide, could lead to loss of rewards to someone else who did serve God.

In the promise to the overcomers Christ speaks of permanence, as today we have "pillars of the community." The "names" here suggest insignias or stamps of ownership, thus the believers in glory will wear, as it were, the name of God (relationship), the name of the New Jerusalem (citizenship) and the new name of Christ (ownership forever).

III. Laodicea: The Lukewarm Church (14-22)
"The Rich Church that Nauseates Christ"

Christ, who is the Amen (the Ending) and the Beginning, finds nothing in this church to commend.

Their lukewarm condition, not hot with fiery zeal nor cold with utter departure from the truth, is utterly distasteful to our Lord. The church claimed wealth and affluence, but in the sight of God had nothing of real value.

These Laodiceans needed the "deity of Christ" (gold tried in fire), and true righteousness of Christ (not merely external values), and the "eyesalve" of spiritual illumination from Christ by the Holy Spirit.

Does not this depict much of professing Christendom today?

Outline of Chapter Three

Christ Speaks to His Churches

OBJECTIVE: To reveal Christ walking in the midst of His churches, appraising, judging, and correcting within, with the aim of stimulating true believers or overcomers to love for Christ in the light of heavenly rewards.

OUTLINE:

I. SARDIS: The Lifeless Church (3:1-6)
A. The Address of the Administrator (1)
  1. An Epistle to the Angel-messenger.
  2. An Epistle to the Sardians (means *remnant*)
  3. An Epistle from Christ
    a. He has the Sevenfold Spirit—source of power
    b. He holds the seven stars—servants who preach
B. The Analysis of the Assembly. (1b-4)
  1. The Appraisal of Christ (1, 2)
    a. Works imperfect (works without worthfulness)
    b. Witness insufficient (reputation without reality—living but dead)
  2. The Appeal of Christ (1, 2)
    a. Be watchful
    b. Strengthen the remaining things
    c. Remember past blessings
    d. Hold fast
    e. Repent
  3. The Approach of the Judge (3) Christ will come as a thief
  4. The Approbation of the Remnant (4)
    a. Garments not defiled ... purity.
    b. To walk in white ... perfection.
    c. They are worthy ... position.
C. The Admonition of the Advocate (5,6)
  1. Promises for the Overcomers (5)
    a. Purity in eternity (white raiment)
    b. Security and certainty (name not blotted out)
    c. Publicity in glory (confessed in heaven)
  2. Plea for "Open ears"

II. PHILADELPHIA: The Loving Church (7-13)
A. The Address of the Administrator (7)
  1. An Epistle to the Angel-messenger (7)
  2. An Epistle to the Philadelphians (means *brotherly love*) (7)
  3. An Epistle from Christ,
    a. He is holy
    b. He is true
    c. He has the key of David (see Isaiah 22:22)
    d. He opens and no man shuts
    e. He shuts and no man opens
B. The Analysis of the Assembly (8-11)
  1. Their Power (8)
    a. An open door promised
    b. A little strength used
    c. A Bible—loyalty kept
    d. A fidelity maintained
  2. Their Protection (9)
    Even false teachers must recognize God's true people.
  3. Their Preservation (10)
    Philadelphians to be kept from the "hour of temptation" i.e. preserved from the Great Tribulation.
  4. Their Prospect (11)
    The Second Coming with its rewards (see 2 Jn 8)
C. The Admonition of the Advocate (12, 13)
  1. Promise to overcomers
    a. Pillars—permanency
    b. Insignias
    . Name of God - relationship
    . Name of city - citizenship
    . Name of Christ - ownership
  2. Plea for "open ears"

III. LAODICEA: The Lukewarm Church (14-22)
A. The Address of the Administrator (14)
  1. An Epistle to the Angel-messenger (14)
  2. An Epistle to the Laodiceans (*rule by the people*) (14)
  3. An Epistle from Christ
    a. He is the Amen
    b. He is the Faithful and True Witness
    c. He is the Beginning of the Creation of God
B. The Analysis of the Assembly (15-20)
  1. The Complaint (15, 16)
    a. Their works known (15)
    b. Their lukewarmness condemned (15, 16)
    c. Their impending judgment (16) To be spewed out ...
  2. The Condition (17)
    a. Professed to be rich, but poor
    b. Knowing not they were
      -Wretched
      -Miserable
      -Poor
      -Blind
      -Naked
  3. The Counsel (18, 19)
    a. Buy gold—typifies Christ's deity
    b. Buy white raiment—typifies spiritual righteousness
    c. Anoint eyes with eyesalve—typifies spiritual illumination
    d. Be zealous
    e. Repent
  4. The Call (20)
    Christ outside the door of His church, knocking to be admitted
C. The Admonition of the Advocate (21, 22)
  1. Promise for overcomers—glorious enthronement
  2. Plea for "open ears"
    Last time "church" appears in the whole book until 22:16.

Observations:
Spiritual lessons and applications from each verse
Chapter Three

1. Let us guard against a profession without possession, a name without life. Many an unsaved church member is in this category.

2. Christ knows our works ... He looks on the heart. Your outside may look good, but it is the inside of your heart that counts.

3. Repentance is the necessary step that leads the erring church back to fellowship with God, but not many are in the mood for that.

4. Notice three uses of "name:" a facade name (1); faithful names (4); future names confessed (5).

5. If we walk with the Lord here, we will there, as well.

6. Notice, the individual in the church is to "hear." Will you open your ears, individual believer?

7. When Christ opens a door, we should enter with faith and zeal.

8. Always be aware that "a little strength" is sufficient when God is in it.

9. Never forget that God loves you. Even our enemies should see that.

10. Keeping His Word patiently is what Christ asks of us. Let us do it.

11. Never let go of God's blessings, clinging to His promises.

12. Take comfort in knowing you belong to God forever.

14. As the "Amen," He will conclude all history; as the "faithful and true witness," He has performed His ministry; as the "beginning of the creation of God," He always has been (see John 1:1-4).

15. Few things are more displeasing in a church than "lukewarmness."

16. Lukewarmness nauseates the Lord.

17. Material wealth is no sign of the true blessing of God, regardless of what some "prosperity teachers" say.

18. Being acceptable to God is the most important part of Christianity.

20. While this verse may be used as a gospel invitation, its true meaning conveys the idea of Christ outside His own church knocking to get in. Is that the case with churches today? Denominations?

22. The conclusion of "the things which are," about the churches and the church age comes with verse 22.

The sum of attitudes and actions, spiritual or unspiritual, creates the character of the assembly. Thus many individuals in each of these churches (there were always some overcomers) have the characteristics of the church described.

How about you? Are you an/a:

Ephesian, who is sound in doctrine, but you've left your first love?

Smyrnan, so dedicated you can either live or die for Christ?

Pergamite, messed up in doctrine and conduct?

Thyatiran, involved in immorality, carnality, even idolatry (hedonism, selfism, occultism)?

Sardian, practically dead, with a reputation without reality?

Philadelphian, loving God and brethren, faithfully serving?

Laodicean, lukewarm, self-satisfied, materialistic?

LIVE LIKE AN OVERCOMER!

Quotations
From Other Expositors
Chapter Three

First, here is a summary, from the prophetic perspective, of all the seven churches:

Chapters Two and Three

"These seven Churches, then besides being literal historical Churches, stand for the entire Christian body, in all periods of its history. But how, or in what respects? Upon this point, let me add a word or two before I close.

"The seven Churches represent seven phases or periods in the Church's history, stretching from the time of the apostles to the coming again of Christ, the characteristics of which are set forth partly in the names of these Churches, but more fully in the epistles addressed to them. There has been an Ephesian period — a period of warmth and love and labor for Christ, dating directly from the apostles, in which defection began by the gradual cooling of the love of some, the false professions of others, and the incoming of undue exaltations of the clergy and Church offices. Then came the Smyrna period — the era of martyrdom, and of the sweet savor unto God of faithfulness unto death, but marked with further developments of defection in the establishment of castes and orders, the licence of Judaizing propensities, and consequent departures from the true simplicities of the Gospel. Then followed the Pergamite period, in which true faith more and more disappeared from view, and clericalism gradually formed itself into a system, and the Church united with the world, and Babylon began to rear itself aloft. Then came the Thyatiran period — the age of purple and glory for the corrupt priesthood, and of darkness for the truth; the age of effeminacy and clerical domination, when the Church usurped the place of Christ, and the witnesses of Jesus were given to dungeons, stakes and inquisitions; the age of the enthronement of the false prophetess, reaching to the days of Luther and the Reformation. Then came the Sardian period — the age of separation and return to the rule of Christ; the age of comparative freedom from Balaam and his doctrines, from the Nicolaitans and their tenets, from Jezebel and her fornications; an age of many worthy names, but marked with deadness withal, and having much of which to repent; an age covering the spiritual lethargy of the Protestant centuries before the great evangelical movements of the last hundred years, which brought us the Philadelphian era, marked by a closer adherence to the written word, and more fraternity among Christians, but now rapidly giving place to Laodicean lukewarmness, self-sufficiency, empty profession, and false peace, in which the day of judgment is to find the unthinking multitude who suppose they are Christians and are not."

– J. A. Seiss

Letter to the Church at Sardis (1-6)

"Sardis means 'a remnant,' or, 'those who have escaped.' This is surely very significant, and tells its own story too plainly to be misunderstood. It brings before us, prophetically, the great State-churches of the Reformation, who escaped from Rome only to fall eventually (alas, that it should be so) into cold, lifeless formalism.

"It is plainly to be seen, from the first verse, that there is a measure of return to early principles. The Lord's introduction of Himself to this church is very similar to that in the letter to Ephesus, and yet the difference is most marked. Here He is said to have the seven stars in His right hand. It is, at least, the recognition that ministry belongs to Christ. Ministers are Christ's ministers, not the Church's. Yet, even in the glorious days of the Reformation, the truth was not fully apprehended that ministers are to be controlled by, and subject to, Christ, without any human intermediary. While the Protestant ministry is very different from the Romish hierarchy, unfortunately human ordination has done much to becloud a proper conception of the servant's responsibility to the Master.

"The Lord declares solemnly, 'I know thy works, that thou hast a name that thou livest, and art dead.' How sad and solemn the indictment! One might well ask in amazement, How can such things be after the blessing and revival of Reformation days? But when we remember that the State-churches were, from the first, intended to include all the population of a given country, who were supposed to be made members of the church and kingdom of Christ by baptism in infancy, one can readily understand why such churches, though, possibly, strictly orthodox, may yet be largely composed of persons still dead in trespasses and in sins. Nothing can be much sadder than vast congregations of people, baptized, banded together as Christians, 'taking the sacrament' of the Lord's Supper, zealous for church and Christianity, and yet largely devoid of personal, saving faith in Christ — trusting rather in forms and ceremonies, and what some have called 'birthright membership,' than in new birth through the Word and Spirit of God.

"What is needed everywhere is a great revival of decided gospel preaching, pressing home on the consciences of men and women their lost condition, despite church membership, if they have not personally received the Lord Jesus Christ."

– H. A. Ironside

Letter to the Church at Philadelphia (7-13)

"Philadelphia is a phase of the Church growing out of the Reformation period. The word means 'brotherly love,' and the Philadelphia Church is made up of the few names that were left in Sardis — the remnant who are keeping themselves unspotted from the world. He that hath the key of David is watching over them. He finds no fault in them, but commends them because they have a little strength, having strengthened the things which remained. 'I will keep thee from the hour of trial, that hour which is to come upon the whole world, to try them that dwell upon the earth.' This is His definite assurance that the Church of God will not pass through, nor even into the terrors of The Great Tribulation. We are delivered from the wrath to come (1 Thess. 1:9,10). 'Behold, I come quickly; hold fast that which thou hast, that no man take thy crown.' "

– William L. Pettingill

"The letter to the church at Philadelphia, like that to the faithful of Smyrna, is designed to reassure and strengthen hearts already courageous, to confirm the faithfulness of minds already loyal. These two churches, at Philadelphia and Smyrna, represent in John's symbolical scheme of seven all completely faithful communities throughout the world. And the two letters, taken together, are intended to put before all loyal Christians the essential nature of their situation.

"The similarity between the messages to Smyrna and Philadelphia is not confined to general approbation; point for point, the letters cover the same ground. In the first place, the fundamental position of each church is the same. Each is confronted with slander and malice from those who style themselves Jews; each has to face direct persecution from the Roman authorities for loyalty to the Name; each is assured that the Jewish persecution, no less than the Roman, is Satanic … To both churches the promise of spiritual security is made, as a reward for continued faithfulness (2:11; 3:10), and in each instance this reward is associated with the crown of final victory. The church at Smyrna is poor, that at Philadelphia weak; in each case their condition enhances the worth of their achievements."

– Martin Kiddle

Letter to the Church at Laodicea (14-22)

"Laodicea means 'The judging or rights of the People.' It is opposite of Nicolaitanism. The domineerers of the people still go on in Rome, but in Protestantism the people (the laity) arise and claim their rights and do the judging. This condition was also foreseen by the Apostle Paul. 'For the time will come when they (the laity) will not endure sound doctrine; but after their own lusts shall they heap to themselves teachers, having itching ears' (2 Timothy 4:3). We see in Laodicea the final religious and apostate conditions of protestant Christendom and the complete rejection of the professing body. 'I will spew thee out of my mouth.' He Himself is seen standing outside, which shows that He is rejected. But infinite Grace! He knocks and is still willing to come in and bestow the riches of His grace. And the Philadelphian-Christian, who is separated from the Laodicean state, whose heart is filled with the Love of Christ can learn a lesson here. If our Lord stands outside and yet knocks and waits in patience, we too with Him outside of the camp, where He is disowned, can try to gain admittance to Laodicean hearts."

– Arno Gaebelein

"The three main characteristic features of Laodicea were their poverty, their nakedness, and their blindness; and these are what the Lord, ever gracious, here offers to meet. He might have commanded, but no, He counsels, 'buy of Me gold purified by fire.' 'Buy' need present no difficulty. Christ has the treasures of grace, the wealth of Heaven at His disposal. He fixes the terms on which He sells: 'Ho, every one that thirsteth, come ye to the waters, and he that hath *no money;* come ye, buy, and eat; yea, come, buy wine and milk *without money,* and *without price'* (Isa. 55:1). Your title to come, to buy, is your need and poverty. 'Gold' purified or refined by fire points to divine righteousness, tested and tried; without it, oh, how poor! with it, how rich! 'White garments' are declared to be the righteousness of saints, i.e., their righteous deeds (Rev. 19:8), which would cover their moral nakedness and the shame of it as well. 'Eye salve' is for spiritual discernment."

– Walter Scott

Christ Forecasts the History of Christianity
An Expository Sermon

Chapter Three

The Things Which Are (Part 2)
Overcomers Forever

Introduction

Continuing with the seven churches of Revelation, we will consider primarily in this message how these three churches depict general conditions in the history of Christianity over the last 500 years. At the same time, there are many practical lessons to be learned that will apply to any church any time in history, including this very time and year.

I. Sardis, the Lifeless Church (1400-1600)
The Age of Reformation (1-6)

Sprawling across Europe, the Roman church had already peaked in power in the 12th century when Hildebrand, a pope, kept a Holy Roman Emperor waiting to see him outside in the snow for three days. But in spite of the general deadness of professing Christianity, there were signs of awakening. John Wycliffe had translated the Bible into English. Some priests had started to preach the gospel. The Eastern Orthodox Church, which had spread Christianity into Eastern Europe and Russia, had no loyalty to the pope of Rome but were fighting off the attacks of Arabs, Turks and other Muslims, who sought to convert whole nations to Islam with the sword. In 1453, Constantinople fell to the Muslims, causing some scholars who truly believed in Christ to flee to the west.

Savonarola, Martin Luther, thousands of others, began to preach the gospel. Anabaptists in the "radical reformation" came out of hiding.

These were some of the "names" in Sardis.

In a parallel event, Columbus, a Bible-believing Explorer with ideas similar to the reformers, concluded that the earth was round and desired to spread the gospel to the whole world, thinking that Christ would return when all the peoples of the earth had the opportunity to know God. This was the real reason he sailed west and accidentally discovered America. The event profoundly affected the future of biblical Christianity.

Remember however that all of these churches were actually historical congregations in 90-100 A.D., but with prophetic overtones.

Likewise, there are practical lessons for us, for any church, in any time period. Let us notice these five imperative admonitions and apply them to our lives, to our churches:

First, "Be watchful." (2). We are to be alert, awake, observant as to our own spiritual lives in the light of prevailing conditions. We are to "wake up," not remaining in a "dead state," even though "they had a name that they lived but were dead!"

Second, we need to "strengthen the things that remain," clinging to the fundamentals of the faith and maintaining devotion to Christ, re-enhancing our love and fervor.

Next, we are to "remember" past blessings. Has there been a time when you were closer to Christ than you are now? O, let us call to remembrance all of the blessings, all of the gifts, all of the experiences we have had in walking with God. Our lives will be reinforced by "stirring up our pure minds by way of remembrance."

In addition we must "hold fast," which means to keep and not to lose anything else spiritually in our lives and in our churches. We must never surrender to theological modernism or be content with dead orthodoxy either.

"Repent," Jesus says again, which calls for a change of mind, heart and attitude that leads to renewal, to a complete turn around, to genuine revival.

If our churches sink into deadness, these are Christ's admonitions to US.

II. Philadelphia, the Loving Church (1600 until ...)
The Age of Evangelization (7-13)

The last several centuries, perhaps until the latter part of the 20th century, has been the era of worldwide evangelism, as Christians have spread the gospel to all the continents. Through the "open door" have gone men like John Clarke in America, later Adoniram Judson to Burma, William Carey to India, and tens of thousands of missionaries carrying the gospel all over the world. Christianity spread from Europe to Africa, Asia, Australia, North America, South America. Hundreds of thousands of churches have been established, many still preaching the gospel. There are tens of millions of true believers worldwide. The period between 1859 and 1950 saw the greatest dissemination of the gospel in all of history. Even today in local churches, on the printed page, through radio and television, more gospel is being proclaimed to more people than ever before in human history.

A rebirth of expectancy concerning the Second Coming arose in the late 1800s and prevails even today. The loving church proclaims His love.

The rapture of believers could occur at any time!

No negative descriptions are forthcoming here, for Jesus finds no fault with this congregation. Look at what Jesus said to this church and would say to ours as we grow a similar congregation:

"I have set before thee an open door." Opportunities to win others in our own land and opportunities to send the gospel to the uttermost part of the earth exist now. Paul once wrote: "For a great door and effectual is opened unto me and there are many adversaries" (1 Cor. 16:9). As God opens doors we must enter!

"I will make them of the synagogue of Satan ... know that I have loved thee" (9). As David said, "Thou anointest my head with oil in the presence of mine enemies" (Ps. 23), so eventually Bible believers shall triumph indeed.

"I will keep thee from the hour of temptation" (10), assures the Saviour, referring in a practical sense to being delivered from a great time of stress and persecution and in the ultimate sense to the pre-tribulational Rapture.

"I will write upon him [the overcomer] my new name" (12). Whatever happens, victory and triumph are the real outcomes for Philadelphian type believers.

III. Laodicea, the Lukewarm Church (1900's until ...)

The Age of Apostasy (14-22)

During the final stages of Christian history on this planet, there will be no great world conversion, no mighty revival that will Christianize civilization. Although powerful revivals could come in the end times, they will be localized, if they occur.

Lukewarmness is the end-time trait of professing Christians. Departing from the faith, particularly belief in the deity of Christ, the infallible truth of the Word, and the importance of genuine righteousness and sincere godliness, characterize the Laodicean mood.

Our church must not sink into Laodicean lukewarmness, laziness and decadence.

They were *spiritually lukewarm,* neither totally cold, devoid of any theological truth or personal dedication, nor fervently hot with enthusiasm and divine power, just in between, nauseating, lethargic, repugnant to God.

They were *materially rich,* having assets, crowds, money, but self-satisfied, complacent and content with a lukewarm status quo.

They were *actually poverty-stricken* in the eyes of God with no real riches laid up in heaven, no real wealth of spirit and soul on earth.

But Christ's love still persists,

"As many as I love, I rebuke and chasten: be zealous therefore and repent."

Yes, revival, in a measure is still possible! But we must confess our lukewarmness and repent.

Conclusion

Notice again the promises to the overcomers, all seven of them.

"To him that overcometh will I give to eat of the tree of life, which is in the midst of the paradise of God" (2:7). There is ETERNAL PROVISION!

"He that overcometh shall not be hurt of the second death (2:11). There is ETERNAL SECURITY!

"To him that overcometh will I give to eat of the hidden manna, and will give him a white stone, and in the stone a new name written, which no man knoweth saving he that receiveth it" (2:17). There is ETERNAL REWARD!

"And he that overcometh, and keepeth my works unto the end, to him will I give power over the nations ... and he shall rule them with a rod of iron; as vessels of a potter shall they be broken to shivers; even as I received of my Father. And I will give him the morning star" (2:26-28). There is ETERNAL AUTHORITY!

"He that overcometh, the same shall be clothed in white raiment; and I will not blot out his name out of the book of life, but I will confess his name before my Father and before his angels" (3:5). There is ETERNAL ACKNOWLEDGMENT!

"Him that overcometh will I make a pillar in the temple of my God, and he shall go no more out: and I will write upon him the name of my God, and the name of the city of my God, which is New Jerusalem, which cometh down out of heaven from God, and I will write upon him my new name" (3:12). There is ETERNAL EXALTATION!

"Who is he that overcometh the world, but he that believeth that Jesus is the Son of God?" (1 John 5:5).

"To him that overcometh will I grant to sit with me in my throne, even as I also overcame, and am set down with my Father in his throne" (3:21).

THERE IS ETERNAL ENTHRONEMENT!

A Commentary on the Revelation
Expository, Exegetical, Devotional and Practical
Greek words from the Textus Receptus

Chapter Three

The Letter to the Church at Sardis (1-6)

1. Sardis, was the ancient capitol of the Kingdom of Lydia which occupied at one time the bulk of Asia Minor and a very important and wealthy city. The word may be derived from *sarda* or the *sardius* stone, a beautiful gem, or may be from a semitic word meaning *remnant* or *escaped few* ... **seven spirits ... seven stars** (*hepta pneumata ... hepta asteros*) — "His having the seven stars or presiding ministers, flows, as a consequence, from His having the seven Spirits, or the fullness of the Holy Spirit (Isa. 11:2). The human ministry is the fruit of Christ's sending down the gifts of the Holy Spirit. Stars imply brilliance and glory," (J.F.B.) ... Godly ministers filled with the Holy Spirit shine as lights in a dark world ... **and art dead** (*kai nekros ei*) — not that they were all "dead in trespasses and sins" (Eph. 2:1), but that they were corporately lifeless, barren, unfruitful, unproductive. Here was reputation without reality, externally seemingly alive, but internally a spiritual corpse, rather than a dynamic "body of Christ ..." **2. be watchful** (*ginou gregoron*) — wake up from deadness, watching continually, alert to duty like a sentry on guard duty ... **strengthen** (*sterison*) — establish or stabilize the things that remain ... "those basic moral principles and apostolic doctrines, stand by them, uphold them" (A. Garner), plus the spiritual character and dedication that should accompany fidelity to truth ... **perfect** (*pepleromena*) — not the same word as in Matthew 5:48, which is *teleois*, but a form of *pleroo*, signifying filled up or complete. Corporately, the church had not fulfilled the requirements of God. **3. Remember** (*mnemoneue*) — what has been received and heard, being reminded of their receiving the Word earlier with joy, when they heard it, for faith comes by hearing ... **hold fast** (*terei*) — not same word as in 2:25, which is *kratesate achri* ... this word means keep, guard, with seriousness of heart and obedience ... **I will come on thee as a thief** (*hekso hos kleptes*) — hence the English word kleptomaniac includes the Greek word for thief, but Jesus will be acting in liberating righteousness, when He comes as a thief to rob the grave of its victory at the resurrection and to "kidnap" His children from the presence of sin. In this verse's context however, the idea is of stealth-like sudden intervention, which could either be bringing chastisement upon a dead church, or His actual coming.

Be watchful and awake (Mark 13:37) ... **4. not defiled their garments** (*hai ouk emolunan ta himatia auton*) — they have not stained and soiled their spiritual testimony, keeping unspotted (Jude 23) ... **5. and I will not blot out his name** (*kai ou me eklsaleipso to onoma autou*) — I will not by any means under any circumstances remove his name, identity or existence is the promise here, not the threat that names could be blotted out, which some writers have interpolated into this verse.

The Letter to the Church at Philadelphia (7-13)

7. Philadelphia, which means "brotherly love," is twenty-eight miles east of Sardis and was built by Attalus Philadelphus, king of Pergamum, who died about 138 B.C. ... **he that is holy** (*tode legei ho hagios*) — similar to the Old Testament title, "The Holy One of Israel" ... the Greek word signifies separate from evil and despising it, in contrast to the "synagogue of Satan ... **true** (*alethinos*) — genuine, not false, truth speaking, truth loving. His nature is as His name (John 14:6; John 1:9; 6:32; 15:1; 17:3) ... **the key of David** (*ten kleida tou David*) — a reference to Isaiah 22:22, which presents in Isaiah's time Eliakim, to whom the key, the emblem of authority over the house of David, was passed from Shebna; who has "the key of David," — authority over the rights and realm of Davidic line of Kings (See Luke 1:32,33). Christ has authority over even a larger "house" (Hebrews 3:2-6), including the gospel era and the future millennium. "Eliakim had the key of the house of David laid upon his shoulders, meaning he was the trusted steward under King Hezekiah of the royal heritage of the Davidic line of kings. His name means "set or appointed by God," which was reflected in his service. He may have been of Davidic descent. Christ is the greater "Eliakim" with the "key" for all time ... **8. open door** (*thuron eneogmenen*) — since Christ has the "key," He can open doors, here a door for spiritual usefulness, evangelism and service. Philadelphian type churches often enter such "doors" to carry the gospel over the world ... **9. I will make** — that is, *cause* ... Here the promise to Philadelphia is greater than that to Smyrna, where the "synagogue of Satan" would not prevail over them. Here some of the "synagogue of Satan" come to Christ and find the truth. Until Christ comes and all Israel shall be saved, there is a remnant who become "Messianic Jews." That was historically the case nineteen centuries ago, but prophetically has been seen during the Philadelphian era of church history … **10. patience** (*tes hupomones*) — meaning patient endurance (same word in verb form, "endures," in Matthew 24:13). **from** (*ek*), meaning out of, "the temptation, the sore temptation which is coming on: the time of great tribulation before Christ's second coming" (J.F.B.). Compare Matthew 24:21; Dan. 12:1; Luke 21:35,36: "For as a snare shall it come on all of them that dwell on the face of the whole earth. Watch ye therefore, and pray always, that ye may be accounted *worthy to escape* all these things that shall come to pass and to stand before the Son of man." "The particular persecutions which befell Philadelphia shortly after, were the earnest of the great last tribulation before Christ's coming, to which the church's attention in all ages is directed" (J.F.B.). A pre-tribulational rapture is here taught … **11. Behold I come quickly** — the great incentive to faithfulness of life. … **that no man take thy crown** … failure to be what God calls us to be results in loss of rewards, which others who are faithful will receive. **12. pillar in the temple**, a metaphor here, since Rev. 21:22 says "I saw no temple …the Lord and the Lamb are the temple" in the New Jerusalem. As His people we will be permanent pillars within, not the New Jerusalem. As His people we will be permanent pillars within, not decorative or supportive pillars without as in many buildings. **No more out** does not mean non-mobility or limitations, but speaks of our eternal place as citizens of heaven … **13. churches** (*ekklesiais*), literally "assemblies."

The Letter to the Church at Laodicea (14-22)

14. Laodiceans, the city was between Colosse and Philadelphia and was destroyed in 62 A.D., but rebuilt in greater splendor by wealthy citizens without help from Rome. Paul must have written a non-canonical and lost epistle to this church (Col. 4:16). Apparently Jesus' message resulted in renewal, for the church flourished and in 361 A.D. a church council was held here to settle on the canon of Scripture as we know it. Only ruins now remain … **Amen** … the Hebrew word for "so be it," or may God's will be affirmed and accomplished, same as "verily" in the Gospel of John … **faithful** (*pistos*) — trustworthy, to be believed … **witness** (*martus*) — hence martyr … Trench says: "Three things are necessary to be a faithful and true witness: (1) to have seen with His own eyes what He attests; (2) to be competent to relate it to others; (3) to be willing to do so perfectly. In Christ all of these conditions meet." … **beginning of the creation of God**, a high title as suggested in John 1:1-3; Col. 1:15-18 … **15.**

cold (*psuchros*) — indicating icy cold, as though never warmed … never originally part of the family of God … **hot** (*zestos*) — hence the English "zest" for fervency (Acts 18:25, Romans 12:11), carrying the idea of boiling hot … **16. lukewarm** (*chilros*) — not icy cold, as the lost might be, who could possibly be won, not fervently warm as Spirit filled believers should be … "But the lukewarm has been brought within the reach of holy fire, without being heated by it into fervor; having religion enough to lull the conscience in false security, but not religion enough to save the soul, as Demas." (J.F.B.). Some Laodiceans were no doubt saved, but there must have been a mix with the merely religious… **spue thee out of my mouth** (*mello se emesai ek tou stomatos mou*) — indicating a rejection with righteous judgment. Note that the word implies the *stomach*, full regurgitation from within. Doctors used to use lukewarm drinks to induce vomiting. Today, who would enjoy a lukewarm Coca-cola? Self sufficiency is the fatal danger of the lukewarm church … **17. because thou sayest** (*hoti legeis*) — How many church members brag about their possessions and accomplishments, but are only lukewarm in God's sight, poor and not rich! **wretched** (*talaiporos*) in a really wretched state, as Paul once was (Romans 7:24) …**miserable** (*eleeinos*) — impoverished spiritually with no spiritual power or heavenly riches (Luke 16:11; Matt. 6:19-21) …**blind** (*tuphlos*) — not absolutely blind or the "eyesalve" would not have remedied them …**naked** (*gumnos*) — unclothed in a spiritually sense, a shameful and sad situation … **18. tried in the fire** — "a striking expression in the Greek: *pepiromenon ek puros* (hence *pyrotechnic* in English), it means 'set on fire, burn.' Clearly the idea here is 'refined by fire'" (Ralph Earle). **19. chasten** (*paideuo*) — meaning discipline, instruct and correct …**20. knock** (*krouo*) — remember the latch is on the inside, whether Christ is knocking at "the church's door" or the heart's door. The person within must open the door by an act of will to admit the Master … **21. throne** (*throno*) — To sit down with Christ in His heavenly throne is the glorious destiny of those who are true, saved overcomers. Perhaps from time to time in eternity, Christ will invite every single person who qualified as an overcomer (1 John 5:4,5) to sit down with Him for a while and share in His omnipotent reign. What a destiny! How sad the unsaved, by contrast, in the lake of fire forever and ever. (Rev. 20: 11-15).

RAINBOWS FROM REVELATION
The Revelation of Jesus Christ

A chapter by chapter, verse by verse study
"There was a rainbow round about the throne like unto an emerald" (4:3)

CHAPTER FOUR: The Rapture of John

References

Rev. 19:11
1 Cor. 15:51,52
1Thes. 4:17,18
Rev. 11:12
Rev. 1:19

Rev. 1:10
2 Cor. 12:2-4
Dan. 7:9

Eze. 1:28

1 Chr. 27:1

Ex. 37:23
Eze. 1:13
Zech. 4:2
Isa. 11:2

Ex. 25:25

1. AFTER this I looked, and, behold, a door was opened in heaven: and the first voice which I heard was as it were of a trumpet talking with me; which said, Come up hither, and I will show thee things which must be hereafter.

2. And immediately I was in the spirit: and, behold, a throne was set in heaven, and one sat on the throne.

3. And he that sat was to look upon like a jasper and a sardine stone: and there was a rainbow round about the throne, in sight like unto an emerald.

4. And round about the throne were four and twenty seats: and upon the seats I saw four and twenty elders sitting, clothed in white raiment; and they had on their heads crowns of gold.

5. And out of the throne proceeded lightnings and thunderings and voices: and there were seven lamps of fire burning before the throne, which are the seven Spirits of God.

6. And before the throne there was a sea of glass like unto crystal: and in the midst of the throne, and round about the throne, were four beasts full of eyes before and behind.

7. And the first beast was like a lion, and the second beast was like a calf, and the third beast had a face as a man, and the fourth beast was like a flying eagle.

8. And the four beasts had each of them six wings about him; and they were full of eyes within: and they rest not day and night, saying, Holy, holy, holy, Lord God Almighty, which was, and is, and is to come.

9. And when those beasts give glory and honor and thanks to him that sat on the throne, who liveth for ever and ever,

10. The four and twenty elders fall down before him that sat on the throne, and worship him that liveth for ever and ever, and cast their crowns before the throne, saying,

11. Thou art worthy, O Lord, to receive glory and honor and power: for thou hast created all things, and for thy pleasure they are and were created.

References

Eze. 1:5

Num. 2:2
Eze. 1:10

Isa. 6:2,3

Rev. 1:6;
5:13,14; 7:12

Rev. 11:15, 16
Rev. 22:5

Gen. 1:1
Jn. 1:3
Col. 1:16
Ps. 19:1

Scriptures for Comparison

Read and compare all of Ezekiel 1-3, Psalm 18:7-15, Psalm 68:4,33 2 Kings 2:1

Ezekiel 1:4-6,10,22,26-28

And I looked, and, behold, a whirlwind came out of the north, a great cloud, and a fire infolding itself, and a brightness was about it, and out of the midst thereof as the color of amber, out of the midst of the fire.

Also out of the midst thereof came the likeness of four living creatures. And this was their appearance; they had the likeness of a man.

And every one had four faces, and every one had four wings.

As for the likeness of their faces, they four had the face of a man, and the face of a lion, on the right side: and they four had the face of an ox on the left side; they four also had the face of an eagle.

And the likeness of the firmament upon the heads of the living creature was as the color of the terrible crystal, stretched forth over their heads above.

And above the firmament that was over their heads was the likeness of a throne, as the appearance of a sapphire stone: and upon the likeness of the throne was the likeness as the appearance of a man above upon it.

And I saw as the color of amber, as the appearance of fire round about within it, from the appearance of his loins even upward, and from the appearance of his loins even downward, I saw as it were the appearance of fire, and it had brightness round about.

As the appearance of the bow that is in the cloud in the day of rain, so was the appearance of the brightness round about. This was the appearance of the likeness of the glory of the Lord. And when I saw it, I fell upon my face, and I heard a voice of one that spake.

Isaiah 6:3

And one cried unto another, and said, Holy, holy, holy, is the Lord of hosts: the whole earth is full of his glory.

Read and compare all of Isaiah 6

Summary of Chapter Four

The Rapture of John

I. The Trumpet (1)
"After this" a trumpet sounds, a voice is heard, an invitation to "come up hither" is issued.

II. The Transition (2)
Even as John the Apostle "was raptured" into heaven to behold the throne of God after the pre-history of the church age is given, so will believers alive at the close of the church age hear the voice of a trumpet, summoning us to "come up hither."

III. The Throne (2,3)
Seeing the glorious rainbow-encircled throne of His splendor moving into place, the apostle beholds an appearance of the Everlasting Father.

IV. The Twenty-Four (4)
John also sees 24 elders, evidently representing the saints of God, the present priesthood of the believers. There were 24 "courses" or teams of priests who served at the tabernacle and at the temple, later, for two-week periods. Some writers suggest that the 12 apostles and 12 patriarchs of Israel are seen here, representing the Old and New Testament saints. This writer is of the opinion that these are the New Testament saints, the royal priesthood. Compare with I Peter 2:9, 10. They surround the throne on lesser thrones, sharing in the divine reign, wearing crowns of gold.

V. The Throne Attendants (5-8)
The four beasts or living creatures (Greek word — zoa) are the constant attendants upon God's throne. They are seen in Ezekiel 1 with only four wings; hence, they may change form. They may somehow participate in God's self-revelation. Some writers indicate that each one is indicative of the four Gospel's presentations of the character of Christ. In Matthew, Christ is the Lion of the Tribe of Judah. In Mark, He is the humble servant; the calf, a sacrificial being. In Luke, Christ is the perfect man. In John, His deity is taught, typified by the "eagle." If this is a correct observation and the beasts do reflect God's revelation of Christ, this does not nullify their reality in any sense.

VI. The Theme (8)
Echoing through heaven "day and night" is the majestic theme of glory, the sublime holiness of the Eternal God.

VII. The Triumphant Testimony (9-11)
When they acclaim the holiness and greatness of God, the 24 elders (saints) cast their crowns at His feet, worshipping Him who is the supreme Creator.

Outline of Chapter Four

A Door in Heaven

OBJECTIVE: To reveal the sovereign majesty of the eternally enthroned and ever-ruling Almighty God.

OUTLINE:

I. The Trumpet (1)
A. John sees an open door (Cf. "doors" 3:8, 20; 19:11)
B. John hears a "talking trumpet" voice. (Compare 1 Cor. 15:51; 1 Thess. 4:17, 18)
C. John records the heavenly invitation (Cf. 11:12; 17:1;21:9) "Come up hither"
D. John to be shown "things which must be hereafter"

II. The Transition (2)
This was like a "rapture," catching up (2 Cor. 12:2)
A. The Suddenness of the Experience - "immediately"
B. The Spirituality of the Experience - "in the spirit"

III. The Throne (2, 3)
A. The Arrangement "was set in heaven" (Ez.1-3)
B. The Almighty
  1. His Position "sitting"
  2. His Appearance
    a. Like a jasper stone — multi-colored yellowish with strong purples
    b. Like a sardius stone — red
C. The Aura - a circular rainbow with emerald color

IV. The Twenty-Four (4)
A. Their Names: elders
B. Their Number: 24 (Cf. I Chronicles 24:4)
C. Their Position: seated on thrones
D. Their Garments: white raiment (Cf. 19:8)
E. Their Crowns: gold (Cf. James 1:12, 1 Peter 5:4)

V. The Throne-Attendants (5-8)
A. Emanating Thunders (5)
B. Burning Lamps of Fire—the Seven Spirits (5) (Cf. Isaiah 11:2)
C. Praising Living Creatures: beasts, cherubim (Ez.1)
  1. Their Place: around the throne (6)
  2. Their Description
    a. One like a lion, calf, man, eagle
  3. Their Characteristics (8)
    a. Full of eyes ... seeing all
    b. Having six wings each; 24 in all

VI. The Theme (8)
HOLINESS IS THE THEME OF HEAVEN

VII. The Triumphant Testimony (9-11)
A. The Worship of the Twenty-four Elders (9, 10) Response to the Praises of the Beasts (zoa)
B. The Worthiness of the Lord (10) Response proclaimed by the elders
  1. The elders hear the praises
  2. The elders fall down to worship
  3. The elders cast their crowns at His feet
C. The Words of the Twenty-four Elders (11) Glory, honor, power suggest Trinity God praised as CREATOR (as REDEEMER in Chapter 5)

Observations:
Spiritual lessons and applications from each verse
Chapter Four

1. Let us listen for the sound of that trumpet that will summon us into His presence at our rapture, which John's being caught up also typifies.

2. The suddenness of John's experience reminds us of the instancy of our own rapture — "in the twinkling of an eye" (1 Corinthians 15:51, 52, 1 Thessalonians 4:13-18).

3. The rainbow (compare Genesis 9) is a symbol of the covenant-keeping God and the promises of God. It surrounds the throne, a complete circle, suggesting both promises and fulfillment. In heaven we shall see the completion of God's program. We must not let those who use rainbows to symbolize their teachings rob us of the enjoyment of God's fantastic multi-colored rainbow of beauty. God's own throne is surrounded by an emerald-hued rainbow. Study Ezekiel 1:26-28.

4. Will you be worthy to wear a crown in that day? Study the five crowns, as found in 1 Corinthians 9:25; James 1:12; 2 Timothy 4:8; 1 Peter 5:4; 1 Thessalonians 2:19.

5. Stand awestruck before the majesty of God's eternal throne. From Ezekiel it appears that this is the portable, movable throne of God which can be "set" where he chooses. See Ezekiel 1.

6. Does not God, do not the angels, see all we do? See Zechariah 4:10.

7. If the living creatures also reflect the character of Christ in the four gospels, then we must read and study often these accounts of His ministry.

8. Let us join with the angels in proclaiming and praising the HOLINESS of God. Compare Exodus 28:36, where the high priest's crown contains the words, "HOLINESS UNTO THE LORD."

9. Thanksgiving to God is always in order. (Compare 1 Thessalonians 5:18).

10. In true humility, we must always credit God with our successes. Worship should be a part of every believer's daily ministry.

11. Learn to worship God in spirit and in truth now. (See John 4:24).

Quotations
From Other Expositors
Chapter Four

John Caught up to Heaven (1,2)
"I have said that this open door in heaven, and this calling up of the Apocalyptic seer through that door into heaven, indicate to us the manner in which Christ intends to fulfill His promise to keep certain of His saints 'out of the hour of temptation;' and by what means it is that those who "watch and pray always" shall 'escape' the dreadful sorrows with which the present world, in its last years, will be visited. Those of them that sleep in their graves, shall be recalled from among the dead; and those of them who shall be found living at the time, 'shall be changed, in a moment, in the twinkling of an eye;' and both classes 'shall be caught up together in the clouds, to meet the Lord in the air.' The same voice which John heard, even "the voice as of a trumpet," whether dead or living, they shall hear, saying to them, 'Come up Hither.' And there shall attend it a change and transfer as sudden and miraculous as in his case."

– J.A. Seiss

The Majestic Throne (3)
"'Behold a throne stood in the Heaven.' This was the first sight beheld by the Seer in this new vision. The throne is the central subject in this heavenly scene. It is the sign and symbol of God's universal government. It 'stood in the Heaven.' The stability of that government is conveyed in the word 'stood' or set; 'the Heaven' fixes definitely and precisely the seat of royal authority. What a contrast to the tottering thrones of earth! Here, at the outset, is an intimation that Jehovah reigneth. The throne is our security and strength. It is, too, the great central fact in the universe. It is the pledge that the fiat of the Eternal shall compel obedience from every created being. It is the sign of order, of rule, of authority. The throne set in Heaven is in contrast to the mutability of all earthly governments."

– Walter Scott

The Rainbow (3)
"The throne in vastness and majesty is one befitting the Lord of hosts. Encircled with a rainbow it is a witness that in the exercise of absolute sovereignty, of all-ruling power, God will graciously remember in covenant mercy His creatures. It is a sign to all in Heaven that God delights in goodness.
"The complete, unbroken circle round the throne proclaims the truth, "His mercy endureth for ever." The bow set in the cloud of old, with its

47

prismatic colours and varied beauties, is the token of God's covenant with the earth (Gen. 9:9-17). It is rarely seen as a complete circle, but generally as an arch, or half-circle, and is God's object lesson for the race, a public sign hung out in the heavens that all may see and learn that God is good, a lesson from God and of God to men. In the last notice of the rainbow it is seen over the head of the Lord when in power He asserts His claim to the earth. He will sweep the defiled scene with the besom of destruction, but even then the old appointed token of divine goodness reappears (Rev. 10:1). Instead of the combination of colours to which we are accustomed in the rainbow the heavenly one over the throne is 'like in appearance to an emerald.' The beautiful green, the characteristic colour of the vegetable world, and the only one which never tires the eye, is the chosen color of the rainbow beheld by the Seer. The glorified saints will have constantly before their never-tiring gaze the rainbow in its entirety; the remembrance of God's grace to the earth even when He is about to deal with the race in judgment."

– Walter Scott

The Twenty Four Elders (4)

"But now the fourth verse brings before us a sight never beheld in heaven on any previous occasion: twenty-four thrones (not merely "seats") surrounding the central throne, and upon them twenty-four elders seated, with victors' crowns (not diadems) upon their heads, and clothed in priestly robes of purest white. Who are these favored ones gathered around the glorious central Being? I do not think we need be in any doubt as to their identity, if we compare scripture with scripture and distrust our own imagination, which can but lead us astray.

"In 1 Chronicles, chapter 24, we read of something very similar; and again I would remind you that many of John's first readers were Hebrews, thoroughly familiar with the Old Testament. Can we question for a moment that every Jewish believer would instantly remember the twenty-four elders appointed by King David to represent the entire Levitical priesthood? He divided the priests into twenty-four courses, each a course to serve for two weeks at a time in the temple which Solomon was to build. The same arrangement was in force when our Lord's forerunner was announced. Zacharias was 'of the course of Abiah,' the eighth in order (Luke 1:5).

"The priests were many thousands in number; they could not all come together at one time, but when the twenty-four elders met in the temple precincts in Jerusalem, the whole priestly house was represented. And this is the explanation, I submit, of the symbol here. The elders in heaven represent the whole heavenly priesthood—that is, all the redeemed who have died in the past, or who shall be living at the Lord's return. In vision they were seen—not as a multitudinous host of millions of saved worshipers, but just twenty-four elders, symbolizing the entire company. The church of the present age and the Old Testament saints are alike included. All are priests. All worship. There were twelve patriarchs in Israel, and twelve apostles introducing the new dispensation. The two together would give the complete four and twenty.

"Then, observe further: these persons are not angels. They are redeemed men who have overcome in the conflict with Satan and the world, for they wear victors' wreaths upon their brows. Angels are never said to be 'crowned,' nor have they known redemption."

– H.A. Ironside

Cherubim-Beasts-Living Creatures (6-9)

"Looking at the cherubim, John is impressed not only with the singularity of their form, he is impressed also with the singleness of their function. It is this which explains why they are so much like Jesus. 'And the four beasts had each of them six wings about him; and they were full of eyes within: and they rest not day and night, saying, Holy, holy, holy, Lord God Almighty, which was, and is, and is to come.' The cherubim are the highest of all created intelligences. They are full of eyes, implying clear insight into matters. These lofty ones employ the resources of their intellects, the deep emotions of their hearts, the ceaseless drive and dynamic of their powerful wills—and they worship! It is the one great, supreme, dominating activity of their lives. All else is counted worthless when compared with the supreme activity of worship. With all their heart and mind and soul and strength they worship Him that sits upon the throne. They acknowledge Him to be the holiest One in the universe. Holy! Holy! Holy! Thrice holy God! Holy Father, Holy Son, and Holy Ghost!"

– John Phillips

Praises To God (8-11)

"In verse 8 the Zoa express their continual praise to God: 'Holy, holy, holy, Lord God Almighty, which was, and is, and is to come.' This is the first of seventeen utterances of the Zoa. When the Zoa are doing this the Elders worship God also and 'cast their crowns before the throne,' saying, 'Thou art worthy, O Lord, to receive glory and honor and power: for this hast created all things, and for thy pleasure they are and were created.'

"Soon the judgments of God will reclaim God's creation for Himself and He will once more be able to enjoy it and have pleasure in it."

– Bill Lawrence

What is it Like to Enter Heaven?
An Expository Sermon

Chapter Four

Introduction

For the first time in sacred Scripture, an actual entry into the portals of glory is described in awe-inspiring images. While ancient apocalyptic fantasies, penned by men who used the names of Old Testament personalities, had been in circulation for a long time, and others would join their ranks, none of these books were ever considered worthy of acceptance as being divinely inspired.

But this masterpiece of truth, the Book of Revelation, is the crowning capstone of the Bible, and these scenes in chapter four lift us up to heavenly realms with John to behold that which Paul in an earlier experience was not permitted to reveal. "Whether in the body or out of the body," he could not tell, but he was "caught up" to the "third heaven," too (2 Corinthians 12:1-4). The first heaven is the atmospheric realm; the second heaven is the stellar universe; the third heaven is the actual abode of God in a different and spiritual but real dimension.

Perhaps at our rapture, when Jesus comes for us, we shall rejoice in similar scenes as we arrive before the throne of God!

I. The Rapture of John (1, 2)

Strongly suggestive of the rapture of believers at the close of the church age, this chapter begins by saying, "after this" after the description of the churches. All this suggests that after this church dispensation is over, the rapture and the future tribulation time, to be explained in this book, will occur.

"Come up hither ..." the invitation of God in trumpet tones summons the aged apostle from Patmos Isle into this heavenly and holy realm.

Here likewise begins the third division of this book, as indicated in the key verse (1:19). Here commences the major section of this prophecy, "the things which must be hereafter."

John, caught up into heaven, is to see and record the grand panorama of end time events which will climax this age!

II. The Realities of Glory (3-8)

"Immediately" in a spiritual realm, entering that door into heaven itself, John, "whether in the body or out of the body," perhaps he could not tell, like Paul, now sees a throne. Psalm 103:19 reads, "The Lord hath prepared his throne in the heavens; and his kingdom ruleth over all."

Ezekiel, 600 years before Christ, saw the same throne, seemingly a center of government which may be mobile, riding upon "wheels," controlled by cherubim.

There by the banks of the river Chebar in Babylon, Ezekiel depicts the throne as being in the midst of a "firmament" on something like a crystalline pavilion, suspended and carried above the heads of the four cherubim.

"And above the firmament that was over their heads was the likeness of a throne, as the appearance of a sapphire stone: and upon the likeness of the throne was the likeness as the appearance of a man above upon it.

"And I saw as the color of amber, as the appearance of fire round about within it, from the appearance of his loins even upward, and from the appearance of his loins even downward. I saw as it were the appearance of fire, and it had brightness round about.

"As the appearance of the bow that is in the cloud in the day of rain, so was the appearance of the brightness round about. This was the appearance of the likeness of the glory of the Lord. And when I saw it, I fell upon my face, and I heard a voice of one that spake" (Ezekiel 1:26-28).

Now "no man has seen God at any time." Therefore, this is "the likeness" or a manifestation of God in His glory. He assumes, as it were, this form to communicate with His people. We are not seeing in any of these the real essence of His divine, omnipotent, omniscient, omnipresent Being.

Notice the similarity of John's and Ezekiel's description of that august and awesome Occupant of the THRONE, the power center of the universe.

Colors of amber and fire, shades of yellowish jasper and reddish sardius stone, flashing lightnings and pealing thunders dazzle the beholder with majestic magnificence. Surrounding the throne, the emerald rainbow with its predominant greens, all combine to draw our attention to the greatness and glory of the Almighty in the exercise of His universal power.

NEXT, our attention is drawn to 24 lesser thrones in heaven, occupied by 24 seated elders, each wearing crowns of gold. Twelve in the Bible is the number of divine government. Twice twelve may speak of government of heaven and government of earth. At any rate, most premillennialists see the elders as representatives of the raptured, redeemed, resurrected and glorified believers who share in the kingdom of God. Since there were 24 courses of priests in Old Testament times, we may see here the royal priesthood, the "kingdom of priests," the "joint heirs with Christ," associated with God's throne forever. (See I Peter 2:9; Romans 8:17, 18).

THEN, John looks at the "seven lamps of fire" which are "seven Spirits of God" (verse 5).

Seven is the number of divine completion and perfection. Hence, the sevenfold perfection of the Holy Spirit is indicated. Isaiah, speaking of Messiah to come, prophesies of His anointing (fulfilled in Matthew 3:16) when the Holy Spirit "like a dove" descended upon Jesus, saying,

"And the *Spirit of the Lord* shall rest upon him, the *spirit of wisdom* and [the *spirit of*] *understanding,* the *spirit of counsel* and [the *spirit of*] *might,* the *spirit of knowledge* and [the *spirit of*] *the fear of the Lord*" (Isaiah 11:12): SEVEN TITLES OF THE HOLY SPIRIT, speaking of His multiple ministries, all most manifest in Christ. Remember, Peter stressed, "how God anointed Jesus of Nazareth with the Holy Ghost and power ..." (Acts 10:38).

In heaven, the Holy Spirit is here symbolized by the SEVEN LAMPS OF FIRE, also reminiscent of the seven-branched candlestick in the Tabernacle of old which symbolized Christ, the Light of the World, endued with the Spirit and shining through the burning oil, often typical of the Spirit's anointing.

IN ADDITION, John describes the four "beasts," or "zoa" as the Greek reads ... "living creatures," the "cherubim" of Ezekiel 1. Many commentators have likened the beasts to the four gospels in succession.

Thus in Matthew he appears as the Lion of the Tribe of Judah, the King of Israel, "the first living creature was like a lion." In Mark He is the devoted Servant, ministering, toiling, submissive to His Father's will, finally laying down His life for others — "the second living creature was like an ox." In Luke He is seen as the Son of Man, the perfect Man, who nevertheless is the representative of a lost race, identified with it and bearing our sins — "the third living creature had a face as of a man." In John He is the Son of God, the Heavenly and Incarnate Word, coming down from heaven and returning to heaven — "the fourth living creature was like a flying eagle."

Ezekiel sees them with a slight difference and the order begins with the Man, followed by the Lion, the Ox and the Eagle. In fact, each has four faces. This shows that they may change form or that John saw each one with a different "face" more prominent. It is possible that these angelic beings, existing in a heavenly realm under vastly different conditions than we experience on earth, are simply not always in exactly the same form. Ezekiel saw four wings; here there are six. Recall that Isaiah saw six wings on the seraphim (Isaiah 6:1-3).

Remember that these are real beings, whatever else they may suggest. They are high and holy attendants, constant, holy courtiers, before the celestial throne. In the ancient tabernacle, embroidered images of cherubim decorated the vail before the Holy of Holies. On the ark of the covenant, two angelic beings, with wings extended above the top center, or "mercy seat," are typical of the real cherubim above and by the "throne of grace" (Exodus 25:20, 21).

Carefully observe the many numbers in this chapter: four "beasts," six wings, seven lamps of fire, twenty-four elders. Mark these for future study.

It was a glorious sight. After all the millennia of time, at last, a human being, John the Apostle, is permitted to draw back the curtain of time and mystery, that we might behold, however fleetingly, a glimpse of the glory world that awaits us!

"Eye hath not seen, nor ear heard, neither have entered into the heart of man, the things which God hath prepared for them that love him. But God hath revealed them unto us by his Spirit: for the Spirit searcheth all things, yea, the deep things of God" (1 Corinthians 2:9, 10).

III. The Refrain of Heaven (8-11)

This great paean of praise, echoing ceaselessly through the celestial realm, magnifies the HOLINESS OF GOD.

Closely notice the words grouped in *threes.* This is indicative of the TRINITY.

Three times the word "Holy" appears. The thrice-holy God is the Father, Son and the Holy Ghost! Holy! Holy! Holy!

Isaiah heard the seraphim, likewise attending the throne of God, as we have seen,

"And one cried unto another, and said, Holy, holy, holy, is the Lord of hosts: the whole earth is full of his glory" (Isaiah 6:3).

It is possible that the cherubim and the seraphim are the same "living creatures," sometimes having a slightly different form. Other commentators think these are two orders of angels. This writer thinks they are the same being because of the basic similarity of their actions.

Observe also the three titles or appellatives of God:

LORD ... He is Lord of the universe.

GOD ... He is the Supreme Being.

ALMIGHTY ... He is the Total Power.

Perhaps Christ, the Holy Spirit and the Father in that order are hinted here in the triple names.

The third threefold emphasis concerns time:

"which was, and is, and is to come."

God has always been, from eternity past; He is NOW; He will continue ceaselessly, forever. He is God of the past, present, future!

Of Jesus it is also written, "Jesus Christ, the same yesterday, and today, and forever" (Hebrews 13:8).

God's universe exists in "trinities," reflections of His supreme character. Genesis 1:1 gives us the basic constitution of creation:

"In the beginning" - TIME;

"God created" - exercised ENERGY;

"the heaven" - SPACE;

"and earth" - MATTER.

Because matter and energy are two forms of the same entity, as proven by atomic science, when matter is transmuted into energy, there are really three basic entities in our universe: TIME, SPACE, MATTER-ENERGY. A trinity of creation, designed by God. Time is in three tenses; space is in three dimensions; matter is in three forms (solid, liquid, gas). Many scientists believe energy is in only three basic forms, but has a variety of manifestations. Because of the highly technical nature of energy, this writer will not discuss that field. The point is that the created universe reveals something of the nature and power of God.

"For the invisible things of him from the creation of the world are clearly seen, being understood by the things which are made, even his eternal power and Godhead ..." (Romans 1:20).

The threefold repetition of "HOLY" emphasizes the HOLINESS OF GOD!

The threefold names of the Deity teach the PERSONALITY OF GOD!

The threefold tenses of time reveal the ETERNALITY OF GOD!

Such is the "refrain of heaven."

Conclusion

When heaven rings with these songs of praise, the four beasts are said to express THREE things: glory, honor and thanks (9).

Then the 24 elders prostrate themselves before the rainbow-encircled throne, casting their crowns before the Almighty. This teaches us that however greatly we may seem to serve God, the glory and praise always belong to Him alone. He alone is worthy!

Imagine for a moment those wondrous crowns promised believers, being cast as an act of supreme homage before the august majesty of the Sovereign of the Universe.

There is a **crown of life,** promised to those who are faithful unto death and to those who love Him so devotedly that they triumphantly resist temptation.

Jesus promised, "Be thou faithful unto death and I will give thee a crown of life" (Rev. 2:10).

"Blessed is the man," wrote James (1:12), "that endureth temptation; for when he is tried, he shall receive the crown of life, which the Lord hath promised to them that love him."

There is the **incorruptible crown** for those who strive for mastery properly, who keep the old sinful nature under control, who run the race for Christ with unwavering consecration. Athletes of old carefully kept to their training schedules and rigid disciplines.

"Now they do it to obtain a corruptible crown; be we an incorruptible" (1 Cor. 9:25).

There is the soul-winner's crown, suggested by Paul in 1 Thessalonians 2:19, as he thinks of the results of his ministry,

"For what is our hope, or joy, or **crown of rejoicing?** Are not even ye in the presence of our Lord Jesus Christ at his coming?"

There is the **crown of righteousness** of which Paul wrote in 2 Timothy 4:8, reserved for those who live in the light of His coming, loving His appearing: "Henceforth there is laid up for me a crown of righteousness, which the Lord, the righteous judge shall give me at that day, and not to me only, but unto all them also that love his appearing."

There is the **crown of glory** for godly and faithful pastors: "And when the chief shepherd shall appear, ye shall receive a crown of glory that fadeth not away" (1 Peter 5:4).

Finally, like a chorus to the angelic and cherubic theme of heaven, the elders say,

"Thou are worthy, O Lord, to receive [three things] glory, honor and power."

This is an accolade of praise to God as CREATOR.

"For thou hast created all things, and for thy pleasure they are and were created" (11).

O my friends who hear or read these words, *these* are the glories to which you are invited by our wonderful Saviour!

Christian brothers and sisters, think of your eternal and glorious destiny. The time yet shall come, when at the rapture and the first resurrection, we shall enter into the fullness of the heavenly realm. "It will be worth it all when we see Jesus."

A Commentary on the Revelation
Expository, Exegetical, Devotional and Practical
Greek words from the Textus Receptus

Chapter Four

Vision of God's Throne in Heaven (1-3)

Chapters 4 and 5 go together, forming the beginning of the revelation proper, an introduction to the unfolding panorama of the end times commencing in chapter 6. As the first three chapters deal with Christ's administration of the churches on earth, so 4 and 5 present Christ's administration over the entire earth and the universe. **1. After this** (*meta tauta*) — After these things marks the transition from "the things which are," the churches and the church age, to "the things which shall be hereafter," meaning the end times ... **I looked** — (*eidon*), saw, perceived and observed ... **a door was opened** — (*idou thura eneogmena*) — the Greek here literally means it was standing open. John is transported through this opened door, where he can see events on earth or in heaven ... **the first voice which I heard** (*kai he phone he prote hen ekousa*) — the voice which he had previously first heard in 1:10 ... **Come up hither** (*anaba hode*) — through the open door into the heavenly realm. How near the other world, the spiritual realm may be! ... **things which must take place hereafter** (*ha dei genesthei meta tauta*) ... in 1:19 the word **shall be** (*mellei*) is used; here **must** (*dei*), a stronger word is used to indicate the absolute certainty of these events ... **2. I was in the spirit** (*egenomen en pneumati*) — literally, I became in the spirit, completely under the control and direction of the Spirit, transported to the heavenly world, "whether in the body or out of the body I cannot tell," as Paul (2 Cor. 12:2) ... **one sat on the throne** (*kai epi ton thronon kathemenos*) — this is the eternal Father and Creator ... While God is invisible (1 Tim. 1:17) and is "Spirit" and is to be worshipped in Spirit and in truth, He does manifest Himself in visible forms, both in the Old and New Testaments, as here. These are called **theophanies**, appearances of God in a visible or human form to communicate His message as in Exodus 24:10 and in Ezekiel 1-3. Old Testament preincarnate appearances of Christ are called **christophanies**, as in Daniel 3:25. Christ on earth was God manifest in the flesh (John 1:14). **3. jasper** (*iaspidi*) — one of the gems in the Aaronic High Priest's breastplate, Exodus 28:20, where it is the last of twelve stones; again in Rev. 21:18, where it is listed first among the jewels adorning the foundations of the New Jerusalem. It is reddish, somewhat wavy in colors, sometimes mingled with hues of yellow or green, translucent ... **sardius stone** (*sardio*) — same as sardius in 21:21, a fiery red, called also a cornelian. Pliny says the stone was named after the city of Sardius. God's visible manifestation is thus a translucent red, with possibly other colors of yellow and green with flashes of fiery crimson, apparently dazzling in brilliance and resembling a human form ... **rainbow** (*iris*) — forming a complete circle, a type of God's eternal verdant youthfulness and perfection. An arch or half-circle would indicate the promise of God as in Gen. 9:13-17, whereas the full circle would include the fulfillment and completion of the promise. The predominating color is **emerald** (*smaragdino*), a deep green, a refreshing and pleasant shade, suggesting life and growth and symbolizing God's consoling promises amid the scenes of judgment which are a prominent feature of this book. Ezekiel beheld a similar rainbow (Ezek. 1:28):

"As the appearance of the bow that is in the cloud in the day of rain, so was the appearance of the brightness round about. This was the appearance of the likeness of the glory of the Lord ..." "The heavenly bow speaks of the shipwreck of the world through sin; it also speaks of calm and sunshine after the storm. The cloud is the holiest place; on Mount Sinai at the giving of the Law; at the Ascension (Acts 1:9); at His coming again (1:7)" (J.F.B.).

The Four and Twenty Elders (4,5)

4. seats (*thronoi*), translated "seats" to indicate lesser and smaller than the grand central throne ... **four and twenty elders** (*eikosi tessaras presbuterous*) — they are not angels, but remind us of the 12 Patriarchs of the nation of Israel and of the 12 Apostles of the Church, the two institutional witnesses from the Old and New Testaments. They have white robes (19:8-the righteousness of saints) and **crowns of gold** (*stephanous chrusous*). The word elders appears 12 times in Revelation. Twelve is the number of divine government. As in 1 Chronicles 24:3-5 and in chapter 25 also, 24 was a significant number, twice 12. We read of 24,000 (1 Chronicles 23:3,4), 24 courses and 24 priests on duty in the Temple. These 24 elders may be viewed as actually 24 saints on duty at that time or as typical and representative of all the people of God glorified in heaven. After the Rapture and Resurrection Old Testament saints from Israel, tracing back to the 12 tribes … and the New Testament saints, tracing back to the 12 Apostles, will be together in heaven. **5. thunderings and voices** (*phonai kai brontai*) — "The thunderings express God's threats against the ungodly: there are voices in the thunders (10:3), that is, not only does He threaten generally, but also predicts special judgments (*Grotius*) … **seven lamps** (*hepta lampades*) … **seven Spirits** (*hepta pneumata*) **seven eyes** (*ophthalmous hepta* in 5:6) … the Holy Spirit in sevenfold completion, perfection and knowledge as in Isaiah 11:2.

The Four Beasts — Living Creatures (6-8)

6. sea of glass like unto crystal (*thalassa hualine krustallo*) — reminiscent of "the paved work of sapphire stone" under the manifestation of God in Exodus 24:10 … and of the "firmament … as the color of terrible crystal" in Ezekiel 1:22. This was typified in Solomon's Temple by the brazen "sea" in front of the sacred structure (1 Kings 7:23, 2 Chronicles 4:2), in which the Shekinah glory of God was manifested. **four beasts** (*tessera zoa*) — "Here we have the plural of *zoon*, which occurs in Heb. 13:11; 2 Peter 2:12, Jude 10 and 20 times in Revelation. It is always translated beasts in the KJV. … these here were heavenly beings, literally 'living creatures' … from *zoe*, life … the 'beast of Revelation' is indicated by the Greek word *therion*, 'wild beast,' which occurs 38 times in this book and is correctly translated 'beast.' (Ralph Earle). These are heavenly living beings, like the four "living creatures" of Ezekiel 1:5, etc., which are essentially the same and are called cherubim in Ezekiel 10:1-14. Each cherub (singular … the "im" in Hebrew is like "s" and means plurality) in Ezekiel supports a corner of the crystal firmament on which appears the sapphire throne and the glowing fiery brilliance of God's personal manifestation. The entire first chapter of Ezekiel should be studied here in detail. Note Ezekiel 10:14: "And every one (of the cherubim or living creatures) had four faces; the first face was the face of a cherub, the second face was the face of a man, and the third face was the face of a lion, and the fourth the face of an eagle." This contrasts with Ezekiel 1:10, where instead of a "cherub," we read "the face of an ox." Here is that passage: "As for the likeness of their faces, they four had the face of a man, and the face of an ox, and the face of a lion, on the right side: and they four had the face of an ox on the left side; the four also had the face of an eagle." This seems to indicate they do not always have the exact same appearance. In Ezekiel they seem to be conveying the movable, portable throne of God, the firmament above their heads with the sapphire throne and the awesome Occu-

pant, their wheels by them. Here is the full passage from Ezekiel 1:12-26:

"**12.** And they went every one straight forward: whither the spirit was to go, they went; and they turned not when they went. **13.** As for the likeness of the living creatures, their appearance was like burning coals of fire, and like the appearance of lamps: it went up and down among the living creatures; and the fire was bright, and out of the fire went forth lightning. **14.** And the living creatures ran and returned as the appearance of a flash of lightning. **15.** Now as I beheld the living creatures, behold one wheel upon the earth by the living creatures, with his four faces. **16.** The appearance of the wheels and their work was like unto the colour of a beryl: and they four had one likeness: and their appearance and their work was as it were a wheel in the middle of a wheel. **17.** When they went, they went upon their four sides; and they turned not when they went. **18.** As for their rings, they were so high that they were dreadful; and their rings were full of eyes round about them four. **19.** And when the living creatures went, the wheels went by them: and when the living creatures were lifted up from the earth, the wheels were lifted up. **20.** Whithersoever the spirit was to go, they went, thither was their spirit to go; and the wheels were lifted up over against them: for the spirit of the living creature was in the wheels. **21.** When those went, these went; and when those stood, these stood; and when those were lifted up from the earth, the wheels were lifted up over against them: for the spirit of the living creature was in the wheels. **22.** And the likeness of the firmament upon the heads of the living creature was as the colour of the terrible crystal, stretched forth over their heads above. **23.** And under the firmament were their wings straight, the one toward the other: every one had two, which covered on this side, and every one had two, which covered on that side, their bodies. **24.** And when they went, I heard the noise of their wings, like the noise of great waters, as the voice of the Almighty, the voice of speech, as the noise of an host: when they stood, they let down their wings. **25.** And there was a voice from the firmament that was over their heads, when they stood, and had let down their wings. **26.** And above the firmament that was over their heads was the likeness of a throne, as the appearance of a sapphire stone: and upon the likeness of the throne was the likeness as the appearance of a man above upon it."

This "chariot of God" is seen there to land, as it were and then take off, described in Ezekiel 3:12,13. Here in Revelation the throne is in place and the cherubim are on the crystal sea (firmament), rather than beneath it and conveying it. **7. like a lion** (*homoron leonti*), symbolizing strength and courage … **calf** (*mascho*), "first a sprout, then the young of animals, then a calf (bullock or heifer) as in Luke 15:23,27, 30 or a full grown ox (Ezekiel 1:10)" (A.T. Robertson). The Greek term can be used for ox or calf … **face as a man** (*prosopon hos anthroupou*) — as the ox indicates service, the man represents intelligence and understanding … **like a flying eagle** (*homion aeto petomeno*) — speaking of soaring into the heavens in victorious flight. Jewish writers tell us, based on Numbers 2, that the flag or banner or standard of each tribe of Israel took the color of the stone which represented it on the High Priest's breastplate (Exodus 28:15-21), and that there was embroidered upon each a particular design a lion for Judah, a young ox for Ephraim, a man for Reuben, and an eagle for Dan. These were the representative tribes and all the rest were organized under four standards with Judah on the east along with Issachar and Zebulon; Reuben on the south along with Simeon and Gad; Ephraim on the west along with Manasseh and Benjamin; and Dan on the north along with Asher and Naphtali. In the center of this quadrangular encampment was the Tabernacle of God with four divisions of Levites forming an inner encampment about it. It was thus that Israel marched through the wilderness under the four banners of the lion, the young ox, the man and flying eagle. These were their ensigns. They were thus a reflection of heavenly things, as we see here (adapted from J.A. Seiss) Since these living creatures are associated with God's revealing Himself, the ancient church fathers and many since have taught that they also suggest the four gospels. In Matthew Christ is the Lion of the Tribe of Judah, the King; in Mark Christ is the Servant-Son of Jehovah, the ox or calf; in Luke, Christ is the Son of Man (face as a man); in John Christ is the Heavenly Incarnate Son of God, who ascended back to heaven, the flying eagle. **8. Six wings** — in Ezekiel there are four wings on each cherub; in Isaiah 6:1-3 there are six wings on each seraph. Some commentators distinguish between the seraphim and cherubim; others, including this writer, think there are two titles for the same beings and that they do not always appear exactly the same, but vary. HOLY, HOLY, HOLY (*hagios, hagios, hagios*), as also in Isaiah 6:3. Compare also Psalm 99:3,5,9. Holiness is the supreme attribute of God. He is the Threefold Holy God as three persons, three tenses (past, present, future), yet One God, a great mystery.

Praises to God (9-11)

9. glory, honor, thanks (*doksan, timen, eucharistan*) — as in the Doxology in English and the origin of the word eucharist in English arises from the Greek word for thanks or thanksgiving.

The latter term is used among liturgical churches in connection with communion. **10. cast their crowns** (*kai balousin tous stephanas*) — thus acknowledging that without Him nothing can be accomplished in the Kingdom of God. All glory and honor belongs to Him. Even rewards bestowed at the Judgment Seat of Christ could not be received apart from His grace and the impartation of His power for service. "To God be the glory …" **11. Worthy are thou O Lord** (*aksios ei ho kurios*) — Only God is truly deserving of **glory, honor,** and **power** (*dunamin*), for He is the Almighty Creator of the Universe, of all things. It was and is for His pleasure that all things in the whole Universe were created. The Father is thus acclaimed as "worthy" as the **Creator,** while in 5:9 the Lamb (the Son) is acclaimed as "worthy" as the **Redeemer.**

There are no less than eleven poetic expressions of praise, Merrill Tenney observes, in the entire book, though not all are called songs. They are found here in 4:8 and 4:11; then there follow acclamations to God in 5:8-10; 5:11,12; 5:13; 7:9,10; 7:11,12; 11:15; 11:16-18; 15:2-4; and 19:1-8, where the four Hallelujahs conclude the series. "An essense of worship pervades the entire Apocalypse. These declarations of praise by the heavenly host, whether angels or redeemed people, serve to show there is a constant background to the shifting scenes of the book. Behind the changing panorama of human history described under the symbolical pictures abides the unchanging reality of an eternal world in which God's purpose is unfailing and in which His Christ is victorious. Numerical structure is prominent in Revelation: **seven churches, seven seals, seven trumpets, seven personages, seven vials, seven dooms** and **seven new things** appear in the text. Seven is emblematic of completeness or perfection" (Tenney). Of significance also are the four "Come hithers": 4:1 and 11:12, where John and then the two witnesses are caught up to heaven (Gr. *anabaino*); and 17:1 and 21:9 (Gr. *deuro*), where John sees first Babylon the harlot, then Jerusalem the Lamb's wife. Besides the seven major "sevens" above, there are seven "lesser sevens": seven stars/angels (1:20); seven Spirits/lamps of fire (4:5); seven angels with judgments (8:1; 16:1); seven thunders (10:4); seven heads/crowns, mountains, kings (12:3; 17:9,10); seven voices (in ch. 14); seven "blessings" or "blesseds" or beatitudes (1:3; 5:13; 7:12; 14:13; 16:15; 20:6; and 22:7) in this wonderful Revelation.

RAINBOWS FROM REVELATION
The Revelation of Jesus Christ
A chapter by chapter, verse by verse study
"There was a rainbow round about the throne like unto an emerald" (4:3)

CHAPTER FIVE: The Seven Sealed Scroll

References

Ezek. 2:9,10
Isa. 29:11
Dan. 12:4

Rev. 4:11
Rev. 5:9

Jn. 1:18

Deut. 29:29

Gen. 49:9,10
Heb. 7:14
Isa. 11:1,10
Rom. 15:12

Isa. 53:7
Jn. 1:29,36
1 Pet. 1:19
Zech. 3:9;4:10
Isa. 11:2

Rev. 4:2

Ps. 141:2

References

Rev. 14:3
Rev. 1:9
1 Pet. 1:18,19

Ex. 19:6
Isa. 61:6
Rev. 1:6

Ps. 68:17
Dan. 7:10

Rev. 4:11

Phil. 2:10
1 Chr. 29:11
Rom. 9:5
1 Tim. 6:16
1 Pet. 4:11

Rev. 4:10
Rev. 7:11
Rev. 11:16

1. AND I saw in the right hand of him that sat on the throne a book written within and on the backside, sealed with seven seals.

2. And I saw a strong angel proclaiming with a loud voice, Who is worthy to open the book, and to loose the seals thereof?

3. And no man in heaven, nor in earth, neither under the earth, was able to open the book, neither to look thereon.

4. And I wept much, because no man was found worthy to open and to read the book, neither to look thereon.

5. And one of the elders saith unto me, Weep not: behold, the Lion of the tribe of Judah, the Root of David, hath prevailed to open the book, and to loose the seven seals thereof.

6. And I beheld, and, lo, in the midst of the throne and of the four beasts, and in the midst of the elders, stood a Lamb as it had been slain, having seven horns and seven eyes, which are the seven Spirits of God sent forth into all the earth.

7. And he came and took the book out of the right hand of him that sat upon the throne.

8. And when he had taken the book, the four beasts and four and twenty elders fell down before the Lamb, having every one of them harps, and golden vials full of odors, which are the prayers of saints.

9. And they sung a new song, saying, Thou art worthy to take the book, and to open the seals thereof: for thou wast slain, and hast redeemed us to God by thy blood out of every kindred, and tongue, and people, and nation:

10. And hast made us unto our God kings and priests: and we shall reign on the earth.

11. And I beheld, and I heard the voice of many angels round about the throne and the beasts and the elders: and the number of them was ten thousand times ten thousand and thousands of thousands;

12. Saying with a loud voice, Worthy is the Lamb that was slain to receive power, and riches, and wisdom, and strength, and honor, and glory, and blessing.

13. And every creature which is in heaven, and on the earth, and under the earth, and such as are in the sea, and all that are in them, heard I saying, Blessing, and honor, and glory, and power, be unto him that sitteth upon the throne, and unto the Lamb for ever and ever.

14. And the four beasts said, Amen. And the four and twenty elders fell down and worshiped him that liveth for ever and ever.

Scriptures for Comparison

Daniel 12:8,9,10

And I heard, but I understood not: then said I, O my Lord, what shall be the end of these things?

And he said, Go thy way, Daniel: for the words are closed up and sealed till the time of the end.

Many shall be purified, and made white, and tried; but the wicked shall do wickedly: and none of the wicked shall understand; but the wise shall understand.

John 1:29:

The next day John seeth Jesus coming unto him, and saith, Behold the Lamb of God which taketh away the sin of the world.

Philippians 2:9-11

Wherefore God also hath highly exalted him, and given him a name which is above every name:

That at the name of Jesus every knee should bow, of things in heaven, and things in earth, and things under the earth;

And that every tongue should confess that Jesus Christ is Lord, to the glory of God the Father.

Summary of Chapter Five

Worthy is the Lamb

I. The Book (1-3)
Continuing the awesome description of heavenly scenes, John beholds a mysterious book, sealed with seven seals in the right hand of the Almighty. After an appeal for some worthy or eligible person to qualify as the opener of the scroll, no one in the universe is found with the proper credentials. Then, as John weeps with overcoming emotion at the overwhelming majesty of it all and lack of a worthy person to loose the seven seals, one of the elders speaks.

II. The Lion Lamb (4-7)
"Weep not: behold the Lion of the Tribe of Judah hath prevailed to open the book." Only Christ is qualified to supervise the end time judgments incorporated in the mysterious scroll. The Greek word indicates the rolled scroll type of volume, common for millennia.

Christ appears, not as the Lion, but as the Lamb, and takes the book.

Walter Scott says, "The 'seven seals' express the perfection with which the hidden counsels of God are securely wrapped up in the divine mind till their disclosure by the Lamb … For as the seven-sealed book, with its full and minute disclosure of the future, is no longer a hidden mystery, prophecy, once a secret, is no longer a secret."

III. Praises and Songs (8-14)
The 24 elders fall down before Him and sing a new song of praise, extolling the worthiness of the Lamb and acclaiming Him as the redeemer and royalizer of His people.

These distinguished elders are evidently representative of the New Testament saints, although some have thought that since there were 12 patriarches of the tribes of Israel and 12 apostles, that they are here in view. It is more likely that these priest-kings with their white robes depict the raptured, glorified believers of this age, commencing their reign with Christ.

Joining the anthem of the elders who represent the saints of God is a vast angel choir of 100,000,000 with thousands of thousands more, who sound a sevenfold acclamation of praise unto the Lamb.

As the chapter closes and the heavenly prelude to the judgment scenes to follow in chapter six concludes, the entire universe and all creatures join in a triumphant accolade of "blessing, honor, glory and power" unto the enthroned manifestation of Deity and to the Lamb.

Outline of Chapter Five

The Seven Sealed Book

OBJECTIVE: To reveal the supreme worthiness of Christ alone to oversee the final destiny of the earth, of mankind, of all things.

OUTLINE:

I. The Seven Sealed Scroll (1)
A. The Source of the Scroll—God
B. The Symbols on the Scroll—written within and without
C. The Seals on the Scroll—it is "shut" and must be opened

II. The Search (2-4)
A. The Question of the Angel: Who is worthy? (2)
B. The Quest for a Worthy One (3)
C. The Tears of John—no one found (4)

III. The Savior (5, 6)
A. The Elder Speaks (5)
B. The One is Worthy (5)
  1. He is Lion of the Tribe of Judah (Isaiah 11:1)
    a. He alone prevails
    b. He will open the book
    c. He will loose the seals
  2. He Is the Lamb, as it had been slain (6)
    a. In the midst of all
    b. Having the Holy Spirit (Isaiah 11:2)

IV. The Solution (7)
The great search ends with the Lamb taking the book.

V. The Songs and Sayings (8-13)
A. The Song of the Redeemed (8-10)
  1. Voiced by the Cherubim and the Elders (8)
  2. Accompanied by the Harp Music (8)
  3. Preceded by the Incense of Prayer (8)
  4. Expressing His Worthiness (9)
  5. Extolling His Work of Redemption (9-10)
    a. He was slain
    b. He has redeemed us by blood
    c. He has called us from all peoples
    d. He has exalted us to His kingdom.
B. The Saying of the Angels and the Redeemed (11, 12)
  1. The Throng that Sang (11)
  2. The Theme of the Song (12)
    Compare "worthy" in 4:11; 5:4, 9, 12; also 3:4 and 16:6)
  3. The Thoughts They Voiced—seven in number (12)
    a. Power   c. Wisdom   e. Honor
    b. Riches   d. Strength f. Glory
                             g. Blessing
C. The Saying (Song?) of all Creation (13)
  1. Four Realms:
    a. Heaven   c. Under the earth
    b. Earth   d. In the sea
  2. Four Words:
    a. Blessing   c. Glory
    b. Honor   d. Power

VI. The Submission (14)
Cherubim and elders fall down and worship.

Observations:
Spiritual lessons and applications from each verse
Chapter Five

1. God operates in His universe by plan, by "books." It is scriptural for us to plan, prayerfully, our lives and future (compare Daniel 12:1-4).

2. Who, indeed, is ever worthy to work the works of God? Certainly not man by his own merits and abilities.

3. No man, however talented, gifted, brilliant or illustrious, is worthy before a holy God to perform either great or small tasks. Yet, God uses sinners saved by grace.

4. Aware of all humanity's shortcomings in all areas, we too might weep in realization of the true lost nature of all mankind. Even angels are not intrinsically worthy.

5. Jesus makes up for our lack. He can banish tears and prevail over everything.

6. Jesus, the Lamb of God, in one sense, is always in the midst of His people ... in the midst of his "elders."

7. Jesus alone is worthy and eligible to supervise the judgments this book contains, control the earth, and rule in splendor.

8. The elders, typifying the saints of God, raptured or resurrected, play their harps and offer, like sweet incense, their prayers (see Pslam 141:2).

9. Heaven is filled with singing and praise. Here, the worthiness of the Lamb who is the source of REDEMPTION is the focus. In 4:11, the elders extol the Lord, who is the source of CREATION.

10. Currently, believers are kings and priests, a kingdom of priests, whose future destiny is to reign on the earth (see I Peter 2:9). A king rules; a priest intercedes for others. Present "sacrifices" believer-priests are to offer include themselves (Romans 12:1) and praise, thanksgiving, good works and gifts (Hebrews 13:15, 16).

11. Angels, invisible to us, but real, are found in heaven and on earth (see Hebrews 1:14).

12. Angels, elders (saints), cherubim can all join in praise. We can praise God today in our hearts, by our lives, through our words. Observe seven points of praise in the acclamation of worthiness.

13. All things glorify God ultimately (see Romans 8:28; I Corinthians 15:24-28).

14. Worship is directing our minds, emotions, our entire beings, toward God in adoration, praise and love. "Falling down" indicates total surrender, allegiance.

Quotations
From Other Expositors
Chapter Five

The Book (1-4)
"Chapter five describes the Lamb and the seven-sealed scroll. It also serves as a prelude to the seven seal judgments. All three series of judgments (seals, trumpets, vials) will be preceded by a prelude ... It is a scroll (the real meaning of the Greek term translated 'book') that is written on both sides and is sealed with seven seals."

–Arthur Frucktenbaum

"Now this scroll is here pictured as being entirely sealed with seven seals. These seals were probably arranged in a row on the outside of the scroll. Thus viewed, they sealed the scroll's enclosure. The meaning is this: The closed scroll indicates the Plan of God unrevealed and unexecuted. If that scroll remains sealed, God's purposes are not realized; His plan is not carried out. To open that scroll by breaking the seals means not merely to reveal but to carry out God's plan."

–William Hendrickson

"This book contains the description of the horrendous judgments to befall the earth in the end times, the apocalyptic conclusion of history, the affirmation of a millenium and a last judgment, and a glimpse of the eternal state. Out of the seventh seal proceed the seven trumpets, from which emerge the seven vial judgments. It has been called a telescopic development, each series opening up the next."

–James O. Combs

The Lion-Lamb (5-7)
"Jesus is the Lion sprung from Judah. He is this Root of David-the foundation on which the Davidic hopes repose. He overcame, in the trials of life, in the temptations of the wilderness, in the agonies of the garden, in the errors of death and in the bonds of the grave. He is victor now over Law, and sin, and death, and hell. He hath paid the redemption price of the forfeited inheritance. He is the true God, who, having so far triumphed and been accepted, will also prove ready and worthy to complete His work ... He who appears here as a Lamb, is the same whom the Elder had just described as a Lion. The two titles might seem to be incongruous. What more opposite than the monarch of the forest, in

strength and majesty, ... and the lamb in its uncomplaining meekness in the hands of the sacrificer. But the two pictures do not conflict. They supplement each other. The opening of the seals is an act of strength ... a going forth of power to take possession of a kingdom ... in the accomplishment of this Christ is a Lion, clothed with power and majesty.

"But the character in which He overcame, and became in that respect qualified for His work, and in which He presents Himself before the throne as a candidate to be adjudged worthy to do it, is that of the sacrificial Lamb, who had innocently and meekly suffered, bearing our sins in His own body, and vanquishing all legal disabilities by His atoning blood ... As the Lamb He hath 'borne our sorrows and carried our iniquities (Isa. 53:4-7) and stands before the throne in passive humiliation and loyal suffering.' As Judah's Lion ... 'in righteousness He will judge and make war.'"

–J.A. Seiss

The Twenty-Four Elders (8-10)

"The moment that the Lamb takes the book, in verse eight the four living ones and the four and twenty elders fall down before Him, having every one of them harps, and golden bowls full of odors, which are the prayers of saints ... It is not merely of themselves they sing, but of all the redeemed; so the living ones join in it too. Note the great throng suggested by the words of the song ... We shall have the society of all the pure and holy, made pure by the blood of Jesus ... They ascribe their redemption entirely to the Lamb and His work. Those are the saints of God."

– H.A. Ironside

"The identity of these twenty-four elders has been much debated ... there are clues in the text by which their identity may be deduced. First, these elders are clothed with *white garments,* which throughout the Revelation are symbols of salvation. Celestial beings do not need salvation for they were never lost ... but these elders were at one time lost and at some point received salvation as is seen by the wearing of white garments.

"The second clue is the fact that they are wearing crowns. These are *stephanos* crowns (not diadem crowns worn by those royal in nature), the crowns of overcomers; the type of crown given as rewards at the Judgment Seat of Christ.

"A third clue lies in the very title *elders.* Nowhere else in Scripture is this term used to describe celestial or angelic beings. This term is used of humans in positions of authority in the synagogue

or the church. Hence, from these three clues, the twenty-four elders represent the church saints. If this is true, then they provide further evidence for a pre-tribulational rapture. The church is already in heaven in chapter four and five before the Tribulation begins in chapter six. Chapters two and three viewed the church on earth with a promise in 3:10 that we will be kept from the very time of tribulation. Now that promise has been kept. The fact of the elders wearing crowns also shows that the events described in chapters four and five occur after the Judgment Seat of Christ and before the Marriage of the Lamb (19)."

– Arthur Fruchtenbaum

The Praises of All Creation (11-14)

"We have heard the voices of 'many angels', the Zoa and the twenty-four elders singing praises to God (4:11; 5:9; 11:1), but here we have an almost unlimited number praising the Lamb with a loud voice ... it is the 'loud voice' of all creation. It is fourfold (blessing, honor, glory, might), because it is connected with the earth, whose number is 'four.'"

– Bill Lawrence

"The number of the angels is stated as one hundred millions and then millions and millions! When they see the Lamb that they saw slain now take the book of the Kingdom, do you wonder that they say with a great voice, 'Worthy is the Lamb that was slain'? Have *you* spoken thus about the Lamb of God?" Eventually, "'when every created thing in heaven and on the earth and under the earth and on the sea and all things that are in them say, 'Unto him that sitteth on the throne and unto the Lamb be blessing and honor and glory and dominion, unto the ages of the ages,' all infidels will be included, all rejectors of Christ, all your family, saved or unsaved, all your loved ones, saved or lost alike ... No creature will be left out. This great universal confession, in its final pronouncement after the Great White Throne judgment, will not be for salvation, but it will be a fulfilling of Philippians 2:9-11: "That at the name of Jesus every knee should bow, of things in heaven, and things on earth and things under the earth, and that every tongue should confess that Jesus Christ is Lord, to the glory of God the Father."

– William R. Newell

The Lion of the Tribe of Judah Hath Prevailed
An Expository Sermon

Chapter Five

Introduction

Amid the shining wonders of this celestial scene, our attention is drawn to the great Sovereign of the universe, seated in enthroned splendor, upon a rainbow-encircled throne. In the right hand of the Almighty is a seven-sealed book or scroll. In those days, books were scrolls made of parchment, rolled up just as the orthodox Hebrews keep their Scriptures today in the synagogues. It was such a scroll with visible writing evident. Some have said that this represents the "title deed of the earth." Adam lost it, they aver. Christ regains it. An illustration of this is found in Jeremiah 32:6-15. Jeremiah is told by the Lord to buy land in Israel which is shortly to fall to the Chaldeans. It was not until Israel returned 70 years later than the property could be possessed again by virtue of the deed.

I rather think that the scroll contains a vivid description of the unfolding panorama of the end times, a concept which, to me, seems self-evident. As seals are opened, events transpire in heaven or on earth, resulting in seven trumpets of judgment being blown after the seventh seal is opened.

"Worthy" is the important word in this chapter, appearing earlier in 4:11:

"Thou art worthy, O Lord, to receive glory and honor and power: for thou hast created all things, and for thy pleasure they are and were created."

The WORTHY CREATOR GOD is thus extolled.

I. The Worthy Receiver of the Book (1-7)

An angel calls for someone to open the seven-sealed book. Who was worthy?

Adam, the first man, is not worthy. He lost his right through sin.

Lucifer was given great liberty and dominion by God as "the anointed cherub that covereth" (Ezekiel 28:14). He rebelled and has not that right (Isaiah 14:12-15).

Abraham, the father of the faithful, was not worthy. He, too, was a sinner.

John, the apostle and revelator, knew he was not worthy.

The elders, representing the saved, are not worthy.

The cherubim are not worthy, for they are created beings, though sinless. Who? Who? Who?

Before the Worthy One is revealed, John weeps because no one is worthy to take the book, to supervise history, destiny, all things.

"Weep not ... behold the Lion of the Tribe of Judah hath prevailed ..." says an elder.

The Lion, symbol and type of Judah and the Messiah prevails.

Jacob, when he lay-a-dying, said, "Judah is a lion's whelp; from the prey my son, thou art gone up: he stooped down, he couched as a lion, and as an old lion; who shall rouse him up? The scepter shall not depart from Judah, not a lawgiver from between his feet, until SHILOH come; [a title of Christ ... meaning REST]; and unto him shall the gathering of the people be" (Genesis 49:9, 10).

A descendent of the tribe of Judah, Jesus was the LION; a descendent of the royal Davidic line, He was the Root of David.

"And there shall come forth a rod out of the stem of Jesse [father of David], and a Branch shall grow out of his roots ... and the Spirit of the Lord shall rest upon Him" (Isaiah 11:1, 2).

As the Lion, He is the rightful ruler of Israel forever.

As the Lamb, He is the Savior of all, Jews and Gentiles, forever.

As the Lion, He is depicted as the Mighty King.

As the Lamb, He is seen as the suffering Savior.

As the Lion, He is designated once to establish His hereditary human title as King of Israel. Twice, he is called "the root." Here and in 22:16: "I am the root and offspring of David and the bright and morning star."

As the Lamb, He is mentioned 28 times. He was THE LAMB slain from the foundation of the world (13:8). And in the eternity future, in the New Jerusalem, "the throne of God and THE LAMB shall continue forever."

No wonder John the Baptist exclaimed, "Behold the Lamb of God which taketh away the sin of the world" (John 1:29).

He prevailed, this LION-LAMB, to open the book ...

He prevailed over Herod, who sought to slay Him after His birth.

He prevailed over Satan atop the mount of

temptation.

He prevailed over every temptation, being in all points tempted like as we are, yet without sin.

He prevailed over disease, as He healed the sick.

He prevailed over nature, as He stilled the storm.

He prevailed over His critics, as He spoke as no man ever spoke.

He prevailed in the garden as He prepared to go to the Cross.

He prevailed over those who came to arrest Him as He repelled them to the ground and then surrendered to His enemies ... to become indeed THE LAMB on the altar of Calvary.

He prevailed over sin on the Cross.

He prevailed over hell as He conquered iniquity and took the keys of hell and death.

He prevailed over death as He arose from the grave.

He prevailed over principalities and powers as He spoiled them and entered into heaven.

He prevailed as He sat down at the right hand of the majesty on high.

He will prevail when He comes at the Rapture and Resurrection.

He will prevail over all enemies when He returns as King of Kings.

"THE LION OF THE TRIBE OF JUDAH HATH PREVAILED ..."

The Lion is worthy to receive the book! To supervise and judge, to rule and reign, to consummate all of history into that eternal destiny planned by the TRIUNE GOD.

But no sooner than the kingly Lion title is heralded, does then the Lamb Himself appear.

And immediately He is identified as the One who had been slain, for it is His solitary sacrificial and vicarious atonement for our sins that makes possible His assumption of supreme power over the end times. Had He not first come as the Lamb..."led as a Lamb to the slaughter, and as a sheep before His shearers is dumb, so he opened not his mouth" (Isa. 53:70, "to take away the sins of the world" (John 1:29), He could not come as the Lion in splendid power to be the Messiah indeed for future Israel and Sovereign of the world. The Old Testament mingles "the sufferings of Christ" and the "glory that should follow" (1 Peter 1:11) in the same prophecies, for the earlier prophets did not foresee with clarity the Dispensation of Grace between the two comings.

This word "lamb" here is a most affectioned one in the Greek, denoting a "pet lamb," sharply contrasting with the wild beasts against whom He will wage war (ch. 13). Yet, as the Lamb He opens the seals, (ch. 6) and precipitates the judgments...

This title harks back into pre-history, for He is "the Lamb slain from the foundation of the world" (13:8) in the mind and plan of God...AND in eternity future, beyond this world's duration, believers will behold "a pure river of water of life, clear as crystal, proceeding out of the throne of God AND OF THE LAMB" (22:1)! This is the destiny of those who are "the wife of the Lamb" (19:7) and whose names are written in "the Lamb's book of life!" (21:27).

"He has seven horns and seven eyes, which are the seven Spirits of God" (6). As for these seven horns, they are the symbols of strength and power. In Zechariah 1:18,19, we read,

"I lifted I up mine eyes, and saw, and behold four horns. And I said unto the angel that talked with me; What be these? And he answered me: These are the horns [powers] which have scattered Judah, Israel, and Jerusalem." The horn stands for power, prestige, might and dominion of Christ as indicated. His "horns" are in sharp contrast to the "horns" of the beast in Daniel 7:7 and Rev. 13:1, where 10 mere earthly powers combine under the Antichrist.

As the horns speak of Christ's imperial dominion, so the "seven eyes" suggest His complete knowledge, for He sees all things..."they are naked and opened unto the eyes of Him with whom we have to do" (Heb. 4:13). Those eyes are the "seven spirits," mentioned in Isaiah 11:2 and reemphasized in Rev. 1:4; 3:1 and 4:5. It is the all-knowing, all wise Holy Spirit, who anointed Christ and whose presence in the Divine Trinity is eternal.

Notice that Jesus, the Lion-Lamb, takes the Book. He alone has the sovereign right to supervise and execute the end time events and to bring all of history into its final consummation. No one else is worthy. No one else can ever qualify.

How important it therefore is for us today to serve Him with selfless devotion and undying love.

How important it is to keep his commandments without spot, "unrebukable," until the appearing of our Lord Jesus Christ,

"Which in His times he shall shew, who is the blessed and only Potentate, the King of Kings and Lord of Lords;

"Who only hath immortality, dwelling in the light which no man can approach unto; whom no man hath seen, nor can see [in His real essence]: to whom be honor and power everlasting. Amen!" (1 Tim. 6:14-16).

II. The Worthy Redeemer of the Saints (8-10)

There will come a glorious day, after the rapture, when we shall, as the elders, sit round about the celestial throne. We shall play the harps of God and offer the incense of prayer. We shall then in joyous voices sing anew of the worthiness of the Lamb. From heaven's vantage point we shall, if we desire, behold the fulfillment of all that the Book of Revelation so vividly describes.

Throughout all eternity, I doubt not but that we shall continue to acclaim His worthiness, wherever we are in His universe.

He is the WORTHY REDEEMER. He was slain before the foundation of the world in the mind and plan of God.

He has redeemed us, not "with corruptible things as silver and gold, but with the precious blood of Christ."

"In whom we have redemption through his blood, the forgiveness of sins, according to the riches of his grace" (Ephesians 1:7).

We have been redeemed out of all peoples everywhere.

Not just the Jews, but all among the Gentiles, who will hear His voice and heed His gospel!

He has paid the price for sin, shedding His blood, His literal blood, worth more than all the sacrifices of all the animals of all the ages past.

"Neither by the blood of goats and calves, but by his own blood he entered in once into the holy place, having obtained eternal redemption for us. For if the blood of bulls and of goats, and of ashes of a heifer sprinkling the unclean, sanctifieth to the purifying of the flesh: How much more shall the blood of Christ, who through the eternal Spirit offered himself without spot to God, purge your conscience from dead works to serve the living God?" (Hebrews 9:12-15).

We dare not, as even some professing Bible believers do, downgrade the blood of Christ!

No! A thousand times, NO!

"Of how much sorer punishment suppose ye shall he be thought worthy, who hath trodden under foot the Son of God, and hath counted the blood of the convenant, wherewith he was sanctified an unholy thing, and hath done despite unto the Spirit of grace?" (Hebrews 10:29).

In heaven we shall sing about the blood!

"Thou hast redeemed us by the blood."

"And they sang a new song, saying, Thou art worthy to take the book, and to open the seals thereof: for thou wast slain, and hast redeemed us to God by thy blood out of every kindred, and tonge and people and nation; and hast made us unto our God kings and priests: and we shall reign on the earth" (9,10).

O, what a glorious time, when we sing the song of blood-redemption before the Throne!

III. The Worthy Ruler of the Universe (11-14)

Our glorious LION-LAMB, symbols and titles of sovereignty and saviourhood, is greater than all

the angels. The largest choir in all the universe, consisting of a hundred million angelic voices and thousands of thousands more, "an innumerable company of angels," blend their voices to praise the Lord of all.

Hebrews 1 speaks of His superiority over all the angels, "Being made so much better than the angels, as he hath by inheritance obtained a more excellent name than they ... Let all the angels of God worship him ..." (1:4, 6).

"Worthy is the Lamb that was slain to receive power, and riches, and wisdom, and strength, and honor, and glory, and blessing" (12).

He is worthy to receive *power* because all things were made by Him.

He is worthy to receive all *riches* because "though he was rich, yet for your sakes he became poor, that ye, through his poverty might be made rich" (2 Corinthians 8:9).

He is worthy to receive *wisdom,* for He is Christ, the wisdom of God (I Corinthians 1:24).

He is worthy to receive *strength,* the power physically to rule with a rod of iron, for this is His divine destiny. He will have power oVER the nations!

"And he shall rule them with a rod of iron; as the vessels of a potter shall he break them to pieces: even as I received of my Father" (2:27).

He is "the Manchild, who is to rule all nations with the rod of iron" (12:5)!

"And out of his mouth goeth a sharp sword, that with it he should smite the nations: and he shall rule them with a rod of iron ..." (19:15).

He is worthy to receive *honor,* because he is the only one qualified for universal honor.

He is worthy to receive *glory,* and we look for "the glorious appearing of the great God and our Savior Jesus Christ."

He is worthy to receive *blessing,* for He is the supremely Blessed One of all the ages.

"Blessing and honor and glory and power, be unto Him," shouts all of creation.

Like the cherubim, let us echo our "Amen!"

Like the elders, which typify the saints, let us fall down before Him and worship Him that liveth for ever and ever.

Some grand and future day, not too far distant, we shall also join with a vast and innumerable host of heaven, as the voice of many waters, as the voice of mighty thunderings, saying,

"Alleluia; for the Lord God omnipotent reigneth!" (19:6).

O, in that glorious moment, where will you be? With Christ in heaven? In fulness of joy? Saved by the blood?

O, if you are unsure of your salvation, come to Christ now. Receive Him as your Savior now. You will become a child of God.

A Commentary on the Revelation
Expository, Exegetical, Devotional and Practical
Greek words from the Textus Receptus
Chapter Five

The Book with Seven Seals (1-4)

1. And I saw in the right hand (*kai eidon epi ten dekisan*) — the hand of authority and power; Alford indicates that the idea here is that the book lay upon the open hand of God, available, ready to be taken by a worthy person, there being no reluctance on God's part to have it opened and unsealed … Remember again that no one actually sees the true essence of His Divine Being ("no one hath seen God at any time" — John 1:18), for Paul states: "Now unto the King eternal, immortal, invisible, the only wise God, be honor and glory forever and ever" (1 Timothy 1:17). God manifests and reveals Himself however at times in a form reminiscent of a glorious human, or He can speak through a "cloud" or a "burning bush" or "in a still small voice" … **a book written within and on the backside** (*biblion gegrammenon esothen kai opisthen*) — ancient books were in the form of rolls or scrolls, as is evident from the discovery of the Dead Sea Scrolls at Qumram. This scroll, some say, may have been so rolled that each time a seal was opened, the cylindrical roll could be unrolled by a new inches OR it may have been so designed that all seals were in a line on the edge of the wrapped document. It is clear that it is sealed with seven seals (*katesphragismenon spagisin hepta*) – Daniel's scroll (12:4), rather than to be opened in his time (536 B.C.), was to be sealed up until "the time of the end." With the Book of Revelation, and especially in the last days, as "the time of the end" approaches, Daniel can better be understood and also "unsealed." The big question here is what the scroll is and just what does it contain? Many expositors think it is the **title deed to the world** (Seiss, Ironside, De Burgh, Phillips, etc.) or to man's inheritance. As proof, Jeremiah, in spite of the impending seventy years of captivity (Jer. 32:6-15), bought a field, receiving the title deed, which was properly sealed. It was then placed in an earthen vessel and thus preserved in order that Jeremiah's heirs might have the property following the long seventy year captivity. Since this "sealed" document was a title deed to land, it is thought that this sealed book is a title deed to the earth, which only Christ is worthy to receive. Although a very interesting view, these concepts do not seem to appear in the context of this passage. What is evident is that this scroll must contain a description and account of events, judgments, and revelations dealing with the period set forth, mainly the Tribulation, the execution of which can only be supervised by a truly worthy Person, namely Christ. **2. A strong angel** (*angelion ischuron*) — an angel of strength; some have suggested that this is Michael, but this is conjecture (See however Jude 9; Rev. 12:7-12; Dan. 12:1; Dan. 8:16; 9:21; Luke 1:19, 26 for information about Michael and Gabriel and their special ministries). **loud voice** (*phone megale*) — like a megaphone … **Who is worthy to open the book and to loose the seals thereof?** Opening the book and breaking the seals seem to be separate actions. It is as though Jesus opens the book and the loosing of the seals (Rev. 6) is the execution of what is written therein. The challenge for a worthy Opener is unanswered. **3. no man** — not even one, no one had the power or ability or qualifications in heaven, on earth, in the realm of departed spirits. No one is ethically, morally, or spiritually able to accept the responsibility and authority to unroll or unleash or execute its contents. **4. And I wept much** (*kai eklaion polu*) — Eager now to learn of these "things which must be hereafter", John is temporarily overcome with disappointment, weeping much, profusely, possibly supposing that he, like Daniel, might be involved with a sealed book. Notice that no angel steps forward. No great Old Testament saint, like Moses or Elijah or Isaiah, is qualified, nor are any of the Apostles already in heaven eligible and qualified for this high and holy honor to open this book. John himself, rather than rashly and proudly imagining that he was worthy, weeps in humility and meekness.

The Lion-Lamb (5-7)

5. Weep not, behold (*me klaie idou*) — one of the elders says, but instead, look, behold, comprehend, for the answer to the quest and question is present … **The Lion of the tribe of Judah, the Root of David, hath prevailed** (*enikesen ho leon ho ek test phules Iouda*) — the word **prevailed** (*enikesen*) is the same word as **overcome** (*nikon*) in chapters two and three with a different prefix and suffix. See Isaiah 11:2. Not only is He the Root, that is the descendant from David, but this also includes the idea that He is Himself the root and origin of David, as is indicated in Matthew 22:42-45, where Jesus quotes Psalm 110 in which David called Him Lord. Thus Christ's question, "If David then call him (the Messiah) Lord, how is he his son?" (22:45). He is at once David's Branch, the Root and Offspring (22:16) David's Son and David's Lord, the Lamb slain and also the Lion (*leon*) of Judah (Gen. 49:9-12). His past victories well qualify Him to open the book and to loose the seals thereof. **6. In the midst** (*en meso*) — The Lamb appears in the midst of the throne, in the midst of the four beasts (*zoa*), in the midst of the elders, in the center, as it were of the celestial circle, beyond which a larger circle of angels and then the whole universe is seen praising God at the end of the chapter. **Lamb** (*arnion*) — not the usual word as in John for Lamb, which is *amnos* (John 1:29), but a word meaning "little lamb"; in contrast to the beast (Rev. 13), where the word is *therion*, a wild ravenous, vicious beast. Notice the Lamb is standing, though He had been slain, as if ready now for service and movement. Once He was led as a Lamb to the slaughter (Isa. 53:7), for He was Christ our Passover (Lamb) sacrificed for us (1 Cor. 5:7), but now He is prepared to open seals and dispense judgments (Rev. 6:1,3,5,7,9,12; 8:1). **Seven horns and seven eyes** (*kerata hepta kai ophthalmous hepta*) — Horns speak of power (contrast the ten horns of the beast — 13:1; 17:12; Daniel 7:7,8), since He is perfect in might and power, seven symbolizing completion and perfection. The number seven occurs fifty-four times in Revelation. Compare with Zechariah 4:2, the seven lamps of the Menorah, the candlestick, and the seven eyes in 4:10: "For who hath despised the day of small things? for they shall rejoice, and shall see the plummet in the hand of Zerubbabel with those seven; they are the eyes of the Lord, which run to and fro through the whole earth." The seven spirits (see Isaiah 11:2) speak of the Holy Spirit, who anointed Christ, and who in omniscience and omnipresence sees all that happens on earth. **7. took the book** — The Lamb takes it from the Father, for He now is fully authorized to propel the wheels of history on through the coming apocalyptic period, gloriously triumphing over Satan and wickedness, and establishing His kingdom and control over this world. He will reign a thousand years and on into eternity forever.

The Twenty-four Elders' Song (8-10)

8. His taking the book precipitates heavenly celebrations unparalleled in biblical history. First the four beasts, living creatures, *zoa,* fall down before the Lamb, for even the cherubim, the highest of angelic creatures must pay obeisance to the mighty Lamb. Then the twenty-four elders prostrate themselves in total submission to the Lamb of God, aware that He will manifest Himself as the Lord of history and the Consumnator of the age, the Lamb, the Lion, the Sacrifice (was slain), the Redeemer, the Royalizer, and supreme Sovereign. **having every one of them harps** (*echontes hekastos kitharan*) — stringed heavenly instruments, which evidently the raptured and glorified saints may play in praise. This is the origin of the concept that people in heaven have harps. Think of a place where the redeemed are all musically endowed beyond imagination ... **and golden vials full of odours** (*kai phialas chrusas gemousas thumiamaton*) — these are golden bowls full of incense, representative of prayer. Psalm 141:2 says, "Let my prayers be set forth as incense: and the lifting up of my hands as the evening sacrifice" ... **which are the prayers of saints** (*hai eisin hai prosevchar ton hagion*). The incense symbolizes prayer, a sweet savour unto the Lord, as in the Old Testament Tabernacle with its Altar of Incense (Ex. 37:25-28). This is further proof that these elders are the saints of God, for angels are not intercessors and do not pray on our behalf. Even in heaven the glorified saints continue to offer prayers to the Father and praise to the Lamb. **9. A new song** — three times in the Apocalypse songs are specifically mentioned. While the "sayings" in the end of this chapter and elsewhere may be musical or nonmusical choral expressions in unison, these are definitely songs: here where the elders-saints sing; in 14:3 where the 144,000 sing "a new song" only they can sing; and in 15:3 where the Tribulation martyrs sing the song of Moses and the song of the Lamb ... **worthy** (*aksios or axios*) — meaning of great value, weight or merit. This Greek word occurs seven times in Revelation: 3:4; 4:11; 5:2; 5:4; 5:9; 5:12; and in a negative sense in 16:6. The fifty-four occurrences of the specific number "seven" and the less obvious listings and sets of "sevens", as here are mentioned cannot be coincidental, but evidence of divine design. **And hast redeemed** (*kai egorasas*) — meaning purchased, perhaps out of a slave market, with a full price being paid ... **by thy blood** (*en haimati sou*) the English **hemoglobin** is derived from the Greek *haima*. In both the Old Testament and the New the idea of redemption by blood is most prominent. The O.T. word *dam* (Heb.) for blood occurs 362 times, with many usages; the New Testament word *haima* appears 98 times in Greek, translated "blood." ... **us** (*hemas*) is used in the Authorized Version. Other

ancient manuscripts read "them," but since there is strong textual evidence for **us**, this exposition retains it. **kindred, tongue, people, nation** — again the four designations here relate to the earth, since four is the number of the world in Scripture. **10. And has made us unto our God** (*kai epoiesas autous to theo hemon*) — in relationship to God believers have been made something very special. Sometimes in Hebrew the third person is used to mean the first person, which may be why some manuscripts read **them** instead of **us**, but on the other hand this was originally written in Greek, but there is no doubt the twenty-four elders mean themselves, i.e. the glorified believers … **kings and priests** (*basileion kai hiereis*) can be interpreted as a kingdom of priests. These priest-kings are a priesthood in heaven, the highest position, and are to be kings on earth, a lesser role, in the millennium. All will reign with Christ forever (22:5) … **reign on the earth** (*basileu somen epi tes ges*) — during the "regeneration", the millennium, the twelve apostles will sit on twelve thrones, judging the twelve tribes of Israel (Matt. 19:28); other believers will exercise authority over the millenial world (See Matt. 5:5; Acts 20:28; Luke 19:17; 2 Tim. 2:12).

Praises to God (11-14)

11. Notice the concentric circles of worshippers: the throne in the midst with the Almighty and the Lamb; then the four living creatures; then the twenty-four elders, the ransomed, raptured, resurrected saints; then an array of angels, myriads of myriads, then all creatures successively, those in heaven, on earth, under the earth, and in the sea, rendering homage to the Almighty and the Lamb … **ten thousand times ten thousand** (*muriades muriadon*) and **thousands** and **thousands** (*chiliades, chiliadon*) — all beyond human calculation … **12. Worthy is the Lamb that was slain** — angels, too, acknowledge the worthiness of the great Redeemer, who also by His death delivered creation from the bondage of corruption (see Romans 8:19-23). We see not yet all things put under Him however (Heb. 2:8) … the sevenfold array of glorious honors of which He is worthy is set forth and is worthy of careful study: **power** (*dunamin*), dynamic and administrative power; **riches** (*plouton*), universal wealth; **wisdom** (*sophian*), infinite knowledge and understanding; **strength** (*ischun*), physical-supernatural ability; **honor** (*timen*), acclaim and recognition; **glory** (*doksan*), incomparable and magnificent; **blessing** (*eulogian*), goodness, favor, kindness, happiness. **13.** A fourfold ascription of praise comes from all who have ever lived or will live on this world (See Phil. 2:9-11). **14. Amen** — the

four living creatures, whereas in 4:11 the twenty-elders have already praised Him who "created all things," now render their praise and ratification to all these ascriptions of glory to "him who sits upon the throne and unto the Lamb." **And the four and twenty elders fell down and worshipped him** (*kai hoi presbuteroi epesan kai prosekunesan*) — The aged Apostle has beheld a sweeping, awesome view of the transcendent and resplendent glory of God as Creator upon His rainbow encircled throne. His executive authority over the entire Universe is delegated to and vested in Jesus Christ, the "Lamb slain from the foundation of the world" and whose ineffable worthiness is magnified so clearly in this chapter. Before Him the elders-saints, the glorified believers, bow in praise and worship, as a panoramic revelation of judgments upon this earth is about to unfold. The prelude is complete; the tribulation time is now to be exhibited before the awestruck gaze of the sainted John. **that liveth forever and ever** — that is, unto the ages of the ages, the *aions* of the *aions*. Because He lives, we shall live also. How glorious will be the future fulfillment and reenactment of these events which John saw, when we are all in the presence of the Lamb. And how much more glorious in the eternal and celestial city, the New Jerusalem, when we shall continue to serve Him and to see His face and to reign with Him forever and ever (22:3-5).

Numbers in Revelation

Since numbers hold so prominent a place in the Apocalypse, it is appropriate at this point to list them, before moving into the bulk of the book. These in order are: 2 (occurs 11 times); 3 (occurs 11 times); $3\frac{1}{2}$ (occurs 2 times); 4 (occurs 30 times); 5 (occurs 3 times); 6 (2 times including 13:18); 7 (occurs 54 times); 12 (occurs 9 times); 12 (occurs 22 times); 24 (occurs seven times); 42 (occurs twice); 144 (occurs 4 times); 666 (occurs 1 time); 1,000 (occurs 9 times); 1,260 (occurs twice); 1,600 (occurs once); 7,000 (occurs once); 12,000 (occurs 13 times); 144,000 (occurs 3 times); 100,000,000 (occurs once—5:11); 200,000,000 (occurs once—9:16). This is a total of 21 different numbers, appearing in this one book, more than in any other book of the Bible. Seven is the predominant number, occurring 54 times with twelve coming next. Seven symbolizes divine completion and perfection. Twelve is the number of government and administration in Scripture (The Companion Bible).

RAINBOWS FROM REVELATION
The Revelation of Jesus Christ

A chapter by chapter, verse by verse study

"There was a rainbow round about the throne like unto an emerald" (4:3)

CHAPTER SIX: Christ Opens the Seals

References

Jn. 1:29

Zech. 1:8; 6:3
Ps. 45:4,5
Mt. 24:5

Rev. 4:7

Zech. 1:8; 6:2,3
Mt. 24:5,7

Zech. 6:2,6
Mt. 24:7

Rev. 4:7

Zech. 6:2,3,6
Jer. 14:12;
15:2; 24:10
Ez. 14:21
Mt. 24:9

2 Tim. 1:8

1. AND I saw when the Lamb opened one of the seals, and I heard, as it were the noise of thunder, one of the four beasts saying, Come and see.

2. And I saw, and behold a white horse: and he that sat on him had a bow; and a crown was given unto him: and he went forth conquering, and to conquer.

3. And when he had opened the second seal, I heard the second beast say, Come and see.

4. And there went out another horse that was red: and power was given to him that sat thereon to take peace from the earth, and that they should kill one another: and there was given unto him a great sword.

5. And when he had opened the third seal, I heard the third beast say, Come and see. And I beheld, and lo a black horse; and he that sat on him had a pair of balances in his hand.

6. And I heard a voice in the midst of the four beasts say, A measure of wheat for a penny, and three measures of barley for a penny; and see thou hurt not the oil and the wine.

7. And when he had opened the fourth seal, I heard the voice of the fourth beast say, Come and see.

8. And I looked, and behold a pale horse: and his name that sat on him was Death, and Hell followed with him. And power was given unto them over the fourth part of the earth, to kill with sword, and with hunger, and with death, and with the beasts of the earth.

9. And when he had opened the fifth seal, I saw under the altar the souls of them that were slain for the word of God, and for the testimony which they held:

10. And they cried with a loud voice, saying, How long, O Lord, holy and true, dost thou not judge and avenge our blood on them that dwell on the earth?

11. And white robes were given unto every one of them; and it was said unto them, that they should rest yet for a little season, until their fellow servants also and their brethren, that should be killed as they were, should be fulfilled.

12. And I beheld when he had opened the sixth seal, and, lo, there was a great earthquake: and the sun became black as sackcloth of hair, and the moon became as blood;

13. And the stars of heaven fell unto the earth, even as a fig tree casteth her untimely figs, when she is shaken of a mighty wind.

14. And the heaven departed as a scroll when it is rolled together; and every mountain and island were moved out of their places.

15. And the kings of the earth, and the great men, and the rich men, and the chief captains, and the mighty men, and every bondman, and every free man, hid themselves in the dens and in the rocks of the mountains;

16. And said to the mountains and rocks, Fall on us, and hide us from the face of him that sitteth on the throne, and from the wrath of the Lamb:

17. For the great day of his wrath is come; and who shall be able to stand?

References

Ps. 13:1,6

Heb. 11:40

Mt. 24:7
Isa. 50:3
Joel 2:10
Isa. 34:4
Mt. 24:29

Mt. 24:29
Mk. 13:25

Nah. 1:5
Isa. 34:4

Jer. 3:23
Ps. 2:4
Ps. 48:4,5
Isa. 2:10-12,19

Hos. 10:8
1 Thes. 1:10
Jer. 30:7
Mal. 3:2
Zeph. 1:14

Nah. 1:6
1 Thes. 5:9

Scriptures for Comparison

Matthew 24:5-8

For many shall come in my name, saying, I am Christ; and shall deceive many.

And ye shall hear of wars and rumors of wars: see that ye be not troubled: for all these things must come to pass, ut the end is not yet.

For nation shall rise against nation, and kingdom against kingdom: and there shall be famines, and pestilences, and earthquakes, in divers places.

All these are the beginning of sorrows.

Ezekiel 14:21

For thus saith the Lord God; How much more when I send my four sore judgments upon Jerusalem, the sword, and the famine, and the noisome beast, and the pestilence, to cut off from it man and beast?

Isaiah 50:3

I clothe the heavens with blackness, and I make sackcloth their covering.

Summary of Chapter Six

The Coming Day of Wrath

In chapters six through nineteen, the TRIBULATION is described. This period occupies 14 of the 22 chapters of the book.

The TRIBULATION, designated "the day of the Lord" in the Old Testament is the climactic era in God's plan for the ages. Satan, under God's permissive hand, is allowed to bring to the earth his evil forces, with the restraining power of God no longer "withholding" his efforts (II Thess. 2:3-9).

As this chapter begins the four living creatures prepare to make their introduction announcement, "Come and see" to John. Christ the Lamb will open the first six of the seven seals. As He opens each seal, a vision appears which signifies an event on the earth, with the exception of the fifth and seventh seals, that trigger events in heaven.

I. First Seal (1,2)

The first seal introduces a rider on a WHITE HORSE, thought by most premillennial expositors to be indicative of the rapid rise of the ANTICHRIST, the world leader, after the rapture of the believers, suggested in chapter four. Paul speaks of his appearance in the end times, "that man of sin, the son of perdition," shall be "revealed" … "who opposeth and exalteth himself above all that is called God, or that is worshiped; so that he as God sitteth in the temple of God, showing himself that he is God … For the mystery of iniquity doth already work: only he who now letteth {hindereth} will let {hinder — meaning of Greek word}, until he be taken out of the way. And then shall that wicked be revealed, whom the Lord shall consume with the spirit of his mouth, and shall destroy with the brightness of his coming" (II Thess. 2:3, 4, 7, 8).

II. Second Seal (3,4)

The second seal brings forth the RED HORSE, representing War. While international conflicts have plagued the earth since the earliest times after the Flood, the last days will bring a great intensification of "wars and rumors of wars" (Mark 13:7). During the 20th century two major world wars engulfed the globe, involving dozens of nations and resulting in the deaths of multiplied millions. It appears that the rider on the white horse, setting forth the rise of the Antichrist, rather rapidly is succeeded by the personification of War, the rider on the red horse. After the Rapture the world will be plunged into a conflict and conflagration, the like of which has never been before (Dan. 12:1).

III. Third Seal (5,6)

The BLACK HORSE is representative of FAMINE and shortages. Even now a billion people on the earth are on the brink of starvation. Even rationing is here suggested with the inference of a day's wages being necessary (a penny - denarius) to pay for a day's food. Special care is given in the disbursement of oil and wine, luxuries of life.

IV. Fourth Seal (7,8)

The fourth horseman, called DEATH, is astride a PALE HORSE. Death and Hell are said to prevail over a fourth part of the earth "to kill with sword [WAR], and with hunger [STARVATION], and with death [PESTILENCE], and with the beasts of the earth." (Compare Ezekiel 14:21: "For thus saith the Lord God; How much more when I send my four sore judgments upon Jerusalem, the sword, and the famine, and the noisesome beast, and the pestilence, to cut off from it man and beast?").

These four horsemen are figurative, but they have a literal application.

V. Fifth Seal (9-11)

When Christ opens the fifth seal, the martyrs in heaven, perhaps of all the ages, are seen under a heavenly altar. They are told to wait a while until other martyrs die in the end times.

History is replete with accounts of multitudes of Christians who refused to renounce Christ before a Caesar; who would not bend to the ecclesiastical or religious regime; who have up their lives under repressive dictatorships, which persecuted believers; and those who die even now in Muslim, communist and other anti-Christian governments.

In the Tribulation, those who turn to Christ, Jews and Gentiles refusing the "mark of the Beast" (Rev. 13:15) will die by the millions.

VI. Sixth Seal (12-17)

"The six seals can be indicated in order: Antichrist, war, famine, deathly pestilence, martyrdom and physical changes," comments Herbert Lockyer. Chaos and disorder reign, but it appears that the Antichrist will reestablish near total control as the Tribulation proceeds.

This chapter somewhat parallels Matthew 24:4-12, which should be studied carefully. Some say that chapter 6 further describes "the beginning of sorrows." Be sure to compare Isaiah 34:4.

This is "the great day of his wrath," certain to come, already in progress as the chapter ends.

Outline of Chapter Six

The Seven Seals are Opened

OBJECTIVE: To introduce and describe the opening stages of the future end time period, when all the apocalyptic pronouncements of the Bible will be fulfilled and history as we know it will come to a close.

OUTLINE:
I. The First Seal: Rise of the Antichrist (1, 2)
A. The Action of the Lamb: He opens the seal
B. The Announcement of the First Beast (zoa): "Come and see"
C. The Appearance of the First Horse (2)
   1. The horse is white (compare Mat. 23:27)
   2. The rider has a bow (threat of power)
   3. The horseman goes forth to conquer

II. The Second Seal: Spread of Worldwide War (3, 4)
A. The Action of the Lamb: He opens the seal
B. The Announcement of the Second Beast (zoa): "Come and see"
C. The Appearance of the Second Horse (4)
   1. The horse is red (color of blood)
   2. The rider has a sword (use of power)
   3. The horseman wages warfare

III. The Third Seal: Increase of Famine (5, 6)
A. The Action of the Lamb: He opens the seal
B. The Announcement of the Third Beast (zoa): "Come and see"
C. The Appearance of the Third Horse (6)
   1. The horse is black (color of judgment)
   2. The rider has a pair of balances
   3. The horseman measures out provisions
A voice among the 4 beasts specifies a day's food for a day's wages (denarius - penny), oil and wine carefully handled. Rationing is indicated here.

IV. The Fourth Seal: Death and Hell (7, 8)
A. The Action of the Lamb: He opens the seal
B. The Announcement of the Fourth Beast (zoa): "Come and see"
C. The Appearance of the Fourth Horse (8)
   1. The horse is pale (greenish parllor)
   2. The rider is DEATH personified
   3. The horseman has the power of death
     a. To kill with sword
     b. To kill with hunger
     c. To kill with death/pestilence
     d. To kill with wild beasts

These are the Four Horsemen of the Apocalypse. In a sense the Antichrist may be the rider of the first three in this symbolic description.

DEATH is the rider of the fourth with HELL following in his awful wake. Compare Ezek. 14:21, where God, who overrules all things, speaks of 4 similar judgments on Israel.

V. The Fifth Seal: Martyrs in Heaven (9-11)
A. The Martyrs' Place: "under the alter"
   1. They were slain for the Word of God
   2. They were slain for their testimonies
Some commentators think these are Tribulation martyrs; others think all martyrs of all ages are seen in this vision, since others are to be slain as they were, in the future.
B. The Martyrs' Prayer: "How long, O Lord?"
   1. Judgment Will Come
   2. Vengeance Is Certain
C. The Martyrs' Patience: they are "to rest a little season"
D. The Martyred Peoples: others will die for Christ.

VI. The Sixth Seal: Cataclysms on Earth (12-17)
A. The Powers of Heaven Shaken (12-14)
   1. Seismic Phenomena: "earthquakes"
   2. Astronomical Phenomena
     a. Sun becomes black
     b. Moon becomes as blood
     c. Stars (meteors) fall
     d. Heaven rolls back
   3. Geological Phenomena
     a. Mountains moved
     b. Islands moved
B. The Powers of Human Leaders Shaken (15,16)
   1. Their Flight (15): afraid of God
     a. Kings
     b. Great Men
     c. Rich Men
     d. Chief Captains
     e. Mighty Men
     f. Bondmen (slaves)
     g. Freemen
   2. Their Plight: under judgment
   3. Their Prayer (16): to rocks and mountains, "Fall on us..."
C. The Power of Christ in Wrath Has Come (17)

Beginning with the Seal Judgments and continuing through the entire seven year Tribulation, the wrath of God is directed toward a wicked world.

Observations:
Spiritual lessons and applications from each verse
Chapter Six

1. Invitations from Christ, offered sometimes in Scripture by angels, are evidences of His grace. He said, "Come unto me" (see 22:17). Contrast "Come up hither" … indicating a rapture (4:1 and 11:12) with "Come and see," which deals with retribution.

2. Christ on His white horse (19:11) is in contrast to this conqueror who leads the four horsemen in judgments and scourges.

3. God's Word and message are well organized, numbered. A good pattern for us to follow.

4. The sword of wrath and evil here contrasts with the Sword of the Scriptures (Hebrews 4:12).

5. The balances here are for measuring out rationed provisions; contrast God's balances mentioned in Daniel 5:27: "Thou art weighed in the balances and found wanting."

6. A penny here is a denarius, a day's wages in Bible times. Oil and wine are reserved for the rich. For Christians, "wine is a mocker, and strong drink is raging" (Proverbs 20:1).

7. As each of the four beasts (*zoa* — living creatures, cherubim) has a work to perform individually; so also do we.

8. How thankful believers should be that we shall escape this awful time of world conflagration when man is allowed to do his worst.

9. As millions have died for Christ throughout the ages, so we ought to live for Christ now until we die by whatever means.

10. Like all the martyrs, we must remember that "vengeance is mine; I will repay, saith the Lord" (Romans 12:19).

11. Waiting patiently is probably harder here on earth than in heaven. In our patience, we should possess our souls.

12. God sometimes uses the forces of nature for his judgments; sometimes He intervenes supernaturally, when it seems like nature's processes. Compare Joel 2:30, 31; Rev. 8:12 and 16:10; and Mat. 24:29.

13. The mighty winds of judgment can be contrasted with the gentle wind of the Holy Spirit's work (John 3:8).

14. God is in control of all the forces of the universe.

15. The pride of man is nothing in the face of the judgment of God.

16. Here is a strange prayer to rocks and mountains; they cannot hide anyone from God.

17. This describes a future time of wrath. We "wait for his Son from heaven, whom he raised from the dead, even Jesus, WHICH DELIVERED US FROM THE WRATH TO COME" (1 Thes. 1:10).

Saved from Wrath

Unquestionably the "wrath" of the Lamb and the judgment of God is operative throughout the Seven Year Tribulation period. As the Book of Revelation is in general chronological order (there are some flashbacks and explanatory passages) the events in this chapter deal with the first year or two of the Seven. If "we shall be saved from wrath through him" (Rms. 5:9); if we really are "delivered from the wrath to come" (1 Thes. 1:10); if "God hath not appointed us to wrath, but to obtain salvation through our Lord Jesus Christ" (1 Thes. 5:9); if some are "counted worthy to escape all these things that shall come to pass and to stand before the Son of man" (Luke 21:36); THEN the Christians of this age will not undergo or experience this time of wrath from its very beginning. The Rapture precedes the Great Tribulation. Were it not so, it would be foolish to "watch" for His imminent return, since He could not come until the Antichrist appeared, the tribulation and other prophesied events had already happened or were in process. Yet, Jesus said, WATCH. Let us heed His words. Jesus may come today! Look for Him!

Quotations
From Other Expositors
Chapter Six

First Seal - White Horse (1,2)

"In the 24th chapter of Matthew our Lord Jesus gave a summary of the judgments of "The Great Tribulation," which we shall find to correspond precisely with the story of the seven seals. He pointed out that in that day there should be, first, false Christs, deceiving many. In connection with the first seal the rider on the white horse is a false Christ, doubtless the Beast-King of Rev. 13, presenting himself as a great and triumphant ruler, having great success, going forth conquering and to conquer."

– *William L. Pettinghill*

"A war-horse is evidently referred to. Now the horseman cannot, as the mass of expositors allege, signify Christ on a career of conquest. Psalm 45, and especially Revelation 19:11, have been confidently alleged in proof of the application of the first Seal to Christ. But both the Psalmist and the Seer direct us to Christ in that grand moment of His Coming to assume the sovereignty of the world, whereas the first Seal epoch refers to a time some years before the introduction of the kingdom in power. In chapter 19 the rider is named; here he is not named. From what part of the earth the Seal horseman emerges we are not informed. We have here a symbol of conquering power. A white horse denotes victorious power. It points to the advent on the prophetic scene of a power bent on conquest. A career of unchecked, brilliant, yet almost bloodless victory lies before this coming royal warrior of worldwide fame. A Cyrus, an Alexander, or a Napoleon in triumphs and conquests, but without bloodshed and slaughter, is the horse and rider of the first Seal."

– *Walter Scott*

Second Seal - Red Horse (3,4)

"The temporary peace which the rider of the white horse will bring in his train will be of short duration, for there can be no permanent peace until the Prince of Peace comes to rule. The people will think they have found the solution for their problems when the Antichrist begins his reign. But alas for them! It will be only a false peace, and will be allowed by war and bloodshed. Not only will there be war between nations, but there will also be war between classes. The world has never seen such conflict as will arise after the restraining power of the Holy Spirit has been removed."

– *Louis T. Talbot*

Third Seal - Black Horse (5,6)

"The black horse is an evident symbol of famine. Black is used to depict famine in other portions of Scripture (Jer. 4:28; Lam. 4:8, 9), and famine often follows war as it did after World War I.

"Inflation also tends to grip the world right after a world war. Such will be the case during the Tribulation. The balances in the hand of the rider on the black horse indicate the scarcity of food. In fact, a penny is the biblical reference to the equivalent of a man's wage for one day (Matt. 20:2,9). Three measures of barley are about a pint, a minimum daily sustenance diet. This, then, indicates that a man will have to work for a whole day just to earn enough money to live, which will leave nothing for his family or the elderly."

– *Tim LaHaye*

Fourth Seal - Pale Horse (7,8)

"Our Lord said the 'pestilences' also would be the condition of this period (Matthew 24:7). 'Death' here symbolized as a person on 'a pale horse.' 'Hell followed him,' because the grave and judgment follow death logically and scripturally. The word 'Hades' describes a region at the earth's center (Matthew 12:40), and those who are therein will be brought up for judgment before the 'Great White Throne' (Revelation 20:11-15).

"The three agencies of Death are 'sword, hunger (famine), and beasts of the earth (pestilences).' These three as agents of judgment are often found associated. See Jeremiah 14:12; 212:7; 24:10; 44:13; Ezekiel 6:11-12; and 5:12. The choice of one of these as judgments was offered to David, in I Chronicles 21:10-12).

"Twenty-five percent of the earth will be destroyed by these three judgments.

"Thus far we have seen 'The Four Horsemen of the Apocalypse': conquering, removing peace, bringing famine, and causing death! These have not yet ridden forth, but during these days of The Tribulation Period they will. Chaos, famine, and death will be common. One out of every four will die!"

– Bill Lawrence

Fifth Seal - Martyrs (9-11)

"To Moses was given a pattern of the things in the heavens (Hebrews 9:23). Therefore, there was an altar in heaven, or rather there is an altar. It was possibly thither that our Lord was going in John 20:17 to present Himself, according to Hebrews 9:12, as the Great High Priest. Underneath this altar in heaven are seen the souls (yet disembodied) of God's martyrs, evidently from Abel on. Their martyrdom has cried to heaven, as did Abel's blood, for vengeance. These souls give expression now to the change of dispensation from grace to judgment: "How long, O Master, the holy and true, dost thou not judge and avenge our blood on them that dwell on the earth?" The answer is, that God is delaying judgment—not for salvation purposes, but that the rest of the martyrs may join their fellows!

"There was given them to each one a white robe (manifested righteousness) and it was said unto them, that they should rest (note this—they are at rest, personally) yet for a little time, until (1) their fellow-servants also and (2) their brethren, who should be killed even as they were, should have fulfilled their course"—(keep these two classes in mind).

"This fifth seal exhibits especially three things: First, the patience of God — 'He proceeds slowly and reluctantly from mercy to judgment.' Second, the change of dispensation evidenced in the character of the prayers of these martyrs for vengeance. Third, the utter wickedness of the earth which is plainly expected to go on martyring the full complement of God's saints.

– William R. Newell

Sixth Seal - Cataclysms (12-17)

"Each series of judgments ends with convulsions of nature, and the sixth seal concludes the first series of judgments with such convulsions. The convulsions begin with an earthquake (verse 12a) followed by a blackout of the sun and moon, followed by a meteor shower (verses 12b-14). As has been stated, the Bible speaks of five blackouts during the end times, and this is the second blackout. Anarchy ensues as men begin to flee from the wrath of God rather than to turn to Him in faith (verses 15-17)." (See Joel 2:31; Rev. 8:12; 16:10; Matthew 24:24.)

– Arnold G. Fruchtenbaum

"It seems evident from these verses that the world will know that this is a judgment from the Lord Jesus Christ, for they refer to Him as the Lamb. They are also fully aware that they are in the Tribulation Period. The fact that the fifth seal delineates the large-scale persecution of Christians during the Tribulation prepares us for the opening of the sixth seal. That is followed suddenly by this great catastrophe, which in turn leads the world to recognize that this is the judgment of God because they have persecuted the followers of the Lamb of God. Suddenly they will recognize that they are being judged and will be conscious that there is no place to hide. Oh, that men in that day will have enough sense to recognize that the Lord is their defense, as did the people in Nahum's day (Nah. 1:5-7) in a similar experience. These sixth-seal catastrophes are only an introduction to the great cataclysms that will come upon the earth during the remainder of the Tribulation Period.

"The first twenty-one months of the Tribulation Period consists of horrifying events. After the Antichrist assumes worldwide control, world war, famine, inflation, and the death of 25 percent of the world's population will follow. Then will occur a great persecution of God's people, followed by the catastrophic judgment of God. If this passage of Scripture teaches anything, it instructs us that the Tribulation is a period no man should enter. The wonderful thing is, you don't have to! If you have received the Lord Jesus Christ as your Savior, you will never go into the Tribulation Period."

– Tim LaHaye

"So then six of the seven seals are broken, but the seventh is not described until later (8:1). Chapter 7 is parenthetical."

– John Phillips

The Four Horsemen are Soon to Come
An Expository Sermon

Chapter Six

Introduction

In chapters 6-19, the future last years of this age are described, a period which we shall see will last seven years and will incorporate all of the apocalyptic teaching of the Old and New Testaments. Fourteen of this book's chapters, two-thirds of the Revelation, deal with this grand finale of history.

Daniel foresaw it. "And at that time shall Michael stand up, the great prince that standeth for the children of thy people: and there shall be a time of trouble, such as never was since there was a nation even to that same time: and at that time thy people shall be delivered, every one that shall be found written in the book" (Daniel 12:1).

This is the Great Tribulation, forecast by Christ, particularly the last half: "For then shall be great tribulation, such as was not since the beginning of the world to this time, no, nor ever shall be" (Matthew 24:21).

Then Satan will be allowed under God's permissive will to bring to the earth the powers of hell in a futile effort to thwart the plan of God. His doom is already sealed, but the sinfulness of men's hearts is here revealed.

Then God will use even the wrath of men to praise Him.

Then the unleashed enmity of man against man, the diabolical worst of Satan, and the overriding judgments of God on the earth, will combine, strangely, to bring about this climactic, horrendous period in the earth's history.

Then the "day of the Lord" of Old Testament truth will take place.

Then the "time of Jacob's trouble" will occur (Jeremiah 30:7).

Then the Antichrist will expand his dominion, as energized by Satan, over practically the whole earth.

Then Israel will experience a final persecution and preservation with the Messiah Jesus coming to conclude the Tribulation and deliver His people.

Beginning after the rapture of this dispensation's believers and the resurrection of the dead in Christ, this prophesied period will run its seven-year course, to be concluded by "the glorious appearing of the great God and our Savior Jesus Christ" (Titus 2:13).

Five times in Daniel (7:25; 9:27; 12:7,11,12), and five times in Revelation (11:2,3; 12:6,14; 13:5), time periods of about 3 $^1/_2$ years are specified, sometimes called 42 months; sometimes 1,260 or 1,290 or 1,335 days. Daniel 9:27 speaks of a week of years, which will later be expounded thoroughly. This "seven" or "week of years" is divided into two segments. Sometimes the 3 $^1/_2$ years refer to the first half; sometimes to the second half. The context usually indicates which half is in view.

Basically, chapters 6-11 deal with the first half, or 1,260 days, with the seal judgments probably running for one or two years.

I. The Four Horsemen (1-8)

After the rapture and resurrection are suggested in chapter 4 and 5, the full account of the end time events commences with the opening of the first four seals on the mysterious book, taken by Christ, the Lion-Lamb, from the right hand of Him who sits upon the throne.

As Christ opens the first seal in heaven, the restraining, withholding power of the Holy Spirit, who has been indwelling believers, is withdrawn. There begins the rapid rise to power of a new world figure in the tradition of a Caesar, a Genghis Kahn, a Napoleon, an Adolph Hitler. Probably from a minor role in world affairs, suddenly this new personality emerges. He seems to have answers to this world's problems and confusion.

Quickly consolidating his power in a technological age, he is able to use the threat of force to take over other countries and lands. He is the last adventurer-conqueror, but he is more than that. He is the prophesied Antichrist, the "beast" (therion) of chapter 13.

This, the rider on the white horse indicates.

But his peaceful conquests in the style, perhaps, of the Hitler takeover of Austria decades ago, evolve into war and conflict. Perhaps, as the rider on the red horse, he precipitates World War III or IV.

This is taught by the vision of the red horse.

The aftermath of war is always famine, shortages and starvation. Even today, there are a billion people or more hungry. During this future time, which God will allow, the shortages will be so acute that it will take a day's wages to buy enough food for that day. Oil, presumably the olive oil of ancient times, but possibly in prophecy the petroleum of today, is in short supply, as will be the wine. Rationing will be the order of the day.

This is the meaning of the vision of the black horse with the balances in the hands of the rider.

The fourth horseman is Death personified with Hell following after. This passage reveals that one-fourth of the world's population will be slain in the international conflagration here foreseen. Only in modern times, in the 20th century, does the awful potential arise to slay a fourth of the world's population, perhaps over a billion people, in a short time. Some think a nuclear holocaust would accomplish exactly that.

Thus, the fourth rider, on the pale horse, is a symbolical presentation of the literal and horrendous conflicts of the end time.

These four horsemen have never yet galloped across the face of the earth, so to speak. Perhaps even now their hoofbeats can be heard just beyond the horizon of future time.

II. The Faithful Martyrs (9-11)

When Christ opens the fifth seal, the scene shifts from an earth under judgment and conflict, to the realms of heaven and the site of a great altar there. Beneath it are, I believe, all the martyrs of all the ages.

In Old Testament times, even the prophets were slain by the earthly chosen people of God. In New Testament days, John the Baptist preceded Christ, who among other things, also died as a martyr for His cause. That, too, was in the providence and plan of God. In the book of Acts, we read the accounts of several deaths for the gospel's sake. For the first three centuries of the Christian era, it was usually dangerous to life and limb to become a Christian. Millions died under the Roman emperors. Some were burned alive; some tortured; some cast to the lions for sport; some were thrust through with a sword; some were beheaded; some were crucified … "of whom the world was not worthy."

Even under the triumph of cultural, catholic Christianity, dissenters and Bible-believers were persecuted and slain.

During the Reformation, multiplied thousands died for their faith.

In the 20th century in many lands under Nazis, Communists, Fascists, religious fanatics of all kinds, political oppression and religious oppression, millions have died for Christ.

"The blood of the martyrs is the seed of the church."

Here John beholds the martyrs crying out for vengeance. They are assured that in due time, other martyrs will die also, even during the tribulation. They are to wait. God's time will come.

III. The Fatal Cataclysms (12-17)

When Christ opens the sixth seal on the myste-

rious book of divine judgments, herein set forth, the planet earth is again the scene of horrendous events.

This is the actual first judgment from heaven under divine direction. The previous first four seals simply reveal what mankind will be doing during the opening stages of the Great Tribulation.

But here are geological occurrences. "Earthquakes," "mountains moving," "islands moving out of the places" all indicate a planet in the throes of subterranean activity. The great tectonic plates on which geologists tell us the continents float atop an inner core of molten materials beneath the earth's thin crust, will be in dynamic agitation.

Christ likewise predicted earthquakes for the end times in the Olivet Discourse (Matt. 24).

There are also astronomical phenomena in our solar system. "Stars," meteors, perhaps, shower the earth, striking fear in the hearts of multitudes. The sky seems to roll back like a scroll (Isa. 34:4).

No wonder many of the world's leaders will be frightened.

Already a vast network of underground tunnels exists in specific places in America and Russia for the protection of political and military leaders in case of a nuclear war.

Incredibly, it seems some have a kind of bizarre prayer meeting, reminiscent of some of the weird events in Hitler's bunker in the last days of World War II. From beneath the surface, in shelters to which they have retreated from the bombardments of the future war and judgments of God, a strange prayer arises to the rocks and mountains,

"Fall on us, and hide us from the face of him that sitteth on the throne, and from the wrath of the Lamb."

There will be kings there who thought they were too mighty for Jesus.

There will be great men who thought they were too great for God.

There will be rich men who thought they were too wealthy for God.

There will be soldiers who thought they were too strong to need God.

There will be mighty men who thought they could live without God.

There will be bond men and free men—all who have rejected Christ.

Notice this last verse: "For the great day of his wrath is come; and who shall be able to stand?"

A Commentary on the Revelation
Expository, Exegetical, Devotional and Practical
Greek words from the Textus Receptus

Chapter Six

Four Horseman (1-8)

1. And I saw when the Lamb opened one of the seals (*kai eidon hote enoiksen to arnion mian ek ton sphragidon*) — Again John personally views from heaven's vantage point a vision of the last years of human history as we know it. The same Lamb who took away the sins of the world, now supervises the dispensing of judgment upon a world which preferred sin to salvation ... **noise of thunder** (*hos phone brontes*) — as the storm gathers on earth, heaven's thunders peal. **2. behold a white horse** (*idou hippos lukos*) — the horse is a symbol of war and white usually signifies purity, but the Pharisees were "whited sepulchres (Matt. 23:27). While many commentators take this rider to be Christ, most dispensationalist see this as depicting the emergence of the Antichrist ... The other horses all have a negative and violent significance; therefore this view fits the context. Compare Zech. 1:8, where colored horses symbolize God's judgments going forth. These four horsemen are also part of the judgments of God, though involving evil, violence, privation and death. This is not Christ, for He is the Lamb, opening seals. **Conquering and to conquer** (*nikon kai hina nikese*) — for the purpose of conquering ... Deceptive treaties and negotiations (innocent white in appearance) may become black in judgment. Initial conquests will be through the threat of power, the bow ... no arrows apparently used. Thus the Antichrist will rise to power and enlarge his influence and control. See Daniel 8:23-27; John 5:43. **The second seal** (*sphragida ten deuteron*) — the first beast (lion-like) calls our "Come" as the first horse gallops forth; the second beast (calf-like) calls "Come" as the second horse appears. **4. Red horse** (*hippos purros*) — crimson, signifying bloodshed, war and death violent and horrible. The rider may be the Antichrists, whose real purposes for world domination becomes evident, as he launches attacks on other nations. The peace and flattery vanishes as slaughter and invasions mount. *Purros* hear means "flaming red" or "crimson" ... **A great sword** (*machaira megale*) — an instrument of death and destruction. A worldwide war will ensue during the Tribulation. **5. Black horse** (*hippos melas*) — typical of woe, mourning, hunger, famine, starvation. These things are always the result of great wars ... **pair of balances** (*echon zugon*) — these scales were for careful measuring, denoting scarcity, rationing, famine ... The followers of the Antichrist-horseman here are promised peace, experience war and instead of plenty must suffer privations. **6. A measure of wheat for a penny** (*choiniks sitou denariou*) — a measure is about a quart and a penny is a denarius, about one day's wages in Bible times. This indicates that today's food would cost a day's wages for one person under the Antichrist's regime and would be under his rationing control. ... **and see thou hurt not the oil and the wine** (*kai to elaion kai ton oinon me adikeses*) — ordinarily a denarius would buy sixteen to twenty quarts of wheat in Bible times; while the oil and wine would be available at inflated prices and reserved for the elite and the leaders. Some have seen liquor and petroleum here. The third creature (manlike) utters the "Come and see" here, but the fourth beast (eagle-like) introduces the pale horse next. **7.** It is interesting that these four angelic beings, **zoa**, beasts participate with the Lamb, who opens the first four seals in these verses. Behind the scenes God's angelic hosts, as in Daniel, participate in the workings of divine providence and divine plans, unknown and unseen by mere earthlings. **8. A pale horse** (*hippos chloros*) — a pale greenish horse, here suggesting famine, pestilence and death. "The livid green color is a term that describes the appearance of one who is terror-stricken, deathly sick, dying" (Albert Garner). **Death** (*thanatos*) — meaning death is presented as a personification. **Hell** (*Hades*) — a personification. **fourth part of the earth** (*tetarton tes ges*) — evidently it is the fourth part of the planet especially effected by this judgment and the first three horseman. Antichrist establishes hegemony over a fourth of the globe, a great number of the people dying as a result of these judgments. Some commentators think an entire fourth of the world's population dies; others think that these judgments at this stage are limited to the fourth part of the earth ... **with the sword** (*en hromphaia*), the bloody instruments of war, including modern weaponry of all kinds ... **and with hunger** (*kai en limo*) — food shortages, famine, privation always follow war, anarchy and killing ... **and with death** (*kai en thanato*) — some commentators equate this word with pestilence, plagues and such like, involving physical, emotional and mental anguish and suffering. Terrible plagues like AIDS afflict in the late 1990's, as many as 250,000,000 people, the majority of whom are in Africa. Deaths from this disease, if a cure is not found, will be the largest of any plague in history. **beasts of the earth** (*therion test ges*) — this is not limited to the usual ravenous wild beasts, but can include not only violent and ferocious attacks, but diseases caught by humans, derived from animals. Some think AIDS arose in monkeys. These four horsemen indicate the horrendous times ahead in the Great Tribulation when Antichrist arises and violence, famine, death and pestilence are rampant. Behind the scenes, God even uses the wickedness of man as a part of His divine judgments. Man's inhumanity to man, though arising from a rebellious will against God, nevertheless becomes self-inflicted punishment by the human race upon the human race.

Martyrs (9-11)

9. The fifth seal (*pempten sphragida*) — no longer do ghastly scenes of earth pass before us, for the view is now in heaven, where an altar is seen. Evidently, the earthly tabernacle reflected heavenly realities (Hebrews 8:4,5). As the blood of sacrificial animals in Old Testament times was poured at the bottom of the altar, so the souls of those who sacrifice their lives for God are represented as under the altar. Some think these martyrs are just the Tribulation martyrs, many of whom doubtless die during the period of the first four seals. Others conclude that these are all the New Testament martyrs of this age, from Steven until the Rapture. Some believe that these are all the martyrs from Abel until the last martyr of the Tribulation, all of whom had not yet arrived. This writer so concludes. That they are under the altar although in heaven, is indicative that they are seen here in that position. It does not follow that they are always there, if they are now in heaven and part of the raptured and resurrected believers. The idea is the emphasis on the fact they died for their faith and that others would also die before full vengeance is poured out on the persecutors. The pouring forth of judgments in this book constitute the times of avenging. **10. How long, O Lord, dost thou not avenge our blood on them that dwell on the earth?** Already, the process had begun, but would be consummated at the final Return of Christ and finalized at the Great White Throne Judgment (Rev. 20:11-15), when all the wicked are consigned to the Lake of Fire. **11. White robes** (*stole leuke*) — Compare Rev. 3:5; 7:9,13; 15:6; 19:8,14. In this verse the white "stoles" are distributed as a symbol of their righteous fidelity to Christ even unto death.

Such will likewise receive a "crown of life" (Rev. 2:11). Special recognition in heaven will be extended to all martyrs and unique rewards.

Wrath (12-17)

12. The sixth seal (*sphragida ten hekten*) — the scene shifts back to earth for a picture of the cataclysms, chaos and confusion which will befall much of the world at this stage of future history. These events occur during the first half of the Tribulation and probably during the first one or two years … **great earthquake** (*seismos megas*) — hence seismic, seismographs, etc. in our English scientific terminology. Additional earthquakes will occur as the end times rush toward the Second Coming and Armageddon … **sun black as sackcloth of hair** (*helios megas hos sakkos trichinos*) — this blackout could occur as a result of volcanic and seismic disturbances, when ash is spewed into the sky. This happened at Mount St. Helens in Washington state in the 1980's. Quakes and volcanic activity are often related … **moon became as blood** (*selene hole egeneto hos haima*) — an awesome reddening of the moon, as when a total eclipse occurs … only here there is another cause, possibly dangerous contamination of the atmosphere could cause this. In addition, meteors, possibly asteroids and other interplanetary matter, pummels the earth. These falling stars can be seen at certain times of the year, but nothing like this future judgment. **14. Mountains and islands were moved.** The seismic, atmospheric, astronomical and geological disturbances all occur during the period. **15. hid themselves** — wicked men of all ranks fearfully seek for shelter. **16. Fall on us** — compare Hosea 10:8. This is a strange prayer meeting, but God is not sought. **17. wrath** (*orges*) — The wrath of the Lamb and the Day of the Lord and the time of tribulation judgment have indeed come. For believers, study 1 Thess. 1:10; 5:9. The idea of some recent commentators that the wrath of God is not actually poured out on the earth until late in the Tribulation has no foundation.

RAINBOWS FROM REVELATION
The Revelation of Jesus Christ
A chapter by chapter, verse by verse study
"There was a rainbow round about the throne like unto an emerald" (4:3)

CHAPTER SEVEN: Believers in the Tribulation

References

Jer. 49:36
Dan. 7:2
Zech. 6:5
Mt. 24:31

2 Tim. 2:19

Ezek. 9:4,6

Gen. 49:1-27
Rev. 14:1,3
Isa. 44:8

Eph. 4:30
2 Cor. 1:22

1. AND after these things I saw four angels standing on the four corners of the earth, holding the four winds of the earth, that the wind should not blow on the earth, nor on the sea, nor on any tree.

2. And I saw another angel ascending from the east, having the seal of the living God: and he cried with a loud voice to the four angels, to whom it was given to hurt the earth and the sea,

3. Saying, Hurt not the earth, neither the sea, nor the trees, till we have sealed the servants of our God in their foreheads.

4. And I heard the number of them which were sealed: and there were sealed a hundred and forty and four thousand of all the tribes of the children of Israel.

5. Of the tribe of Judah were sealed twelve thousand. Of the tribe of Reuben were sealed twelve thousand. Of the tribe of Gad were sealed twelve thousand.

6. Of the tribe of Asher were sealed twelve thousand. Of the tribe of Naphtali were sealed twelve thousand. Of the tribe of Manasseh were sealed twelve thousand.

7. Of the tribe of Simeon were sealed twelve thousand. Of the tribe of Levi were sealed twelve thousand. Of the tribe of Issachar were sealed twelve thousand.

8. Of the tribe of Zebulun were sealed twelve thousand. Of the tribe of Joseph were sealed twelve thousand. Of the tribe of Benjamin were sealed twelve thousand.

9. After this I beheld, and, lo, a great multitude, which no man could number, of all nations, and kindreds, and people, and tongues, stood before the throne, and before the Lamb, clothed with white robes, and palms in their hands;

10. And cried with a loud voice, saying, Salvation to our God which sitteth upon the throne, and unto the Lamb.

11. And all the angels stood round about the throne, and about the elders and the four beasts, and fell before the throne on their faces, and worshiped God,

12. Saying, Amen: Blessing, and glory, and wisdom, and thanksgiving, and honor, and power, and might, be unto our God for ever and ever. Amen.

13. And one of the elders answered, saying unto me, What are these which are arrayed in white robes? and whence came they?

14. And I said unto him, Sir, thou knowest. And he said to me, These are they which came out of great tribulation, and have washed their robes, and made them white in the blood of the Lamb.

15. Therefore are they before the throne of God, and serve him day and night in his temple: and he that sitteth on the throne shall dwell among them.

16. They shall hunger no more, neither thirst any more; neither shall the sun light on them, nor any heat.

17. For the Lamb which is in the midst of the throne shall feed them, and shall lead them unto living fountains of waters: and God shall wipe away all tears from their eyes.

References

Isa. 60:1-5
Rms. 11:25
Lev. 23:40

Isa. 43:11
Ps. 3:8

Rev. 4:6,11;
5:9,12,14;
11:16

Rev. 5:13,14

Rev. 7:9
Dan. 12:10

Gen. 49:11
Mt. 24:21
Isa. 1:18
Rev. 6:9

Is. 4:5,6
Lev. 26:11

Ps. 121:5,6
Is. 49:10

Ps. 23:1,2
Ez. 34:23
Rev. 21:4

Scriptures for Comparison

Micah 2:12
I will surely assemble, O Jacob, all of thee; I will surely gather the remnant of Israel; I will put them together as the sheep of Bosrah, as the flock in the midst of their fold: they shall make great noise by reason of the multitude of men.

Matthew 24:14
And this gospel of the kingdom shall be preached in all the world for a witness unto all nations; and then shall the end come.

Revelation 12:17
And the dragon was wroth with the woman, and went to make war with the remnant of her seed, which keep the commandments of God, and have the testimony of Jesus Christ.

Summary of Chapter Seven

In Wrath God Has Mercy

I. Angels (1-3)

Between the sixth seal and the seventh seal, an interlude appears, consisting here of the entire chapter. It is a moment of pause, as John is shown a vision of those who will come to Christ during the forthcoming "day of his wrath."

Before the introduction of the ecological judgments in chapter eight, over which some angelic administration is to be involved, the call to wait for the special sealing of God's elect is made. The "servants of God" are to be sealed in their foreheads. Like the familiar seal of a notary upon a document, this sealing implies protection, legalization, authority and authenticity. Regardless of "the winds of adversity," they will fulfill their ministry.

II. Israelites (4-8)

As incredible as it may seem, the majority of commentators attempt to "spiritualize away" the literal, obvious meaning of the plain and positive designation of the first company. There are "144,000 of all the tribes of the children of Israel."

God who knows which Jew or Israelite is a descendent of which tribe, makes it even clearer by giving a listing of the 12 tribes.

These are the Israelites who accept Christ as Messiah and Savior AFTER the rapture and resurrection, becoming "the godly remnant" of the end times. During the first half of the coming TRIBULATION, some 3 1/2 years, they will become the dynamic witnesses of God, proclaimers of the gospel, spiritually and supernaturally protected while they spread the gospel.

Combining the meanings of the tribal names in order gives us this succession of ideas that thus describe their character and ministry.

Confessors or praisers of God (Judah), looking upon the Son (Reuben), a band of blessed ones (Gad and Asher), wrestling with forgetfulness (Naphtali and Manasseh), hearing and obeying the Word (Simeon), cleaving unto the rewards of a heavenly home and dwelling place (Levi, Issachar and Zebulun) an addition (Joseph), sons of God's right hand, begotten in the extremity of this age (Benjamin).

Dan is omitted with both Joseph (father of Ephraim) and Manasseh (son of Joseph) mentioned. Clues might be found in Genesis 49:16-18,

Joshua 19:40-48; Judges 18. Some have speculated that the antichrist might be a Jew from the Tribe of Dan. That is not likely.

III. Gentiles (9-17)

Beginning in verse nine is the description of a vast multitude of Gentiles from all peoples, who "come out of GREAT TRIBULATION." Doubtless, these are the Gentiles, tribulation saints, people who accept Christ through the preaching of the 144,000 and their converts during the coming time of judgment.

They are a separate group from the raptured and resurrected saints. Evidently they had no clear presentation of the gospel before the rapture.

People will get saved, even in the coming climactic judgment time, but most will die martyr's deaths.

God in judgment still shows mercy. Amazingly, one of the purposes of the Great Tribulation is to spark a worldwide revival. These hosts are the result.

In my judgment they are not part of the raptured, resurrected saints of God, the wife of the Lamb. They are a distinct group, although what is said about them applies in some ways to all believers. Since only a small part of the world's population has clearly heard the gospel, it is God's plan that a final message be proclaimed, by these 144,000 Israelites and their converts all over the world. "This gospel of the kingdom must be preached in all the world, and then shall the end come," (Matthew 24:14) shall be fulfilled.

These Gentiles are in heaven, many dying martyr's deaths, too; they are before the throne of God; clothed in white robes, they carry palm branches and serve God day and night. They are not said to reign with Christ. They are known of God and blessed by Him, but crowns exceed palm branches; kings are above servants; and the wife of the Lamb enjoys a more glorious destiny.

These are seen as a vast throng in heaven. In conversation with one of the elders John learns they are washed in the blood of the Lamb, eternally blessed with provision and shelter. The Greek use of the word d*well*, for God dwells with them, always indicates the protection of a roof or the spreading of a roof for shelter. Thus, this "great multitude" will enjoy the protection of God forever with all the privileges listed here.

Outline of Chapter Seven

Those Saved During the Tribulation

OBJECTIVE: To describe the Tribulation saints

OUTLINE:

I. The Special Angels (1-3)
A. The Four Angels of Judgment
  1. Their Place (1) on four corners of earth
  2. Their Power (1)
    a. Control meteorological forces
    b. Oversee geological judgments
      1.) Earth
      2.) Sea
      3.) Trees
B. The Angel from the East (2)
  1. His Possession: "the seal of the living God"
  2. His Pronouncements
    a. Delivered in a loud voice
    b. Directed to the four angels
    c. Decreeing a hiatus before further judgments (see Chapter 8)

II. The Sealed 144,000 (Israelites) (4-8)
  No question about these being Israelites.
A. The Total Number: 144,000
B. The Twelve Tribes: 12,000 each tribe
  Translated meanings of theHebrew names:
  1. Judah: "praise of God"
  2. Reuben: "Viewing of the son"
  3. Gad: "a company"
  4. Asher: "blessed"
  5. Naphtali: "a wrestler" or "striving"
  6. Manasseh: "Forgetfulness"
  7. Simeon: "hearing and obeying"
  8. Levi: "joining or cleaving to"
  9. Issachar: "reward" or "given by way of reward"
  10. Zebulun: "a home" or "dwelling place"
  11. Joseph: "added" or "an addition"
  12. Benjamin: "a son or the right hand" or "a son of old age"

III. The Saved Multitude (Gentiles) (9-18)
A. Their Number: innumerable (9)
  1. Of all Nations
  2. Of all Kindreds
  3. Of all People
  4. Of all Tongues
B. Their Place: heaven
C. Their Theme: salvation (10)
D. The Angels' Beatitude (11, 12)
  AMEN
  1. Blessing
  2. Glory
  3. Wisdom
  4. Thanksgiving
  5. Honor
  6. Power
  7. Might
  AMEN
E. The Elder's Question (13) Who are these?
F. Their Identity (13, 14)
  1. They come out of the GREAT TRIBULATION
  2. They washed their robes
  3. They made them white in the Lamb's blood
  4. They are before the throne of God
  5. They serve Him day and night
  6. God dwells with them
G. Their Privileges (16-17)
  1. Forever sustained (hunger no more)
  2. Forever refreshed (thirst no more)
  3. Forever sheltered (no sun or heat)
  4. Forever nourished (Lamb shall feed)
  5. Forever led (shall lead them)
  6. Forever supplied (fountains of waters)
  7. Forever comforted (every tear wiped away)

The Gospel During the Tribulation
"By means of the 144,000 Jews, God will accomplish the second purpose of the Great Tribulation, that of bringing about a world-wide revival.

The connecting link after these things is chronological and also shows a cause and effect relationship between the first and the second parts of Revelation."

– Arnold G. Fruchtenbaum

"Revelation 7:9-17 assures us that a great number from every nation will finally become believers during the Great Tribulation. They are gathered together as the returing Messiah's 'elect,' when the angels bring them from the four corners of the earth. Matthew 24:31, 39-42 tells us that this gathering will occur at the end of the Tribulation period as Christ returns in power and glory to defeat the armies of Antichrist in the Battle of Armageddon. When Christ appears, He will be accompanied by the pre-tribulation Christians who have been in Heaven. Jude 14 reveals that 'The Lord cometh with ten thousands [millions] of His saints.'"

– Grant R. Jeffrey

Observations:
Spiritual lessons and applications from each verse
Chapter Seven

1. Invisible to human eyes, angelic beings may exercise influence and power over the elements even in our times. Christ can still storms.

2. The seal speaks of possession, authority and legality.

3. Believers of this age are "sealed with that Holy Spirit of promise" unto the day of redemption. See Ephesians 1:13; 4:30; II Corinthians 1:22.

4. God never leaves Himself without witnesses. When the saints of this age are removed, God raises up new witnesses.

5. Let us praise God (Judah), look at the Son (Reuben), and confess we are His company (Gad).

6. In this age, we believers, also enjoy being blessed (Asher), should wrestle with the old enemy-Ephesians 6:12 (Naphtali), and need to "forget not the Lord," but "forget the things that are behind" (Manasseh), like the 144,000 will.

7. Christians always should hear and obey the Word (Simeon), cleave to the Lord (Levi), and know we shall receive rewards for obedience (Issachar), even as the 144,000.

8. How we can rejoice in a heavenly dwelling place (Zebulun), add spiritual virtues — II Peter 1:5-7 (Joseph), and appreciate being sons of His right hand — Romans 4:17 (Benjamin).

9. This vast multitude of believers, Tribulation saints, like the believers of all ages, stand before the throne, a place of indescribable glory.

10. Praise to God is the theme of heaven.

11. Worship continues beyond earth; its ultimate form is in heaven.

12. Let us echo the sevenfold blessing, beatitude of praise: blessing, glory, wisdom, thanksgiving, honor, power, might ... every day of our lives.

13. God asks us to consider great questions and truths in His Word.

14. How important is the blood of Christ! It should never be downgraded as "just symbolical" or a "figure of speech."

15. When God says He will "dwell" among His people, the idea is "tabernacle," including the concepts of protection, possession, shelter, covering over His own people by His pervasive presence.

16. Contemplate the eternal protection here, not only for the Tribulation saints, but for all believers of every age.

17. Believers will be fed and led and comforted forever, this multitude and all Christians.

Saved in the Tribulation

A most important passage in 1 Thessalonians 2:9-12 indicates that the Antichrist's coming "is after the working of Satan with all power, signs and lying wonders, and with all deceivableness of unrighteousness in them that perish; because they received not the love of the truth that they might be saved. And for this cause God shall send them strong delusion, that they should believe a lie: that they all might be damned who believed not the truth, but had pleasure in unrighteousness." This passage teaches that those Gentiles who have heard the gospel and not acted on it, who receive not … that they might be saved … will experience a strong delusion and follow the Antichrist, because they believed not the truth. Hence, in this writer's judgment, those who hear and refuse or neglect the gospel will seal their own doom and will not receive the message of the gospel in the Tribulation. The great multitude here have not clearly heard the gospel in this age. They will have an opportunity. Christ-rejectors now, after the Rapture, are not found in this great multitude.

Quotations
From Other Expositors
Chapter Seven

Angels (1-3)

"A detailed study of the work of angels in the book of Revelation would reveal that they are the special ministers of God, administering His plans for the earth. In chapter 8 they are observed presenting the trumpet judgments. Here we find that they control the forces of nature. Actually, in the seventh chapter the angels supervise the administration of two things:

"1. They control the wind from the four corners of the earth. 'And after these things I saw four angels standing on the four corners of the earth, holding the four winds of the earth, that the wind should not blow on the earth, nor on the sea, nor on any tree' (Rev. 7:1).

"2. They seal the servants of God, the 144,000 tribulation witnesses. Since the sixth seal takes place toward the end of the first quarter of the Tribulation, we find that the destroying angel is ordered to wait until the works of sealing are finished. This would indicate that at the beginning of the Tribulation, the 144,000 servants of God will be sealed and begin their ministry of preaching the Gospel, attended by a mighty worldwide soul harvest which will culminate in a severe time of persecution for believers, inspired by the Antichrist. This would accord with the breaking of the fifth seal; at this time the sealing angel will have finished his work and the destroying angel will be permitted to hurt the earth and the sea ushering in the sixth seal."

– Tim LaHaye

Israelites (4-8)

"I am sure that many of my hearers have often been perplexed by conflicting theories regarding the hundred and forty-four thousand. The way in which so many unscriptural and often positively heretical sects arrogate to themselves this title would be amusing, if it were not so sad. You are perhaps aware that the Seventh-Day Adventists apply it to the faithful of their communion, who will be found observing the Jewish Sabbath at the Lord's return. They suppose that these will be raptured when the Lord descends, and judgment poured out upon the rest of the church. Then we have the followers of the late 'Pastor' Russell who teach that

the hundred and forty-four thousand include only the 'overcomers' of their persuasion who continue faithful to the end, following the teaching of the system commonly called Jehovah's Witnesses. Besides these, there are many other sects, whose leaders consider their own peculiar followers will be the hundred and forty-four thousand sealed ones at the time of the end. All of these, however, overlook a very simple fact, which, if observed, would save them from their folly. That is, the hundred and forty-four thousand are composed of twelve thousand from each tribe of the children of Israel. There is not a Gentile among them, nor is there confusion as to tribe.

– H. A. Ironside

"A. The Holy Spirit will most assuredly be here to empower the ministry ot the 144,000. The prophet Joel foresaw this ministry of the Spirit of God in Joel 2:28,29:

"And it shall come to pass afterward, that I will pour out my Spirit upon all flesh; and your sons and your daughters shall prophesy, your old men shall dream dreams, your young men shall see visions; and, also, upon the servants and upon the handmaids in those days will I pour out my Spirit.

"This passage makes it clear that the outpouring of the Holy Spirit experienced on the day of Pentecost (referred to by Peter in Acts 2) will be the type of outpouring experienced by the 144,000 witnesses of the Tribulation.

"B. For some strange reason, good and able Bible scholars have been confused about the kind of message the 144,000 will preach. Some have suggested that they will preach 'the Gospel of the kingdom,' meaning they will revert to the same message that John the Baptist preached. This cannot be so, for since Jesus Christ died on Calvary's cross and rose again, there has only been one way and one person of salvation!

"Some have tried to stipulate that several gospels are referred to in the Scriptures. Let us look at some of them:

1. 'The gospel of the grace of God' (Acts 20:24)
2. 'My gospel' (Rom. 2:16)
3. 'The gospel of God' (Rom. 15:16)

4. 'The gospel of peace' (Eph. 6:15)
5. 'The gospel of Christ' (Rom. 1:16)
6. 'The everlasting gospel' (Rev. 14:6).

"A careful examination of these passages will indicate that these terms are interchangeable and refer consistently to one Gospel. In fact, at the close of the book of Acts (28:30,31) we find, 'And Paul dwelt two whole years in his own hired house, and received all that came in unto him, preaching the kingdom of God, and teaching those things which concern the Lord Jesus Christ, with all confidence, no man forbidding him ...'

"It is apparent from this that the 144,000 witnesses will be preaching the same message that the Apostle Paul or the Apostle Peter preached, the same message that we preach."

– Tim LaHaye

Gentiles (9-17)

"In verses 9-10 John sees a multitude of Gentiles from every nationality standing before the throne of God. The expression "after these things" means that the salvation of these myriads of Gentiles follows chronologically the 144,000 Jews and there is a cause and effect relationship.

"After describing the worship of the one on the throne (verses 11-12), the text proceeds to identify who these Gentiles are that are found around the throne (verses 13-14). These Gentiles are identified as those who have come out of the Great Tribulation. They are saved Gentiles for they have washed their robes in the blood of the Lamb. Since they follow chronologically the ministry of the 144,000 Jews, the implication is that they are the Gentiles who come to Christ as a result of the preaching of the 144,000 Jews. Included are the fifth seal saints who suffered martyrdom. Because of the massive persecution that these tribulation saints have undergone, this passage concludes with a description of the comfort they now enjoy in the presence of God (verses 15-17).

"From this chapter it should be evident that the Holy Spirit will be still at work in the tribulation, for the work of regeneration is His peculiar ministry. While the work of restraining evil is removed allowing the Antichrist to begin his evil rise to power, the Holy Spirit Himself will still be in the world and will have an active ministry."

– Arnold G. Fruchtenbaum

"They are people who were living on the earth in the period of the Judgment. The great tribulation times are everywhere inseparably linked with the judgment times (see Dan. 12, Matt. 24, Mark 13,

Rev. 1:7); and this whole multitude is made up of those who come out of the great tribulation. This is positively stated by the Elder, and so recorded by John. It is therefore true, and no man is at liberty to question it. There are other saved ones, of several classes, who subsequently come out of the after-parts of this great tribulation—the 144,000 for instance, the two witnesses, and those which refuse to worship the Beast or to receive his mark— but they are not of this particular company."

– J. A. Seiss

"John does not know who these are, as his answer to the elder's question 'Who are they and when came they?' plainly shows. We feel he would have known them if Old Testament saints, as he and Peter and James knew Elijah and Moses on the Transfiguration Mount. Also, he would have known them if Church saints. He is told that they 'came out of the great tribulation.' Also that they 'washed their robes, and made them white in the blood of the Lamb.' That means salvation, and salvation by faith in God's Word regarding the blood of Christ. These are not of the Church, yet they are in heaven."

– William R. Newell

"It is significant to note here that this multitude of Gentiles who are saved during the Tribulation carry palms in their hands. There appears to be a distinction between this group and the Christians earlier caught up in the Rapture. This group apparently has no crowns at this point ... yet they hold palms, a symbol of rejoicing and gladness.

"Because this assemblage in white robes is gathered from out of the Tribulation Period, many will consequently suffer martyrdom and wear the crown of martyrs. Those who were previously caught up in the Rapture seem to be represented by those sitting AROUND the throne (Rev. 4:4). Those, however, who are saved in the Tribulation Period are here seen standing BEFORE the throne (Revelation 7:9).

"These verses make it evident to us that worldwide preaching will somehow occur during the Tribulation for this "multitude, which no man could number of all nations" will come to Christ."

– Salem Kirban

"The saved Gentile multitude is assured that the privations of life, hunger and thirst, and persecution and tribulation, sun and burning heat, shall never again be their sad lot. There shall be no recurrence of past evils."

– Walter Scott

Can People Be Saved During the Tribulation?
An Expository Sermon

Chapter Seven

Introduction

In describing the climax of the age, Jesus Christ told his apostles, "For then shall be great tribulation, such as was not since the beginning of the world to this time, no, nor ever shall be, and except those days should be shortened" (Matthew 24:21, 22).

Of course, people can be saved in any age. However, there is a most serious warning issued by the Apostle Paul in 2 Thessalonians 2:7-12. In explaining the deceptive power of the future man of sin, son of perdition, antichrist, the Wicked One, Paul speaks of his followers as those who "received not the love of the truth, that they might be saved." He continues, "and for this cause God shall send them strong delusion, that they should believe a lie [THE LIE]: that they all might be damned who believed not the truth, but had pleasure in unrighteousness."

This Scripture seems to indicate that those who hear the gospel in this age and reject Christ are ripe prospects to follow the new world leader, when he arises after the Rapture.

Those who receive not the truth, after hearing it, that they might be saved, will all "be damned."

It is a very serious matter to keep on refusing Christ time after time. Should the Rapture occur, such a person will have sealed his own eternal doom.

Those who do get saved during the Tribulation will be those who have never heard or scarcely heard the gospel. Even now, half the world's population hardly know who Jesus is. It is out of that vast number that the "great multitude" of this chapter will emerge.

Remember also that God's earthly chosen people, the Jews, will be a special case.

I. The Might of the Angels (1-3)

No book in the Bible more extensively describes the powerful ministry of the angels than Revelation. The four angels "holding the four corners of the earth" are poised in preparation for the horrendous events of chapter 8, when the trumpet judgments begin. Four in the Bible is the number of the world. The "four horsemen" will ravage the earth in the opening stages of the Tribulation. The "four angels" may be the "four angels" bound in the river Euphrates (9:14) which are all involved in judgments on the world, profound events that will be literal.

But God's saving grace is indicated in the special call to hold back wrath until God's 144,000 special servants are "sealed." That spiritual sealing is doubtless by the Holy Spirit, who stamps these witnesses with the mark of divine possession, protection and blessing, as in 2 Corinthians 1:22.

Angels are "ministering spirits, sent forth to minister to them who are to be the heirs of salvation" (Hebrews 1:14).

II. The Marvel of the 144,000 Israelites (4-8)

Applying the meaning of the names of the Twelve Patriarchs, as listed and as arranged in order, to the work and character of these 144,000, the great 19th-century expositor Joseph Seiss says:

"All Jewish names are significant, and the meaning of those which are here given are not hard to trace. Judah means 'confession or praise of God'; Reuben, 'viewing the son'; Gad, 'a company'; Asher, 'blessed'; Nephthalim, 'a wrestler or striving with'; Manassah, 'forgetfulness'; Simeon, 'hearing and obeying'; Levi, 'joining or cleaving to'; Issachar, 'reward' or 'what is given by way of reward'; Zebulon, a 'home' or 'dwelling place'; Joseph, 'added' or an 'addition'; Benjamin, 'a son of the right hand, a son of old age.' Now put these several ideas in order and it is evident who they are and what they do.

"These 144,000, then, are Israelites, living in the period of judgment, who only then are brought to be confessors and praisers of God, whilst most of their kindred continue in unbelief and rebellion. Viewing the Son, as their fathers would never view Him, they acknowledge Him as their Messiah and Judge. As Jews, they thus constitute a distinct company to themselves, and are blessed. As the result of their conversion, they are also very active in practical righteousness. They strive and wrestle

81

against their own and their nation's long oblivious-ness to the truth as it is in Jesus, hearing and obeying now the voice of the Lord, cleaving unto the shelter and heavenly home promised by the prophets as the portion of those who call upon the name of the Lord even at that late hour. They are not the church proper; for their repentance comes too late for that. They are a super-addition to the Church — a supplementary body — near and precious to Christ, but made up after the Church has finished its course. As Paul in his apostleship was like one born out of due time, so they are in the position of children belated in their birth: sons of God indeed, and destined to follow the Lamb whithersoever He goeth, but sons begotten in the day of God's right hand, in the period of His power and judgment, in the last extremity of the age. All this comes out naturally and distinctly, without the least straining of a single word."

These mighty, sealed, anointed witnesses will be God's remnant, the remnant of the woman's seed, "which keep the commandments of God, and have the testimony of Jesus Christ" (12:17). They will be Messianic Jews, still by and large rejected by the nation Israel, but able to participate even in the Tribulation time in a large-scale evangelistic effort. Their ministry will probably result in the salvation of the great multitude of Gentiles who accept Christ after the Rapture. Evidently, these die martyr's deaths as a result of Satan's war against them (12:17), since they are seen in heaven early in chapter 14.

III. The Multitude of Gentile Tribulation Saints (9-17)

Since over half the world's population has never clearly heard the gospel, God will reach forth in grace and mercy, even in this future time of wrath. While this writer would never say anything is totally impossible, the likelihood of anyone who has never heard the gospel before the Rapture having a second chance is very remote.

But think of those who have never heard. They are from all nations, kindreds, peoples and tongues. They will have the opportunity of clearly hearing the gospel. Even though the new world leader will eventually attempt to put all such professing Chris-tians to death, millions upon millions will turn to Christ and be saved.

Picture this vast and glorious multitude of souls in heaven. They come from every continent, from all races, from many cultures. Betokening God's grace at all times, they find the truth under dire and difficult circumstances. The pains of the Great Tribulation they do not escape, but the joys of being with Christ forever will be theirs.

"For when God's judgments are in the earth, the inhabitants of the world will learn righteous-ness" (Isaiah 16:9).

By the end of the Tribulation their numbers will swell. But think of the blessedness, the peace, the joy, the comfort, the everlasting satisfaction of these Palm-bearers!

Their home will be happy and wholesome, under the everlasting protection of the Eternal Father. Their privilege will be to serve and honor the Lamb, who will provide for their rest and peace throughout eternity. Their view of the throne of God in its awesome majesty will be eternal. They, too, are washed in the blood of the Lamb.

Link the two "greats" in this chapter. A GREAT MULTITUDE (9) "… these are they which came out of the GREAT TRIBULATION, and have washed their robes, and made them white in the blood of the Lamb" (14).

No, they are not "the Church." They are a vast company of redeemed believers, who, like the 144,000, constitute a special class of saved people who will enjoy all the blessings of heaven, as will also the Old Testament saints.

But let us consider this glorious assembly of victors. They are destined to enjoy a high and holy dignity. Three things, John Phillips says, will be in store for them. They are to enjoy God's broadest protection, for over them God stretches His taber-nacle. They enjoy God's boundless provision, for no negative influences can ever touch them. They enjoy God's blessed presence, for their reward is to be close to the Lamb, who promises their welfare, happiness and undying bliss.

They are special servants, commissioned to serve in the heavenly temple, and whose privileged role will doubtless continue in the days when God makes a new heaven and a new earth to endure forever.

Conclusion

Do not suppose, gentle reader, that you can keep on rejecting Christ until after the Rapture, and then, if these things all really happen, accept Christ.

You will be a prime prospect for Satanic delu-sion. You will be ready to follow the antichrist, to worship his image, to submit to the devil and evil.

O, this is the day of salvation! Now is the accepted time. Come to Christ now. Repent of your sins. Receive Him as your Savior. You will be saved from the wrath which is to come.

A Commentary on the Revelation
Expository, Exegetical, Devotional and Practical
Greek words from the Textus Receptus

Chapter Seven

Angels (1-3)

1. And after these things I saw four angels (*meta touto eidon tessaras angellous*) — Here John observes four angels in four directions, indicating the entire world. Four is the number of the world in Scripture, used relative to nature, creation, the earth and God's relationships to the earth ... **standing on the four corners of the earth** (*hestotas epi tas tessaras gonias tes ges*) — meaning four directions from which the wind blows and not implying that the earth is square ... **holding the four winds of the earth** (*kratountas tous tessarras anemous tes ges*) — firmly holding back, grasping or controlling the four winds. Judgment is to come from all directions in succeeding chapters, but here is a preliminary calm before the storm. See also Daniel 7:2; Matt. 24:31 ... **earth** (*ges*), **sea** (*thalasses*), **tree** (*dendron*) — in chapter eight the ecology suffers from judgment, involving all three, but that is after the sealing of this elect group. In part these judgments will be in response to the prayer of the martyrs in 6:10. **2. And I saw another angel** — this is the fifth, whose message of restraint introduces the sealing of the 144,000 ... **ascending from the east** (*anabainonta apo anatoles heliou*) — literally ascending from the sun (*heliou*) rising (*anatoles*). He comes from the East, the direction from which Christ will return as the Sun of Righteousness (Mal. 4:2). "For as the lightning cometh out of the east and shineth even unto the west: so shall the coming of the Son of Man be" (Matt. 24:27). **having the seal of the living God** (*echonta sphragida theou zontes*) — having, holding, bearing the seal, which indicates ownership, security and protection for certain people of God. Undoubtedly, the Holy Spirit is involved here (Eph. 1:13) **3. loud voice** (*phone megalone*) — a very loud announcement heard by all of heaven. See 5:9, 12; 8:13; 19:10; 14:7,9,15 for other uses of this expression **3. hurt not** (*me adikesete*) — do not harm disturb, or disarrange the earth, sea or trees yet (compare Ex. 12:13; 14:30) ... **till we have sealed the servants of our God in their foreheads** (*metaphon auton*). Evidently, this is a visible mark in contrast to the mark of the beast (Rev. 13:16).

Israelites (4-8)

4. And there were sealed an hundred and forty and four thousand (*hekaton tesserakonta tessares chiliades*) — here is a specific number (*armithmon*); therefore to spiritualize this passage to say that the meaning is indefinite and applies to an indeterminate multitude of Christians or the "church" is **prima facie** absurd ... **of all the tribes of the children of Israel** — "originating out of every tribe of Israel, documented and enumerated, tribe by tribe" (A. Garner). These are a believing remnant of Israelites in the end times, who become God's special witnesses during the Tribulation. In the 1900s at least 100,000 Messianic Jews worship Christ. After the Rapture, this elect remnant believes in Jesus, person by person. God knows which Jew is a descendent of which tribe. There is no problem with Him. **4-8 Of the tribe of Judah ... of Ruben ... of Gad ... of Asher ... of Naphtali ... of Manasseh ... of Simeon ... of Levi ... of Issachar ... of Zebulon ... of Joseph ... of Benjamin, twelve thousand sealed from each tribe** — The birth order appears in Genesis 49 with Reuben the eldest, followed by Simeon, Levi and Judah with Joseph and Benjamin being last. Here Judah is placed first, since he was the ancestor of Christ, Lion of the Tribe of Judah. Thus Jesus is entitled to the scepter of power and is Shiloh (rest). See Gen. 49:8-12 for Messianic prophecies. The order here in Revelation is so arranged to suggest in order by the meaning of the names the work of the 144,000. Two alterations appear in this listing. Dan is omitted, possibly because they were the first to lapse into idolatry (Judges 18); Joseph appears rather than Ephraim, perhaps because of the same reason (Judges 17, Hosea 4:17). Ephraim and Manasseh were both Joseph's sons and had territories among the twelve tribal provinces. Levi, the priestly tribe, had no provincial land, but dwelt in cities. Study Genesis 49:13-22 for background on these two sons of Joseph and their descendents. Each received territory to preserve the plan of having twelve province-states for all of Israel. Both Dan and Ephraim, along with Manasseh have provincial status in the millennium with new territories, all parallel as assigned. See Ezekiel 48:1-8. Levi has a special portion as in Ezekiel 48:22. These 144,000 Israelites proclaim the gospel, particularly the gospel of the kingdom (Matthew 24:14) during the Tribulation, being supernaturally protected for a time. As a result of their testimony and preaching, the great multitude of Gentiles in the latter part of this chapter come to Christ. Many martyrs sacrifice their lives for Christ during this time. However, some view this multitude as the raptured, resurrected believers, since they are in heaven and the 144,000 are obviously on earth, but this writer does not share this opinion.

The Great Multitude of Gentiles (9-17)

9. **A great multitude which no man could number** (*ochlos polus hon arithesai auton oudeis edunato*) — this does not mean billions, but does indicate a vast number (*arithesai*) in the many millions, which could not be counted by an observer. It is this commentator's view that these are Tribulation saints, Gentiles mostly, but might include a few Jews who were not in the 144,000, since these are from all nations, kindreds, people and tongues. They are in heaven, hence they have died and may not have resurrected bodies until the end of the Tribulation (Rev. 20:4,5) and the conclusion of the First Resurrection ... **stood before the throne** — they are standing, not seated as the elders in Revelation 4 and 5, but like a vast army stand in review before the Lamb. That they are clothed with white robes shows that they are saved, washed in the blood, cleansed of sin. **The palms in their hands** speak of victory. 10. **And cried with a loud voice** (*kai krazousin phone megale legontes*) — it is their continuing ceaseless employment to praise God, saying **Salvation to our God** (*he soteria to theo hemon*) — to Him is the credit for their deliverance, and to the Lamb. 11. **And all the angels stood round about the throne, and about the elders and about the four beasts and fell before the throne** — this praise comes from the angels and is expressed in the presence of the twenty-four elders, who represent the raptured and resurrected believers in this writer's opinion. 12. **Saying Amen,** (*So be it*), **blessing** (*he eulogia*), **glory** (*doksa*), **wisdom** (*sophia*), **thanksgiving** (*eucharistia*), **honor** (*time*), **power** (*dunamis*), **might** (*ischus*), **be unto our God** (*to thee hemon*). Certainly, this is a most illustrious assembly of saints, since angels voice a chorus of praise, when they display their palms of victory. 13. **And one of the elders answered ... What are these which are arrayed in white robes? and whence came they?** This is not a question for information, but for emphasis. 14. **And I said unto him, Sir, thou knowest** — It is interesting that John did not recognize any of these, which would have been the case were they Old or New Testament saints, as Peter, James and John recognized Moses and Elijah on the mount of Transfiguration (Matthew 17). **These are they which came out of great tribu-**lation (*hoitoi eisin hoi erchomenoi ek tes thlipseos tes megales*) — literally "the tribulation, the great one." This would seem to indicate that this is not the general tribulation which all believers may suffer. "In the world ye shall have tribulation, but be of good cheer, I have overcome the world" (John 16:33). Rather they have been in and have come out of the Great Tribulation having **washed their robes and made them white in the blood of the Lamb. 15. Therefore are they before the throne of God** — they are redeemed, cleansed, a special multitude of saved people, evidently distinct from the saints of the church age who have lived during these 2,000 years. They seem to have special privileges and assignments, remaining in God's presence and serving in the heavenly and Temple day and night in worship, praise and fellowship ... **he that sitteth on the throne shall dwell with them** — the idea of **dwell** (*skenosei*) is to spread a tent or tabernacle over them. He will protect them from any harm, personally abiding in their midst and overshadowing them with His presence. See 21:3, where **the tabernacle** (*skene*) **of God is with men and he will dwell** (*skenosei*) **with them. 16. They shall hunger no more** — having access to the water of life forever (see 22:1,17) ... **neither shall the sun light on them nor any heat** — no scorching, burning rays, no unbearable, blistering heat (see 21:21-24). **17. The Lamb shall feed them ... lead them unto living fountains** — all provisions will be made for them then and forever, as again in 22:1-3. **17. And God shall wipe away all tears** — Not only this great company, but all believers of all ages will enjoy these everlasting blessings. Paul wrote: "I reckon that the sufferings of this present time are not worthy to be compared with the glory that shall be revealed in us" (Romans 8:18). While this passage relates to this Gentile crowd, note the promises for all the redeemed in the eternal state: "And God shall wipe away all tears from their eyes, and there shall be no more death, neither sorrow, nor crying, neither shall there be any more pain, for the former things are passed away. And he that sat upon the throne said, Behold, I make all things new ... It is done. I am Alpha and Omega, the beginning and the end. I will give unto him that is athirst of the fountain of the water of life freely. He that overcometh shall inherit all things: and I will be his God and he shall be my son" (21:4-7). "And there shall be no more curse: but the throne of God and of the Lamb shall be in it: and his servants shall serve him" (22:3).

RAINBOWS FROM REVELATION
The Revelation of Jesus Christ
A chapter by chapter, verse by verse study
"There was a rainbow round about the throne like unto an emerald" (4:3)

CHAPTER EIGHT: Four Trumpets/Cataclysms

References

Rev. 6:1
Acts 21:40

Num. 10:9
Luke 1:19
Dan. 12:1

Rev. 5:8
Heb. 7:25; 9:24
Ex. 30:1
Ps. 141:2
1 Tim. 2:5

Luke 1:10

Ex. 19:16
Rev. 11:19; 16:18
2 Sam 22:8
1 Kings 19:11

Rev. 15:1

Ex. 9:23
Is. 28:2
Ezek. 38:22
Joel 2:30
Rev. 7:1,3
Is. 2:13

1. AND when he had opened the seventh seal, there was silence in heaven about the space of half an hour.

2. And I saw the seven angels which stood before God; and to them were given seven trumpets.

3. And another angel came and stood at the altar, having a golden censer; and there was given unto him much incense, that he should offer it with the prayers of all saints upon the golden altar which was before the throne.

4. And the smoke of the incense, which came with the prayers of the saints, ascended up before God out of the angel's hand.

5. And the angel took the censer, and filled it with fire of the altar, and cast it into the earth: and there were voices, and thunderings, and lightnings, and an earthquake.

6. And the seven angels which had the seven trumpets prepared themselves to sound.

7. The first angel sounded, and there followed hail and fire mingled with blood, and they were cast upon the earth: and the third part of trees was burnt up, and all green grass was burnt up.

8. And the second angel sounded, and as it were a great mountain burning with fire was cast into the sea: and the third part of the sea became blood;

9. And the third part of the creatures which were in the sea, and had life, died; and the third part of the ships were destroyed.

10. And the third angel sounded, and there fell a great star from heaven, burning as it were a lamp, and it fell upon the third part of the rivers, and upon the fountains of waters;

11. And the name of the star is called Wormwood: and third part of the waters became wormwood; and many men died of the waters, because they were made bitter.

12. And the fourth angel sounded, and the third part of the sun was smitten, and the third part of the moon, and the third part of the stars; so as the third part of them was darkened, and the day shone not for a third part of it, and the night likewise.

13. And I beheld, and heard an angel flying through the midst of heaven, saying with a loud voice, Woe, woe, woe, to the inhabiters of the earth by reason of the other voices of the trumpet of the three angels, which are yet to sound!

References

Ezek. 14:19

Rev. 6:13;
14:9; 16:4

Jer. 9:15
Ex. 15:23
Amos 5:7

Is. 13:10
Joel 2:31
Amos 8:9
Mt. 24:29
Rev. 6:12

Is. 5:11
Rev. 14:6;
19:17
Rev. 9:12;
11:14; 12:12

Scriptures for Comparison

Exodus 9:22-26

And the LORD said unto Moses, Stretch forth thine hand toward heaven, that there may be hail in all the land of Egypt, upon man, and upon beast, and upon every herb of the field, throughout the land of Egypt.

And Moses stretched forth his rod toward heaven: and the LORD sent thunder and hail, and the fire ran along upon the ground; and the LORD rained hail upon the land of Egypt.

So there was hail, and fire mingled with the hail, very grievous, such as there was none like it in all the land of Egypt since it became a nation.

And the hail smote throughout all the land of Egypt all that was in the field, both man and beast; and the hail smote every herb of the field, and brake every tree of the field.

Only in the land of Goshen, where the children of Israel were, was there no hail.

Exodus 7:20-21

And Moses and Aaron did so, as the LORD commanded; and he lifted up the rod, and smote the waters that were in the river, in the sight of Pharaoh, and in the sight of his servants; and all the waters that were in the river were turned to blood.

And the fish that was in the river died; and the river stank, and the Egyptians could not drink of the water of the river; and there was blood throughout all the land of Egypt.

Summary of Chapter Eight

Great Tribulation and Cataclysms Rock the Earth

I. Angels (1-6)

Following the interval between the sixth and seventh seal in which the 144,000 and other Tribulation saints are described, the Savior opens the seventh and last seal. A silence ensues, strange, mysterious, a calm before the storm.

Seven angels appear, to whom are given seven trumpets. As a trumpet is blown in heaven, a judgment occurs on earth, in the case of the first six. The trumpets herald or declare a powerful occasion, event or fact.

Suddenly, "another angel," who can be none other than the Angel of the Lord, Jesus Christ, appears. Only Christ is the Mediator between God and man (1 Timothy 2:5). Thus, no mere created angel would presume to serve as an intercessor.

Christ offers the prayers of saints (see Hebrews 7:25) before God's throne, particularly those for deliverance and vengeance. Then He symbolically casts the golden censer of prayers and incense to the earth, picturing the truth that though He is our Intercessor now, He will be our avenger in the future time of judgment.

II. Trumpets (7-13)

The angels then prepare to sound.

When the first angel sounds his trumpet, unheard on earth, of course, the ecology on earth is effected. As the judgments on ancient Egypt were literal, so also are these.

When the second angel sounds his trumpet, a great comet-like object or meteor impacts the earth, splashing into the sea, causing a chemical and color change, for one-third of the waters turn to blood, one-third of the sea creatures die, and one-third of all ships are destroyed.

When the third angel sounds his trumpet, another comet-like object or star falls to the earth in such a way that one third of the fresh water streams are poisoned. The star is called "Wormwood." Wormwood, or absinthe, is a bitter, intoxicating and poisonous herb. Many die as a result of this quintessence of all wormwood.

When the fourth angel sounds his trumpet, the atmosphere is so filled with smog, debris and contaminants, that the light of the sun, moon and stars is diminished by one-third. This, too, is a literal judgment on the Christ-rejecting world.

Finally, an angel flies across heaven, unseen on earth, announcing the three WOES yet to come.

Outline of Chapter Eight

The Seven Trumpets (first four)

OBJECTIVE: To reveal Christ as the Dispenser of Divine Judgment.

OUTLINE:

I. The Strange Silence (1)
 A. Seventh Seal Opened
 B. Short Silence Occasioned

II. The Savior's Supplication (2-6)
 A. The Sovereign Angel of the Lord Intercedes— CHRIST (3-5)
  1. His Place: at a heavenly altar (3)
  2. His Possession: a golden censer (3)
  3. His Prayers: as incense offered (3)
  4. The Prayers of saints: from angel's hand (4)
  5. The Preparation for judgment (5)
   a. Censer filled with fire (judgment)
   b. Censer cast to earth (catastrophes)
   c. Commotion in the universe
 B. The Seven Angels Prepare to Sound (6)

III. The Seven Sounds (first four) (7-12)
  ECOLOGY TO BE AFFECTED
 A. First Trumpet—Consumed Vegetation
  1. Hail, fire, blood cast upon earth
  2. One-third trees, all grass, consumed
   VEGETATION AFFECTED
 B. Second Trumpet—Colored Seas (8, 9)
  1. Comet—mountain falls in sea
  2. Color—chemical changes in one-third of sea
  3. Catastrophes in ocean
   a. One-third sea life die
   b. One-third ships destroyed
    OCEANS AFFECTED
 C. Third Trumpet—Contaminated Waters (10, 11)
  1. Burning star falls
  2. Bitter waters result
   FRESH WATERS AFFECTED
 D. Fourth Trumpet—Curtailed Light (12), light diminished by one-third
  1. Sun smitten
  2. Moonlight affected
  3. Starlight affected
  4. Daylight reduced
   ATMOSPHERE AFFECTED

IV. The Somber Statement (13)
 A. The Flying Angel's Appearance
 B. The Triple Woe Announcement
 C. The Three Trumpet Judgments Approaching

Observations:
Spiritual lessons and applications from each verse
Chapter Eight

1. Sometimes when it seems God is silent, remember such occasions will not last long. In this case, it was only half an hour.

2. God has work for angels, even those of highest rank. God has work for each of us, as well.

3. Consider the incense of prayer, as suggested in Psalm 141:2; Malachi 1:11; Ephesians 5:2.

4. Only Christ is the one Mediator and the Advocate (1 Timothy 2:5; 1 John 2:1, 2); thus Christ, the Angel of the Lord, offers the prayers of saints to God. He mingles our prayers with His own.

5. The same Christ who hears prayers of saints and martyrs from all ages will supervise the fiery judgments of the last days.

6. Even angels must prepare for great exploits and efforts; how much more should we prepare ourselves always to better serve our God.

7. God controls the forces of the universe by "natural processes" and can intervene supernaturally for the accomplishment of His purposes.

8. God, who created the world, has the right to alter its constituency. He is all powerful.

9. Death is a reality of life and time. The wages of sin is death. Confusion, chaos, destruction, are results of sin; God can use such forces to punish.

10. Poisonous waters await the Tribulation generation, but there is a water of life now.

11. Wormwood, a bitter herb, is the name by which this object will be called. Turning from God always brings bitter results. See Jeremiah 9:14, 15.

12. As in New Testament times, so now also are there worshippers of the sun, moon and stars. Even astrologers approach this kind of false worship. It is appropriate that these celestial creations, as objects of worship, should be obscured … This will be a literal event.

13. The word "woe" calls for a solemn, somber realization of an impending judgment or execution of punishment as a consequence of sin.

Quotations
From Other Expositors
Chapter Eight

The Great Silence (1)

"We read in Acts of 'a great silence,' induced by Paul, as he waved his hand to his boisterous accusers, from the stairs of the castle at Jerusalem, and began to speak to them in their sacred tongue. It was the silence of surprise, wonder, and interest to catch what was being said.

"The Lion-Lamb of God has been engaged breaking the seals of the mysterious roll, which He only was worthy to touch or look upon. Six of those seals had been broken, enacting events of the most stupendous moment. But one more remained—the last in the series—and involving the final consummation of the great mystery of God. And as that seal is broken, an interest and awful expectancy rises in the hearts of the celestial orders, which renders them as silent as the grave. All heaven becomes mute and breathless. Saints and angels hush their songs to look and wait for the results. And even the Almighty pauses before the action proceeds."

–J. A. Seiss

The Seven Angels (2-6)

"After this awful pause, the action of the throne is resumed. A company of angels make their appearance on the heavenly arena. They are seven in number. They are of particular rank and distinction, for not all angels are of the same dignity and office. Paul enumerates 'dominions, principalities, and powers" among the celestial orders. Daniel speaks of some chief princes. Paul and Jude refer to archangels. Angelic beings are not, therefore, of one and the same grade. The sons of God, in general, come before him only at appointed times (Job 1:6), but the Saviour speaks of some angels who 'do always behold the face of the Father which is in heaven' (Matt. 18:10). And the sublime agents which John beheld after the opening of the seventh seal, are described as 'the seven angels who stand in the presence of God.'"

–J. A. Seiss

The Angel Priest (3-5)

"The scene before us is one of profound interest, and cast moreover in the mould of familiar Jewish imagery. "Another angel." Who is he? We are satisfied that the angel priest is Christ, our great High Priest. The service at the altars proves it, for both the brazen altar and the golden altar are referred to. No mere creature could add efficacy to the prayers of saints, for that could only be effected by One having in Himself independent right and competency. Further, the action recorded at the altars is of a mediatorial character, one between suffering and praying saints on earth and God; and as Christianity knows of but 'one Mediator between God and men, the Man Christ Jesus' (I Tim. 2:5), the proof is undeniable that the angel priest is Christ and Christ alone, not a representative person or company, as some expositors understand it. There is a pretty general consensus of thought amongst the early expositors of the Apocalypse in rightly regarding the angel here as meaning Christ to the exclusion of all others. 'Another angel' is three times used of Christ in the apocalyptic visions (chaps. 8:3;10:1;18:1). This title is one which supposes reserve and distance."

–Walter Scott

The Seven Trumpets (6)

"Trumpets are typical of convocation, and the judgment of the trumpets is preparatory to the regathering of Israel to their own land. The seige of Jericho, when the seven blasts upon seven trumpets by the seven priests after the sevenfold march about the city on the seventh day were followed by the destruction of the city, finds its antitype in the trumpet judgments of the Apocalypse. Jericho, the accursed city, is ever a type of this world abiding under the curse and wrath of God.

"There is great danger in supposing everything in The Revelation to be symbolical. While there is no doubt that symbols abound in the book, they are carefully distinguished, and our rule of interpretation holds good here as elsewhere. 'If the plain sense make good sense, seek no other sense.'

"The seven trumpets judgments, as in the case of the seals, are divided into two groups. Four is the Earth or world number, and the first four judgments are seen to affect the natural world, and men only indirectly. The phenomena are such as are usually explained away as due to natural causes, leaving God out of the calculation. The last three, and three is the Trinity number, are called the woe judgments, and are such as cannot thus be explained, as in them the hand of God is more directly discernible. God cannot always be explained away, much as His enemies may desire it."

–W.L. Pettingill

"Trumpets are most interesting, being connected with war (Num. 10:9; Jer. 4:19); with convocations and movements of ancient Israel (Numbers 8); with festivals and celebrations and ceremonies (Num. 10:10; Lev. 23:24; 25:9; 2 Chr. 29:27); with royalty (1 Kings 1:34, 39; 2 Kings 9:13); with the manifestation of the terrible majesty and power of God (Ex. 19:16; Amos 3:6); with the overthrow of the ungodly (Joshua 6:13-16); with events related to the Second Coming (Matthew 24:31); with the Rapture (1 Cor. 15:51, 52; 1 Thes. 4:16). A close study of these passages shows not only that the trumpet is the most mentioned instrument in the Word, but can signify many things.

"These trumpets are all angelic and supernatural, not heard by the peoples of earth at the time, the first six being preliminary to ongoing judgments, the last (7th) announcing the grand finale of earth's history."

–James O. Combs

First Four Trumpets (7-12)

"Hail and fire, mingled with the blood of man and animals. All green grass and one third of the trees destroyed. One third of the creatures of the Sea and one third of all the ships destroyed. A great star, Wormwood (a symbol of bitterness), falls and embitters a third part of the river and the fountains of water. Many die from water pollution. The third part of the Sun, Moon and the Stars are darkened and do not shine for a third of the time. This indescribable holocaust, as terrible as it is, is about to be surpassed, according to the Angel, by the three Trumpets yet to sound. Impossible! yet true, for now Hell (the bottomless pit) is to be unlocked."

–C.C. Gosey

The Angel's Announcement (13)

"The thirteenth verse introduces, in a very solemn way, the three trumpets yet to follow, which are distinguished from the four we have already commented upon, as 'woe' trumpets. They speak of a more intensified form of judgment than any previously portrayed. I only desire now to call your attention to the expression, 'the inhabiters of the earth.' A similar term we find frequently in this book, 'Them that dwell upon the earth.' Upon these the heaviest judgments fall. They are not merely they that live here upon earth, but they form a distinctive class. They are the people who have rejected the heavenly calling. When God offered them full and free salvation through death of His beloved Son, they turned away from Him, because to have closed in with Christ would have meant to give up their worldly desires and love of sin, therefore they become the 'dwellers on the earth.' "

–H.A. Ironside

A Planet Amid Fire and Smoke
An Expository Sermon

Chapter Eight

Introduction

Approaching the Book of Revelation from a basically literalist viewpoint, requires the acceptance of language for what it says, unless obvious figures of speech are used. Of course, the scenes in heaven, described in John's vision, are precisely that. They are true and actual events, beheld by the Revelator, but taking place in heaven. They have a significance and convey lessons—which do not detract from the fact that John saw these things in a very real sense.

I. The Time of Silence (1)

Often before a great storm strikes, there is a stillness in the air, a foreboding quietness, suddenly broken by the crash of thunder and the howling of tempestuous winds. So here, heaven pauses in a silence of surprise, wonder and interest. It is a holy hush in anticipation of the heavenly ministry of Christ and the earthly judgments about to fall.

Sometimes it is well for us, viewing the things coming upon this earth, to stop, to be still and to know that God is indeed the Lord.

Christ, the righteous Judge, completes the opening of the seven seals, precipitating that awesome heavenly music, which in turn heralds seven judgments and the events that occur during the first half of the forthcoming Tribulation. The exception is the final trumpet, the seventh, which encompasses all of the events of chapters 12-19. These are the "days of the voice of the seventh trumpet, when the mystery of God will be finished" (10:7).

II. The Truth of the Savior's Intercession (2-5)

None other than Jesus Christ is this "another angel" in verse 5, seen here in His capacity as our great High Priest. Through Him we offer sacrifices of praise to God continually (Hebrews 13:15: 1 Peter 2:5). He is our Advocate with the Father, Jesus Christ the righteous (1 John 2:1). The incense, as indicated in 5:8, comes from "golden vials full of odours, which are the prayers of the saints." Mingling the prayers of God's people with His own intercessory ministry, He offers such sweet incense, as the one Mediator between God and man (1 Timothy 2:5).

Some have speculated that this angel is actually a created being of high rank, since Christ is the Opener of the seals. But it seems inconceivable in the light of the whole tenor of Scripture that angels are somehow involved in presenting or answering prayers. Only Christ is the Great High Priest. He is also the Angel of the Lord (see Genesis 16:7; Exodus 3:2; Numbers 22:22; Judges 2:1; 1 Kings 19:7; Psalm 34:7; Isaiah 37:36).

To interpret otherwise is to open a door for angels to be intercessors, to hear the prayers of the saints, to participate some way in a priestly function on behalf of believers, as the Roman Catholics suggest.

But the heavenly angels and deceased "saints" do not pray for us, any more than Mary, the human mother of our Lord, prays for us (John 14:6).

The incense is an emblem of prayer, as Psalm 141:2 so clearly teaches: "Let my prayer be set forth before thee as incense; and the lifting up of my hands as the evening sacrifice."

It appears that this beautiful passage occurs in connection with the "heavenly Tabernacle," after which the earthly Tabernacle was designed, for, "See, saith he, that thou make all things according to the pattern shown thee in the mount" (Hebrews 8:5).

Hence this is the "altar of incense" in heaven, reflected in the golden altar of incense set forth in Exodus 37:25-28. As that altar was a place for sweet smelling incense to ascend unto God, so the heavenly altar is a place where prayers are presented by our High Priest, like incense, sweet and aromatic, before the Eternal Father.

This ministry is continual, effective also during the Tribulation, when the cries of martyrs and persecuted believers rise to the throne of God.

In response (see 6:9-11), Christ casts the golden censer to the earth, thus signifying that His judgments and the time of vengeance are at hand.

III. The Trumpets of Judgment (first four) (6-11)

Always a time of solemnity or celebration in biblical times, the blowing of trumpets signaled a time for people to bestir themselves. Trumpets are associated with war (Jeremiah 4:19); with assembling and marching (Numbers 10:1); with festivals (Leviticus 23:24); with introduction of royalty (2 Kings 9:13); with the power of God (Exodus 19:16); with overthrow of the ungodly (Joshua 6); with the coming of Christ (1 Thessalonians 4:17, 18).

These seven angels that "stand" in the presence of God, whose responsibility it is to sound the trumpets, seem to occupy a high, heavenly station. Some have speculated that Michael and Gabriel are in their number. See Daniel 12:1; Luke 1:19.

As the angels prepare to sound, the world's ecology is in view. There have been many fanciful and varied interpretations of these surroundings, attempting to make each one a symbolical presentation of some event in history, spiritualizing away any literal meaning.

We reject that view.

"When the plain sense of Scripture makes common sense, seek no other sense ..."

The first trumpet touches the ground, the trees, the green grass. This could be a by-product of a nuclear holocaust. In any event, the vegetation is affected. This is the beginning of the end of the ecology as we have known it. There will be firestorms of incredible magnitude.

Heralding the turning of one-third of the oceans to blood, the second angel sounds his trumpet. A great mountain burning with fire, a giant meteor, comet or planetoid streaks across the sky, plunging and splashing into the ocean with a mighty impact. That such events have happened in the history of this planet is evident from the great meteor crater in Arizona, which is 4000 feet wide. There is evidence, too, geologically, that even more massive objects have crashed onto the earth.

Recent scientific speculations and calculations have pointed out the danger of an asteroid or a comet colliding with the earth, or in a near miss, causing great catastrophes on earth. One astronomer points to a time, with very intricate computations and computer calculations, in the 3100s A.D. when an asteroid will probably pass near the earth or fall into the sea with horrendous consequences.

Articles appear in popular and scientific journals from time to time raising the serious possibility of such planet changing events.

That is precisely what will happen during the Tribulation. In this chapter two comet-like objects or asteroids, of which there are thousands upon thousands between our Earth and the planet Jupiter, plunging from outer space, contaminate the waters of this world and produce ecological destruction of immense magnitude.

Nor must we wait a thousand years for this to happen. In 1991 there was considerable apprehension among astronomers about an asteroid which came within a million miles of earth. Had it been captured by the earth's gravity, it could have either fallen to earth or been caught in an orbit as a new small moon.

When the third angel sounds, another great star burning as a lamp falls upon this planet, a second meteor or comet-like object, contaminating and poisoning the fresh waters. Portending such a possibility is the serious contamination of earth's fresh water streams now by chemicals, radioactivity, unprocessed refuse and acid rain.

Perhaps because of the burning trees and grass, the gasses released by the falling objects upon impact and by other contaminants in the atmosphere, the light of the sun, moon and stars is diminished by one-third. This, too, may be portended by the heavy clouds of dirty gray smog that hang like an acrid curtain above many of the world's major cities.

Thus, the fourth trumpet completes the effect on the ecology; land, water and air.

These calamities and distresses, befalling a planet embroiled in wicked wars, led by the coming Antichrist, and rushing pell-mell toward destruction are the preludes of even more intense woes.

Conclusion (13)

Unseen by earthlings, an angel flies through heaven, proclaiming the woes to come, as will be described in chapters 9 and 12.

A "woe" is a biblical term, an interjection, an exclamation of grief or a proclamation of impending tragedy. It can apply to an individual who is approaching a time of suffering, as when Jesus said, "Woe unto them that are with child ... for then shall be great tribulation" (Matthew 24:19,21).

When Jesus pronounced eight "woes" upon the hypocritical scribes and Pharisees, He was forecasting their doom under divine judgment (Matthew 23).

When Isaiah pronounced six "woes" on the ancient Israelites (Isaiah 5), he decried the wicked sins and evil attitudes of his contemporaries, predicting divine judgment upon that sinful society.

When Habakkuk pronounced five "woes" upon backslidden Judah in 626 B.C. (Hab. 2), he both pointed out their sins and prophesied judgment. Yet in the midst of his vigorous denunciations of sin, He reminded the people that the time would come when "the earth shall be filled with the knowledge of the Lord, as the waters cover the sea" (Hab. 2:14).

But these last "woes" affect the whole world.

A Commentary on the Revelation
Expository, Exegetical, Devotional and Practical
Greek words from the Textus Receptus

Chapter Eight

The Opening of the Seventh Seal (1-5)

1. And when he had opened the seventh seal, there was silence in heaven about the space of half an hour *(kai hotan enoiksen ten sphragida ten hebdomen, egeneto sige en to ourano hos hemior on)* — During this "seventh" opening a great silence settles upon the heavenly company, including God the Father, the Son, the Spirit, the elders, the angels and the souls in heaven, contrasting with the jubilation and praise of chapters 4,5, and 7. It is a calm before a storm; it is a quietness springing from the awe of beholding the workings of God; it is a frozen silence in anticipation of the trumpet judgments being introduced by the opening of the seventh seal. Out of the last seal proceed the seven trumpets, the last of which is the grand announcement of those events to culminate in the "Kingdoms of this world becoming the kingdoms of our God and His Christ…" The "days of the voice of the 7th angel (10:7) include the last half of the Tribulation, the seven vials of judgment and the destruction of Antichrist, all of which issues in the Second Advent in glory and power. **2. Seven angels** *(eidon tous hepta angellous)* — In the non-inspired Apocryphal books, which are part of pre-Christian Jewish literature and which used to appear in most English Bibles prior to the 20th century and are still used by Catholics is an interesting passage: "I am Raphael, one of the seven holy angels, which present prayers of the saints and which go in and out before the glory of the Holy One" (Tobit 12:15). All this does is reveal the fact that the Jews believed in 7 special angels. Other names are given in the non-canonical pseudopigryphal book of Enoch: Uriel, Raguel, Sarakiel and Raphael, besides Michael and Gabriel, which is here reported as a matter of interest only … **which stood before God** *(hoi enopion tou theou hestekasin)* — only Michael and Gabriel are said to "stand" (Dan. 12:1); Luke 1:19) and are the only angels mentioned by name in the Word, both employed on the most distinguished missions with Michael also designated "the archangel" (Jude 9). **3. And another angel came and stood at the altar, having a golden censer** — both the altar and censer are heavenly realities, part of the cere-

mony in the presence of God of which the earthly tabernacle and temple were reflections. See Exodus 37:25-29. In Hebrews 7-10 the typology and meaning of the earthly tabernacle, ceremonies and offerings are clearly set forth as fulfilled by our Great High Priest both on earth and in heaven. This Angel of the Lord is, I think, Christ, who is mingling the sweet incense of His intercessory prayers with the prayers of the saints and offering, as our Advocate, our petitions before the throne. Compare I John 2:1,2; Hebrews 7:25-27 and 9:1-10. **5. And the angel took the censer and filled it with fire of the altar and cast it into the earth** *(kai eilephen tou ho angelos libanoton kai egemisen auton ek tou puros thusiasteriou kai ebelen eis ten gen)* — "the censer was a small vessel employed for presenting incense to the Lord in the sanctuary and which was appointed to be set every morning on the altar of incense when the priest went in to dress the candlestick (lampstand). Live coals from the altar of burnt offering were put into it, and a quantity of incense was thrown on them, causing a cloud of sweet perfume to ascend and fill the tabernacle" (Fairbairn). Here the Angel-Priest, Christ, takes the censer, filling it with hot coals from the altar and then casts them into the earth. This signifies that the prayers of the martyrs in Rev. 6:9,10 are being answered along with all the prayers of the saints in heaven already and those new believing saints on earth. Christ has the authority to respond in fiery judgment, which the succeeding chapters describe … and there were **voices** *(phonai)* and **thunderings** *(brontai)* and **lightnings** *(astrapai)* and an **earthquake** *(seismos)* — phenomena in heaven trigger in the succeeding judgments and similar events on earth.

The First Four Trumpets (6-12)

6. And the seven angels prepared themselves to sound — they make themselves alert, ready, prepared and poised to sound their trumpets. As each sounds, a judgment transpires on earth. These chronologically proceed from the 7th seal and brings us to the midpoint of the Tribulation Period, since 3 $\frac{1}{2}$ year periods are specified in chapters 11 and 12 in conjunction with events subsequent to the first six trumpets. **7. And the first angle sounded** *(kai ho protos esalpisen)* — he blows his trumpet. Imagine the haunting melody of a heavenly horn reverberating through the spiritual realm and sparking events in the earthly realm. It must have been beautiful, yet solemn, not a trumpet sound of joy, but of august and martial majesty … "The common feature of the first four trumpets is, the judgments under them effect natural objects, the accessories of life, the earth, trees, grass, the sea, rivers, fountains, the light of the sun, moon and stars. The last three, the woe trumpets (vs. 13) effect men's life with pain, death and hell. The language is evidently drawn from the plagues of Egypt, five or six out of the ten seem to correspond: the hail, the fire (Ex. 9:24), the water turned to blood (Ex. 7:19); the darkness (Ex. 10:12), and even death, as in Rev. 9:18" (J.F.B.). In the seal judgments, the trumpet judgments and the vial judgments, the first four in each case are related with a change in the remaining three, as we shall see. The sounding of these trumpets remind us of the fall of Jericho, when great consequences accompanied the blasts (Josh. 6) … **and there followed hail and fire, mingled with blood** *(kai egento chalaksa kai pur memigmena en haimati)* — this also reminds us of the fire which fell on Sodom and Gomorrah (Gen. 19:24). What sparks this conflagration is not clearly stated. Various theories have been advanced, such as a nuclear war, volcanic eruptions world wide, the approach of the comets or asteroids very close to the earth or some scientific device in space, possibly from a space station. Of course, God might mysteriously with no evident cause known to man, bring this judgment to pass. The results effect the ecology with a third of the trees being consumed. Even now the destruction of great oxygen producing green forests and jungles world wide is of great concern to scientists, whose dire predictions for the future of this planet sound apocalyptic. While all the grass is consumed, it evidently will grow back to some extent during the Tribulation. **8. And the second angel sounded and as it were a great mountain burning with fire was cast into the sea,: and the third part of the sea became blood** — This seems to depict a great comet or an asteroid/meteor plunging into the sea, causing great destruction. Science in the late 20th century began to warn of the possible collision of asteroids with the earth. It need not be more than a few miles wide to cause great tidal waves, destroying a third of the ships of the sea and by disintegrating cause discoloration of the oceans and produce poisons, lethal to sea life. **10. And the third angel sounded and there fell a great star from heaven, burning as it were a lamp, and it fell upon the third part of the rivers, and upon the fountains of waters —**

In this writer's judgment this is a second meteor/asteroid falling on the earth in such a way as to poison the fresh water streams and the fountain heads of great rivers. This would be the supreme pollution. Trying to spiritualize this passage and make the star mean Satan strains this text. Now in chapter 9, we are specifically told that "the star" is a "he". Not so here. "If the plain sense of Scripture makes common sense, seek no other sense." This is literal. **11. And the name of the star is called Wormwood** *(kai to onoma tou asteros legetai ho apsinthos)* — from the wormwood plant a bitter herb can be extracted, actually absinthe as from the Greek word above. In minute amounts it has been used for medicinal purposes or for mixing with wines, but it can be fatal if consumed in large amounts. This star is simply named Wormwood, because of the poisonous substance diffused into the eco-system and the water supply from its falling upon the planet and the waters. **12. And the fourth angel sounded and the third part of the sun was smitten, and the third part of the moon, and the third part of the stars; so as the third part of them was darkened and the day shown not for a third part of it and the night likewise** — So contaminated may be the atmosphere because of the fumes, smoke and debris from the first three trumpet judgments that the light of the heavenly bodies is diminished by one third. Notice the word "third" occurs 9 times.

The Flying Angel (13)

13. And I beheld, and heard an angel flying through the midst of heaven, saying with a loud voice, Woe, woe, woe to the inhabiters of the earth … While some ancient Greek manuscripts read eagle for angel, it does seem out of context and character to have a talking eagle here. This is an angel, flying like an eagle, but solemnly announcing the coming judgments as "Woes." The word **heaven** here is *mesouranemati* and is only used in the Apocalypse. It signifies the mid-heaven or the meridian, high in the sky. Rather than being an angel of normal appearance, he seems in flight to be "swift and certain in swooping down upon its prey" (Garner) … **loud voice** here is *phono megale,* like a megaphone … the word **woe** is in the Greek *ouai,* thrice repeated. The first is easily discernible, the fifth trumpet judgment being the unleashing of demon creatures (9); the second woe will include the sixth trumpet and all events leading up to the earthquake in Jerusalem (11:13,14); the third woe for the inhabiters of the earth is Satan's last three and a half years on earth (Rev. 12:12-14).

RAINBOWS FROM REVELATION
The Revelation of Jesus Christ

A chapter by chapter, verse by verse study

"There was a rainbow round about the throne like unto an emerald" (4:3)

CHAPTER NINE: Trumpets/Judgments

References

Isa. 14:12
Lk. 10:18;
Rev. 17:8

Joel 2:2,10

Ex. 10:4
Jud. 7:12

Rev. 6:6
Rev. 8:7
Ex. 12:23
Ezek. 9:4
Rev. 7:2,3

Rev. 11:7

Job 3:21; 7:15
Isa. 2:19
Jer. 8:3

Joel 2:4
Nah. 3:17
Dan. 7:8

Joel 1:6

Jer. 47:3
Joel 2:5-7

Eph. 2:2; 6:12

1. AND the fifth angel sounded, and I saw a star fall from heaven unto the earth: and to him was given the key of the bottomless pit.

2. And he opened the bottomless pit; and there arose a smoke out of the pit, as the smoke of a great furnace; and the sun and the air were darkened by reason of the smoke of the pit.

3. And there came out of the smoke locusts upon the earth: and unto them was given power, as the scorpions of the earth have power.

4. And it was commanded them that they should not hurt the grass of the earth, neither any green thing, neither any tree; but only those men which have not the seal of God in their foreheads.

5. And to them it was given that they should not kill them, but that they should be tormented five months: and their torment was as the torment of a scorpion, when he striketh a man.

6. And in those days shall men seek death, and shall not find it; and shall desire to die, and death shall flee from them.

7. And the shapes of the locusts were like unto horses prepared unto battle; and on their heads were as it were crowns like gold, and their faces were as the faces of men.

8. And they had hair as the hair of women, and their teeth were as the teeth of lions.

9. And they had breastplates, as it were breastplates of iron; and the sound of their wings was as the sound of chariots of many horses running to battle.

10. And they had tails like unto scorpions, and there were stings in their tails: and their power was to hurt men five months.

11. And they had a king over them, which is the angel of the bottomless pit, whose name in the Hebrew tongue is Abaddon, but in the Greek tongue hath his name Apollyon.

12. One woe is past; and, behold, there came two woes more hereafter.

13. And the sixth angel sounded, and I heard a voice from the four horns of the golden altar which is before God,

14. Saying to the sixth angel which had the trumpet, Loose the four angels which are bound in the great river Euphrates.

15. And the four angels were loosed, which were prepared for an hour, and a day, and a month, and a year, for to slay the third part of men.

16. And the number of the army of the horsemen were two hundred thousand thousand: and I heard the number of them.

17. And thus I saw the horses in the vision, and them that sat on them, having breastplates of fire, and of jacinth, and brimstone: and the heads of the horses were as the heads of lions; and out of their mouths issued fire and smoke and brimstone.

18. By these three was the third part of men killed, by the fire, and by the smoke, and by the brimstone, which issued out of their mouths.

19. For their power is in their mouth, and in their tails: for their tails were like unto serpents, and had heads, and with them they do hurt.

20. And the rest of the men which were not killed by these plagues yet repented not of the works of their hands, that they should not worship devils, and idols of gold, and silver, and brass, and stone, and of wood: which neither can see, nor hear, nor walk:

21. Neither repented they of their murders, nor of their sorceries, nor of their fornication, nor of their thefts.

References

Rev. 8:13
Rev. 11:14

Rev. 8:3

Rev. 16:12

Ps. 68:17
Rev. 7:4
Ez. 38:4

1 Chr. 12:8
Isa. 5:28,29

Isa. 9:15

Deut. 31:29
Lev. 17:7
Ps 106:37
Ps 115:4-7
Ps 135:15-17

Scriptures for Comparison

Isaiah 14:12-15

How art thou fallen from heaven, O Lucifer, son of the morning! how art thou cut down to the ground, which didst weaken the nations! For thou hast said in thine heart, I will ascend into heaven, I will exalt my throne above the stars of God: I will sit also upon the mount of the congregation, in the sides of the north: I will ascend above the heights of the clouds; I will be like the most High.

Yet thou shalt be brought down to hell, to the sides of the pit.

Summary of Chapter Nine

The Woes on the World

I. The Fifth Trumpet (1-12)

These fifth and sixth trumpets are also the first and second of three "woes on the world," announced by the flying angel at the close of chapter 8. People on earth will not behold this herald of approaching dooms, but John saw him and records all of this for information. The second woe, which involves the armada of 200,000,000 in the midst of Asia and concludes with the earthquake of 11:14, is followed by the third "woe" (12:12), when Satan, confined primarily to earth intensifies his evil endeavors, knowing he has but a short time. That "time" is the last half of the Tribulation period.

The first woe and fifth trumpet judgment begins with a falling star, who is Lucifer or Satan (see Luke 10:18), since to that "star" is given the key of the bottomless pit. He opens the pit and unleashes on the earth a terrible scourge of demon creatures.

Probably they are invisible to human eyes, but they torment men on earth for five months. People even seek death during that fearsome five-month period, but cannot find it. That they are supernatural demon creatures is evident from the fact that they have a king who is the angel of the bottomless pit. His name is Abaddon or Apollyon, both of which mean "destroyer." This may be a fallen "principality" (Ephesians 6:12) and not Satan himself, but rather a high-ranking fallen angel, a follower of Satan in his original rebellion (Isaiah 14:12-14).

Attempts to make these demon creatures, horrible in their appearance, symbolical of modern mechanized and computerized warfare, are fanciful and not indicated at all in the text.

II. The Sixth Trumpet (13-21)

When the sixth angel sounds his trumpet, the four angels said to be found in the river Euphrates are unloosed.

A vast armada of 200,000,000 equipped and armored soldiers, are in figurative and literal terms, seen pillaging the world. A third of the world's population is slain as a result of the Tribulation Wars, now centered in the Middle East in this prophetic foreview.

Due to description here some expositors think these are also demonic beings, while others see in the hellish horsemen some future form of armor and equipment, worn by actual soldiers from the Far East, clashing with armies and nations, causing widespread death and destruction on a massive scale.

In spite of the horrendous nature of this great "woe," people on earth continue in their hardness and sinfulness without repentance.

Outline of Chapter Nine

The Seven Trumpets (fifth and sixth)

OBJECTIVE: To reveal that sinful human beings, regardless of sin's consequences, yet harden their hearts.

OUTLINE:

I. The First Woe on the World (1-12)

 E. Fifth Trumpet: Crowned Demon-Creatures (1-12)
  1. The Opener of the Pit—Satan
  2. The Origin of the Judgment—from beneath (2)
  3. The Operation of the Locusts (3-10)
   a. They have power (3)
   b. They torment unsaved men (4)
   c. They do not kill (5)
  4. The Result of the Judgment (6). A death wish unresolved.
  5. The Appearance of the Locusts (7-10)
  6. The Time of the Torment—5 months (10)
  7. The Ruler of the Creatures: Apollyon (11)
  ONE WOE IS PAST: TWO MORE ARE TO COME

II. The Second Woe on the World (13-19) (13-19; Compare 11:1-14)

 F. Sixth Trumpet – Hellish Horsemen
  1. A Voice from Heaven (13)
  2. A Command for Angels (14)
  3. A Destiny of Death (15)
  4. An Armada in Asia (16)
  5. The Tools of Destruction (17, 18)
   a. Fire
   b. Smoke
   c. Brimstone
  6. The Vision of their Power (19)
  7. The Purpose of their Efforts—to hurt (19)

III. The Sinful Wickedness of the World (20,21)

  1. No Repentance of Idolatry (20)
  2. No Repentance of Murders (21)
  3. No Repentance of Sorceries (*pharmakia* - or drug abuse)
  4. No Repentance of Fornication
  5. No Repentance of Thefts

(Six of the seven trumpets in Chapters 8 and 9 are listed as "A" through "F.")

Observations:
Spiritual lessons and applications from each verse
Chapter Nine

1. God allows Satan certain latitude in his evil dealings, but uses even his wicked plans as a part of His own righteous judgment. See 1 Corinthians 10:13.

2. There are evil forces in the nether world, fallen angels and demons that, under certain circumstances, can be unleashed on earth.

3. Locusts in Old Testament times were literal tools of judgment (see Joel 1 and 2:1-10). These locusts of Revelation are real but demonic, far more powerful than those Joel described.

4. How important it is in any age to have "the seal of God." See Ephesians 4:30.

5. It is always a path of suffering and eventual torment when people turn from God.

6. Seeking death and not finding it will be a future experience of sad consequences, but people today are seeking death, unwittingly, in so many ways, so often with chemical substances.

7. This description can only be of demonic beings.

8. How fierce are the forces of evil … But God is greater than the devil!

9. Evil forces can move with great speed.

10. Times of turmoil and torment today are indicative of worse times to come.

11. Unquestionably, the ruler of these fallen angelic beings, seduced by Satan at the time of his fall at the dawn of time as we know it, is a high-ranking subordinate of Satan.

12. Study the other woes of Habakkuk 2 and Isaiah 5. Look up the word in the concordance and see how God uses it.

13. God's power and voice are still heard above all the forces of evil.

14. Angels are involved in God's invisible government.

15. God is very specific about a certain time and place. He handles details.

16. As John hears the words of truth, let us hear them as well.

17. Notice the horses are in a "vision." The armada is real, but is symbolically described.

18. Perhaps the 200,000,000 coming from the Far East involve the Asian multitudes — even China or India. The imagery here may indicate fiery destruction, possibly by sophisticated weaponry.

19. "Serpents" usually connote evil.

20. Idolatry continues in spite of God's prohibition and judgment.

21. Notice that hardened multitudes of the world continue in the four wicked sins of (1) violence, (2) drug addiction-sorcery, (3) immorality, and (4) stealing. These sociological ills are with us today. They will be intensified in the Tribulation.

No Repentance

"There is a lack of repentance manward. John tells us, 'Neither repented they of their murders, nor of their sorceries, nor of their fornication, nor of their thefts.' What a picture of a crime-oriented culture! Man has finally arrived at his goal — a government and culture in which permissiveness is the accepted norm and where all kinds of deviation and misbehavior are applauded and encouraged, a government presided over by a fascinating but foul individual called the man of sin (2 Th. 2:3).

"The word rendered 'sorceries,' incidentally, literally means 'use of drugs' and is derived from the Greek word from which we get our English word 'pharmacy.' The word is primarily used to signify medicine, drugs, spells, then poisoning and sorcery. Drugs were used in sorcery, generally accompanied by incantations and the use of various charms. Today's world is fast becoming a drug- and demon-oriented world."

– John Phillips

Quotations
From Other Expositors
Chapter Nine

The Pit Opened (1)

"The first verse of Chapter 9 does not record the fall itself, but rather the star is seen as already fallen from heaven to the earth. It would seem likely, therefore, that the person referred to as the star is none other than Satan himself. J. B. Smith believes the star is an angel:

'That a literal star is not meant is evident from the part that to him was given the key, that is, the authority (Matthew 16:19; Revelation 1:18), to open the bottomless pit. An intelligent being must be intended. It has been observed that a star is used as a symbol of the angel, 1:20. As early as the days of Job, there is a similar use of the word (Job 38:7).'

"To this personage is given the key of the bottomless pit, or pit of abyss. This is the first instance of this expression in Scripture mentioned three times in this chapter and four additional times later in Revelation. The 'bottomless pit' (Gr,. *abyssos*) is the abode of demons according to Luke 8:31. The Greek word is found seven times in Revelation (9:1,2,11; 11:7; 17:8; 20:1,3). The opening verse of this chapter, therefore, presents Satan as having the key to the pit of the abyss with power to release those who are confined there."

– John F. Walvoord

The Locust Creatures (2-12)

"As soon as the mouth of the pit is opened, a thick blackness issues from it like the black smoke of a great furnace — a blackness which fills the air and obscures the sun; and out of the smoky blackness proceed living things, horrible in shape, malignant in disposition, and armed with power to afflict and torment men's bodies. John calls them locusts; but they are supernatural, infernal, not earthly locusts. They neither consume nor injure any of the grass of the earth, or any green thing, or any tree. They do not appear to eat at all, though they have teeth like the teeth of lions. They are winged creatures, and their flight is noisy, sounding like chariots and horses rushing into battle. They seem to dwell mostly in the air and in the smoke and darkness. Neither is there any indication that they are capable of being caught or killed.

"The forms of these creatures are particularly described. They are a sort of infernal cherubim — antipodes of the Living ones conjoined with the heavenly throne. The horse, the man, the lion, the scorpion, are combined in them. Their general appearance is like horses caparisoned for battle. Their heads are surmounted by the semblance of crowns seemingly of gold. They have faces resembling the faces of men. They are hairy, with hair like women's hair. Their backs and breasts are encased as if with iron plates, after the manner of a Roman soldier, and they have tails of the size and shape of a scorpion."

– J.A. Seiss

The Hellish Horsemen (13-21)

"There is no direct statement as to the origin of this army, but the implication is, from the fact that the angels of verse 14 were bound 'in' or at the Euphrates, that the army may come from the East. A similar and later development mentioned in Revelation 16:12 following the outpouring of the sixth vial also depicts an invasion from the East. Chronologically the trumpets involved closely succeed one another and their judgments seem to fall like trip-hammer blows as the great tribulation comes to its close. It may be that the army here described continues to fight until the time of the second coming of Christ, and the number slain is the total number involved in the conflict.

"John also gives a graphic description of the horses as well as of the warriors who sit upon them. They are declared to have breastplates of fire and of jacinth and brimstone. Some have interpreted the description as John's understanding of a scene in which modern warfare is under way. Further, the heads of the horses are compared to heads of lions out of whose mouths fire, smoke, and brimstone issue. This again is a description that might be comparable to modern mechanical warfare. Whether these are symbols or the best description John can give of modern warfare, this is an awesome picture of an almost irresistible military force destroying all that opposes it. The terms 'horses,' 'lions,' and 'serpents' all speak of deadly warfare. The mention of lions can be compared to that in Revelation 10:3 where lions roar, and to the description of the locusts in 9:8 as having teeth of lions, and to the beast of Revelation 13:2, which has the mouth of a lion. As king of beasts the lion speaks of victorious conquest."

– John F. Walvoord

They Came from the Bottomless Pit
An Expository Sermon

Chapter Nine

Introduction

Up to now, the first four trumpets have affected the natural world, working great effects on nature as we know it. But this trumpet now before us touches on the spiritual realm, the unseen but real world, where principalities and powers and rulers of the darkness of this world conduct their visible warfare against God and truth and justice.

These woes are indeed of a most mysterious character.

Many people have sought to interpret these two trumpets as being figures of speech that relate to sophisticated weapons and crafts of our times. Our basic approach is literal, but with the realization that figures of speech and symbols are here in this style of literature. To distinguish between the strictly literal interpretation of a judgment and the symbolical significance of a vision is the task of the Bible student. Heavenly wisdom should be sought. "The secret things belong unto God ..."

Following the principle that "if the plain sense of Scripture makes common sense, seek no other sense" and that "God says what He means and means what He says," necessitates understanding a passage such as this as literally as possible. When a symbol is used in Revelation, it is either explained within the book itself or can be understood by comparing other prophetic and apocalyptic material within the wide range of Sacred Scripture.

Let us look at these two trumpets and the events they herald.

I. Demonic Creatures (1-12)

Even Satan, Lucifer, the fallen angel, has great power and is here given the key of the bottomless pit. In the coming time of Tribulation, God will allow Satan to open up that nether world of imprisonment, unleashing a terrible plague of invisible but diabolical creatures. They will torment men for five months.

It is not easy to imagine a "bottomless pit," which, when uncapped, spews forth like a volcano a darkening smoke that obscures the sun and fills the air.

However, the 1980 volcanic blast and eruption at Mt. St. Helens in Washington State furnishes a powerful illustration. There an overshadowing darkness and falling ash turned midday into a midnight and fresh air into an almost poisonous and noxious mixture of air, gases and ash.

The pit is an *abyss,* the word in the Greek. An abyss is a great shaft like a well. Seven times in Revelation the term bottomless pit/abyss occurs. In Luke 8;31, the word *abyss* is translated "the deep," where demons cast out of possessed men were loathe to go.

Evidently, this spiritual realm is encased in the interior of this planet and is the prison of fallen angelic creatures, who are now demons. But some are loose now and many will be loosed in the future Tribulation, as we see here.

Imagine those who would seek death and be unable to die! Some expositors think that no death will occur for this five-month span anywhere.

The souls of men are in torment, even before plunging into a fiery hell. Yes, there is a fiery abyss with myriads of evil beings within it. Sometimes in the dark recesses of witchcraft and sorcery, real contact is made with the foul realm. How we ought to avoid anything that smacks of Satanism or evil magical powers, whether in today's rock music or in the secret covens of witches and warlocks. It is a dangerous curiosity that leads men and women to delve into the depths of Satan. No one ever wins who links his soul and mind to Satan's forces.

These infernal locusts have the mobility of a grasshopper and the terrible sting of a scorpion. Could we see them with mortal eyes, they would have the terrible appearance herein described, but remember these are invisible but real vile and demonic beings. Even now, those who embrace Satanism and the Occult often utilize horrible, ugly faced representations of demons or the devil, both in pictures, on clothing and even in tattoos on the body.

Evil and devilish practices of Voodooism, spiritualism and other Satanically spawned heathen practices are widespread in Latin America and in Africa. Truly the planet is ripe for intensified demonic activity.

Leading the evil empire of demonic creatures is their king, whose name, "Abaddon," meaning in Hebrew "destroyer" or "destruction," as it is used in Job 28:22 ("destruction and death"). The equivalent Greek word is *Apollyon,* meaning "the one who is destroying."

Most likely, this is not Satan, who opens the pit, but a fallen angelic being of previous high rank, who followed the devil's original rebellion.

But in the TRIBULATION, this awful worldwide surge of demonism and torment will result in pain and suffering. All this is covered by the fifth angel's announcement in trumpet tones of impending doom.

II. Destructive Conflicts (12-19)

Again the scene shifts to heaven. For even as Satan's power is rife, so God's power is universal.

As we approach in our study the midpoint of the Tribulation, the wars intensify. The vastness of Asia is in view with its billions of inhabitants. China itself has one billion today. India boasts nearly 700 million.

Obviously, the four angels who have been "bound in the great river Euphrates" are divine messengers of judgment. Whether that is their present locale or not is not specified, but I would conclude that they arrive at this strategic location during the first half of the Tribulation and await God's directive.

At the appointed time, these invisible angelic beings, who are instruments of divine judgment, initiate a series of events that results in the slaying of the third part of men. They have restrained the forces of evil until the appointed time. Now they let loose the forces that result in one of the great battles of future history. They were prepared for the specific hour, day, month and year when this carnage is to begin.

We have mentioned the hordes of China and India, which are "beyond the River Euphrates to the East." We would not omit the "Muslim" nations of Pakistan, Afghanistan, Iran, Iraq and newly freed former countries within the old defunct Soviet Union, such as Kazakhstan, etc.

Here it seems more likely that the description of the horsemen may depict human warfare.

Verse 18 declares, "By these three was the third part of men killed, by the fire, and by the smoke, by the brimstone, which issued out of their mouths."

This indeed may depict a mechanized force with cavalry elements, using fiery weapons of destruction, poison gas (smoke) and "brimstone," which can be a description of colossal explosive power, such as nuclear bombs. Many of the aforementioned countries now possess nuclear capability and its unleashing on the Asian continent could end in the slaughter of over a billion people.

Thank God, the true believers of this Age will not be present. They will have been delivered by the Rapture from the wrath that is to come.

Bear in mind that these horrendous events will occur during the latter part of the first half of the Tribulation. The idea that a long false peace will characterize the first three and a half years of the "Seventieth Week (of years) of Daniel" finds little support in Scripture.

God will allow these things to happen, as man's inhumanity against man is intensified and the invisible conflict between God's forces of righteousness and Satan's evil powers continues. In all of this, however, the judgment of God is at work. Evil brings evil in the natural and supernatural course of events, until God brings it to a halt.

III. Doomed Unrepentants (20-21)

Resisting the grace of God and refusing the Gospel of God issues in man denying that sin fosters evil results. Today's sex perverts, aspiring to political power, deny that their evil conduct has made AIDS a worldwide plague of death. The civilization of the future clings to its sins.

"And the rest of the men which were not killed by these plagues (the first six trumpet judgments, up to this point) YET REPENTED NOT OF THE WORKS OF THEIR HANDS" (20a). Devotion to idols is rampant among billions today with the New Age movement promoting both pantheism, which is worshipping all creation and nature as god, and literal and symbolical idolatry with people worshipping images or idols and "mother earth" and "the unseen force."

Besides idolatry, there are four evils which the world of the future will refuse to forsake in spite of God's judgments. "Neither repented they of their murders, nor of their sorceries (drug use and abuse), nor of their fornication (immorality, free sex, perversion, homosexuality, lesbianism, beastiality, etc.), nor of their thefts" (21).

Can anyone doubt that these ills confront us TODAY!

Conclusion

There is still time to repent now before the Rapture and the Tribulation come. There is still time to believe the gospel. If anyone reads of this chapter's horrendous plagues, dismiss it not as fanciful allegory. While some of these truths are shrouded in mystery, their fulfillment is certain and sure.

Now is the time for you to turn to Christ.

You can be saved from the "wrath which is to come."

Right now, bow your head and invite Jesus Christ to come into your heart and life and save you today!

A Commentary on the Revelation
Expository, Exegetical, Devotional and Practical
Greek words from the Textus Receptus

Chapter Nine

The Fifth Trumpet/The First Woe (1-12)

1. And the fifth angel sounded and I saw a star fall from heaven unto the earth *(Kai ho pemptos angelos esalpisen kai eidon astera ek ouranou peptokota eis ges tes)* – What John saw here was in a sense a flashback, since the Greek word *peptokota* indicates the past tense, showing the star had already fallen, as described in Isaiah 14:12, where Lucifer, son of the morning, is seen fallen from heaven after his original rebellion, prior to the creation of man. He was guilty of the sin of pride, as demonstrated by his excessive use of "I will," in opposition to God. Primarily Satan's activities are focused upon the human race on this planet, although he has limited access to the throne of God, as clearly taught in Job 1,2. Not actually imprisoned in hell as yet, the evil accuser walks to and fro and seeks some to devour (1 Peter 5:8)...as god of this world, he blinds the unsaved (2 Cor. 4:3,4)...**And to him was given the key of the bottomless pit** *(kai edothe auto he kleis tou phreatos tes abussou)* – Unlike the falling star and mountain in chapter 8, this "star" is a "he", a personality, whereas the previous star is a comet-like object literally falling into the sea. In 12:4, where Satan is "the dragon", he is depicted as "drawing a third part of the stars of heaven" in his rebellion, which in 12:7,8,9 are seen to be angels who followed his infernal leadership. Thus "a star" can emblematize angelic beings, including fallen ones. Here Lucifer is allowed to open the bottomless pit, where demonic beings, also fallen angels, are imprisoned and to which he will be consigned in the millennium (20:1-3). The Greek word for bottomless pit is *abussou,* transliterated as abyss in English. It is translated "the deep" in Luke 8:31, where the demons exiting from the maniac of Gadara, were loathe to go back to the abyss, actually the bottomless pit. **2. And he opened the bottomless pit** *(kai enoiksen to phrean tes abussou)* – Some expositors think that this is presently Satan's abode, but, while he might have occasional access there, he is not bound but active in the Universe. At this particular time he is given the key to open this prison in order to unleash his demons … **and there arose a smoke out of the pit** *(kai anebe kapnos kaminou megales)* – Out of the shaft opening arises evidently a visible smoke, reminiscent of a volcanic explosion - **As the smoke of a great furnace** *(hos kapnos kaminou megales)* – Forth from this smoke filled abyss, evidently in a spiritual realm within the bowels of the earth, the demons and fallen angels may periodically arise, but the huge onrush here described of demon creatures exceeds anything in history...**and the sun and the air were darkened by reason of the smoke of the pit** *(kai eskotothe ho helios kai ho aer ek tou kapnou tou phreatos)* – This appears to be quite literal, but from whence geographically this foul smoke erupts remains to be seen. Notice there is an interplay between the coexistent and contemporaneous spiritual realm, where Satan and his angels function, as well as God's angels, and the material realm, which we humans see. There is a visible world and an invisible world side by side in God's universe, another dimension undetected by scientific investigations, but nevertheless real, present and inescapable. In this book this interplay between the two realms is most evident … **3. And there came out of the smoke locusts upon the earth** *(kai ek tou kapnou ekselthon akrides eis tes geo)* – John is able to see and discern both the visible and the invisible, which human beings cannot now see. Initially they are described as locusts *(akrides)* and remind us of the devastating plagues of the past where literal locusts consumed life-giving crops (See Exodus 10:12-15; Judges 7:12; Joel 2:3) ... **And unto them was given power, as the scorpions of the earth have power** *(kai edothe autois eksousia hos echousin eksousian hoi skorpioi tes ges)* – Ordinary locusts or grasshopper-like creatures and stinging scorpions two to six inches long are not in view here, but rather powerful, pain-inflicting invisible beings capable of tormenting the wicked lost of that time. Strange indeed that God uses even the forces of evil unleashed to punish an ungodly world, for He makes the "wrath of man to praise him," as well. No compassion or love abides in Satan's corrupted heart, but only hatred even for those who yield to his vile leadership. **4. And it was commanded them that they should not hurt the grass of the earth, neither any green thing, neither any tree, but only to those men which have not the seal of God in their foreheads.** – While insects assail the grass and the crops, these demon-crea-

99

tures are limited to attacking human beings. Perhaps filled with resentment and vengeance and driven by an evil rage which knows no bounds, these released prisoners, from the pit, lash out in inflicting awful torment upon the unsaved. Protected supernaturally are those with the "seal of God" in their foreheads, which must designate the "sealed 144,000" of chapter 7, the Israelite witnesses for the truth. At this stage the 144,000 have not fulfilled their destiny and must be preserved for their world-wide ministry to those who have not heard the gospel. **5. And to them was given that they should not kill them by that they should be tormented five months and their torment was the torment of a scorpion when he striketh a man** *(kai edothe autois hina me apokteinosin autous all hina basanishthesontai menas pente kai ho basanismos auton hos basanismos skorpiou)* – Notice the word *basanismos* in the Greek which means to distress, vex, or rub on a touchstone or put to the test and then to examine by torture. This is both physical and mental torment, like the extreme pain that usually comes from actual scorpion bites and their chemical poison, excruciating and agonizing. **6. And in those days shall men seek death and shall not find it and shall desire to die and death shall flee from them** *(kai en tois hemerais ekeinas zetesousin hoi anthropoi ton thanaton kai oume heuresousin auton kai epithumesousin apothanein kai pheugei ho thanatos ap auton)* – Note the word *thanatos* or death, not merely a biological phenomena, but a transition to an after-life, for this word is frequently used by Paul to describe the death of Christ. The other word most used (133 times in the NT for death) is *nekros* and is used in the majority of cases in association with the death and resurrection of Christ. But in this future period of five literal months in the latter part of the first half (1260 days) of the Tribulation will be a time when people cannot die. The terminology may not mean that no death occurs, but that some men will seek death and yet live on in torment. **7. And the shapes of the locusts were like unto horses prepared unto battle and on their heads were as it were crowns of gold and their faces were as the faces of men** *(kai ta homoiomata ton akridon homoioi hippois hetoimasmenois ploemen kai epi tas kephales auton hos stephanoi homoioi chruso kai ta prosopa auton hos prosopa anthropon)* – Here begins a vivid description of what these demonic beings are seen to be, certainly no mere insect creatures, but bizarre spirit beings, possibly yet bearing a slight, but corrupted resemblance to what they once were as unfallen angels, now frightful and ugly. They are a combination of locusts, scorpions, horses prepared for battle, crowned rulers, man-like visages with streaming woman-like hair with teeth like lions...truly a depiction of warped onetime beauty, now forever twisted by rebellion against God into evil and sadistic spiritual creatures. **8. And they had hair as the hair of women and their teeth were as the teeth of lions** – ready to tear and inflict pain. Notice that God is allowing this to happen, but the torment is inflicted by Satan's fallen angels. The description of how they were seen by John continues. **9. And they had breastplates as it were breastplates of iron; and the sound of their wings was as the sound of chariots of many horses running to battle.** – These beings are protected by breastplates *(thorakas)*, or so it appeared as is indicated by the expression "as it were." Their wings evidently make it possible for them to traverse the earth visibly assaulting men and initiating torment in their human bodies. **10. And they had tails like unto scorpions and there were stings in their tails: and their power was to hurt men five months** – Scorpions do have stingers in their tails, but these ghastly creatures inject far more than a chemical poison; their torturous sting in the souls and bodies of the unsaved is far greater than any mere insect-caused discomfort. **11. And they had a king over them, which is the angel of the bottomless pit whose name in the Hebrew tongue is Abaddon but in the Greek tongue hath his name Apollyon** *(echousin ep' auton basilea ton angelon test abussou onoma auto Hebraisti Abaddon kai en te Hellenike onoma echei Apollvon)* – Indisputably, the fact that a king is over these monstrous spiritual beings, who is the fallen angel of the abyss, proves that these are indeed not some poetic or symbolical description of modern mechanized warfare, but real demons. Both Abaddon in Hebrew (see Prov. 27:20 and Job 26:6 for this very word in Hebrew) and Apollyon in Greek mean "destruction" or "destroyer" and the evil spirits he unleashes will afflict men with this plague of excruciating pain. Whether this king is Satan himself or a high-ranking fallen angel presently imprisoned in the bottomless pit is matter of varying opinions with this writer leaning toward the latter. **12. One woe is past and behold there come two woes more hereafter.** – For comparison with Chapters 8 and 9, Joel 1:2-7; 2:1-11 is strictly parallel and expressly refers (2-11) to The Day of the Lord Great and Terrible. Vs. 10 (Joel 2) gives the portents accompanying the day of the Lord coming, a period of time, when the earth, the heavens, the sun, moon and stars are all involved. During the entire seven years of Tribulation horrendous events occur, most of which are mentioned or at least hinted in the Old Testament prophecies. Also see Rev. 11:14 and 12:12 for the end of the second woe and beginning of the third.

The Sixth Trumpet/The Second Woe (13-19)

13. And the sixth angel sounded and I heard a voice from the four horns of the golden altar which is before God, – Whereas the fifth trumpet resulted in divine judgment emerging from the bottomless pit, the sixth angel introduced judgment proceeding from heaven's golden altar (See Rev. 6:9; 8:3; Ex. 30:3) by divine command. This altar is evidently the same altar of incense from chapter 8, from which coals of fire were cast on the earth, followed by the first four trumpet judgments effecting the ecology. **14. Saying to the sixth angel** (*legonta to kekto angelo*) – This divine order proceeds from the exalted and glorified Christ, who is worthy to take the book of judgments sealed and to open the seven seals; who is eligible to cast the fiery coals from the altar in heaven upon earth; and who is in command, directing the sixth angel to dispatch four specific angels "bound in the River Euphrates" to precipitate events leading to one of the great battle of the Tribulation Wars ... **Loose the four angels which are bound in the great river Euphrates** – This quartet may be the same four angels from 7:1-4 who are instructed to suspend the ecological judgments of chapter 8 until the 144,000 Israelites are divinely sealed. Here it is not implied that these angels have been chained to the river for all time, but that they are at that time, waiting, bound by obedience to God until the proper time. **15. And the four angels were loosed which were prepared for an hour and a day and a month and year** – until the specific foreordained time for their intervention on earth had arrived. It is still future ... **for to slay the third part of men** – This would be an enormous number still, if the world's population is 6 billion. Apparently, it is the warring soldiers involved here. Now the actual judgment is not conducted directly by the four angels, but rather they participate in allowing the huge armada and the enormous cavalry hordes to amass in the Middle East. **16. And the number of the army of the horsemen were two hundred thousand thousand** (*dismuriades muriadon*) – myriads of myriads, some 200,000,000 soldiers doing battle against one another ... **and I heard the number of them. 17. And thus I saw the horses in the vision** - Bear in mind this is a vision (*horasei*) in which John sees the interplay between the visible and invisible world. He then proceeds to describe the conflicting armies. **17. And thus I saw the horses in the vision and them that sat upon them having breastplates of fire and of jacinth (a dusky red) and of brimstone and the heads of the horses were as the heads of lions and out of their mouths issued fire and smoke and brimstone.** – It is possible that in this case John is seeing some sort of scientific or mechanized calvary with sophisticated weapons and thus describes them, since this seems to be an actual battle or series of battles involving these huge hordes of horsemen. **18. By these three** (*apo ton triton plegon touton*) **was the third part of men killed, by the fire and by the smoke and by the brimstone** – suggesting fiery detonations and conflagrations caused by weaponry, gas and smoke, and sulphurous burning weapons used by men against men. Some expositors think that the "third of men" refers to all mankind, while others limit the meaning to the 200,000,000 engaged in these Asian battles. Even now, in the 1990's, the Middle East is fraught with the danger of nuclear war. This may be a portent of things to come. A proliferation of nuclear weapons in this area constitutes a major problem already in existence. **19. For their power is in their mouth and in their tails: for their tails were like unto serpents, and had heads and with them they do hurt.** – This picture could easily apply to futuristic scientific and mechanized warfare, but only the actual fulfillment will reveal the true nature of the hellish horseman and the cursed calvary.

Summary Observations on Sinful Man (20,21)

20. And the rest of the men which were not killed by these plagues (all six of the trumpet judgments) yet repented not of the works of their hands, that they should not worship devils – this is the true nature of false worship, the adoration of devils whether represented by idols as here described or their ideas like Mother Earth or pantheistic theories that all of the Universe Is God. **21. Neither repented they of their murders** (*ek ton phonon auton*) – violence, premeditated murder, babykilling, infanticide, euthanasia, slaughters as in World War II gassing of the Jews ... **sorceries** (*pharmakeion*) – use and abuse of drugs, pharmaceutical hallucinogenic substances not only used for chemical highs but for Satanic and heathenish visions and worship ... **fornication** (*porneias*) – all kinds of sexual sin such as adultery, promiscuity, homosexuality, lesbianism, perversions, beastiality, pornography and such like, all rampant in society today ... **thefts** (*klemmaton*) – thievery, extortion, bribery, stealing of all kinds, cheating, etc. All of these conditions exist today throughout the world and seem to be increasing.

Supplemental Summary
A Futurist Outline of the Book of Revelation
Part One: Chapters 1-11

KEY VERSE: 1:19

I. THE THINGS WHICH THOU HAST SEEN, Chapter 1 — John sees Jesus on Patmos
A. Preview and Prologue, Vs. 1-8
B. Interview – Christ in His glory among His candlesticks, Vs. 9-18
C. Foreview of the Book, Vs. 19, 20

II. THE THINGS WHICH ARE, Chapters 2, 3

THE SEVEN CHURCHES	THE CHURCH AGE
A. Ephesus	Apostolic Age
B. Smyrna	Persecution Age, 2nd, 3rd Centuries
C. Pergamos	Rise of Ritualism, 4th - 6th Centuries
D. Thyatira	Dark Ages, 7th - 14th Centuries
E. Sardis	Renaissance-Reformation, 15th - 17th Centuries
F. Philadelphia	World Evangelism, 17th - 20th Centuries
E. Laodicea	Decline and Decay, ?

Not all futurists see the suggestion of periods of time in the message to the 7 churches, but believe that primarily these were historic congregations typifying all kinds of churches during this entire period between the 1st and 2nd Comings … that is, there are always congregations of each type (Ephesian, Smyrnan, etc.).

III. THE THINGS WHICH SHALL BE HEREAFTER, Chapters 4 - 22
The heavenly phenoma or sign or symbol is understood to be figurative, but the application or resultant phenomena or event <u>on earth</u> is thought to be usually literal, unless very obviously a metaphor.

THE SEVEN SEALS — Events taking place in beginning months or years of Tribulation.
A. FIRST SEAL: Antichrist, 6:1,2
B. SECOND SEAL: World Wide War, 6:3,4
C. THIRD SEAL: Famine, Result of War
D. FOURTH SEAL: Destruction and Death, 6:8
E. FIFTH SEAL: Martyrs (more must die in the Tribulation), 6:9-11
F. SIXTH SEAL: Cataclysms (horrendous end-time events), 6:12-18
    INTERLUDE —　　144,000 Israelis converted and sealed.
                       Many Gentiles come to Christ in Tribulation time, 7:9-15
G. SEVENTH SEAL: Silence, 8:1
    INTERLUDE —　　The High Priest in Heaven, 8:2-4. Seven trumpets issue from 7th seal.

THE SEVEN TRUMPETS —　　Thought to be mostly literal with actual falling objects,
**　　　　　　　　　　　　　　　real damage to ecology; some seemingly natural events.**
A. FIRST TRUMPET: Hail and Fire, 8:1-7
B. SECOND TRUMPET: Mountain Falls into Sea, 8:8,9
C. THIRD TRUMPET: Star Wormwood Pollutes Streams, 8:10,11
D. FOURTH TRUMPET: Heavenly Bodies Affected, 8:12,13
E. FIFTH TRUMPET: Demon Creatures Unleashed, 9:1-8
F. SIXTH TRUMPET: 200,000,000 "Hellish Horsemen" (thought to mean Asian Wars of the Tribulation), 9:9-17
    INTERLUDE —　　The Mighty Angel and the Proclamation, Ch. 10
                       The Temple Rebuilt in Israel, 11:1,2
                       The Two Witnesses for <u>First</u> 1,260 Days, 11:3-14
G. SEVENTH TRUMPET: Incorporates Final "Days," <u>Last</u> 3 $^1/_2$ Years, 11:15-19; Chapters 12-19

Chapters 10, 11, 12 mark the mid-point of the Seven Year Tribulation Period (the Seventieth Week of Daniel, 9:20-27) with 3 $^1/_2$ year time periods referring either to the first half or the second half mentioned.

RAINBOWS FROM REVELATION
The Revelation of Jesus Christ

A chapter by chapter, verse by verse study

"There was a rainbow round about the throne like unto an emerald" (4:3)

CHAPTER TEN: Time No Longer!

References

Ezek. 1:28

Ezek. 2:9,10
Ps. 95:5

Ps. 29:3-8
Rev. 4:5
Rev. 8:5

Dan. 8:26
Dan. 12:4,9
Deut. 29:29

Dan. 12:6

Gen. 1:1
Ex. 20:11

1. AND I saw another mighty angel come down from heaven, clothed with a cloud: and a rainbow was upon his head, and his face was as it were the sun, and his feet as pillars of fire:

2. And he had in his hand a little book open: and he set his right foot upon the sea, and his left foot on the earth,

3. And cried with a loud voice, as when a lion roareth: and when he had cried, seven thunders uttered their voices.

4. And when the seven thunders had uttered their voices, I was about to write: and I heard a voice from heaven saying unto me, Seal up those things which the seven thunders uttered, and write them not.

5. And the angel which I saw stand upon the sea and upon the earth lifted up his hand to heaven,

6. And sware by him that liveth for ever and ever, who created heaven, and the things that therein are, and the earth, and the things that therein are, and the sea, and the things which are therein, that there should be time no longer:

7. But in the days of the voice of the seventh angel, when he shall begin to sound, the mystery of God should be finished, as he hath declared to his servants the prophets.

8. And the voice which I heard from heaven spake unto me again, and said, Go and take the little book which is open in the hand of the angel which standeth upon the sea and upon the earth.

9. And I went unto the angel, and said unto him, Give me the little book. And he said unto me, Take it, and eat it up; and it shall make thy belly bitter, and it shall be in thy mouth sweet as honey.

10. And I took the little book out of the angel's hand, and ate it up; and it was in my mouth sweet as honey: and as soon as I had eaten it, my belly was bitter.

11. And he said unto me, Thou must prophesy again before many peoples, and nations, and tongues, and kings.

References

Rev. 4:11
Dan. 7:25

Dan. 12:7
Rev. 11:15
Dan. 12:10-11

Ezek. 2:8-10

Ezek. 3:1-3

Jer. 15:16

Rev. 11:9
Rev. 13:7
Rev. 17:15

Scriptures for Comparison

Daniel 12:5-7; 12:10-12

Then I Daniel looked, and behold, there stood other two, the one on this side of the bank of the river, and the other on that side of the bank of the river.

And one said to the man clothed in linen, which was upon the waters of the river, How long shall it be to the end of these wonders?

And I heard the man clothed in linen, which was upon the waters of the river, when he held up his right hand and his left hand unto heaven, and sware by him that liveth for ever that it shall be for a time, times, and a half; and when he shall have accomplished to scatter the power of the holy people, all these things shall be finished ...

Many shall be purified, and made white, and tried; but the wicked shall do wickedly: and none of the wicked shall understand; but the wise shall understand.

And from the time that the daily sacrifice shall be taken away, and the abomination that maketh desolate set up, there shall be a thousand two hundred and ninety days.

Blessed is he that waiteth, and cometh to the thousand three hundred and five and thirty days.

Ezekiel 2:9,10

And when I looked, behold, a hand was sent unto me; and, lo, a roll of a book was therein;

And he spread it before me; and it was written within and without: and there was written therein lamentations, and mourning, and woe.

Ezekiel 3:1-3

Moreover he said unto me, Son of man, eat that thou findest; eat this roll, and go speak unto the house of Israel.

So I opened my mouth, and he caused me to eat that roll.

And he said unto me, Son of man, cause thy belly to eat, and fill thy bowels with this roll that I give thee. Then did I eat it; and it was in my mouth as honey for sweetness.

Summary of Chapter Ten

Summary of Chapter Ten

Time No Longer

I. Angel and the Thunders (1-4)

As there was an interval between the sixth seal and the seventh seal back in Chapter 7, where the 144,000 and the Great Multitude of Gentile saints introduced, so there is an interval between the sixth trumpet and the sounding of the seventh trumpet in 11:15.

Chapters 10 and 11 are not only the middle of the book, but the middle of the 7 year Tribulation. A close comparison with Daniel 7:25, 9:27 and 12:7, 11, 12 will be most helpful.

Many expositors believe that the "mighty angel:" here is an appearance of Christ, the Angel-Messanger, as in 8:3,4, because of the similar description of this personality with Christ's appearance in chapter 1.

Others hold this is as indicated: "a mighty angel" with high rank, who compares with the 2 angels in Daniel 12.

When the angel-messenger cries with a loud voice like a roaring lion, seven thunders sound. No one knows for sure what they proclaimed, but it likely relates to the horrendous future times. Their voices are "sealed."

II. The Proclamation of Time Ending (5-7)

When the angel announces in an oath there will be Time no longer, this is thought by some to mean "delay no longer," that is, that time will be consummated, that the end-time days, here designated the "days of the voice of the seventh angel" and indicating the last half of the Tribulation (12-19) will quickly occur.

This writer thinks that "time" is a good translation of the Greek *chronos,* that while these aforesaid things are true, that the normal flow of time as we have known it with its normal flow of history will be changed by the events precipitated by the seventh angel's trumpet.

III. The Little Book (8-11)

In the angel's hand is this mysterious book (scroll), which contains a description of the events to be described. It is to be ingested by John, after which he continues to prophesy before peoples, nations, tongues and kinds. He is to absorb the information contained in the book into his mind and being. Sweet are the promises and plans of God, but often the judgments and justice of God, also predicted, are bitter in results.

The Mighty Angel and the Little Book

OBJECTIVE: To reveal that God is Lord of time and will supervise its consummation.

OUTLINE:

I. The Person of the Mighty Angel (1, 2)
A. Attire: a cloud (1)
B. Adornment: a rainbow (2)
C. Appearance (1)
　1. Face like the sun
　2. Feet as fire
D. Actions (2)
　1. His hand holds a little book
　2. One foot placed on sea
　3. One foot place on earth
E. Announcement: Like a Lion Roaring (3)

II. The Pronouncements of the Mysterious Thunders (3, 4)
A. Their Sound: like thunderings
B. Their Secrets: not revealed
C. Their Sealing: ordered by God (Compare Daniel 12:4, 9)

III. The Proclamation of the Mighty Angel (5-7)
A. The Sight: angel lifts hand to heaven (5)
B. The Swearing: invokes the Lord as Creator (6)
C. The Substance of the oath (6) TIME (Gk. *chronos*) NO LONGER

IV. The Performance of Eating the Mystery Book (8-11)
A. The Order of the Voice (8). Take the little book.
B. The Order of the Angel (9)
　1. Take the little book
　2. Eat the little book
　a. Sweet to taste
　b. Bitter in results
C. The Obedience of John (10)
D. The Obligation of John—to prophesy (11)
　1. Before many peoples
　2. Before many nations
　3. Before many tongues
　4. Before many kings

Observations:
Spiritual lessons and applications from each verse
Chapter Ten

1. God and His angels are supreme in God's Universe, as John beholds. Some think this is Christ; others that he is like an archangel. In either event God overrules in contrast to 9:20-21.

2. He who created all things can control all things on sea and land.

3. Seven thunders, awesome and majestic convey a mysterious message. Not everything about God or His plan has been revealed, but "all things work together for good to them that believe God."

4. That the "secret things belong unto God" is evident; any effort to find a meaning of the 7 thunders outside the Bible is wrong.

5. If even mighty angels look up to God in heaven, how foolish we saved mortals be, if we fail in adoration and praise to Him.

6. Since Time will ultimately end, we do well to "redeem the time" in these evil days, using it well for God and His glory.

7. Christ "finished" redemption on the Cross; He will "finish" His mysterious program for the Universe as well.

8. As John took the little book and ate it, so we should spiritually "eat" the Word of God: "Thy words were found and I did eat them ..." (Jer. 15:16).

9. God's promises and prophecies are bittersweet with both positive and negative truth.

10. Obedience to God is not conducive to health, happiness and prosperity; there may be a price to pay for service; we must take the bitter with the sweet.

11. Since John was told to continue His prophetic ministry and his words are preached even today, we must continue our service for Christ, again witnessing to truth.

Quotations
From Other Expositors
Chapter Ten

The Mighty Angel (1,2)

"The identity of this strong angel is debated by Bible teachers. Some contend that this is Christ. Since Christ appeared as the angel of God in the Old Testament, this would be another occasion in which He appears to the nation of Israel. Others say it is not Christ but an unidentified angel.

"The Lord Jesus Christ does not appear in the book of Revelation as an angel. In fact, we will look in vain for a presentation of Him as an angel after the incarnation. Ever since Jesus took on flesh, died for the sins of men, was crucified, was resurrected, and ascended into heaven, He has always appeared as the Son of God in His essential deity. Although this angel possesses some Godlike characteristics, he is not God. Part of the problem could well be a failure to understand the nature of angels. Although far beneath the character of God, they are created beings of unusually high order.

"It is rather interesting to see that angels play a prominent part in the book of Revelation. They are mentioned more than sixty-six times throughout the book, always in a position of service. They do not create things, but fulfill the administration of God in the affairs of men. This is not the first time we have been introduced to a mighty angel, for in chapter 5:2 we find the same word used, though there it is translated "strong".

"Don't be deceived by glorious description of this angel — 'clothed with a cloud; and a rainbow was upon his head, and his face was as though it were the sun, and his feet as pillars of fire' (10:1). Actually, in 18:1 we find another angel, pronouncing doom on Babylon, having great power and so much glory that "the earth was made bright with his glory." No one seems pressed to identify this angel as the Lord Jesus Christ; consequently we should not think it strange that God could have other mighty angels that could easily fit the description of the one in our text."

– Tim LaHaye

Thunders and Mystery (3-7)

"The Prophet was about to record the words of the thunders. He heard and understood. This vision is full of voices: that of the angel of the thunders, and another 'out of Heaven.' This was a voice of authority, 'Seal what the seven thunders have spoken, and write them not.' Those unrevealed communications were to be sealed from us. It was not the time to make them known. The exact import of these revelations has not been disclosed; probably they are embodied in the after communications directly concerning the end. There are two commands addressed to the Seer: first, to seal up the sayings of the thunder; second, to write them not (compare with Dan. 8:26; 12:90. It may be, as in the case of the Hebrew prophet, that this part of the apocalyptic vision, containing the unwritten words of the angel and of the seven thunders, is 'closed up and sealed till the time of the end.' Sealing these prophetic revelations supposes that the end is a long way off. If the end is near, then the prophecies are not to be sealed. In one case words are sealed, for the end is far off (Dan. 12:9); in another the sayings are not sealed, for the end is nigh (Rev. 22:10)."

– Walter Scott

"Chapter ten is the story of the little book. John saw a strong angel carrying a little book or scroll (verses 1-2). This is the second scroll mentioned in Revelation. The first was the seven sealed book or scroll that contained the seven seal and the seven trumpet judgments which described the events of the first half of the tribulation. Now a second scroll comes into the picture, the content of which will shortly be revealed.

"Up to this point six of the seven trumpets have sounded, so there is yet one more remaining. The results of the seventh trumpet are now announced by the strong angel (verses 5-7). In the days of the seventh angel the judgments of God will be completed. The seventh seal judgment contains the seven bowl judgments which will finish the judgments of God declared by the prophets. All the prophecies dealing with the tribulation's second half will then be fulfilled. That the seventh trumpet will not be an all-at-once judgment but a process is evident from the statement, "in the days of the voice of the seventh angel is the mystery of God finished." The plural number shows that a time period is involved. The bowl judgments all come towards the end of the tribulation and with them the mystery of God is finished. The seventh trumpet that contains the seven bowl judgments is the third woe. For this reason, it is the worst of all.

"The little book contains all the information regarding the seventh trumpet with the bowl judgments as found in Revelation 15: 16.

"Attention is focused on the little book in verses 8-10. John was commanded to eat the book. In his mouth the taste was as sweet as honey but it became bitter in the belly. The clue to the meaning of this symbolic act is found in verse 11 which states what the content of the book is: 'And they say unto me, Thou must prophesy again over many peoples and nations and tongues and kings.'"

– Arnold G. Fruchtenbaum

The Little Book (8-11)

"The second division of this chapter has a practical message for us all. John was told to take the book and 'eat' it; and when he did so, he found it sweet to his taste, but his inward parts became very bitter.

"What are we to understand from this? The Word of God is likened to food. Jesus said, 'Man shall not live by bread alone, but by every word that proceedeth out of the mouth of God.' The message of the 'blessed hope' of our Lord's return is 'sweet' to those who 'love his appearing'; but if this blessed message is really 'eaten,' it leads to a pathway of separation which is oftentimes fraught with bitter experiences."

– Louis T. Talbot

"God's words, to one who loves them, are always sweet, as David says, 'sweeter also than honey and the … honeycomb.' Jeremiah said, 'Thy words were found, and I did eat them.' But, while to Jeremiah, God's words became 'a joy and the rejoicing of my heart,' to John, upon digesting this little book, they became bitter.

"Its contents were such as, when pondered and understood, were of anguish to the prophet. It evidently contained the revelation found in chapter 11 concerning the future awful 'Sodom and Egypt' spiritual state of Israel (11:8) and the Remnant's experiences under the rage of Satan and his vassals, in chapters 12 and 13. 'They say unto me, Thou must prophesy again over many peoples and nations and tongues and kings.'

"Now this is exactly what John goes on to do, ending up with the ten kings allied with the Beast: their career and doom, in chapters 13, 17, and 19."

– William R. Newell

The Mystery of God
An Expository Sermon

Chapter Ten

Introduction

Millions of people believe that the world is out of control, careening headlong into confusion and anarchy. While this may seem to be true for the present, the overreaching plan of God for the ages will be consummated. True, the Great Tribulation, as we have seen, must rage when God allows the human race to intensify violence and evil, under the impetus of Satan's power. True, evil men and seducers will wax worse, as Paul declared (2 Tim. 3:13). True, the final Antichrist will reach the zenith of his power in the end times.

But over and above all the Lord of History will fulfill His ultimate will and design, as prophesied in the infallible Word of God. The mystery of God, His plan to consummate history and establish the millennial reign of Christ will be fulfilled.

I. The Mighty Angel (1-4)

While in the Old Testament the Son of God is frequently described as "the angel of the Lord," "Jehovah-Angel," the title is not used in the New Testament. Only in Revelation 8:3-5, where an angel offers prayers up to God, is the appellation applicable to Jesus Christ, the only Mediator.

Many biblical scholars identify this "mighty angel" with Christ, particularly because of the magnificent description, similar to the portrayal of Christ in the first chapter.

In my view this august and distinguished angel is one of the high ranking unfallen "principalities and powers" above whom Christ is exalted. He is the "head of all principality and power" (Col. 2:10). "For by him (Christ) were all things created, that are in heaven and that are in earth, visible and invisible, whether they be thrones or dominions or principalities or powers: ALL THINGS WERE CREATED BY HIM AND FOR HIM" (Col. 1:16).

This majestic angel has a cloud for clothing, a rainbow-like aura above his head, a shining face like the sun and fiery feet like brass.

Doubtless this is the same angel Daniel saw (10:5,6): "Then I lifted up mine eyes, and looked, and behold a certain man clothed in linen, whose loins were girded with fine gold of Uphaz: His body was like the beryl, and his face as the appearance of lightning and his eyes as lamps of fire, and his arms and his feet as lamps of fire, and his arms and his feet like in color to polished brass, and the voice of his words like the voice of a multitude."

This angelic being, resplendent though he was before Daniel, speaks of his need for the aid of Michael in verse 13, something the pre-Incarnate Christ would never require.

Again this angelic being is seen in Daniel 12, as we shall see. In a comparable fashion this angel is one of two who are standing by waters, one of whom makes the preliminary proclamation, which is reemphasized in this chapter.

After the mighty angel takes his stance before John in this vision, he "cries with a loud voice."

Seven thunders then utter their voices.

Seven times in the Book of Revelation besides this occasion, thunders are mentioned and some interpreters think they are the seven thunders.

In 4:5, in connection with the throne of God we read "out of the throne proceeded lightnings and thunderings and voices ..."

In 6:1, when the Lamb opens the first seal, John says, "I heard, as it were, the noise of thunder, one of the four beasts saying, Come and see."

In 8:5, as the angel (who may be Christ) casts the fire from the heavenly golden altar into the earth, John says, "And there were voices, and thunderings, and lightnings and an earthquake."

In 11:19, when John beholds the ark of the covenant in the heavenly temple, "there were lightnings, and voices, and thunderings, and an earthquake and great hail."

In 14:2, when John sees the 144,000 in heaven, he writes, "And I heard a voice from heaven as the voice of many waters, and as the voice of great thunder…"

In 16:18, as the seventh angel pours out his vial of wrath in the closing days of the Great Tribulation and a great voice from the heavenly temple and the throne declares, "It is done," we then read, "And there voices and thunders and lightnings …"

Finally, in 19:6, in heaven, as the marriage supper of the Lamb is held and as preparations for the glorious appearing are being consummated as praises rise to God, John writes, "And I heard as it were the voice of a great multitude, and as the voice of many waters, and as the voice of mighty thunderings, saying, ALLELUIA: for the Lord God omnipotent reigneth."

Another suggestion compares the seven thunders with Psalm 29 and the "voice of the Lord" (vs. 3-9), used seven times:

"The voice of the Lord is upon the waters…

"The voice of the Lord is powerful…

"The voice of the Lord is full of majesty…

"The voice of the Lord breaketh the cedars…

"The voice of the Lord divideth the flames…

"The voice of the Lord shaketh the wilderness…

"The voice of the Lord maketh the hinds to calve…"

As interesting as these comparisons may be, the fact is that what the seven thunders uttered was sealed up. "The secret things belong unto the Lord, but the things that are revealed belong unto us …" (Deut. 29:29).

But they must have to do with the horrendous events of the Great Tribulation. This we will understand better by and by.

II. The Mandating Oath (5-7)

This mighty angel utters a profound pronouncement that corresponds with Daniel 12:7: "And I heard the man clothed with linen, which was upon the waters of the river, when he held up right hand unto heaven, and sware by him that liveth forever and ever that it shall be for a time, times, and an half: and when he shall begin to sound, the mystery of God should be FINISHED, as he hath declared to his servants the prophets" (7).

The span of time denoted as "the days of the voice of the seventh angel" covers the last $3\frac{1}{2}$ years of the total Tribulation Period.

This brings us to the glorious appearing and time when "the kingdoms of this world are to become the kingdoms of our Lord and His Christ."

All the mysterious prophecies concerning the kingdom of Christ will be fulfilled and clarified. This "mystery of God" is the final sum of all God's dealings in judgment and restoration for Israel, leading to the reign of the Messiah. It is the unveiling of God's plan for the bride of Christ and the reign of the New Testament saints as co-regents (Rev. 20:6). It is the completion of the plan of God for a golden age on this earth, involving both Jews and Gentiles.

The process by which God concludes history as we know it is given in chapters 12-19.

How glorious to know that His people are on the winning side.

III. The Mysterious Book (8-11)

In the right hand of the "mighty angel" is this little book.

To this writer it must contain a detailed description of what John is to describe in successive visions beginning in chapter 11.

John takes the book, and accepts the Word of God and the words of God. Like Jeremiah of old, he "eats" — absorbs, ingests, swallows — the message of God.

"The words were found and I did eat them and thy words were unto me the joy and rejoicing of my heart" (Jeremiah 15:16).

The promises are sweet, like honey, as it were in John's mouth, but the judgments he must record make "his belly bitter."

The results of sin and judgment are bitter indeed. Even to the faithful preacher of all the counsel of God, there comes an inner sadness, a lament that judgments must come, that evil must be punished, that justice must prevail.

John does not relish beholding the vision or recording on parchment the catastrophes and cataclysms of the last half of the 70th Week of Daniel. But he must prophesy. He must speak the truth. He will not flag.

Conclusion

As John continued his prophetic witness, so must we.

The Bible speaks of a heaven to gain and a hell to shun.

O respond to that message now. Come to Christ before all of these things come to pass. You will "escape all these things" (Luke 21:36). "For God hath not appointed us to wrath, but to obtain salvation by our Lord Jesus Christ" (1 Thess. 5:9).

A Commentary on the Revelation
Expository, Exegetical, Devotional and Practical
Greek words from the Textus Receptus

Chapter Ten

The Mighty Angel and the Seven Thunders (1-4)

1. And I saw another mighty angel *(kai eidon allon angelon ischuron)* — Viewpoints vary among biblical scholars as to the identity of this "mighty angel": some think this is Christ; others believe this personality is another like the "strong angel" *(angelon ischuron* - same words in Greek as here)* in 5:2 who asks who is worthy to open the seven sealed scroll. It is this expositor's view that this "mighty angel" and the "strong angel" are both high ranking angelic beings, possibly the same two seen in Daniel 12:5-7. However, excellent commentators compare this "mighty angel's" appearance with Christ in chapter 1 and with Daniel 10:5,6, which they think is a Christophany rather than an illustrious angelic being. As there was an interval with additional truth revealed in its proper sequence between the sixth and seventh seals (chapter 7), so there is here after the sixth and before the seventh (11:15-19). Rather than designate these episodes as parenthetical, as does Scofield, I regard them as explanatory revelations necessary to the sequential understanding of this unfolding account of the end times. **Come down from heaven** — This is "another mighty angel," comparable to the first "strong angel" (5:2), as I have said; whereas the first remains in heaven, the second, at least in vision, descends to the earth ... **clothed with a cloud** - signifying mystery and dark judgments from a heavenly origin ... **and a rainbow upon his head and his face as it were the sun and his feet as pillars of fire** — true it is that this description is most similar to that of Christ in Chapter 1, a fact the reader must consider in making an interpretive judgment ... rainbows symbolize the covenant of mercy God made with Noah and the human race (Gen. 9:11-16) ... "his face was like the sun (in brilliance), as surrounded by the rainbow of promise, of mercy and resurrection hope and assurance to Israel and the church to come" (Albert Garneer). **2. And he had in his hand a little book open** *(kai echon en te cheiri biblaridion eneogmenon)* — some have understood this to be the same book which Christ received in 5:8, now open. The seven-sealed book is taken by Christ and now "reversed" to read the back side which contains the rest of the Tribulation judgments and which are here recorded. That view this expositor does not share, since that would make this mighty angel Jesus Christ. But this would be strange indeed, for this is a "little book" and is passed to an Apostle to absorb. There is a parallel in Ezekiel 2:9; 3:1,2, but the scroll Ezekiel "ate" and the one John "ingested" are obviously different ... **And he set his right foot upon the sea and his left foot on the earth** — showing divine dominion and control, even though the Antichrist rises out of "the sea" and the false prophet "out of the earth" (13:1,11). **3. And cried with a loud voice** *(kai ekraksen phone megale)* — the same expression as for the first "mighty-strong" angel (5:2), who asks "who is worthy to open the book"... the expression *phone megale* or loud voice like a megaphone occurs 13 times in Revelation (5:2,12; 6:10; 7:2,10; 8:13; 10:3; 12:10; 14:2,9,15,18; 19:17) ... **as when a lion roareth** *(hosper leon mukatai)* — similar in shock or effect as a lion's roar (See Jer. 51:38; Hos. 11:10 and I Pet. 5:8 - where Satan is compared to a roaring lion) ... **and when he had cried seven thunders uttered their voices** *(kai hote ekraksen elalesan hai hepta brontai tas heauton phonas)* — articulating in reverberating tones a sevenfold message, indicating completion or divine perfection, as the number seven often does. The Psalmist in 29:3-11 speaks of the voice of the Lord seven times, the first introducing thunder. **4. And when the seven thunders had uttered their voices, I was about to write: and I heard a voice from heaven saying unto me, Seal up the things which the seven thunders uttered and write them not** — much has been written about what these seven thunders signify, but the fact is no one knows ... it is not revealed ... wild speculations are out of order. Seven other occasions of thunders are mentioned in Revelation (4:5; 6:1; 8:5; 11:19; 14:2; 16:18; 19:6), but these are different. Though John heard them and could have written down their messages, he is prohibited from so doing, since there are some things so horrendous they will occur only in their time and without warning. Deut. 29:29 tells us that "the secret things belong unto God..." We dare not try to unseal what God has sealed.

The Oath and Mystery of God (5-7)

5. And the angel which I saw stand upon the sea and upon the earth lifted up his hand to heaven — Here turn to Daniel 12:5-7 for comparison. **6. And sware by him that liveth forever and ever who created heaven and the things that therein are, and the earth and the things that therein are, and the sea and the things that are therein, that there should be time no longer** (the last clause in Greek *hoti chronos ouketi estai*) — some expositors take the word *chronos* to mean "delay," although the principal meaning is "time," hence the word "chronology." I submit that the mighty angel is announcing that time as we know it, measured time from the dawn of history, is about to change radically, that a process involving 3 $\frac{1}{2}$ more years will now commence, consummating in the ultimate establishment of the millennial reign and the final judgments of Israel, the nations and unbelievers. It is true that any presumed delay in the consummation is over, but that does not appear to be the emphasis here. Note the comparative Scriptures: "Then I Daniel looked, and behold, there stood two, the one of this side of the river, and the other on that side of the bank of the river (Euphrates in 534 B.C. in Babylon, when Daniel wrote). And one said the man clothed in linen, which upon the waters of the river, How long shall it be to the end of these wonders? And I heard the man clothed in linen, which was upon the waters of the river, when he held up his right hand and his left hand unto heaven and sware by him that liveth forever and ever, that it shall be FOR A TIME, TIMES, AND A HALF (emphasis ours ... 3 $\frac{1}{2}$ years); and when he shall have accomplished to scatter the power of the holy people (Israel), all things shall be "FINISHED" (12:5-7). **7. But in the days of the voice of the seventh angel, when he shall begin to sound, the mystery of God should be finished, as he hath declared to his servants the prophets** (all *en tais hemerais tes phones tou hebdomou angelou hotan melle salpizein kai etelesthe to musterion tou theou hos evengelisen tous heartou doulos tous prophetas)* — Notice carefully that the expression "days of the voice of the seventh" indicates a period of time, which I identify with the entire last half of the Tribulation period and the establishment of Christ's Kingdom on earth (chapter 12-20). Closely compare this with Daniel 12:11: "And from the time that the daily sacrifice shall be taken away, and the abomination of desolation set up, there shall be a thousand two hundred and ninety days." "The 'abomination of desolation,' spoken of by the prophet Daniel" (Matthew 24:15) is to be set up at the midpoint of the 7 year Tribulation Period; therefore, the last half runs three and a half years as 12:7 indicates, moving over into the millennial kingdom.

John Eats the Little Book (8-11)

8. And the voice which I heard from heaven spake unto me again and said, Go and take the little book, which is open in the hand of the angel which standeth upon the sea and upon the earth — John in this vision then approaches the mighty angel in obedience. **9. And I went unto the angel and said unto him, Give me the little book, And he said unto me, Take it, and eat it up, and it shall make thy belly** *(Gr.- koilian* or stomach) **bitter, but it shall be in thy mouth sweet as honey.** Compare Jer. 15:16; Ezek. 2:8; 3:3; Ps. 19:9,10. While John in the vision actually consumed the *biblaridion*, God's servants are to eat by reading, marking, learning and inwardly digesting truth from the Word. Such assimilation requires concentration, thinking, faith and prayer. **10. And I took the little book out of the angel's hand and ate it up; and it was in my mouth as sweet as honey; and as soon as I had eaten it, my belly was bitter** — sweet prophetic truth delights the soul, but, like Ezekiel's eaten book, "There was written therein lamentations and mourning and woes" (Ezek. 2:10), bitter things indeed. **11. And he said unto me, Thou must prophesy again before many peoples and nations and tongues and kings** — This John proceeds to do in recording the remainder of the great Apocalypse. Chapters 10, 11 and 12 constitute the center fulcrum of both the whole book and the 7-year Tribulation, as we shall see.

CHAPTER ELEVEN: The Two Witnesses

References

Ezek. 40:3
Ezek. 42:20
Zech. 2:1
Num. 23:18

Ezek. 40:17,20
Luke 21:24
Dan. 7:25
Dan. 12:7,11,12
Rev. 12:6; 13:5

Acts 14:17
Deut. 17:6

Zech.
4:2,3,11,14

2 Kings 1:10-12
Num. 16:29
Hos. 6:5

1 Kings 17:1
Luke 4:25
James 5:16

Rev. 13:1,7
Dan. 7:21

Heb. 13:12
John 19:16-19
Isa. 1:10

Rev. 17:15
Ps. 79:2,3

Esther 9:19,22
Rev. 16:10

1. AND there was given me a reed like unto a rod: and the angel stood, saying, Rise, and measure the temple of God, and the altar, and them that worship therein.

2. But the court which is without the temple leave out, and measure it not; for it is given unto the Gentiles: and the holy city shall they tread under foot forty and two months.

3. And I will give power unto my two witnesses, and they shall prophesy a thousand two hundred and three-score days, clothed in sackcloth.

4. These are the two olive trees, and the two candlesticks standing before the God of the earth.

5. And if any man will hurt them, fire proceedeth out of their mouth, and devoureth their enemies: and if any man will hurt them, he must in this manner be killed.

6. These have power to shut heaven, that it rain not in the days of their prophecy: and have power over waters to turn them to blood, and to smite the earth with all plagues, as often as they will.

7. And when they shall have finished their testimony, the beast that ascendeth out of the bottomless pit shall make war against them, and shall overcome them, and kill them.

8. And their dead bodies shall lie in the street of the great city, which spiritually is called Sodom and Egypt, where also our Lord was crucified.

9. And they of the people and kindreds and tongues and nations shall see their dead bodies three days and a half, and shall not suffer their dead bodies to be put in graves.

10. And they that dwell upon the earth shall rejoice over them, and make merry, and shall send gifts one to another; because these two prophets tormented them that dwelt on the earth.

11. And after three days and a half the spirit of life from God entered into them, and they stood upon their feet; and great fear fell upon them which saw them.

12. And they heard a great voice from heaven saying unto them, Come up hither. And they ascended up to heaven in a cloud; and their enemies beheld them.

13. And the same hour was there a great earthquake, and the tenth part of the city fell, and in the earthquake were slain of men seven thousand: and the remnant were affrighted, and gave glory to the God of heaven.

14. The second woe is past; and, behold, the third woe cometh quickly.

15. And the seventh angel sounded; and there were great voices in heaven, saying, The kingdoms of this world are become the kingdoms of our Lord, and of his Christ; and he shall reign for ever and ever.

16. And the four and twenty elders, which sat before God on their seats, fell upon their faces, and worshiped God,

17. Saying, We give thee thanks, O Lord God Almighty, which art, and wast, and art to come; because thou hast taken to thee thy great power, and hast reigned.

18. And the nations were angry, and thy wrath is come, and the time of the dead, that they should be judged, and that thou shouldest give reward unto thy servants the prophets, and to the saints, and them that fear thy name, small and great: and shouldest destroy them which destroy the earth.

19. And the temple of God was opened in heaven, and there was seen in his temple the ark of his testament: and there were lightnings, and voices, and thunderings, and an earthquake, and great hail.

References

Rev. 4:1
Acts 1:9

Rev. 6:12;8:5;
11:19; 16:18;
12:17

Rev. 8:13; 9:12

Rev. 10:7
Dan. 2:44

Rev. 4:4

Rev. 16:5
Rev. 19:6

Ps. 2:1-4
Ps. 99:1
Rev. 6:17
Dan. 11:3
2 Cor. 5:10

Rev. 15:5,8
Num. 4:5
Heb. 9:4

Scriptures for Comparison

Zechariah 4:11-14

Then answered I, and said unto him, What are these two olive trees upon the right side of the candlestick and upon the left side thereof?

And he answered me and said, Knowest thou not what these be? And I said, No my lord. Then said he, These are the two anointed ones, that stand by the Lord of the whole earth.

Summary of Chapter Eleven

When the Seventh Trumpet Sounds

I. The Temple on Earth (1,2)

As this chapter opens, John has just "eaten" the little book from the angel's hand, given him in Chapter 10. He is to prophesy "again before many peoples, and nations, and tongues, and kings."

Then the Revelator is ordered to rise, take a measuring instrument called a reed, which was about 10 feet long, and to measure the temple. This presupposes its reconstruction prior to or during the coming time of Tribulation.

II. Time Periods (2,3)

But, though temple worship in Jerusalem is to be restored, it will be interrupted once more by the invasion of Gentiles, the forces of Antichrist who will dominate the Middle East and Jerusalem for 42 months, a period of 3 1/2 years. This corresponds with the last half of the "seventieth week" (of years), in Daniel 9:27.

"And he shall confirm the covenant [the new world leader, the Antichrist, will make a treaty with the Jews in Israel] with many for one week" [a seven-year period, the last of 70 seven-year periods]. The first 69 seven-year periods ended with Christ's ministry. There has been a long interregnum between the 69th and 70th week (of years) during which the "Times of the Gentiles" have been in progress. That time is rapidly coming to a close.

Daniel 9:27 continues: "And in the midst of the week [of years], he shall cause the sacrifice and the oblation to cease [Antichrist will terminate the temple ceremonies after 3 1/2 years and set up the abomination of desolation], and for the overspreading of abominations, he shall make it desolate, even until the consummation and that determined shall be poured out upon the desolate [or the desolator]."

For the first 3 1/2 years, the new world leader will maintain warm and friendly relations with Israel, guaranteeing their integrity and autonomy. But then he will break his treaty, invade Jerusalem, slay the two witnesses about whom we will now study, and continue his evil domination for 42 months. This is the last half of the seven-year Tribulation. Jesus commented on this in Matthew 24:15: "When ye therefore shall see the abomination of desolation, spoken of by the prophet Daniel, stand in the holy place [in Jerusalem, in the temple area—probably the image of the beast discussed in Chapter 13] THEN ... flee into the mountains ... THEN shall be great tribulation, such as was not since the beginning of the world, to this day; no, nor ever shall be" (Matthew 24:21).

III. Two Witnesses (3-14)

The two witnesses prophesy during the first (relatively peaceful for Israel) half of the seven years and are supernaturally protected.

They preach in Jerusalem, announce the awesome judgments described in the first half of this book, but have little response from the Israelites, except possibly the conversion of the 144,000 mentioned in Chapter 7.

When the Antichrist (the beast) breaks his treaty with Israel and invades Jerusalem, the witnesses are slain. The whole world rejoices, viewing their bodies everywhere through television, in all probability. But they are resurrected and ascend up to heaven. This is the midpoint of the final 7 years.

Jerusalem is struck by an earthquake, concluding the "second woe." Read 8:11 and 9:12.

In the final verses of this chapter, the scene shifts to heaven.

IV. The Seventh Trumpet (15-19)

The seventh angel sounds the seventh and final trumpet in the series. This trumpet encompasses the whole time period of 42 months, described in detail in the next chapters through 19. This final 1,260 days, or "time, times and a half time," is called in 10:7 "the days of the voice of the seventh angel."

In heaven, the 24 elders representing the raptured, glorified saints and the resurrected New Testament saints, rejoice and worship, proclaiming that indeed the time of rewards in heaven is at hand, and the time of judgments on earth is in process.

When the heavenly temple is opened, the true Ark of the Covenant is seen, a symbol of the fact that He is present in power with them.

The following chapters describe the conclusion of history, the "Great Tribulation" proper, when civilization as we know it will destroy itself under the judgment of God, and Christ will intervene in majesty and glory.

Truly, the kingdoms of this world will become the kingdoms of our Lord and his Christ (messiah), and he shall reign for ever and ever.

Outline of Chapter Eleven

The Two Witnesses

OBJECTIVE: To reveal that Christ will triumph over all.

OUTLINE: The chapter begins with the temple on earth and ends with the temple in heaven.

I. The Temple on Earth (1, 2)
A. An Instrument Given: a reed (10 feet long)
B. An Instruction Spoken: "Rise and measure" (Compare Ezekiel 40:108).
C. An Intention Expressed: measure only (1)
  1. The temple of God
  2. The altar
  3. The worshippers
D. An Enclosure Omitted: the outer court (2)
  1. Temple court to be dominated by Gentiles
  2. Jerusalem to be under a 42-month domination

II. The Time Periods (2, 3)
A. 42 months; 3 1/2 years, second half of the TRIBULATION
B. 1,260 days; 3 1/2 years, first half of the TRIBULATION

III. The Two Witnesses (3-12)
A. Their Time, 1,260 days (3)
B. Their Empowerment (3)
C. Their Emblems—olive trees and candlesticks (4) (compare Zechariah 4:1-14)
D. Their Protection (5)
E. Their Actions (6)
F. Their Enemy (7)
G. Their Martyrdom (7-10)
H. Their Resurrection (11)
I. Their Ascension (12)

IV. The Terrible Earthquake (13, 14)
A. Jerusalem Smitten
B. Seven Thousand Slain
C. Remnant (144,000) Glorify God
D. Second "woe" Ends

V. The Triumphant Seventh Trumpet (15)
The crowned Christ to reign forever

VI. The Thankful People (16-18)
A. The Elders Worship (16)
B. The Praise is Offered (17)
C. The Conclusion of History is Coming (18)
  1. Nations are angry
  2. God's wrath has come
  3. Resurrection is at hand
  4. Judgment is coming
  5. Rewards will be given
  6. Destruction is for the destroyers

VII. The Temple in Heaven (19)
A. Temple Opened in Heaven
B. Ark of the Covenant is Seen
C. Universe Responds with Wonders

1990's Temple Mount Activities

In the latter part of this century, since Israel has controlled the old Jerusalem, many Jewish organizations have been researching and planning to rebuild and reinstitute the Temple (Third).

The "Temple Mount Faithful" has desired to place a cornerstone near the Dome of the Rock, the Muslim shrine since 691 A.D., but have been unable to do so. "The Society for the Preparation of the Temple" is making artifacts and vessels according to biblical and Talmudical patterns. "The Ateret Cohanim" has established a yeshiva (religious school) to train and educate Temple priests.

"The Institute for Talmudic Commentaries," located in the nearest synagogue to the Western Wall, is pursuing research with respect to the Temple and its worship. Many rabbis and others claim descent from the priestly line.

Other organizations have manufactured "Clothing for the Third Temple Era" and biblical-type ten stringed harps, such as were used in ancient times. Sooner or later all of these efforts will come to fruition.

"Given the obstacles, we might conclude that every preparation to rebuild the Temple at present is an exercise in futility. The same was once said of the attempts of the early Zionist movement to reestablish a Jewish presence in the Holy Land. Who at that time would have dreamed that an independent Jewish State, almost five million strong, would have risen and stood against the sea of hostile Arab nations for more than four decades? The very fact that Scripture affirms that the Temple will be rebuilt indicates that a way will be found to rebuild"!

–Tommy Ice

Observations:
Spiritual lessons and applications from each verse
Chapter Eleven

1. When God gives a command, such as "Rise" in this case, the servant of God needs to obey.

2. The details of God's instructions are always important.

3. God gives power to His people to accomplish His will.

4. The olive tree, source of oil, is an emblematic anointing; the candlestick is a symbol of testimony or witness; it is also the symbol of Israel, the Menorah.

5. Occasionally in various ways and times, God intervenes supernaturally to protect His servants until their old work was done.

6. Like Elijah of old, the witnesses shut heaven for 3 $^1/_2$ years (James 5:17).

7. Every servant of God is immortal until his work is finished.

8. Think of the contrast: Jerusalem, place of peace, place of propitiation, where Christ died; Jerusalem, resistant to God's will, like Sodom and Egypt in ancient times.

9. The revengeful resentment of the lost and guilty against the righteous can be very intense.

10. Evil rejoicing of the wicked, like a "devil's Christmas party" does not last long.

11. It behooves all to fear God, whether supernatural events occur or not.

12. Like the two ascending into heaven after their resurrection, so believers will be caught up at the Rapture earlier.

13. In all circumstances the true believers ought to give glory to God.

14. Sometimes God's judgments come in rapid succession.

15. Christ is now and will be revealed as the Supreme Sovereign of the Universe.

16. Let us worship God as we think of His kingdom.

17. Thanksgiving for all things is always in order. "In every thing give thanks."

18. This world in its wickedness is rushing people toward the last times and judgments.

19. In heaven, the true ark, symbol of God's powerful presence with His people, is testimony to His eternal love, provision for sin, and covenant-keeping nature. At the beginning of this chapter is the earthly temple, at the end the heavenly temple.

Rebuilding the Temple

"For two thousand years Jews have longed to return to the Promised Land and rebuild their beloved Temple on the Temple Mount. During these centuries of exile, three times a day, righteous Jews turned toward Jerusalem, the Holy City, and prayed to God that He would return the divine Shekinah Presence to their rebuilt Temple: "May the Temple be rebuilt speedily in our day!" All this time it was impossible for most Jews even to visit the ruins of the Temple, so their longing had to be limited to studying its features and to prayer. Since 1948, however, a growing number of Israelites have begun to transform this longing into a practical plan of action that may lead to the rebuilding of the Temple in our generation."

–Grant R. Jeffrey

Quotations
From Other Expositors
Chapter Eleven

The Temple (1, 2)

"What, then, is the implication, but that when this period is once reached, Jerusalem will have been largely repopulated by the children of its ancient inhabitants, its temple rebuilt, and its ancient worship restored. God is not yet done with the Jews as a distinct people. In their half-faith and 'blindness in part,' they will seek and find their way back to a revival of their ancient metropolis, temple, and ritual. Some of the most striking passages of holy Scripture assert this with a clearness and positiveness which no fair exegesis can ever set aside. The New Testament constantly assumes it. And when it is accomplished, as it certainly will be, Jerusalem will still be 'the holy city,' because of the consecration it of old received. The temple will also be in some sort God's temple, though at first unacknowledged and unappropriated by Christ. And among the worshippers will also be many true servants of God; for already under the sixth seal we were called to contemplate a movement among the tribes of Israel by which 144,000 were marked as the Lord's, and singled out as the objects of His gracious protection."

– J.A. Seiss

The Forty-two Months (2)

"'Forty and two months' is the holy city to be trampled; that is, three years and a half, no more, and no less. It is a literal city that is trampled and defiled; it is a literal oppression and affliction that befalls it; and so the months which compute the duration of the trouble are also literal months. These great chronological scaffoldings which men build around prophetic dates, is mere fancy-work — 'wood, hay, and stubble' — nothing but rubbish and obscurations of the truth of God. When it is meant that we should take numbers and dates in some other way than as they read, He gives us intimation of it; and in the absence of such divine hints, as in this case, there is no warrant for taking them any otherwise than as they stand written. 'Forty and two months' are forty and two months, and not twelve hundred and sixty years."

– J.A. Seiss

The Two Witnesses (3)

"The fourth event transpiring throughout the first half of the tribulation is the ministry of the Two Witnesses in Revelation 11:3-6. In verse three the timing of the ministry is given as 1,260 days which is the equivalent of $3\frac{1}{2}$ years. These $3\frac{1}{2}$ years cover the first half of the tribulation period. Their identity is given in verse four, and they are said to be the fulfillment of Zechariah 4:11-14.

"These Two Witnesses have been subject to much speculation. Many prophetic teachers try to identify them with two men that have lived in the past. One is always said to be Elijah, while the other is said to be either Moses or Enoch. Those who claim them to be Enoch and Elijah base it on the fact that these two men have never died, and so they will return to die in the tribulation. Often Hebrews 9:27 is used as evidence, 'for it is appointed unto men once to die.' But this is a general principle and not an absolute. For example, take the word 'once.' Yet some people have died twice, namely, all those who had been resurrected in the Old and New Testaments apart from Christ. Furthermore, what about the living church saints? If indeed Hebrews 9:27 is an absolute rule, it would mean that all living church saints at the Rapture will also have to die some time. Those who wish to make them Elijah and Moses fall back on the fact that these were the two who appeared with Christ at the Transfiguration. But this is very flimsy evidence and hardly shows a cause and effect relationship. Others say it is because these men had unfinished ministries, and they will return to finish it this time. This is a very subjective judgment, and many from the Old Testament could be nominated for the same reason. The fact that the miracles performed by the Two Witnesses are similar to those of Moses and Elijah is hardly sufficient evidence, for God can use others to perform these same miracles."

– Arnold G. Fruchtenbaum

"Moreover Hippolytus places the final week at the end of the world and divides it into the period of Elias and the period of Antichrist, so that during the [first] three and a half years of the last week the knowledge of God is established. And as for the statement, 'He shall establish a compact with many for a week' (Dan. 9:27), during the other three years under the Antichrist the sacrifice and offering shall cease. But when Christ shall come and shall slay the wicked one by the breath of His mouth, desolation shall hold sway till the end."

– Jerome, 400 A.D.
Translated by Gleason L. Archer, Jr.

"Moses and Elijah performed these very miracles in Old Testament times — another reason which leads us to believe that they will doubtless be the 'two witnesses' of Jehovah during the closing days of the seventieth week of Daniel. Moreover, Elijah went to heaven without dying; and God buried Moses, no man knowing where his body lay in a 'valley' near Mt. Nebo. Satan contended with Michael for the body of Moses, as Jude tells us. Did he want to hinder God's plan for the last days? At least, these are interesting questions."

– Louis T. Talbot

"The two witnesses of chapter 11 are probably Elijah and Enoch, who were translated without death in view of their coming death in the streets of Jerusalem in the great Day of Tribulation."

– William L. Pettingill

The Seventh Trumpet (15)

"Thus the angels will announce in heaven at the beginning of the last half of the Tribulation Period that the one-world kingdom of the Antichrist will be conquered by the kingdom of Christ."

– Tim LaHaye

"The question that remains, however, is how can the kingdoms of the world become at this point the kingdoms of Christ when, as a matter of fact, the seven vials seemingly are still to be poured out? The answer as indicated previously seems to be that just as the seven trumpets are comprehended in the seventh seal so the seven vials are comprehended in the seventh trumpet. The process of destruction of earthly power is therefore already under way."

—John F. Walvoord

The Heavenly Scene (16-19)

"Let us now study humbly the fivefold results of God's 'taking' His power.

"1. 'The nations were wroth.' The anger of earth at heaven's beginning royal interruption is unbounded. It is a great subject of prophecy — 'why do the nations rage?' (Psalm 2; Psalm 83; Joel 3:9-13; Zechariah 14:2-4) … When man's long carnival and carousal of selfishness is confronted by a will that is resistless, so that nations must bow to it or be stricken off the earth — then shall we see the events that lead to 'the war of the great day of God,

the Almighty';

"2. 'And thy wrath came.' God's wrath has been postponed so long that men deny altogether a God capable of anger and vengeance. Paul disposes of this in one searching question: 'Is God unrighteous who visiteth with wrath? Be it not! for then how shall God judge the world?' (Romans 3:5,6). God is Love; but God also is Light; and He hates sin with all the infinite eternal abhorrence of His infinitely holy being and nature!

"3. 'And the time of the dead to be judged.' The 'coming' of divine wrath involves that measuring out to each (unsaved) creature, that recompense due, in view of light had, and attitude and deeds. This is called judgment. Only the unbelieving will be judged, as we see in John 5:24, and John 3:18. Thus only the lost are in view in the words, 'the time of the dead to be judged.'

"4. 'And the time to give their reward.' This seventh trumpet ushers in the glad day of rewards! 'To thy servants the prophets.' The prophets are first; and do we wonder? The prophets of God were first in time, and peculiar in duty and suffering … 'And to the saints.' Probably all the saints of God are here included. The rapture of the Church (1 Thess. 4) occurs, we believe, at chapter 4:1. We know that Paul, Moses, David and Abraham are looking to a 'day' of rewards. That day has not come yet, though they have been eagerly awaiting it for centuries. Rewards are connected with the kingdom, as Paul shows in 2 Timothy 4:18.

"5. 'And to destroy them that destroy the earth.' The seventh angel's trumpet does not say that all these things have been brought to pass; nor (as do the prophets) merely that they shall come to pass; but, as Alford says, 'the hour is come, for it all to take place' … This passage, if simply believed, becomes a key to seven chapters, Revelation 10-16:

"1. There is a literal temple in heaven. The one on earth was a pattern of the things in heaven (Hebrews 8:5; 9:22).

"2. The real 'ark of his covenant,' which declares His purposes and His faithfulness, is there.

"3. This ark's pattern was given to Israel, not to the Church: the Church does not have to do with earthly temple-worship, nor with those governmental affairs of earth with which God has connected Israel."

– W. R. Newell

God is Never Without His Witness
An Expository Sermon

Chapter Eleven

Introduction

After the Rapture of believers (4:1), the world would be without witness for His truth, were not God to dispatch these two Spirit-filled, supernaturally empowered witnesses to Jerusalem, Israel and the world. Probably through their 3 1/2 year ministry during the first half of the future seven-year Tribulation, the 144,000 Israelites (chapter 7) come to Christ, likewise becoming the end-time remnant and witnessing servant-prophets. Through their ministries a great multitude of Gentiles (7:14) come to Christ and come out of the "great tribulation."

I. The Warning about the Gentiles (1, 2)

In his vision John measures the rebuilt and future temple, like Ezekiel in chapter 40. But the circumstances are different. The temple here during the Tribulation might be called the Third Temple, possibly the very structure now being planned by Temple Mount groups in Jerusalem at this time (1990s). What Ezekiel measured was vastly greater, being the Fourth Temple or Millennial Temple, which will be the world center of worship during the 1,000 year reign of Christ.

When Christ said in Luke 21:24, "And they shall fall by the edge of the sword, and shall be led away captive into all nations," He was referring to the fall of Jerusalem and the dispersion of the Jews following 70 A.D. From then until 1967, Jerusalem was under the control of Gentile world powers: the Roman Empire, the Eastern (Byzantine) Roman Empire, the Muslims (from 636 A.D.), the Crusaders from Europe (1099-1187 A.D.), the Turkish and Ottoman Empires until 1917-18, and, finally, the British Empire from 1918-48. From 1948 until 1967 the Jordanians controlled old Jerusalem and the temple area.

Jesus said, "Jerusalem shall be trodden down of the Gentiles UNTIL THE TIMES OF THE GENTILES BE FULFILLED." Evidently that period is at its close, since Jerusalem is under the Israeli government. However, the temple area is still basically under the control of the Muslims who are Arabs.

Apparently, though the Jews will have their rebuilt temple, possibly even before the Rapture, the "outer court" will still be trodden down of the Gentiles for a short period of 42 months, the last half of the coming Tribulation, when the "beast" — Antichrist — takes over and sets up the "abomination of desolation," as both Daniel (9:27) and Christ indicate (Matthew 24:15).

It is conceivable that the Jews and Muslim Gentiles might somehow share the Temple Mount area in an accommodation arranged by the new world leader shortly after his rapid rise to power following the Rapture.

Here is the appropriate time to reemphasize the importance of the numbers here presented in the light of Daniel 9:27, to which we have just referred. Look again at this key and vital verse; let me expand upon it and expound it as we carefully consider its content: "And he" the prince that shall come, the beast, the Antichrist, "shall confirm," impose, enforce, "the covenant," an agreement, a treaty, "with many," the Israelis living in the land in the last days, "for one week," that is for a week of years, a seven year period ... this seven years is divided into two sections of 3 1/2 years each, as is obvious ... "and in the midst of the week," after 1,260 days (Rev. 11:3), "he shall cause the sacrifice and the oblation to cease," that is, the Jewish worship in a rebuilt Third Temple, which is to be instituted in the end times ... "and for the overspreading of abominations he, the coming prince-beast-ruler Antichrist, "shall make it desolate."

To this Jesus refers specifically in Matthew 24:15: "When ye (Jews) shall see the abomination of desolation, spoken of by Daniel the prophet, stand," [that is, actually erected] "in the holy place" or the temple itself (whoso readeth let him understand) ... THEN, let them which be in Jerusalem flee into the mountains ..." (24:16) ... "For then shall be great tribulation, such as was not since the beginning of the world, to this time, no, nor ever shall be" (24:21).

This second half of the "tribulation period" is The Great Tribulation proper.

Each half lasts for 1,260 days or 42 months.

Speaking of this same time, Paul tells us that the "man of sin, the son of perdition," will "oppose and exalt himself above all that is called God, or that is worshipped: so that he as God sitteth in the temple of God, showing himself that he is God" (2 Thess. 2:3,4).

Thus, the "outer court" will be given unto the Gentiles, who will tread under foot the holy city (Jerusalem) for 42 months, the last half of the seven year period. Chapters 12 and 13 will furnish further details, as we shall see.

II. The Witnesses on Earth (3-12)

Now we come to these two witnesses who are to prophesy for half of the seven year period. The issue is, do they prophesy during the first half or the second half?

My view is that right here in the middle of the Book of Revelation where these time periods are repeated from Daniel's writings, we find a review of what has been happening during the first half, prior to the unveiling of the Antichrist as "the beast that ascendeth out of the bottomless pit" in his true Satanic character (vs. 7).

Acts 14:17 indicates that God does not "leave himself without a witness."

If all believers are caught up to be with Christ at the Rapture, just before this final seven year period begins, there would be no witness other than nature and written records, unless He sends to the world these two witnesses at that time to proclaim His message.

It was the great second-third century writer Hippolytus, a pupil of Irenaeus, who was a follower of Polycarp, who was a disciple of John the Apostle, who taught that the first half of "Daniel's Seventieth Week" of years could be called the "time of Elijah," since he believed he would be one of the two witnesses; while the second half could be known as the "time of the Antichrist," who then would achieve supreme worldwide dominion.

I believe these two witnesses exercise their ministry in Jerusalem until the seven year treaty is broken and the Antichrist invades Jerusalem and claims divinity for himself, putting to death God's prophets. I think this fits best in the prophetic plan, as revealed.

Now, notice they are compared to olive trees and candlesticks.

In Zechariah's time, the high priest Joshua (about 520 B.C.) and Prince Zerubbabel of the Davidic royal family, were the anointing oil, as it were, of the Holy Spirit; as candlesticks, living "menorah," they shine as Spirit-filled witnesses with the light of God's message to Israel during the coming time of tribulation. God has often used two witnesses confirming truth, both in ancient times and finally in future prophetic times.

Now who are these two witnesses?

I am convinced that Elijah, whose return is prophesied in Malachi, is one of the two.

"Behold, I will send you Elijah the prophet before the coming of the great and dreadful day of the LORD (the last half of the Tribulation): and he shall turn the heart of the fathers to the children, and the heart of the children to the fathers, lest I come and smite the earth with a curse" (Mal. 4:5,6).

So deeply ingrained in the minds of practicing religious Jews is this prophecy, that they provide an empty chair symbolically for Elijah at the Passover-Seder meal in the home each year.

As to the identity of the others, some say Moses, who turned water to blood, as these witnesses do; others say Enoch, who like Elijah, never died.

Writing in 1993, Rabbi Harold S. Kushner presents the Jewish view: "We believe that one day he (Elijah) will come to announce the imminent arrival of the Messiah and the delivery of the world from all imperfection."

This expositor accepts the case for Elijah and Enoch.

Another theory suggests Daniel, who is to "stand in his lot at the end of the days" (Daniel 12:13) and John, who was to "prophesy again" (Rev. 10:11). Arnold Fruchtenbaum thinks they will be none of these, but rather two powerful Jewish prophet-witnesses God will raise up.

In any event, they preach, prophesy, predict the awesome judgments in the first part of this book (the seal and trumpet judgments) and continue until the Antichrist invades Jerusalem and they are slain.

Until then, they are supernaturally preserved from death and harm. There can be no question but that Jerusalem is the scene of their endeavors.

When the Antichrist slays them, their dead bodies are displayed publicly for $3\frac{1}{2}$ days, while the wicked of the world rejoice in their demise, because "these two prophets tormented them that dwell on the earth."

No doubt their proclamations of divine wrath receive worldwide notice through television and pictures of their corpses will be seen by people and kindreds and tongues and nations.

Partying and celebrations will break out over the world, complete with Christmas-like gift-giving, prompting one preacher to call this "the devil's Christmas party."

Can you imagine then the utter consternation of the viewing peoples, who might see on their screens these two prophets rising up from the streets of Jerusalem and ascending before their very eyes up into heaven!

Like John in 4:1, they will hear a voice from heaven, saying, "Come up hither," and their enemies will behold them ...

III. The Woe in Jerusalem (13,14)

The first woe (the unleashing of the demonic creatures in 9:1-12) is followed by the second woe, which includes the Tribulation Wars of 9:13-21 and concludes with the great Jerusalem earthquake. Israel is still in darkness spiritually and will suffer under Antichrist in the second half of the Tribulation as chapter 12 makes clear.

IV. The World Kingdom of Christ (15)

After this interval between the sixth and seventh trumpet, which includes the angelic proclamation of the "mystery of God being finished during the days of the voice of the seventh angel, AND the descriptions of the remarkable ministry of the two witnesses during the first 1,260 days of the future seven years, "the SEVENTH ANGEL SOUNDED: AND THERE WERE GREAT VOICES IN HEAVEN, SAYING, THE KINGDOMS OF THIS WORLD ARE BECOME THE KINGDOMS OF OUR LORD AND HIS CHRIST AND HE SHALL REIGN FOREVER AND EVER."

This angel's trumpet and the resulting voices announcing the climax of the age cover a three-and-a-half-year timespan insofar as the fulfillment is concerned.

The "days of the voice of the seventh angel" (10:7) constitute an overall (3 1/2 years) period, wherein the Antichrist achieves the zenith of power, the vial judgments are poured out (16) and Babylon falls (18), which precedes the glorious appearing, the battle of Armageddon and the actual establishment of Christ's Kingdom (19, 20).

This is a process running 3 1/2 years (See also Daniel 12:7,11,12).

V. The Worshippers in Heaven (16-19)

While horrendous events befall the earth in the throes of divine wrath and in the midst of unbridled wickedness, the heavens ring with the praises of the saints. The twenty-four elders, again representative of the raptured and resurrected saints, extol the greatness of the Almighty.

They rejoice that God is orchestrating the climax of history (time), as we know it.

They acknowledge the wrath of the evil nations and the full impact of the wrath of God.

They announce the judgment and rewards for the servants, prophets and saints, who in heaven appear before the judgment seat of Christ.

They pronounce the destruction which is to come upon the destroyers of the earth.

Then, in heaven itself, in the true temple there, the ark of the covenant is seen. Whether there is in heaven an original Ark, which Moses copied, as shown in the mount so long ago, or perchance the true Ark has been transported to heaven, we will not fully comprehend until that time.

But the Ark is the symbol of God's presence with Israel and their destiny is sure.

Now impressively, and majestically, John beholds lightnings and hears thunders and sees an earthquake and great hail, all of which presage the additional judgments to rain down upon the earth as the "days of the voices of the seventh angel" continue toward the grand finale of history and the glorious appearing of the great God and our Savior Jesus Christ.

Conclusion

Christians are on the winning side.

If you are not a Christian, you are lost and a loser, on the losing side ... COME TO CHRIST TODAY.

"Verily, verily I say unto you, He that heareth my word and believeth on him that sent me, hath everlasting life" (John 5:24). You can be preserved from going through the final catastrophic judgments on this earth. You will not come into condemnation, judgment or damnation (as the Greek word means), but you will be counted "worthy to escape all these things that shall come to pass."

You will be with Christ during the Tribulation on earth, appearing before the judgment seat of Christ (2 Cor. 5:10).

If you have never made the decision to receive Christ, NOW IS THE TIME.

A Commentary on the Revelation
Expository, Exegetical, Devotional and Practical
Greek words from the Textus Receptus

Chapter Eleven

The Temple (1,2)

1. **And there was given unto me a reed like unto a rod** *(kai edothe moi kalamos homois hrabdo)* — John receives a reed *(kalamos)*, also translated staff (Matt. 27:29,30) ... this is a walking staff, a support, a protection and a measuring stick, also compared to a rod *(hrabdo)*, like a pilgrim's staff, usually 6 to 10 feet long, though no indication as to its length is given ... **and the angel stood saying ... Rise and measure the temple of God** *(eguire kai metreson ton naon tou theou)* — the Greek word here is not *hieron*, which means the temple area (Mark 11:15), but the sanctuary itself, *naos* ... **and the altar** *(kai to thusiasterion)* — not the outside altar for sacrifices, but the inside altar of incense actually within the temple building ... **and them that worship therein** *(kai tous proskunountas en auto)* — **and those worshipping in it** ... measuring the people here means to number them, identify them ... these are likely some of the 144,000, who in a rebuilt Third Temple will have access to the interior of the building, but not the Holy of Holies. All of this presupposes the erection of a Jewish Temple in Jerusalem in the future. As of this writing (1990's) plans and models for a Third Temple have been made in Jerusalem and dozens of artifacts for Temple worship already completed. Temple Mount groups of Jews have pioneered this effort in the last part of the 20th century (detailed in *Ready to Rebuild* by Thomas Ice and Randall Price, 1992). 2. **But the court which is without the temple leave out and measure it not, for it is given unto the Gentiles: and the holy city shall they tread under foot forty and two months** — this evidently refers to the Temple Mount area itself, which in ancient times included a "court of Gentiles," an area in which Gentiles could have limited access. If the Temple were to be constructed north of the Dome of the Rock, some accommodation with the Muslims might exist, giving them rights to their area. However, the Antichrist is to appear in the Temple (2 Thess. 2:4), when he breaks his 7-year treaty with Israel and the court will be under control of Gentiles for the final 42 months of the Tribulation period. Compare Luke 21:24. When this was written in about 95 A.D. the Jewish Temple had long since been destroyed (70 A.D.); therefore, this speaks of the future beyond controversy.

The Two Witnesses (3-12)

3. **And I will give power unto my two witnesses** *(kai doso dusin martusin mou)* — the actual word *power* is not in the Greek, but is implied; hence the word is in italics in the King James Version. These empowered witnesses are present for temple worship during the first half of the 7 years, evidently ministering to the Israelis ... **and they shall prophesy** *(kai propheteusousin)* **a thousand two hundred and threescore (1,260) days** — the biblical prophetic year is 360 days, 12 months of 30 days each; hence this equals 42 months. These are literal days, not figurative years. God sends His witness to Israel and to the world ... clothed in sackcloth *(peribeblemenoi sakkous)*, garments of repentance and sorrow. They will cause no small stir and may be the instruments to win the 144,000 of chapter 7 to Jesus the Messiah and who also become witnesses in the end times to God's truth. 4. **These are the two olive trees and the two candlesticks** *(elaiai* and *luchniai)* — this a reference to Zechariah 4, where trees upon the right side and the left side of the candlestick in the ancient prophecy show that the High Priest Joshua and the Prince of the Royal House of David, Zerubbabel, both anointed of God (olive oil symbolizing the Holy Spirit, Zech. 4:6) are meant by the trees; however, God has two other "olive trees" for the Tribulation Period. In Zechariah there is only one candlestick — lampstand — "menorah," whereas, here are two candlesticks. In Zechariah the one candlestick (lampstand) represented Israel; here the two candlesticks are the witnesses, shining forth for Israel. Zechariah said, "These are the two anointed ones, that stand" ... this is paraphrased by John in verse 4. Who they are is the profound question. Some have thought they were the Old and New Testaments, but the

Scriptures could not be "slain." Others have suggested Daniel and John returning. Many 2nd and 3rd century expositors and many recent premillennial writers have believed them to be either Elijah and Moses or Elijah and Enoch (See Malachi 4:5,6, and Jude 9 and Matthew 17:1-13). **5. And if any man will hurt them** (*kai ei tis autous thelei adikesai*) — that is, if anyone determines by a strong will to harm them ... **fire proceedeth out of their mouth and devoureth their enemies and if any man will hurt them, he must in this manner be killed** — since Elijah had a similar power (2 Kings 1:10), many have thus identified one of the witnesses with him, besides the reference of Jesus that Elijah truly would "come and restore all things" (Matt. 17:11, alluding to Malachi 4:5,6, as indicated earlier). This supernatural protective power will prevent anyone from harming them unit they finish their ministries. **6. These have power to shut heaven that it rain not in the days of their prophecy** — a further indication that Elijah, who did this in Old Testament times is one of the witnesses (See 2 Kings 17:1 and James 5:17) ... in both cases a 3 1/2 year period is indicated for drought ... **and have power over waters to turn them to blood, and to smite the earth with all plagues, as often as they will** — as Moses and Aaron did in ancient Egypt (Exodus 7:19; 20-25 and Exodus 8-14, where the plagues were literal divine judgments). These prophets doubtlessly announce the judgments of chapters 8 and 9, which also involve water turned to blood and horrendous plagues. Some think Moses, as in Jude 9, is one of the two witnesses. Others, including many early writers point to the fact that neither Elijah nor Enoch died and that it is logical for these translated saints to return (Heb. 9:27). **7. And when they have finished their testimony** (*kai hotan telesosin ten marturian auton*) — at the conclusion of the 1,260 days and in the midst of the "week" of Daniel 9:27 ... **the beast that ascendeth out of the bottomless pit** (*to therion to anabainon ek tes abusson*) — this is the first time in Revelation he is actually mentioned, except for the rider on the white horse in 6:1,2; this is the Antichrist, now breaking his treaty with Israel and invading Jerusalem, a campaign to result in his setting up the abomination of desolation (chapter 13) ... **shall make war with them, and shall overcome them, and kill them** — this Satan-energized personality, more completely described in Chapter 13, derives his power from the abyss, a matter to be discussed at length later. These two witnesses are slain and publicly exhibited in Jerusalem for all the world (by television) to see. **8. And**

their dead bodies (*ptoma auton*) — not *nekros* (a dead body), but their corpse-form ... **shall lie in the streets of the great city, which spiritually** (*pneumatikos*) **is called Sodom and Egypt** — a reference to Isaiah 1:9,10 where corrupt Jerusalem is compared to Sodom, indicating a city of moral and ethical evil, debauchery and rebellion against God, as with Egypt. Does this indicate that the evil of sodomy will be so widespread in the end-times that it will even permeate Jerusalem? ... **where also our Lord was crucified** — See John 19:17,18; Acts 7:58; Heb. 13:12. Though this is the "holy city," with some true believers and moral Israelis, the wickedness of the ungodly and the hatred against these truth-telling, judgment announcing prophets will be intense and vicious. **9. And they of the people and kindreds and tongues and nations shall see their dead bodies three days and an half and shall not suffer their dead bodies** (*ptoma auton*) **to be put in graves** — immortal until their work is done, these mighty witness-prophets are on ignominious display, as God's martyrs in other eras have often been. **10. And they that dwell on the earth shall rejoice over them and make merry and shall send gifts one to another, because these two prophets tormented them that dwell on the earth** — only in our times when television can screen anywhere on earth events occurring any place instantly, could this be fulfilled. Because they have preached against sin and evil and proclaimed God's wrath, predicting the judgments of the first half of the Tribulation, they will, in a sense, be blamed. God's servants are always blamed when they prick the consciences of the wicked, who harden their hearts against truth. Partying and gift-giving all over the world will prevail as the ungodly rejoice over the murder of the righteous. How often the world despises God's prophets and God's people! Prophets were stoned, sawn asunder, assassinated; Apostles were martyred, crucified, slaughtered; and Christ was taken and by wicked hands was crucified. So it was; so it shall be until ... **11. And after three days and an half** — a miniature of the 3 1/2 years of their powerful public ministry ... **the Spirit of life** (*pneuma zoes*) from God (*ek tou theou*) — proceeding out of and originating with God ... **entered into them** — this is the Spirit, wind, breath of God, which will also bring life into Israel's dry bones (Ezekiel 37:10,11), which speaks of genuine spiritual life entering into Israel itself at the climax of history. The resurrection of the two witnesses presages the spiritual resurrection of all Israel, when they see the Messiah coming in glory (Rev. 1:7) ... **and they stood**

upon their feet — these words are from Ezekiel 37:10, which deals with the close of the "times of the Gentiles" wherein the holy city is trodden under foot ... **and great fear fell upon them which saw them** — which includes not only Jews and Gentiles in the city, but peoples of the world through television. **12. And they heard a great voice** (*phones megales*) ... **Come up hither** — as in 4:1, when John was summoned into heaven ... **and they ascended up to heaven in a cloud** — possible the Shekinah Cloud (Ex. 40:34; Matt. 17:5; Acts 1:9).

Second Woe Ends (13,14)

13. And the same hour was there a great earthquake (*egeneto seismos megas*) — a calamitous judgment in the Middle East ... **and the tenth part of the city fell** — this is Jerusalem... **and in the earthquake were slain of men seven thousand** — these are doubtless among the followers of the Antichrist, whom even many Jews earlier acclaim ... **and the remnant were afrighted and gave glory to the God of heaven** — this is the 144,000 or at least some from among them. **14. Second woe** (*ouai deutera*) — see 9:12-21 as well as this chapter ... **third woe** (*ouai he trite*) — Satan's descent to earth for the last half of the Tribulation Period (12:7-12).

Seventh Trumpet (15-18)

15. And the seventh angel sounds — as the seventh seal (8:1) introduced and encompassed the seven trumpets, so this seventh trumpet incorporates the remainder of the process, continuing 3 $^1/_2$ years and climaxing in the glorious kingdom being established. **16. Four and twenty elders** — the raptured and resurrected saints, reigning and worshipping, then proclaiming events on earth and in heaven taking place during the "days of the voice of the seventh angel" (10:7) ... **17. thou hast taken to thee thy great power and hast reigned** — here the proclamation acknowledges the active intervention of God and Christ in consummating history. **18. nations angry** — how "petty man's impotent anger, standing here side by side with the wrath of the omnipotent God" ... **time of the dead that they should be judged** — includes the judgment seat of Christ (2 Cor. 5:10), which occurs in heaven while the Tribulation is on earth ... and the giving of **reward unto thy servants the prophets** — the resurrection of the Old Testament saints and the Tribulation martyrs appears to take place after the Glorious Appearing (Rev. 20:1-6) ... **and to them that fear thy name small and great** — compare the judgment of the

nations in Matthew 25:31-46).

Temple in Heaven (19)

19. And the temple of God was opened in heaven — that there is a temple in heaven is evident, as in 14:15; 15:5,6,8; 16:1,17, wherein is the Ark of the Covenant, evidently the original in heaven, which Moses copied. (See Hebrews 8:5; 9:23,24) ... In heaven meteorological phenomena occur, a preview of what will continue to happen on earth in the Tribulation.

No less than five temples, recognized by God and explained in Scripture are mentioned, plus three special or spiritual temples. These latter include, first, the actual body of Jesus Christ, who said, "Destroy this temple, and in three days I will raise it up" (John 2:19) ... "But he spake of the temple of his body" (2:21).

Second, the body of the believer in this Dispensation is the temple of the Holy Spirit: "What? know ye not that your body is the temple of the Holy Ghost ...?" (1 Cor. 6:19).

Third, the church is a temple: "In whom (Christ) all the building, fitly framed together groweth into an holy temple in the Lord" (Eph. 2:21).

But, as related solely to Israel in the past and in the future, four temples are depicted: Solomon's Temple, or the First Temple (1 Kings 6-8); the Second Temple, first rebuilt after the 70 years captivity following the destruction of the First Temple in 586 B.C. Later this temple was enlarged and expanded by Herod prior to the time of Christ (See Ezra 6; Haggai 1, 2; John 2:20). This temple was destroyed in 70 A.D.

The Third Temple is to be built prior to or during the future Tribulation Period as in this chapter ... Antichrist will desecrate it with "the abomination of desolation" (See 2 Thes. 2:4).

The Fourth Temple will be built and used during the millennium as described in Ezekiel 40-43. The Temple here (19) and in the other references listed above exists in heaven now. In the New Jerusalem, eternal home of the redeemed, John says, "And I saw no temple therein: for the Lord God Almighty and the Lamb are the temple of it" (Rev. 21:33). No special holy places need to be dedicated for worship, since our adoration will be directly to Him!

RAINBOWS FROM REVELATION
The Revelation of Jesus Christ
A chapter by chapter, verse by verse study
"There was a rainbow round about the throne like unto an emerald" (4:3)

CHAPTER TWELVE: War in Heaven

References

Gen. 37:9

John 16:21
Micah 5:2,3
Gal. 4:19

Rev. 13:1;
17:3,7,9

Dan. 8:10
Ex. 1:16
Matt. 2:16

Ps. 2:9
Rev. 2:27;19:15
Luke 24:51
Acts 1:9-11
Rev. 11:3
Rev. 12:4,14
Dan. 7:25

Dan. 10:13
Luke 10:18

Isa. 14:12-14
Job 1:6

Gen. 3:1-4
2 Cor. 11:3
Eph. 6:12

References

Job 1:9,11; 2:5
Zech. 3:1
John 12:31
Rom. 8:37

Rom. 16:20
Luke 14:26

Ps. 96:11
Isa. 44:23
Rev. 18:20

Rev. 12:4,5

Ex. 19:4
Deut. 32:11
Isa. 40:31
Dan. 7:25

Isa. 59:19

Isa. 10:20-21

1. AND there appeared a great wonder in heaven; a woman clothed with the sun, and the moon under her feet, and upon her head a crown of twelve stars:

2. And she being with child cried, travailing in birth, and pained to be delivered.

3. And there appeared another wonder in heaven; and behold a great red dragon, having seven heads and ten horns, and seven crowns upon his heads.

4. And his tail drew the third part of the stars of heaven, and did cast them to the earth: and the dragon stood before the woman which was ready to be delivered, for to devour her child as soon as it was born.

5. And she brought forth a man child, who was to rule all nations with a rod of iron: and her child was caught up unto God, and to his throne.

6. And the woman fled into the wilderness, where she hath a place prepared of God, that they should feed her there a thousand two hundred and threescore days.

7. And there was war in heaven: Michael and his angels fought against the dragon; and the dragon fought and his angels.

8. And prevailed not; neither was their place found any more in heaven.

9. And the great dragon was cast out, that old serpent, called the Devil, and Satan, which deceiveth the whole world: he was cast out into the earth, and his angels were cast out with him.

10. And I heard a loud voice saying in heaven, Now is come salvation, and strength, and the kingdom of our God, and the power of his Christ: for the accuser of our brethren is cast down, which accused them before our God day and night.

11. And they overcame him by the blood of the Lamb, and by the word of their testimony; and they loved not their lives unto the death.

12. Therefore rejoice, ye heavens, and ye that dwell in them. Woe to the inhabiters of the earth and of the sea! for the devil is come down unto you, having great wrath, because he knoweth that he hath but a short time.

13. And when the dragon saw that he was cast unto the earth, he persecuted the woman which brought forth the man child.

14. And to the woman were given two wings of a great eagle, that she might fly into the wilderness, into her place, where she is nourished for a time, and times, and half a time, from the face of the serpent.

15. And the serpent cast out of his mouth water as a flood after the woman, that he might cause her to be carried away of the flood.

16. And the earth helped the woman, and the earth opened her mouth, and swallowed up the flood which the dragon cast out of his mouth.

17. And the dragon was wroth with the woman, and went to make war with the remnant of her seed, which keep the commandments of God, and have the testimony of Jesus Christ.

Scriptures for Comparison

Genesis 37:9

And he dreamed yet another dream, and told it his brethren, and said, Behold, I have dreamed a dream more; and behold, the sun and the moon and the eleven stars made obeisance to me.

Psalm 2:7-9

I will declare the decree: the LORD hath said unto me, Thou art my Son; this day have I begotten thee. Ask of me, and I shall give thee the heathen for thine inheritance, and the uttermost parts of the earth for thy possession. Thou shalt break them with a rod of iron; thou shalt dash them in pieces like a potter's vessel.

Daniel 7:25

And he shall speak great words against the most High, and shall wear out the saints of the most High, and think to change times and laws: and they shall be given into his hand until a time a times and the dividing of time.

Summary of Chapter Twelve

The War in Heaven

I. The Woman vs. the Dragon (1-5)

Thus far, our studies have brought us to the end of the seven trumpets, the final one encompassing the "days of the voice of the seventh trumpet," a period of time lasting the 1,260 days from the midpoint of the Tribulation until the glorious appearing.

As the twelfth chapter opens, a "flashback" occurs for the purpose of identifying and explaining the first of seven personages or characters of the end times set forth in this and the next chapter.

Reverting back to the first coming of Christ, the woman clothed with the sun denotes Israel in history and prophecy. From Genesis 37 and Joseph's dream, the symbology of the "sun, moon and eleven stars" (Joseph was the 12th star) is evident. The "great wonder," a woman crowned with 12 stars is ISRAEL, not the church, not the Virgin Mary, not some feminine religious teacher.

Out of Israel came the "wonder child," Jesus, the Messiah of Israel and the Savior of the world.

Threatening the birth of the "manchild" is the "great, red dragon," obviously identified as Satan. His seven heads depict the evil perfection of his influence on civilization's progress and the ten horns indicate the final form of Gentile world power, as Satan will work through ten nations to enthrone his "antichrist" as the world ruler.

But this is basically a "flashback." The dragon's drawing a "third of the stars of heaven" speaks of his primeval rebellion (Isaiah 14:12-15; Ezekiel 28:12-17) when a third of the angels followed his rebellion. These fallen angels are the principalities and powers against which we wrestle (Ephesians 6:12). This reference carries us even further back in time.

But the reader's attention is focused on the dragon's efforts to thwart the birth of the "manchild," Jesus, who is to rule all nations with a rod of iron (see Psalm 2:7-9 and Revelation 19:15). This is still part of the "flashback."

After the birth of the "manchild," which Satan opposed (Matthew 2:16-18), Christ fulfilled his destiny and ascended to heaven (Acts 1:9-11). Three factors about Him are evident: (1) His birth, (2) His ascension, (3) His future rule.

That is the end of the "flashback."

II. Michael vs. the Dragon (6-12)

The narrative resumes at the midpoint of the future TRIBULATION. The new world ruler, the beast, has severed his seven-year covenant with Israel, slain the two witnesses in Jerusalem (chapter 11), whose ministry ran the first 1,260 days or 3 1/2 year period. Now Israel, the woman, is persecuted. Many flee to "a place in the wilderness," perhaps hundreds of thousands of God's earthly chosen people, who still have not received Jesus as Messiah. They are protected as they flee from the "floods" sent out by the devil. They are preserved and sustained for 1,260 days, or "a time, times and half a time" from the face of the serpent, Satan, lest he destroy God's earthly chosen people.

At this same time of their flight (see Matthew 24:15-26), Satan is totally expelled from heaven, denied even the limited access he presently experiences as revealed in Job 1 and 2. Satan is then confined primarily to earth for the last 1,260 days of the Tribulation. Heaven rejoices. Satan energizes the antichrist with supernatural power (13:5) and he reaches the zenith and high plateau of his evil career, continuing for "42 months," before his destruction.

III. Israel vs. the Dragon (13-16)

"The persecution, desperate and deadly, by the enemy of the nation Israel, is now before us — 'the time of Jacob's trouble.' Satan hates Israel: first because they are God's elect royal people; next, because of that nation IS CHRIST (Romans 9:5), who is to have the kingdom upon Satan's final overthrow; and finally because Israel is the perpetual proof before the eyes of men of the truth of the Scriptures and of the fact of Jehovah God" (W. R. Newell).

In the meanwhile, the godly "remnant" who "have the testimony of Jesus Christ," the saved 144,000 Israelite witnesses, come under the warring attacks of Satan. Most probably they die martyr's deaths, since in Chapter 14, they are seen in heaven.

IV. The Remnant vs. the Dragon (17)

In the meanwhile, the godly "remnant," who "have the testimony of Jesus Christ," the saved 144,000 Israelite witnesses (Chapter 7) come under the warring attacks of Satan. Most probably they die martyr's deaths, since in Chapter 14, they are seen in heaven. This is further proof that the "woman" is Israel, since they are the "remnant of her seed."

Outline of Chapter Twelve

The Seven Personages (first five)

OBJECTIVE: To predict the expulsion of Satan as the accuser of the brethren in preparation for Christ's supreme conquests.

OUTLINE:

I. The Wondrous Woman: Israel (1-2)
A. Her Appearance (1)
B. Her Apparel (1)
   1. Clothed with sun
   2. Covering the moon (under her feet)
   3. Crowned with 12 stars
      THE WOMAN REPRESENTS ISRAEL
      (Gen. 37)
C. Her Approach to Childbirth

II. The Wondrous Dragon: Satan (3, 4)
A. His Character: great (powerful)
B. His Color: red (emblematic of evil, blood, etc.)
C. His Crowns: spiritual and political influence
   1. Seven heads — civilization in stages
   2. Ten horns — final political influence
D. His Cruelty
   1. Misled a third of the angels (stars)
   2. Minded to destroy the manchild (Christ)

III. The Wonderful Manchild: Christ (5)
A. About Christ
   1. He came from Israel (first coming)
   2. He will conquer the nations (second coming)
   3. He was caught up to heaven (ascension)
B. About Israel in Tribulation (6)
   1. Passage from Palestine into the wilderness
   2. Place prepared of God in the wilderness (Petra?)
   3. Period of preservation: 1,260 days of protective safety

IV. The Warring Archangel: Michael (7-12)
A. The Expulsion of Satan (7-9)
   1. The Violence—war in heaven
   2. The Victory—Satan defeated
   3. The Vanquishing—Satan cast out
B. The Exclamation (10)
   1. The Acclaim for Christ
      a. Salvation
      b. Strength
      c. Kingdom of our God
      d. Power of his Christ
   2. The Accuser in Defeat

C. The Encouragement (11) (All God's people in view)
   1. They overcame Satan by the blood
   2. They overcame Satan by the word of testimony
   3. They overcame Satan by loving Christ unto death
D. The Exhortation (12): Rejoice, ye heavens

V. The World Wide Woe (12-16)
A. The Exclamation (12): WOE to the inhabitants of the earth!
THIS IS THE THIRD WOE (9:13, 10:12; 11:14)
SATAN VICIOUSLY VIOLENT ON EARTH FOR A SHORT TIME, 3 1/2 years. He continues for the rest of the Tribulation.
B. The Explanation of Satan's Ire (13-16)
   1. Satan attacks Israel
   2. Israel protected for 3 1/2 years in "the place"
   3. Satan sends a "flood"
   4. Israel protected by "the earth."

VI. The Witnessing Remnant: 144,000 (see Chapter 7)
A. Satan Angry at the Woman, Israel
B. Satan Attacks the Remnant of her Seed
   1. They keep God's commandments
   2. They have Jesus' testimony

Israel brought to her knees

"In Daniel 12 the prophet discusses the latter half of the Tribulation, stating that there shall be a time of trouble, such as never was since there was a nation even to that same time, 'and at that time thy people shall be delivered, everyone that is found written in the book' (vs. 1).

"Someone asked the angelic being who was present in 12:6, 'How long shall it be to the end of these wonders?' The answer: 'For a time, times and a half; and when they shall have made an end of breaking the power of the holy people, all these things shall be finished' (7). The drift of this passage shows that the purposes of the judgments of the Tribulation — at least the last half — are designed to bring Israel to their knees."

– David L. Cooper

Observations:
Spiritual lessons and applications from each verse
Chapter Twelve

1. When God speaks in symbols (wonders or signs — the Greek word *semeion* means sign, mark, indication, token, usually involving something unusual, symbolical, or even supernatural), the meanings can often be found either in the same book or in a reference somewhere else in the Bible.

2. Even as the woman travailed prior to birth, so all achievements require travail of one kind or another.

3. Satan is a real and powerful foe, challenging even Jesus Christ.

4. In alliance with Satan is an evil host of fallen angels, loose in the world, and doing his bidding.

5. Since Christ, the Manchild, is to rule all nations, we should let Him rule our hearts and lives every day now.

6. God often prepares a place for His people in every age, a place of repair, strength, love. That place can be found by drawing night to God.

7. We are to fight the good fight of faith, resisting Satan now. The war between God and Satan, good and evil, is even now in progress, reaching a peak when this verse is fulfilled.

8. Christ prevails (5:5); Satan "prevailed not."

9. Satan is always the deceiver, projecting evil as good (see Isa. 5:20, 21).

10. Even now Satan accuses us, but Christ is the Advocate (1 John 2:1,2)

11. Here is the formula for overcoming Satan: (1) the blood of the Lamb — plead the blood; (2) maintain your testimony — by word and deed; (3) love God more than life itself.

12. Since heaven rejoices in spiritual victories, we should rejoice in the Lord alway.

13. Satan's animosity is always directed toward the objects of His favor.

14. God can give us "wings" on occasion, to help us flee from Satan. See Isaiah 40:31, "they shall mount up with wings as eagles."

15. Satan can use supernatural, natural and circumstantial pressures against the people of God. But God is bigger than the devil.

16. God moves in mysterious and unusual ways to protect His own.

17. God's people in every age should keep his commandments and have a strong testimony for Jesus Christ. Even as the godly Jewish remnant, the 144,000, suffer serious persecution in the future, so in the days before the rapture, much discrimination and persecution may befall God's faithful people with many dying martyr's deaths. Millions have died in the 20th century, victims of both political and religious persecution.

The enemy cast out forever

"Upon the occasion of casting down to the earth, all the Scripture names are announced: 'The great red dragon … the old serpent' (his hideous character and malignant, poisonous deceit as God sees it), he that is called the Devil (slanderer) and Satan (God's absolute adversary and ours), the deceiver of the whole world' — what a list! If the back yard of your home were a den of rattlesnakes, headed by a king cobra, and they had been there all your life, hissing and threatening, and you should come home some evening to find that they had at last been driven out, to return no more at all, would you not rejoice? So will heaven when the enemy and his host are cast out forever."

— *W. R. Newell*

Quotations
From Other Expositors
Chapter Twelve

The Woman (1-6)

"Revelation 12:1-17 is the central passage describing Satan's relationship to Israel during the tribulation. At that time there will be an all-out satanically organized campaign to wipe out the Jews once and for all.

"Verses 1-5 lay out a historical summary from the birth to the ascension of Christ. Verse six pictures Israel in flight just as Matthew 24:16-20 did. The picture of Jews on the run is followed by the reason why in verses 7-12. Satan will be cast down to the earth, and he will set out to destroy the Jews. Verses 13-14 further explain verse six where Israel is in flight. Finally in verses 15-17 the passage concludes by describing Satan's persecution of the Jews, especially the believing remnant."

– Arnold G. Fruchtenbaum

"That this woman represents Israel is evident, for:

"1. The place in the prophecy is Israelitish: The two witnesses have been stationed at Jerusalem, where temple-worship is again going on.

"2. The words, 'sun,' 'moon,' and 'stars' immediately remind us of Joseph's dream, Genesis 37:9 — "Behold, the sun and the moon and the eleven stars made obeisance to me," — a forecast of Israel, in the last days.

"3. The Church cannot be spoken of in this language, for she was chosen 'before the foundation of the world' and her glory is not at all describable in terms of this present creation. She has union with Him who has gone 'far above all the heavens'; whereas this woman's connection is plainly with what we call the 'solar system,' — that is, as viewed from earth.

"4. That she is clothed with the sun, with the moon under her feet, and on her feet, and on her head a twelve-star crown, indicates the subjection of earth to her governmental glory: 'The splendor and fulness of governmental glory: 'The splendor and fulness of governmental authority on earth,' belong, by God's sovereign appointment, to Israel: and the restoring of the Kingdom to Israel, under Christ, is the subject before us in this part of The Revelation.

"5. Israel is described in the prophets as travailing in birth; the Church never is (Micah 5:2,3; Israel 9:6; 7:14).

"6. Israel, not the Church, gave birth to Christ (Roman 9; Micah 5; Isaiah 9:6; Hebrew 7:14). In no possible sense did the Church do so.

"7. It is very evident, and is most important to recognize, that this woman's real history is on earth, persecuted by the enemy.

"8. The subsequent earthly history (Revelation 12) of the woman, corresponds exactly with what other prophets tell us concerning the trouble of Israel in the last days.

"9. The period of that trouble, as we see in Revelation 12:6, coincides also with the last of Daniel's seventieth week — The Great Tribulation of three and one-half years."

– W.R. Newell

The Dragon (1-17)

"The dragon, then, is Satan (verse 9). We have here the beginning of the end of the great warfare between God and His adversary begun in Eden. There the Serpent beguiled the woman, and God declared He would put enmity between the Serpent and the Woman, and between her Seed and his seed. Now her Seed is Christ, and none other, as Paul shows in Galatians 3:16. 'Unto us a child is born' cries Isaiah (9:6,7), 'of the increase of whose government and of peace there should be no end,' which is the exact subject before us in Revelation 12. Satan's enmity and jealousy was against Christ, who was to 'rule all the nations': for had not Satan himself been their prince and god?"

– W.R. Newell

The Man Child (2-5)

"Alford concludes, 'The man-child is the Lord Jesus Christ, and none other.' He is described as destined to rule all nations with a rod of iron. This is an allusion to Psalm 2:9, where in connection with Christ's reign over the earth, it is declared, 'Thou shalt break them with a rod of iron;' the same thou found in Revelation 19:15, where it is stated of Christ, "He shall rule them with a rod of iron." His rule over all nations with a rod of iron is to be distinguished from His rule over Israel which is of more benevolent character (Luke 1:32-33).

"The catching up of the man-child to God and to His throne seems to be a portayal of the ascension of Christ. Alford interprets this as meaning that 'after a conflict with the Prince of this world, who come and tried Him, but found nothing in Him, the Son of the woman was taken up to heaven and sat on the right hand of God. Words can hardly be plainer than these.'"

– John F. Walvoord

Michael (7-9)

"The adversaries of the dragon are Michael and his angels, which initiate war against the old serpent and his angels. Will heaven always be a place of peace? Decidedly not, for war of the intensest and fiercest kind rages during this battle. Michael is introduced and described to us as one of great power, who fights for 'the Woman.' He is 'one of the chief princes' (Daniel 10:13); Israel's prince (Daniel 10:21); 'the great prince which standeth for thy people' (Daniel 12:10); and 'the archangel,' or highest angel (Jude 9). He is a worthy adversary!"

– Bill Lawrence

Place in the Wilderness (6, 13-16)

"A prophecy in the Psalms suggests that the ancient rock city of Petra, Jordan, will be one of the places of refuge for the Jews in that time of trial. 'Who will bring me into the strong city? Who will lead me to Edom?' (Psalm 60:9). The prophet Isaiah also refers to Israel escaping to Moab (Jordan): 'Let My outcasts dwell with you, O Moab; be a shelter to them from the face of the spoiler. For the extortioner is at an end, devastation ceases, the oppressors are consumed out of the land' (Isaiah 16:4). However, Petra is not large enough to hold a significant part of the population of the nation Israel. Many nations, including Africa, North America and others may be part of the 'wilderness' where the Jews will flee for protection from the Antichrist. Isaiah prophesied that five cities in Egypt that will have so many Jews in the last days that the common language will be Hebrew. Christ declared in Matthew 25 that He will judge the nations of the earth on the basis of how they treat the Jews and Gentile tribulation believers who flee the Mark of the Beast system. If the citizens of our nations provide refuge for the Jews, they will be blessed and allowed to participate in the blessings of Christ's millennial Kingdom. Sinful individuals in the nations that join in the persecution will be cast into darkness and hell."

– Grant R. Jeffrey

The Remnant (17)

The remnant will be the witnessing body of 144,000 Jews.

– Louis T. Talbot

"Two classes appear to be referred to. Abraham was promised a twofold seed: an earthly, likened to the sands of the sea; and a heavenly, likened to the stars of the sky. And from the beginning of the gospel there have always been two classes of believers: the Jewish and the Gentiles. So 'the commandments of God' suggest to us God's older revelation by Moses, and the Law given through him: and 'the testimony of Jesus' calls to mind the Christian profession. The allusion would, therefore, seem to be (1) to Jewish believers, the 144,000 of whom, described in chapter 7, are then still on the earth; and (2) Gentile servants of God who hold fast the confession of Christ over against the prevalent abominations of the time. These are now sought out with desperate hate, wherever they may be, and proceeded against with determination to conquer them to the worship of the Beast, or failing in that, to cut off the heads of all who refuse to yield."

– J.A. Seiss

"Satan cannot win. Just as the blood of the martyrs has proved to be the seed of the church, so during the Tribulation, persecution will but drive many Jewish people into the arms of the Lord Jesus. He has tried persecution many times before, and it has always failed to deter faith and conversion. That he tries it again is a mute confession of failure, the last resort of a desperate and darkened mind. The godly Jews will not recant. They will only scatter far and wide, bearing as they go the gospel of the kingdom, and their triumph will be complete."

– John Phillips

"These tribulation saints will prove their faith by martyrdom during the severe persecution, first, from the Great Whore church and later, from the Antichrist. In Revelation 7:9 John saw "a great multitude which no one could number, of all nations, tribes, peoples, and tongues, standing before the throne and before the Lamb." The angel told John that these are the tribulation martyrs who will form the last great harvest of souls. They will pay the supreme price of martyrdom for their faith.

–Grant R. Jeffrey

When Satan is Cast Out
An Expository Sermon

Chapter Twelve

Introduction

Since before the pristine days of Adam and Eve, the archenemy of God, the one-time "anointed cherub that covereth," perhaps the highest of the created angels, has waged a nefarious battle against God, His creation, and the human race, after man was created.

At Calvary, he sustained a powerful blow when Jesus died for all sin. "Now is the judgment of this world: now shall the prince of this world be cast out" (John 12:31). "And I, if I be lifted up from the earth, will draw all men unto me" (John 12:32).

But he still persists as a roaring lion, walking about, seeking whom he may devour (1 Peter 5:8). As he persists, we are to resist (1 Peter 5:9).

But at the midpoint of the coming Tribulation, he will receive a further defeat, being totally cast out of any limited access to God, which he yet exercises as the accuser of the brethren as is exemplified in the case of Job (Job 1, 2).

At the close of the Tribulation and the beginning of the Millennium, he will be enchained and confined to the bottomless pit. After his last and futile, final rebellion (Revelation 20:10), he will be forever consigned to the lake of fire, a place prepared for the devil and his angels.

This chapter speaks of many truths which we shall examine and compare with many other passages.

I. The Wonders (1-6)

Emblematic of Israel, the sun-clothed woman, wearing the 12 stars that suggest the 12 tribes of Israel, is seen as the source of the Savior Messiah. This is a flashback to the first coming of Christ. This is the first wonder. That this woman symbolizes Israel is evident from Genesis 37:9, where Joseph saw the sun, moon and 12 stars, representative of Jacob and his family, in an illuminating dream.

The second is the great red dragon, Satan, threatening Israel in the past and in the future, ever violently antagonistic to the coming Manchild — Messiah, who will rule all nations. After Bethlehem and the coming of the wise men, Satan stirred up Herod to slay the male children in an attempt to "devour" the manchild.

But Christ performed His ministry and ascended to heaven, from "henceforth expecting until his enemies be made his footstool" (Heb. 10:13).

This is the end of the "flashback" which furnishes additional information to identify and focus on "the Christchild," (vs. 5) moving from His birth through to His ascension and succession at the right hand of the throne of God:

"Who being the brightness of his glory, and the express image of his person, and upholding all things by the word of his power, when he had by himself purged our sins, sat down on the right hand of the Majesty on high" (Heb. 1:3).

The scene quickly changes to the midpoint of the Seven Year Tribulation Period. The first 1,260 days have expired with the martyrdom and resurrection of the two witnesses and their subsequent resurrection and ascension. Antichrist, the beast, (11:7) now has broken his covenant with the many Jews living in Israel and turns upon God's earthly chosen people. Multitudes flee into the wilderness to an especially prepared place amid both mountains and deserts, characteristic of the whole Middle East.

Chronologically, this mid-point of the whole period introduces "the great tribulation" proper, the last three and a half years. As described in the next chapter, the "abomination of desolation" is set up in the temple area.

Here now are Jesus' words descriptive of this very event:

"When ye see therefore the abomination of desolation, spoken of by Daniel the prophet, stand [standing up, erected] in the holy place [which can be nothing else but the temple area], (whoso readeth, let him understand)," a reference to Daniel 9:27 and 12:11, as we have seen ... "then let them which be in Jerusalem flee into the mountains: let him which is on the housetop not come down to take anything out of his house: neither let him which is in the field return back to take his clothes. And woe unto them that are with child, and to them that give suck in those days! But pray ye that your flight be not in winter, neither on the sabbath day;

FOR THEN SHALL BE GREAT TRIBULATION, SUCH AS WAS NOT SINCE THE BEGINNING OF THE WORLD TO THIS TIME, NO, NOR EVER SHALL BE. And except those days should be shortened, there should no flesh be saved: but for the elect's sake those days shall be shortened. Then if any man shall say unto you, Lo, here is Christ [Messiah], or there; believe it not …" (Matthew 24:15-23).

The flight of the people of Judea and the flight of the woman into the wilderness both describe the same event.

II. The War (7-11)

Satan then fights in heaven against the archangel Michael, mentioned in the book of Daniel in 12:1: "And at that time Michael shall stand up, the great prince which standeth for the children of thy people: and THERE SHALL BE A TIME OF TROUBLE, SUCH AS NEVER WAS SINCE THERE WAS A NATION EVEN TO THAT SAME TIME: AND AT THAT TIME, THY PEOPLE SHALL BE DELIVERED, EVERY ONE THAT SHALL BE FOUND WRITTEN IN THE BOOK."

Notice Satan is called the great red dragon, suggesting his diabolical dealings behind the scenes in world and political affairs. He is the prince of the power of the air, as Paul so designates (Eph. 2:2). He is called the serpent, for he subtly deceives, as in Genesis 3.

He is called the devil, which means "accuser," for he accuses the brethren even now, day and night, before God in his limited access. But thank God, our Advocate Jesus Christ defends us. He has never lost a case. The whole book of Job unveils Satan in this role.

He is named Satan, which means "adversary," for so he is, the adversary of God and good and all that is right and holy and pure. He is no friend, even to the enemies of God.

Satan wars against God and the holy angels.

Satan wages war against believers as the accuser now.

Satan loses in these wars and is finally cast out.

Satan will foster a violent wave of evil during the last days of the TRIBULATION, for he knows he will have a short time … actually only 1,260 days or a time, times and half a time until his imprisonment in the bottomless pit.

In a sense this war originated in the primeval past, when Lucifer (light-bearer) rebelled against God, as recorded in Isaiah 14:12-15:

"How art thou fallen from heaven, O Lucifer, son of the morning! how art thou cut down, which didst weaken the nations! For thou hast said in thine heart,
I will ascend into heaven,
I will exalt my throne above the stars of God:
I will sit also upon the mount of the congregation, in the sides of the north:
I will ascend above the heights of the clouds;
I will be like the most High.
Yet thou shalt be brought down to hell, to the sides of the pit." That original sin occurred prior to the creation of Adam and Eve. Since the existence of humankind, he has been the source of evil, wickedness and temptation, playing upon fallen human nature.

A furthur description of his magnificence as the highest of created angelic beings is set forth in Ezekiel 28:12-15:

"Thus saith the Lord God: Thou sealest up the sum, full of wisdom, and perfect in beauty. Thou has been in Eden the garden of God; every precious stone was thy covering, the sardis, topaz, and the diamond, the beryl, the onyx, and the jasper, the sapphire, the emerald, and the carbuncle, and gold: the workmanship of thy tabrets and of thy pipes was prepared in thee in the day that thou was created. Thou art the ANOINTED CHERUB THAT COVERETH; and I have set thee so: thou wast upon the holy mountain of God; thou walkest up and down in the midst of the stones of fire. Thou wast perfect in all thy ways from the day that thou wast created, till iniquity was found in thee."

Pride was Satan's great sin, prompting him to even attempt to become as great as God Himself, possibly even dethroning the Almighty, imagining that might even be attainable.

But now, in the midpoint of the Tribulation, Satan is denied even limited access to God. Evidently, a third of the angels did participate in his ancient rebellion (the dragon's tail "drew a third part of the stars of heaven and cast them into the earth" vs. 4).

For the last half of the Seven Years Satan and his fallen angels are confined to the earth.

At this triumphal expulsion the hosts of heaven lift their voices in praise and adoration, for at last the "accuser of our brethren is cast down, which accused them before our God day and night."

"AND THEY OVERCAME HIM
BY THE BLOOD OF THE LAMB!
BY THE WORD OF THEIR TESTIMONY!
AND THEY LOVED NOT THEIR LIVES UNTO DEATH!"

III. The Woe (12-17)

This third in a series of woes mentioned earlier (8:13; 9:12; 11:14) involves the inhabiters of the earth

(12); the fleeing Israelites who seek refuge against the invading armies of the beast in the land of Israel (11:7-13) and the "remnant." God prepares a "place in the wilderness" where many Israelis are nourished for a time, times and half a time from the face of the serpent. This again means 3 $\frac{1}{2}$ years. As to the place, some have conjectured that this is the highly inaccessible rose red rocky place called PETRA. Of course, this may not be the place at all, but many prophecy scholars for the last 100 years have thought it to be a possibility. Carved in the red sheer cliffs are dozens of amazing structures, either quarried out by the ancient Idumeans, descendents of Esau, or by a Roman garrison stationed there in the first century.

On land, the isolated valley, surrounded by nearly perpendicular escarpments, can be entered only through a narrow canyon. It is a tourist attraction now with a luxury hotel nearby. Currently located in Jordanian territory (1990s), Petra has been the site of Christian books and Bibles, buried there, for the possible discovery by the fleeing Israelites of the future Tribulation. Of course, some other place, known only to God, may fit the biblical description.

With remote and uninhabited desert areas in the vast Arabian peninsula which God might "prepare in the wilderness," the exact place, there or elsewhere, remains unidentified. Whether their protection is supernatural, diplomatic, military or something beyond our present ability to understand also remains a future mystery.

The "wings of an eagle" might connote a vast aerial evacuation of hundreds of thousands of Israelis, maybe millions. Against all of Satan's evil efforts, they are protected and preserved. They will be the nucleus of Israelites who will accept Christ as their Messiah indeed at the Second Coming to the Mount of Olives, as predicted by the prophet Zechariah (chapter 14).

But the "remnant," evidently the 144,000 of chapter 7, suffer the cruelty and persecution of Satan. A most interesting passage in Isaiah 10:20-23 may be applicable to the time of Tribulation and this same "remnant:"

"And it shall come to pass in that day, that the remnant of Israel, and such as are escaped of the house of Jacob, shall no more stay upon them that smote them; but shall stay upon the Lord, the Holy One of Israel in truth. The remnant shall return, even the remnant of Jacob, unto the mighty God. For though thy people Israel be as the sand of the sea, yet a remnant shall return: the consumption decreed shall overflow with righteousness. For the Lord God of hosts shall make a consumption, even determined, in the midst of the land."

"For yet a little while, and the indignation shall cease, and mine anger in their destruction" (Isa.10:25).

Whether the "flood" cast out of Satan's mouth against the fleeing woman (Israelites) is literal here, involving some unusual meteorological and geological phenomena, or these expressions are figures of speech, has been discussed by many prophecy scholars, but remains a matter of conjecture. Some think that flowing armies are meant by 'the river' with other forces intercepting (the earth swallowing the flood).

In any event all of Satan's evil machinations are unable to destroy God's earthly chosen people, but then he turns his attention to the believing remnant, who are undoubtedly saved Israelis, because they "keep the commandments of God and have the testimony Jesus Christ."

We shall see them again in chapter 14, where they are in the presence of the Lamb of God.

Conclusion

Remember that these events all transpire from the "middle of the week" of seven years. Our attention will be drawn in chapter 13 to the beast out of the sea, the antichrist and his political domain, and the beast out of the earth, the false prophet.

But let us remember again that we are "saved from the wrath which is to come."

While these final 42 months of this world's history, as we know it, pass with horrendous fury, as described through chapter 19, the resurrected, raptured New Testament saints will be "with the Lord." We must appear before the judgment seat of Christ.

Friend, if you have read these words and yet have not come to Christ, there is still time. "Now is the day of salvation; now is the accepted time."

To be saved from wrath, to be saved from your sins, to be saved from everlasting perdition, to be saved for heaven and a glorious, blessed destiny, to be with Christ forever in the New Jerusalem, THERE IS BUT ONE WAY.

You must realize you are a sinner and receive Christ as the One who died on the cross for your sins. That is God's plan of salvation.

"But as many as received him, to them gave he power to become the sons of God, even to them that believe on his name" (John 1:12). Come to Christ now!

A Commentary on the Revelation
Expository, Exegetical, Devotional and Practical
Greek words from the Textus Receptus

Chapter Twelve

The Woman, the Manchild and the Dragon (1-6)

1. And there appeared a great wonder in heaven *(kai semeion mega ophthe en to ourano)* — the word *semeion* means "sign," the same word as in Matt. 16:1,3 — "sign of thy coming..." it is here translated "wonder," signifying something symbolical, mysterious and important ... **a woman** *(gune)* — She is Israel, both in the past and the future. Out of Israel Christ came (Isa. 7:14; 9:6; 66:7,8; Micah 5:2) and Israel is the target of Satan's attacks in the future Tribulation, as here described ... **clothed with the sun and the moon under her feet** — a reference to Gen. 37:9 ... **a crown of twelve stars** — 12 is a reference to the 12 tribes with Jacob (the sun) or Israel, the original progenitor of the earthly chosen people ... the moon is representative of their mothers. **2. And she being with child ... travailing in birth** — this is a flashback to the first coming in order to review and identify both Israel and the promised Messiah and to highlight His birth. **Travailing in birth** is one word in Greek, *(odinousa)*, suffering birthpangs ... Israel suffered birthpangs, awaiting the Messiah for centuries, but when He came they knew Him not. **3. Another wonder in heaven** *(allo semeion en to ourano)* ... **a great red dragon** *(drakon megas purros)* — the Greek word is found only in Revelation (13 times, 8 times in this chapter), meaning "serpent, dragon or sea monster" (Foerster), "the key image for Satan in the whole book." (See Gen. 3:14 for "serpent"). *Diabolos* (slanderer - accuser), devil, appears 38 times in the New Testament; *Satanas* (adversary) occurs 36 times. *Drakon* first is used here in all of Scripture for Satan, indicating his fierce and ravenous character ... **seven heads** and **ten horns** speak of his political influence in history (see 13:1, 17:3-7) and prophecy, for he will energize the antichrist (beast) and the final false church (great whore). **4. His tail drew the third part of the stars of heaven** — Stars here represent angels falling with Satan (compare Job 38:7).

This verse refers to the devil, demon spirits and fallen angels who participated in the rebellion, possibly between Gen. 1:1 and 2. See Ezekiel 28:14-19, where the "king of Tyrus" must be Lucifer, as "the king of Babylon" in Isaiah 14:12-14. The prophets look beyond the evil human leaders to Satan, source of their power. ... **and the dragon stood before the woman to devour her child** — this is also part of a flashback to Satan's fall and his subsequent attempt to attack Jesus through Herod in the slaughter of the infants of Bethlehem (Matt. 2:16). **5. And she brought forth a manchild** *(kai eteken huion arsen)* — literally a son, a male ... **rule all nations with a rod of iron** *(hos mellei poimainein panta ta ethne en hrabdo sidera)* — **rule** means "to tend as a shepherd," a role only the Messiah-King can fulfill with his rod: "a rod is for long-continued obstinacy until they submit themselves to obedience" (Bengel). Compare Ps. 2:9; Isa. 2:1-5; Rev. 2:27; 19:15. This ruling son, a male, can only be Christ Himself ... **and her child was caught up unto God and to his throne** — not a reference to the rapture of believers, but a plain statement of the ascension (Luke 24:50-53). Here the flashback ends and the narrative of the end-times resumes in the next verse at the midpoint of the Tribulation. **6. And the woman fled into the wilderness** — (Matt. 24:15-26) **where she hath a place prepared of God** — the rose red rock city of Petra in Jordan may be a part of this place, but no Scripture definitely so says ... the fulfillment will reveal what the place really is (see Isaiah 26:20) ... **a thousand, two hundred and three-score days** — the last half of the Seven Years of Daniel 9:27.

Satan's Expulsion by Michael from Heaven (7-12)

7. And there was war in heaven — in a sense this conflict has been going on since Satan's attempted coup d'etat, but Michael, the archangel (Jude 9) intensifies this spiritual warfare and rids even the "outskirts" of heaven of Satan's intrusions (Job 1:6,7). **8. And prevailed not** *(kai ouk ischusen)* — even as they did not prevail in the original rebellion, when sin was initiated into the Universe. **9. And the dragon was cast out** — "There are four gradations in the ever deeper downfall of Satan: (1) He is deprived of his heavenly excellency, though having still access to heaven as man's accuser; (2) He is judicially 'cast out' by Christ when He died on the Cross (John 12:31-33), thus defeating him by dying for all mankind's sins, but he is still the accuser and loose; (3) He is bound during the millennium (20:1-3); (4) After having been loosed for a while he is cast forever into the lake of fire (20:10)" (Adapted from Canon Fausset) ... **dragon** *(drakon)* — his political influence and power over civilization are connoted by this term ... **serpent** *(ophis)* — his subtlety, ulterior and destructive motives, active evil tempting tactics are indicated ... **devil** *(diabolos)* — meaning accuser, slanderer, in Greek ... **Satan** *(Satanos)* — The Hebrew word is also *satan*, which means adversary and was tranliterated into Greek ... **deceiveth the whole world** *(ho planon ten oikoumenen holen)* — he is the "god of this age" and blinds the unbelieving (2 Cor. 4:3,4; I Jn. 5:19). **10. And I heard a loud voice** *(phone megale)* — amplified as through a megaphone ... **Now is come salvation** *(soteria)* — meaning here deliverance from the continual accusations of Satan ... **strength** *(dunamis)* — from which we get dynamic, dynamite, dynamo and other words. The verb form is in Phil. 4:13, where Christ strengthens *(dynamizes)* us ... **kingdom** *(basilea)* — hence the word basilica, where a king resided in ancient times ... Satan is still accusing the brethren and will be able to do so until this expulsion. **11. And they overcame** *(enikesan)* — the same word is translated "prevailed" in 5:5 concerning Christ ... **by the blood** *(idia to haima)* — by reason of the Lamb's blood ... His blood is not only sufficient for atoning for our sins, but its power abides and can be used by the believer as a weapon against Satan. His blood is never to be downgraded ... **word of their testimony** *(logon tes marturias auton)* — the root word is *martyreo*, translated "witness," "testify" and "testimony" ... ... **loved not their lives unto death** — did not love in priority their own lives more than Christ, His Word, His cause, being willing to serve Christ until death, however it might come, either by violent martyrdom or natu-

ral causes. **12. Woe to the inhabiters of the earth and of the sea** — This is the third "Woe" (11:14) and spans the last half of the Tribulation time, with Satan confined primarily to this planet, affecting all peoples including those on the islands of sea ... **great wrath** *(thumon megan)* — filled with vicious animosity and antagonism ... **a short time** *(olion kairon)* — only about 1260 days remain before his imprisonment. (20:1-3).

The Flight of the Woman (13-16)

Here the narrative resumes concerning fleeing Israel, already introduced in vs. 6. **13. And when the dragon saw that he was cast into the earth, he persecuted the woman** — the word <u>persecuted</u> here is *dioko*, sometimes translated "pursue" or "follow after" as is used in that sense in Phil. 3:12 concerning pursuing Christ's will for one's life, but here it carries the idea of pursue to persecute. **14. And to the woman were given two wings of an eagle that she might fly into the wilderness into her place** — if this is a figure of speech it speaks of swiftness in getting to safety, but if more literally, it may mean a massive aerial evacuation to the place, where God will protect and provide for them for the last half of the Seven Years, that is, the <u>time, and times, and half a time</u> (compare Daniel 12:7). **15. Water as a flood after the woman** — the word for flood is *potamos* and is usually translated "river." **16. the earth helped the woman** — whether this is figurative or possibly the opening of a dam to let waters flow to drown the fleeing Israelites, which is counteracted by some geological phenomena is a matter of conjecture.

The Remnant (17)

17. The dragon — unable to destroy the protected Israelis ... **went to make war with the remnant of her seed** — they are Jews (Israelis) and keep the commandments and **have the testimony of Jesus Christ** — they are the 144,000. **Remnant** is *loipon* here, but the idea of the godly remnant is found in both Testaments.

Supplemental Summary
A Futurist Outline of the Book of Revelation
Part Two: Chapters 12-22

The first part of this outline is found at the conclusion of Chapter 9 concluding with the Seventh Trumpet, which introduces and incorporates the rest of the Book of Revelation.

I. THE SEVEN PERSONALITIES: Here are key figures in the latter half of the Tribulation, the last 1,260 days.
A. FIRST PERSONALITY: The Woman, Israel in History and Prophecy (12:1)
B. SECOND PERSONALITY: The Manchild Who Is To Rule, Christ (in a "flashback") (12:2,5)
C. THIRD PERSONALITY: The Dragon, Satan (12:3)
D. FOURTH PERSONALITY: Michael, the Archangel (12:17)
E. FIFTH PERSONALITY: The Remnant, 144,000 (12:17)
F. SIXTH PERSONALITY: The Beast out of the Sea, The Antichrist (13:1-10)
G. SEVENTH PERSONALITY: The Beast out of the Earth, the False Prophet (13:11-18)

II. THE SEVEN VOICES: In this chapter 7 voices are heard: by the 144,000, by 5 angels, by the Spirit; the Son of Man is seen at the close acting in judgment.
A. FIRST VOICE: The 144,000 and Their Song 14:1-5
B. SECOND VOICE: An Angel Proclaiming the Everlasting Gospel 14:6,7
C. THIRD VOICE: An Angel Announcing the Fall of Babylon 14:8
D. FOURTH VOICE: An Angel Pronouncing Judgment on the Beast Worsippers 14:9-12
E. FIFTH VOICE: The Holy Spirit Assuring the Blessedness of the Martyrs 14:13
F. SIXTH VOICE: An Angel Calls for Christ to Thrust in His Sharp Sickle 14:14-16
G. SEVENTH VOICE: Another Angel Instructs an Additional Angel to Use His Sickle 14:17-20

III. THE SEVEN VIALS: These are the seven last plagues coming on earth in the closing stages of the Great Tribulation.
INTRODUCTION — Seven angels given the seven vials (bowls), filled up with the wrath of God 15:1-8
A. FIRST VIAL: Disease 16:2
B. SECOND VIAL: Seas to Blood 16:3
C. THIRD VIAL: Rivers and Streams to Blood 16:4-7
D. FOURTH VIAL: Solar Light Intensified 16:8,9
E. FIFTH VIAL: Darkness over Antichrist's Domain 16:10,11
F. SIXTH VIAL: River Euphrates Dries up; Kings of East to come to ARMAGEDDON 16:12-16
G. SEVENTH VIAL: Babylon Falls (Rome? Rebuilt Babylon? Western Civilization?) 16:17-21
    INTERLUDE — Babylon Presented 17:1-18; 18:1-24
Woman is the city ruling the earth, and her philosophy and religion.
The Beast is the person and dominion of the last world ruler.
It is important to distinguish between religious/political and commercial Babylon.

IV. THE SEVEN TRIUMPHS: No less than seven glorious triumphant victories are described in the last 4 chapters.
A. FIRST TRIUMPH: The Church Triumphant 19:1-10
B. SECOND TRIUMPH: The King of Kings Triumphant 19:11-21
C. THIRD TRIUMPH: Triumphant Imprisonment of Satan 20:1-3
D. FOURTH TRIUMPH: Triumphant Victory over Death 20:4-6
E. FIFTH TRIUMPH: Triumphant Dominion over Earth 20:6
F. SIXTH TRIUMPH: Triumphant Victory over Last Rebellion and Sin 20:7-10
G. SEVENTH TRIUMPH: Triumphant Eternal Kingdom of God 21:1-27; 22:1-6

CONCLUSION — The final message from Jesus Christ to His people, the world, 22:7-21.

RAINBOWS FROM REVELATION
The Revelation of Jesus Christ

A chapter by chapter, verse by verse study

"There was a rainbow round about the throne like unto an emerald" (4:3)

CHAPTER THIRTEEN: The Two Beasts

References

Dan. 7:2,7,8
Rev. 12:3
Rev. 17:3

Dan. 7:6
Rev. 12:9

Rev. 13:12,14
Rev. 17:8
2 Thes. 2:3

Ex. 15: 11
Isa. 46:5

Dan. 7:20,24,25

John 1:14
Col. 2:9
1 John 2: 18

Dan. 7:21-23

Dan. 12:1
1 Pet. 1:19,20

Rev. 2:7

1. AND I stood upon the sand of the sea, and saw a beast rise up out of the sea, having seven heads and ten horns, and upon his horns ten crowns, and upon his heads the name of blasphemy.

2. And the beast which I saw was like unto a leopard, and his feet were as the feet of a bear, and his mouth as the mouth of a lion: and the dragon gave him his power, and his seat, and great authority.

3. And I saw one of his heads as it were wounded to death; and his deadly wound was healed: and all the world wondered after the beast.

4. And they worshiped the dragon which gave power unto the beast: and they worshiped the beast, saying, Who is like unto the beast? who is able to make war with him?

5. And there was given unto him a mouth speaking great things and blasphemies; and power was given unto him to continue forty and two months.

6. And he opened his mouth in blasphemy against God, to blaspheme his name, and his tabernacle, and them that dwell in heaven.

7. And it was given unto him to make war with the saints, and to overcome them: and power was given him over the kindreds, and tongues, and nations.

8. And all that dwell upon the earth shall worship him, whose names are not written in the book of life of the Lamb slain from the foundation of the world.

9. If any man have an ear, let him hear.

10. He that leadeth into captivity shall go into captivity: he that killeth with the sword must be killed with the sword. Here is the patience and the faith of the saints.

11. And I beheld another beast coming up out of the earth; and he had two horns like a lamb, and he spake as a dragon.

12. And he exerciseth all the power of the first beast before him, and causeth the earth and them which dwell therein to worship the first beast, whose deadly wound was healed.

13. And he doeth great wonders, so that he maketh fire come down from heaven on the earth in the sight of men,

14. And deceiveth them that dwell on the earth by the means of those miracles which he had power to do in the sight of the bast; saying to them that dwell on the earth, that they should make an image to the beast, which had the wound by a sword, and did live.

15. And he had power to give life unto the image of the beast, that the image of the beast should both speak, and cause that as many as would not worship the image of the beast should be killed.

16. And he causeth all, both small and great, rich and poor, free and bond, to receive a mark in their right hand, or in their foreheads:

17. And that no man might buy or sell, save he that had the mark, or the name of the beast, or the number of his name.

18. Here is wisdom. Let him that hath understanding count the number of the beast: for it is the number of a man; and his number is Six hundred threescore and six.

References
Isa. 33:1
Jer.15:2; 43:11
Mt. 26:52
Heb. 6:12
Rev. 14:12

Rev. 12:4

Rev. 13:3,4

1 Kings 18:38
2 Kings 1:10
2 Thes. 2:9

2 Kings 20:7

Rev. 20:4

Gal. 6:17
Rev. 7:3

Rev. 14:9-11

1 Cor. 2:14
Rev. 15:2

Scriptures for Comparison

Daniel 7:7-8

After this I saw in the night visions, and behold a fourth beast, dreadful and terrible, and strong exceedingly; and it had great iron teeth: it devoured and brake in pieces, and stamped the residue with the feet of it: and it was diverse from all the beasts that were before it; and it had ten horns.

I considered the horns, and, behold, there came up among them another little horn, before whom there were three of the first horns plucked up by the roots: and, behold, in this horn were eyes like the eyes of man, and a mouth speaking great things.

Summary of Chapter Thirteen

The Beast and the False Prophet

I. The First Beast, Politically Viewed (1-10)

Still at the midpoint of the future seven years of tribulation, this chapter describes the beast-king, elsewhere designated as the "antichrist" (1 John 2:28, 3:3), the man of sin and son of perdition (2 Thessalonians 2:3-10), the little horn-king (Daniel 7:8, 25), the prince that shall come (Daniel 9:26, 27) and "the abomination of desolation" (Matthew 15:25).

The figurative description of him as "the beast" includes the culmination of Western Civilization which he will dominate in the spirit of the powerful kings of Babylon, Medo-Persia, Greece and Rome. In effect the first three verses seem to fuse the final world government with the final world ruler in one "beast."

A comparison of Daniel 7 is essential to the understanding of these verses. This final "one world" government will be the ultimate development of Western Civilization, incorporating characteristics of world empires over the last 2,500 years, as prophesied in Daniel 2 and 7.

The mouth like a lion (2) reminds us of the winged lion of Daniel 7:4 that symbolized Babylon, at the time (600 B.C.) the greatest empire in ancient history.

The feet of a bear suggests the Medo-Persian Empire of Cyrus and Darius (Daniel 7:5), the largest ancient empire up to that time (536 B.C. - 300 B.C.).

The leopard appearance speaks of the Greek civilization and empire of Alexander the Great, which powerfully affected Western Civilization with its language, culture, ideas, and philosophy, all of which continue today.

The beast himself is equivalent to the beast of Daniel 7:7, which represented the Roman Empire which began its rapid rise to dominance about 150 B.C. and held sway through the centuries beyond the fall of Rome in 476 A.D. in the form of the Holy Roman Empire which existed from 800 A.D. until 1806 when Napoleon ended it for good. At Constantinople the Eastern Romans (Byzantines) had a "Roman Emperor" until 1453 A.D.

Greco-Roman civilization has influenced the whole world. This beast in Revelation 13 is the culmination of history with domination by this powerful leader, who embodies the ultimate in human, but Satanically inspired leadership.

The ten horns parallel the ten horns of Daniel 7:7 and represent 10 end time nations that merge to give full power to the "beast" (Chapter 17:12).

II. The First Beast, Personally Viewed (4-10)

Possibly tantamount to a revived Roman Empire, this "beast" speaks of both the dictator and his dominion.

Surviving, some think, an assassination attempt, the new world leader rapidly becomes the object of world wide support and even worship. His career reaches a peak at the midpoint of the seven years and continues for 42 months, 3 1/2 years.

III. The Second Beast Arises (11-18)

The second beast (11-14) is the false prophet (19:20), a religious leader with supernatural and perhaps scientific powers. Coming up out of the earth may intimate he has a connection with Israel, but he is the devil's messenger with horns like a Lamb in imitation of Christ, but he speaks with "dragon" power.

He directs the world's worship to the great supernaturally animated "image of the beast," the abomination of desolation, probably a statue of the antichrist in the Holy Place, which is the temple in Jerusalem (Matthew 24:15).

All people are compelled to worship the (first) beast and his image or suffer the death penalty.

In order to buy or sell in a "cashless" society, it will be necessary to have the "mark of the beast," possibly a laser imprint on the hand or forehead, visible only by a scanner.

The term 666 has been thought to mean the triple concentration on the number six, or the number of man, indicating this "superman" of the end times. It may be the actual use of the numbers as a logo. The original Greek looks like this Cxßv. In Greek, letters, like in Latin, represent numbers. The "chi," X, is the abbreviation of Christ; the "xi" looks like a serpent coiled; the "sigma" is an "s." The idea may be the serpent in a false Christ, Satan incarnate. In Greek the "chi" is 600; the "xi" is 60; the "sigma" is 6. It is pronounced "chi-xi-sigma." (Use a hard "c" as in Christ.)

Many theories have been advanced. "Let him that hath understanding count the number of the beast for it is the number of a man; and his number is six hundred, threescore and six."

Outline of Chapter Thirteen
(Continues from Chapter Twelve)

The Seven Personages (sixth and seventh)

OBJECTIVE: To reveal the power and dominion of the antichrist in the end times and encourage the saints under persecution

OUTLINE:
VI. The Wicked Antichrist (1-10)
The first beast out of the sea

A. The Description of the Beast (1, 2)

B. The Death of the One Head (3)

C. The Deception of the World (4)

D. The Dynamic from Satan (5)

E. The Denunciation of God (6)

F. The Domination of the Earth (7)

G. The Delusion of the People (8)

H. The Declaration by God (9, 10)

VII. The Worst False Prophet (11-18)
The second beast out of the earth

A. His Presence (11)

B. His Powers (13, 14, 16, 17)
Religious-political-miraculous-universal-economic-scientific-totalitarian

C. His Project—the image (14, 15)

D. His Program (14, 15)
1. False religious worship (15)
2. Total economic control (16, 17)

E. God's Pronouncement (18)
"Here is wisdom."
This mystery has not been fully solved.

The Seven Year Period

"When was it perceived that the '70th week of Daniel' related to the apocalyptic end times, according to church history? Writing about 400 A.D., Jerome, translator of the Latin Vulgate, discussed Daniel 9 in his commentary on the book.

"Citing the writings of Hippolytus (circa 225 A.D.), he remarks, 'Moreover Hyppolytus places the final week at the end of the world and divides it into the period of Elijah and the period of Antichrist, so that during the first three and a half years of the last week the knowledge of God is established. And as for the statement, 'he shall establish a compact with many for a week' (Daniel 9:27), during the other three years under the Antichrist, the sacrifice and offering shall cease. But when Christ shall come and slay the Wicked One by the breath of His mouth, desolation shall hold sway till the end' (From Jerome's Commentary on Daniel, translated by Gleason L. Archer).

"Regrettably, many of the writings of Hippolytus have been lost, but some have been found and published in volumes of the Anti-Nicene Fathers (the expositors who wrote before the Council of Nicea in 323 A.D.).

"Now who was Hippolytus? He was a disciple of Irenaeus who wrote several works between 160 and 200 A.D.

"Irenaeus was a disciple of Polycarp, who died as a martyr in 155 A.D. and was the pastor of the church at Smyrna.

"Polycarp was a disciple of John the Apostle, who wrote the book of Revelation.

"There is a possible direct line of conveyed teachings from John through to a third generation, Hippolytus.

"That the concept of the seven year tribulation and the harmonization of Daniel's and John's time period prophecies was extant in the second century is therefore indisputable.

– James O. Combs

Observations:
Spiritual lessons and applications from each verse
Chapter Thirteen

1. The sea represents peoples, nations, kindreds, tongues (17:14 and Isaiah 57:20, 21).

2. The dragon (Satan) supernaturally empowers the new world leader. Satan never sleeps.

3. Either the wounded head represents the restoration of the Roman Empire (not necessarily with that name) or the resuscitation of the antichrist after an assassination or both.

4. It is always easier to follow false religion than the truth.

5. Satan's power, like the antichrist's, is limited in time.

6. Satan loves blasphemy against God and His name. That is why it is prevalent now.

7. Those who do accept Christ in the tribulation are under persecution.

8. God knows beforehand who will truly believe and also those who names are not written in the Lamb's book of life.

9. Bible mysteries are not easily understood; some only the future will reveal.

10. Saints in all ages need patience and faith.

11. This second beast is a false religious leader; false religion has a thousand forms, but none acknowledge Christ as the only Savior. (See 1 John 4:1-6.)

12. People are by nature religious and will worship something.

13. Satan's evil supernatural power works even now on occasion.

14. Satan's false prophet is a master deceiver as are many false prophets now.

15. Motivation to worship the beast is not love, as with Christ, but the fear of death, the threat of murder. How evil indeed is this!

16. Religious and economic dominance is tied to receiving the "mark of the beast," the numbers or symbols necessary to buy and sell. Contrast 7:3.

17. Ponder the three things: (1)The mark, (2) the name, (3) the number.

18. The full meaning of 666 may not be known until the tribulation is in progress. but we know that the beast, the antichrist, is a man, supernaturally empowered, Satanically indwelt and nearly universally worshipped in the end times. His military, economic, religious and political power will be absolute.

One View on the mystic 666
"All I can say is that SIX is the number of man, and THREE is the number of manifestation. In these three sixes I see the full manifestation of what is in the heart of man-man's last effort to attain divinity and deity, to rob God of His glory and to exalt himself. But undoubtedly, when the Anti-christ actually appears and the first Beast is manifested, the meaning will be so plain that everyone who turns to God in that day will be warned thereby to have 'no fellowship with the unfruitful works of darkness,' but will cleave to the Lord more earnestly because they know the end has drawn nigh. Guesses as to the meaning of 666 have been innumerable; I shall not add another."

- H. A. Ironside

Quotations
From Other Expositors
Chapter Thirteen

The First Beast, A Political Power (1-3)

"The first beast represents the revived Roman Empire (vs. 3), the ten toes of Daniel 2, which have not been historically fulfilled. So united with Satan is this beast-like leader that what is written of Satan in 12:3 is here ascribed to the political leader (Dan. 7:8).

"This verse throws much light on Daniel 7:1-12. There the first beast was a lion (eagles' wings are added to bring out added truth), namely, Babylon; the second was a bear, that is, Medo-Persia; the third was a leopard (birds' wings and heads are included to set forth additional truths), Greece. The fourth beast is not likened to any known animal in nature; hence, it is called nondescript. Now it is clear why the fourth beast is not named, because there is no beast that combines the features of a leopard, bear, and lion. But the revived Roman Empire will incorporate the features of the preceding three empires. Ancient Rome boasted that no matter how many powers she subjugated in her conquests, she could always assimilate them into her hegemony. That political power is being emphasized here is certain from the mention of his power, and his seat (the whole earth), and great authority."

– Charles L. Feinberg

"The beast, however, is not only a real person, he is a representative person. Totalitarian states have frequently arisen in which the state and the head of the state have been closely identified. The beast, as head of state, is the state. The beast of Revelation 13 is both an emperor and an empire.

"All modern totalitarism governments— Fascist Italy, Nazi Germany, Communist Russia and China— have been modeled upon these ideas. In a complete dictatorship, the head of state is the state. When people thought of Germany under Hitler, they thought of Hitler. This trend will be consummated in the beast, who will be a truly representative person. He will not only head the revived Roman Empire, he will be the empire. He will speak for it, act for it, think for it, decide for it."

– John Phillips

The First Beast and Personal Dictator

"Future Activities of Antichrist

"1. His rise to Power. As already seen in Revelation 6:2, the Antichrist will come on the scene in the "latter times" and assume power by the stealth of diplomacy. He will not gain control by war but by the stealth of diplomacy. He will not gain control by war but by tricking the leaders of the world into the idea that he can offer peace and by gaining enough support from each of the ten kings of the earth. Eventually he will end up with control of all of them.

"2. His one-world government. This one-world government is predicted in the image of Nebuchadnezzar (Dan. 2). The ten toes of the image represent an amalgamation of the ten kings under the dominance of the Antichrist. Revelation 17:12-15 reveals that the kings of the earth will finally come to the conclusion that they are not capable of governing themselves in peace with other nations of the world; thus they 'shall give their power and strength unto the beast.' Verse 13 suggests that for the sake of the world peace they will establish a world government that they will consider the solution to the world's problems. That we have already entered into a day when man's political concept of government is one world in scope can scarcely be doubted.

"3. The Antichrist will dominate world economy. When Revelation 17:13 states that the kings of the earth 'shall give their power ... unto the beast,' this means not only their armies but also their economic power. It is inconceivable that a one-world government be established without an interrelated one-world economy.

"4. The Antichrist's religion. The religion of the Antichrist appears in several places in Scripture, primarily Daniel 11:36-39 and 2 Thessalonians 2:1-12. These passages teach that the Antichrist will exalt himself 'above all that is called God,

139

showing himself that he is God' (2 Thess. 2:4). This evil personage will be a master of deceit even in the religious realm.

"5. His covenant with Israel. Daniel 9:27 indicates that he will make a covenant with Israel for seven years which, as we have already seen, will be broken in the middle of the Tribulation when it suits his purposes.

"6. His death and resurrection. As already seen, the Antichrist will die and be resurrected. Revelation 17:8 states that 'The beast that thou sawest was, and is not; and shall ascend out of the bottomless pit, and go into perdition; and they that dwell in the earth shall wonder, whose names were not written in the book of life from the foundations of the world, when they behold the beast that was, and is not, and yet is.' This verse indicates that the Antichrist will die in the middle of the Tribulation. Since we have already seen that Satan will be cast out of heaven, aware that his time is short, he will indwell the Antichrist and duplicate the resurrection. Thus he will come up out of perdition and again contrast the supernatural work of Christ. From that point on, indwelt by Satan himself, he will have power to perform 'signs and lying wonders' (2 Thess. 2:9-12) and could potentially deceive 'even the very elect.'"

– Tim LaHaye

The Second Beast the False Prophet (11-18)

"The second beast is seen coming up out of the Earth, which probably intimates his connection with Israel, the earthly people. He poses as a prophet. He is the Devil's messenger, coming forth as an angel of light and a minister of righteousness. There are two horns, like a lamb, in imitation of the Lamb of God, but his speech savors of the fires of Hell — 'he spake like a dragon.' He directs the worship of the world to the Beast-King. He does great miracles, even calling down fire from Heaven. Finally he sets up an image of the Beast-King in the Holy Place of the Temple of God at Jerusalem, causes the image to breathe and to speak. This is the Abomination of Desolation spoken of by Daniel the Prophet and by our Lord Jesus. All people are compelled to worship the image on pain of death and to receive the mark of the beast upon their hands and foreheads. Those who refuse find themselves unable to buy or sell anything anywhere.

"The number of the beast, 666, is, of course, symbolical, being the number of incompleteness thrice repeated. It is ever short of the perfect seven, showing that however the Beast-King may try to show himself forth as God, he will fail to deceive at least the very elect. It is significant that the numerical equivalent of the name of Jesus is 888, eight being the number of resurrection and eternal triumph."

– William L. Pettingill

"Proper interpretation must regard these two Beasts of Revelation 13 as two men. They are on the scene at the same time; both have fearful energies of evil; but the second does nothing independently of the first. We read, 'he exerciseth all the authority of the first beast in his sight' (or presence). He also works wonderful 'signs' which are done 'in the sight' (presence) of the first Beast. The word means just what the same word (*enopion*) means in John 20:30, where our Lord's miracles are said to have been wrought 'in the presence' of His disciples,—emphasizing that fact!

"Practically common consent regards 'the man of sin' of 2 Thessalonians 2 as the Antichrist. But of him it is said, 'he ... opposeth and exalteth himself against all that is called God or that is worshipped; so that he sitteth in the temple of God, setting himself forth as God.' But this is the exact contrary of the actings of the second beast in Revelation 13:12,14, who 'maketh the earth and them that dwell therein to worship the first beast, whose 'death-stroke' was healed ... saying to them that dwell on the earth, that they should make an image to the beast who hath the 'stroke of the sword' and lived.' The second beast is nothing but the 'prophet' of the first Beast. Once admitted (which we shall find we must do) that the first Beast is a man, and not any kind of a system, not even the Fourth Empire as such (Revelation 13:18) and we are driven to conclude that the first Beast of Revelation 13 is 'the man of sin' of 2 Thessalonians 2 — the 'lawless one:' for he owns no one but himself. He could not be described as leading the earth to worship another, — as does the false prophet, the second beast of Revelation 13."

– William R. Newell

Is the Antichrist Alive and Well and Living on the Planet Earth?
An Expository Sermon
Chapter Thirteen

Introduction

While the last great world ruler, the Antichrist is described in many passages of Scripture to which we will allude, the 13th chapter of Revelation is the major passage, bringing everything about him into sharp focus.

God has given us decipherable clues in Daniel 2 and 7 to understanding the great Beast-King of the end times and his regime. None of what is described here has already occurred, nor have any events in history ever been really similar to this account. With high drama John stands on the sand of the sea, like Daniel of old, and beholds a mysterious beast rising forth, herein depicting both the regime and the rulership of that last supreme world ruler who will exalt himself above all that is called God and exercise dominion over the entire earth in the closing days of this age.

I. The World-wide Dominion (1-3)

As vividly set forth in the 2nd chapter of Daniel, the "times of the Gentiles" are symbolized by a gigantic metallic image in the bizarre dream of Nebuchadnezzar, as interpreted by the youthful prophet Daniel. By this term is meant the period during which the Jews are scattered among the Gentiles, the times in which the nations hold sway over the land of Canaan.

Nebuchadnezzar and Babylon are represented by the glistening head of gold (606-538 B.C.), although Babylonian regimes had risen and fallen since the ancient days of Nimrod after the Flood (Gen. 10:8-10). At this time however the pinnacle of ancient Babylonian civilization is reached.

Then followed the rule of the Medes and Persians, symbolized by the chest and arms of silver (about 538-330 B.C.) .

Greek political and cultural domination is depicted in the belly and thighs of brass with Alexander the Great as the great conqueror, spreading the language of the Greeks throughout the ancient world. His successors established Greek speaking governments, which dominated Western Civilization until the rise of Rome.

The legs of iron reveal that the Roman Empire would indeed have two legs, a Western and an Eastern. The Western Roman Empire suffered a "broken leg" in 476 A.D., when the Germanic tribes overran Rome, establishing their own kingdoms on the foundation of the earlier regime. Roman culture, Latin languages, the Roman Catholic religion continued, melding with northern European cultures until a Roman Pontiff crowned the Frankish King Charlemagne as Holy Roman Emperor in 800 A.D. Within a century and a half the Holy Roman Empire was a great Western power, lasting until 1806, when Napoleon's armies swept across Europe.

Though the Empire passed through various stages, Roman principles prevailed throughout the greater part of Europe, becoming the basis of Western Greco-Roman Civilization, as we now know it.

Out of the Western Roman Empire and its continuation as the Holy Roman Empire emerged the modern nations of Europe, which adopted the imperial idea of spreading their dominion, power and control to other parts of the world, especially over the last 500 years. North and South America, Africa and Asia were thus powerfully influenced by Greco-Roman civilization. New empires arose.

These include the Italian Empire, which involves papal power extended worldwide, as well as 19th and 20th century conquests in Africa; the French Empire of Napoleon, later expanding under the Third Republic to control vast territories in Africa, Southeast Asia, South America and the islands of the sea; the Spanish Empire, which spread Latin culture throughout the Western Hemisphere after Columbus and to the Far East as well; the Portuguese Empire which spawned Brazil in South America; the Dutch Empire, which once controlled all of Indonesia and colonies in the Western Hemisphere; the Belgian Empire which colonized the heart of Africa, the Congo; the British Empire on which in the 19th century "the sun

141

never set;" and out of England came forth America and its political, economic and cultural imperialism, reaching its peak in the 20th century; the German Empire, the continuation of the Holy Roman Empire under its Kaisers (Ceasars) and even Adolph Hitler with his Third Reich (the first was the Holy Roman Empire; the second was Germany under the Kaisers).

After the fall of Constantinople in the East came the rise of the Russian Empire under the Czars (Ceasars), who considered Moscow to be "The Third Rome," and themselves to be the successors of the Byzantine emperors. Thus I view Russia and the nations of Eastern Europe to be the ongoing development of the Eastern leg of the Great Image.

Finally, the "feet of the image" consist of iron mixed with clay and the ten toes symbolizing the last ten nations which will give their kingdom to the beast, paralleling the 10 horns both Daniel and John describe. This is yet future.

A second description follows in Daniel 7, wherein Babylon is represented by a winged lion; Medo-Persia by a bear; Greek civilization by a four winged, four headed leopard (the successors of Alexander ruled over 4 major kingdoms); the Roman Empire, then being symbolized by a nondescript beast "diverse from all the others, exceeding dreadful," with ten horns (Dan 7:19,20).

It is this last beast, epitomizing Roman Western Civilization in its final stage that reappears here in Revelation, embodying the character and heritage of all the previously described empires.

Now there is a blend here in these first verses of both the dominion itself and the dynamic and diabolical leader who will dominate the world in the end times. In Daniel's vision, the Antichrist is the "little horn," springing up among the ten horns (nations) of the end times. John, on the other hand, beholds the beast-empire and segues into a depiction of its leader, who embodies the whole regime as supreme dictator and is therefore "the beast." It is a dual designation.

II. The World Dictator (3-10)

In the end times there will come a dynamic genius, forecast in Scripture, who will be a powerful personal dictator. THE ANTICHRIST.

Paul vividly describes this future world ruler in 2 Thessalonians 2:1-12: "Now we beseech you brethren by the coming [parousia] of our Lord Jesus Christ, and by our gathering together unto him [the Rapture], that ye be not soon shaken in mind, or be troubled, neither by spirit, nor by word, nor by letter as from us, as that the day of Christ is at hand [that the day of the Lord has arrived and is now present, that is, that the Great Tribulation was already in progress].

"Let no man deceive you by any means: for that day [the day of the Lord or the Great Tribulation] shall not come except there come a falling away [apostasia-thought to be a great departure or apostasy from the faith in the last days] first, and that man of sin be revealed, the son of perdition; who opposeth and exalteth himself above all that is called God, or that is worshipped; so that he as God sitteth in the temple of God [at Jerusalem], showing himself that he is God. [While he first appears as the rider on the white horse (6:1,2), he is seen in his true and evil character at the midpoint of the future 7 years, when he invades Jerusalem, 11:7].

"Remember ye not, that when I was yet with you, I told you these things?

"And ye know what withholdeth [katechon-restrains] that he might be revealed in his [appointed] time.

"For the mystery of iniquity [Satan's hidden principle of rebellion against God and proper authority] doth already work: only he who now letteth [katechon-restrains] for the present will let [restrain], until he be taken out of the way [the Holy Spirit is the hindering, restraining influence in the world, indwelling true believers, but He will cease this restraint after the Rapture].

"And then shall that Wicked [One] be revealed, whom the Lord shall consume with the spirit of his mouth, and shall destroy with the brightness of his coming [the epiphany of his parousia]: even him whose coming is after the working of Satan with all power and signs and lying wonders, and with all deceivableness of unrighteousness in them that perish; because they received not the truth, that they might be saved.

"And for this cause God shall send them strong delusion, that they should believe a Lie: that they all might be damned who believed not the truth, but had pleasure in unrighteousness."

He will "have a mouth speaking great things" (5), as we read also in Daniel 7:20: "and a mouth that spake very great things, whose look was more stout than his fellows."

He will "continue for forty and two months (5), as likewise Daniel declares: "and they shall be given into his hand until a time and times and the dividing of time" (7:25).

He will "make war with the saints" (7), those who are saved during the Tribulation, Jews and Gentiles, as also Daniel declares (7:21): "I beheld, and the same horn made war with the saints, and prevailed against them."

Throughout the last 3 ½ years of this final period, the whole world will worship this Antichrist, as he has power not only over "the Revived Roman Empire", but "over all kindreds, and tongues, and nations" (7).

III. The World Religion (11-15)

Ahead is an all-inclusive one world universal religion, absorbing the other religions into a great convergence, which will eventually focus on the great image of the beast to be erected in Jerusalem in the temple area, where the Jewish Temple will be rebuilt and the Islamic Dome of the Rock has been for thirteen centuries....in the city where Christ died and rose again. This image is the "abomination of desolation, spoken of by the prophet Daniel (Matthew 24:15) standing in the holy place," as Jesus prophesied.

Spearheading this abominable false and Satanic religion will be the "second beast" or the "false prophet," colleague and co-ruler with the Antichrist.

Central to this final religion is the animated, perhaps supernaturally activated, statue of the Antichrist in Jerusalem right in that sacred mount recognized by Jews, Muslims and Christians as the place where God has manifested his power.

No wonder it is the abomination that maketh desolate!

IV. The World Economic System (16-18)

There is coming a controlled world economy, so rigid that none can buy or sell without the right numbers, logos, computer symbols or "the mark of the beast "

Writes Grant Jeffrey: "An enormous and sophisticated computer system in Europe will provide the initial consolidated financial integration of the economic systems of the advanced nations. Already an 18 digit number has been assigned to virtually every citizen of the western world. Your number includes your year of birth, sex, your current social insurance number, and a code identifying the street you live on. The cities and towns of the entire western world have been assigned digital codes for this purpose (based on satellite photo reconnaissance). The technology already exists. However none of this is the Mark of the Beast system. These are just signs of how close we are to the Great Tribulation. The 666 system will not be introduced until the Antichrist is killed and resurrected at the mid-point of the seven year treaty period. The Christians will be raptured by Christ before the introduction of this diabolical Mark of the Beast system by the False Prophet."

Highly sophisticated computerized commercial and business transactions, directly dependent on microchips, point in the direction of a cashless society, where no one could buy or sell without the right access code or the correct computer read symbols on merchandise. Automatic deposits and instant automatic debiting of bank accounts reveal how all of this could be accomplished in the end times. "Here is wisdom. Let him that hath understanding count the number of the beast: for it is the number of a man; and his number is Six hundred three score and six." (18).

While many theories have been advanced to explain this cryptic truth, two things are certain. The Antichrist, the Beast-King is a human being, although energized by Satan, and when he is revealed, he will be associated with 666, using these numbers (they are the Greek letters CHI, XI and SIGMA in the Greek method of assigning each number a letter of the alphabet, since there were no Arabic numerals in existence for use when this was written).

Conclusion

Many wild and fanciful attempts to identify the Antichrist have been circulated throughout the history of Christianity. All such speculation is in vain. Though he might indeed be alive and well and living now on the planet earth, HE WILL NOT BE REVEALED UNTIL AFTER THE RAPTURE.

Let us therefore not look for the Antichrist, but rather look for Jesus Christ, who will deliver us from the wrath to come.

A Commentary on the Revelation
Expository, Exegetical, Devotional and Practical
Greek words from the Textus Receptus

Chapter Thirteen

The First Beast Out of The Sea (1-10)

1. And I stood upon the sand of the sea (*kai estathe epi ten ammon tes thalasses*) — John in a similar manner as Daniel (7:2) beholds the sea of humanity (Isa. 57:20,21) out of which arises the beast (*therion anabainon*). Notice again this wild beast is Greek *therion*, not *zoa* as the living creatures in Rev. 4 and 5. Daniel saw the great world powers seeking their own glory and not God's. Nebuchadnezzar became like a beast (Dan. 4) because of his self-deifying pride, for he forgot that "the Most High ruleth in the kingdom of men." The four successive beasts of Daniel 7 depicted Babylon, Medo-Persia, Greece and Rome; here the beast is a restored "Roman Empire," though it will probably not be so called, but is politically the final culmination of Greco-Roman civilization spread over the world and under a ruler so powerful that he could say as some powerful kings of the past, "I am the state." **Seven heads and ten horns** (*kephalas hepta ... kerata deka*) — The dragon in 12:3 is also so described, indicating the political domination of the prince of the power of the air, which is manifested in the regime of the *therion* here, which culminates in the end times, but the dragon's crowns are on his heads, whereas the beast's are on his horns. This writer believes the 7 heads are the 7 major world powers of biblical and prophetical history: Egypt, Assyria, Babylon, Medo-Persia, Greece, Rome, "the seventh," and the eighth which is one of the seven, a restored Roman-western regime. The ten are still future (Dan. 7:24; Rev. 17:10-13) and will be dominated by the antichrist or first beast here. **Names of blasphemy** (*onomata blasphemias*) — signifying the opposition against the true God the beast and his co-kings or horns will instigate. **2. beast** (*therion*) **was like unto a leopard** (*en homoion pardalei*) — alluding to Dan. 7:6, where the fast moving imperial builder Alexander the Great and his Greek successors are prophesied ... **feet as a bear** (*podes autou hos arkou*), a reference to Dan. 7:5 and the Medo-Persian realm ... **mouth as a lion** (*hos stoma leontes*) — recalling the Babylonian lion in the days of Nebudchadnezzar. Hence the beast here politically is the outgrowth and final stage of the spreading western civilization, based on the former world kingdoms of ancient times. The dragon gave him his power ... seat ... authority (*dunomin, thronon, eksousian*) — this political power under the personal power of the antichrist is all granted by Satan, the dragon (*drakon*) **3. And I saw one of his heads ... wounded to death** (*esphagmenen eis thanaton*) — obviously there is a blend of the whole regime and the personal leadership of the antichrist in "the beast" Scriptures here. Therefore differences in interpretation of the **deadly wound ... healed** exist: some say that this is the death and revival of the Roman Empire (European world domination) in the Tribulation; others say that the beast himself, the Antichrist, suffers an assassination and is resuscitated either with sophisticated technology or supernaturally. Both concepts may be correct. Old Rome was wounded unto death in the final fall of both the Eastern Roman Empire (1453 A.D.) and the Holy Roman Empire in the west (1806 A.D.), but will be restored in the end times. That is quite evident. **And all the world wondered after the beast** (*hole he geo*-whole earth) **4. they worshipped the dragon** (*prosekunesan to drakonti*)— Satan worship is spreading in the late 20th century, whereas the idea was ridiculed earlier. When the true God is rejected the heart is opened to Satan worship ... **they worshipped the beast** (*prosekunesan to therio*) — the antichrist will appear in the temple at Jerusalem, setting up "the abomination of desolation" and will claim to be God (II Thes. 2:3,4). This occurs at the midpoint of the 7 years of the total tribulation (11:7), when he invades Israel, breaking his treaty and slaying the two witnesses (Daniel 9:27). It is then that the Israelis realize that he is not a substitute messiah or their friend, but is their enemy, resulting in their fleeing into the wilderness. **Who is like unto the beast? Who is able to make war with him?** Compare Ex. 15:11, where a similar expression is used of God. Some suggest this is a parody of the name of Michael (the archangel), whose name means, "Who is like unto God?" **5. And there was given unto him a mouth speaking great things and blasphemies** — a very obvious allusion to Daniel 7:20: "And the ten horns that were in his head, and of the other which came up, before whom three fell: even of that horn that had eyes and a mouth that spake very great things, whose look was more stout than his fellows" ... and Daniel 7:25: "And the horns of this kingdom are ten kings that shall arise: and another shall rise after them; and he shall be diverse from the first, and he shall subdue three kings. And he shall speak great words against the Most High, and think to change times and laws: and they shall be given into his hand until a time, times and the dividing of time." In Daniel's vision the antichrist is "the little horn," whereas John sees him as fused with the beast political, but still separate, a dual significance. Daniel says three kings are uprooted, but they probably are replaced by three others, as the ten are still seen in chapter 17, thus suggesting that the final ten may not be the same nations. That this powerful person and his whole Roman regime reach a zenith of power and continue for 42 months or a "time, times and dividing of times" is crystal clear in both passages, thus indicating that the Great Tribulation proper is the last $3^1/_2$ years (11:2,3; 12:6; 12:14). **6. And he opened his mouth in blasphemy against God, to blaspheme his name, and his tabernacle, and them that dwell in heaven** — His blasphemous attacks, ridicule and hatred are directed toward God Himself, His name (Jesus Christ, Jehovah, Lord God, Almighty God, etc.), his tabernacle (*skenen*) dwelling place — very likely the true worship place which Israel will have established in connection with the Third Temple), and the saints dwelling (tabernacling ... *skenoutas*) in heaven. These latter are the raptured and resurrected saints, now joined by Tribulation martyrs. Some may recall the rantings of Hitler in the 20th century, but that is only a faint shadow of what the antichrist will do with far more skill and convincing logic. **7. And it was given unto him to make war with the saints and to overcome them** — these are not members of the church, who are in heaven already, but rather those who accept Christ through the preaching of the 144,000 and the two witnesses and their converts, also mentioned in 6:9; 14:12; 15:3; 16:6;17:6;18:24). The "church" is nowhere mentioned from chapter 3 to chapter 22. Many of these saints are Jewish believers who reject the antichrist — false Messiah and receive Jesus. Notice also Daniel 7:21: "I beheld and the same horn made war with the saints, and prevailed against them." ... almost the same terminology and both refer to Tribulation saints, not the church or believers of this age. In 12:17 the dragon goes

to make war against the "remnant of her seed, which keep the commandments of God and have the testimony of Jesus Christ," evidently the 144,000, who came from "the woman," who is Israel **And power was given unto him over all kindreds and tongues and nations** — (Power here is *eksousia* meaning authority, rather than power *dunamis* — dynamic energy.) His absolute dominion extends from his ten nation nucleous to the entire world, every tribe, tongue and nation, none excluded. No one ever achieved this total control in history and only the antichrist shall until he comes whose right it is to rule all nations with a rod of iron, King of Kings, Jesus Christ. **8. And all that dwell upon the earth shall worship him** — his absolute political power will be augmented by absolute religious power, merging the religions of the world under his supreme guidance, somehow gaining the worshipful allegiance and divine stature of unsaved professing Christians (left behind after the Rapture), Muslims, Hindus, Buddhists, etc. That does not mean that all other deities are totally eliminated, but that he claims to be the supreme god, showing himself in the temple that he is god (2 Thes. 2:3,4). Exceptions will be those whose names are **written in the book of life of the Lamb, slain from the foundation of the world.** God knows precisely who will accept Christ and has so recorded it. During the Tribulation some who refuse to worship the beast will be saved either during the Tribulation, or as the Jews who finally receive Jesus when they see Him (Zech. 12:10-14;13:1;13:6,7;Rev. 1:7) coming in glory and establishing His kingdom. Compare also 1 Peter 1:19,20. **9. If any man have an ear, let him hear** — Compare 2:7,11,17,29; 3:6,13,22, where the believer is to hear what the Spirit says to the churches. Here any man on earth is to hear the truth that those who are written in the Lamb's book of life will not worship the antichrist, an idea that may cause Jews and others to think before giving over to the antichrist's world-wide religion and evil worship **10. He that leadeth into captivity shall go into captivity; he that killeth with the sword must be killed with the sword**— this consoling passage is a variation of what Jesus said, when he told Peter after the apostle cut off Malchus' ear; "all they that take the sword shall perish by the sword." It is true that those who conquer and take captives will themselves be conquered and taken captives, as the Germans during the close of World War II. Those who kill by weapons are to be killed by weapons ... reaping what they have sown. This word of reassurance is written not only for the people persecuted in the Tribulation, but in a larger sense for all suffering saints of any age. **Herein is the patience and faith of the saints.** Knowing that in bearing their appointed sufferings and in being aware of ultimate divine retribution, these suffering believers could with patience and faith face the worst the devil and the antichrist can dispense. What a comfort in a time of great distress.

The Second Beast our of the Earth (11-18)

11. And I beheld another beast (*kai eidon allo therion*) this second beast is also a personality, as is the first (who is also the whole regime), but this *therion* comes from the earth and has no counterpart in O.T. prophecy. Some expositors supppose this second beast is the antichrist, rather than the first, but, since he is of a secondary character and if obviously subservient to and loyal to the first beast, this writer believes this second one is "the false prophet," who exalts the antichrist with deification … **coming up out of the earth** (*anabainon ek tes geo*) — some suppose that this means he arises from God's earthly chosen people, the Israelites, but the argument is weak. Arising not from the political "seas" of humanity, but from the culture and civilization of this earth is how this may be interpreted. Modern emphasis on "mother earth" and mystic nature religions as in the New Age movement is a common occurence in the late 1990s. He has horns like a lamb, thus is an imitation in part of the Lamb of God, even as the first beast has a deadly wound and is healed, also reminiscent of Jesus the Lamb's sufferings and resurrection. Satanic power from the dragon enables him to speak and act most remarkably, as we shall see. **12. And he exerciseth all the power** (*eksousian* — authority) **of the first beast before him…** an evil co–regent — **And causeth the earth and them that dwell therein to worship the first beast whose deadly wound was healed** — whereas the first beast is a deified political leader, the second beast is a religious and economic ruler. In Roman times before Constantine the emperor was to be revered as a god, since it was supposed people would be more loyal to a diety than to a mere human. If the antichrist is apparently resurrected, it will be much easier to attribute divinity to him. Some early Roman Christians thought Nero might be resurrected and reign again on the basis of this idea known as the Nero revivus theory. Of course, the restoration of Roman world domination on a much larger than the ancient scale may parallel all of this. **13. And he doeth great wonders** (*semeia megala*) — miraculous deeds that are signs of his claimed divine but really Satanic power. As Satanism, witchcraft, spiritism, and other bizarre phenomena prevail, where magic and miracle are presumed possible to humans, the mindset is created to accept without a real scientific analysis amazing supernatural feats … **so that he maketh fire come down from heaven in the sight of men** — thus imitating what Elijah did and doing what the disciples foolishly suggested to Jesus be done in the case of a city's rejection of the Lord. Ability to work miracles is no sign of God's approbation or direction, for Satan's emissaries, as in the case of Janes and Jambres in Moses' day, can duplicate some divine miracles. **14. And deceiveth them that dwell on the earth by means of those miracles which he had power to do in the sight of the beast; saying that they should make an image to the beast, which had the wound by a sword and did live.** — this image of the beast is to be the "abomination that maketh desolate" as in Daniel 9:27, 12:11 and Matthew 24:15, and it will stand in "the holy place," the Temple area in Jerusalem, focus of world-wide worship. **15. And he had power to give life unto the image of the beast, that the image of the beast should both speak, and cause that as many as would not worship the image of the beast** (*eikon tou theriou*) **should be killed** — hence the word icon. This will be a real statue, possibly similar to that in Daniel 3, but supernaturally (and perhaps electronically) activated to speak. **16. a mark in their right hand, or in their forehead** — this may be invisible except to a scanner, but is necessary for buying or selling, so complete is the economic control over the world's commerce. **17. mark** (*charagma*) — an insignia, logos or symbol … **name** (*onoma*) … doubtless an impressive title or designation … **number** (*arithmon*) — hence arithmatic. **18. count the number of the beast: for it is the number of a man: and his number is six hundred, threescore and six.** — theories abound on what this means, but most likely its full significance will only be revealed when the antichrist is revealed. The image in Daniel 3, probably of Nebuchadnezzar, foreshadows this future event. It measured 60 cubits high (a cubit was either 18 or 22 inches in length) and 6 cubits wide… six is man's number in his depravity, short of seven, which is the number of divine completion and perfection, often associated with God. (See 1 Samuel 17:4). In the Greek text, certain letters represent numbers, as here: six hundred (chi) sixty (xi) and six (sigma).

RAINBOWS FROM REVELATION
The Revelation of Jesus Christ
A chapter by chapter, verse by verse study
"There was a rainbow round about the throne like unto an emerald" (4:3)

CHAPTER FOURTEEN: The Seven Voices

References

Rev. 5:6
Rev. 7:3,4
Ex. 12:3
Ezek. 9:4
Rev. 22:4

Rev. 1:15
Rev. 19:6

Rev. 5:9

Mt. 19:12
2 Cor. 11:2
Eph. 5:27
Heb. 12:23
James 1:18

Ps. 32:2
Zeph. 3:13
Mal. 2:6
1 Pet. 2:22
Rev. 8:13
Rev. 13:7

Rev. 11:18
Neh. 9:6
Ps. 33:6
Ps. 95:5
Ps. 124:8

Isa. 21:9
Jer. 51:7,8
Rev. 18:2

Rev. 13:14,15

Ps. 75:8
Rev. 18:6
Rev. 16:19
Gen. 19:24
2 Thes. 1:7-9

1. AND I looked, and, lo, a Lamb stood on the mount Zion, and with him a hundred forty and four thousand, having his Father's name written in their foreheads.

2. And I heard a voice from heaven, as the voice of many waters, and as the voice of a great thunder: and I heard the voice of harpers harping with their harps:

3. And they sung as it were a new song before the throne, and before the four beasts, and the elders: and no man could hear that song but the hundred and forty and four thousand, which were redeemed from the earth.

4. These are they which were not defiled with women; for they are virgins. These are they which follow the Lamb whithersoever he goeth. These were redeemed from among men, being the first fruits unto God and to the Lamb.

5. And in their mouth was fond no guile: for they are without fault before the throne of God.

6. And I saw another angel fly in the midst of heaven, having the everlasting gospel to preach unto them that dwell on the earth, and to every nation, and kindred, and tongue, and people.

7. Saying with a loud voice, Fear God, and give glory to him; for the hour of his judgment is come: and worship him that made heaven, and earth, and the sea, and the fountains of waters.

8. And there followed another angel, saying, Babylon is fallen, is fallen, that great city, because she made all nations drink of the wine of the wrath of her fornication.

9. And the third angel followed them, saying with a loud voice, If any man worship the beast and his image, and receive his mark in his forehead, or in his hand,

10. The same shall drink of the wine of the wrath of God, which is poured out without mixture into the cup of his indignation; and he shall be tormented with fire and brimstone in the presence of the holy angels, and in the presence of the Lamb:

11. And the smoke of their torment ascendeth up for ever and ever: and they have no rest day nor night, who worship the beast and his image, and whosoever receiveth the mark of his name.

12. Here is the patience of the saints: here are they that keep the commandments of God, and the faith of Jesus.

13. And I heard a voice from heaven saying unto me, Write, Blessed are the dead which die in the Lord from henceforth: Yea, saith the Spirit, that they may rest from their labors; and their works do follow them.

14. And I looked, and behold a white cloud, and upon the cloud one sat like unto the Son of man, having on his head a golden crown, and in his hand a sharp sickle.

15. And another angel came out of the temple, crying with a loud voice to him that sat on the cloud, Thrust in thy sickle, and reap: for the time is come for thee to reap; for the harvest of the earth is ripe.

16. And he that sat on the cloud thrust in his sickle on the earth; and the earth was reaped.

17. And another angel came out of the temple which is in heaven, he also having a sharp sickle.

18. And another angel came out from the altar, which had power over fire; and cried with a loud cry to him that had the sharp sickle, saying, Thrust in thy sharp sickle, and gather the clusters of the vine of the earth; for her grapes are fully ripe.

19. And the angel thrust in his sickle into the earth, and gathered the vine of the earth, and cast it into the great winepress of the wrath of God.

20. And the winepress was trodden without the city, and blood came out of the winepress, even unto the horse bridles, by the space of a thousand and six hundred furlongs.

References

Isa. 34:8-10
Rev. 18:9,18

Rev. 13:10
Rev. 12:17

1 Cor. 15:18
Heb. 4:9,10
Isa. 57:1,2

Dan. 7:13

Joel 3:13
Mark 4:29
Jer. 51:33
Mt. 13:39-41

Rev. 16:8
Joel 3:13

Rev. 19:15

Isa. 63:3
Heb. 13:12
Rev. 19:14

Summary of Chapter Fourteen

The Six Angels of Judgment

The opening paragraph of Chapter 14 introduces us again to the 144,000 (see Chapter 7) who have the name of the Father on their foreheads. This is the "seal" mentioned in 7:3. Now they are seen in heaven, for probably they die martyr's deaths when Satan, "the dragon," makes war with the "remnant" (12:7). Their purity is proclaimed ... "they are virgins," not that they have never married, but that they are pure and holy through Christ and in spiritual character, undefiled by immorality.

"These are the firstfruits ... unto God." They are the first of the Tribulation saints, for a great multitude (chapter 7) will come to Christ even in these awful judgment times, those who have not heard the true gospel of Christ until the 144,000 and their converts proclaim it.

The succeeding verses describe the activities of the angels who give warnings and execute judgment with the Holy Spirit's message after the first three and before the final three. Notice and underline the words "voice" or "voices," "an angel," or "another angel" and "saying."

I. The First Angel

The first of the six angels announces the everlasting gospel, "Fear God and give glory to him ... for the hour of his judgment is come" (6, 7).

II. The Second Angel

The second angel (8) proclaims the doom of "Babylon," the city, system, the regime of the final times.

III. The Third Angel

The third angel (9) issues the warning of doom for those who worship the Antichrist, and his image or receive his "mark."

Then the Holy Spirit speaks (13): "Blessed are the dead which die in the Lord henceforth ..." This verse has blessed many believers of all ages, but really relates to the vast numbers of end time martyrs who refuse the mark of the beast and die for their faith.

In the closing section of the chapter (14) the Son of man (see Daniel 7:13, 14) is seen seated on a cloud, holding the sharp sickle of wrath and judgment.

IV. The Fourth Angel

"And another angel," the fourth, cries with a loud voice, "Thrust in thy sickle and reap ... for the time is come ... for the harvest of the earth is ripe." (See Matthew 13:40-43). The wicked are to be bound together for the final fiery judgment at Armageddon and at the Glorious Appearing.

V. The Fifth Angel

The fifth angel (17) emerges from the heavenly temple also carrying a sharp sickle for judgment on "the vine of the earth."

VI. The Sixth Angel

"Another angel" (18) comes from the heavenly altar with "power over fire," speaking of the fiery wrath of the end time (see 2 Thessalonians 1:7-10). This sixth angel directs the fifth angel to thrust in his sharp sickle. "The vine of the earth" is the false vine. Christ is the true vine (John 15:1). The Antichrist is "the vine of Sodom." Moses spake of this long ago in Deuteronomy 32:31-35: "Their rock is not our rock, even our enemies themselves being judges. For their vine is of the vine of Sodom and all the fields of Gomorrah: Their grapes are grapes of gall, their clusters are bitter: Their wine is the poison of serpents, and the cruel venom of asps. Is not this laid up in store with me, sealed among my treasures? Vengeance is mine, and recompense, at the time their foot shall slide: for the day of their calamity is at hand, and the things that are to come upon them shall make haste."

When this angel thrusts in his sickle the Lord Christ will tread the winepress of divine wrath (see Isaiah 63:1-6 for the day of vengeance; Joel 3:12-14 for description of Armageddon and the sickle and the winepress; and Revelation 19:15 for treading the "winepress" of judgment.)

So great will be the carnage at the final battle that the blood will flow like a river up to the horses bridles for 600 furlongs, about 200 miles outside the city of Jerusalem.

Outline of Chapter Fourteen

The Seven Voices

OBJECTIVE: To reveal Christ as the "Son of man" coming to consummate the wrath of the Lamb upon this earth at Armageddon and the Glorious Appearing.

OUTLINE:

I. The First Voice: The New Song of the 144,000 (1-5)

    Compare Chapter 7 now

A. Where They Are (1)

  1. Upon Zion (Hebrews 12:22-24)

  2. Redeemed from the earth

  3. Before the throne

B. Who is With Them (1, 3)

  1. The Lamb (1)

  2. The Father (3)

  3. The four beasts (3)

  4. The elders (3) See 5:9.

C. Who They Are (3) THE 144,000

  1. Their purity (4)

  2. Their perfection (4)

  3. Their place (5) "before the throne"

D. What They Do (4, 5)

  1. They sing the new song (3)

  2. They follow the Lamb (5)

II. The Second Voice: The Everlasting Gospel (6, 7)

    The first angel speaks

A. The Appearance of the Angel

B. The Appeal of the Angel

C. The Announcement of the Angel

III. The Third Voice: Babylon's Fall (8)

    The second angel speaks

A. The City - Babylon (17:18)

B. The System - Babylon (17:5)

C. The Sin - Babylon (18:9-19)

IV. The Fourth Voice: Beast-worshippers' Doom (9-12)

    The third angel speaks

A. The Awful Sins (9)

  1. Worshiping the beast

  2. Worshiping his image

  3. Receiving his mark

B. The Announced Sentence (10, 11)

  1. Drink of wine of wrath

  2. Torment with fire

  3. No rest day or night

C. The Alternative for Saints (12) Patience

V. The Fifth Voice: Blessedness of Dying in the Lord (13)

    This is the voice of the Holy Spirit speaking

A. Blessing and Happiness

B. Bliss and Rest

VI. The Sixth Voice: "Thrust in ... Sickle" 13-16)

    The fourth angel speaks

A. The Scene (14)

B. The Son of Man (14)

C. The Statement: Thrust in the Sickle (15)

D. The Sickle (first one)

VII. The Seventh Voice (17): "Thrust in Sickle" (second) (17-20)

    The fifth and sixth angel (the last one speaks)

A. The Angel Appears (sixth) (17)

B. The Angel with the Sickle (17)

C. The Angel (sixth) with a Command (18)

D. The Angel (fifth) Casts the "Vine of the Earth" into the Winepress (19)

E. The Winepress of Judgment (20)

    Uniformly used symbol of the apocalyptic climax at Armageddon and Second Advent.

God's Dealings in End Time Events

"In this chapter, then, we have the full outline of the dealings of God in the latter-day crisis. There are seven divisions of it. First, there is the full remnant of godly Jews associated with the Lamb on mount Zion, in sympathy with His sufferings and waiting for the kingdom. Secondly, a testimony to the Gentile nations scattered all over the world as well as to those seated on the prophetic earth. Thirdly, the fall of Babylon. Fourthly, the fearful doom, both in this world and in the next, of such as should worship the beast and his image, or receive the mark of his name. Fifthly, the blessedness from that time of those that die in the Lord. Sixthly, the discriminating process of the harvest. And seventhly, the awful infliction of vengeance on religious apostasy; the first, at least, of these two last acts of judgment being executed by the Son of man, which necessarily supposes the very close of the age; the wrath, not of God only, but of the Lamb."

– William Kelly

Observations:
Spiritual lessons and applications from each verse
Chapter Fourteen

1. What a blessing for each believer in every age to belong to the Father.

2. "Voices" reiterated three times speak of Christ's voice (1:15) and of thunderous judgment voices (11:19); and heavenly harp music (15:2).

3. Heavenly groups will include the New Testament saints, the Old Testament saints, the tribulation martyrs and the 144,000 special servants for the end times ... each separate but all part of the family of God. Are you in God's family?

4. Following the Lamb should be the aim of all even now.

5. Through Christ we, too, are without fault before the throne of God.

6. No other place in the Bible does an angel "preach" to the world. How this will occur is a matter of interesting speculation.

7. As in every age, the fear of the Lord is the beginning of wisdom.

8. The wicked world system, consummated in the future Tribulation under the Antichrist, will be vile indeed, but judgment always comes.

9. False worship exists now, but will be almost universal in the Tribulation.

10. Eternal torment is the destiny of those who follow the false worship of the Antichrist. Eternal torment is for all who reject Christ. Which shall it be? Christ or Antichrist, for you?

11. No reprieve from everlasting perdition will be granted.

12. Patience is the solace of saints in all ages, AND in these end times described.

13. The Holy Spirit always speaks comfort to the believers in every age.

14. The Son of man is not here meek and lowly, but mighty and lethal.

15. Earth's judgment for sin is certain and sure. How will you fare then?

16. Christ is the wielder of the sickle of judgment. He is the Savior now; He will be the Avenger then.

17. There are angelic forces at work in earth and in time that are invisible to our eyes.

18. Angels understand the plan and order of God; we ought to learn and obey.

19. During the end times Christ Himself will tread "the winepress of wrath," but now you can bow before Him and be saved.

20. Rejecting the blood of Christ for sin and sinners can result in going through a terrible time of man's wickedness against man, when human blood will flow like a river at Armageddon. DON'T let that be your destiny. Receive Christ today.

The Spirit's Words (13)

When the Holy Spirit says, "Blessed are they that die in the Lord from henceforth," He refers to Tribulation martyrs prophetically, but the principle in that truth applies to all believers in every age, for it is indeed "blessed" and "better" to depart and be with Christ (Phil. 1:23) than to abide on earth. "To be absent from the body" is to be "present with the Lord" (2 Cor. 5:8).

Quotations
From Other Expositors
Chapter Fourteen

The 144,000 (1-5)

"The opening paragraph of chapter 14 shows us the Lamb standing on Mount Zion and with Him 144,000 having His name and the name of His Father written on their foreheads. There seems to be no reasonable doubt that this company is the same as the 144,000 sealed Israelites seen in chapter 7. They are doubtless the Jewish remnant so often seen in the Psalms and Prophecies. There is great joy in Heaven manifested by the music heard by John, for the time is come for Israel to 'blossom and bud and fill the face of the world with fruit' (Isa. 27:6). They turn to the Lord during the time of The Great Tribulation and follow the Lamb withersoever He goeth. The vision of the Lord Jesus *on Mount Zion in Jerusalem*, the place of God's earthly rest and the place of grace for Israel, is *anticipative*, and is given just here as showing the sharp contrast between God's King upon His holy hill of Zion, and Satan's creation, the Abomination of Desolation, in the Temple of God, showing himself forth as God (2 Thess. 2:4)."

– W.L. Pettingill

"The company on Mt. Zion are next described as undefiled, a virgin band, who have kept themselves from the uncleanness everywhere prevailing in those fearful days. It is to be their hallowed privilege to follow the Lamb wherever He goes, for they are described as being redeemed from among men, being the firstfruits of the kingdom age, even as our Lord Himself is described as the firstfruits of the present dispensation, and His church, associated with Him, is 'a kind of firstfruits of His creatures.'"

– H.A. Ironside

"Here in Revelation 14, we are not told the words of the 'new song.' But we know it was of rapturous, thunderous exultation. All heaven has been looking forward eagerly to it. It is connected directly with the setting up of the glorious reign on earth: for the prophetic appearance of the Lamb on Mount Zion with the 144,000 is the signal for it. Only one other event outdoes it in the rapture it gives to heaven, and that is the marriage of the Lamb, in chapter 19. Therefore we ought to wait here; to let our hearts be filled full, as it were, with the spirit of this song and its occasion. If we are in tune with heaven, what gives heaven such ecstasy, must move us deeply!"

– William R. Newell

"It was a custom among the ancients for servants to receive the mark of their master, and soldiers of their general, and those who were devoted to any particular idol the mark of that particular idol. These marks were usually impressed on their right hands, or on their foreheads (Rev. 13 and 16), and consisted of some hieroglyphical character, or of the name expressed in vulgar letters, or in numerical characters. Gal. 5:17: 'The marks of the Lord Jesus.' What these marks were, the Apostle explains by the stripes, etc, mentioned in 2 Cor. 11:23. There is beautiful allusion to the stigmata — marks which were sometimes fixed on servants and soldiers, to show to whom they belonged. How strikingly do these two remarks illustrate the scene of Jesus the Lamb of God, the all-conquering Redeemer, standing as the great Captain of Salvation at the head of His brave army of saints on Mount Sion. 'I looked, and, lo, a Lamb stood on the Mount Sion, and with Him an hundred forty and four thousand, having His Father's name written in their foreheads.'"

– Biblical Treasury

The Everlasting Gospel (6-7)

"This angel will warn the people to fear God instead of Antichrist, to give glory to God instead of Antichrist, and he will instruct them how to do it. Otherwise, he would be proclaiming a message of doom instead of good tidings. The word Gospel means 'good tidings,' and the only way we can offer men eternal good tidings is to show them how to receive the Lord Jesus Christ by faith. A message concerning the judgment of God is only a partial presentation of the gospel of Christ. The complete story of the gospel not only clarifies that man is a sinner, but according to 1 Corinthians 15:3,4 also includes God's remedy for sin through Christ, who died for our sins 'according to the scriptures; and that he was buried, and that he rose again the third day.' This seems to be God's last offer to mankind to flee the wrath to come before they accept Antichrist. There is no evidence that this angel will be any more successful in preaching the eternal gospel than was Noah, the preacher of righteousness before the Flood. On the contrary, it seems that man will pit his will against God and succumb to the lying tongues of Satan's chief tools during that period, Antichrist and the False Prophet."

– *Tim LaHaye*

Babylon's Fall (8)

"The announcement here is prophetic as the actual fall of Babylon probably comes later if the reference is to the physical city. The destruction of the city of Babylon itself, whether a reference to Rome, as is commonly held, or to a rebuilt city of Babylon on the ancient site of historic Babylon, does not take place until the end of the Great Tribulation. Inasmuch as the context here seems to deal primarily with the end of the Great Tribulation and the beginning of the Millennial Kingdom, the reference seems to be to the literal city."

– *John F. Walvoord*

Beast-Worshippers (9-11)

"There be those who mock and jeer at the idea of an eternal hell for the wicked. Many are the jests they perpetrate at the expense of these preachers of fire and brimstone. But here a great and mighty Angel from heaven is the preacher, and his sermon from beginning to end is nothing but fire and brimstone, even everlasting burning and torment for all who take the mark of Antichrist! Shall we believe our modern sentimental philosophers, or abide by the word of our God and of his holy angels? Alas, alas, for the infatuated people who comfort themselves with the belief that perdition is a myth — the bugbear of antiquated superstition!"

–*J.A. Seiss*

Saint's Blessings (12-13)

"It is always true that those who die in the Lord are blessed; but this Scripture is for the Lord's suffering ones in the awful scenes of The Great Tribulation."

– *William L. Pettingill*

Armageddon (14-20)

"The verdict of commentators is very much divided. There are circumstances in the context which tell both ways. The parallelism with the vintage which follows, seems to favor a harvest of the wicked: but then on the other hand, if so, what is the distinction between the two ingatherings? And why do we read of the casting into the winepress of God's wrath in the second case, and of no corresponding feature in the other? Again, why is the agency so different — the Son of man on the white cloud with a golden crown in the one case, the mere angel in the other? Besides, the two gatherings seem quite distinct. The former is over before the other begins. On the whole then, though I would not pronounce decidedly, I must incline to think that the harvest is the ingathering of the saints, God's harvest, reaped from the earth: described here thus generally, before the vintage of wrath which follows."

– *Henry Alford*

"These verses describe what will take place at the Battle of Armageddon, the last great war on earth. Just as Satan, through the Antichrist and the God-defying armies of the world, is persecuting the Jews; just as each nation is seeking to destroy the others, the Lord Himself will return in glory to put an end to these wicked devices. The picture is graphically told in Rev. 19:11-1, and this we shall study in a later lesson. In the verses before us, however, the emphasis is place upon the terrible harvest of that day.

"The Lord Himself described the scene when, in Matt. 13:30, He said of the wheat and the tares: 'Let both grow together until the harvest: and in the time of harvest I will say to the reapers, Gather ye together first the tare, and bind them in bundles to burn them: but gather the wheat into my barn.'"

– *Louis T. Talbot*

God's Last Warnings for the Last Times
An Expository Sermon

Chapter Fourteen

Introduction

From the primeval days of the Garden of Eden God has issued warnings of the dire consequences of sin and evil. All through the Old Testament, godly priests and anointed prophets have called upon the wicked to turn from their iniquity.

Our Lord Jesus Christ preached repentance as a strong element in salvation: "Except ye repent, ye shall all likewise perish" (Luke 13:5).

In the closing stages of the forthcoming Great Tribulation God issues His last warnings of impending doom. Those who have not clearly heard the gospel in this age can heed that call, if they have refused to follow the Antichrist, not receiving his ultimately lethal mark.

Today God warns all sinners to repent and believe the gospel before the climactic end times at last unfold.

This rich chapter may be examined from different aspects.

Seven voices are obviously discernible: (1) the voice of the 144,000 on Mount Zion; (2) the voice of the first of six angels, announcing the "everlasting gospel;" (3) the voice of another angel proclaiming the doom of Babylon; (4) the voice of the third angel pronouncing the doom of the beast-worshippers; (5) the voice of the Holy Spirit assuring the blessedness of dying a martyr's death; (6) the voice of another (the fourth angel), speaking to the Son of Man, Jesus; (7) the voice of another (the sixth angel), addressing the fifth angel and instructing him to thrust in his sharp sickle of judgment.

But our consideration in this message focuses first on *the singing witnesses,* then examine the truth of *the saving lamb* before moving on to the *six warnings* of verses 6-21.

I. The Singing Witnesses (1-5)

Now the primary question here is simply, "Who are these 144,000 spiritual and godly persons?"

Most premillennial, literalist scholars and teachers view this illustrious company as identical to the 144,000 sealed witnesses from the twelve tribes of Israel (7:1-8), who become God's proclaimers of truth after the Rapture and whose preaching results in the salvation of the "great multitude, which no man could number, of all nations, and kindreds, and people, and tongues," the Gentile Tribulation saints (7:9-17).

Both William R. Newell, one of the most extensive commentators on the Apocalypse in the first half of the 20th century and Tim LaHaye, a best selling author of the latter part of this century, suggest that these are not Jews or Israelites at all here, since they are not so designated, but are said to "be purchased out of the earth" and are the "firstfruits unto God and the Lamb" (4).

To adopt this interpretation, it must be assumed that *Mount Zion* here is a heavenly usage of the term, not the literal center of Israel's worship during the upcoming Millennium. (Hebrews 12:22: "But ye are come unto Mount Zion, and unto the city of the Living God, the new Jerusalem …").

Newell offers the possibility that these are "especially devoted saints of all ages." Tim LaHaye in his illustrated exposition makes a strong case for the concept that these 144,000 are the outstanding, elite and best Christians of this Dispensation.

However the majority of premillennial commentators and communicators regard this distinguished crowd as identical to the listing in chapter seven.

Thus, this passage could be interpreted as anticipative of their position with Christ on the literal Mount Zion in Jerusalem, following the Glorious Appearing. Another possibility is that, since they are "the remnant" of chapter 12:17, who "keep the commandments of God, and have the testimony of Jesus Christ," and are evidently under severe attack by Satan, that they die martyr's deaths and are here seen with the Lamb in the heavenly Mount Zion. Some suggestions that they experience a "rapture" distinct from all others have no real basis in Scripture.

My view is that these are the same 144,000 Israelite believers, saved and sealed by the Spirit in the first half of the last seven years.

They are led by the Lamb of God.

They have their Father's name "written in their foreheads," which I take to mean the "seal of God," as in 7:3.

They alone can sing an anthem of glorious deliverance, accompanied by an orchestra of harps, before the throne of God and in the presence of the living creatures and the elders

They are "redeemed from the earth," a glorious truth, which must be the theme of their new song.

They are pure, "virgins," for they have not indulged in the spiritual adultery which is friendship with a wicked world system (James 4:4). Nor have they been involved in the false religion of Babylon (Rev. 17:1-5), the "mother of harlots and abominations of the earth."

They follow the Lamb wherever He goes.

They are the "firstfruits unto God and to the Lamb," the first ones who are saved out of Israel and out of the world in the Tribulation, whose lives, testimony and ministry result in the salvation of millions of Gentiles and perhaps many Jews, prior to the appearance of the Messiah at the close of these future times and the national conversion of God's earthly people (Rev. 1:7; Zechariah 13:1, 6,7).

They are without fault before the throne.

What a blessed company they are!

What a wonderful destiny they will enjoy!

II. The Saving Lamb (1, 4, 10)

No less than 28 times in the Book of Revelation is Christ called "the Lamb," his most repeated title. Since four is the number of the world and seven is the number of perfection, 28 may suggest that He is the perfect Savior for all the world.

At the outset of His earthly ministry, John the Baptist pointed to Him, saying, "Behold the Lamb of God, which taketh away the sin of the world" (John 1:29). He was, He is the Great Pascal Lamb, typified in every Passover commemoration since the deliverance from Egypt 1,500 years before His human birth. As He went to the Cross, "he was oppressed, and he was afflicted, yet he opened not his mouth: he is brought as a lamb to the slaughter, and as a sheep before his shearers is dumb, so he openeth not his mouth" (Isa. 53:7).

Today, He is still the Lamb of God who suffered in our place for our sins.

In the future and throughout eternity, He continues to be exalted as the Lamb, worthy to open the sealed book of judgments (5:6), worthy to receive the supreme acclaim of all heaven (5:12), worthy to dispense wrath upon a wicked world (6:17). Throughout eternity in the New Jerusalem, the names of all the true believers of all ages are inscribed in the Lamb's Book of Life (21:2 7).

In this chapter, verse one, the Lamb is the Leader.

In verse four the Lamb is the Redeemer.

In verse ten the Lamb is the Judge.

And you and I will someday behold and hear "the voice of many angels round about the throne and the beasts and the elders: and the number of them was ten thousand times ten thousand, and thousands of thousands: saying with a loud voice:

"Worthy is the Lamb that was slain to receive power, and riches, and wisdom, and strength, and honor, and glory and blessing!"

"And every creature, which is in heaven, and on the earth, and under the earth, and such as are in the sea, and all that are in them, heard I saying, Blessing, and honour, and glory, and power, be unto him that sitteth upon the throne and unto the Lamb forever and ever!" (5:14).

III. The Six Warnings (6-21)

These six alarming warnings (seven, if you count 15:1, which announces the final seven impending vials of wrath), precede the closing days of the future tribulation and the consummation of the age (aion).

First, there appears in mid-heaven an angel, "having the everlasting gospel to preach unto them that dwell on the earth, and to every nation, and kindred, and tongue and people" (6).

Just how this angel will communicate the message to every person is not clear, but a major element of his message is to "Fear God and give glory to him: for the hour of his judgment is come ..." Basically, there is only one gospel, although it is presented in varying biblical forms, all drawn from the central truth of the death, burial and resurrection of Christ, who died for our sins.

This appears to be a last chance invitation to get right with God, but there is little evidence that his message will be heeded to any great degree, any more than the proclamation of the gospel is now.

Second comes the warning about the final fall of Babylon (8), to be more explicitly described in chapter 18. Not only the termination of the Antichrist's religious, political and economic system in view, in my judgment, but also the collapse of all ungodly civilization. Evidently, since the first of three angels flies through the heaven, so also does this angel, crying, "Babylon is fallen, is fallen!"

When the **third** angel follows the others in flight, he utters a solemn and awful **warning** about the beast-worshippers, saying with a loud voice, "If any man worship the beast and his image and receive his mark in his forehead, or in his hand, the same shall drink of the wine of the wrath of God, which is poured out without mixture into the cup of his indignation; and he shall be tormented with fire and brimstone in the presence of the holy angels and in the presence of the Lamb" (9, 10).

What a terrible alternative will be presented to men in those days of horror! A choice must be made between worshipping the Devil and the Antichrist on the one hand and worshipping God and His Christ on the other. In order to buy and sell, the mark of the beast or the number of his name will be required, but to accept the mark is to seal one's own eternal doom.

The **fourth** warning is a promise. It is the Holy Spirit next who utters His voice audibly, instructing John to record this assurance: "Blessed are the dead which die in the Lord henceforth" (13), for they will "rest from their labors and their works do follow them."

While these words have been an immeasurable blessing to believers of this entire age, it specifically applies to those Tribulation martyrs, who refuse the mark of the beast, remain loyal to Christ and die for His sake. How blessed indeed they will be, for they share in the First Resurrection and the sovereign reign of King Jesus on this Earth (Rev. 20:6)! This is a warning for believers.

The **fifth** warning deals with the final harvest of this earth, wrought with the sharp sickle of judgment held by the Son of Man (1-20).

Seen here seated upon a cloud, wearing the golden crown of His authority, He seems poised to lower the sickle, so to speak, to the earth, to separate the wheat from tares. In Matthew 13 we read, "The harvest is the end of the world (age-*aion*). The Son of Man shall send forth His angels, and they shall gather out of His Kingdom all things that cause stumbling, and them that do iniquity, and shall cast them into the furnace of fire; there shall be weeping and gnashing of teeth. Then shall the righteous shine forth as the sun in the kingdom of their Father. He that hath ears, let him hear." This is a detailed description of how the Lord will proceed to assemble for the final harvest

of judgment the wicked of this world.

Another angel with a loud voice announced that it is time to cut a swath of judgment with His sickle (15, 16). The reaping process occurs.

Two more angels appear (the fifth and sixth), the first with another sharp sickle of judgment, the second to utter the command to thrust in his sickle, that the clusters of the "vine of the earth" may be gathered. Since Christ is the true vine (John 15:5), Antichrist may be "the vine of the earth," ready now to be drawn to Armageddon in Israel for the final holocaust. These angelic pronouncements constitute **the sixth warning,** for the wrath of God now will reach its most intense level in the concluding judgments on this earth. All of this follows the Old Testament symbolism of the winepress. As grapes in the winepress were trodden by the feet of the workers, so God will tread down and crush like grapes His enemies.

Gathered in vast armies from around the world (16:16), the forces of the last Beast-King, the Antichrist, challenged perhaps by the "kings of the East," will finally invade Israel and besiege Jerusalem, only to met and conquered by the triumphant armies out of heaven, led by the King of Kings, who vanquishes all the forces of evil by His Glorious Appearing. As we continue through this book, the details will be unfolded.

Conclusion

While these things relate to the future, the principles are timeless. God issues His warnings to turn from sin now. Heed that warning today.

Accept Christ right now before He comes to rapture His people and to resurrect the dead in Christ, otherwise you may be left to go through the horrendous judgments ahead and still, since you have heard the gospel, follow the lie of the Antichrist and then suffer the eternal and irremediable consequences.

It will be too late, when these come to pass, if you have heard the gospel and refused it.

Now is the time to come to Christ. Now. "Believe on the Lord Jesus Christ and thou shalt be saved."

A Commentary on the Revelation
Expository, Exegetical, Devotional and Practical
Greek words from the Textus Receptus

Chapter Fourteen

The 144,000 on Mount Zion (1-5)

1. And I looked and lo, a Lamb stood on the mount Zion (*Kai eidon, kai idou to arnion hestos epi to horos Sion*). Again John views a contrasting scene to the multitudes paying obeisance to the image of the beast, with the 144,000 seen on Mount Zion. While some commentators interpret this crowd as distinct from the Israelite witnesses in chapter seven, most see them as identical. Either they are seen prospectively and prophetically as actually on the literal Mount Zion at the outset of the millennium, following Christ's return, or here the heavenly Mount Zion is meant (Hebrews 12:22) and they are now beyond earth, having died martyr's deaths as the suffering remnant (Rev. 12:17). Since they are "before the throne of God" (3,5), the latter seems more logical. They are with the Lamb, awaiting the completion of the First Resurrection and the Glorious Return ... an **hundred and forty four thousand** — it would seem unusual for the Spirit to use these numbers for two distinct crowds ... **having his father's name written in their foreheads** appears to be related to the sealing of 7:3. **2. And I heard a voice from heaven, as the voice of many waters, and as the voice of mighty thunder: and I heard the voice of harpers harping with their harps** (*hos kitharodon kitharizonton*) — notice that voice (*phone*) occurs four times. Here is an endorsement of instrumental music in this Dispensation and beyond, for harps or stringed instruments will be a part of heaven's symphonic chords (See Ps. 87:5-7 and Rev. 15:2). **3. And they sung as it were a new song before the throne, and before the four beasts, and the elders: and no man could learn that song but the one hundred and forty and four thousand, which were redeemed from the earth.** "Not even the angels can learn that song, for they know not experientially what it is to have come out of 'great tribulation' and to make their robes white in the blood of the Lamb." A special exclusivity pertains to this elite company of blood–washed believers, especially selected and commissioned to spread the gospel in the Tribulation period in the face of the greatest persecution yet experienced. Redemption must be the theme, but not even the "ransomed church of God" will voice the words of this special anthem of praise, this new song, accompanied by a heavenly orchestra ... but only the 144,000. **4. They are virgins** (*parthemoi gar eisen*) — meaning they are pure of heart, godly, unsullied by immorality. Likewise, they have not consorted with the harlots of religion or bowed to worship the beast (compare Daniel 3:1-18; Rev. 13:12, 15-18) ... **they follow the Lamb** — they are in His close proximity, a fitting reward for those who followed so dedicatedly on earth ... **redeemed** (*egorasthesan*) — purchased by the blood of Christ ... **firstfruits unto God and to the Lamb** — the first Tribulation saints appear here. **5. And in their mouth was found no guile: for they are without fault** ... the purity and piety in their spiritual character is evidenced by their speech, their words. While it is only through Christ that redeemed persons can be "without fault," these future Israelite "remnant" saints set a shining example for all to pursue.

The Everlasting Gospel (6,7)

6. And I saw another angel fly in the midst of heaven, having the everlasting gospel to preach unto them that dwell on the earth, and to every nation, and kindred, and tongue and people. Scofield and others suggest that first there was The Gospel of the Kingdom. This is the good news that God purposes to set up a kingdom on earth in fulfillment of the Davidic Covenant (2 Sam. 7:16) ... Second, The Gospel of the Grace of God, centered in Christ's death and resurrection, became the main message (1 Cor. 15:1-4). A further aspect, the Everlasting Gospel, is proclaimed by an angel. Evidently, judgment is part of the message. Just how this angel communicates to the entire world this message is simply not clear; therefore its full understanding may await its actual fulfillment. **7. Saying with a loud voice** (*phone megale*), **Fear God, and give glory to him; for the hour of his judgment is come: and the sea, and the fountains of waters.** When Christ first came, he sent forth His disciples to join Him in preaching the gospel of the Kingdom, that the King had arrived and would eventually establish a spiritual and material kingdom. Israel rejected that good news, but in the divine plan of God the gospel assumed a different form, namely the message of individual salvation through faith in the crucified and risen Savior. The believers of this age and the church are charged with sharing this message worldwide. After the Rapture, God will raise up the 144,000 to proclaim Christ's saving Gospel, also incorporating a renewal of the kingdom message for Israel and the world. They will be joined by a great multitude of Gentiles as in 7:9,14. But most of the world will follow not God, but Satan; not Christ, but Antichrist; not worshipping God, but the image of the beast. Here is the final warning, the final opportunity, the final presentation this time by an angel of the true message of Christ. As in all other ages, the response is meager, as mankind plunges deeper into sin. Nevertheless, the message is somehow given.

Doom of the Wicked (8-11)

8. And there followed another angel *(kai allos angelos deuteros ekolouthesen)* — While the first angel proclaims the everlasting gospel, this second announces the fall of wicked Babylon, which I take to mean the final capitol city (be it Rome or a rebuilt literal Babylon) of the Antichrist, the religious apostate system, the political-economic empire of the end times and the consummation of a wicked world-system ... **Babylon is fallen, is fallen, that great city, because she made all nations drink of the wine of the wrath of her fornication** — in particular view here is the religious aspect, however, since 17:2 uses similar expressions. **9. And the third angel followed them** — this pronouncement of doom encompasses all of the beast-worshippers. It appears the first angel offers salvation; the second condemns false religion; the third dooms the followers of Antichrist ... **if any man worship the beast and his image, and receive this mark in his forehead, or in his hand** ... doubtless through sophisticated end time technology, total visibility of all Antichrist's's activities will be telecast worldwide; programs at the image of the beast shrine in the temple area will be likewise seen everywhere; an imprinted mark, possibly invisible except for a scanner, will be required to engage in commerce or buy anything, thus indicating total economic controls. Believers of this age have no reason to be apprehensive about "the mark," as all of this deals with Tribulation times of wrath, from which New Testament saints are delivered. Saints have a "seal," while the wicked have a "mark." What a contrast,

but Satan, the imitator is at work. **10. The same shall drink of the wine of the wrath of God, which is poured out without mixture into the cup of his indignation** *(kai autos pietai ek tou oinou tou thurou tou theou tou kekerasmenou akratou)* — Jesus took "the cup" in the Garden of Gethsemane containing, as it were, the sins of the world. Those who finally refuse must drink themselves of the wine of God's wrath ... **and he shall be tormented with fire and brimstone in the presence of the holy angels, and in the presence of the Lamb** *(kai basanisthesetai en puri kai theio enopion angelon hagion kai enopion tou arniou)* — the solemn and sad destiny of the lost with no reprieve, no cessation of eternal torment as here described, applies not only to the followers of Antichrist, but to the rejecters of Christ of all ages. For eternity, while the passage does not say the saints will see them, both the Lamb and the holy angels are eternally witnesses of their doom. **11. And the smoke of their torment** *(kai hokapnos tou basanismou auton)* — like sulfuric fog ... **ascendeth up** *(anabainei)* — present tense, continuing in an eternal present, never ending ... **forever and ever** *(eis aionas aionon)* — into the ages of the ages, aeons of aeons, an expression for the everlasting in Greek ... **and they have no rest day nor night** *(kai ouk echousin anapausin hemeras kai nuktos)* — evidently the heinous final rejection of Christ by the Satanically deluded followers of Antichrist is so wicked, that these descriptive terms are used particularly for them, but in general for all ... **who worship the beast and his image and whosoever receiveth the mark of his name** — no possibility of salvation exists in the Tribulation time for those who thus manifest their spiritual allegiance to this archenemy of God, the dragon, that old serpent, the Devil, who doles out devilish powers to the two earthly Beasts of Revelation 13. All idolaters shall have their part in the lake of fire and brimstone as well (21:8; 16:2; 13:16,17).

Blessedness of the Believers (12-13)

12. Here is the patience of the saints: here are they that keep the commandments of God, and the faith of Jesus Christ — The Tribulation martyrs and saints may be comforted by the fact of final victory and the abolition of the wicked in the lake of fire forever. In contrast to the worshippers of the beast and their destiny are the saints who keep the commandments of God and the faith of Jesus Christ. In the next verse the blessedness of those who die in the Lord is assured by the Holy Spirit. The wicked are thus doomed and the godly are blessed. These saints will be rewarded at their resurrection and share in the reign of Christ during the millennium (20:4). **13. And I heard a voice from heaven saying unto me** — the only time in which the Holy Spirit specifically speaks in this Book, although in 22:17, the Spirit with and through the bride, says, "Come" … **write** (graphon) **Blessed** (makarioui) **are the dead** (hoi nekroi) **which die in the Lord from henceforth** — there is a special happiness or blessedness in dying as a martyr, as these Tribulation saints in view shall do. Such receive a crown of life (2:10), as all other martyrs shall at the judgment. Especially does this passage apply to the many believing Gentiles and perhaps also many Jews, who accept Christ after the Rapture and must suffer under the beast. In a larger sense, all who "die in the Lord" are blessed, since to "die is gain" and "to depart and be with Christ is far better," as Paul says (Phil. 1:21-24) … Yea, **saith the Spirit, that they may rest from their labors and their works do follow them** — rest and rewards are blessings indeed.

The Angels and Armageddon (14-20)

14. And I looked and behold a white cloud (kai eidon kai idou nephele leuke) — similar to the cloud which overshadowed Christ at His Transfiguration (Matt. 17) and the cloud which received Him at His ascension (Acts 1:11) and those with which He will return in glory (Rev. 1:7) … **and upon the cloud one sat like unto the Son of man** (homoion huion anthropou) **having on his head a golden crown** — this is Christ the King, who is similarly seen in Daniel 7:13,14: … **and in his hand is a sharp sickle** — having received the authority the Son of man now exercises it, supervising the end time judgments that will issue in His supreme and sovereign reign. Ideas differ as to the "sickle" here, some thinking that He is seen reaping the harvest of the saved, but my opinion is that this is a sickle of judgment, that by this symbolic act, He will reap, as it were, the harvest of the wicked to be put in bundles to be burned (Matthew 13:30, 40, 41, 49, 50), a process involving these final judgments and the battle of Armageddon. **15. And another angel** — the first of 3 more angels all involved in judgment … **came out of the temple (in heaven), crying with a loud voice to him that sat on the cloud, Thrust in thy sickle and reap: for the time is come for thee to reap; for the harvest of the earth is fully ripe** — says Joseph Seiss: "There is nowhere a description or holding forth of the instruments in any harvest

scene referring to the gracious homegoing of the good. The earth is to be cleared of its ill products now, therefore only a cutting implement is in hand, and so conspicuously displayed. The work is one of vengeance and sore judgment, therefore it is sharp!" **16. And he that sat on the cloud thrust in his sharp sickle on the earth and the earth was reaped** — details of this heavenly enactment will be reflected in the subsequent events on the earth, moving through the vial judgments, the fall of Babylon, the battle of Armageddon and the arrival of the Conquering King (Rev. 19). Again observe the sharpness, the thrusting in of the cutting implement, hardly a description of gathering in the saints. **17. And another angel came out of the temple which is in heaven** — the second of the series of three angels, participating in Christ's administration of these closing events (Matt. 13:41-43) … **he also having a sharp sickle** — an emblem of cutting down, so to speak, the evil forces of earth, especially then the Antichrist and his followers. **18. And another angel** (a third) **came out from the altar, which had power over fire** — compare here Rev. 8:5; "and the angel took the censer, and filled it with fire of the altar and cast it into the earth." Evidently the altar here is the heavenly altar of incense where prayers are heard and offered; therefore this angel's action is in response to the prayers of persecuted saints … **and cried with a loud cry to him that had the sharp sickle, Thrust in thy sharp sickle, and gather the clusters of the vine of the earth: for her grapes are fully ripe** — some think that the "vine of the earth" is Antichrist, since Christ is the "true vine" (John 15:5). In any event this a picture of the wicked under his control. **19. And the angel** (the second one) **thrust in his sickle into the earth, and gathered the vine of the earth, and cast it into the winepress of the wrath of God** — picturesque description of divine and angelic action concluding with the battle of Armageddon (Rev. 16:16). **20. And the winepress was trodden without the city** (Jerusalem)**, and blood came out of the winepress, even unto the horse bridles, by the space of a thousand and six hundred furlongs** — as all nations gather for the final battle (Zechariah 14:1-3), the land of Israel will be bathed in blood, as rivers of blood flow from the carnage of man's inhumanity against man, and a result of God's final judgment and Christ's return. One thousand six hundred furlongs is about 200 miles … what a red river of death! This is a result of "Armageddon."

RAINBOWS FROM REVELATION
The Revelation of Jesus Christ
A chapter by chapter, verse by verse study
"There was a rainbow round about the throne like unto an emerald" (4:3)

CHAPTER FIFTEEN: Vials of Wrath

References

Rev. 16:1
Rev. 14:10

Rev. 4:6
Matt. 3:11
Rev. 13:14,15
Rev. 13:17
Rev. 5:8

Ex. 15:1-21
Deut. 32:3, 4
Ps. 145:17

Ps. 8:9,7
Jer. 10:7
Isa. 66:23

References

Rev. 11:9
Num. 1:50

Ex. 28:6

Rev. 4:6
2 Thes. 1:9

Ex. 19:18
Lev. 11:44
Ex. 40:34
1 Ki. 8:10
Deut. 33:2
Isa. 2:19

1. AND I saw another sign in heaven, great and marvelous, seven angels having the seven last plagues; for in them is filled up the wrath of God.

2. And I saw as it were a sea of glass mingled with fire: and them that had gotten the victory over the beast, and over his image, and over his mark, and over the number of his name, stand on the sea of glass, having the harps of God.

3. And they sing the song of Moses the servant of God, and the song of the Lamb, saying Great and marvelous are thy works, Lord God Almighty; just and true and thy ways, thou King of saints.

4. Who shall not fear thee, O Lord, and glorify thy name? For thou only art holy: for all nations shall come and worship before thee; for thy judgments are made manifest.

5. And after that I looked, and, behold, the temple of the tabernacle of the testimony in heaven was opened:

6. And the seven angels came out of the temple, having the seven plagues, clothed in pure and white linen, and having their breasts girded with golden girdles.

7. And one of the four beasts gave unto the seven angels seven golden vials full of the wrath of God, who liveth for ever and ever.

8. And the temple was filled with smoke from the glory of God, and from his power; and no man was able to enter into the temple, till the seven plagues of the seven angels were fulfilled.

Scriptures for Comparison

Exodus 15:1-13

Then sang Moses and the children of Israel this song unto the LORD, and spake, saying, I will sing unto the LORD, for he hath triumphed gloriously: the horse and his rider hath he thrown into the sea.

The LORD is my strength and song, and he is become my salvation: he is my God, and I will prepare him an habitation; my father's God, and I will exalt him.

The LORD is a man of war: the LORD is his name.

Pharaoh's chariots and his host hath he cast into the sea: his chosen captains also are drowned in the Red sea.

The depths have covered them: they sank into the bottom as a stone.

Thy right hand, O LORD, is become glorious in power: thy right hand, O LORD, hath dashed in pieces the enemy.

And in the greatness of thine excellency thou hast overthrown them that rose up against thee: thou sentest forth thy wrath, which consumed them as stubble.

And with the blast of thy nostrils the waters were gathered together, the floods stood upright as an heap, and the depths were congealed in the heart of the sea.

The enemy said, I will pursue, I will overtake, I will divide the spoil; my lust shall be satisfied upon them; I will draw my sword, my hand shall destroy them.

Thou didst blow with thy wind, the sea covered them: they sank as lead in the mighty waters.

Who is like unto thee, O LORD, among the gods? Who is like thee, glorious in holiness, fearful in praises, doing wonders?

Thou stretchedst out thy right hand, the earth swallowed them.

Thou in thy mercy hast led forth the people which thou hast redeemed: thou hast guided them in thy strength unto thy holy habitation.

Summary of Chapter Fifteen

The Victory of Saints and the Vials of Judgment

I. The Vision (1)

Great and marvelous is the somber and majestic scene to which we are introduced here. John sees a great sign and a beautiful sea of glass, the crystalline pavilion that surrounds the throne of God. The sign is the vision of the angels receiving the last plagues to cast upon the earth, as the chapter describes.

II. The Victors (2-4)

Upon the sea of glass stand the martyrs of the Tribulation Period, those who die in victory under the cruel persecution of the Antichrist. They are a second company, besides the 144,000 seen in the previous chapter, who are saved Israelites (7 and 14).

They lift their voices in anthems of praise to the King of Saints.

III. The Vials (5-8)

Notice that John sees the heavenly temple of the tabernacle in heaven opened. Forth from its inner recesses emerge the seven angels, perhaps the same seven who earlier blew the trumpets (8-11). They are most elevated and distinguished angels, clad in white and gold.

When they pause before the temple, one of the four angelic beings, the cherubim of Ezekiel 1, the "beasts" (Greek word *zoa*), presents to the seven angels seven vials or bowls full of the wrath of God. Incidentally, the Greek word for "the beast" meaning the Antichrist is *therion,* a completely different word than the four "beasts," *zoa,* meaning living creature. This again illustrates the importance of simple Greek research for the serious Bible student.

So powerful and profound and final are to be these horrendous seven last plagues that the heavenly temple is filled with smoke, as John sees it, closing any access to this heavenly sanctuary until the seven plagues as described in Chapter 16 are fulfilled.

None of the raptured or resurrected saints of this age will suffer under this final outpouring of wrath. The "wrath" of the Lamb commences with the four horsemen of Chapter 6. (See 6:17).

160

Outline of Chapter Fifteen

The Seven Last Plagues Introduced

OBJECTIVE: To reveal Christ, the King of Saints, acting in judgment.

OUTLINE:

I. The Vision of the Seven Angels (1)
   A. The Sign Great and Marvelous
   B. The Seven Angels of Wrath

II. The Victors over the Beast (2-5)
   A. The Pavilion: a sea of glass (2)
   B. The People Who are Martyrs (2)
      1. Victors over the Antichrist
      2. Victors over the image
      3. Victors over the mark
      4. Victors over the number
   C. The Praises (3, 4)
      1. The Title of the Song (3)
         The song of Moses ... the son of the Lamb
      2. The Text of the Song (3-4)
      Great and marvelous are thy works,
         Lord God Almighty;
      True and just are thy ways,
         Thou King of saints.
      Who shall not fear thee,
         O Lord,
      And glorify thy name?
         for Thou only are holy;
      For all nations shall come and worship before Thee;
      For thy judgments are made manifest.
      These are the Tribulation martyrs seen in heaven

III. The Vials of Wrath and Judgment (5-8)
   A. The Heavenly Temple Opened (5)
   B. The Holy Angels Emerge (6)
   C. The Horrible Vials Received (7)
   D. The Heavenly Temple Closed (8)

The Wrath of God in Revelation

The Rapture is "Pre-Wrath," but the entire period of seven years described in Revelation 6-19 is a time of wrath.

- Rev. 6:16: "wrath of the Lamb."
- Rev. 6:17: "day of his wrath."
- Rev. 11:18: "Thy wrath is come."
- Rev. 14:8: "wine of wrath."
- Rev. 14:10: "wine of the wrath."
- Rev. 15:1: "the wrath of God."
- Rev. 16:1: "vials of the wrath ..."
- Rev. 16:19: "fierceness of his wrath."
- Rev. 19:15: "fierceness of the wrath of Almighty God."

Observations:
Spiritual lessons and applications from each verse
Chapter Fifteen

1. God's grace and God's judgment are both great and marvelous.

2. While those in this verse are Tribulation victors, we too are to be victorious over evil through Christ. "This is the victory that overcometh the world, even our faith" (1 John 5:4).

3. God's people can always sing of his glory and power under any and all circumstances. We are to "offer the sacrifice of praise to God continually" (Hebrews 13:15).

4. In the future millennium, when sin is suppressed for a thousand years, all nations will serve God. We ought to come and worship before Him now every day.

5. As there is a heavenly temple now, so also the people of God on earth, assembled, are a temple of the Lord. We need to experience the power and presence of God in our midst.

6. God's angels, emerging from the temple to do the will of God in that future time remind us that we should emerge from meeting with the temple of believers on earth, ready to do the bidding of God now.

7. As God's angels work in beautiful harmony, so should God's servants on earth work together in harmony and order, each performing our work and ministry for God.

8. Unseen on earth, not even imagined by man, the program of God, as ordered and ordained in heaven, moves on, often with man less concerned about heaven than is heaven with man. Nevertheless, on this final somber occasion some heavenly activity halts while judgments are dispensed.

Quotations
From Other Expositors
Chapter Fifteen

The Sign in Heaven (1)

"Chapters 15 and 16 belong together. They form one whole, touching one important subject, to wit: the third or last woe. The contents bear a close analogy to the conclusion of chapter 11, if they be not indeed the continuation and amplification of what was there summarily introduced; for all these visions are very intimately related, both in general subject and time. There the temple in heaven was opened, and lightning, voices, thunders, earthquakes, and great hail followed. Here the same temple is opened, and out of it issue seven angels, with the seven last plagues, who empty their bowls of the wrath of God in calamities upon the wicked world, culminating in the very things named as the result of the opening there. There the Elders said that the nations were enraged, that God's wrath had come, and that the time to destroy them that corrupt the earth had been reached. Here we are shown the pouring out of that wrath, its particular instruments, subjects, operations, and results.

"John begins by telling of 'another sign in heaven.' In chapter 12 he told of two signs: the sign of the sun-clad Woman, and the sign of the great Red Dragon. It is with reference to them that he calls this 'another sign.' Three signs were given to Moses, Gideon, Saul, and Elijah. Three signs are mentioned in Matthew 24 as heralding the Lord's coming — the sign of the Son of man in heaven, the putting forth of leaves by the withered fig tree, and the lapse of the world into the condition in which it was at the time to destroy them that corrupt the earth had been reached. Here we are shown the pouring out of that wrath, its particular instruments, subjects, operations and results."

– J.A. Seiss

The Multitude (2-4)

"How could these folk standing on the sea of glass in the presence of God be victorious when they will have been killed during the Tribulation Period by the wave of persecution inspired by Antichrist? The answer is found in 1 Corinthians 15:55-57: 'O death, where is thy sting? O grave, where is thy victory? The sting of death is sin; and the strength of sin is the law. But thanks be to God, which giveth us the victory through our Lord Jesus Christ.' Death at the hands of a murderous dictator or anti-Christian persecutor is only defeat as man looks upon the situation. People living during the Tribulation will think the Antichrist is overcoming the saints, but in reality he will be sending them out into eternity to be with their Lord. Man's vision when unenlightened by the Holy Spirit renders him incapable of understanding the eternal blessings of God. If man does not incur blessings in this life, he considers that defeat, not realizing that what man gains in this life is inconsequential in comparison to what he gains in the life to come. One great blessing bestowed upon these souls is the martyr's crown (James 1:12; Rev. 2:10), which will provide them with a special position of authority during the Millennial kingdom and probably throughout the eternal ages to come.

"'Having the harps of God' would indicate that they are playing the heavenly instruments in a beautiful symphony of praise and worship. In addition to the heavenly harp, they will also sing 'the song of Moses ... and the song of the Lamb.'"

– Tim LaHaye

"The hymn of praise sung by the martyred saints in glory is identified as 'the song of Moses the servant of God, and the song of the Lamb.' The fact that 'song' is repeated with a definite article in both cases would lead to the conclusion that two songs are in view rather than one, both being sung by the martyred throng. The former recounts the faithfulness of God to Israel as a nation in recognition that a large number of Israelites are among these martyred dead. The song of the Lamb speaks of redemption from sin made possible by the sacrifice of the Lamb of God, and would include all the saints.

"There has been difference of opinion as to what song is meant by 'the song of Moses.' Walter Scott follows the traditional interpretation in referring it to the song of Exodus 15 sung by Moses and the children of Israel on the occasion of their triumph over the host of Pharaoh at the Red Sea. The alternative view advanced by J.B. Smith has much to commend it, however. He suggests that the song of Moses is the one recorded in Deuteronomy 32, a song personally written and spoken to the children of Israel by Moses himself at the close of his career. It is a comprehensive picture of God's faithfulness to Israel and His ultimate purpose to defeat their enemies. This latter song more nearly corresponds to the situation found here in Revelation 15. Both passages, however, ascribe praise to God and are similar in many ways to the hymn here recorded."

– John Walvoord

Seven Angels (5-8)

"The opening words of this vision constitute a technical expression signifying a complete break, introductory of an entirely new subject (see chap. 4:1). Thus the Vial plagues are altogether unique,

and form a body of special judgments by themselves. There are two important respects in which they differ from the Seal and Trumpet chastisements: the throne in 'the Heaven' is the source and authority of these latter, while the temple is the scene from whence the Vials of wrath are poured out. The fact that the temple takes the place of the throne changes the situation entirely, and introduces a severer course of dealing, one flowing from what God is in His righteous and holy character. Hence the second marked difference of the Vials from preceding judgments is that in them the wrath of God against the organized systems of evil is finished up or completed. 'After these things' is a technical formula several times found in the Apocalypse."

– Walter Scott

The Temple (8)

"1. There is a literal temple of God in heaven. Unless this is clearly seen and believed, much will be obscure. Was not Moses commanded when he was to make the tabernacle, 'see that thou make them after their pattern, which hath been showed thee in the mount' (Exodus 25:40)? Now these tabernacle things are distinctly called, in Hebrews 9:23, 'patterns of the things in the heavens.'

"We saw in Revelation 11:19, that 'there was opened the temple of God that is in heaven; and there was seen in his temple the ark of his covenant.' Also, in chapter 8:3, we find a golden altar before the throne of heaven.

"2. It is true that in the New Jerusalem John beholds no temple; and the reason is given that our Lord God, the Almighty, and the Lamb, are the temple thereof. In that city they will see His face directly. All formal matters are past — especially governmental matters such as are connected with the temple of which we read in The Revelation.

"3. With the heavenly temple in The Revelation, only judgment matters are connected. Even in 8:3-5, where the prayers of God's saints come up, it is with the effect upon earth of thunders, and voices, and lightnings, and an earthquake! Again in 11:19, upon the opening of the temple of God in heaven, and the vision of the ark of His covenant, there follow 'lightnings, and voices, and thunders, and an earthquake, and great hail.' And now, upon the opening of the temple there came forth the seven angels with the seven last plagues.

"4. We find in the temple, in 11:19, the ark of God's covenant; and again, in 15:5, the remarkable expression 'the temple of the tabernacle of the testimony in heaven.'

"This indicates that God is about to fulfill His covenanted promises toward Israel, for to Israel belong the covenanted things (Romans 9:4)."

– William Newell

Our Victory is FOREVER!
An Expository Sermon

Chapter Fifteen

Introduction

Win or lose? Victory or defeat? Heaven or hell?

These abrupt and challenging contrasts are relevant right now to the people of this earth.

You are either on the Lord's side by faith in Christ or you are on the devil's side, going on in sin. There is no neutral ground. As to whether you are on the winning side or the losing side, God's side or Satan's side, is up to you.

The wages of sin is always death, separation from God, the sad and tragic consequences of evil.

But there is salvation right now. If you are lost, you are a loser. If you are saved, you are a winner, a victor.

This contrast is most evident in Revelation 15, where we see the future martyrs of the Tribulation in glorious, victorious song, while the wicked world of the future must fall under divine wrath and judgment. Notice first of all:

I. The Sign (1)

There are other "signs," that is, symbols of great importance in this sacred book. The "wonders" in Revelation 12, referring to the sunclothed woman (Israel) and to the great red dragon (Satan) is this same Greek word *(semion)*, here translated "sign." It signifies that what is seen has a powerful effect on events to take place on earth. The sign here is the august emergence of the seven angels, who will dispense and supervise the last and final judgments on this earth as the Tribulation's seven year cycle comes to a close.

The sign is indeed "great," for in these vials is the finished wrath of God. The angelic procession, carrying the vials of judgment, proceeds from the heavenly temple, for all patience is now exhausted.

This sign is "marvelous," for these most horrendous judgment-events issue in the full consummation of history as we know it.

In the resulting catastrophic occurrences on earth are found the details of "reaping" at the close of the 14th chapter and of the "treading" of the "great winepress of the wrath of God" (14:19,20). Hundreds of years earlier the eloquent Isaiah, prophet of the Messiah and the Millennium, re-

corded the thoughts of Christ at the close of the yet future Tribulation:

"Who is this that cometh from Edom, with dyed garments from Bozrah? This that is glorious in his apparel, traveling in the greatness of this strength?

"I that speak in righteousness, mighty to save. Wherefore art thou red in thine apparel, and thy garments like him that treadeth the winefat?

"I have trodden the winepress alone; and of the people there was none with me: for I will tread them in mine anger, and trample them in my fury: and their blood shall be sprinkled upon my garments, and I will stain all my raiment. For the day of vengeance is in mine heart, and the year of my redeemed is come" (Isaiah 63:1-4).

The "wrath of God" is general, worldwide, and in view of man's iniquity and idolatry and rebellion. The "wrath of the Lamb" seems to be more particular (6:17), directed especially toward the Antichrist and his forces, as the 19th chapter reveals.

But before the extensive prophetic and dramatic description of the pouring out of the vials of wrath, this magnificent scene of the victors over Antichrist, who die gloriously rather than deny their faith, is set forth …

II. The Song (2-4)

Already, those faithful witnesses, those Israelite evangelists of the end times, who shall proclaim God's message to those who have not heard clearly the gospel in this age, are seen in heaven, back in chapter 14. They are all singing their special song, as the "firstfruits" from the spiritual harvest that will occur even during this last time of judgment …

Now, the martyrs, Gentiles as well as Jews (compare 7:9-17), who refuse the mark of the beast and who pay for their fidelity to God with their lives (14:13), blend their voices together in heaven to sing the song of Moses and of the Lamb, saying,

"Great and marvelous are thy works
  Lord God Almighty:
Just and pure are thy ways,
  Thou King of Saints.
Who shall not fear thee,

O Lord and glorify thy name?
For thou only art holy:
For all nations shall come
and worship before Thee
For thy judgments are made manifest."

As the Israelites among them sing, they will doubtless remember the Song of Moses in Exodus 15, an anthem of praise for deliverance from Egypt and the Pharaoh and slavery and death, intoned by the emancipated people of God after the Exodus.

As the Gentile martyrs praise the Lamb in their hearts, they will doubtless rejoice in that "all nations" will be under the rule of the Lion of the tribe of Judah and of the Lamb who takes away the sins of the whole world.

They are not resurrected yet, but will come forth at the close of the Tribulation with glorified bodies, reunited with all the glorified souls at the First Resurrection (20:4):

"And I saw the souls of them that were beheaded for the witness of Jesus, and for the Word of God, and which had not worshipped the beast, neither his image, neither had received his mark in their foreheads, or in their hands; and they lived and reigned with Christ a thousand years."

Doubtless, the already raptured and resurrected saints, caught up to be with Christ before the Tribulation bursts upon this globe, will watch, as did John the Revelator in the vision, as a rejoicing audience, listening to this beautiful song.

Of course, the Antichrist and the forces of this world falsely assume that the victory is theirs when the saints are slain, but by their martyr's deaths they gain crowns of victory forever ... "Be thou faithful unto death and I will give thee a crown of life" (2:10).

III. The Seven (1, 5-8)

Comes now the full description of the seven angels marching out of the temple of God in heaven and receiving from one of the four beasts (*zoa* - living creatures, the cherubim of Ezekiel 1) the seven golden vials, large bowl-like receptacles, "full of the wrath of God."

Man never gets away with sin and rebellion. In the final stages of the Tribulation, these "seven last plagues" are poured out on a Christ-rejecting world, run amok after Satan and the false religious worship that focuses on the image of the beast. The seven angels, perhaps the same seven, who earlier blew the seven trumpets (8, 9, and

11:15-19), now prepare to administer this end time wrath. "True and righteous are His judgments," for the world will be engaged in mutual slaughter, the persecution of God's earthly chosen people (Israel), and the slaying of millions of true Christians for refusing the mark of the beast.

Again the New Testament saints of this age are not in view here, since they are "saved from the wrath which is to come" (1 Thes. 1:10).

They are "kept from the hour of temptation which shall come upon all the world to try them that dwell therein" (3:10).

"The temple was filled with smoke from the glory of God." This reminds us of the glory of the Lord which filled the temple of Solomon thousands of years ago, when it was completed and dedicated (2 Chr. 7:1-4). But that was an earthly scene.

Here is a stark and startling contrast. In that earthly temple the glory of God betokened blessings and bounty and beauty. But here in the heavenly temple at this crucial stage in future judgment events, the glory of God produces not light and loveliness, but smoke, proceeding from His power. Since this symbolizes in heaven the judgments to occur on earth, this smoke is not to be entered by any heavenly beings or saints. No one is to enter this real, heavenly temple as long as the smoke of wrath pervades the place. "The seven plagues of the seven angels must be fulfilled."

In view of these awesome scenes of both victory and wrath, it behooves all who read or hear these words to consider their own fate. When these things are fulfilled, where will you be? Where will you stand?

Conclusion

Are you prepared for the future? Whether these things come to pass in the very near or the yet remote future, YOU need to be right with God.

You can become a part of the family of God by the new birth now. To continue to reject Christ until after the Rapture will mean you will be left to pass into the horrendous judgments that will culminate in these seven last plagues.

Realizing you are a sinner if you have never accepted Christ, come to Him now, believing that He died for your sins on the cross. Out of the depths of a sincere heart, pray that simple but profound prayer, "God be merciful to me, a sinner. Save me now, for I do receive Jesus Christ as my own personal Savior."

A Commentary on the Revelation
Expository, Exegetical, Devotional and Practical
Greek words from the Textus Receptus

Chapter Fifteen

The Seven Last Plagues Introduced (1)

1. And I saw another sign in heaven *(kai eidon allo semeion en to ouranou)* — John uses the word *semion*, translated <u>sign</u>, which is translated <u>wonder</u> in 12:1,3. Israel as the woman is a <u>sign</u>, a wondrous manifestation of God's divine choice of a people ... The dragon is a <u>sign</u>, a strange and evil personality, who is the devil and Satan ... This third "sign," deals with the punishment of sin ... thus we have seen good, evil and punishment ... **great and marvelous** *(mega kai thaumaston)* — something to arouse awe and amazement ... **seven angels having the seven last plagues** *(angelous hepta tas eschatos)* — some commentators think that the seals, the trumpets and judgments are contemporaneous, describing in different terms events that happen simultaneously through the 7 year tribulation with all the first judgments occurring at the same time and so through the seven, but it seems to this writer that the 7 last plagues are so designated to indicate that each set of judgments runs its course, followed by the next, that the three major rounds of seven judgments are sequential, these being the last and final series ... **for in them is filled up** *(hoti en autais etelesthe)* — which literally means they finish up the divine dispensing of wrath, fulfilling the proclamation involved in the seventh trumpet (11:15-18) and leading up to the glorious appearing of Christ (Rev. 19) ... **the wrath of God** *(ho thumos tou theou)* ... this verse summarizes what is to follow in this chapter ... There are no more plagues after these until Christ comes in power and glory. Details related to these judgments and the content of chapter 14 are further explained in chapters 17, 18. (Compare Psalm 75:7,8).

The Martyrs' Song (2-4)

2. And I saw as it were a sea of glass *(kai eidon hos thalassan hualinen)* — this compares with the brazen laver for the cleansing of the O.T. Priests (Ex. 38:8; 1 Kings 7:44), thus speaking of the cleansed believers who appear before God

(compare Rev. 4:6) ... **mingled with fire** *(memigmene puri)* — notice that the word for fire has produced "purify" in English. This perhaps indicates the fiery trials through which they had passed in dying as martyrs ... **and them that had gotten the victory over the beast** *(kai tous nikontas ek tou therion)* — their victory was an emancipation from the beast's domain, albeit through the door of martyrdom. Rev. 14:1-5 depicts many of these as the 144,000, but others, perhaps many millions will die for Christ during the Tribulation and they are seen here in heaven, although not yet resurrected until Rev. 20:4 comes to pass ... **and over his image and over his mark** *(kai ek tes eikonos autou)* — thus they resist the mark of the beast and refuse to worship the image of the beast, the abomination of desolation (Matthew 24:15; Rev. 13:7,15), but notice the contrast in the destiny of the beast-worshippers (Rev. 14:9,10) ... **and over the number of his name** *(kai ek tou arithmou tou onomatos autou)* — they have refused all 3 of the beast's demands, giving allegiance rather to the supreme Name, He who is Alpha and Omega (Compare Acts 4:12; Romans 14:11,12; Phil. 2:9-11) ... **stand on the sea of glass** *(hestotas epi ten thalassan ten hualinen)* — they can stand not merely as victorious Israel at the Red Sea (Ex. 15), and as John upon the sand of the sea, but upon the great SEA itself before the throne of the Almighty, a sea firm and reflecting their glory as glass; their past conflict shedding the brighter luster on their present and future triumph. Their happiness is heightened by the retrospect of the dangers through which they passed" (JFB) ... **having the harps of God** *(echontas kitharas tou theou)* — how much more beautiful their tones than the timbrels of Moses' sister, Miriam, and her great women's choir! **3. And they sing the song of Moses** *(kai adousin ten hoden Moseos)* — this short but glorious song which follows is reminiscent of the song of liberation in Exodus 15, but could, as some say, also refer to Moses' song in Deut. 32. The martyred Jews who know the Messiah would sing with special feelings of tradition ... **the servant of God** *(tou doulou tou theou)* — while only the 144,000 could sing the melody and words spoken of in 14:3, all the martyrs in heaven can join in this anthem, but the saved Israelite martyrs would rejoice in their remembrance of Moses, who doubtless will be a spectator to all of this ... **and the song of the Lamb, saying** *(kai ten oden tou arniou)* — perhaps 5:12 gives us the words of this song, which might be repeated, but the song here unites both Israelite and Gentile martyrs for Christ in celebrative harmony ... **Great and marvelous are thy works** *(megala kai thaumasta ta erga sou)* — many of His great works are extolled in Moses' last song (Duet. 32) ... Moses' 40-year-long leadership in the wilderness begins and closes with "a song of Moses" ... **Lord God Almighty** *(kurie ho theos ho pantokrator)* — a full presentation of His person in this line ... each phrase or clause is a line in this poetic song ... **just and true are thy ways** *(dikaiai kai alethniai hai hodoi sou)* — His justice and truth are unimpeachable ... **thou King of Saints** *(ho basileus ton ethnon)* — He is King of His people and will be king of all nations and peoples. **4. Who shall not fear thee, O Lord?** *(tis ou me phobethe)* — who would dare to refuse Him homage, reverential awe and spiritual respect? (See Deut. 6:2; 10:2; Eccl. 12:13,14; Matthew 10:28; 2 Cor. 5:11) ... **and glorify thy name** *(kai doksasei to onoma sou)* — Angels, elders, glorified and redeemed believers, martyrs, all the universe? ... **for thou only art holy** *(hoti monos hosios)* — in the song we hear that He is almighty, just, true, and holy ... **for all nations shall come and worship before thee** *(hoti panta ta ethne heksousin kai proskun sousin enopion sou)* — His divine judgments and justice will triumph before the whole universe.

The Temple, the Angels, the Vials (5-8)

5. After that I looked and behold was opened *(kai meta tauta eidon kai ennoige)* — previously we have seen the temple in 11:19 opened to see the ark of the covenant therein, the original, emblematic of Christ's presence and perfect compliance with the laws of God, as the Bread of Life and Rod of God, but here it is not His Covenant keeping and presence which is in view, but His wrath proceeding from the temple, a place of heavenly holiness and worship ... **the temple of the tabernacle of the testimony in heaven** *(ho naos tes skenes tou marturiou en to ouranou)* — notice

that three words, temple, tabernacle (dwelling place) and witness (martyr) are associated. From a place of holiness, the dwelling place of God, where He Himself witnesses to truth and inspires saved men to witness in their words and lives, even to the point of giving up their lives for Christ. **6. And the seven angels came out of the temple** *(kai eksethon hoi hepta angeloi ek tou naou)* — possibly the same seven distinguished angels which "stand" before God (8:2), including perhaps Gabriel (Luke 1:19). Only two angels are named in Scripture; the other being Michael the archangel (Jude 9). The Jews thought of seven "presence angels," high ranking beings, standing in God's presence, ready to do his bidding, even in their writing supplying other names ... that of course was not inspired Holy Writ, but worthy of thought ... **having the seven plagues** *(hoi echontes tas hepta plegas)* — possessing, holding these final judgment events which will plague and befall the planet, not merely diseases, but serious consequences of sin ... **clothed in pure and white linen and having their breasts girded with golden girdles** — so illustrious are these seven angels that their heavenly attire resembles that of Christ (Rev. 1:13). Compare the "mighty angel" of chapter 10, and in Daniel 10 is a majestic angel, as well. **7. And one of the four beasts** — the same *zoa* of chapters 4 and 5 and 6:1-8, exalted cherubim, attendants upon God's universal throne (see Ezekiel 1) ... **gave unto the seven angels** — delivered to them for their use and service ... **seven golden vials** *(hepta phialas chrusas)* — golden containers ... **full of the wrath of God** *(gemousas tou thumou tou theou)* — brimful, completely filled, containing the accumulated wrath of the Almighty long held back (see Romans 4:5) ... **who liveth forever and ever** — the everlasting ruler of the universe. **8. And the temple was filled with smoke** — not the Shekinah cloud of God's glory (see 1 Kings 8:10,11), but the dark smoke of wrath this time coming from that glory (see Ex. 29:42,43; Ex. 19:18) ... **and from his power** *(dunameos)* — his dynamic power ... **and no man was able to enter the temple till the seven plagues of the seven angels were fulfilled** — it is as though heavenly worship pauses as the last stages of judgment are dispatched to earth. This is the last year of the Great Tribulation.

RAINBOWS FROM REVELATION
The Revelation of Jesus Christ
A chapter by chapter, verse by verse study
"There was a rainbow round about the throne like unto an emerald" (4:3)

CHAPTER SIXTEEN: The Vials Poured Out

References

Rev. 1:10
Rev. 11:12
Rev. 11:15
Rev. 16:17
Rev. 19:1
Rev. 21:3
Rev. 8:7
Ex. 9:9
Rev. 13:14

Ex. 7:17
Rev. 8:9

Rev. 6:3,4
Rev. 8:10,11

Gen. 18:25
Ps. 97:2

Mt. 23:34
Isa. 49:26
Rev. 5:12

Rev. 14:10

Rev. 6:7,8
Rev. 8:12

II Chr. 28:22
I Sa. 8:21
Num. 1:50

Ex. 28:6

Rev. 9:21

1. AND I heard a great voice out of the temple saying to the seven angels, Go your ways, and pour out the vials of the wrath of God upon the earth.

2. And the first went, and poured out his vial upon the earth; and there fell a noisome and grievous sore upon the men which had the mark of the beast, and upon them which worshiped his image.

3. And the second angel poured out his vial upon the sea; and it became as the blood of a dead man: and every living soul died in the sea.

4. And the third angel poured out his vial upon the rivers and fountains of waters; and they became blood.

5. And I heard the angel of the waters say, Thou art righteous, O Lord, which art, and wast, and shall be, because thou hast judged thus.

6. For they have shed the blood of saints and prophets, and thou hast given them blood to drink; for they are worthy.

7. And I heard another out of the altar say, Even so, Lord God Almighty, true and righteous are thy judgments.

8. And the fourth angel poured out his vial upon the sun; and power was given unto him to scorch men with fire.

9. And men were scorched with great heat, and blasphemed the name of God, which hath power over these plagues: and they repented not to give him glory.

10. And the fifth angel poured out his vial upon the seat of the beast; and his kingdom was full of darkness; and they gnawed their tongues for pain,

11. And blasphemed the God of heaven because of their pains and their sores, and repented not of their deeds.

12. And the sixth angel poured out

his vial upon the great river Euphrates; and the water thereof was dried up, that the way of the kings of the east might be prepared.

13. And I saw three unclean spirits like frogs come out of the mouth of the dragon, and out of the mouth of the beast, and out of the mouth of the false prophet.

14. For they are the spirits of devils, working miracles, which go forth unto the kings of the earth and of the whole world, to gather them to the battle of that great day of God Almighty.

15. Behold, I come as a thief. Blessed is he that watcheth, and keepeth his garments, lest he walk naked, and they see his shame.

16. And he gathered them together into a place called in the Hebrew tongue Armageddon.

17. And the seventh angel poured out his vial into the air; and there came a great voice out of the temple of heaven, from the throne, saying, It is done.

18. And there were voices, and thunders, and lightnings; and there was a great earthquake, such as was not since men were upon the earth, so mighty an earthquake, and so great.

19. And the great city was divided into three parts, and the cities of the nations fell: and great Babylon came in remembrance before God, to give unto her the cup of the wine of the fierceness of his wrath.

20. And every island fled away, and the mountains were not found.

21. And there fell upon men a great hail out of heaven, every stone about the weight of a talent: and men blasphemed God because of the plague of the hail; for the plague thereof was exceeding great.

References

Isa. 41:2
Rev. 9:14

I Jn. 4:1
I Tim. 4:1
Ex. 8:1-6

Rev. 20:8

I Thes. 5:2

Rev. 19:11-21
Zech. 14:1-3

Rev. 15:8

Dan. 12:1
Rev. 11:19

Isa. 51:17

Rev. 6:14

Rev. 11:19

Scriptures for Comparison

Exodus 7:17, 18

Thus saith the Lord, In this thou shalt know that I am the Lord: behold, I will smite with the rod that is in mine hand upon the waters which are in the river, and they shall be turned to blood.

And the fish that is in the river shall die, and the river shall stink; and the Egyptians shall loathe to drink of the water of the river.

Summary of Chapter Sixteen

It's Done! Civilization Ends!

The numerical key to the book of Revelation is the number seven. Since seven is the number of divine completion and perfection, the book is made up of sets of sevens. Again the sevens relating to judgment are divided into groups of four and three. The first four show God working indirectly in judgment using other means; the last three reveal God working directly in such a way that men must see the hand of God and He cannot be explained away.

Again the seals, the trumpets and vials are structured in sixes and ones with an interval or parenthetical passage between the sixth and seventh in each set.

All that is seen in the sixteenth chapter, as we approach the close of the second 1,260 day or three and a half year period, occurs in the Great Tribulation proper.

I. The First Vial

When the first vial of wrath is poured out on the earth, a terrible sore, an awful disease affects the followers of the Antichrist. Perhaps such scourges as AIDS presage this final plague.

II. The Second Vial

When the second angel pours out his vial on the oceans, they undergo a complete change of chemical constituency, whereas in the earlier trumpet judgment only a third of the seas were affected. "It became as the blood of a dead man."

III. The Third Vial

The rivers and springs are next in order, the third plague turning all of them into blood. As this happens, the "angel of the waters" proclaims the justice of the judgment, since multiplied millions of saints and prophets have shed their blood for the truth through the centuries.

IV. The Fourth Vial

Intensification of the sun's light and heat is the result of the fourth vial. "For our God is a consuming fire."

V. The Fifth Vial

A strange, cosmic darkness follows this scorching heat, possibly caused by powerful solar disturbances with giant burning flares, followed by dark clouds of interplanetary debris. The fifth vial especially affects the throne and domain of the Antichrist with this strange darkness.

VI. The Sixth Vial

The sixth judgment dries up the Euphrates to prepare the way for the kings of the east (sunrising) to march their armies toward the final battle of that great day of God Almighty. Notice the Satanic trinity — dragon, beast, false prophet — influencing the gathering of the forces for the battle of Armageddon.

Yet it is God who actually gathers them to the land of Israel, "against Jerusalem to battle" (Zechariah 14:2) with vast forces converging in the plain of Esdraelon, the valley of Armageddon.

Then comes the parenthetical call of Christ in verse 15, as the Savior encourages the endtime believers under the awful duress of the final days.

VII. The Seventh Vial

Finally, the seventh angel pours out his vial into the air with a "great voice" proclaiming from the throne, "It is done!" The climactic conclusion of the Tribulation is at hand. The cities of the nations will fall as civilization collapses. Huge hail stones of over a hundred pounds each will pummel the planet. All these judgments are punitive, not remedial, in their effect, for mankind continues blaspheming God.

The Mountain of Megiddo

"What is Armageddon or 'Har-Magedon? Its name means "Mountain of Megiddo." It was here the Lord so marvelously helped Barak overthrow the Canaanites (Judges 5:19). The region is named from Megiddo, a royal Canaanite city (Joshua 12:21). To the northwest is Mount Carmel where, at the mouth of the Kishon River, Elijah killed the hundreds of Baal's prophets. Mount Gilboa, where King Saul, the persecutor of God's king-David fell, is southwest. And on the north or northwest, overlooking all, is Mount Tabor, where Barak assembled the hosts of the Lord against the enemy. From Judges 4:6, 12, 14, and Jeremiah 48:18, I feel that the 'mountain' (Hebrew - Har) in Har Megedon is Tabor. 'Megiddo' is named 12 times, the governmental number in Scripture; and the last time is almost the form we have it here: Megiddon in Zech. 12:11."

— W. R. Newell

Outline of Chapter Sixteen

The Seven Vials of Wrath

OBJECTIVE: To reveal the seven past plagues to befall the earth at the close of the Tribulation.

OUTLINE: First "Great Voice" out of heavenly temple "Go your ways and pour out the vials of the wrath of God upon the earth."

I. The First Vial: Sores Effect Beast-worshippers (2)
A. The Painful Plague
1. Noisome
2. Grievous
B. The Punished People
1. They have the mark of the beast
2. They worship the beast's image

II. The Second Vial: Seas Turn to Blood (3)
A. That Comparison: as the blood of a dead man
B. That Completion: all life in the seas dies

III. The Third Vial: Streams to Blood (4-7)
A. A Reddening Judgment (4)
B. A Retributive Judgment (5, 6)
C. A Righteous Judgment (7)

IV. The Fourth Vial: Sun's Heat Increased (8, 9)
A. The Scorching (8)
B. The Scorning (9)
1. Blasphemy continues
2. Repentance rejected

V. The Fifth Vial: Seat (throne) of the Beast Darkened (10, 11)
A. The Coverage of Darkness: throne and kingdom (10)
B. The Cursing of the Unrepentant (11)
1. They blaspheme because of pains
2. They repent not of their deeds

VI. The Sixth Vial: Stoppage of Euphrates River Effected (12)
A. The Result of the Event: drying up
B. The Reason for the Event: to prepare the way for "kings of east" to move toward Armageddon (13-16)
1. Demonic Forces Loosed (13)
2. Satanic Trinity Suggested (13)
   a. Anti-God: the dragon, Satan
   b. Anti-Christ: the beast, man of sin
   c. Anti-Holy Spirit: the false prophet, beast out of earth — see (Chapter 13:11)

3. Worldwide Battle Indicated (14)
4. Christ's Blessing Promised (15)
5. Final Battleground Named (16) "Armageddon,"Second "GAreat Voice" out of Heavenly temple "It is done."

VII. The Seventh Vial: Shaking of World Described (17-21)
A. Announced Doom (7)
B. Atmospheric Disturbances (18)
C. Awesome Disruptions (18-21)
1. Mighty earthquake strikes (18 19)
2. "Great city" divided (19)
3. Cities destroyed (19)
4. "Babylon" collapses (19)
5. Geography altered (20)
6. Hail falls (21)
7. Men blaspheme (21)

The Vials and The Judgments on Ancient Egypt Before The Exodus

"The seven vials judgments and their effects are literal, just as the plagues on Egypt were literal. Six of the seven vial judgments are similar to those plagues put upon Egypt. Compare:

• 1st vial and sixth plague, boils (Ex. 9:8-12).

• 2nd and 3rd vials and 1st plague, blood (Ex. 7:10-21).

• 5th vial and 9th plague, darkness (Ex. 10:21-23).

• 6th vial and 2nd plague, frogs (Ex. 8:6-11).

• 7th vial and 7th plague, hail (Ex. 9:22-26)."
— *Bill Lawrence*

"As these judgments in olden times were literal, so shall these divine demonstrations of wrath be literal. Only the "frogs" in Revelation are symbolic, as the passage clearly teaches, for they represent evil demonic spirits,"
— *James O. Combs*

Observations:
Spiritual lessons and applications from each verse
Chapter Sixteen

1. As the angels are obedient, so also should believers be now.

2. True worship must be directed toward God who is a Spirit (John 4:24), never to an "image."

3. All are dead in sins (Ephesians 2:1); thus it is appropriate that the seas, like the human race, should reflect the conditions of a "dead man."

4. Refusing the water of life from the heavenly stream of salvation ultimately can result in having only "blood to drink."

5. The eternal God is always righteous.

6. The Lamb is worthy of worship; wicked mankind is worthy of judgment.

7. God's judgments are true, never based on false assumptions.

8. God can exercise special power over His creation.

9. Scorched, but sin-hardened mankind, is steeped in blasphemy and rebellion.

10. Physical and spiritual pain are results of choosing sin and Satan (and Antichrist) instead of righteousness and Christ.

11. Human depravity is sometimes most evident when people suffer, blaming God for their self-generated suffering, the consequences of their own immorality and love of sin.

12. God moves in the affairs of men, fulfilling His will.

13. This final Satanic trinity (Satan, Antichrist, and false prophet) will have supernatural demonic strength, a factor in today's world, too.

14. Resisting Satanic power in any age is necessary.

15. Both in this future time and now, true believers are urged to keep watching for Christ.

16. Behind the scenes, both divine providence and human circumstances work toward the culmination of the age. Finally the process is accelerated until Armageddon occurs.

17. When God announces something is finished, it is.

18. God's power over all elements is total and complete.

19. Evil Babylonianism in all of its forms will be judged (false religion, Satan and beast worship, new ageism, spiritism, totalitarianism, materialism, etc.). God can execute horrendous judgment.

21. God's judgments are "exceedingly great."

Saved From Wrath

"For those who may be troubled by the teaching that the church must pass through the Great Tribulation before she is caught away to meet her Lord, it should be sufficient to observe that, according to the Word of God, the Great Tribulation is a visitation of God's wrath upon His enemies. In the seven plagues "is completed the wrath of God" (Rev. 15:1; and the seven vials connected with these plagues are "the vials of the wrath of God" 16:1).

This begins with "the wrath of the Lamb" (Rev. 6:16, 17), which is recognized as in progress by even many of the wicked, during the time when the seven seals are opened and the "four horsemen" ride forth, following the Rapture.

This is "the wrath to come" from which our Lord delivers us (I Thes. 1:9, 10; 5:8 - 10).

It is true that tribulation is our appointed portion here (John 16:33), and Paul declared that "through much tribulation we must enter the kingdom (Acts 14:22); but the Great Tribulation is quite another matter, for it comes from God Himself and is His judgment upon His enemies."

– W. L. Pettingill

Quotations
From Other Expositors
Chapter Sixteen

The Voice (1)

"Why is it that these seven angels that pour out the seven last plagues are represented as coming out of the temple or tabernacle? The temple and the tabernacle remind one of Israel; and the event refers to the time when the 'man of sin,' the Antichrist, is upon the earth attempting to persecute to the death the Jewish remnant. No person can do that without bringing judgment upon himself, for God made a covenant with Abraham, saying, 'I will bless them that bless thee, and curse him that curseth thee' (Genesis 12:3). The latter portion of this covenant will be the part the enemies of Israel will bring upon themselves. Consequently the angels who are to execute those judgments are portrayed as coming out of the temple and out of the tabernacle, which represent the covenants of God with Israel. In other words, here is a picture of the fulfilling of the covenants that God made with Abraham.

"Rome, Spain, Germany, France, Russia and all the other nations that have persecuted the children of Israel have, in consequence, suffered sorrow and national shame. And the end is not yet. These seven last plagues are judgments that will be meted out, mainly because of the persecution that will be directed against Israel."

– Louis T. Talbot

The First Angel's Vial (2)

"The first bowl judgment introduces grievous or painful sores upon men. Dr. Wilbur Smith notes that the same word is used by the Old Testament translators of the Greek Septuagint for boils when telling the story of the Egyptian plagues. For this reason many have called it the plague of boils. This judgment delineates two essential points:

"**1. The time** — when Antichrist is worshipped. Further confirmation that the three judgments, the seals, the trumpets, and the vials, are sequential, not concurrent, as some Bible teachers suggest, is clarified in the same judgment. Antichrist will not be set up as the object of worship

until the middle of the Tribulation Period. This judgment will fall on men because of their worship of Antichrist, which could only occur after the middle of the Tribulation Period as we saw in chapter 13. The time of this judgment, then, will probably commence within the first one to three months of the last half of the Tribulation Period.

"**2. The recipients** — beast worshipers. The selection from among the peoples on the earth is clearly seen in this passage: only those containing the mark of the beast and worshipping his image will be selected for those awful sores. This would indicate that God in His marvelous grace will not bring judgment on believers during this latter half of Tribulation, but will protect them as He did the children of Israel during the plagues of Egypt. This further confirms our assumption that in the previous judgments, when He slays 25 percent and one–third of the world's population, He will exempt believers."

– Tim LaHaye

The Second Angel's Vial (3)

"And the second angel poured out his vial upon the sea; and it became as the blood of a dead man: and every living soul died in the sea" (16:3).

"The second vial is poured out upon the sea with the result that the sea becomes as blood (literally 'it became blood as of a dead man'), and every living soul in the sea dies. As in the second trumpet in 8:8, the analogy seems to be to the first of the ten plagues in Egypt (Exodus 7:20–25) which killed all the fish in the Nile River and made the water unfit to drink. In all these cases it is possible that the sea does not become literally human blood but that it corresponds to it in appearance and loathsomeness. The area of the judgment is similar to that of the second trumpet where one-third of the sea is turned to blood and one-third of the creatures of the sea die. Here the judgment is universal. The reference to the sea may be limited to the Mediterranean, but the same word would be used if the judgment extended to all large bodies of

171

water. In the latter event, a major portion of the earth would be involved in the judgment as most of the earth is covered with water."

– John Walvoord

The Third Angel's Vial (4-7)

"The rivers and springs are next in order and the third plague turns all their waters into blood. The angel of the waters is heard justifying this awful catastrophe as a righteous act of God in judgment upon the world which has poured out the lifeblood of saints and prophets; it is now meet that the blood–shedders should have blood to drink. The altar of the Temple is also heard speaking out, saying, 'Yea, O Lord God, the Almighty, true and righteous are Thy judgments.' In this Day of Grace the altar is speaking out better things than the blood of Abel; but we are studying the Day of Judgment, when the doors of grace shall have been shut, and in that Day the only judgment for men will be righteous judgment; and who shall be able to stand?"

– W. L. Pettingill

The Fourth Angel's Vial (8,9)

"Men have from the ages tended to worship the sun, that which has been created, rather than the creator (Romans 1:18–23; Ezekiel 8:16). Even today, when scientists lecture on the effects of solar heat and on photosynthesis the sun, rather than God, is usually made into the worshipped World Santa Claus who gives us everything. Now with this plague God shows the Antichrist and his earth full of followers, that He, not the sun, is the Sustainer of the earth (Colossians 1:16–17). God here, as in the other judgments, show all who follow the Beast the utter futility of depending on any one but God to control the world in which we dwell."

– Salem Kirban

The Fifth Angel's Vial (10,11)

"Darkness and anguish do not tend to soften men's hearts, or to lead them to confess their sins. Their very suffering but stirs them up to blaspheme God the more. And so, in the outer darkness of a lost eternity, our Lord has told us there shall not only be weeping and wailing because of suffering endured, but there will be the gnashing of teeth, which implies rage and indignation against God. With permanency of character he who re-

jects Christ is guilty of eternal sin, and eternal punishment necessarily follows."

– H.A.Ironside

The Sixth Angel's Vial, (12-16)

"The sixth angel pours his Vial upon the actual River Euphrates, which dries it. Consider that this great River is 1,800 miles in length, and from Mohammarah to the Sea is 3,600 feet wide and 30 feet deep! With one judgment act of God its bed becomes dry ground!

"Why does God do this? It is simply stated: "that the way of the Kings from the East might be prepared." God is preparing for the great Battle of Armageddon, bringing the forces of Satan across the dry River bed to be utterly destroyed by Jesus, followed by His heavenly forces (Revelation 16:16 and Chapter 19). The River Euphrates is spoken of in similar terms in Is. 11:15 and Zech. 10:10–11."

– Bill Lawrence

The Seventh Angel's Vial (17-21)

"The next two chapters of the Apocalypse will give a detailed description of Babylon and of all that is centered there. Expositors have ranged far and wide in their efforts to interpret the significance of Babylon in the Apocalypse. Some have thought it to be Rome; some have seen it as a symbol for Jerusalem; some conceive a rebuilt, literal Babylon; some have gone so far as to see it as a symbolic reference to the United States of America."

– John Phillips

"We cannot emphasize too strongly that the three series of divine judgments — first the seals, second the trumpets, third the vials of wrath — we have those preliminary hardening actions of God upon an impenitent world, by which he prepares that world for the Great Day of Wrath — at Christ's coming as King of Kings, as seen in Rev. 19:11-15."

– William R. Newell

"Here is recorded the world's greatest earthquake, causing seismographs all over the world to spin like tops as the planet shakes in it's deaththroes, but unregenerate men curse God all the more, as the earthquake, plagues and great hail, described as weighing from 85 to 125 pounds, pummel the earth."

– G. C. Gosey

God's Wrath Upon His Enemies
An Expository Sermon

Chapter Sixteen

Introduction

Finally comes the full force of God's divine wrath upon a wicked, Christ–rejecting, sin–loving, rebellious world in these seven vials of wrath upon this earth.

That they are literal should be beyond doubt, even as the horrendous judgments on ancient Egypt were real catastrophes and awesome events.

This is *"the wrath to come"* from which our Lord delivers us.

"…Wait for his Son from heaven, whom he raised from the dead, even Jesus, which delivered us from the *wrath* to come" (1 Thessalonians 1:10).

"For God hath not appointed us *to wrath,* but to obtain salvation by our Lord Jesus Christ" (1 Thessalonians 5:9).

Beginning after the Rapture, this time of wrath commences, continuing through the middle of the Tribulation and looking onward to the climax of the Glorious appearing.

Seven times the expressions *"wrath of the Lamb"* or *"wrath of God"* are used, the first being in connection with the Seven Seals.

"… Fall on us, and hide us from the face of Him that sitteth upon the throne, and from the *wrath of the Lamb"* (6:6). Here God and Christ are involved in this first mention of wrath.

Concerning the wicked worshippers of the Beast, the Antichrist during the Tribulation, we read, "The same shall drink of the wine of the *wrath of God,* which is poured out without mixture into the cup of his indignation …" (14:10).

Depicting the judgments upon "the vine of the earth" (possibly the Antichrist in opposition to Christ the true vine – John 15:1). John writes that an angel thrust in a sickle into the vine of the earth and cast it into the great winepress of the *"wrath of God"* (16:19).

Setting forth the prelude to these events of chapter 16, John says, "and I saw another sign, great and marvelous, seven angels, having the seven last plagues; for in them is filled up the *wrath of God"* (15:1).

"And again, one of the four beasts [living creatures] gave unto the seven angels seven golden vials full of the *wrath of God"* (15:7).

Here in verse one of this chapter comes the awful command, "Go your ways, and pour out the vials of the *wrath of God* upon the earth" (16:1).

When at the end of the Seven Year Tribulation the King of Kings returns, "he treadeth the winepress of the fierceness and *wrath of Almighty God"* (19:15). Again God and Christ are specifically involved in the last mention of wrath.

Besides these seven, other references without the full expression concerning *His wrath* are found in 6:17: the great day of *His wrath* is come, in 11:18: *thy wrath* is come, in 16:19: the wine of the fierceness of *His wrath.*

Truly the whole Tribulation is a period of His wrath; consequently, the Pre–wrath Rapture is really a Pre-Tribulational Rapture.

Any idea that the Rapture occurs in the midst of this Tribulation period or three quarters of the way through, in connection with this chapter, must ignore all the other passages dealing with the subject of divine wrath and judgment to come.

I. The Plagues (1–21)

Whereas in heaven the true tabernacle–temple has always dealt with redemption and prayers and forgiveness, a solemn transition now occurs. It becomes the divine court of judgment and justice with the terrible penalties for rejection of redemption and prayers and forgiveness at last dispensed.

The **first vial** results in disease. Again invisible to human eyes, the angels of wrath pour out these results of men's sins. Thousands of years earlier, prior to the Exodus, Moses and Aaron sprinkled the ashes of the furnace upward (about 1450 B.C.) and it became small dust over all the land of Egypt, and became a boil breaking forth with blains upon man and beast.

Now terrible sores, noisome and grievous, break out on the followers of the Antichrist. Awful plagues, like the black plague, the bubonic plague, and other ravaging diseases have wiped out millions of people in centuries gone by. At the close of the 20th century the plague of sexually transmitted diseases has spread to every continent with AIDS being the worst, a death–dealing disease, fearful and fatal, which comes, most often, as a consequence of immorality and sin.

This plague will be worse, but evidently does not result in quick death.

The **second vial** causes the seas to become as the blood of a dead man. Earlier in the Tribulation, one third of the seas was affected, but now the oceans become contaminated and polluted as they undergo a chemical change, which appears "as the blood of a dead man."

This is the end of the ecology as we have known it, as this whole era comes to an end.

When the **third vial** is poured out, the rivers and fountains of their waters become blood.

It is a just and appropriate retribution for the shedding of the blood of millions of martyrs during the Tribulation and throughout history.

As the **fourth vial** is released, the light and heat of the sun is intensified and the human race is scorched by fire.

Whether the earth careens off its orbit and nears the sun, or some huge solar flare erupts from the solar surface out into space, or some other unknown phenomena takes place, no one now can be sure.

The heat will not be so intense as to consume, but rather to scorch.

Following the intense heat, the **fifth angel** pours out his vial on the seat–throne–headquarters of the Antichrist, and over his vast realms comes a bizarre and strange darkness.

Possibly, some explosion on the earth could be followed by a thick cloud of debris which could blot out the sun.

In the 1980s when Mount St. Helens in Washington state exploded in a volcanic convulsion, the ashes formed a thick cloud that turned midday into the darkest night for thousands of square miles, an illustration of the feasibility of this judgment. Of course, it also occurred in Egypt (Exodus 10:21–23) ages ago.

Notice that the capitol of the Antichrist is the center of this phenomena, perhaps a rebuilt Babylon on the shores of the Euphrates, where Wickedness is to be set on its base in the end–time

(Compare with Zechariah 5:5-10).

In preparation for the Battle of Armageddon, the **sixth vial** is poured on the River Euphrates, and the water dries up.

That this is the literal river is beyond doubt. Twenty–one times in Scripture is the river mentioned, five times called "the great river." When the Roman Empire was at its peak in territorial dominion, it was the eastern boundary. Nearly 1,800 miles in length, it rises in the Armenian mountains and flows through Baghdad and the site of ancient Babylon.

What means God will use to stop its flow, the fulfillment will reveal, but the way is clear for the land armies of the vast eastern Asian continent to surge through the Middle East enroute to the Land of Israel and the final battle of the Great Tribulation.

These "kings of the east" could include leaders from Russia, Iran, India, China, Japan and other Far Eastern powers. Evidently, the Antichrist may not be able to hold total control of these Asian powers, even though "the whole world" is wondering after the beast.

Somehow Israel becomes a major issue again, as history moves to its grand finale.

Involved in the process leading up to the Battle of Armageddon are demonic, invisible forces, said to proceed out of the mouth of the dragon, the beast and the false prophet, the evil Satanic trinity. All the armies of the world thus move, perhaps over a period of months or weeks, toward the Middle East and the final confrontation.

When the **seventh angel** pours out his vial into the air, again there issues a great voice out of the temple of heaven, announcing, IT IS DONE!

Thus, civilization, as we have known it, comes to its crashing conclusion. The earth is to rock and reel "like a drunkard" (Isaiah 24:20) under cataclysmic earthquakes and a "plague of hail," exceeding great. These events may stretch out over some period of time, since this summarizes the events described in greater detail in chapters 17, 18, and 19.

Consider the appropriateness of these judgments.

Since Christ, the cure for soul disease, is rejected and not worshipped, the sores afflict the acceptors of Antichrist as described under the judgment of the **first vial** (2).

Since Christ's blood is for the sins of the world (the wicked are like the troubled sea) — Isaiah 57:20 — the seas turn to blood under the **second vial** of wrath, dispensed by the second angel. These are literal judgments, as were the plagues on ancient Egypt, but how ironically just (3).

Since Christ's servants, offering the water of life, have been martyred by the millions through the centuries, shedding their blood like a river of undying love, the waters now turn to blood. "True and righteous are his judgments." This is the **third vial** (4–7).

Since men loved darkness rather than light (John 3:19) and inasmuch as the Light did shine into the darkness and the darkness comprehended it not (John 1:5), a strange and painful darkness overshadows the capitol, the headquarters and the whole realm of the Antichrist. "If our gospel be hid, it is hid to them that are lost: in whom the god of this world hath blinded the minds of them that believe not, lest the light of the glorious gospel of Christ, who is the image of God, should shine unto them" (2 Corinthians 4:3,4). This is the **fifth vial** (10,11).

Since Christ, the Prince of Peace, has been refused, the circumstances, even the geography of the world is altered to prepare for the advent of Christ, the Warrior (19:11) at the battle of Armageddon. The water of the Euphrates, already turned to blood, dries up, clearing the way for land armies to come from the East toward the final battle of the great day of God Almighty. This is the **sixth vial** (12-14).

Since Christ cried "IT IS FINISHED" from the cross (John 19:30) and His work of redemption has been so refused by the world in general, God announced "IT IS DONE" (17), as His work of judgment nears completion, great geological and meteorological events attend the fall of civilization. Babylon, the city, the system, the whole regime of the Antichrist, is struck by divine wrath (18-21).

Three times in the chapter the human race is seen blaspheming instead of repenting (9, 11, 21).

Those who have earlier heard the gospel of Christ and refused it will be congealed in their awful violent rejection of God and His gospel.

All of this results from the **seventh vial.**

II. The Plea (15)

Because there will be those who have heard the gospel before the Rapture, who will accept Christ during the Tribulation, this word of Christ especially applies to them:

"Behold, I come as a thief, Blessed is he that watcheth, and keepeth his garments, lest he walk naked and they see his shame."

Yet, this plea of Christ is appropriate for us today.

It is important that we walk with Christ, wait for Christ, watch for Christ daily, for He will come for us as "a thief in the night" (1 Thessalonians 5:2).

III. The Place (16)

Armageddon is a vast valley in Palestine, connecting the Plain of Esdraelon, the Valley of Jezreel and the Valley of Jehoshaphat. In the Old Testament Joel 3 and Zechariah 14 are among the passages that describe this battle and its aftermath. These Scriptures should be pondered carefully. The third chapter of Habakkuk gives a poetic picture of Christ's glorious return in splendor to establish His kingdom and put down His enemies, as does Isaiah 34.

Napoleon Bonaparte, nearly 200 years ago, marveled at the vast valley, commenting that all the world's armies could fight there; his words were almost prophetic.

Though it may be initially a battle to establish the Antichrist's power over some possible rebels, the showdown, in reality, will be between Christ and the Antichrist with our Lord gloriously triumphant.

Conclusion

Now friend, how do you stand in God's program?

Sooner of later the plagues of wrath will fall.

Sooner of later Christ will come for His people.

Sooner or later the battle of Armageddon will be fought.

You, gentle reader, must someday die and stand before God at the judgment.

Are you saved or lost?

Come to Christ now.

A Commentary on the Revelation
Expository, Exegetical, Devotional and Practical
Greek words from the Textus Receptus

Chapter Sixteen

Angels commanded to Go Forth (1)

1. **And I heard a great voice** *(Kai ekousa megales phones)* — the voice of God out of the heavenly temple speaks the command to execute the seven last plagues, all of the results of which occur in the last stages of the Tribulation. The first four affect the earth, sea, springs and the sun, whereas the last three affect the throne of the beast, the river Euphrates in preparation for the final battle of Armageddon and the horrendous conclusion of the whole judgment period ... **Go your ways and pour out** *(hupagete kai ekcheete)* — the thought is that all of the contents would be drained from these receptacles ... **the vials of the wrath of God upon the earth** *(kas hepta phialas tou theou eis ten gen)* — "This wrath is reserved for rebels (Psalm 79:6); persecutors (Jeremiah 10:25); heathen nations (Zephaniah 3:8,9); despising unbelievers (Romans 2:4,5). It will be as literal as God's judgment upon the pre–flood world, Sodom and Gomorrah, and as the plagues of Egypt" (A. Garner).

The Seven Vials (2-21).

2. **And the first went and poured out his vial upon the earth and there fell a noisome and grievous sore upon the men** — these are foul and painful ulcers ... **noisome** *(kakon* – meaning evil or bad*)* ... **grievous** *(poneron* – painful, hurtful, heavy*)* ... **which had the mark of the beast upon them which worshipped his image** — this terrible disease is reminiscent of the boils that afflicted the Egyptians in the sixth judgment (Exodus 9:8–12). The devotees to beast worship, like the magicians who withstood Moses, suffer from this plague. 3. **Upon the sea; as it became as the blood of a dead man** *(eis ten thalassan kai egeneto haima hos nekrou)* — this means that the sea becomes similar to the blood of a dead corpse, coagulated, polluted, with no normal flow ... **and every living soul died in the sea** — literally "soul of life." This is the end of the marine ecology. Compare Revelation 8:8,9, where one third of the

seas are so affected and the O.T. references to a similar smaller phenomena in Egypt: Exodus 7:20,21; Psalm 78:44; Psalm 105:29. 4. **And the third angel poured out his vial upon the rivers** *(potamous)* **and the fountains of waters** *(pegas ton hudaton)* **and they became blood** — this near universal contamination and pollution of the earth's water supply must be at the near end of the Tribulation, since there are survivors of these judgments and consumption of these "bloody" waters would further endanger human life. 5. **And I heard the angel of the waters say, Thou art righteous, O Lord, which art and wast and shalt be, because thou hast judged thus** — Unsaved, sin–hardened, beast-worshipping humans would blame God for many of these judgments, refusing to acknowledge that they are experiencing the just punishment of their evil deeds, but in God's divine and presently invisible government, the "angel of the waters" makes the solemn pronunciation here, affirming the absolute righteousness and judgment for their sin. 6. **For they have shed the blood of saints and prophets and thou hast given them blood to drink, for they are worthy** — while the human race generally has persecuted the people of God throughout history, shedding the blood of martyrs freely in every century of this Dispensation, this passage primarily may refer to the Jewish believers who receive Christ after the Rapture under the preaching of the Two Witnesses and the 144,000 who refuse, like the saved Jews, to worship the image of the beast. Yet, the human race is guilty, wicked leaders in particular of rejecting God, martyring Christians and hating those who follow Him. In all of these dire and destructive judgments, God is still just and holy and righteous in all of His dealings. When God's grace is refused, God's wrath must eventually fall. The wicked are worthy of the punishment they receive. 7. **And I heard another voice out of the altar say, Even so, Lord God Almighty, true and righteous are thy judgments** — those who impugn God for His justice do not desire forgiveness, but approval of their sins. **8. And the fourth angel poured his vial upon the sun and power was given unto him to scorch men with fire** *(en puri)* — Earlier under the fourth trumpet (8:12), the heavenly bodies were diminished in brilliance by one third, but here the light, heat and rays of the sun are increased. This is no mere extreme peak of temperature, as might be found in the hottest deserts, but rather a special phenomena, wherein solar rays feel like torches. Isaiah may have foreseen this in 24:5,6, a chapter dealing with the end times: "The earth mourneth and fadeth away, the haughty people of the earth do languish. The earth also is defiled under the inhabitants thereof; because they have transgressed the laws, changed the ordinance, broken the everlasting covenant. Therefore the curse defileth the earth, and they that dwell therein are desolate: therefore the inhabitants of the earth are burned, and few men left." **9. And men were scorched with great heat, and blasphemed the name of God, which hath power over these plagues: and they repented not to give him glory.** — "We would think it impossible for people with souls in them to hold out against such exhibitions of angry almightiness. But no; they only blaspheme the name of God having command of the plagues, and repent not to give Him glory. They have sold themselves to hell and received the sacrament and seal of it upon their bodies, and they only dare and sin on to their inevitable damnation" (Seiss). **10. And the fifth angel poured his vial upon the seat** *(epi ton thronon)* **of the beast** *(tou theriou)* — some authorities think that Rome in its final stages will be the world capital of the Antichrist, an idea held in early centuries before the so called conversion of the Empire to Christianity, when Rome became the center of ecclesiastical authority – and still is. The Reformers four centuries ago believed that Rome and Babylon and the Pope were the Antichrist. Other writers see a rebuilt Babylon in view here with the last capital–headquarters–throne of the Antichrist situated on the banks of the ancient Euphrates ... **and his kingdom was full of darkness** *(kai egeneto he basileia autou eskotomene)* — whether a literal Babylon or Rome itself, the whole central regime of the Antichrist experiences a mysterious and strange darkness. If some solar disturbance causes the increased scorching rays, its aftermath might be a cloud of debris, hurtling through space and beclouding a portion of the earth's surface. Compare Exodus 10:21 ... **and they gnawed their tongues for pain** — the same tongues which had blasphemed God they now bite in pain. **11. And blasphemed the God of heaven** *(kai eblasphemesan ton tou ouranou)* — as is also indicated in vs. 9,21 ... **because of their pains and their sores and repented not of their deeds** *(ek ton panon auton kai ek ton helkon auton kai ou metemoesan ek ton ergon auton)* — suffering, polluted, covered with sores and burns, vast numbers go on in their self–delusions, blaming God, blaspheming God, refusing God. While this is future, the pattern exists now, as can be seen in multitudes dying with incurable diseases at a relatively young age, such as those suffering from AIDS in the 1990's, clinging to their sin, refusing the truth of God and hating those who rebuke them and urge them to repent. Yet God would have them repent, that none might perish eternally (II Peter 3:9, Amos 4:11, Romans 2:5), but He will force His will on no one. **12. And the sixth angel poured out his vial upon the great river Euphrates** — first mentioned in Genesis 2:14, it is designated by name twenty–one times in Scripture, called "the great river" five times. It is some 1,800 miles long, arising in the Armenian Mountains, first flowing south toward Israel, about 100 miles from the Mediterranean. Turning eastward, it becomes a navigable waterway. It flowed through old Babylon, modern Bagdad and other communities, finally emptying in the Persian Gulf ... **and the water thereof was dried up** *(kai ekseranthe to hudor autou)* — a different and miraculous event was the parting of the Red Sea for the passage of the Israelites (Exodus 14:16) ... this event is not for deliverance, but is rather a part of divine judgment, opening up easy access to Israel and the battle of Armageddon for the foot soldiers, armored vehicles and land forces of all kinds ... **that the way of kings of the east might be prepared** *(hina he hodos ton basileon ton apo anatoles heliou hetoimasthe)* — note that east is literally sun–rising *(heliou)*. The majority of the human race is east of the Euphrates: the 60,000,000 of Persia, the 150,000,000 of Pakistan, the 900,000,000 of India, the 125,000,000 of Bangladesh, the 1,200,000,000 of China, 125,000,000 of Japan (land of the rising sun), plus Korea, Southeast Asia and the 200,000,000 in Indonesia. Vast hordes, huge armies, in spite of the devastation thus far in the Tribulation, will still marshal their forces and sweep across the southern Asian continent. Possibly technological inventions which short circuit electronic and computer devices by laser beams or some other method will result in a return to land armies and foot soldiers. In any event, they will come, as indicated in other Scriptures (Joel 3:9–14; Zephaniah 3:8; Zechariah 1:3,9; Isaiah 24:1,2,8). Whether the ruling Antichrist must attempt to keep these Eastern peoples under his sway or they perhaps think they can rebel is an open question. In any event, Israel will be an issue and God, behind the scenes, allows them access to the Middle East for the conclusion of time as we know it. **13. And I saw three unclean spirits like frogs** *(kai eidon pneuma-tria akatharta hos batrachoi)* **come out of the mouth of the dragon and out of the mouth of the beast and out of the mouth of the false prophet.** — This is reminiscent of the frogs of Exodus 8:1–6, but is a spiritual phenomena, not animal occurrence, since these evil spirits are like frogs. They are said to proceed from the mouths of the Satanic trinity: the dragon – anti–God– Satan; the beast – Antichrist; and the false prophet – anti–Holy Spirit, thus revealing this is a spiritual warfare, with these frog-like demonic beings going forth to deceive and draw these kings of the east and other armies of the world to their own destruction. God can even use the wrath and evil of the wicked one and his cohorts to precipitate divine judgment. **14. For they are the spirits of devils** *(pneumata daimonian)* **working miracles, which go forth unto the kings of the earth and the whole world to gather them to the battle of that great day of God Almighty** — "These demon spirits are the elect agents to walk in the world to attempt to abolish God from the earth; and they are frog–like in that they come forth out of the pestiferous quagmires of the universe, do their work amid the world's evening shadows, and creep and croak and defile the ears of the nations with noisy demonstrations, till they set all the kings and armies of the whole earth in enthusiastic commotion for the final crushing of the Lamb and all His powers" (Seiss). Miraculous events will occur by Satanic power, impressing the nations of the world to assemble for the final battle. **15. Behold I come as a thief, Blessed is he that keepeth his garments, lest he walk naked and they see his shame** — right in the midst of this vivid depiction of Satanic influence and power appears this encouraging motivational word from the Lord. This is especially applicable to Tribulation time believers, those who come to Christ after the Rapture, Jews and Gentiles, who did not previously hear and refuse the gospel. Christ's Glorious Appearing is just about to occur. However, it is always an appropriate outlook even now. This is a parentheti-

cal word from the Lord, as the next verse continues the thought of the previous verse. **16. And he gathered them together into a place called in the Hebrew tongue Armageddon** *(kai sunagagen autous eis ton topon ton kaloumenon hebraisti Armagedon)* — overruling the evil activities of the demon–spirits, God gathers these multitudes to a topographical place *(topon)*, an actual location, known as the "valley of slaughter," (Judges 5:19; 2 Kings 23:29; 2 Chronicles 35:22). This is the vast area in central Israel (Samaria – also known in the 90s as the "occupied territories" with the valleys connecting and leading toward Jerusalem. Study also "the Valley of Jehoshaphat in a Bible atlas. **17. And the seventh angel poured out his vial into the air and there came a great voice out of the temple of God from the throne saying, It is done.** — Forth like a great sound from a megaphone comes this powerful divine proclamation, which encompasses the concluding and climactic events of the whole seven year Tribulation. It is now at a close. Earthly judgments on the wicked and the trials of Israel now are culminating and will conclude with Christ's appearing (Revelation 1:7). Contrast this with Christ's words in finishing His atoning work on the cross, when He said, "It is finished." **18. And there were voices** *(kai phonai)* **and thunders** *(ka brontai)* **and lightnings** *(kai astrapai)* **and there was a great earthquake** *(kai seismos egeneto megas)* **such as was not since men were upon the earth, so mighty an earthquake and so great** — these events take place in the last stages of the Tribulation, just before the battle of Armageddon. **19. And the great city was divided into three parts** — Babylon which then falls with the cities of the nations. **20. Every island fled away** — great geological and seismological convulsions occur on the planet … **and the mountains were not found. 21. And there fell upon men a great hail … every stone about the weight of a talent** — talents in ancient times ranged between about 85 pounds and 125 or more … **men blasphemed God,** these wicked millions never humble themselves, never seek God, but only continue to reject and blaspheme and blame and hate God.

RAINBOWS FROM REVELATION
The Revelation of Jesus Christ
A chapter by chapter, verse by verse study
"There was a rainbow round about the throne like unto an emerald" (4:3)

CHAPTER SEVENTEEN: Mystery Babylon

References

Rev. 15:1,6
Rev. 21:9
Nah. 3:4
Jer. 51:13

Jer. 51:7
Rev. 14:8

Zech. 5:5-11
Rev. 13:1

Ezek. 28:13
Dan. 11:38

2 Thes. 2:7

Rev. 13:15
Rev. 6:9
Acts 22:20

Rev. 13:1
Dan. 7:14,21

Rev. 17:11
Rev. 13:10
Rev. 9:1,2

References

Rev. 13:1

Luke 2:1

Rev. 13:3,12,14

Dan. 7:20

Rom. 8:7

Deut. 10:17
1 Tim. 6:15
Rev. 19:16
Jer. 50:44

Isa. 8:7
Isa. 57:20,21

Jer. 50:41
Ezek. 16:37,39

2 Thes. 2:11
Rev. 10:7

Rev. 16:19

1. AND there came one of the seven angels which had the seven vials, and talked with me, saying unto me, Come hither; I will show unto thee the judgment of the great whore that sitteth upon many waters:

2. With whom the kings of the earth have committed fornication, and the inhabitants of the earth have been made drunk with the wine of her fornication.

3. So he carried her away in the spirit into the wilderness: and I saw a woman sit upon a scarlet-colored beast, full of names of blasphemy, having seven heads and ten horns.

4. And the woman was arrayed in purple and scarlet color, and decked with gold and precious stones and pearls, having a golden cup in her hand full of abomination and filthiness of her fornication:

5. And upon her forehead was a name written, MYSTERY, BABYLON THE GREAT, THE MOTHER OF HARLOTS AND ABOMINATIONS OF THE EARTH.

6. And I saw the woman drunken with the blood of the saints, and with the blood of the martyrs of Jesus: and when I saw her, I wondered with great admiration.

7. And the angel said unto me, Wherefore didst thou marvel? I will tell thee the mystery of the woman, and of the beast that carrieth her, which hath the seven heads and ten horns.

8. The beast that thou sawest was, and is not; and shall ascend out of the bottomless pit, and go into perdition: and they that dwell on the earth shall wonder, whose names were not written in the book of life from the foundation of the world, when they behold the beast that was, and is not, and yet it.

9. And here is the mind which hath wisdom. The seven heads are seven mountains, on which the woman sitteth.

10. And there are seven kings: five are fallen, and one is, and the other is not yet come; and when he cometh, he must continue a short space.

11. And the beast that was, and is not, even he is the eighth, and is of the seven, and goeth into perdition.

12. And the ten horns which thou sawest are ten kings, which have received no kingdom as yet; but receive power as kings one hour with the beast.

13. These have one mind, and shall give their power and strength unto the beast.

14. These shall make war with the Lamb, and the Lamb shall overcome them: for he is Lord of lords, and King of kings: and they that are with him are called, and chosen, and faithful.

15. And he saith unto me, The waters which thou sawest, where the whore sitteth, are peoples, and multitudes, and nations, and tongues.

16. And the ten horns which thou sawest upon the beast, these shall hate the whore, and shall make her desolate and naked, and shall eat her flesh, and but her with fire.

17. For God hath put in their hearts to fulfill his will, and to agree, and give their kingdom unto the beast, until the words of God shall be fulfilled.

18. And the woman which thou sawest is that great city, which reigneth over the kings of the earth.

Scriptures for Comparison

Zechariah 5:6-8,10-11

And I said, What is it? And he said, This is an ephah that goeth forth. He said moreover, This is their resemblance through all the earth.

And behold, there was lifted up a talent of lead: and this is a woman that sitteth in the midst of the ephah.

And he said, This is wickedness. And he cast it into the midst of the ephah; and he cast the weight of lead upon the mouth thereof.

Then said I to the angel that talked with me, Whither do these bear the ephah?

And he said unto me, To build it a house in the land of Shinar: and it shall be established, and set there upon her own base.

Summary of Chapter Seventeen

Mystery, Babylon the Great

I. The Woman on the Beast (1-7)

Both in Chapter 14:8 and in Chapter 16:19, the fall of Babylon is announced prior to this detailed description in Chapters 17 and 18. In these later chapters Babylon appears as a "woman" and as a "city."

It is important to distinguish between ecclesiastical, religious Babylon and political, commercial Babylon.

In the second century almost all commentators identified Babylon as a cryptic name for Rome, capital of the Empire and center of world religion and government. It was the culmination of all previous western civilizations with its domain extending from most of the British Isles all across Southern and Central Europe, all of North Africa, and on the east to encompass a large portion of Arabia and practically all of what had been the old Babylonian Empire and much of the Medo-Persian Empire, as described in Daniel 7, 8 and 11. It extended to the Persian Gulf.

Greco-Roman culture, customs, languages (Latin and Greek) laws, architecture and general thought dominated the Western World for centuries. Adaptations and variations in languages, religion and culture continued through the centuries with the Byzantine Empire in the east, its capital at Constantinople (Istanbul) continuing until 1453, when the East Roman Empire fell. But the Orthodox religion and much of the Eastern culture was continued by the Czars (Caesars) of Russia. Moscow has been known as the Third Rome (after Constantinople, the second).

In the West the Roman Empire suffered a severe blow in 476 A.D., when Germanic tribes crushed the Western Empire, but gradually the conquerors absorbed the Latin language and culture and the Holy Roman Empire lasted for a thousand years with varying relationships between the Holy Roman Emperor and the Pope of Rome. Napoleon Bonaparte finally abolished the Holy Roman Empire in 1806 A.D.

As this chapter opens John is shown a woman arrayed in costly apparel, but drunk with the blood of the martyrs of Jesus. Pagan Rome persecuted early Christians; papal Rome later through the suppression of "heretics" and finally the "inquisition" followed suit, persecuting true believing Christians, including many "Anabaptists."

Mystery Babylon is false religion, with corrupted Christianity, absorbing many of the idolatrous ideas of ancient Roman and Greek religion, which in turn, drew heavily from Babylonian and Egyptian models. It includes apostate Catholicism, as Martin Luther taught, corrupted Eastern Orthodox Christianity and, through the centuries, decadent Protestantism which departs from the faith once and for all delivered to the saints.

II. The Meaning of the Vision (8-17)

Mystery Babylon in the last days is the culmination of ecumenicalism without true Christianity. After the Rapture, only the shell of "the Christian religion" is left. Everything resembling Christianity culminates in this final false world superchurch, including unsaved, lost professing Christians (1-7).

The chapter defines the woman as a city; the beast as a person and a system with mysterious origins ... "the beast that was, is not, and yet is." Some think this refers to Roman civilization, its eclipse and restoration; others believe it refers only to the person of the Antichrist.

A twofold interpretation is offered for the vision of the beast's seven heads. First they are seven mountains, an unmistakable reference to the famous seven hills on which Rome was built and which carry seven names unto this day.

Second, the seven heads are said to be seven kings, five of whom have fallen. One was said to be, the other was to come and continue for "a short space." The beast is the eighth, but is one of the seven.

This writer holds to the seven great world civilizations of biblical history as the seven heads: Egypt, Assyria, Babylon, Medo-Persia, Greece, Rome (in all of its forms), covering about 2,000 years until the early 1800's. Either Anglo-American civilization or possibly communistic European domination of the world being the seventh, is the final form of Gentile world dominion, when the ten horns (10 final powerful rulers) will give their sovereignty over to the beast (Antichrist).

Finally, they destroy the apostate world superchurch and its influence.

The woman is the great city (Rome), and the whole system it represents.

Outline of Chapter Seventeen

Vision of the Symbols Explained

OBJECTIVE: To reveal the judgment of the great harlot church in the end times.

OUTLINE:
Note: the invitation COME HITHER
  Compare:
  "Come up hither" (4:1)"
  "Come up hither" (11:12)
  "Come hither" (17:1)
  "Come hither" (21:9)

I. The Harlot Woman: Apostate Christianity in End Times (1-6)
  A. Angel's Ministry (1-3)
    1. Angel's invitation to see "Babylon" (1)
    2. Angel's depiction of "Babylon" (2)
    3. Angel's transportation of John to see "Babylon" (3)
  B. Astonishing Mystery (3-6) "Babylon"
    1. Description (3, 4)
        a. Astride a scarlet beast
        b. Arrayed in luxury
        c. Accustomed to abominations
    2. Designation (5)
      MYSTERY, BABYLON THE GREAT
      "The woman is that great city, which reigneth over the kings of the earth."
    3. Doom (16)

II. The Scarlet Beast: Antichrist and His Empire (3, 7, 8)
  A. He Was
    The Roman empire has been (possibly Antichrist was also alive before).
  B. He is Not
    The Roman empire goes into eclipse (possibly Antichrist is in the bottomless pit).
  C. He Yet Is
    Roman Western civilization continues and will finally dominate the world again (possibly the Antichrist will be someone who lived before who emerges again) (See 11:17).

III. The Seven Heads (first interpretation): Seven Hills of Rome (9) History books list the seven hills frequently by name.

IV. The Seven Heads (second interpretation): Seven Successive World Civilizations (10, 11)
  A. Five are Fallen
    1. Egypt
    2. Assyria
    3. Babylon (Daniel 7) 606-536 B.C.
    4. Medo-Persia (Daniel 7) 536-330 B.C.
    5. Greek (Daniel 7, 8, 11) 330-150 B.C.
  B. One Is
    6. Rome 150 B.C., 476 A.D., 1453 A.D., 1806 A.D.
  C. One to Continue a Short Space
    7. Anglo-American civilization? 1800-2000 A.D.?
  D. One of Seven Restored
    Roman-European world domination

V. The Ten Horns: Alliance of 10 Powerful Western Nations (12, 13)
  A. Their Leadership is Future
  B. Their Power is with the Beast (Antichrist and his realm)
  C. Their Desire is to Give Power to the Beast

VI. The Victorious Lamb: the Coming King (14)
  A. He Will Overcome Wicked Rulers
  B. He Is Called Lord of Lords and King of Kings
  C. He Has His People
    1. Called
    2. Chosen
    3. Faithful

VII. The Many Waters: Vast Population (15-18)
  A. People
  B. Multitudes
  C. Nations
  D. Tongues
    Compare Isaiah 57:20. This false religion will dominate the world. Refer here to point I, number 3; consider again the doom of the woman
      a. Hated by the government
      b. Destroyed by the government
      c. Dominated by the beast
Babylon, the city, can be none other here than Rome, both pagan and papal, as well as political, in the end time (18).

Observations:
Spiritual lessons and applications from each verse
Chapter Seventeen

1. We are invited to study God's judgments and prophecies even now.

2. Alliances of the world and the church have often been made, but are always dangerous and damaging to true religion.

3. Think of the contrast between this "woman" and the "Lamb's wife" (19:7).

4. Luxury, idolatry and immorality often go together.

5. "Babylon" is the mother of other false religion, here a final combination and culmination of apostate Christianity, mixed with all kinds of evils and errors.

6. Persecuting and massacring true Christians is a mark of false religion.

7. God wants us to understand many of His mysteries. Study them.

8. Be sure your name is written now in the Lamb's book of life.

9. It takes illuminated wisdom to understand God's truths. See James 1:5.

10. God understands and designs future history.

11. Wicked advocates of error and sin ultimately go into perdition, always.

12. God in His providence allows political alliances.

13. When several wicked leaders conspire together, great evil follows, as in the history of Nazism, fascism, communism, etc.

14. Always the Lamb overcomes evil, sooner or later.

15. Waters often represent the "sea of humanity."

16. God sometimes designs that wicked men destroy other wickedness, using even "the wrath of man to praise him."

17. God's words will always be fulfilled in the showdown.

18. Cities like Rome in history and prophecy become the centers of good or evil. Contrast Babylon, which epitomizes worldly, earthly, devilish civilization at its peak, with New Jerusalem, the city of God.

The Babylonish System

"The next two chapters (17, 18) of Revelation deal with the whole question of Babylon. In chapter 17 we have the Babylonish system to consider; in the next one, the Babylonish city. Thus there are two Babylons, and the one grows out of the other. The beast (Antichrist) controls the first and creates the second.

"The Babylonish system is both religious and political. The religious system paves the way for the political system. In the beginning, the religious system supports the political system, but in the end the political system supplants the religious one. The religious system is symbolized in Revelation 17 and the Babylonian mother; the political system is symbolized by the Babylonian monster …

"The scarlet woman has one master craving — power. To get that power she has abandoned every principle. Do the kings of the earth have power? She will court them, cajole them, command them; she will give them anything they want as long as they give her power in exchange … the name of the woman is printed out in bold capitals. Her name is **BABYLON.** Her home is the city of seven hills (9, 18), and she is identified prophetically with Rome. She is an apostate religious system linked with Rome, but in fact is far older than Rome. In her final form she gathers up into her embrace all the false religions of earth. From Babylon (Gen. 10, 11) they first began their migration across the globe; to Babylon they will return."

— John Phillips

Quotations
From Other Expositors
Chapter Seventeen

The Woman on the Beast (1-7)

"The first six verses of our chapter reveal to us a most astounding and awful scene, portraying through symbols two great forces, one religious, the other governmental.

"This vision comes from 'one of the seven angels who had the seven bowls.' Though it is not stated by John, the context locates this judgment scene as taking place in the middle of the Tribulation Period. It is a controlling influence in the Antichrist's government.

"Ten details delineate this woman:

"1. 'The great harlot'

"2. 'That sitteth upon many waters'

"3. 'With whom the kings of the earth have committed fornication'

"4. 'And the inhabitants of the earth have been made drunk with the wine of her fornication'

"5. 'A woman (in the wilderness) sitting upon a scarlet-colored beast'

"6. 'Arrayed in purple and scarlet'

"7. 'Bedecked with gold and precious stones'

"8. 'Having a golden cup in her hand, full of abominations and filthiness of her fornication'

"9. 'Upon her forehead was a name written, MYSTERY, BABYLON THE GREAT, MOTHER OF HARLOTS AND ABOMINATIONS OF THE EARTH'

"10. 'Drunk with the blood of saints, and with the blood of the martyrs of Jesus.'

"Even before we come to the angel's interpretation of this vision, it is clear that we are not dealing with a human being, for no one woman could commit fornication with the kings of the earth, nor could a woman be 'drunk with the blood of the saints and with the blood of the martyrs of Jesus.' Our rule for Bible interpretation is that when the plain sense of Scripture makes common sense, seek no other sense. Fortunately, the angel gave John the interpretation to this vision, which we will consult after examining the vision of the beast."

– *Tim LaHaye*

"We are not able to resist the conclusion that there is here a double destruction before our eyes.

"1. The overthrow of the woman in chapter 17 is accomplished by the Beast and his ten kings.

"2. The Beast and his ten kings are being at the time adulated by the earth, the Beast himself universally worshipped (except by God's elect). All the kings and powers of the earth are subject to him, as we saw in chapter 13.

"3. The Beast, his kings, and of course the whole earth with them, join in the destruction of the harlot, whom we see at the beginning of chapter 17 riding the revived Roman Beast.

"4. Evidently Romanism, with its situation on the seven hills of Rome, is indicated by this woman, 'drunken with the blood of the saints, and with the blood of the martyrs of Jesus.' The whole earth, with its kings, is delighted at the removal of the last vestige of this hateful harlot, who really has been a burden, spiritual, mental, political, and financial, to all the nations over which she held sway; although they committed spiritual 'fornication' with her: that is, she pronounced them 'Christian,' and they gave her money and 'reverence.'"

– *William R. Newell*

"In the last, tragic world–drama of 'the things which shall be hereafter' (Revelation 1:19); that is, after the translation of the church, forever to be with the Lord — in this approaching, terrific drama of sin and blood and tears, one of the chief 'personages' will be 'the great whore ... MYSTERY, BABYLON THE GREAT, THE MOTHER OF HARLOTS AND ABOMINATIONS OF THE EARTH.' As we shall see from this study of Revelation 17:1–19:4, the 'great whore' which John saw, a 'woman ... upon a scarlet coloured beast,' is a symbol of none other than apostate Christendom in its final form. This spectacular organization will include those, both Catholic and Protestant, who profess the name of Christ, yet deny 'the faith once for all delivered unto the saints.'"

– *Louis T. Talbot*

"Mystery Babylon! The system has survived the centuries, and it lives on in many a pagan religion in the world today and reigns supreme in Rome. Rome is certainly not the mother of harlots and abominations, for that title belongs to ancient Babylon — but she certainly is included. The intoxicating wine of idolatry with all its accompanying vileness was already bottled and labeled three thousand years before Rome was dreamed of; but Rome is a major purveyor of this merchandise. The whole worldwide system of idolatry, possibly coached and led by Rome, will unite at last under the beast. Idolatry will be the cornerstone of his world religion; once the beast rids himself of the Roman system, it will all be headed up in himself and his image. Twice in Revelation seventeen, the woman is identified with Rome. The fact that she sheds the blood of the martyrs of Jesus aids in her prophetic identification, for certainly ancient Babylon did not shed the blood of Christian martyrs. In the last days Rome, as a religious system, is clearly linked with Babylon and Babylon with Rome.

– *John Phillips*

The Meaning of the Vision (8-18)

"The angel turns from the woman to the Beast when the vision is explained. John would cease to wonder at the appalling picture.

"1. The ancient empire beheld in vision **'was;'** that is, it existed in its imperial form in John's day.

"2. **'And is not.'** It has no present political existence [now]. The kingdoms which composed it of course remain, but the empire as such no longer exists. Modern Europe, with its many conflicting interests, jealousies, and separate kingdoms, is the result of the complete breakup of the once undivided empire of the Caesars. The western part of the empire, which fell last, is by far the guiltiest, as being the scene of Christian light and grace. These two phases of the empire are simple matters of history, but the remaining features are prophetic, and are only written in the pages of the Sacred Volume. God lifts the veil, and we see, after the lapse of many centuries, the empire once more filling the gaze of men — an astonishment to apostate Christendom.

"3. **'Is about to come up out of the abyss.'** Satan will revive the empire, and then stamp his own character upon it. The human rise of the Beast must be carefully distinguished from its satanic revival in the midst of the seventieth prophetic week at the epoch of Satan's expulsion from Heaven (chapter 12). The Seer beholds it in vision on the eve of its revival. 'Is about to come up.' The abyss produces this monster of iniquity — the Beast. Heaven opens and gives forth the Church — the bride of the Lamb.

"4. **'Go into destruction.'** This is the final phase of Gentile power. Rome came into existence 753 B.C. It passed through many trials, weathered many political storms, till it reached the zenith of its glory in the time of Christ. Its connection with Christ and Judah is the great crisis in the history of the empire. Subsequently the blood of the people was shed in such multitudes that millions were involved in the most awful slaughter recorded in history.

"When the empire reappears in its last and satanic form it will be an object of universal wonder, save to the redeemed. What a state of things we have arrived at! Satan brings out of the darkness of the pit a power which he fashions and controls, outwardly like the empire, yet diabolically featured. Men then will wonder and worship both Satan and his human instruments."

– *Walter Scott*

"John's words in Revelation 17:9 declares: 'There are also seven kings.' This statement reveals that there are seven kingdoms or empires whose destiny is to rule the world curing the thousands of years comprising the Times of the Gentiles. 'Five have fallen, one is and the other has not yet come. And when he comes, he must continue a short time. The beast that was, and is not, is himself also the eighth, and is of the seven, and is going to perdition' (Revelation 17:9–11). Five empires ruled the known world in succession before John the Apostle wrote his book of Revelation. The empires of Egypt, Assyria, Babylon, Media–Persia and Greece each ruled the known world. Each empire in its turn oppressed the Children of Israel. John wrote, 'one is and the other is not yet come' describing the sixth kingdom, the Roman Empire that ruled the world in John's day. Rome, the sixth kingdom, will return in the last days as the seventh kingdom, the Revived Roman Empire with its ten–nation confederacy."

– *Grant R. Jeffrey*

The Role and Rule of Rome in End Times
An Expository Sermon

Chapter Seventeen

Introduction

A proper understanding of this chapter arises from an understanding of everything that precedes it in the book of Revelation, studied in the light of Daniel's interpretation of Nebuchadnezzar's great metallic image (Daniel 2) with its 10 toes and Daniel's vision of the beasts in the seventh chapter of his book with special attention given to the fourth beast with the 10 horns. The toes and the horns in all instances relate to the 10 nations in the end times that constitute the nucleus of Antichrist's regime ... in the future.

The Woman is the final world superchurch, incorporating idolatrous and erroneous religious ideas from heathenism, as developed over all the history of time.

Most Bible scholars see Rome as Babylon in this chapter. Many Bible scholars see political and commercial Babylon as being a rebuilt actual city which will be the Antichrist's final capital in the Tribulation, perhaps even Babylon itself, where civilization began. See Genesis 11.

In this message we will look at the Woman, the Beast and the Lamb.

I. The Woman (1-8)

Satan has had a diabolical plan in motion since the dawn of human civilization. Its final culmination will occur during the forthcoming time of Tribulation in the rise to supreme recognition of a worldwide religious system, which will participate with the last world ruler in dominating the world until "Babylon" itself is destroyed.

Now we have here in this chapter a woman who is a city, but more than that, who is a system, a philosophy, a religious power.

Why is this city called "Babylon"? For the same reason that old Jerusalem is called "Sodom and Gomorrah" in chapter 11. Jerusalem had become so blinded, that when the Lord came the first time, He was rejected and crucified. Like those two ancient cities, the supernatural power of God was refused along with God's messengers.

Rome in its history and final state partakes of the spirit of Babylon.

Babel, or Babylon, was founded thousands of years ago by Nimrod, the mighty hunter, the rebellious panther, the first king, who was imperialistic in ambitions and highly organized in his plans. Throughout the Old Testament Babylon is seen as a place in opposition to God, His people and true religion. It is mentioned 260 times in the Bible and is depicted as the center of pride, human wisdom and human religion.

According to many ancient records and modern research studies, Nimrod and his wife Semiramis founded a religious system which spawned idolatry. Their son, Tammuz, is said to have died and then been restored to life. Some ancient traditions even set forth a "virgin birth" for Tammuz. This Babylonian cult focused on the central idea of a mother and tiny child, but added gods and goddesses of all kinds to be revered and worshipped. This was the fountainhead of idolatry in the world.

Such associated concepts as idols and images, vestal virgins, holy water, priestly celibacy, ceremonial cleansing, prayer beads and wheels, plus dozens of other varying religious practices were interwoven into the fabric of this religious system.

In the process of time this "Babylonian cult" spread over the ancient world with different names used for the gods and goddesses including the Mother and the Child.

As Babylon itself was eclipsed in political power by other imperial regimes, the center of the system passed to Pergamos, where "Satan's seat" was. In time, ancient Babylonian religion and customs began to infiltrate Christianity, bringing in idolatry and false doctrine.

Pagan Rome under the Caesars persecuted Christians for centuries, shedding the blood of many martyrs. Later, after the presumed conversion of Constantine, who became the Roman emperor in the early 300's, Christianity became the official religion of the Roman Empire, *but* all kinds of idolatrous ideas and practices, carried over from ancient Babylon and spread throughout the civilized world, were simply absorbed and adapted to the new Christian religion, names being changed in many cases, but the customs maintained.

Much of these errors were superimposed upon the Christian religion.

In time, Papal Rome (Rome ruled by the popes, who were known as Pontifex Maximus, a title traceable to the heathen days of the Empire) also persecuted true Christians in the inquisitions and branding of heretics.

In the future, the final merger of Catholicism, Eastern Orthodox Catholics, apostate Protestantism and a wide variety of false religions will result in the completion of Mystery, Babylon the Great.

In the 20th century, ecumenical movements, parliaments of religion, dialogue with religionists of all persuasions have taken place. Ultimately all of this will blend into the final state of BABYLON THE GREAT, MOTHER OF HARLOTS AND ABOMINATIONS OF THE EARTH.

A GREAT WORLD SUPERCHURCH WILL DEVELOP, WHICH WILL EXERCISE GREAT INFLUENCE, AFTER THE RAPTURE OF ALL TRUE BELIEVERS FROM CHRISTENDOM. ALREADY, THE TRENDS AND PATTERNS, LEADING TO THIS ULTIMATE STATE, ARE IN PROCESS.

BUT, AS HERE DELINEATED, THIS VAST WORLD SUPERCHURCH ITSELF WILL BE DESTROYED BY THE POLITICAL POWERS OF THE END TIMES. ONLY THE BEAST, THE ANTICHRIST, WILL REMAIN TO BE THE OBJECT OF UNIVERSAL UNGODLY WORSHIP.

H. A. Ironside, a great expositor of this century, has well summarized these future developments:

"We have already seen in our study of the 13th chapter that this Beast sets forth the Roman Empire as revived in a Satanic-inspired league of nations after the church dispensation is over.

"This will be very different from anything that is formed in our own times, and may result from events occurring while the believers are still here. This federation of the future will be utterly godless and God-defiant. When that league is formed it will be natural that a confederacy of all religious systems will be wrought out, and this too will be Satanic in character.

"It will be a union of Christless professors of Christianity, inheriting all the human and diabolical mysteries of Babylon. In other words, all sects will be swallowed up in the one distinctively Babylonism system that has ever maintained the cult of the mother and the child. This system will, for the first part of the Tribulation Period, dominate the civil power. Thus the woman will be in the saddle again and ride the beast! He who has eyes to see and a heart to understand can readily discern the preparation now in progress, with this very end in view."

In a fascinating book, published in 1990, a prominent Catholic historian, novelist and former priest describes what he foresaw as the "struggle for world dominion between Pope John Paul II, Mikhail Gorbachev and the Capitalist West." The book is entitled, *The Keys of this Blood.*

He advanced the thesis that the Roman Pontiff was a keen and perceptive analyst of world trends and had set upon a calculated agenda to reestablish and exalt the Roman Church as the supreme world power.

As he saw it, three forces were struggling for world domination in the continuing swirl of world events. There was the "Red International," or Communism, as orchestrated by Gorbachev; the "Golden International," the politicians, bankers, industrialists, leaders of international commerce, and other advocates of the international capitalist system; and the "Purpose International," the worldwide hierarchical system of the Roman Catholic Church.

Red Communism as we have known it has practically disintegrated and Gorbachev is no longer a world figure, although Chinese Communism controls one fourth of the world's population.

Author Malachi Martin suggests that in this struggle for world domination the Roman Pontiff and such religious systems as unite with it can be the supreme power on this earth. Yet the "capitalists," which Revelation calls the "merchants of the earth," are forging ahead to build a New World Order.

As Martin views it, the present conflicting forces are playing for the high stakes of world control.

Does this resemble in any way what appears to be an alliance between religion and the last great world government under the Antichrist, which certainly, as one reads Revelation, does seem to exist in a capitalist society?

Time will tell.

II. The Beast (8-18)

Now this beast is both the final personality who is to rule and his regime, his empire.

It is said that he "was" and "is not," but shall "ascend out of the bottomless pit and go into perdition."

Some prophecy scholars therefore believe that this applies primarily to a personality. Theories that Judas Iscariot, who died and went to his own place (Acts 1), is to be resurrected and fulfill this role, have been advanced.

In my view the primary reference is to the Roman Empire, which was the dominant power for a thousand years on earth. As a united empire it is not now, but is to be revived and restored, if not in name, at least in substance and reality.

Originally founded in 753 B.C. Rome rose to

power and by 150 B.C. was establishing control over the civilized world.

From the days of Augustus Caesar and the time of Christ until 476 A.D. Rome was supreme, although a second and more magnificent capital was built in the East, the fabled Constantinople. The Western leg of the Empire was broken by invading tribes from the north and east in 476 A.D., but Rome continued to be the seat of the Supreme Pontiff of the Roman Catholic Church. The Holy Roman Empire, founded in 800 A.D., was the continuation of Roman Western Civilization, while Eastern Roman Empire with its capital at Constantinople continued until 1453 A.D. When it fell, the Eastern imperial tradition was taken up by the Czars (caesars) of Russia, complete with the Russian Orthodox Church.

Rome itself was a city built on Seven Hills, and unmistakably, second century Christians, reading the Revelation, would understand that Rome was intended, when verse nine so clearly states, "The seven heads are seven mountains on which the woman sitteth."

The seven hills of Rome are the Palantine, near the center of the city; the Capitoline, to the northwest; and lying in a curve stretching north to southwest, the Quirinale, the Viminal, the Esquiline, the Caeline, and the Aventine, so designated for nearly twenty-five centuries.

But the heads also symbolize seven kings, which in this writer's judgment signify the seven great world civilizations of (1) Egypt, (2) Assyria, (3) Babylon, (4) Medo-Persia, (5) Greece, (6) Rome, and a seventh not specified.

The last Holy Roman Emperor ceased using the title in 1806, but even after the fall of Rome in 476 A.D., the Eastern Roman Empire in 1435 A.D. and the abolition by Napoleon of the Holy Roman Empire in 1806, Graeco-Roman civilization has continued and is to be revived in full flower.

The "beast" is the "eighth," a restoration of the Roman Empire, in fact if not in name.

As for the "ten horns," these are ten powerful nations in the End Times, which "give their kingdom unto the beast."

Presumably, these are ten countries, once under the Roman Empire in its various stages, nations which continue the language (Latin languages are Spanish, French, Italian, Portuguese, Romanian and several lesser known tongues. Even English is filled with words drawn from Latin roots.)

In 1957 the Treaty of Rome was signed, which brought into existence the European Economic Community, beginning with six nations and now numbering twelve in 1945 (Italy, France, Germany,

Holland, Belgium, Luxembourg, England, Ireland, Denmark, Spain, Portugal, Greece-only Denmark and Ireland were not under either the Roman or Holy Roman Empires).

What the final ten will be and how widespread their territorial dominion will be is a matter of conjecture, but in my judgment, it will be the outgrowth of the present European unity effort and eventually include much of the Middle East.

From this central union of nations, the Antichrist will establish world dominion.

But this world's civilization is destined to fall under the judgment of God.

The "woman," the final religious system, will be destroyed by the last political power, probably so beast worship can have no rivals.

III. The Lamb (14)

As the Tribulation comes to a close, the forces of the beast and the ten kings of the end times will oppose all that is called God, or that is worshipped. Antichrist will show himself in the temple of God at Jerusalem, claiming to be God (2 Thes. 2:1-12).

But the Lamb will triumph in power.

All the judgments of the Tribulation from chapter six through chapter nineteen constitute the wrath of the Lamb (6:16).

At the battle of Armageddon the Lamb will be victorious.

We read, "These (the beast and the ten kings) shall make war with the Lamb, and the Lamb shall overcome them; for he is Lord of Lords and King of Kings; and they that are with him are called, and chosen, and faithful."

"Worthy is the Lamb that was slain to receive power and riches and wisdom and strength and honor and glory and blessing" (5:12).

Conclusion

If you want to be saved from the wrath to come, if you want to have eternal life, if you want to be on the winning side, look to the Lamb of God.

"Behold the Lamb of God, that taketh away the sin of the world" (John 1:29).

You can be a part of the family of God and be in the Bride of Christ. On the opposite side, you might become a member of the harlot-church, Mystery, Babylon the Great, which will be linked with the Antichrist.

Come to Jesus today!

A Commentary on the Revelation
Expository, Exegetical, Devotional and Practical
Greek words from the Textus Receptus
Chapter Seventeen

The Woman Riding the Beast (1–7)

1. And there came one of the seven angels which had the seven vials, and talked with me, saying unto me (*Kai eithen eis ek ton hepta angelon ton echonoton tas hepta philias kai elalesen met emou legon*) — in the prior chapter the fall of Babylon (16:19) is introduced in connection with the seventh vial judgment ; so chapters 17 and 18 give a detailed account, much the same as chapter 19 describes the judgment on the beast and the false prophet, summarily alluded to in 16:13–15 and in the sixth vial judgment. Probably the seventh angel is the spokesman, who reveals the doom of Babylon in all of its aspects … **Come hither: I will shew unto thee the judgment of the great whore that sitteth upon many waters** (*deuro deikso soi to krima tes pornes test megales tes kathemenes epi hudaton pollon*) — **pornes**, from which also comes the English word **pornography**, is translated as **harlot** and **whore**, as also in vs. 5, 15, 16, not a complimentary description, but spiritual immorality is here intended, departing from the truth. This kind of figure of speech is often used by the Old Testament prophets. (See Hosea 4:12; Jeremiah 2:20; Ezekiel 16:15,16,41, etc.) Of course the woman on many waters is interpreted later as a "city" and as having dominion over "peoples, nations, kindred and tongues" (v. 15,18). **2. With whom the kings of the earth have committed fornication** (*meth hes hoi baseleis tes ges eporneusan*) — again the last word in Greek here is a verb form of *pornen,* practicing immorality. **Drunk with** — that is their *emethusthesan,* their drunk condition spiritually, is owing to the mutual corruption of wicked political systems and wicked religious systems. In part, this must refer to pagan Rome, which perpetrated ten major persecutions on Christians in the first three centuries of this Dispensation and many lesser ones; later Papal Rome is included, but not exclusively, since

Romanism, Greek Catholicism and apostate Protestantism have all been involved in turning from true biblical faith to idolatry, immortality and compromise. **3. So he carried me away into the wilderness: and I saw a woman upon a scarlet colored beast** — (*therion*) — in this vision John is transported into the wilderness of a wicked world, a moral wilderness. The beast here is the same as in chapter 13, but is here seen as scarlet. Rome is seen astride the world power, ruling it by its claim of supremacy. Heathen religion, emperor worship, idolatry and immorality characterized Pagan Rome, but Papan Rome over the centuries has continued with false religious ideas, carried over from ancient Babylonian paganism, which also permeated other world empires of long ago. As the dragon is fiery red, so the beast is blood–red, suggest blood guiltiness and violence … **having seven heads and ten horns** (*echonta kephalas hepta kai kerata deka*) — some commentators think that the seven-head kings represent the seven forms of Roman leadership: (1) kings; (2) consuls; (3) dictators; (4) decemvirs; (5) military tribunes; (6) emperors (all of which were involved in Roman history prior to Christ's birth, although emperors continued for centuries both in the East and the West); (7) the final beast, who is also the 8th. Other schemes have been suggested. Some commentators suggest that the writer has in mind seven Roman emperors, of which the last and 8th would be the Antichrist, but that necessitates a great gap in time from about 100 A.D. to the very last days. The ten horns are ten contemporaneous last day regimes that support the Antichrist, giving "their kingdom to the beast." **4. And the woman was arrayed in purple and scarlet and bedecked with gold and precious stones and pearls, having a golden cup in her hand full of abomination and filthiness of the wine of her fornication.** — This vivid description was applicable to the wealth and wickedness of Imperial Rome during its pagan days under a succession of emperors prior to 313 A.D. and the accession of the Emperor Constantine. Later during the long centuries of Roman religious domination over Roman and former Roman territories, wealth and prestige continued with little or no gospel being preached. Many concerned Roman Catholics perceived that the harlot was Rome. For instance in 1200 A.D., an English abbot told King Richard the Lionhearted, concerning Antichrist, "he was born long ago at Rome and is now exalting himself above all that is called God ... the harlot arrayed in gold is the church of Rome." So said Joachin of Calabria. During and after the Reformation, Lutherans and others likewise identified the woman here as the Church of Rome, filled with wealth and wickedness and blasphemies. That is not to say that genuine believers could not be found in its ranks, for Luther and many of his contemporaries remained in "the church" in hopes of reforming it. **5. And upon her forehead was a name written, MYSTERY, BABYLON THE GREAT, MOTHER OF HARLOTS AND ABOMINATIONS OF THE EARTH** — the capitalized title in Greek: *(musterion Babulon, he megale he meter ton pornon, kai bdelugmaton tes ges).* — The word **mystery** indicates a spiritual fact, previously concealed and not perceived until divinely revealed. It was Rome that crucified Christ; that destroyed Jerusalem and scattered the Jews; that persecuted the early Christians in Pagan times; that persecuted Protestant Christians in Papal times; that will again be restored to grandeur before the burning of the harlot. **Mother of harlots** extends beyond Rome itself to all of Christendom ... for the harlot sits "upon many waters," influencing the whole world. When astride the beast in the end times, this mixed Babylonian–Roman–Christian religion of error will rise to an apex of power for a time. It is all rooted, however, in the early Babylonian religion of ancient times, originated by Nimrod (Genesis 10:11). See Hislop's "The Two Babylons." **6. And I saw the woman, drunken with the blood of saints, and with the blood of the martyrs of Jesus** — what John here sees is what has happened to true believers throughout this age, beginning in his own times. The word "admiration" here is in Greek *thauma,* which in verb form is the word "wondered" or *ethaumasa;*

hence do not interpret this as admiration in the conventional sense, but rather think of it as consternation or amazement. John is amazed that the religious Roman system is united to the beast–political system. **7. And the angel said unto me, Wherefore didst thou marvel? I will tell thee the mystery of the woman, and of the beast that carrieth her, which hath seven heads and ten horns.** — The remainder of this chapter then gives an explanation, partially cryptic and symbolical of course.

The Vision Explained (8–18)

8. The beast that thou sawest was, and is not; and shall ascend out of the bottomless pit, and go into perdition — Some regard the beast here as the Antichrist personally, rather than the culmination of all wicked world–systems, and certainly "beast" can mean either or both of these concepts. A dual interpretation is correct. If this means the Antichrist himself, then some have conjectured that Judas was, is not, and, as a son of perdition (Acts 1:25 and John 17:12), was placed in the bottomless pit and is to arise as the Antichrist, resuscitated by Satan (compare 13:3). Some 2nd century Christians thought Nero might be raised up to be the Antichrist, though he had been dead for decades. My view is that the beast as a political and personal entity is meant. The Roman Empire itself did exist, would not exist for a time and then exist again, but that does not nullify the possibility that the Antichrist himself also passes though a stage of being, then not being, then living again. Some authorities think that he will be slain during the Tribulation, then resuscitated, with additional powerful Satanic energy, becoming practically Satan incarnate. This would fulfill the rest of the verse ... **And they that dwell on the earth shall wonder, whose names were not written in the book of life from the foundation of the world, when they behold the beast that was, and is not, and yet is. 9. And here is the mind which hath wisdom. The seven heads are seven mountains on which the woman sitteth.** — Here is an obvious dual interpretation of these seven heads, symbolizing both seven mountains and seven kings. These seven hills of Rome have been well known for over 2,000 years, a fact not lost on readers of this book for many centuries. They are called: the Palantine, the Capitoline, the

Quirinale, the Viminal, the Esquiline, the Caeline and the Aventine. Ancient Roman literature, coinage and tradition join as testimonies that this concept is correct. **10. And there are seven kings: five are fallen, and one is, and the other is not yet come; and when he cometh he must continue a short space.** — This is the further symbolic meaning. Some have thought (even Newell) that Roman emperors are in view, prior to John's writing this book. They are (1) Augustus Caesar; (2) Tiberias; (3) Caligula; (4) Claudius; (5) Nero; the 6th would be Domitian, who was in power in John's day. The 7th might be some later ruler, but the Antichrist in the future would be the 8th. That seems to me to necessitate some rather extensive bending of this verse, since 19 centuries have elapsed since the sixth in this list. The other view not accepted here is that previous Roman forms of government are indicated. Many of us believe that since the beast in Revelation 13 is a composite and the outgrowth of the previous great world empires (the face of a lion suggesting Babylon, the feet of the bear indicating Medo-Persia, the similarity to the leopard symbolizing the Greek Empire founded under Alexander the Great — study Daniel 7:1–8; 17–28 for comparisons) that what is meant are the FIVE major world empires of ancient times, namely, Egypt, Assyria, Babylon (both early and the neo-Babylonian Empire under Nebuchadnezzar), Greece (Alexander the Great and his successors), making five which had fallen. Rome, in my judgment was the sixth, and continued beyond 476 A.D. in the Roman, Western world with religion and traditions coming led with Germanic and Frankish and Anglo-Saxon tribes, later in the form of the Holy Roman Empire (until 1806). The Eastern Roman Empire, which fell in 1453 A.D., was followed by the Russian Empire and a succession of Czars (Caesars) with Eastern Catholic (Orthodox) religion. The 7th head theoretically might be the Anglo-American civilization of the 19th and 20th centuries. The 8th is the restoration of the sixth: Roman, Western Civilization, dominating Europe and the Middle East. **11. And the beast that was, and is not, even he is the eighth, and is of the seven and goeth into perdition. 12. And the ten horns which thou sawest are ten kings which have received no kingdom as yet.** — this final alliance has not yet developed into its final state, but awaits the Tribulation … **but they receive power as kings one hour with the beast.** — These are not ten kingdoms which are formed out of the western half of the Roman Empire in the 5th and 6th centuries, as some have taught, but rather ten countries united under Antichrist at a specific time or "hour" in the future, a definite time of short duration, during the 7 year Tribulation. **13. These have one mind, and shall give their power and strength unto the beast** (*houtoi mian gnomen echousin kai ten dunamin kai eksousian auton didoasin to therio*) — submitting totally to the Antichrist in his role as supreme ruler. **14. These shall make war with the Lamb, and the Lamb shall overcome them: for HE is Lord of Lords** (*kurios kurion*) **and King of Kings** (*basileres basileon*) — this will occur at the close of the Tribulation (Revelation 19:11–21), when He comes in glory and power, smiting His enemies at the Battle of Armageddon (16:16) … **and they that are with him are called** (*kletoi*) **and chosen** (*ekletoi*), **and faithful** (*pistoi*) — the raptured and resurrected and glorified saints returning as the "armies of heaven." **15. And he saith unto me, The waters which thou sawest, where the whore sitteth are peoples and multitudes and nations and tongues.** — The power of the final harlot church extends all over the world. **16. And the ten horns which thou sawest upon the beast shall hate the whore, and shall make her desolate and naked, and shall eat her flesh, and burn her with fire.** — The political power will suppress and destroy this religious power as only the Antichrist is to be worshipped in the end. **17. For God hath put in their hearts to fulfill his will, and to agree and to give their kingdom unto the beast, until the words of God shall be fulfilled.** — Overruling Satan's diabolical schemes, God sets the stage for the final fulfillment of all the prophecies in the Bible of the end time, causing these 10 leaders to render full allegiance and submission to the Antichrist. **18. And the woman which thou sawest is that great city which reigneth over the kings of the earth.** — That was the case when this was written and continued so for centuries; then religiously it continues unto this day. This can be nothing else than Rome.

RAINBOWS FROM REVELATION
The Revelation of Jesus Christ
A chapter by chapter, verse by verse study
"There was a rainbow round about the throne like unto an emerald" (4:3)

CHAPTER EIGHTEEN: Babylon Falls!

References

Rev. 10:1
Ezek. 43:2

Isa. 21:9
Rev. 14:8
Rev. 16:19
Isa. 13:19-21
Jer. 50:8
Jer. 50:39

Jer. 51:7
Isa. 47:14,15
Jer. 51:34

Isa. 48:20
Jer. 50:8
Rev. 15:1

Gen. 18:20

Ps. 137:8
Jer. 50:15
Jer. 50:29

Ezek. 28:2-8
Isa. 47:7,8

Isa. 47:9
Jer. 50:31
Jer. 50:34

Ezek. 26:16
Jer. 50:46

Jer. 50:40
Gen. 19:28

Ezek. 27:27-34

Ezek. 27:12-22

1. AND after these things I saw another angel come down from heaven, having great power; and the earth was lightened with his glory.

2. And he cried mightily with a strong voice, saying, Babylon the great is fallen, is fallen, and is become the habitation of devils, and the hold of every foul spirit, and a cage of every unclean and hateful bird.

3. For all nations have drunk of the wine of the wrath of her fornication, and the kings of the earth have committed fornication with her, and the merchants of the earth are waxed rich through the abundance of her delicacies.

4. And I heard another voice from heaven, saying, Come out of her, my people, that ye be not partakers of her sins, and that ye receive not of her plagues.

5. For her sins have reached unto heaven, and God hath remembered her iniquities.

6. Reward her even as she rewarded you, and double unto her double according to her works: in the cup which she hath filled fill to her double.

7. How much she hath glorified herself, and lived deliciously, so much torment and sorrow give her: for she saith in her heart, I sit a queen, and am no widow, and shall see no sorrow.

8. Therefore shall her plagues come in one day, death, and mourning, and famine; and she shall be utterly burned with fire: for strong is the Lord God who judgeth her.

9. And the kings of the earth, who have committed fornication and lived deliciously with her, shall bewail her, and lament for her, when they shall see the smoke of her burning,

10. Standing afar off for the fear of her torment, saying, Alas, alas, that great city Babylon, that mighty city! for in one hour is thy judgment come.

11. And the merchants of the earth shall weep and mourn over her; for no man buyeth their merchandise any more:

12. The merchandise of gold, and silver, and precious stones, and of pearls, and fine linen, and purple, and silk, and scarlet, and all thyine wood, and all manner vessels of ivory, and all manner vessels of most precious wood, and of brass, and iron, and marble,

13. And cinnamon, and odors, and ointments, and frankincense, and wine, and oil, and fine flour, and wheat, and beasts, and sheep, and horses, and chariots, and slaves, and souls of men.

14. And the fruits that thy soul lusted after are departed from thee, and all things which were dainty and goodly are departed from thee, and thou shalt find them no more at all.

15. The merchants of these things, which were made rich by her, shall stand afar off for the fear of her torment, weeping and wailing,

16. And saying, Alas, alas, that great city, that was clothed in fine linen, and purple, and scarlet, and decked with gold, and precious stones, and pearls!

17. For in one hour so great riches is come to nought. And every shipmaster, and all the company in ships, and sailors, and as many as trade by sea, stood afar off.

18. And cried when they saw the smoke of her burning, saying, What city is like unto this great city!

19. And they cast dust on their heads, and cried, weeping and wailing, saying, Alas, alas, that great city, wherein were made rich all that had ships in the sea by reason of her costliness! for in one hour is she made desolate.

20. Rejoice over her, thou heaven, and ye holy apostles and prophets; for God hath avenged you on her.

21. And a mighty angel took up a stone like a great millstone, and cast it into the sea, saying, Thus with violence shall that great city Babylon be thrown down, and shall be found no more at all.

22. And the voice of harpers, and musicians, and of pipers, and trumpeters, shall be heard no more at all in thee; and no craftsman, of whatsoever craft he be, shall be found any more in thee; and the sound of a millstone shall be heard no more at all in thee;

23. And the light of a candle shall shine no more at all in thee; and the voice of the bridegroom and of the bride shall be heard no more at all in thee: for thy merchants were the great men of the earth; for by thy sorceries were all nations deceived.

24. And in her was found the blood of prophets, and of saints, and of all that were slain upon the earth.

References

Deut. 24:7

1 Jn. 2:15,16

Ezek. 27:27-31

Rev. 17:4

Isa. 23:14

Ezek. 27:30

Josh. 7:6

Isa. 44:23
Rev. 12:12
Luke 11:49
Jer. 51:63,64

Jer. 7:34
Isa. 14:11

Isa. 47:9,10
Rev. 9:21

Rev. 16:6
Jer. 51:49

Summary of Chapter Eighteen

Babylon Under Judgment

I. The Fall of Babylon (1–8)

The collapse of the ancient Babylonian Empire of Nebuchadnezzar and his successors, described in Daniel 5, is a faint foreshadowing of the awesome end of the final Babylon the Great.

After the ten kings under the Antichrist have destroyed the ecclesiastical segment (the final world religion and superchurch) of Babylon, the remainder, including the capital city, the whole system and culture, comes under divine judgment in Chapter 18. Evidently, Chapter 17 deals with the religious aspect of Babylon, while Chapter 18 focuses on the social, financial, and commercial side of the last great government and the whole system it represents.

At the outset of the chapter, John beholds "another angel" crying "mightily with a strong voice," announcing the final doom of the wicked city, system and regime of the end times.

There follows then, "another voice," appealing to any who have been saved during the Tribulation and who have not perished under the Antichrist's persecution, to separate themselves from Babylon. In a sense, believers of all ages are urged to "come out" of "Babylonianism," which throughout Scripture exemplifies opposition to God, beginning in Genesis 11 and the Tower of Babel.

While Chapter 17 seems a thinly veiled depiction of Rome in history and prophecy, this chapter is thought by many scholars to describe a rebuilt Babylon in the Middle East, serving as the final capital of the Antichrist. These conservative scholars see a "religious Babylon" in Rome and all that the city has been and stands for and a "commercial Babylon" beginning in Chapter 18. Others believe that all of the prophecy relates to Rome itself, figuratively called "Babylon," and that the prophecies of Babylon's ruin in Isaiah, Jeremiah and Ezekiel have already been fulfilled, thus prohibiting an actual reconstruction of the literal city.

In either event Babylon in all of its aspects, relationships and significance will indeed FALL.

II. The Future of Babylon (9–20)

It is certain that the catastrophe described here has not yet been fulfilled. Nothing like this has ever occurred with either Rome or Babylon or the empires they headed or will head again.

Three times the expression "one hour" occurs (10, 17, 19), indicating a sudden and total destruction. Verse 8 uses the expression, "her plagues shall come in one day …" The final capital will be consumed by fire in a short span of time, reminiscent of a nuclear inferno. This whole passage may be called a "dirge," some of it being poetic in nature and much of it rooted in similar expressions as in Isaiah, Jeremiah and Ezekiel, relating to Babylon the ancient city.

Monarchs, merchants and mariners are caught up in the holocaust destruction. While they lament these horrendous events, the saints, apostles and prophets in heaven are said to rejoice.

Nothing else like this is found in the annals of literature.

A long list of merchandise is set forth, some twenty–seven separate things, arranged in seven classes: (1) costly ornaments, (2) costly clothes, (3) costly furniture, (4) costly perfumes, (5) costly food, (6) costly military accoutrements, (7) the bodies and souls of men. The last two summarize the whole (14), since materialistic hedonism (personal pleasure, luxury and physical things are the supreme good in life) and spiritual (soulish) error are prominent in a wicked world system. All of these things relate not to communism but to capitalism in its final form.

III. The Fate of Babylon (21–24)

This chapter contains three prolonged statements by angels, this being the last. Then there are recorded statements from three classes on earth: the kings, the merchants and the sailors.

The final vividly demonstrated proclamation by a "mighty angel" is easily arranged in poetic form:
"Thus with violence shall that great city
   Babylon be thrown down,
And shall be found no more at all.
And the voice of harpers and musicians,
   and the pipers and trumpeters, shall
   be heard no more in thee at all;
And no craftsman of whatsoever craft,
   shall be found any more in thee;
And the sound of a millstone
   shall be heard no more in thee …"

Outline of Chapter Eighteen

The Final Fall of Babylon

OBJECTIVE: To reveal the ultimate end of godless civilization, headed up under the Babylonian system in all of its aspects, from the capital city to its culture, ideologies and practices.

OUTLINE:

I. The Declaration of the Angel (1-3)
  A. The Arrival of the Angel (1)
  B. The Announcement of the Angel (2-3)
    BABYLON THE GREAT IS FALLEN, IS FALLEN
    1. Babylon's Punishment (2)
      a. To become the habitation of demons
      b. To become the hold of foul spirits
      c. To be a cage for unclean, hateful birds
    2. Babylon's Past (3)
      a. Moral sins: "nations drunk of wine of her fornication"
      b. Political sins: "kings of earth committed fornication with her."
      c. Commercial sins: "merchants waxed rich"

II. The Degradation of Babylon (4-7)
  A. The Call for Separation (4)
    Surviving believers urged to separate from the city
  B. The Consequences of Her Sins (5, 6)
    To be rewarded "double" according to her works
  C. The Complacency of Her Pride (7)
    Supposes she "will see no sorrow"

III. The Destruction of Babylon (8)
  A. Plagues to Strike
    1. Death
    2. Mourning
    3. Famine
  B. Fiery Fall in One Day
  C. Divine Judgment is Strong

IV. The Dirge for Babylon (9-19)
  A. Rulers Lament the Destruction (9, 10)
    1. Much Mourning
    2. No Merchandise

  B. Merchants Mourn over Destruction (11-16)

  C. Seven Classes of Articles (11,13)
    1. Valuables and Ornaments
      a. Gold
      b. Silver
      c. Precious Stones
      d. Pearls

    2. Costly Array
      a. Fine Linen
      b. Purple
      c. Silk
      d. Scarlet

    3. Luxurious Furnishings
      a. Thine Wood
      b. Vessels of Ivory
      c. Vessels of Precious Wood
      d. Vessels of Brass
      e. Vessels of Iron
      f. Marble

    4. Rich Aromas and Ointments
      a. Cinnamon
      b. Frankincense
      c. Ointments

    5. Abundant Life-styles (with)
      a. Wine
      b. Oil
      c. Fine Flour
      d. Wheat
      e. Animals
      f. Sheep

    6. Transportation
      a. Horses
      b. Chariots

    7. Evil Domination
      a. Slaves
      b. Souls of Men
    (27 different products and entities)

  D. Transporters Cry over Destruction (17-19)

V. The Desolation of Babylon (20-24)
  A. Heaven Rejoices (20)

  B. An Angel Demonstrates the Fall (21)

  C. City and System in Ruins (22, 23)
    1. No Music
      a. No Harpers
      b. No Musicians
      c. No Pipers
      d. No Trumpeters

    2. No Manufacturing
      a. No Craftsmen
      b. No Industry

  D. Babylon's Blood-guiltiness Stated (24)

Observations:
Spiritual lessons and applications from each verse
Chapter Eighteen

1. Invisible to our eyes, spiritual forces are at work in the universe, a conflict between God's angels and Satan's angels, even now.

2. No matter how high a city or system may rise, it is doomed by its own sins.

3. Spiritual immorality is false religion with a crass emphasis on material gain and prosperity.

4. God wants His people in all times to be separated.

5. God's remembrance of sin is total, except for those who come to Christ.

6. Double judgment can fall upon most wicked activities.

7. Arrogant pride and refusal to recognize the possible judgments of God for sin do not nullify God's wrath.

8. Judgment on sin can come quickly, in one hour.

9. The world always laments judgment for sin, but does not repent as usual.

10. Fear of torment alone is not enough to bring repentance.

11. Weeping and mourning over earthly loss is nothing compared to the weeping and mourning that will take place in hell.

12. Excessive materialism imagines that "things" will last forever.

13. Traffic in the souls of men is the worst of sins ... that is, false teaching that brings the lost into a deluded bondage instead of to Christ.

14. There will be an end to worldly things; they all pass away.

15. Riches without true Christianity are nothing.

16. All the crying of "alas" in the world cannot bring back the destroyed luxuries of this world.

17. What shall it profit if one gains the whole world and loses his soul?

18. Even the whole world at the passing of the millennium will also be burned away. What really endures?

19. Let us be warned never to set our hearts upon mere riches, even if they increase, but to be good stewards of all God gives us.

20. Heaven rejoices when God avenges His own.

21. God uses visual illustrations to emphasize a major truth.

22. Babylon's desolation is a reminder of the ultimate fruits of sin.

23. "Sorceries," addictive drug misuse, is always an awful evil.

24. God's people have often shed their blood for Christ; they will again.

Babylon vs. Jerusalem
A fascinating contrast between Babylon, as representing all that the world and a wicked civilization in all of its ramifications and Jerusalem, representing God's plan for civilization and for blessings on the world through righteousness, can be drawn. Babylon means "confusion" and Jerusalem means "possession of peace." Babylon will be destroyed forever; Jerusalem in a new form will endure forever.

Quotations
From Other Expositors
Chapter Eighteen

Babylon's Doom (1-4)

"The first three verses set forth a condition which is an excellent picture of the past and present history of the papacy. As we saw in our study of Chapter 17, we need only turn to the annals of the Roman Catholic Church to read of fiendish deeds committed in the name of the Lord. We saw that the Inquisition was established by the papacy. With its torture chambers, its deeds of unspeakable cruelty, its slaying of men, sparing not even helpless women and children, yet they called it 'The Holy Office.' When we read these things, we may well believe that the description of Babylon, which God's Word says, 'has become the habitation of devils, and the hold of every foul spirit, and a cage of every unclean and hateful bird,' refers to that system!

"If a union of Protestantism and Romanism should ever be formed, at that moment we should be compelled to give up the Bible, because Rome has not changed one whit in her attitude toward liberty of conscience and freedom to study God's Word. Not only that, but we should also be compelled to exchange the great doctrine of justification by faith and all that it includes for the mysteries that were invested in the wife of Nimrod, the consort of one of the mightiest apostates who ever lived in the Old Testament days. Men like Luther, Huss, John Knox called mightily to the people to come out from the system and be separated from it. Let us lift high the torch which they have put in our hands, and magnify the grace of God which alone brings salvation. We need to contend earnestly for the faith in this day when tens of thousands are wending their way back to spiritual bondage, from which the gospel of the Reformers delivers men."

– Louis T. Talbot

"If we are to understand the book of Revelation we must carefully differentiate between these two Babylons. While 'Mystery Babylon' will be destroyed at the midpoint of the seven-year Tribulation period by the Antichrist and his ten kings, the city of Babylon will be destroyed three–and–a–half years later by God at Armageddon, the Day of the Lord. Revelation records that John 'wondered' at the false Babylonian church because it is still in our future. However, he did not wonder at the city of Babylon because he was already familiar with its role as an opponent of God. While the destruction of the city of Babylon is a major part of the Old Testament's prophecies, Chapter 17 of Revelation is the only place in the Scripture where we find prophecies about the end–time false church. The ecumenical church is called 'the Great Harlot' and 'the woman' while the city of Babylon is never described as a woman. Another difference is that the false Babylon church makes herself rich and is 'arrayed in purple and scarlet and adorned with gold and precious stones and pearls' (Revelation 17:4). On the other hand, the city of Babylon will make others rich, as Revelation declares: 'The merchants of the earth have become rich through the abundance of her luxury' (Revelation 18:3)."

– Grant R. Jeffrey

"A comparison of the prophecies of Isaiah and Jeremiah in regard to the fall of ancient Babylon will show how plainly the doom of the spiritual counterpart is there prefigured. In several instances the same identical figures are used, and this has led some commentators to suppose that the doom of the literal city was not final; and so it is taught by some that Babylon is to be rebuilt on her ancient site, to flourish for a few years as the religious and commercial metropolis of the world, only to be again destroyed, and that, finally, at or immediately preceding the Lord's second coming. These teachers generally agree in making this restored Babylon the seat of the Antichrist, whom they, as a rule, identify with the future world–emperor. But I think we have already shown that a careful comparison of the Old and New Testament Scriptures on these subjects makes this view untenable. The city of old has fallen to rise no more."

– H.A. Ironside

Believer's Deliverance (4,5)

"Come forth, My people, out of her."

"While these words have a real application to the believer to come forth to Jesus outside the spiritual Babylon — ecclesiasticism, Nicolaitanism and the false promises for 'mystery' Babylon in its various forms; yet the particular *interpretation* of the words is not to the saints, who will have been raptured before this call goes forth. The call to 'come forth' from this great commercial Sodom of the last days — rebuilt Babylon — is evidently issued to those individuals living in or doing business in that capital of the Antichrist in the last days. In Isaiah 52:11 and Jeremiah 50:8; 51:6, 9, 45, we see that it will be especially Jewish saints and those attached to them that are warned; for they are bidden in Jeremiah 51:50 to 'Remember Jehovah from afar, and let Jerusalem come into your mind.'"

– William R. Newell

Babylon or Rome? (6 - 19)

"We must remember that the Beast and his ten kings of chapter seventeen made desolate the woman that sat on the seven mountains — Romanism (17:9,16). But the overthrow of Chapter 18 is directly from God: 'in one day,' 'in one hour,' (18:10, 17, 19). This overthrow is lamented by the kings of the earth.

"If you desire to know the last and final form of iniquity, behold the two women of Zechariah 5 bearing an ephah, covered with a talent of lead. The woman, called Wickedness, sits in the ephah. 'Whither do these bear the ephah?' asks the prophet, and the angel answers: 'To build her a house in the land of Shinar: and when it is prepared, she shall be set there in her own place.' Now Babylon is that land of Shinar (Genesis 10:10).

"Notice in Revelation 18:3, 11, 15, 23, 'the merchants of the earth,' also 'merchandise,' (Greek 'cargo' — showing these things will be carried by ships, as see verse 17). Rome has no market and the Tiber has no harbor, to speak of. Naming the articles of the cargo begins with verse 12: 'Merchandise of gold, and silver, and precious stone,' etc. Nearly thirty kinds are enumerated, and it is all a story of luxury upon luxury! It must be *pearls*; it must be *fine linen*; it must be *silk*; it must be vessels of most

precious wood; it must be *fragrant spices*; it must be *wine and olive oil*; it must be *fine flour*; it must be *slaves*; it must be things that are *dainty* and *sumptuous*. This city must be 'decked' with *fine* linen, *scarlet*, gold and pearls!"

– William R. Newell

"In the angel's explanation to John we find that the seven heads stand not only for seven kings, but also for seven mountains on which the woman sitteth. Then in verse eighteen we see that the woman is the great city which reigneth over the kings of the earth. This cannot mean the literal ancient Babylon, for that city was built not upon mountains, but on the plain of Shinar, and it had, long before John's day, ceased to reign over the kings of the earth. The city which wielded universal sovereignty in John's time was Rome, and everybody knows that Rome was built upon seven hills."

– William L. Pettingill

Babylon, Past or Future? (20-14)

"The action is significant and prophetic, and sublime withal. A similar dramatic proceeding pointing to the overthrow of Babylon of old is described in Jeremiah 51:60–64; there however, Seraiah was the actor; here an angel of might. Both the literal and mystical cities were to be utterly and suddenly destroyed by violence. The two chapters, Jeremiah 51 and Revelation 18, should be carefully studied and compared. Then follows in verse 22 and 23 a beautifully descriptive and touching account, poetically expressed, of her utter desolation. How complete the ruin! Joyless, dark, and silent, Babylon stands out as a monument of the utmost vengeance of God. Wickedness had sat enthroned in the midst of that city professedly bearing the Name of Christ; but at last, when she had filled to the full her cup of iniquity, God rises in His fierce anger, His indignation burns, and Babylon falls to rise no more. Her destruction is irremediable. The chapter closes with a reiteration of the bloody character of the system, (see chapters 17:6; 18:24)."

– Walter Scott

Alas, Alas, Babylon is Fallen, is Fallen
An Expository Sermon

Chapter Eighteen

Introduction

Earlier in Revelation 14:8 we read, "Babylon is fallen, is fallen, that great city, because she made all nations drink of the wine of the wrath of her fornication." Now in this chapter we see the prior announcement by a holy angel completely fulfilled.

What then is "Babylon?"

Certainly, it is "that great city, which reigneth over the kings of the earth" (17:18).

Almost certainly second century Christians understood the title "Babylon" as a thinly veiled description of "the eternal city of Rome," grand capital of the whole Western world and center of Greco–Roman civilization. Many believed that Rome was indeed the fourth world empire, which Daniel foresaw, beginning with Babylon on the Euphrates and proceeding through the Persian Empire and the seceding cultural empire of Greece, sparked by Alexander the Great.

This view faded after the Christianization of the Roman Empire and the political and ecclesiastical triumph of what we now call Roman Catholicism. But the Reformers, led by Martin Luther, breaking with Catholicism, saw "Babylon" here as corrupted Christianity, centered at Rome under the pontiffs. Many conservatives hold that view today, but see an all–inclusive corrupted Christianity with apostate Protestantism, Roman Catholicism, and possibly the Eastern Orthodox and other elements blended into one final ecumenical superchurch.

In the larger sense Babylon, first called Babel in Genesis 11, where man instituted the first city, the first humanistic civilization with its attempt to climb up to heaven on a great tower by human effort and skill, is more than either the ancient city or Rome itself. It does mean the final capital of the Antichrist, but there is more.

It signifies the city, the system, the civilization of this world, culminating in the anti-Christian philosophy of the end times.

This does not nullify the literal nature of the great city. Today hundreds of millions of religious people look to Rome for leadership.

But there is quite obviously a difference in the way Babylon is described in Chapter 17 and in Chapter 18. A "city," falling over a vast area, is indicated in both chapters. But the ten kings under the Antichrist destroy "the whore, the woman."

But in Chapter 18 the city itself is devastated by divine judgment.

One possible scenario, envisioned by some, is that Rome will be destroyed by the Antichrist in order to wipe out all vestiges of even corrupt Christianity, thus opening the way for universal worship of the image of the beast in Jerusalem (13:11–18 with Daniel 9:27 and Matthew 24:15). Therefore the capital would move to a literal rebuilt Babylon.

One interesting passage in Zechariah might refer to an event such as is here predicted. In the prophet's fifth chapter and in his ninth vision, these facts are recorded:

"Then the angel that talked with me went forth, and said unto me, Lift up now thine eyes, and see what is this that goeth forth.

"And I said, What is it? And he said, This is an ephah [an ephah is a measurement a little more than a bushel, but this passage could mean a container which can hold an ephah] that goeth forth. He said moreover, This is their resemblance through all the earth.

"And, behold, there was lifted up a talent of lead: and this is a woman that sitteth in the midst of the ephah.

"And he said, This is wickedness. And he cast it into the midst of the ephah; and he cast the weight of lead upon the mouth thereof.

"Then lifted I up mine eyes, and looked, and, behold, there came out two women, and the wind was in their wings; for they had wings like the wings of a stork: and they lifted up the ephah between the earth and the heaven.

"Then said I to the angel that talked with me, Whither do these bear the ephah?

"And he said unto me, To build it an house in the land of Shinar: [Babylonia–Iraq] and it shall be established, and set there upon her own base" (Zechariah 5:5,11).

While scholars differ as to the exact meaning and application of this prophecy, written 600 years before Revelation, one view is that the Woman, called Wickedness here, is to be identified with the Woman in Revelation 17. It is suggested that in the end times — and much of Zechariah deals with the future coming of the Messiah — the Woman will be moved from Rome to Shinar or Babylon. In other words, it will be the final headquarters of apostate Christianity, much weakened, and probably under total domination by the Antichrist after the "burning with fire" (17:16). Thus a Rome–Babylon axis would be instituted, resulting in Revelation 18 referring to a literal, rebuilt Babylon. Other commentators think this view too fanciful.

Whether or not the Zechariah passage relates to a rebuilt Babylon, many scholars believe that the final Babylon will replace Rome as the future capital of the world and that it will be reconstructed on the same site where civilization began after the flood. History would then run full cycle. Evidence is produced to indicate that the dire prophecies of Babylon's ruin in Isaiah, Jeremiah and Ezekiel have only been partially fulfilled or not at all.

Other scholars think that judgments set forth in Jeremiah 50 and 51, for instance, written, among other things, to encourage the Jews in a time when Babylon was overrunning their land in the 6th century B.C., have been fulfilled, along with other similar predictions. They see Rome, or just possibly some other city, as the last capital of the world under Antichrist.

My position is that Rome was and is "Babylon," but that during the Tribulation Wars, the city may very well be destroyed by the ten kings of Chapters 13 and 17, but that then a final Babylon on the ancient site is altogether possible. Frankly, my mind is open on this question.

Before we move briefly through this chapter, here is an interesting opinion from a Catholic commentary on Revelation, published in 1955, entitled *The Book of Destiny* and written by Bernard Leonard. Amazingly, according to Grant Jeffrey, a prophetic researcher who found the book, it was approved by Catholic censors and bears the proper "Imprimatur."

"In this interesting book," comments Jeffrey, "the writer interprets the language of prophecy in an unusually literal manner. He arrives at some startling conclusions for a Catholic religious writer about the identity of the Great Whore of Babylon. After carefully examining the issue, he reluctantly concludes that the Bible declares that Rome and the Roman Catholic Church will be taken over by

Satan during the last days, leading up to the return of Christ. Referring to Revelation 17, Leonard wrote:

"'Hence this great harlot is a city whose apostasy from the true faith is a monstrous thing. This may point to Rome ... And the apostasy of this city, and her becoming the head of an empire that would lead all possible nations and peoples into Antichrist worship, would indeed merit for her the title of THE GREAT HARLOT. The apostles called ancient Rome BABYLON (1 Peter 5:13). So the conclusion is that the great harlot of the future shall be Rome.'"

Whether the final Babylon is Rome or the rebuilt city, several things are very evident in this fascinating chapter.

I. The Doom of Babylon (1–8)

Three angelic proclamations are set forth in this chapter. This initial angel comes "down from heaven, having great power; and the earth was lightened with his glory. And he cried mightily with a strong voice ... saying BABYLON THE GREAT IS FALLEN, IS FALLEN ..." These are the exact words uttered by the second angel in a series of six back in 14:8. The identical expression appears in Isaiah 21:9, written 700 years before Christ, but generally thought to refer to Babylon's conquest by the Medes and Persians (21:2). "And behold, here cometh a chariot of men with a couple of horsemen, And he answered and said, BABYLON IS FALLEN, IS FALLEN; and all the graven images of her gods he hath broken unto the ground."

Continuing in 18:2, the angel adds, "... and is become the habitation of devils, and hold of every foul spirit, and a cage for every unclean and hateful bird. For all nations have drunk of the wine of her fornication, and the kings of the earth have committed fornication with her, and the merchants of the earth are waxed rich through the abundance of her delicacies."

Writing in the 1990's, William R. Newell joined such writers as Joseph Seiss and Clarence Larkin in adopting the view that Babylon would be rebuilt. His analysis:

"It is the last phase of Babylon, which is seen from Genesis 11 to Revelation; being the city on the Euphrates which practiced idolatry and opposed God's city, Jerusalem; then in continuing Babylon's ancient trinity of father, mother and son, under Christian names; and finally, after the church is raptured (Revelation 4:1), the reestablished world-capital at Babylon on the Euphrates, whose prophesied destruction, like Sodom, has not yet taken place. Thus the human race would combine to set up Babylon, which becomes the center of commercial world activity … While the nations rush to rebuild Babylon and it becomes the Beast's capital, then at last will be the full 'power of her luxury,' as described in Revelation 18:3."

The second angel to make a profound proclamation invites an exodus from Babylon. It is possible that it is the Lord Himself in verse four, since the expression, "my people" is used:

"Come out of her, my people, that ye be not partakers of her sins, and that ye receive not of her plagues."

Contextually, this has to do with the Tribulation saints, who are being urged to leave Babylon, but in a larger sense, the appeal is always applicable to extricate themselves from Babylonianism, be it ecclesiastical or hedonistic. True believers are not to swept up by an evil culture with its attendant sins and wickedness.

Babylon the city and the system is doomed to experience divine judgment, but those who know Christ are destined to be ultimately victorious.

II. The Dirge Over Babylon (9–20)

Three groups with great mourning and lamentation cry aloud and weep over the fall of Babylon in all of its aspects and in all of its grandeur.

First the monarchs, beholding the smoke rising from the flaming city, plaintively cry, "Alas, alas, that great city Babylon, that mighty city! For in one hour is thy judgment come" (10).

Second the merchants, the capitalists of the earth, weep and mourn because of the obliteration of this economic and financial world center. Twenty–seven different products or entities are mentioned. They too speak of "one hour" in which the great riches there come to naught (17).

Third, the mariners, those who are involved in the transportation of goods world wide, intone the same "Alas, Alas" (vs. 10, 16, 19) and bewail the fact that "in one hour she is made desolate" (19).

In forecasting these agonizing cries of grief the Holy Spirit arranges it in a quasi–poetic form. Hence it may be called a dirge, and is here so arranged!

Alas, alas, that great city Babylon
That mighty city!
For in one hour is that judgment come...
And the fruits that thy soul lusted after
     are departed from thee,
And all things which were dainty and goodly are

departed from thee,
And thou shalt find them no more at all...

Alas, alas, that great city,
Wherein were made rich all that had ships in the
     sea by reason of her costliness!
For in one hour is she made desolate,
And ye holy apostles and prophets
For God hath avenged you on her!

III. The Destruction of Babylon (20–24)

Dramatically demonstrating the fate of Babylon, a mighty angel casts a great millstone into the sea, saying,

"Thus with violence shall that great city Babylon be thrown down …"

At long last all that Babylon has ever stood for — religion, materialism, opposition to God, wickedness of every kind — is overthrown.

Babylon the final capital of the Antichrist and his system stands in sharp contrast to the heavenly city, the New Jerusalem.

All through history the conflict has continued: Babylon (from Genesis 11) versus Jerusalem (Genesis 14).

But the everlasting Jerusalem is our destiny.

Those who reject Christ and live only for this world and any form of Babylonianism seal their own everlasting doom.

Babylon is fallen, is fallen!

Jerusalem will abide forever and ever.

Conclusion

Which is your destiny?

Are you a citizen of that city which hath foundations whose Builder and Maker is God?

Will you live only for this world, perhaps to live under the Antichrist and his "Babylonian regime" in the coming time of Tribulation?

The fate of Babylon is certain and sure, both the city and system. It will fall.

The city of Jerusalem will be the heavenly home of God's people forever.

Come to Christ and let Him be your Savior now.

A Commentary on the Revelation
Expository, Exegetical, Devotional and Practical
Greek words from the Textus Receptus

Chapter Eighteen

Babylon's Fall (1–3)

1. After these thing I saw another angel *(meta touta eidon allos angelon)* — "The great whore, ecclesiastical Babylon, was hated and destroyed by the ten-nation empire of the beast — Antichrist — 17:18 — and the commercial center of the woman known as the cities of Babylon and Rome were burned. Political Babylon is finally destroyed at Armageddon" (A. Garner) ... **come down from heaven having great power and the earth was lightened** *(ephostisthe)* **with his glory** — this angel — three **mighty** *(ischuros)* angels are mentioned in this book, here in 18:21, and in 10:1, evidently angels of higher rank, since the descriptions are similar to accounts of Christ Himself. **2. And he cried mightily with a loud voice saying** — how appropriate that this proclamation of the fall of Babylon, including the city, the culture, the system, the philosophy, the historical heritage of Babylonianism in opposition to the city of God should be so grandly and dramatically introduced! **Babylon the great is fallen, is fallen** — two principal views are held among conservative historians, theologians and prophetic writers: (1) Some say Babylon the city is Rome, including most of the Reformers since Luther, and also such writers as W.L. Pettingill, H.A. Ironside, Louis T. Talbot, and a multitude of others. All however do not confine the prophecies merely to the literal city, but to the whole system and regime, emanating from the city. (2) Other writers envision a rebuilding of Babylon itself as the final capital, commentators such as Joseph Seiss, Clarence Larkin, John Walvoord, David L. Cooper, Grant Jeffery and Charles Dyer, the latter two providing up-to-date information and statistics in late 20th century publications. These and many others believe prophecies in Isaiah and Jeremiah about Babylon's ruin are not yet fulfilled (See Isaiah 21:9; Jeremiah 51:8 and consult marginal references and the *Treasury of Biblical Knowledge* for all such passages.) Those who interpret Babylon as Rome in both chapters seventeen and eighteen believe that according to these O.T. books, Babylon can never be rebuilt. As many premillennialists hold one view as the other. This commentator leans toward the restoration of Babylon in the end times position, but without dogmatism ... **and is become the habitation of devils** *(daimoniaon)* **and the hold of every foul spirit** *(pneumatos akathartou)* **and a cage of every unclean and hateful bird** — a scene of desolation, evil and demonic spirits is envisioned by the passage. **3. For all nations have drunk of the wine of the wrath of her fornication** *(porneias)* **with her and the merchants of the earth are waxed rich through the abundance of her delicacies** — To a great extent this was true of Rome and the Roman Empire in days when this was first penned, but these conditions are revived and intensified in the end time. Fornication here is to be understood as physical and spiritual immorality in the total framework of endtime Babylonianism.

Call for Separation from Babylon (4,5)

4. And I heard another voice from heaven saying — either the voice of God himself or an angel authorized to speak for Him ... **Come out of her my people** *(ekselthate ho laos mou eks autes)* — see Jeremiah 50:8; 51:6, 45 where similar ideas are expressed relevant to ancient Israel. Today in many world-conforming, apostate or non conservative churches there are still true people of God who ought to respond to this call even now. In the future, during the Tribulation, those who come to Christ are summoned to separate themselves from the final Babylonian religious and political system ... **that ye be not partakers of her sins, and that ye receive not of her plagues** — evidently this deals especially with Babylon in its religious significance. **5. For her sins have reached unto heaven and God hath remembered her iniquities** — Albert Garner comments, "The cities of Rome,

Babylon and ancient Babel seem to be assimilated in a one (final) Gentile world empire, presided over by the Dragon empowered beast or Antichrist in consort with a religious state mistress called Mystery Babylon the Great, the mother of harlots, with illicit offspring, worshipping at different altars. God calls his people, both Israel and the church, to come or to abide outside of her corporate being, her organizations and her degraded forms of worship."

Announcement of Doom (6–8)

6. Reward her even as she rewarded you — evidently, God is issuing this directive, which the angels of judgment execute, for Babylon in all of its aspects is to be punished … **and double unto her double according to her works: in the cup which he hath filled, fill to her double** — three times the word *diplosate* or forms of the word is used; hence English "duplicate." **7. For she saith in her heart, I sit a queen and am no widow and shall see no sorrow** — or "I shall never have to mourn, as one bereft of her husband." "As Babylon was queen of the East, so Rome has been queen of the West and is called on imperial coins, 'the eternal city.' Ammian Marcellin wrote, 'Babylon is a former Rome and Rome a latter Babylon.' Rome is a daughter of Babylon and by her, as her mother, God has been pleased to subdue the world under one sway, so said Augustine in the 5th Century" (J.F.B. Commentary). **8. Therefore shall her plagues come in one day** (see 6:17), **death** *(thanatos)*, **and mourning** *(kai penthos)* **and famine** *(kai limos)*; **she shall be utterly burned with fire: for strong is the Lord who judgeth her** — literal fire will burn the literal city. As the ground was cursed after Adam's fall, the earth in Noah's day was judged by water, the city of Sodom was engulfed in flames, so shall the destiny of Babylon be as here depicted.

Dirge over Babylon (9–19)

9. And the kings of the earth who have committed fornication and lived deliciously with her shall bewail her and lament for her, when they shall see the smoke of her burning. — Man's fleshly, carnal mind relishes a religion, like that of the apostate church, which gives an opiate to conscience, while leaving the sinner license to indulge his lusts. **10. Standing afar off for the fear of her torment, saying, Alas, alas, the great city Babylon, that mighty city! for in one hour thy judgment is come** — the word **Alas** *(ousai)* carries the idea of "woe." Again see vs. 16 and 19, where it is repeated like a refrain. This whole passage is a form of poetic writing and can be considered a dirge. **11. And the merchants of the earth shall weep and mourn over her: for no man buyeth their merchandise anymore** — the "stock market of the ages is closed." The society will be capitalistic. **12. And the merchandise of gold** *(chrusou)* **and silver** *(argurou)*, **and precious stones** *(lithou timou)*, **and of pearls** *(margariton)*, **and fine linen** *(bussinou)*, **and of purple** *(porphuras)*, **and silk** *(serikou)*, **and scarlet** *(kokkinou)*, **and all thine wood** *(pan ulon thuinon)*, **and all manner of vessels of ivory** *(skeuous elephantinon)*, **and all manner of most precious wood** *(ksulou timiontatou)*, **and of brass** *(chalkou)*, **and iron** *(siderou)*, **and of marble** *(marmarou)*. **13. And cinnamon** *(kinnamomon)*, **and odours** *(thumaimata*–incense, aromas*)*, **and ointments** *(muron)*, **and frankincense** *(libanon)*, **and wine** *(oinon)*, **and oil** *(elaion)*, **and fine flower** *(semidalin)*, **and wheat** *(siton)*, **and beasts** *(ktene*–cattle*)*, **and sheep** *(probata)*, **and horses** *(hippon)*, **and chariots** *(hredon*–carriages, vehicles*)*, **and slaves** *(somaton*–bodies*)*, **and souls of men** *(psuchas anthropon)* — twenty–seven separate entities or products. Trafficking in the bodies and souls of human beings is the worst of these. Not only historic slavery, but slavery to merchandised drugs may be intended. The "consumer society" here is under judgment. **14. And the fruits that thy soul lusteth after are departed from thee, and all things which were dainty and goodly are departed from thee, and thou shalt find them no more at all** — here is a picture of luxuries and wealth forever gone, which have been so long prized by pleasure–seeking humanity. **15. And the merchants of these things, which were made rich by her, shall stand afar off for the fear of her torment, weeping and wailing** — not that this account has little to do with religious aspect of Babylon, but rather with an economic regime, which in the end time will not be communist or socialistic, but rather capitalistic in an extreme, corrupted and greedy form. **16. And saying, Alas, alas** *(ouai)* **that great city that was clothed in fine linen and**

purple and scarlet and decked with gold and precious stones and pearls — royal vestments, ecclesiastical regalia and fine clothing and equipages characterize the wealth and grandeur of the final Babylon. **17. For in one hour** *(hoti mia hora)* **so great riches is come to nought. And every shipmaster, and all the company of ships, and sailors, and as many as trade by sea, stood afar off** — again the transportation industry's leaders lament the destruction of this center of world trade. Notice the destruction has occurred in "one hour," a very short period of time. **18. And cried when they saw the smoke of her burning, saying, What city is like unto this city?** — if this is literal Rome, then a vast expansion of its economy is slated for the future with the probable headquarters of the "revived Roman Empire" centered there. Should the late 20th century North Atlantic Treaty Organization (NATO) and the European Economic Community (EEC) evolve into the great world power of the Antichrist, "the eternal city" is slated for doom. If Babylon here is a rebuilt city on the Euphrates, then the oil rich Middle East may finance this final capital, to which the Antichrist may move, tying Europe and Asia together with a central capital. Alexander the Great thought to do exactly that over three centuries before Christ. **19. And they cast dust on their heads and cried, weeping and wailing, Saying, Alas, alas that great city wherein we were made rich all that had ships in the sea by reason of her costliness! for in one hour is she made desolate** — in some Bibles this chapter is arranged as poetry, rather than in the traditional numbered verse style, because this is poetic in form, but this in no wise detracts from its inspiration. Much of the Scripture is in poetical form.

Angelic Vision of Babylon (20–24)

20. Rejoice over her, thou heaven and ye holy saints and prophets *(hagioi apostoloi kai prophetas)* — in heaven the great prophets of Old and New Testament times and the Apostles of the Lamb can rejoice in the judgment on the entire evil Babylonian system, beginning in Genesis 11 at Babel and continuing through the ages. What a contrast between the reaction of monarchs, merchants and mariners on earth and the jubilation in heaven. See also 19:2 ... **for god hath avenged you on**

her — God has always said, "Vengeance is mine; I will repay" (Deuteronomy 32:35 and Romans 12:19). **21. And a mighty angel took up a stone like a great millstone** *(hos mulinon megan)* — compare here Jeremiah 51:60–64, which dealt with Jeremiah's times, but has possible future prophetic ramifications. Here an angel casts a great millstone which represents the end time Babylon dramatically and symbolically into the sea ... **and cast it into the sea, saying, Thus with violence shall that great city Babylon be thrown down and shall be found no more at all** — historically a great millstone *(mulos)* consisted of two large stones that would grind against each other, refining wheat or grain. Some were large enough to need two people working them, while still larger ones were turned by a mule or ass. They might weigh in excess of 100 pounds and would plunge quickly into the sea, sinking rapidly to the bottom. This is the picture here. People of all ages and times, even a modern age like ours, can comprehend what is here set forth. The Bible is for all people at all times in history and in the future. This destruction of Babylon occurs toward the very close of the Tribulation Period, immediately prior to the Battle of Armageddon. The concluding verses are arranged in poetic form:

Thus with violence shall that great city
  Babylon be thrown down,
And shall be found no more at all.
And the voice of harpers, and musicians
  and of pipers, and trumpeters, shall
  be heard no more issues at all in thee
And no craftsman, of whatsoever craft he
  be, shall be found no more in thee;
And the sound of a millstone shall be
  heard no more in thee;
And the light of a candle shall shine no
  more at all in thee;
And the voice of the bridegroom and of
  the bride shall be heard no more at all
  in thee;
For thy merchants were the great men of
  the earth;
For by thy sorceries were all nations
  deceived.
And in her was found the blood of
  prophets and of saints,
And of all that were slain upon the earth.

RAINBOWS FROM REVELATION
The Revelation of Jesus Christ
A chapter by chapter, verse by verse study
"There was a rainbow round about the throne like unto an emerald" (4:3)

CHAPTER NINETEEN: Christ Victorious

1. AND after these things I heard a great voice of much people in heaven, saying Alleluia; Salvation, and glory, and honor, and power, unto the Lord our God:

2. For true and righteous are his judgments; for he hath judged the great whore, which did corrupt the earth with her fornication, and hath avenged the blood of his servants at her hand.

3. And again they said, Alleluia. And her smoke rose up for ever and ever.

4. And the four and twenty elders and the four beasts fell down and worshiped God that sat on the throne, saying, Amen; Alleluia.

5. And a voice came out of the throne saying, Praise our God, all ye his servants, and ye that fear him, both small and great.

6. And I heard as it were the voice of a great multitude, and as the voice of many waters, and as the voice of mighty thunderings, saying, Alleluia: for the Lord God omnipotent reigneth.

7. Let us be glad and rejoice, and give honor to him: for the marriage of the Lamb is come, and his wife hath made herself ready.

8. And to her was granted that she should be arrayed in fine linen, clean and white: for the fine linen is the righteousness of saints.

9. And he saith unto me, Write, Blessed are they which are called unto the marriage supper of the Lamb. And he saith unto me, These are the true sayings of God.

10. And I fell at his feet to worship him. And he said unto me, See thou do it not: I am thy fellow servant, and of thy brethren that have the testimony of Jesus: worship God: for the testimony of Jesus is the spirit of prophecy.

11. And I saw heaven opened, and behold a white horse; and he that sat upon him was called Faithful and True, and in righteousness he doth judge and make war.

12. His eyes were as a flame of fire, and on his head were many crowns; and he had a name written, that no man knew but he himself.

13. And he was clothed with a vesture dipped in blood: and his name is called The Word of God.

14. And the armies which were in heaven followed him upon white horses, clothed in fine linen, white and clean.

15. And out of his mouth goeth a sharp sword, that with it he should smite the nations: and he shall rule them with a rod of iron: and he treadeth the winepress of the fierceness and wrath of Almighty God.

16. And he hath on his vesture and on his thigh a name written, KING OF KINGS, AND LORD OF LORDS.

17. And I saw an angel standing in the sun; and he cried with a loud voice, saying to all the fowls that fly in the midst of heaven, Come and gather yourselves together unto the supper of the great God;

18. That ye may eat the flesh of kings, and the flesh of captains, and the flesh of mighty men, and the flesh of horses, and of them that sit on them, and the flesh of all men, both free and bond, both small and great.

19. And I saw the beast, and the kings of the earth, and their armies, gathered together to make war against him that sat on the horse, and against his army.

20. And the beast was taken, and with him the false prophet that wrought miracles before him, with which he deceived them that had received the mark of the beast, and them that worshiped his image. These both were cast alive into a lake of fire burning with brimstone.

21. And the remnant were slain with the sword of him that sat upon the horse, which sword proceeded out of his mouth: and all the fowls were filled with their flesh.

Summary of Chapter Nineteen

The Two Great Suppers

I. Heavenly Hallelujahs (1–6)

Opening with a grand "Hallelujah chorus" in sharp contrast to the wailing and weeping of the world over the fall of Babylon in chapter 18, the four "Alleluias," or "Praise the Lords" acclaim the triumph of heaven, the judgment of the false and final superchurch and the whole Babylonian system. God now will take unto Him His great power and reign.

Notice the two occasions when "the great voice" is heard, the voice of much people. Their poetic hymn of triumph begins and ends with Alleluia. Next, in verse four the beasts and elders are mentioned for the last time, saying "Amen; Alleluia," joining the "much people" of verse one. A voice out of the throne, perhaps in unison calls for praise from all believers.

Finally, the voice of a great multitude, all of the redeemed of all the ages, sounding the last "Alleluia" here and proclaiming the eternal reign of God, then announcing the marriage of the Lamb.

II. Heavenly Wedding (7–10)

Segueing from the fourth "Alleluia" comes the presentation of the Lamb's wife, the ransomed, glorified bride of Christ in all of her spotless purity after the judgment seat of Christ event earlier.

This the first of the two suppers in this climactic chapter.

It is the marriage of the Lamb, not the bride, which is emphasized. Though we may speak among ourselves of the marriage of the *bride,* it is here the marriage of the *Lamb,* because His is the chief joy. When all of the redeemed are around Him in heaven, then will He see the travail of His soul and be satisfied. After the bridal banquet, the triumphant saints go forth to participate in the glorious appearing and the establishment of His Kingdom.

Here, I believe, is "the general assembly and church of the firstborn which are written in heaven," Hebrews 12:23. Here are the redeemed of this Age rewarded and glorified, now ready to be exalted with Christ in heavenly splendor.

Guests at the marriage feast will include John the Baptist, friend of the bridegroom (John 3:29), the Old Testament saints and the Tribulation Martyrs.

The marriage supper will be a joyous celebration to honor the Lamb and the Lamb's wife before all of heaven.

III. Heaven Opened (11–16)

After this will be a glorious appearing, the like of which this world has never seen. In verse eleven heaven opens, a door from that heavenly and spiritual dimension, where God reigns, will appear. Forth from that divine realm comes the all conquering Christ.

His names are listed, six here in connection with His majestic revelation, but another preceded these in this chapter, making seven. He is the (1) Lamb (7,9); (2) Faithful (11); (3) True; (4) Mysterious Name (no one knows but He Himself (12); (5) The Word of God (13); (6) King of Kings (16); (7) Lord of Lords (16).

This epochal event is the fulfillment of both Old and New Testament prophecies concerning Messiah's sudden and majestic coming in "The Day of the Lord."

It is a literal, personal, visible, physical and spiritual return of the "same Jesus" who ascended up into heaven (Acts 1:11).

IV. Horrific Armageddon (17–21)

John's attention turns from the vision of the mighty King of Kings, followed by His heavenly armies, the White Cavalry of Heaven, to the sun. There an angel appears, summoning the birds of prey, the scavengers and vultures, from all over the world to gather for "the supper of the great God."

They are to devour the carrion left from the slaughter of the armies of the world, following Armageddon. The Messiah will come to stop the Battle of Armageddon by His own conquest, to smite the nations, to rescue the earthly chosen Israelites, to defeat the Antichrist, to bring final judgment on the earth and to establish His kingdom and reign for a thousand years.

The beast (Antichrist) and the false prophet are seized and cast alive into the lake of fire by the heavenly invading armies of angels and saints of God.

Then the course of civilization, which by and large has rejected God and His Word, comes to a close, and a new era will be at hand.

Outline of Chapter Nineteen

The King of Kings Conquers All

OBJECTIVE: To reveal Christ coming in the clouds of heaven with power and great glory to end the Tribulation and establish His Kingdom.

OUTLINE:

I. Great Rejoicing in Heaven (1–10)
 A. Rejoicing Over the Coming Victories (1–6)
  1. The Time: "After" the Tribulation (1)
  2. The Place: "Heaven"
  3. The Acclaim (1,2)
   a. His glory is praised (1)
   b. His judgments are righteous (2)
   c. His punishments are just (2)
  4. The People (1,3)
   "Much people in heaven"
  5. The Worshippers (4)
   Elders and living creatures
  6. The Voice from the Throne (5)
  7. The Proclamation (6)
   "The Lord God omnipotent reigneth"
 Note: the Four Alleluias (1,3,4,6)

 B. Rejoicing Over the Marriage of the Lamb (7–10)
  1. The Lamb (7)
  2. The Wife (7,8)
   a. She has made herself ready
   b. She is arrayed in fine linen (righteousness of saints)
  3. The Guests (9)
  4. John's Reaction (10)

II. Glorious Return of Christ (11-16)
 A. His Arrival (11)
  1. His Steed: a White Horse
  2. His Names:
   a. Faithful
   b. True
  3. His Character: Righteous
  4. His Purpose: Judgment

 B. His Appearance (11–12)
  1. His Eyes: Aflame
  2. His Head: Crowned
  3. His Name: a Secret

 C. His Attire (13)
  1. A Vesture
  2. Dipped in Blood

 D. His Armies (14)
  1. From Heaven
  2. On White Horses
  3. Clothed in White Linen

 E. His Attack (15)
  1. The Word–Sword Used
  2. The Nations Smitten
  3. The Rod of Iron Employed
  4. The Winepress of Wrath Trodden

 F. His Appellation (16)
  1. His Name Inscribed on His Garment
  2. His Supreme Title: King of Kings and Lord of Lords

III. God's Retribution on the Wicked (17–21)
 A. The Angel's Invitation (17,18)
  1. Seen in the Sun
  2. Heard in a Loud Voice
  3. Addressed the Vultures
  4. Invites the Fowls to Feast
  5. Announces the Slaughter

 B. The Antichrist's Opposition (19)
  1. The Beast Himself
  2. The Beast's Allied Rulers
  3. The Beast's Armies
  4. Their Aim: Fight Christ and His Armies

 C. The Awesome Defeat (20)
  1. Beast Defeated
  2. False Prophets Defeated
   a. The miracle workers
   b. The mark of the Beast origination
   c. The image of the Beast creator
  3. Both Consigned Alive to the Lake of Fire

 D. The Annihilated Enemies (21)
  1. Evil Remnant of Beast's Armies Slain
  2. Christ Victorious
  3. Fowls Filled with Flesh

Observations:
Spiritual lessons and applications from each verse
Chapter Nineteen

1. The saints of God, raptured and glorified, will join in the great hallelujah chorus in the heavens.

2. God's judgments are always true and righteous.

3. Punishment of sin and sinners is eternal, forever and ever.

4. Worship of God is always in order.

5. God has all kinds of servants, "small and great," and all should praise Him every day and forever.

6. Never forget that behind the scenes the Lord God Omnipotent reigneth; but it will be the more manifest before the whole universe when Christ returns.

7. Christians should become more like Christ by intention and by the work of the indwelling Holy Spirit, even now, as part of the Lamb's wife, making ourselves ready.

8. After the judgment seat of Christ experience, which happens in heaven while the Tribulation occurs on earth, the "wife of the Lamb" will indeed be "clean and white."

9. The true sayings of God, in all the Bible, are worthy of our acceptance and obedience.

10. "Worship God," is a command not only applicable to the overwhelmed John, but to all believers.

11. Christ is always Faithful and True; He is the Way, the Truth and the Life.

12. The many crowns of Christ speak of His universal dominion in all realms.

13. Christ's vesture dipped in blood reminds us of Isaiah 63, where the avenging Messiah is seen triumphant over His enemies.

14. Glorified believers, "clothed in fine linen, white and clean," not only constitute the wife of the Lamb, but also the armies of heaven.

15. Christ shall rule all nations with a rod of iron, as Psalm 2:8, 9 indicate.

16. No higher title can be imagined than KING OF KINGS AND LORD OF LORDS.

17. A strange invitation this, in contrast to the sweet invitations to come to Christ, for here the invitation is for vultures and fowls of the air to partake of the supper of the great God, devouring the carrion left from the Battle of Armageddon.

18. No matter how high and mighty a military conqueror can be, death is the final conqueror of even the greatest.

19. How strange that Satan, knowing he is defeated, yet presses against the King of Kings through his "beast" and his followers.

20. Both the Antichrist and the false prophet are cast alive into the lake of fire and are seen there a thousand years later (20:10) ... suggesting no end of punishment in hell.

21. The Word-Sword of Christ is all powerful.

Christ Rides the Colt, Then the Horse

The prophecy in Zechariah 9:9: "Behold thy King cometh unto thee: he is just and having salvation: lowly, and riding upon an ass, upon a colt, the foal of an ass" was literally fulfilled, as Matthew 21:4-11 describes. Whey then should it be thought a thing incredible, as some do, that the prediction here of "this same Jesus" depicts Him as riding on a white horse? He came the first time on an ass, a lowly and peaceful beast, as some ancient kings did when they came in peace. He comes the second time on a white stallion for war and judgment.

Quotations
From Other Expositors
Chapter Nineteen

Hallelujah Chorus (1-6)

"Hence, 19:1–10 causes us to hear the hallelujahs of heaven when Christ has come in glory to take unto himself his bride, the church, 19:7. Heaven celebrates God's victory over the harlot, Babylon. John hears, first a great sound of a great multitude. The hosts of angels ascribe salvation and glory and power unto God. They declare that in judging the great harlot God has perfected the salvation of his people. Thus, the glory of his attributes has become manifest, and his power has been revealed. It is God, He alone, who has wrought salvation. Cf. Rev. 5:11,12; 12;10; 18:20; Jer. 51:10. Moreover, in bringing about the fall of Babylon Jehovah's righteousness has been displayed — cf. Rev. 15:3,4; 16:7,15 — for this harlot had corrupted the entire earth with her whoring. Cf. Rev. 14:8; 17:2,4; 18:3,7,9; Jer. 51:7. Self–exaltation, leading people farther and farther away from God, had been her chief delight. Besides, she had brought about the slaughter of the saints, Rev. 17:6; 18:24. Now God has rendered vengeance, Rev. 6:10; 8:5; Jer. 50:13. The angels rejoice exceedingly in the salvation of God's people. They are filled with gladness of heart when they ponder the fact that all opposition has been quenched forever. Hence, again they give expression to this joy by saying, 'Hallelujah.' Their hearts seem to be filled with ecstasy to the very breaking point, and in their rapture they say, 'Praise Jehovah.' That is the meaning of 'hallelujah,' which is found only here in the N.T. Babylon's smoke goes up for ever and ever, Rev. 14:11; 18:8,9,18,21 ff; Is. 13:20 ff; Matt. 25;46. Never again will she rise to vex the church.

"Next, the twenty–four elders, symbolizing the entire church, praise God, and so do the four cherubim, representing all cherubim, Rev. 4;2–6; 5;14; 7:15. So filled are they with thanksgiving that they can utter but two words, 'Amen' [in response to the acclaim of the angels, vs. 13] and 'Hallelujah!' They express their adoration to God who is seated upon the Throne, that is, highly exalted, glorious, sovereign.

"Then, John hears a solo–voice — one of the cherubim or one of the other angels? — coming forth from the region of the Throne, saying:

"'Give praise to our God, all you servants of his, Those fearing him, the small and the great!'

"The lowliest angel and the highest saint, all are summoned to glorify God, the Author of salvation; for all serve him out of reverence.

"Hence, John now hears the voice of all the hosts of heaven: both angels and men. It resembled the sound of many waters and mighty thunders, for these hallelujahs are spontaneous, majestic, and issue from lips innumerable, 14:2.

"These voices proclaim in unison that the Lord, God, the Almighty has now revealed himself in the full majesty of his royal glory and power, verse 6. Each exhorts his neighbor to rejoice and to be glad exceedingly, and above all else, to ascribe unto God all the glory, Rev. 1:6; 14:7."

– William Hendricksen

Happy Wedding Time (7–10)

"The 'Marriage of the Lamb' evidently occurs immediately upon the destruction of Babylon, for these events seem to follow closely upon one another. After the destruction of Babylon in Chapters 17 and 18, the rejoicing over this takes place in 19:1–5, that the Lord reigns and the 'Marriage of the Lamb is come …'

"The marriage takes place 'in heaven' (verse 1), because we are not on earth until 19:17. They must, therefore, be heavenly, and not earthly. The 'wife' of verse 7 is 'the Bride, the Lamb's wife' of Revelation 21:9, which peoples, and is called, 'the New Jerusalem' (Revelation 21:9–21). The husband and wife relationship described in Ephesians 5:21–32 is 'a great mystery,' because it describes the marriage relationship of Christ and the Church (the Bride and Wife).

"The Bride is 'arrayed in fine linen, clean and white,' which is the righteous of the saints (verse 8) — 'a glorious church, not having spot, or wrinkle, or any such thing …' (Ephesians 5:27).

"The 'bride' and 'wife' is not Israel. We are in heaven for the wedding. Besides, Israel is 'divorced' (Jeremiah 3:8) and a 'widow' (Isaiah 54:4), who needs to be restored (Hosea 2:1–170 and will be restored with blessing on the earth. See Isaiah 62:4–5 and 54:4–5).

"Verse 8 and 9 of Revelation 19 indicates that there is a distinction between 'the Marriage' and 'the Marriage Supper.' The 'wife' of verse 8 and 'they which are called' constitute different persons. The 'wife' is the church, but who are those 'which are called unto the Marriage Supper'? They are probably those saints which are not in the 'Bride,' but are in heaven."

– Bill Lawrence

Heaven Opened (11-12)

"When the Lord Jesus is revealed from heaven, in flaming fire taking vengeance upon them that know not God and that obey not the gospel, he does not come alone. He is married now, and his Bride is with him. Even before the flood, Enoch prophesied of this epiphany of the promised One, and said, 'Behold the Lord cometh with ten thousand of his saints to execute judgment upon all' (Jude 14:15). They are with him now, therefore they must have been taken before. John saw, and writes, 'The armies, the ones in the heaven, were following him.' Christ is the Head and Leader, and he goes before; his saints follow in his train. The promise from the beginning was, that the seed of the woman would bruise the serpent's head, and here it is emphasized that, 'He himself treadeth the winepress of the wine of he anger of the wrath of God, the All–Ruler.' He himself is the Great Hero and Conqueror in this battle. But he is 'Jehovah of hosts.' He has many under his command. The armies of the sky are his, and he brings them with him, even 'the called and chosen, and faithful,' (Chapter 17:14).

"ON WHITE HORSES. The great Captain is mounted, and they are mounted too. He comes as the Warrior, Judge, and King, and they share with him in the same character. They are warrior judges and kings with him. In chapter 9, we were introduced to a cavalry from the underworld, of spirit horses from beneath; why not then celestial horses also? Horses and chariots of fire protected Elisha at Dothan; horses of fire took up Elijah into heaven. And heavenly horses bring the saints from heaven when they come with their great leader for the final subjugation of the world to his authority. It is up to the bridle–bits of these horses that the blood in the battle is to flow (Chap. 14:20). These horses are all white, the same as the Great Captain rides. Everything is in harmony. The riders all are royal and righteous ones, and the same is expressed in the color of their horses.

"They wear no armor. They are immortal, and cannot be hurt; and they are not the executors of this vengeance. It is Christ's own personal victory, in accordance with the Apostolic declaration, that 'for this purpose the Son of God was manifested, that he might destroy the works of the Devil,' (1 John 3:8). He bears the only sword, and he alone uses it. He treadeth the wine press alone. Those who accompany him in the scene of conflict therefore need no weapons. The sword of the great Captain is enough. Their defense is in him, and their victory is in him. They follow up the achievements of his sword. They ride through the blood it causes to flow. They 'wash their feet in it,' for it is up to the horses' bridles. But it is David who slays Goliath, and the hosts of God's Israel have only to follow up the mighty triumph, shouting their songs along the path of the victory. When the wicked are cut off, they shall see it; they shall diligently consider the place of the wicked, and it shall not be; but the meek shall inherit the earth, and delight themselves in the abundance of peace (Ps. 37:10,11,34). But who are the armies encountered?"

– J.A. Seiss

Hosts of Christ (14-21)

"'The armies that were in heaven followed him upon white horses, clothed in fine linen, white and clean' (v. 14). The armies of heaven consist of the angelic hosts, the Old Testament saints, the Church, and the tribulation saints. The most significant truth, however, is the garb of this army. They are 'clothed in fine linen, white and clean.'

"'And out of his mouth goeth a sharp sword, that with it he should smite the nations, and he shall rule them with a rod of iron.' The sharp sword here has lead some to believe that it is the Sword of the Spirit, the Word of God. But Dr. John Walvoord states concerning this expression:

The word for sword indicates a long Thracian sword, of one which is unusually large and longer than most swords. The same word is sometimes used to describe a javelin, a sword sufficiently light and long to be thrown as a spear. Here the word is used symbolically to represent a sharp instrument of war, with which Christ will smite the nations and establish His absolute rule. The expression of ruling 'with a rod of iron' is also found in Psalm 2:9 and Revelation 2:27, with a similar expression, 'the rod of His mouth,' in Isaiah 11:4. It represents absolute, unyielding government under which men are required to conform to the righteous standard of God.

"The coming of Christ in His glorious appearing with the heavenly armies will not only bring to consummation the enmity of Satan, his Antichrist, the False Prophet, and the millions they deceive, but will usher in the millennial kingdom; the righteous reign of Christ upon the earth. This fact is seen clearly in the name given to Christ in the next verse.

"And he hath on his vesture and on his thigh a name written, KING OF KINGS, AND LORD OF LORDS." A warrior goes into battle with his sword on his thigh. Christ's sword will be his spoken word. The word that called the world into being will call the leaders of men and the armies of all nations into control. Instead of a sword on His thigh is the name, "KING OF KINGS AND LORD OF LORDS." Christ Jesus , the living Lord, will be established in that day for what He is in reality, King above all kings, Lord above all lords.

– Tim LaHaye

The Coming Invasion from Outer Space
An Expository Sermon

Chapter Nineteen

Introduction

Saint Paul urged Titus (2:13) to be "looking for that blessed hope and the glorious appearing of the great God and our Saviour Jesus Christ."

Writing to the Thessalonian church, Paul encouraged those new Christians, saying:

"And to you who are troubled, rest with us, when the Lord Jesus shall be revealed from heaven with his mighty angels, in flaming fire taking vengeance on them that know not God, and that obey not the gospel of our Lord Jesus Christ: who shall be punished with everlasting destruction from the presence of the Lord and from the glory of his power" (2 Thessalonians 1:7-9).

In the short epistle of the Apostle Jude appears this promise:

"And Enoch also, the seventh from Adam, prophesied of these, saying, Behold the Lord cometh with ten thousands of his saints, to execute judgment upon all and to convince all that are ungodly among them of all their ungodly deeds which they have ungodly committed, and of all their hard speeches, which ungodly sinners have spoken against him" (Jude 14,15).

Speaking of the Tribulation time, Jesus Christ Himself told His disciples about the end:

"And there shall be signs in the sun and in the moon, and in the stars; and upon the earth distress of nations, with perplexity; the sea and the waves roaring; men's hearts failing them for fear, and for looking after those things which are coming on the earth: for the powers of heaven shall be shaken. **And then shall they see the Son of Man coming in a cloud with power and great glory"** (Luke 21:25-27).

"For as the lightning cometh out of the east and shineth even unto the west, so shall the coming of the Son of Man be. For wheresoever the carcase is, there shall the eagles be gathered together. Immediately after the tribulation of those days shall the sun be darkened, and moon shall not give her light, and the stars shall fall from heaven and powers of the heavens shall be shaken; and **then shall the tribes of the earth mourn,** and they shall see the Son of Man coming in the clouds of heaven with power and great glory" (Matthew 24:27-30).

This sublime, majestic and magnificent event, the great revelation of Christ Himself in splendid and illustrious glory and beauty is set forth in this chapter.

Dark, dismal and gloomy as the world outlook may today appear, especially considering the somber calamities to befall the earth during the Tribulation, the radiant effulgence of His glory will be revealed. The long human rebellion, culminating in the dire and dreadful career of Antichrist, empowered by Lucifer, will be terminated.

Human achievement will never solve all of the wickedness of a godless world. It cannot. **"But be of good cheer."** He who is to come will come.

The Second Coming of Christ is no idle figment of a deranged imagination.

It is glorious future reality.

Jesus Christ is coming again!

We shall consider this chapter under these three headings: the Omnipotence of the Almighty, the Opening of Heaven, and the Overthrow of the Antichrist:

I. The Omnipotence of the Almighty (1–10)

"After these things I heard a great voice of much people in heaven, **Alleluia ..."** (1).

In sharp contrast with the dismal dirge of chapter 18, where Babylon's fall on earth is so vividly portrayed, heaven rings with the exultant praises of God.

Four "Alleluias" in this anthem are intoned in heaven in a crescendo of adulation, climaxing with the wondrous declaration,

"Alleluia; for the Lord God omnipotent reigneth" (6).

Here the passage is arranged in poetic form:

Alleluia; Salvation, and glory, and honor and
power unto the Lord our God.
For true and righteous are his judgments;
For he hath judged the great whore,
which did corrupt the earth with her
fornication,
And hath avenged the blood of his servants at
her hand.
And again they said,

Alleluia. And her smoke rose up forever and ever.

And the four and twenty elders and the four beasts fell down and worshipped God, that sat on the throne, saying, Amen, **Alleluia.**

And a voice came out of the throne saying,
Praise our God, all ye his servants,
And ye that fear him, both small and great.

And I heard as it were the voice of a great multitude, and as the voice of the mighty thunderings, saying,

Alleluia: for the Lord God omnipotent reigneth!

This glorious repeated word means "Praise to Jehovah" and here appears in the Greek form. It is the Hebrew expression **Hallelujah,** frequently appearing in the Psalms. The last five Psalms begin with the word, translated as "Praise the Lord."

These four occasions are the only ones in which the expression occurs in the New Testament.

Following the first **Hallelujah,** the fall and ruin of Babylon, the city and the system with its history, culture and rebellion is the occasion for such rejoicing. At last, the evil empire of all false religion and all wicked world systems is at an end.

The second **Hallelujah** acknowledges Babylon's everlasting punishment.

The elders and four living creatures join the celebration of victory with the third **Hallelujah.**

Then comes a call from the throne of God for universal and jubilant praise. This is a limitless expression of eternal ecstasy at the sovereign and supreme reign of God Almighty.

Perhaps this paean of praise segues into the poetic passage about the marriage of the Lamb:

"Alleluia: for the Lord God Omnipotent reigneth.
Let us be glad and rejoice, and give honor to him:
For the marriage of the Lamb is come.
And his wife hath made herself ready,
And to her was granted that she should be arrayed in fine linen, clean and white:
For the fine linen is the righteousness of saints."

This celestial marriage occurs in heaven itself, when the Lamb as the bridegroom, receives his bride, the ransomed, raptured and resurrected saints of the New Testament Age, as His eternal queenly co–regent in the divine government of the Universe.

It happens in heaven at the close of the Tribulation on earth and after Babylon falls.

It must follow the Judgment Seat of Christ, which occupies the attention of heaven and the glorified saints during the earthly Tribulation. "For we must all appear before the judgment seat of Christ, that everyone may receive the things done in the body, according to that he hath done, whether it be good or bad" (2 Corinthians 5;10).

"For we shall stand before the Judgment [Bema] Seat of Christ" (Romans 14:10).

Back in Revelation 11:18, contrasting the events on earth and the heavenly time of rewards, we read,

"And the nations were angry, and thy wrath is come, and the time of the dead, that they should be judged, and thou shouldest give reward unto thy servants the prophets, and to the saints, and them that fear thy name, small and great, and shouldest destroy them which destroy the earth."

The judgment seat of Christ is now over, having taken place in heaven during the Tribulation. Our works have been tried by fire and the good works further purified while the bad works have been consumed (1 Corinthians 3:12–15).

The "saints" the true believers of this age are now to constitute the bride. Her white raiment consists of the righteousness (or righteous acts) of the saints.

A marriage supper follows the ceremony. My opinion is that the invited guests consist of the Old Testament saints, John the Baptist as the friend of the groom, and the Tribulation martyrs, not yet resurrected until chapter 20.

Overwhelmed, John almost worships the angel who shows him these things, but is commanded to "Worship God: for the testimony of Jesus is the spirit of prophecy" (10).

II. The Opening of Heaven (11–16)

At the appointed time, foreseen before the foundation of the world, the mighty Conqueror, the sublime Hero of the ages, emerges from heaven, through the portals of space and time, from the invisible realm of the spiritual, now appearing most gloriously.

The Lamb, being married now, comes forth to claim what is rightly His own.

He is astride the White Stallion from the heavenly stables, the steed suggesting royalty, judgment and war and white signifying righteousness and justice.

He is Faithful and True. Two well deserved

names are added to His redemptive title of "Lamb."

Faithful He is, always fulfilling His every promise.

True is He indeed, for He is "the Way, the Truth and the Life" (John 14:6).

He judges and makes war, for He alone is worthy to enact retribution upon the wicked of the world in righteousness.

His eyes are a flame of fire, searching all depths, penetrating all darkness, illuminating all that He beholds.

His head is adorned with many crowns, for all the kingdoms of this world and all the dominions of the whole Universe are now under his absolute sway. "The kingdoms of this world are become the kingdoms of our Lord and of His Christ, and he shall reign forever and ever" (Revelation 11:15).

He has a mysterious and wonderful name, known only to Him, but will doubtless be revealed. Perhaps it is a wondrous name by which we will address Him throughout eternity.

He is clothed with a vesture dipped in blood, the stains from treading the winepress of the wrath of God (14:19,20; Isaiah 63:1–4).

His name is called (the fifth name indicated in this chapter) **the Word of God.** His is the Word which was in the beginning with God and was God. He is the Word who became flesh and dwelt among men for a third of a century. He is the *logos*, the manifest expression of eternal Deity. He is followed by the armies of heaven, the glorified saints on white horses and clad in that white and clean linen that betokens their righteousness in Christ.

He wields the word–sword of His power, smiting the nations, then to rule them with a rod of iron (Psalms 2:7–9) and to tread that winepress of the fierceness and wrath of Almighty God.

As he thus appears "in his times" **He is shown to be the "Blessed and only Potentate, the King of Kings and Lord of Lords"** (1 Timothy 6:15).

This then is the mighty and majestic Hero who rides forth from heavenly dimension to fight this "battle of the great day of God Almighty."

III. The Overthrow of the Antichrist (17–21)

While the combined armies of the world have gathered against Jerusalem to battle, the mass of the forces are in the vast Valley of Armageddon, there in the heart of Israel, between the Jordan River and the Mediterranean Sea.

"And he gathered them together into a place called in the Hebrew tongue, Armageddon" (16:16).

Apparently, the nations of the world have their armies so assembled, with Israel as part of the issue. It seems that the world ruler may have some difficulty maintaining his total power over the globe. Some of "the kings of the east" (16:12–16) may even challenge his supremacy, but the battle quickly becomes a conflict between the Antichrist and his forces of earth against Christ and the armies of heaven.

Here is how Zechariah describes the coming of the Messiah:

"Behold the day of the Lord cometh ... and I will gather all nations against Jerusalem to battle ... Then shall the Lord go forth and fight against those nations, as when he fought in the Day of battle ... and his feet shall stand in that day upon the Mount of Olives, which is before Jerusalem on the east ... and this shall be the plague wherewith the Lord will smite all the people that have fought against Jerusalem: Their flesh shall consume away while they stand upon their feet, and their eyes shall consume away in their holes, and their tongues shall consume away in their mouth ..." (Zechariah 14:1,2,3,4,12).

An angel standing in the sun is said to summon all of the vultures of the air to come and devour what is left of the flesh of the hundreds of millions in the huge army.

In a powerful and dramatic stroke of justice and judgment, the Antichrist and the false prophet are seized and cast alive into the lake of fire.

King Jesus needs no help even from His armies. He is the sole and supreme Conqueror. All of the combined forces of evil and iniquity shall be shattered in this climactic clash between good and evil.

But the saints of God, and all the redeemed of the ages then share in the glorious Kingdom which cannot be moved. Christ, forever victorious!

Conclusion

But if you know not Christ, no such eternal and marvelous future awaits you. Come to the Lamb of God now and receive Him as your Savior and be born into the Kingdom of God!

A Commentary on the Revelation
Expository, Exegetical, Devotional and Practical
Greek words from the Textus Receptus

Chapter Nineteen

The Marriage Supper (1–10)

1. And after these things *(Kai meta tauta)* — past now are the seal, trumpet and vial judgments; past now is the destruction of Babylon, the city, the system, worldwide in its religious and political and commercial forms; the Tribulation has now run its course ... **I heard a great voice** *(phone megalen)* **of much people in heaven** — this multitudinous company in heaven may include the martyrs under the altar (6:9–11), the 144,000 saved Israelites (7:3), the great multitude that no man can number (7:9), perhaps all of the redeemed, but we are not told specifically ... **saying Alleluia** — in Hebrew "Praise ye Jah," the shorter title for God. Jehovah (Yahweh) means "He who will be, is and was," whereas just Jah (Yah) means "He who is." So sacred was the name to the Jews that they would scarcely ever say it. In our English version, LORD in all caps in the Old Testament always indicates "Jehovah" as it appears in Hebrew. This is the first and only time in the N.T. that the expression "Praise ye Jah" appears, here four times. Compare Psalm 149:4–9 for a very similar passage ... **Salvation** *(soteria)* — He is the great Savior and Deliverer ... **honor** *(doksa)* — worthy of praise and recognition, hence the doxology ... **power** *(dunamis)* — dynamic, exercised energy ... **unto the Lord our God. 2. For true and righteous are his judgments** — although fleshly human wisdom wants to think of God as so merciful, if He exists, that He would not execute just punishment for sin ... **for he hath judged the great whore** *(pornen ten megalen)* — "not until Babylon the harlot (ecclesiastical, religious system) is completely overthrown as in Revelation 17; and not until literal Babylon (18) is completely gone, and all things Babylonian have disappeared, does "Alleluia" burst forth from all holy hearts" (W. Newell) ... **which did corrupt the earth with her fornication** — physical immorality, symbolical immorality, spiritual adultery (see James 4:4 — "friendship with the world's system = enmity with God" ... all involved in prostituting truth and justice ... **and hath avenged the blood of his servants at her hand** — "avenged" here *(eksedikesen)* means to exact in retribution, to render just and appropriate punishment, suitable to the crime or sin. Servants *(doulon)* — in the Old Testament Babylonian, anti–God philosophy and religion (beginning at Babel in Genesis 11) resulted in the slaughter of God's people. During Roman times, millions were slain; and in Roman religious times, many true believers were slain as enemies of the church, and in modern times anti–God Babylonianism has resulted in many being martyrs, a condition that will intensify in the Tribulation under Antichrist. **3. Alleluia** — second mention ... **her smoke rose up** *(ho kaptos autes anabainei)* — continual judgment on evil Babylon the harlot; everlasting joy for the Savior's pure bride, the wife of the Lamb. **4. And the four and twenty elders and the four beasts** — last mention of the elders and the zoa, the four living creatures or cherubim ... **fell down and worshipped God that sat on the throne, saying Amen, Alleluia!** The twenty–four elders are thought to represent the raptured and glorified saints as in chapters 4 and 5, while the four living creatures are constant attendants before the rainbow–encircled throne. They join that "much people" group (1) in uttering this third Alleluia. Just as the dirges and lamentations in chapter 18 can be arranged in poetic form, so these Alleluia passages seem to be inspired poetry. **5. And a voice came out of the throne, saying, Praise our God, all ye his servants, and ye that fear him, both small and great.** Compare 1 Chronicles 16:36 and 23;5 with 2 Chronicles 5:13. This voice out of the throne may be that of Christ Himself, as prophetically in Psalm 22:22, 23: "I will declare thy name unto my brethren: in the midst of the congregation will I praise thee. Ye that fear the Lord praise him ..." **6. And I heard the voice of a great multitude** *(phonen ochlou pollu)* **and as the voice of many waters** *(hudaton pollon)*, **and as the voice of mighty thundering** *(bronton ischuron)*, **saying, Alleluia: for the Lord God omnipotent reigneth** — present tense. He always has and always will reign, though not all recognize His sovereignty. **7. Let us be glad and rejoice, and give honour to him: for the marriage of the Lamb is come, and his wife hath made herself ready** — marriage (gamos) means a wedding and usually the events connected with it, as in John 2:1–3, the marriage in Cana of Galilee. Abbott–Smith defines the word as meaning "a wedding, especially a wedding feast …" The wife of the Lamb consists of the redeemed of this Age; some say also the Old Testament saints, but this writer thinks they are invited as guests and that only the New Testament saints from the ministry of Jesus to the Rapture/Resurrection are included, the "church of the firstborn, whose names are written in heaven" (Hebrews 12:23 where several groups are mentioned). Being made ready by the judgment seat of Christ, which is in session in heaven during the Tribulation on earth (see 2 Corinthians 5:10; 1 Corinthians 3:11–15), the saints are now qualified to be a pure and spotless bride without blemish (Ephesians 5:26,27). **8. And to her was granted to be arrayed in fine linen** (peribaletai bussinon), **clean and white: for the fine linen is the righteousness of the saints** — this fine white linen is emblematic of the righteous acts and works of the saints. The same characterization is made of the uniforms of the armies, accompanying Jesus from heaven (14). Hence, they are the same crowd: godly, glorified believers as the wife of the Lamb and an army with Christ. Israel was the "wife of Jehovah" as in Jeremiah 3:8; 31:32; Hosea 2 and 3, who will be restored on earth during the millennium (Hosea 14). **9. And he saith unto me, Write, Blessed are they which are called unto the marriage supper of the Lamb. And he saith unto me, These are the true sayings of God** — These guests would include "the spirits of just men made perfect" or Old Testament saints (Hebrews 12:24), Tribulation martyrs, the 144,000, etc. John the Baptist as friend of the Bridegroom is "best man." The marriage itself is His presentation to himself of the glorious church, not having spot or wrinkle, saved and cleansed by His blood, rewarded for service; and all shortcomings, already forgiven by grace, are consumed as it were by the fire of His scrutinizing, examining eyes at the judgment seat of Christ. Wood, hay and stubble, those things not pleasing to Him, are forever gone forever (1 Corinthians 3:12,15). **10. And I fell at his feet to worship him. And he said unto me, See thou do it not: I am thy fellow servant** (sundoulos) **and of thy brethren that have the testimony of Jesus: Worship God: for the testimony of Jesus is the spirit of prophecy** — it is as though he says, "We angels, and you apostles all alike have the testimony or bear testimony concerning Jesus by the operation of that one and the selfsame Spirit, who enables me to show you these revelations, and enables you to record them; wherefore we are fellowservants, not I your lord to be worshipped" (J.F.B.). God alone is worthy of worship, not the angels, not the departed saints, not the Apostles. The command is Worship God!

The Messiah's Second Coming (11–16)

11. And I saw heaven opened (kai eidon ton ouranon eneogmenon) — this is the perfect passive participle of anoigo, open. Hence the meaning is that the door opened and stayed open. The perfect tense indicates a continuing state, resulting from a completed act. Heaven's spiritual but literal realm is now connected to the earthly, physical literal realm. Concourse between the two realms will then be the case during the millennium, through which opening some may have passage, especially Christ's co–regents, the saints … **and behold a white horse** (kai idou hippos leukos) — the first white horse (6:1,2) was ridden by the imitator–imposter deceiver, the false messiah, Antichrist, but here we have Christ the conquering King and General of the armies of heaven, leading a divine military expedition from another world … **and he that sat upon him is called Faithful** (pistos) **and True** (alethinos) — not counterfeit, not false, but genuine … **and in righteousness he doth judge and make war** — no unjust, illegal or improper act can ever be performed by this just and righteous Ruler. His judgments are perfect and his wars against evil are just and correct. **12. His eyes were as a flame of fire** — eyes can be used as powerful instruments in communication by strong personalities. Christ's luminous, flaming, awesome eyes, flashing and furious, can penetrate to the deepest confines of the human soul; nothing can be hidden from omniscient, all–seeing gaze. Perhaps the wrath of the Lamb flashes in righteous fury from his fiery eyes … **and on his head were many crowns** (diademata) — not the lesser crown or stephanos, which is mentioned eight times in Revelation (2:10; 3:11; 4:4, 10; 6:2; 9:7; 12:1; 14:14), but diadema, a royal crown as in 12:3; 13:1; 19:12 — here. Christ wears both kinds of crowns … **and he had a name written, that no man knew, but he Himself** … evidently inscribed on one of His crowns is the mysterious and cryptic name, no doubt a blessed and wonderful appellation, which will be known by His own in time and perhaps used forever. **13. And he was clothed with a vesture** (himation) **dipped in**

blood — his garment is a long flowing robe, stained with the blood of His enemies, as in Isaiah 63:1–4. He sheds the blood, not of the godly, as did both the Beast and Babylon, but the blood of the ungodly … **his name is called the Word of God** *(hos Logos tou theou)* — a divine title, when used of Christ, speaking of His being the Person and Power which speaks to humankind; the expression of God and His thought, manifested in the Incarnation (John 1:1–14; 1 John 1:1; 5:7). Here He returns as the Word, not as in the original Incarnation as the Babe in Bethlehem, but as the crowned Son of God, the eternal Word. **14. And the armies which were in heaven followed him upon white horses, clothed in fine linen, white and clean** — the uniform of the armies is the same as the clothing of the wife of the Lamb (8), hence the saints are soldiers in this army (Jude 14,15), but also in the armies must be the angels (Matthew 25:31). **15. And out of his mouth goeth a sharp sword** *(hroma okseia)* — this is the word–sword of His power, His voice (see Isaiah 11:4; 1 Thessalonians 2:8) … **he shall rule them with a rod of iron** *(autos poimanei autous en hrabdo sidera)* — *poimanei* means "shall shepherd" … since He was refused as the Good Shepherd, who gave His life for the sheep (John 10:11), He now will punitively, powerfully enforce His shepherdhood, not with the pastoral rod, but with a rod of iron (See Revelation 2:27; Psalms 2:9; Daniel 2:35, 44, 45; Revelation 12:5), as a benevolent absolute Sovereign … **and he treadeth the winepress of the fierceness and wrath of Almighty God** — a figurative expression, of course, but he shall indeed tread down His enemies, as in Isaiah 63:3 … the entire period of wrath begins in Revelation 6 with the wrath of the Lamb and is here being concluded. "The fierceness of Christ's wrath against His foes will be executed with the resources of omnipotence" (J.F.B.) **16. And he hath on his vesture** *(himation* — outer flowing garment or robe) **and on his thigh** — that lower side portion of His majestic appearance where His robe flows in white radiance, a vesture long enough to include the grand title **King of Kings and Lord of Lords.** The use of the word "thigh" suggests His humanity, as having come from the loins of David, humanly speaking, but now appears in glorious splendor to sit on the throne of His father David (see Luke 1:32,33), ruling over Israel and the whole world … yea over the whole Universe.

The Multitudes Slain (17–21)

17. And I saw an angel standing in the sun — John sees this in his vision; thus whether the angel will be visible by the wicked on earth is a question, since the call is extended to the fowls of the air. No longer is the sun darkened (Revelation 8:12; 9:2; 16:8) … **and he cried with a loud voice** *(phone megale)* **saying to all the fowls** *(orneios* — hence ornothology in English, a study of birds) — many birds are carrion scavengers, carnivorous, declared unclean in Leviticus 11:14. Compare Ezekiel 39:17–22 … **Come and gather yourselves together unto the supper of the great God** — contrast the marriage supper of the Lamb. See Job 39:27–30 for a depiction of a bird of prey. **18. That ye may eat the flesh of kings** *(basileos)*, **and the flesh of captains** *(chiliarchos* — an officer in charge of a thousand), **and the flesh of mighty men** *(kai sarkas ischuron* — flesh from the bodies of strong men), **and the flesh of horses** — indicative that sophisticated technology may be developed to short circuit mechanized equipment by laser beams or other exotic weaponry, thus requiring military horses again … **and of them that sit on them and the flesh of all men both free and bond, both small and great** — for further descriptions of this Battle of Armageddon in Israel, see Revelation 16:12–16; Zechariah 12:1–9; Joel 2:2,3,11–15; Isaiah 34:1–9; Habakkuk 3:3–6; Jeremiah 7:33). **19. And I saw the beast, and the kings of the earth, and their armies gathered together to make war against him that sat on the horse and against his army** — whatever the original causes of this vast mustered army's gathering, the issue now is clear: it is Christ vs. Antichrist. **20. And the beast was taken, and with him the false prophet that wrought miracles before him … these both were cast alive into a lake of fire burning with brimstone** *(eis ten limnen tou puros tes kaiomenes en theio)* — Daniel foresaw this event in 7:11 of his prophecy. The beast is the political power, while the false prophet is the religious power, both embodied in these final leaders of the Antichrist movement. Here is their destiny! **21. And the remnant** *(loipoi* — rest or remainder) **were slain with the sword of him that sat upon the horse, which sword proceeded out of his mouth, and all the fowls were filled with their flesh** — thus ends the Battle of Armageddon; thus ends the Great Tribulation; thus ends this age and this Dispensation; thus ends the long rebellion against God, initiated and precipitated by humanity's fall and organized at Babel after the Flood. A new and glorious age next begins.

RAINBOWS FROM REVELATION
The Revelation of Jesus Christ
A chapter by chapter, verse by verse study
"There was a rainbow round about the throne like unto an emerald" (4:3)

CHAPTER TWENTY: The Millennium

References

Rev. 1:18

Isa. 24:22
2 Pet. 2:4
Rev. 12:9

Dan. 6:17
Mt. 27:66

Dan. 7:9
Mt. 19:28
Lk. 22:30
Rev. 13:12,15
Jn. 14:19
Rom. 8:17
2 Tim. 2:12
Rev. 5:9,10

Dan. 12:2,3
Jn. 5:28,29
Rev. 20:12

Rev. 2:11
Rev. 20:14
Isa. 61:6
1 Pet. 2:9
Rev. 1:6

1 Pet. 5:8

1. AND I saw an angel come down from heaven, having the key of the bottomless pit and a great chain in his hand.

2. And he laid hold on the dragon, that old serpent, which is the Devil, and Satan, and bound him a thousand years,

3. And cast him into the bottomless pit, and shut him up, and set a seal upon him, that he should deceive the nations no more, till the thousand years should be fulfilled: and after that he must be loosed a little season.

4. And I saw thrones, and they sat upon them, and judgment was given unto them: and I saw the souls of them that were beheaded for the witness of Jesus, and for the word of God, and which had not worshiped the beast, neither his image, neither had receive his mark upon their foreheads, or in their hands; and they lived and reigned with Christ a thousand years.

5. But the rest of the dead lived not again until the thousand years were finished. This is the first resurrection.

6. Blessed and holy is he that hath part in the first resurrection: on such the second death hath no power, but they shall be priests of God and of Christ, and shall reign with him a thousand years.

7. And when the thousand years are expired, Satan shall be loosed out of his prison,

8. And shall go out to deceive the nations which are in the four quarters of the earth, Gog and Magog, to gather them together to battle: the number of whom is as the sand of the sea.

9. And they went up on the breadth of the earth, and compassed the camp of the saints about, and the beloved city: and fire came down from God out of heaven, and devoured them.

10. And the devil that deceived them was cast into the lake of fire and brimstone, where the beast and the false prophet are, and shall be tormented day and night for ever and ever.

11. And I saw a great white throne, and him that sat on it, from whose face the earth and the heaven fled away; and there was found no place for them.

12. And I saw the dead, small and great, stand before God; and the books were opened: and another book was opened, which is the book of life: and the dead were judged out of those things which were written in the books, according to their works.

13. And the sea gave up the dead which were in it; and death and hell delivered up the dead which were in them: and they were judged every man according to their works.

14. And death and hell were cast into the lake of fire. This is the second death.

15. And whosoever was not found written in the book of life was cast into the lake of fire.

References

Isa. 65:20
Ezek. 38:2

Isa. 8:8
Ps. 87:2
Ps. 132:13
Gen. 19:24
Ps. 9:15-17

Rev. 19:20
Isa. 66:24

Ps. 9:3
2 Pet. 3:7
Mt. 24:35

Ps. 69:28
Mt. 16:26,27
Rom. 14:12
Phil. 2:9-11

Hos. 13:14
Lk. 16:23-31

1 Cor. 15:26

Jn. 3:16
Rev. 19:20;
20:10,14; 21:8

Scriptures for Comparison

Daniel 12:2
And many of them that sleep in the dust of the earth shall awake, some to everlasting life, and some to shame and everlasting contempt.

John 5:28,29
Marvel not at this: for the hour is coming, in the which all that are in the graves shall hear his voice, And shall come forth; they that have done good, unto the resurrection of life; and they that have done evil, unto the resurrection of damnation.

Isaiah 35:8-10
And an highway shall be there, and a way, and it shall be called The way of holiness; the unclean shall not pass over it; but it shall be for those: the wayfaring men, though fools, shall not err therein. No lion shall be there, nor any ravenous beast shall go up thereon, it shall not be found there; but the redeemed shall walk there: And the ransomed of the LORD shall return, and come to Zion with songs and everlasting joy upon their heads: they shall obtain joy and gladness, and sorrow and sighing shall flee away.

Summary of Chapter Twenty

How History Will Conclude

I. Removal of Satan (1–3)

Following the Rapture and the Resurrection of the New Testament saints, there will be in heaven the judgment seat of Christ, an evaluation of believers' works for rewards. This is described in 1 Corinthians 5:10. After this will come the marriage of the Lamb. On earth the great epoch, called the "Day of the Lord" will occur, as has been fully described in the preceding chapters.

As the Tribulation closes, Christ returns in splendor. There follows the imprisonment of Satan. In this chapter we see (1) Satan bound; (2) the first resurrection; (3) the millennium, mentioned six times; (4) Satan loosed; (5) the last and final war; (6) Satan consigned to the lake of fire; (7) the second resurrection and the second death.

Coming down from heaven is a special angel, authorized to arrest Satan, binding him for a thousand years with a great chain and casting him into the bottomless pit, the Abyss, (Greek word for bottomless pit).

Notice that six times in the first six verses is the 100 year period designated. The Latin word is *millennium*, which has come into popular use.

God will have one further use for even this archenemy. He will test and tempt the descendents of the survivors of the Tribulation to see whether their allegiance during the millennium is merely an outward submission to His supreme rule or a heartfelt dedication to the Savior–King.

II. The Resurrection unto Life (4–5)

Enthroned during this glorious future age will be the resurrected and raptured saints of this age, who will reign with Him. Likewise the Old Testament saints will rule with the Savior. "Judgment is given unto them."

Another special class of believers is designated, which I take to include all the martyrs for Christ in all of history, those beheaded or otherwise slain for the witness of Jesus. A third group will include the Tribulation martyrs, who refuse the mark of the beast and thereby die for Christ.

All of these are included in the first resurrection therefore: the Old and New Testament saints, and all of the martyrs who die during the Tribulation Period.

The first part of verse four refers to those already resurrected, raptured ones, who are kept from the Tribulation by Christ's coming for them, prior to its beginning.

III. Reign of Christ (6)

How glorious will be the victory of Christ and His saints! Only saved people are involved in the First Resurrection.

There will be survivors on earth after the Tribulation is over. The Old Testament speaks of all nations bringing their glory to Jerusalem (Isaiah 2 and 11). "All Israel will be saved" (Romans 11:26), by which is meant that all Israelites alive at the close of the Tribulation will accept Christ as their Savior and Messiah, according to Zechariah 12,13,14.

Many saved Gentiles will escape the antichrist's sword and be the "sheep nations," or Gentiles, as described in Matthew 25;31–46. All unsaved survivors are classified individually as among the "goat nations," or Gentiles and will be banished to hell (gehenna) before the kingdom is fully established.

The whole world will be under the dominion of King Jesus and with the glorified saints associated with Him in His supreme reign.

Sitting on twelve thrones, judging the twelve tribes of Israel will be the twelve Apostles (Matthew 19:28).

While glorified saints neither marry nor are given in marriage, the survivors of the Tribulation will do both — repopulating the world and living indefinitely in ideal environmental conditions in natural but super–healthy bodies (Isaiah 65:20).

But a vast number of descendents of the saved survivors of the Tribulation will have only an outward allegiance without saving faith in Him. That is why Satan is loosed out of his prison. These have never experienced temptation from the devil. They will yield when the moment comes.

IV. Rebellion of Satan (7–10)

Thus Satan amasses a huge army and assaults the capital of the world, the earthly Jerusalem. These attackers are consumed by the fire of God, then raised later with all of the unsaved dead, to stand before the august majesty of the Judge of the Universe to receive their just and eternal retribution.

V. The Resurrection unto Damnation (11–15)

Only the lost and doomed and damned appear here to receive their eternal sentence of separation from God in the lake of fire.

216

Outline of Chapter Twenty

The End of Time

OBJECTIVE: To reveal Christ coming back in the clouds of heaven with power and great glory to end the Tribulation, banish Satan and reign for a thousand years with his first resurrection saints; then to describe the second resurrection (of the lost) and their eternal doom.

OUTLINE:
I. The Removal of Satan (1–3)
A. The Angel with the Key (1)
  1. He descends from heaven
  2. He carries the key to the Abyss
  3. He brings a great chain in his hand

B. The Archenemy Bound (2,3)
  1. His Arrest (2)
  2. His Names (2)
    a. Dragon — evil power behind evil civilization
    b. Serpent — deceiver of the human race
    c. Devil — accuser of the brethren
    d. Satan — adversary of God and man
  3. His Confinement (2) — A thousand years.

C. The Assignment to the Pit (3)
  1. He is cast into the Abyss
  2. He is shut up
  3. He is sealed
  4. He cannot deceive the nations for a thousand years.
  5. He will be loosed a little season

II. The Resurrection unto Life (4,5)
A. Those First on Thrones (4)
  1. Raptured saints included
  2. Resurrected (New Testament) saints included
  3. Raised (Old Testament) saints included

B. Those Raised at the Return: The Martyrs of the Tribulation Period
    a. They were beheaded for their witness
    b. They refused to worship the beast or his image
    c. They did not receive his mark

C. Those Reign With Christ — This is the **First Resurrection**

III. The Reign of Christ (6)
A. First Resurrection Saints Reign

B. Second Death has No Power Over Them

C. They shall be Priests of God

D. They Reign a Thousand Years

IV. The Release of Satan (7–10)
A. His Final Attempt at Rebellion (7,8)

B. His Final Army (8)
  1. Deceived descendents of Tribulation survivors
  2. Drawn from all over Earth
  3. Designated as "Gog and Magog"

C. His Final Attack on Jerusalem (9)
  1. Camp of the saints surrounded
  2. Beloved City surrounded
  3. Devouring fire consumes them
    a. proceeds from God
    b. descends from heaven

D. His Final Abolition (10)
  1. Devil cast into the lake of fire
  2. Beast and false prophet are there
  3. Torment will continue forever

V. The Resurrection unto Damnation (11–15)
John 5:28,29:
  "Marvel not at this: for the hour is coming, in the which all that are in the graves shall hear his voice, And shall come forth; they that have done good, unto the resurrection of life; and they that have done evil, unto the resurrection of damnation."

A. The Throne (great and white) (11)

B. The Time (after earth's passing) (11)

C. The Tomes (books) (12)

D. The Throngs (lost dead) (12)
  1. The Small
  2. The Great — None will escape

E. The Tragedy (condemnation and doom) (13,14)

F. The Test (Name in the Book of Life?) (15)

G. The Torment (lake of fire forever) (15)

Observations:
Spiritual lessons and applications from each verse
Chapter Twenty

1. While Christ has the keys of death and hell (1:18), a mere angel here has custody of the key to the bottomless pit, the abyss. God exercises control over his whole universe.

2. Satan will be bound indeed. Resist him even now, in view of his future doom.

3. Satan has always been the master of deception from the garden of Eden unto this day and until the end of the millennium.

4. Christ's people are the victors, who shall reign with Him.

5. Unsaved deceased souls are in hell, while their bodies are in graves, but they shall "live again."

6. We are priests of God now and will reign as kings with Him in the future.

7. God moves strangely sometimes to fulfill His purposes.

8. In spite of a thousand years of peace, prosperity and beauty, Satan can still find in unregenerate hearts a ripe mood for sin, rebellion and evil war against God.

9. God's first world wide judgment was by water. This purging or destruction of the earth will be by fire.

10. Even after 1,000 years the beast and false prophet are still in the lake of fire, its first occupants. There is no annihilation in view, but rather a continuous separation from God in conscious exile.

11. At the very last, at the end of time as we know it, the great Judge of the Universe will examine the life and deeds of every person who has ever lived on this planet.

12. The "dead in trespasses and sins" must some day give a full account before God.

13. Every person who has ever lived must stand either before the judgment seat of Christ or before the great white throne. No one will be excused.

14. Hell, a temporary place of punishment, is merged with the lake of fire, the final penitentiary of the universe. This second death means eternal separation from God, not the end of existence.

15. This sad verse, the saddest in the Bible, contains a "whosoever." Remember "whosoever believed in him should not perish ..." (John 3:16) in contrast to this: "whosoever is not found written in the book of life."

The Eternal State

This horrible punishment, though prepared for the devil and his angels is nevertheless surely in store for those who will not receive the love of the truth that they might be saved.

People are going down to hell like a flock only because they hate God and heaven. The carnal mind is enmity against God, and an unregenerate person would soon turn a heaven into a hell. Whoever goes down to the pit will have himself to blame for it, for no man will suffer damnation except for the one sin of rejecting the light of the knowledge of God, which lighteth every man that cometh into the world. (See John 1:9; 3:18; 1 John 5:9–12). Jesus bore all the sins of the human race in his own body on the tree and the only sin which can now consign the soul to perdition is the sin of making a God a liar and counting the blood of the covenant an unholy thing.

Everything depends upon this greatest of all questions: What will you do with Jesus?

Come as you are and whoever you are, for He has said, "Him that cometh to me, I will in no wise cast out" (John 6:37).

"For whosoever shall call upon the name of the Lord shall be saved" (Romans 10:13).

Quotations
From Other Expositors
Chapter Twenty

Satan Bound (1–3)

"The twentieth chapter of Revelation introduces the marvelous reign of Christ on earth. This period of time is the utopia man has yearned for and never found. That coming kingdom age is to be an age of righteousness. History proves that the only means to secure a righteous era is for Satan to be bound; as long as he is loose, man will have trouble.

"Naturally there are those who ridicule the idea of a literal angel and chain and literal binding of Satan. As one seminary professor said, 'How big a chain would it take to bind Satan and how heavy should it be? We can't take this passage literally or we introduce many problems we cannot solve.' Really? What does it matter how big or heavy the chain? Is anything too hard for God? Dr. Walvoord, another seminary professor and president has noted, 'The four instances in Scripture of the word for "chain" in Revelation 20:1 give no reason for interpreting the word in other than it ordinary sense. Whatever the physical character of the chain, the obvious teaching of the passage is that the action is so designed as to render Satan inactive.'

"The binding of Satan will restrict him from doing the thing he does best, for the third verse says that he should deceive the nations no more till the thousand years shall be fulfilled. During the millennium Satan will not deceive men about themselves, God, Christ, or eternity. For this reason we conclude that the majority of people living then will be believers. But Satan will be released at the end of the period for one last bit of deception, after which he, too, will be cast into the lake of fire."

– Tim LaHaye

First Resurrection (4, 5)

"'I saw thrones …' The two exiled prophets, Daniel and John, beheld in vision the *same* thrones. The former saw them unoccupied. The heavenly sitters thereon constitute a revelation peculiar to the New Testament, and hence John supplements the vision of Daniel by adding, 'they sat upon them.' Both scenes refer to the commencement of the millennial reign. Nor must the thrones in our text be confounded with the twenty–four thrones of Revelation 4:4. Those seen in vision by Daniel (7:9) and by John (Revelation 20:4) relate to the millennial government of the earth. Those beheld in the earlier vision (chapter 4) grouped around the throne of the Eternal are set in Heaven. The twelve thrones on which the apostles are to sit in sessional judgment upon Israel (Matthew 19:28) are no doubt included in the larger and more comprehensive governing idea conveyed by the Seer (Revelation 20:4).

"The 'they' evidently refers to a well–known class. We have already seen, more than once, the redeemed in Heaven represented by the twenty–four elders taking part in scenes unfolded from chapters four to nineteen. They are the sum of Old Testament and New Testament believers raised or changed at the Coming into the air (1 Thessalonians 4:15–17). This is a much larger body of saints than the martyrs, and hence you have nowhere to locate them in the reign, save as included in the two plural pronouns 'they' and 'them.'"

– Walter Scott

"To what did he thus refer but these very dignities, and to the true people of God as the inheritors of them? Daniel, in a vision, saw the judgment seat, and the dominion of the Beast taken away by the mighty power of God, and declares that then, 'the Kingdom and dominion, and the greatness of the Kingdom under the whole heaven, shall be given to the people of the saints of the Most High' (Daniel 7:26,27). What did he mean but the very thing here beheld by John, and that the sitters on these thrones are the saints of God? Paul wrote, 'a crown,' for which he strove, which is to be the possession of all 'good soldiers of Jesus Christ,' and which the Lord, the righteous judge, would give him, 'at that day,' and 'unto all them that love his appearing' (2 Timothy 2:3–5; 4:7,8). And so the Savior himself exhorts his 'little flock' not to fear, as it is the Father's good pleasure to give them the kingdom (Luke 12:32), enjoins upon his disciples to hold fast that no one take their crown (Revelation 3:11), and promises every faithful and good servant to 'make him ruler over all his goods' (Matthew 24:46,47). Is it also an inevitable prin-

219

ciple, that the conquerors take the dominion? The Sitter on the white horse conquers in the Battle of the Great Day, and by virtue of that triumph he becomes the Supreme King. But with him through all the mighty engagements were his glorified saints, in white apparel, on white horses, indicative of their character of associates, governors and judges, (Judges 5:10). With him in the fight, they are with him in the victory, and share the sovereignty which that victory secures. He conquers, and therefore reigns; they conquer with him, and therefore they 'reign with him.' Thus the sitters on these thrones are none other than Christ's saints whom John saw following their Lord when he came forth to make an end of the anti-Christian domination, and inaugurate his own shepherdizing of the nations."

– J.A. Seiss

The Millennium (6)

"The millennium has to do with the kingdom dispensation, or the establishment of the kingdom of Heaven upon earth. It is the time when 'the kingdoms of this world are become the kingdoms of our Lord and of his Christ.' It will be a time when all nations will dwell under the blessing of God (Isaiah 19:23–25); a time when the nations will learn war no more, but will beat their swords into plowshares (Isaiah 2:4); a time when the world will have an administration of righteousness (Isaiah 32:1); a time when life will be lengthened and when death will be the exception (Isaiah 65:20–23); a time when the inhabitant shall not say, 'I am sick'; when 'the eyes of the blind shall be opened, and the ears of the deaf shall be unstopped. Then shall the lame man leap as an hart, and the tongue of the dumb sing' — in other words, a time when human sickness, suffering and affliction shall be done away (Isaiah 33:24; 35:5,6)."

– Robert L. Moyer

Satan Loosed (7–9)

"During the millennial reign of Christ children will be born into the world, and it will be just as necessary for these to be born again as it is for children in this age to receive a new birth. That children will be born into the world during the reign of Christ, is made clear from Isaiah 11:8, 'And the suckling child shall play on the hole of the asp, and the weaned child shall put his hand on the cockatrice's den.' Many children of godly parents during this age are gospel hardened, and many children in that day will take a similar attitude toward the things of God. They will render, however, feigned obedience to the King, and will sub-

mit to His rule simply because they must. Then when the reign of peace is over, and Satan is loosed from his prison, the King will veil His glory, in order that these may openly declare themselves. That rebellion is described in verses seven through nine."

– Louis T. Talbot

The Last Judgment (11–15)

"'The Judge of all the earth shall do right.' And there shall be no appeal from his decisions, for His is the Supreme Court of the Universe. 'What a magnificent conception,' exclaims Thomas Carlyle, 'is that of a last judgment! A righting of all the wrongs of the ages.' And, I may add, the tracing back of every evil act to its source, and the placing of responsibility for every offence against the moral law, where it belongs.

"None will be great enough to escape that assize; none too insignificant to be overlooked. The dead, 'small and great,' will be there. Even though their bodies had been buried for centuries, yea, for millennia in the depths of the sea, they shall come forth at His bidding, who when he speaks will not be denied. Death, the grave which has claimed what was mortal of man, his body, will give up its prey. Hades, the world unseen, will surrender the undying spirits and souls of the lost. Body, soul and spirit reunited, the man will stand trembling before that judgment bar. The books of record will be opened. Memory will respond to every charge. The word of God too will be opened there; for Jesus declared that Moses' words and His words should judge men in the last day. And the book of life too will be unfolded there; for many in that vast throng had taken it for granted their names were there because, perchance, they had been listed on the roll of some church or religious society. Let them search and look. It will bear witness against them. The Lamb has not inscribed their name in that book. 'And whosoever was not found written,' in that book will be 'cast into the lake of fire.'

"Will any be saved who stand before the great white throne? Not one, if we read the account right; for death and Hades are to be 'emptied into the lake of fire.' All the lost, whose spirits and bodies they have held in durance so long, will be emptied out into the pit of woe. And says God's Word, 'This is the second death.' Death is the separation of the body and spirit, we are told in James 2:26. The second death is the final separation of the lost from the God who created man."

– H.A. Ironside

There is a Great Day Coming
An Expository Sermon

Chapter Twenty

Introduction:

"He is coming! He is coming!"
Not as once He came before
Wailing infant, born in weakness,
On a lonely stable floor;
But upon a cloud of glory,
In the crimson–tainted sky.
Where we see the golden sunrise
In the rose distant lie.

"He is coming! He is coming!"
Not in pain and shame and woe;
With the thorn crown on his forehead
And the blood drops trickling slow;
But with diadem upon Him
And a scepter in His hand,
And the saints all ranged before Him,
A transfigured happy band.

"He is coming! He is coming!"
Not as once He wandered through
All the hostile land of Judah
With His followers poor and few;
But with all the holy angels
Waiting round His judgment seat,
And the chosen twelve apostles,
Sitting, crowned, at His feet.

I. The Jailing of Satan (1–3)

Figuring largely in the Scriptures is this mysterious and evil personality, known by the four designations in verse 2: the dragon, the old serpent, the devil and Satan.

In order to deceive the nations today, Satan often employs two subterfuges: first, that he is only a myth, an outmoded concept unacceptable to an enlightened age; or second, that he is real, powerful and worthy of worship and can impart supernatural abilities. Being a liar from the beginning, he manufactures these approaches to delude the lost. Only those who actually worship him — and an increasing number of people from all walks of life do — please him more than those who say, "There is no devil."

The Apostle Paul well describes his diabolical activity during this and early ages, when he says, "But if our gospel be hid, it is hid to them that are lost: in whom the god of this world [age] hath blinded the minds of them that believe not, lest the light of the glorious gospel of Christ, who is the image of God, should shine unto them" (2 Cor.4:3,4).

He is a real person, evidently the one time "anointed cherub that covereth" (Ezekiel 28:14), and archangel–like being, who was lifted up with pride and, tempting himself, sinned and fell (Isaiah 14:12–14).

He is "the spirit that now worketh in the children of disobedience" (Ephesians 2:2).

He has a kingdom and Jesus spoke of it in Matthew 12:26: "And if Satan cast out Satan, he is divided against himself: how then shall his kingdom stand?"

He has evil agents in the unseen world, including angels, principalities, powers, rulers, spiritual wickedness in high places (Ephesians 6:12), and demons.

He also has tools in the visible world, the men and women who are in rebellion against God and are called "the children of disobedience" (Ephesians 2:2).

He is the prince of the power of the air, the prince of this world (Ephesians 2:2; John 12:31), and the god of this world (2 Corinthians 4:4).

He has ministers, who transform themselves into angels of light (2 Corinthians 11:13–15), claiming to be apostles or messengers of truth, but are really of the devil.

He is called "the dragon," speaking of his diabolical activities on the political and world scene.

He is called "the old serpent," reminding of his deceitfulness in the Garden of Eden.

He is called "the devil," which means "accuser," for he accuses the brethren (Revelation 12:10).

He is called "Satan," meaning "adversary," which indeed he is, of God and of the human race.

At the midpoint of the Great Tribulation he is "cast out" of even limited access to heaven and confined primarily to the planet earth for the final three and a half years before the glorious appearing (Revelation 12:7–12).

But now in this chapter his sinister and vile rebellion is halted.

An angel descends from heaven, seizes him, binds him, shuts him up and sets a seal upon him.

221

He is cast into the bottomless pit, the Abyss, for a thousand years.

He was cut off from his high and holy position, when he originally fell (Isaiah 14:12–14). He has, err since, "walked about as a roaring lion, seeking whom he may devour," (1 Peter 5:8), deceiving the nations, the peoples of the world. He will be cast out of heaven completely during the Tribulation, as we have said. He will be cast into the bottomless pit first and will be cast ultimately into the lake of fire. Thus will end his perfidious, sin–fomenting, evil career.

During the millennium he will tempt no one, but await his final doom.

II. The Jews Born Anew

While this chapter does not depict the future glory of Israel in the millennium, many other Scriptures do.

Ezekiel says, "And I will set up one shepherd over them, even my servant David: he shall feed them, and he shall be their shepherd, And I the LORD will be their God, and my servant David a prince among them; I the LORD hath spoken it" (37:23,24).

Paul declares, "And so all Israel shall be saved: as it is written, There shall come out of Zion a Deliverer, and shall turn away the ungodliness from Jacob. For this is my covenant unto them, when I shall take away their sins" (Romans 11:6).

Isaiah writes, "Shall the earth be made to bring forth in one day? or shall a nation be born at once? for as soon as Zion travailed, she brought forth her children" (6:8).

When they look on him whom they have pierced (Revelation 1:7), they shall ask, "What are these wounds in thy hands? Then shall he answer, Those with which I was wounded in the house of my friends" (Zechariah 13:6).

Zechariah also describes in the twelfth chapter how there will be a great outpouring of the Holy Spirit and all the Israelites shall repent and turn to the house of David, even Jesus, David's son, who will sit upon "the throne of David and reign forever." See Luke 1:32,33.

Did not Jesus promise that the twelve apostles would "sit upon twelve thrones, judging the twelve tribes of Israel?" (Matthew 19:28).

It will be a glorious era, when all of the promises to the Israelites will be fulfilled and Jerusalem will be the capital of the world and Israel His holy nation indeed.

III. The Judgment of the Nations

"When the Son of man shall come in his glory, and all the holy angels with him, them shall he sit upon the throne of his glory: and before him shall be gathered all nations (Gentiles): and he shall separate them one from another, as a shepherd divideth his sheep from the goats: and he shall set the sheep on this right hand, but the goats on the left. Then shall the king say unto them on his right hand, Come, ye blessed of my Father, inherit the kingdom prepared for you from the foundation of the world ... then shall he say unto them on the left hand, Depart from me ye cursed into everlasting fire, prepared for the devil and his angels ..." (Matthew 25:31-34, 41).

When Christ returns, he will gather all of the survivors of the Tribulation from all nations — Gentiles, not Jews — before Him; those, who, during the Tribulation have not received the mark of the beast, but now have treated the Jews, his brethren, under terrible persecution, with kindness and thus be brought over into the millennial age.

Those who follow the beast, who mistreat His brethren, the Jews, doubtless receiving the "mark" and following the Antichrist, are cast out at the beginning of the millennial age.

Only saved Gentiles, probably those who respond to the preaching of the 144,000 and their converts, go over into the Kingdom Age. They are not, however, glorified or made like Christ, as are the raptured and resurrected believers.

IV. The Joys of the Millennium (4–6)

How glorious this era of peace and prosperity shall be!

Time forbids rehearsing all of the thousands of verses in the Old Testament, depicting this Golden Age of the future.

But here are some passages to ponder: Isaiah says, "The wilderness and the solitary place shall be glad for them; and the desert shall blossom as the rose ... And a highway shall be there [in Israel], and it shall be called the way of holiness ... No lion shall be there, nor any ravenous beast go up thereon; it shall not be found there; but the redeemed shall walk there; and the ransomed of the Lord shall return and come to Zion with songs and everlasting joy upon their heads; they shall obtain joy and gladness, and sorrow and sighing shall flee away" (Isaiah 35:1,8–10).

Jeremiah writes, "Behold, the days come, saith the LORD, that I will raise unto David a righteous Branch, and a King shall reign and prosper, and shall execute judgment and justice in the earth. In his days Judah shall be saved, and Israel shall dwell safely: and this is his name whereby he shall be called, THE LORD OUR RIGHTEOUSNESS"

(Jeremiah 23:5,6).

Ezekiel describes the wondrous millennial temple (41–44) and tells us how the land will be divided among the tribes (48), concluding his book with a new title for Jerusalem, "and the name of the city from that day shall be, THE LORD IS THERE [Hebrew — JEHOVAH-SHAMMAH]" (48:35).

Daniel speaks of a stone cut without hands, which will smite the great image that symbolizes the wicked world civilization of history and prophecy. That rock is Christ. "And in the days of these [last days] kings shall the God of heaven set up a kingdom which shall never be destroyed: and the kingdom shall not be left to other people, but it shall break in pieces and consume all these kingdoms and it shall stand forever" (2:44).

In the Pentateuch and in the Psalms and in all the writings of the prophets there are clear predictions, "And the LORD shall be king over all the earth" (14:9). Malachi poetically speaks of the Messiah's coming, saying, "The Sun of righteousness shall arise with healing in his wings" (4:2).

Isaiah 65 and 66 well depict the glory, grandeur, peace and bliss of the coming Millennium and the returning Messiah.

V. Jerusalem the World Capital

This beloved city, where Jesus will sit upon the throne of His father David, shall be the center of world government.

Isaiah is very clear: "2 And it shall come to pass in the last days, that the mountain of the LORD'S house shall be established in the top of the mountains, and shall be exalted above the hills; and all nations shall flow unto it … for out of Zion shall go forth the law, and the word of the LORD from Jerusalem" (Isaiah 2:2,3).

VI. The Justice of God (7–10)

At the end of this golden era God will allow Satan one final fling. He will be released and permitted once more to tempt the peoples of all nations.

Now who are these multitudes?

They are the descendents of the saved survivors of the Tribulation, who have never known temptation from Satan. Although under Christ's rule, they are not exempt from actually accepting Christ as their Savior. Thus, many do not trust Him at all. Thus God is just, allowing Satan this last assault, that the decision of each descendent of the saved survivors may show whether he or she has accepted or rejected Christ.

Alas, a vast multitude rebels, having never truly known the Lord, even though their lifespan has been dramatically increased (if a "child" dies at one hundred, it will be unusual — Isaiah 65:20), with health and strength.

This futile and final assault against "the camp of the saints" and "the beloved city" ends in a fiery conflagration and destruction. The earth as we know it passes away.

Satan himself is then cast finally into the lake of fire.

VII. The Judgment of the Almighty (11–15)

Somewhere on the brink of eternity the great God of the Universe will convene the last supreme court session. Out of what is left of a fire–engulfed earth will be raised all of the unsaved dead of all the ages past.

Picture a vast and innumerable throng of lost souls, reunited with bodies in which they once lived and sinned and died. See that sad array of multiplied billions, each of whom must stand personally before the awesome presence of the eternal God of the Universe to be reminded of all that was ever done in life, every sin, every failure, every missed opportunity to draw nigh to God.

Without excuse, condemned, just tried and seen guilty, each person will hear the sad sentence of exile from God.

No second chance! No last door of escape from the damnation of hell will open.

The test is simple. Where might have been inscribed each name in the book of life, there is not but a blank.

"Whosoever was not found written in the book of life was cast into the lake of fire."

That need not be your destiny.

Think of that other "whosoever": "For God so loved the world that he gave his only begotten Son that whosoever believeth in him should not perish but have everlasting life."

A Commentary on the Revelation
Expository, Exegetical, Devotional and Practical
Greek words from the Textus Receptus

Chapter Twenty

The Last Thousand Years (1-6)

1. And I saw an angel come down from heaven *(kai eidon angelon katabainonta ek tou ouranou)* — he comes from an earlier battle (12:7,8), when under Michael's lead, Satan is cast out of limited access to heaven 1,260 days earlier ... **having the key of the bottomless pit** *(echonta ten klein tes abussou)* — now transferred from Satan who had it in 9:1, being permitted by God there to let loose plagues on earth ... **and a great chain in his hand** — now that the beast and false prophet are cast into the lake of fire, its first occupants, Satan is to be bound and placed in a different pit or abyss, imprisoned and impotent. **2. And he laid hold on the dragon** *(drakonta)*, **that old serpent** *(ho ophis ho archaios)*, **which is the devil** *(diabolos)* **and Satan** *(Satanos — adversary)* **and bound him a thousand years** *(chilia ete)* — a full array of designations showing his draconic evil in the political realm, his ancient deceptive and lying nature as the serpent, his accusative libel against God and the saints as the devil, and his adversarial opposition to God and humans with the name of Satan. The premillennialists for centuries were called chiliasts (pronounced like kiliasts), people who believed in a one thousand year reign. *Millennium* is the Latin word for a thousand years, as it appears in the Latin translation of Scripture, called the Vulgate (from 400 A.D.). **3. And cast him into the bottomless pit** *(kai ebalen auton eis ten abusson)* — we get our word *abyss* from *abyssos*, a term occuring in Romans 10:7 for the abode of the dead — common Greek usage. In Luke 8:31, it refers to the abode of demons. It occurs seven times in Revelation (9:1,2,11; 11:7; 17:8; 20:1,3). In classical Greek *abyssos* was an adjective meaning "bottomless" ... **and shut him up** *(kai ekleisen)* — it cannot be opened nor can Satan escape ... **and set a seal upon him** *(kai esphragisen)* — implies sealing up the door above his head in Greek, a surer seal than that which was applied to the tomb of the Savior ... **that he should deceive the nations no more til the thousand years should be fulfilled** — some expositors attempt to spiritualize the thousand year reign to indicate an indeterminate length of time; others imagine that the millennium is the Christian age, but Satan is not bound now, nor are saints reigning with Christ in the full flower of blessing ... **after that he must be loosed a little season** — Satan's final rebellion fails (verse 7-10) and he is consigned forever to the lake of fire. **4. And I saw thrones and they that sat upon them** — here are the raptured and resurrected saints (1 Thessalonians 4:17, 18; 1 Corinthians 15:51,52) who have been in heaven during the Tribulation and return with him (19:14), now rewarded and reigning with Christ. Foremost are the twelve apostles on twelve thrones, judging the twelve tribes of Israel (Matthew 19:28). This is literal ... **and judgment was given to them** — if we suffer with him, we shall reign with him (2 Timothy 2:12). See also Revelation 2:25-28; 3:21. **And I saw the souls of them which were beheaded for the witness of Jesus and for the Word of God, and which had not worshipped the beast, neither his image, neither had received his mark upon their foreheads, or in their hands; and they lived and reigned with Christ a thousand years** — early ante-Nicene fathers, (from 100 to 313 A.D.) Papias, Justin Martyr, Irenaeus, Cyprian and others all held the doctrine of a literal millennial kingdom on earth. Some extremist millennial views later depicted a gross and carnal concept of the millennium, but after Augustine, much of professing Christianity adopted a spiritualized view of the millennium, equating it with the church age (after about 400 A.D.). After the Reformation (about 1525 A.D.) a revival of the pre-millennialism began. Hundreds of Old Testament Scriptures support and depict this truth, but only here is its length specified. Tribulation martyrs seem to have a special role in the Millennium, as in this verse. **5. But the rest of the dead** — all the unsaved — **lived not again** *(ouk ezesan)* **until the thousand years were finished** — *(ezesan* means "come to life") ... **this is the first resurrection** *(anastasis ho prote)* — hence the English prefix **proto** as in prototype.

1 Corinthians 15:22,23 show the progression of resurrections: "But every man in his own order (or rank or turn): Christ the firstfruits; afterward they are Christ's at his coming (the raptured and resurrected saints prior to the Tribulation, plus the Tribulation martyrs and possibly the Old Testament saints at the close of the Tribulation and the beginning of the millennium), Then cometh the end" … the final and second resurrection (of the wicked—John 5:29). The first resurrection is unto life, for the saved, as here and earlier, since there are stages; the second resurrection is unto damnation as at the end of this chapter. **6. Blessed** *(makarios)* **and holy** *(hagios)* **is he that hath part in the first resurrection** — there is no hint here of "general resurrection" of both saved and lost, which is nowhere taught in Scripture. Happy, holy, prosperous and eternally glorified are the participants in the first resurrection, for they are like Christ in incorruptible bodies (1 Corinthians 15:35–50) … **on such the second death hath no power** — the first death is common to all Christians (except the raptured who are alive at His coming) and to the lost, who also die, but the second death is not physical, the separation of the soul from the body, but eternal, the separation of the body and soul from God forever … **but they shall be priests of God and Christ** — they are the administrators of work and worship, those with immediate access to His presence on behalf of others. All believers are and shall be priests, not merely a select class, and are to rule in love and minister blessings over the whole earth as king–priests. But those who suffer with Him and those who are loyal, life–long, to Him merit special rewards, while there are some who may lose their reward or their crowns, but not their salvation (see Revelation 2:10; 3:11; 2 John 3), **and shall reign with him a thousand years** — Christ will sit on the throne of His father David (Luke 1:32,33; Isaiah 9:6,7), but also on the throne of his glory over all Gentiles (Matthew 25:31). Glorified saints may have access to both earth and heaven and while visible and tangible, are also not subject to the usual laws of physics, as was Christ after His resurrection. He could be visible, invisible, appear and vanish to another place, ascend to heaven with no effect from gravity, yet, he could eat, be touched, and communicate in every way. Israel will be the great nation during this era (Isaiah 20:19–25, etc.), but the Gentiles (sheep) nations. Evidently, life is extended (Isaiah 65:20) indefinitely for all of the Jews and Gentiles who go over into the millennium in natural, but enhanced and rejuvenated, nearly perfect bodies.

The Last Rebellion (7-10)

7. And when the thousand years are expired Satan shall be loosed out of his prison and shall go to deceive the nations which are in the four quarters of the earth, Gog and Magog, to gather them together to battle, the number of whom is as the sand of the sea — the purpose of this release is to allow Satan to tempt the descendents of the saved survivors of the Tribulation, to determine publicly whether they are true believers in the King and Savior, or only have an outward submission. Never have they experienced active temptation from Satan. Their response to him reveals their true state and character, with millions flocking to Satan in a final rebellion. The vast area of Asia, to be thickly populated, Gog and Magog, produces an immense number of rebels. This is not the same as the Ezekiel 38, 39 battle, which occurs in conjunction with the Tribulation before Christ's return. **9. camp of the saints** — abode of glorified and ruling believers … **beloved city** — Jerusalem … **and fire came down from God out of heaven and devoured them** — this is where 2 Peter 3:10–12 will be fulfilled, "wherein the heavens being on fire shall be dissolved, and the elements shall melt with a fervent heat." The faithful nations and Israelites on earth will be preserved and carried over into the new earth, as in Revelation 21:26. **10. And the devil that deceived them was cast into the lake of fire** — notice his stages in falling: (1) before the human race was created (Isaiah 14:12–14); (2) cast out of heaven completely (Revelation 12:7); (3) cast into the bottomless pit (vs. 3); (4) cast into the lake of fire … **where the beast and the false prophet are** — hell is not a place of annihilation, but conscious torment continues forever, for these two wicked personalities are still there after a thousand years in the lake of fire.

The Last Judgment (11–15)

11. I saw a great white throne *(kai eidon thronon megan leukon)* — it is great, far more imposing and important than all of the previously mentioned thrones of the millennial age … white is the emblem of purity and justice here … the seat of the supreme Judge of all the Universe … **and him that sat on it** — the Father … some say the Son, as the Father has committed all judgment unto the Son; possibly the Father and Son in some kind of supernatural joint presence … **from whose face the earth and heaven fled away and there was**

found no place for them — some expositors think the earth and heavens are renovated by fire; others believe they totally pass away to be replaced by a brand new heaven and earth, as in Revelation 21:22. This last judgment, unlike the judgement of the nations is not on earth; nor is it in heaven where the judgment seat of Christ has already taken place (2 Corinthians 5:10; Revelation 11:15–18) over a thousand years earlier. **12. And I saw the dead** (*kai eidon tous nekrous*) — the rest of the dead who were not in the first resurrection, all of the unsaved. The wicked who had died from time of Adam to the end of the Millennium, shall then have their eternal retribution assigned to them ... **small and great stand before God** — individual and all inclusive examination of all peoples of all ranks and stations of all times. Time here will be irrelevant, since this is beyond time as we know it ... **and the books were opened, and another book was opened which is the book of life** — every thought, word and deed is fully recorded for every person who has ever lived ... **and the dead were judged out of those things which were written in the books, according to their works** — this judgment will be true, righteous, honest, fair, complete, just and without respect of persons. **13. And the sea gave up the dead which were in it** — showing that the planet is not totally gone at this stage, since those who drowned or were buried at sea are raised for final judgment ... **and death** (*thanatos*) **and hell** (*hades*) **delivered up the dead which were in them** — out of the sea and from the land of death, where bodies are buried, plus the souls of the dead from hell are brought up to be reunited, body and soul ... **and they were judged every man according to their works** — that there will be degrees of punishment is evident from Matthew 11:22,24. The more light of truth, the more responsible for evil deeds and rejection of Christ ... **14. And death and hell were cast into the lake of fire. This is the second death** – no reprieve, even the factor of death and the nature of the present hell are cast into the lake of fire. This is eternal separation from God. **15. And whosoever was not found written in the book of life was cast into the lake of fire** — notice the four "castings": beast and false prophet (19:20); Satan (20:10); death and hell (14) and all the unsaved (15). Contrast John 3:16; 6:37; and Romans 10:13.

The Millennium: some things scheduled to occur, here in probable order:

1. Christ comes to Mount of Olives (Ze. 14:1–9).

2. All the wicked are gathered (Isaiah 13:9; 33:14; Matthew 13:30,41).

3. Christ (Messiah) judges his own people, the Jews (Romans 11:26; Zechariah 12:10–14; 13:6; Revelation 1:7). Living Israelites receive Jesus as Messiah.

4. Gentile nations of the earth are judged as to how they treated Israel in their trouble (Matthew 25:31–46; Joel 3:2,12; Acts 17:31).

5. Tribes of Israel are examined, judged and restored (Ezekiel 20:33–38; Amos 9:9,10).

6. All of Israel brought into the land (Isa. 11:11,12; 49:12,13; Ez. 39:15,18; 20:40-42; 36:24; Amos 9:14-15).

7. Twelve Apostles sit on twelve thrones judging twelve tribes (Matthew 19:28).

8. Tribes become one nation (no longer 10 tribes and 2 tribes) (Isa. 11:13; Ezek. 37:15–25; Hos. 1:11).

9. The Lord makes a new covenant (Jer. 31:31–33; 32:40; 50:4,5; Ezekiel 37:26; Romans 11:26,27).

10. The Lord forgives their sin and iniquity, remembering it no more (Isa. 60:21; Jer. 31:34; 33:8; 50:20; Ezekiel 36:25–33; Micah 7:18,19; Hebrews 8:12).

11. The Lord's enemies will have been punished (Isaiah 2:17–21; 26:9; 32:4; Ezek. 28:26; Micah 5:15; Neh. 1:8).

12. The Israelites come into full possession of all their promised land (Ezekiel 47:13–48:19; Genesis 15:18; Deuteronomy 11:24; Joshua 1:4).

13. The desert will blossom as a rose (Isaiah 32:15; 35:1–10; 51:3; Ezekiel 36:33–36).

14. The temple, as described by Ezekiel, will be built (Ezekiel 40:1–43:17).

15. The city of Jerusalem is restored, enlarged and established (Isaiah 60:10; Jeremiah 31:38,40; Ezekiel 48:15–17,30–35; Zechariah 14:10,11).

16. The Levitical sacrifices as memorials, with modifications, are restored (Ezek. 43:18–46:24; Mal. 3:3,4).

17. Then nothing shall hurt or destroy in all of His Holy Mountain (Isaiah 11:6–9; 33:24; 35:9; 55:13; 65:25; Ezekiel 34;25).

18. The Lord will be in the midst of his people (Ezekiel 48:35; Joel 3:17–21; Zephaniah 3:15–17; Zechariah 2:10).

19. Christ shall reign a thousand years on the throne of His father David (Luke 1:32,33; Isaiah 9:6,7; 60:1–3 18–22; Zechariah 2:5; 10–13).

20. The New Testament saints, the Old Testament saints and the Tribulation martyrs shall reign with Christ a thousand years (Revelation 20:4–6; 1 Corinthians 6:2; 2 Timothy 2:12).

21. All nations shall come up to worship God at Jerusalem (Isaiah 2:1–3, 66:18–21; Jeremiah 3:17; Micah 4:2; Zechariah 8:20–22, 14:16).

22. The earth will be full of the Glory of the Lord (Numbers 24:21; Psalms 72:19; Isa. 11:9; Hab. 2:14).

CHAPTER TWENTY-ONE: The New Jerusalem

References

2 Pet. 3:13
Isa. 65:17
Isa. 57:20
Heb. 12:26,27

Isa. 12:1
Gal. 4:26
Heb. 11:10
2 Cor. 11:2

Lev. 26:11
Rev. 7:15
Ex. 29:46
Jn. 14:2,3

Isa. 25:8
1 Cor. 15:26,54
Isa. 35:10
Isa. 51:11
Isa. 65:19

Rev. 4:2,9
Isa. 43:19
2 Cor. 5:17
Rev. 14:9; 22:6

Rev. 1:8,11
Rev. 22: 13
Jn. 1:1-3
Isa. 12:3
Jn. 7:37
Rom. 8:17,32
Rev.
2:7,11,17,26
Rev. 3:5,12,21

1 Cor. 6:9
Eph. 5:5
1 Tim. 1:9
Heb. 12:14
Rev. 22:11,15

Rev. 15:1
Rev. 19:7
Rev. 21:2
Eph. 5:31,32

Rev. 10:1
Gal. 4:26
Heb. 12:22-
24,28

Isa. 60:1
Rev. 15:8
Rev. 21:23
Rev. 22:5

Rev. 7:5-8

1. AND I saw a new heaven and a new earth: for the first heaven and the first earth were passed away; and there was no more sea.

2. And I John saw the holy city, new Jerusalem, coming down from God out of heaven, prepared as a bride adorned for her husband.

3. And I heard a great voice out of heaven, saying, Behold, the tabernacle of God is with men, and he will dwell with them, and they shall be his people, and God himself shall be with them, and be their God.

4. And God shall wipe away all tears from their eyes; and there shall be no more death, neither sorrow, nor crying, neither shall there be any more pain: for the former things are passed away.

5. And he that sat upon the throne said, Behold, I make all things new. And he said unto me, Write: for these words are true and faithful.

6. And he said unto me, It is done. I am Alpha and Omega, the beginning and the end. I will give unto him that is athirst of the fountain of the water of life freely.

7. He that overcometh shall inherit all things; and I will be his God, and he shall be my son.

8. But the fearful, and unbelieving, and the abominable, and murderers, and sorcerers, and idolators, and all liars, shall have their part in the lake which burneth with fire and brimstone: which is the second death.

9. And there came unto me one of the seven angels which had the seven vials full of the seven last plagues, and talked with me, saying, Come hither, I will show thee the bride, the Lamb's wife.

10. And he carried me away in the spirit to a great and high mountain, and showed me that great city, the holy Jerusalem, descending out of heaven from God,

11. Having the glory of God: and her light was like unto a stone most precious, even like a jasperstone, clear as crystal;

12. And had a wall great and high, and had twelve gates, and at the gates twelve angels, and names written thereon, which are the names of the twelve tribes of the children of Israel:

13. On the east three gates; on the north three gates; on the south three gates; and on the west three gates.

14. And the wall of the city had twelve foundations, and in them the names of the twelve apostles of the Lamb.

15. And he that talked with me had a golden reed to measure the city, and the gates thereof, and the wall thereof.

16. And the city lieth foursquare, and the length is as large as the breadth: and he measured the city with the reed, twelve thousand furlongs. The length and the breadth and the height of it are equal.

17. And he measured the wall thereof, a hundred and forty and four cubits, according to the measure of man, that is, of the angel.

18. And the building of the wall of it was of jasper: and the city was pure gold, like unto clear glass.

19. And the foundations of the wall of the city were garnished with all manner of precious stones. The first foundation was jasper; the second, sapphire; the third, a chalcedony; the fourth, an emerald;

20. The fifth, sardonyx; the sixth, sardius; the seventh, chrysolite; the eighth, beryl; the ninth, a topaz; the tenth, a chrysoprasus; the eleventh, a jacinth; the twelfth, an amethyst.

21. And the twelve gates were twelve pearls; every several gate was of one pearl: and the street of the city was pure gold, as it were transparent glass.

22. And I saw no temple therein: for the Lord God Almighty and the Lamb are the temple of it.

23. And the city had no need of the sun, neither of the moon, to shine in it: for the glory of God did lighten it, and the Lamb is the light thereof.

24. And the nations of them which are saved shall walk in the light of it: and the kings of the earth do bring their glory and honor into it.

25. And the gates of it shall not be shut at all by day: for there shall be no night there.

26. And they shall bring the glory and honor of the nations into it.

27. And there shall in no wise enter into it any thing that defileth, neither whatsoever worketh abomination, or maketh a lie: but they which are written in the Lamb's book of life.

References

Ezek. 48:30-35

Eph. 2:20
Act. 1:13,26

Zech. 2:1
Rev. 11:1,2

1 Kings 6:20

Heb. 1:4

2 Chr. 3:8

Isa. 54:11,12
Ex. 39:10,14

1 Pet. 2:5-9

Mat. 13:35,46

Jn. 4:21-24

Isa. 24:23
Isa. 60:19

Isa. 60:3,5,10
Mt. 25:31-46
Rev. 20:9

Isa. 60:20
Rev. 22:5

Isa. 35:8
Ps. 69:28
Dan. 12:1
Rev. 3:5;13:8;
20:12,15

Summary of Chapter Twenty-one

The New Heaven and the New Earth

I. What John Saw (1,2)

The last two chapters of this dramatic prophetic apocalypse describe the Celestial City, as John Bunyan called it, the glowing and glorious capital of the Universe and the place with heavenly mansions dwelling places Jesus has gone to prepare for His own.

Reaching the lofty pinnacle of this remarkable vision, this time trip into the future and into eternity, which John experienced in his latter days, the New Heaven and the New Earth are now unveiled before the aged Apostle's eyes. Forty times in this Apocalypse, John specifically states that these were all things that he saw.

Thus these are no more wild flights of a vivid imagination, but the divinely revealed panorama of the ages, unfolded before the sainted Apostle to see and record, completing the message of the Word of God.

Some say that the first heaven and the first earth are renovated by fire (2 Peter 3:10–14) and continue into eternity, basing that conclusion in part on the Scriptures which speak of the eternal foundations of the earth. Others, this writer, included, believe that much of the present spiritual heaven, perhaps all of the Cosmos now as we understand it to exist, and the very planet on which we dwell, completely pass away.

My view is that all things are created brand new, that all trace of Lucifer's rebellion is forever erased, that a genuine New Creation occurs. Since Jesus is preparing a place for us, this program is in process even now.

There will be no sea on the New Planet Earth, neither a vast expanse of water, as now with island continents, nor a foaming sea of wicked humanity of which the book of Isaiah speaks. "For the wicked are like the troubled sea, when it cannot rest" (Isaiah 57:20).

Beholding the descending Holy City, hovering above the new earth, John compares the majestic metropolis to a bride, adorned for her husband. Indeed, the huge city will be populated by the redeemed, the wife of the Lamb, the true queen of heaven.

II. What John Heard (3–8)

A great voice from heaven announces that God will tabernacle (dwell) with men, the saved of all the ages, including those peoples who are loyal to the King and do not yield to Satan's seductive last temptation (20:7–10) and may live on the New Earth. Israel also will live on the New Earth.

All tears will be gone. No more death, sorrow, crying or pain will ever be experienced on the New Earth or in the New Jerusalem. Overcomers, true believers in Christ will inherit all things, all of God's vast and infinite Universe. By contrast, all of the wicked shall remain forever in the lake of fire, which is the second death.

III. What the Angel Showed John (9–27)

From verse nine through verse twenty–seven is a fascinating description of the New Jerusalem, which this writer takes as basically literal. But it will doubtless exceed immeasurably even the inspired language depicting its sublime beauty.

From the summit of a great and high mountain John beholds the decending city. Perhaps it will float above the New Earth, rather than rest upon it.

Shining and shimmering in iridescent radiance, the city glows with the glory of God with a golden hue, like a jasper stone, clear as crystal.

Round about the cosmic metropolis is a wall of jasper, adorned with twelve gates inscribed with the names of the twelve tribes of Israel. God will never forget His earthly covenant people, who will have access to the city to worship Jehovah God and the Lamb.

How wide and how high this urban center will be is difficult to comprehend. Twelve thousand furlongs, if we understand it right, would measure at least 1,600 miles, as we humans might calculate. This is not all of heaven, but rather the City of God … Whether it is somewhat like a cube or a pyramid is a matter of conjecture, but it will have ample space for multiplied millions of the redeemed from all ages. Twelve is the number of government in Scripture; therefore this is the eternal centre of divine rule.

No temple is necessary, for God and Christ are the Temple.

The saved and faithful Gentiles of the millennial age, as well as the Israelites, are brought to this New Earth and they shall likewise worship.

None but the saved shall ever enter. There will be no second chance.

Outline of Chapter Twenty-one

The Seven New Things

OBJECTIVE: To reveal the eternal home of the redeemed, the overcomers, who by faith are rightly related to God, His eternal children.

OUTLINE:

I. The New Heaven (1,2)
   A. Beheld by John
   B. First Heaven Passed Away

II. The New Earth (1,2)
   A. Beheld by John

   B. First Earth Passed Away

   C. Sea is No More

III. The New Peoples (3–8)
   A. God Promises His Eternal Presence (3)

   B. God Claims His People Forever (3)

   C. God is Their God Indeed (3)

   D. God Wipes Away All Tears (4)
      1. No More Death
      2. No More Sorrow
      3. No More Crying
      4. No More Pain
      • Former Things Passed Away

   E. God Creates All Things "New" (5)
      1. This John was to record
      2. These words are true and faithful

   F. God Announces, "It is Done" (completed) (6)
      1. He is the Alpha and Omega
      2. He still offers now the water of Life

   G. God Bestows All Things Upon Overcomers (7)
      1. He is God of the overcomers forever
      2. The overcomers are God's Children forever

   H. God warns of another destiny (8)
      1. Description of the Eternally Lost
         a. The fearful (cowardly)
         b. The unbelieving (faithless)
         c. The abominable (depraved)
         d. The murderers (killers)
         e. The whoremongers (immoral)
         f. The sorcerers (drug addicts,
             evil magicians)
         g. The idolaters (worshippers of false gods)
      2. Destiny of the Eternally Lost

         a. The Lake of Fire
         b. The Second Death

IV. The New Jerusalem (9–21)
   A. Its Glorious Descent (9,10)
      1. Shown by the Angel (9)
      2. Seen by John (10)

   B. Its Grand Description (11–21)
      1. The Illuminating Radiance of the City (11)
         a. Shines with God's glory
         b. Resembles a clear crystaline jasper.
      2. The Pearly Gates of the City (12,13,21)
         • Inscribed with twelve tribes' names
      3. The Jeweled Foundations of the City (14)
         • Inscribed with twelve Apostles' names
      4. The Jasper Walls of the City (12,17)
         • 144 cubits (12x12 cubits) high
      5. The Immense Dimensions of the City (16)
         a. Twelve thousand furlongs long
         b. Twelve thousand furlongs broad
         c. Twelve thousand furlongs high
      6. The Golden Hue of the City (18,21)
      7. The Muticolored Jewels on the City's
         Foundation (19–20)
         a. First Foundation: Jasper
         b. Second Foundation: Sapphire
         c. Third Foundation: Chalcedony
         d. Fourth Foundation: Emerald
         e. Fifth Foundation: Sardonyx
         f. Sixth Foundation: Sardius
         g. Seventh Foundation: Chrysolite
         h. Eighth Foundation: Beryl
         i. Ninth Foundation: Topaz
         j. Tenth Foundation: Chrysoprasus
         k. Eleventh Foundation: Jacinth
         l. Twelth Foundation: Amethyst
      8. The Golden Street of the City (21)

V. The New Temple (22)
   • God and Christ; Not a Building

VI. The New Light (23–27)
   A. The Illumination is from God's Glory (23)

   B. The Saved Nations Enjoy its Light (24–26)

   C. The Lost Shall Never Enter the City (27)

VII. The New River (22:1)
   A. Living Water

   B. Crystaline Water

   C. Divinely Provided Water

Observations:
Spiritual lessons and applications from each verse
Chapter Twenty-One

1. This first verse introduces a new and eternal era, realm, time and place, where the redeemed shall forever enjoy the riches of His grace forever.

2. Like a radiant, white-clad bride on a happy wedding day, the New Jerusalem, home of the bride of Christ, shines with splendor .

3. Far beyond the wars and famines and evil of the times we have known will come in the future the everlasting blessing of God's benevolent presence, unveiled and open, filled with love and joy.

4. No tears will outlast the tender touch of the hand of God, wiping away forever the results and ravages of sin that plagued the universe from the fall of Satan and the subsequent fall of man until the Great White Throne.

5. Lest it seem too good to be true that God will make all things new indeed, the affirmation is added, "these words are true and faithful."

6. God is now ready to give the water of life freely to anyone who will receive it, thus making possible a home in this new paradise of God.

7. Here is the eighth and final promise to the "overcomers," indicating that both "all things," the universe, and God's sublime Fatherhood toward His children, will be ours forever.

8. Amid all of these spectacular promises is couched the sad warning that not all will enjoy His blessings forever, but a vast unbelieving and iniquitious multitude will experience the lake of fire.

9. Because the New Jerusalem is the abode of the bride of Christ, to see the city is to see the bride.

10. Whether the city of God floats above the New Earth or actually comes to rest upon it is unclear, but access from Earth to the City is open.

11. With shimmering, yellowish golden beauty, the City of God shines with radiant illumination.

12. That redeemed Israelites will inhabit the city there can be no doubt; yea, Abraham looked for a city which hath foundations, whose Builder and Maker is God.

13. This is no ethereal phantasm of a city, but rather a real magnificent metropolis.

14. The twelve apostles were not only part of the church's foundation with Jesus Christ Himself being the Chief Cornerstone, but also their names are forever inscribed on the foundations of the vast abode of the redeemed.

15. In Revelation 11 a small area is measured, but here an angel measures the heavenly city.

16. The city is foursquare, extending in three dimensions and enormous distance, all symmetrical, possibly either like a cube or a pyramid with towering residences for the redeemed.

17. The wall is 12 x 12 cubits or 144 cubits in height, surrounding the entire capital.

18. The jasper walls encompass a reflectant and transparent crystalline appearing city.

19. The jasper has a yellowish hue ; the sapphire may be bluer or other colors; the chalcedony is pale and translucent quartz; the emerald is glorious green … these stones remind us of the jewels on the High Priest's breastplate (Exodus 28:16-20.)

20. Sardonix is reddish in color as is the sardius; the chrysolyte is yellowish, like a topaz; the beryl is probably bluish green; the topaz may be white or yellow or have bluish hue; the chrysoprasus is likely whitish; the jacinth is red or purple; the amethyst is purple. Notice that the reds suggest the blood of Christ; white speaks of His righteousness; yellow of glory; purple of royalty; green of eternal life and blue of heaven.

21. Only the gates of pearl are not divinely designed minerals, but rather the product of life and suffering, indicative of Christ's suffering by which He became the Way, the Truth, and the Life.

22. In the New Jerusalem worship is direct with no need of a temple.

23. Heavenly and divine illumination replaces the sun.

24. The saved nations, the millennial people, Jews and Gentiles, who are loyal to Christ through all the thousand years will dwell on the New Earth.

25. God never shuts the doors of His city.

26. If glory and honor is to be brought to God in the future, let us bring glory and honor to Him now.

27. The greatest, most momentous issue of life is whether or not one's name is written in the Lamb's Book of Life.

Quotations
From Other Expositors
Chapter Twenty-One

A New Creation (1,2)

"Three great passages, Isaiah 65:17; 66:22; 2 Peter 3:10–13 and the present Revelation passage, deal with this stupendous subject, the new creation. The definite and repeated statements that the old earth and heaven 'flee away,' 'pass away with a great noise,' (2 Peter 3:10–13) and are 'burned up;' Together with the statement that that 'there was found no place for them,' compel the conclusion that those who argue that these words indicate only a 'cleansing by fire,' and not actual eternal dissolution and disappearance, shrink from the searching realities of this subject. The word 'create' is a solemn word to modify or trifle with! We know that create in Genesis 1:1 cannot mean anything but the calling into existence of that which did not before have being (Hebrews 11:3). And certainly Revelation 21:1 is just as new a beginning!

"The first creation was the shore and scene of what the highest of the creatures, challenging the will of the Creator as the creature's highest good, came in to mar, ruin, and wreck the first creation. Now comes at last, based upon Christ and His work, and wholly new creation which will never pass away, and in which the apostle Peter announces that 'righteousness will be at home' (2 Peter 3:13, Greek). Even the temptation to evil will be eternally absent, for every opportunity of rebellion against the rule of the Most High will have been thwarted, every such rebellion having been proved by experiment disastrous to the creature, as well as dishonoring the Creator."

– William R. Newell

Two Destinies (3-8)

"A voice from the throne cries, 'Behold, I make all things new.' And John is again commanded to write, and assured that 'these words are true and faithful.' It is a proclamation that all the ways of God have found their final issue in the full glory of His blessed Son, who is the first and the last.

"In verse eight we are told of those who shall never enter the holy city, who will have no part in the bright glories depicted above. But, are giving the awful list the Lord graciously extends another gospel invitation, that all to whom these words shall come may know that there is mercy still if they will but avail themselves of it. 'I will give unto him,' He says, 'that is athirst of the fountain of the water of life freely.' And He follows this with a word of encouragement to the overcomer, 'He that overcometh shall inherit all things; and I will be his God and he shall be my son.' The world may bid for us now, and the treacherous flesh within may seek to act in concert with that world and its god, and thus woo our souls from Christ, but who with the glorious promises of this book before him, but must long to rise above the power of present things, and, in the energy of the Holy Spirit overcome the world by faith, in view of what He is preparing for those who love Him!

"How gladly would we believe that no soul of man will fail of the joy that is kept in store for those who know Christ; but, alas, alas, sin has made this impossible of realization; so this part of our chapter closes with the tremendously solemn announcement that, 'the fearful, and unbelieving, and the abominable, and murderers, and whoremongers, and sorcerers, and idolators, and all liars, shall have their part in the lake which burneth with fire and brimstone: which is the second death,' (Revelation 21:8). The list includes not only those who are generally looked upon as discreditable sinners but, the cowardly — who were fearful of confessing Christ, because, perhaps, of the sneers of professed friends, or the consequences of turning from the world; together with the unbelieving — who refused to credit the testimony God had given, and to rest their souls upon the work of Chist — these both are linked up with the unclean and unholy of all classes, inasmuch as 'all have sinned, and come short of the glory of God,' there can be no difference in their final doom if Christ is rejected, though, every transgression and disobedience will receive its just recompense of reward."

– H.A. Ironside

The City of God (9-26)

"That a real City, as well as a perfected moral system, is here to be understood, I see not how we can otherwise conclude. Great Babylon, to which it stands as the exact antithesis, came out finally in a real universally potent city; so, therefore, must this. All elements of a city are indicated. It has specific dimensions. It has foundations, walls, gates, and streets. It has guards outside and inhabitants within, both distinct from what characterizes it as a real construction. It is called a city — 'The Holy City.' It is named as a city, 'The Holy Jerusalem,' It is called, 'The New Jerusalem,' as over against an old Jerusalem, which was a material city. Among the highest promises to the saints of all ages was the promise of a special place and economy answering to a heavenly city, and which is continually referred to as an enduring, God–built city. Abraham, 'looked for a city which hath foundations, whose maker and builder is God,' (Hebrews 11:10). Of all the ancient saints it is written, that, 'God hath prepared for them a city,' (Hebrews 11:16). Jesus assured the disciples from whom he was about to be separated, 'I go to prepare a place for you. And if I go and prepare a place for you, I will come again, and receive you unto myself; that where I am there ye may be also' (John 14:2,3). Hence the Apsotle, in the name of all Christians of his day, said, 'Here we have no continuing city, but we seek one to come,' (Hebrews 13:14). Hence also it is given as one of the great exaltations of true believers, even here on earth, that they 'are come unto the city of the living God, the heavenly Jerusalem,' (Hebrews 12:22); not indeed as to actual possession as yet, but as having attained the title to it and to citizenship in it by faith, hope, and sure anticipation. And whatever difficulty we may have in taking it in, or in reconciling it to our prepossessions, I do not see how we can be just and fair to God's Word, and the faith of the saints of former ages, and not see and admit that we here have to do, not with a mere ideal and fantastic city, but with a true, real, God–built city, substantial and eternal albeit there has never been another like it.

"It has 'a wall great and high,' which is not only like jasper, but which is built of jasper itself. And that wall stands on twelve foundation–stones, and each of those twelve immense stones is a separate and distinct jewel in itself. There are certain substances in nature, found in very small fragments, which are so scarce, rare, beautiful, and enduring that they are called gems, or precious stones; so precious that the prices of them are almost fabulous, and hence they are used almost exclusively for rich and costly ornament. Twelve kinds of these, each a vast, apportioned, and solid mass, make up the foundations on which the jasper walls of this city are built. Through these walls are twelve openings or gateways, with twelve gates; and each of these twelve gates is made of one solid pearl.

"From these gates inward there are as many main streetways, and all the streetway is gold — gold with in purity, such as cannot be reached by any earthly refinement — gold with a peculiar heavenly quality beyond what is ever seen in our gold — transparent gold like the most perfect glass.

"It is a true crystal palace, made of transparent gold. An object is thus presented, the splendor of which far outshines the most sublime creations of which the human imagination ever dreamed.

"The golden city for which the Church of the first–born is taught to look as its eternal home, is 1,500 miles square; for 12,000 stadia make 1,500 miles. John saw it measured, and this was the measure of it, just as wide as it is long, and just as high as it is wide; for the 'length and the breadth and the height of it are equal.' Here would be streets over streets, and stories over stories, up, up, up, to the height of 1,500 miles, and each street 1,500 miles long."

– J.A. Seiss

"In that city which Christ has prepared for His own there will be no created light, simply because Christ Himself, who is the uncreated light (John 8:12), will be there … The created lights of God and of men are as darkness when compared with our Blessed Lord. The light of His own Holy presence. In consequence of the fullness of that light, there shall be no night."

– Lehman Strauss

Those excluded from the Holy City (27)

"'And there shall in no way enter into it anything that defileth, neither he that worketh abomination, or maketh a lie, but they who are written in the Lamb's book of life,' (Revelation 21:27). As a reminder of God's consistent pattern in dealing with men, those who reject His Son will not be admitted to His city. For we learn that 'anything that defileth' or 'he that worketh abomination, or maketh a lie' will not be admitted. That would include everyone in human history who has not received Christ. Thus all those who die in their defilement and lies and abominations are excluded from the city. In essence, only by acceptance of Jesus Christ does man have access to the ultimate blessing that God has prepared for him. This closing scene of chapter 21, with its inspired presentation of the glories that God has established for men in the eternal order, should inspire every man to receive Jesus Christ and thus have his name written in the Lamb's Book of Life."

When God Makes All Things New
An Expository Sermon

Chapter Twenty-One

Chapter Twenty-One
Introduction

Beyond the trials and tragedies of life,
Beyond the valley of the shadow of death,
Beyond the veil of tears through which we pass,
Beyond the Tribulation time of the future,
Beyond the glorious reign of Christ on earth,
Beyond the last judgment of the unsaved dead,
Beyond time as we know it,

There shall be a glorious and eternal age of everlasting splendor and holy happiness, where the redeemed of all the ages shall bask eternally in the divine light of God and of the Lamb, where sorrow and sighing shall be no more where joy and blessing will continue through the immensity of God's universe, then cleansed of sin, and through infinity without end.

Here in the closing two chapters of Revelation is God's last grand invitation to join Him in eternal bliss and blessing. Coupled with that heavenly destiny is the sad but certain warning of perpetual doom and gloom for the lost in a place called the "lake of fire."

I. The New Creation (1–8)

"And I saw a new heaven and a new earth: for the first heaven and the first earth were passed away" (1) It is over now. The long rebellion, initiated by Satan, perhaps before the foundation of the world. The multiplied tragedies of human history with its triumphs and tragedies, its victories and defeats, its sufferings and sorrows, its sin and death. It is over forever. All of the prophesied events to climax this planet's speckled history in fiery judgment and wrath are fulfilled. Now the wonders and beauties of even the golden millennial age have passed into the tomb of time. All that vast throng of lost and doomed and damned souls has stood before God in the most just trial that shall ever be, receiving the sentence of eternal perdition in the lake of fire. It is over now.

This world, as we have known it, as it has been since the first creation, has passed away. Peter's prophecy of desolation has been fulfilled: "But the day of the Lord will come as a thief in the night; in the which the heavens shall pass away with a great noise, and the elements shall melt with a fervent heat, the earth also and the works that are therein shall be burned up.

"Seeing that all these things shall be dissolved, what manner of persons ought we to be in all holy conversation and godliness, looking for and hasting unto the coming of the day of God, wherein the heavens being on fire shall be dissolved, and the elements shall melt with fervent heat?

"Nevertheless, we, according to his promise, look for new heavens and a new earth, wherein dwelleth righteousness" (2 Peter 3:10–13).

O, the wonder of eternity with God! May the Holy Spirit enable us just to catch a fleeting glimpse of those things, which our natural eye "hath not seen, nor ear heard, neither hath entered into the heart of man … the things which God hath prepared for them that love Him" (1 Corinthians 2:9).

"And I saw …" — seven times the expression occurs from 19:11, where the King of Kings gallops forth on His heavenly white stallion. Thirty–nine times he uses the expression, after introducing the truth that these are things which he saw (1:2).

How extensive will be the new heaven He creates? Will it include the entire universe with its galaxies and nebula or just our own region of God's Cosmos or does the expression refer to the invisible heaven, where presently God reigns? Who can say for sure? But suffice it to say that God promises, "I make all things new …"

Heaven, both the abode of God and the universe we see, will be made new.

There will be a new earth, based on some different principle that this planet's environmental canopy, for there will be no need of a sea of water to sustain life.

II. The New Capital (9–23)

One of the very august angels, whose solemn assigned task was to pour out the vials of God's wrath upon a wicked and evil world comes now as a messenger of hope and glory for the righteous and the saved. To the sainted and aged Apostle John, he beckons, uttering the fourth and final "Come hither" invitation.

In 4:1, John is invited to "Come up hither" to behold the things which shall be hereafter.

In 11:12 the two witnesses, who prophesy during the first half of the Tribulation, respond to a "great voice from heaven," following their resurrection after three and a half days of being dead. **"Come up hither,"** is the invitation and they ascend into heaven before the awestruck gaze of the multitudes in Jerusalem on the earth.

In 17:1 the beloved disciple is called ... **"Come hither,** I will show unto thee the judgment of the great whore ..."** by one of those seven angels with the vials.

Now, John is told, **"Come hither,** I will show thee the bride, the Lamb's wife."

Carried in the Spirit to the lofty pinnacle of a high mountain on the New Earth, John beholds "the Holy Jerusalem, descending out of heaven from God."

Abraham of old, four thousand years ago, looked for this city, "which hath foundations, whose builder and maker is God," (Hebrews 11:10).

Paul spoke of the "Jerusalem which is above and is free, which is the mother of us all," (Galatians 4:26).

Now John can more fully grasp the profundity of Jesus' words the night before His crucifixion:

"In my Father's house are many mansions: if it were not so, I would have told you. I go to prepare a place for you. And if I go and prepare a place for you, I will come again, and receive you unto myself; that where I am, there ye may be also" (John 14:2,3).

Effulgent with the glory of God, shining with the iridescent radiance of stone most precious, the huge heavenly metropolis, floats through space, cleansed now of all stains and sin, toward the New Earth.

Described here is a real place, a real city, the home of the bride of Christ forever.

Joseph A. Seiss well answers those who would spiritualize this passage by saying,

"An incorporeal and immaterial eternity for man is aside from the teachings of God's Word ... It has no substance, no reality, for the soul to hold on to God, nothing but a world of shadows, of mists, of dim visions of blessedness, with which it is impossible for a being who is not mere spirit and never will be mere spirit, who knows only to live in a body and shall live forever in a (glorified) body, to feel fellowship or sympathy. But such are not the ideas of our futurity, which the Bible holds out to our faith and hope."

What is depicted here is a shimmering golden citadel of radiant massive beauty, surpassing a thousand fold the vast cities man has built. Enclosed in yellow jasper walls, rising high above

bejeweled foundations, garnished with stones of every color and hue, precious stones, divinely crafted in tender love! Here is the capital of the Universe, New Jerusalem, extending as far as human or glorified eye can see, 12,000 furlongs from corner to corner.

Twelve gates of pearl, each of a single divinely designed variety, give access to the City of God. Each of the gates is named after one of the twelve tribes of the children of Israel, for His earthly chosen people, who know their true Messiah will dwell there. From the listing in chapter seven, I presume that those names will be Judah, Reuben, Gad, Assher, Napthali, Manasseh, Simeon, Levi, Issachar, Zebulon, Joseph and Benjamin.

Mansions and palaces, castles and dwelling places, transparent golden streets, lined with evergreen leaves and ever yielding fruits, hanging from the tree of life, are some of the wonders of this grand central core of God's Universe.

Beneath the wall encompassing the city foursquare, are twelve enormous foundations, adorned with precious stones of all the colors of the rainbow. In them the names of the Twelve Apostles of the Lamb are inscribed, one of each of the twelve. I suppose these are Peter, James, John, Andrew, Phillip, Thomas, Bartholomew, Nathaniel, Matthew, James the less (our Lord's brother) Simon the Zealot, Jude and Matthias (Acts 1:13,26).

Remember that the church is built on "the foundation of the apostles and prophets, Jesus Christ Himself being the chief cornerstone" (Ephesians 2:20).

Populated by the redeemed saints of God of all ages, the city will afford full access for the redeemed earth people. They are millennial believers transported to the New Earth, like Noah and his family of old. They will be subjects of the King forever on a planet where sin will never be known, where peace and joy will never cease.

No longer will there be any need for a great temple, a center for worship, from which praise and thanksgiving might ascend up to the throne of God from a great company of believers. Now the Lord God Almighty Himself and the Lamb are the temple.

Worship and adoration from redeemed hearts will focus upon the God who is love in all of His magnificence and beneficence.

"What is a city without lights!" exclaims Joseph Seiss, "This city is itself a grand prism of inherent light, the Light of God, and of the Lamb, which illuminates at once the eyes of the body and of the soul, and shines not only on the objects without, but on the understandings within, making everything light in the Lord. The glory of God's brightness envelopes it like an unclouded halo, permeates it, and radiates through it and from it so that there is not a dark place about it. It shines like a new sun, inside and out, sending abroad its rays all over the earth, and into the depths of space.

"On the Mount of Transfiguration that same light streamed forth form His body and his raiment."

Truly in the Celestial City we shall understand completely that "God is light and in Him is no darkness at all" (1 John 1:5).

My friend, is this cosmic city of divine creation your eternal home? Will you enjoy the eternal life vouchsafed to those who know the Savior?

III. The Great Contrasts (24–27)

Think of the believers of the Old Testament Age from the days of Abel (Hebrews 11:4) in a golden city, where the names of the Twelve Tribes of Israel are engraved upon gates of pearl.

Think of the believers of the New Testament Age living in the New Jerusalem, the foundations of which are inscribed with the names of the Twelve Apostles.

Think of the nations of the saved from the Tribulation (the sheep of Matthew 25:31–46) and from the millennial time, who will bring the glory and honor of the newly created world into the City of God.

Then, think of the lost, the defiling, the workers of abominations, the makers of lies, those not written in the Lamb's Book of Life.

What is your destiny?

The Holy City, New Jerusalem …?

The Lake of Fire which burneth with fire and brimstone forever and ever?

Conclusion

The choice of your eternity is yours to make. "He that believeth on the Son hath everlasting life, but he that believeth not the Son shall not see life, but the wrath of God abideth on him" (John 3:36).

How tragic to suffer the slings and arrows of outrageous fortune on this earth, sinning and rejecting God's grace, then to spend eternity in the lake of fire!

What then does God offer you.

Consider the things which will be "no more," when the dwelling place of God is with men. There are seven:

"And God shall wipe away all tears from their eyes" (21:4) … thus there will be:

1. **No More Tears** in heaven fair…

2. "And there shall be **No More Death** …": "for the wages of sin is death and the last enemy that shall be destroyed is death" (1 Corinthians 15:26).

Never again a funeral procession, never again the separation and despair accompanying the coming of the Grim Reaper.

3. **"Neither Sorrow"** of any kind in the Celestial City with all the grief, regret and tragedy often involved …

4. **"Nor Crying"** over the setbacks and sad circumstances of life, whether expressed in words or in the heart …

5. **"neither shall** there be **Any More Pain,"** which banishes sickness and disease and all the ills befalling and mortal bodies, wherein we all now dwell. Pain and suffering will be forever exiled, banished from the glorified body, the heavenly environment, and the presence of the Lord on His throne.

6. "And there shall be **No More Curse,"** for all the consequences of sin in all the ages past are gone forever.

7. "And there shall be **No Night** there, and they need no candle, neither light of the sun; for the Lord God giveth them light and they shall reign forever and ever" (22:5).

This sweet and blessed destiny is what God and the Lamb offer you.

Satan, seductive and tempting, will seek to make you think that the pleasures of sin will last, but they are only for a season. Those who follow him, refusing Christ, will spend eternity with him in everlasting torment.

The invitation is simple.

Come to Christ, receiving Him as Savior and Lord and receive eternal life.

If you have never accepted Him, come now to Him!

A Commentary on the Revelation
Expository, Exegetical, Devotional and Practical
Greek words from the Textus Receptus

Chapter Twenty-One

The New Heaven and the New Earth (1–8)
1. And I saw a new heaven and a new earth *(kai eidon ouranon kainon kai gen kainen)* — some insist that the present universe and the spiritual heaven and the earth will be cleansed by fire (2 Peter 3), but not actually annihilated. Others, including this commentator believe that the planet earth will pass away completely to be replaced by a new and more wonderful world, fresh from the hand of the Creator. However the city of God is evidently now in preparation (John 14:2,3) and comes down from "heaven" from God. Whether or not God recreates the entire universe is a puzzling question, later to be fully understood ... **for the first heaven and the first earth were passed away** — which may mean destroyed, dissolved or purged. Literally, "passed away" means, from Greek *apelthan,* "were departed" ... **and there was no more sea** *(kai he thalassa ouk estin eti)* — no doubt basically literal, since a vast expanse of water on the new earth, unlike our present world, will not be needed for environmental and weather phenomena to preserve life... but the sea is also a type of perpetual unrest (Isaiah 57:20,21); it can symbolize the vast mass of humanity (Revelation 17:15 and 13:1) **2. And I John saw the holy city, New Jerusalem, coming down from God out of heaven** — "Jerusalem which is above" (Revelation 3:12; Galatians 4:26, Hebrews 11:10; 12:22; 13;14) ... this descending city is in stark contrast to the earthly "beloved city" (20:9), the "Jerusalem which now is" (Galations 4:25), the ancient and modern and prophetic city of Scripture. In Greek *Hierousaleem* is always used for the heavenly city; when referring to the earthly city as in Galations 4, a differant spelling *Hierosoluma,* is sometimes used... **prepared as a bride, adorned for her husband** (Revelation 19:7–9; 2 Corinthians 11:2; Revelations 22:17; Ephesians 5:25–27) — true "queen of heaven." Not an Eden, not a mystery, not a vague phantasmagoric "spiritual realm," but a real place, inhabited by the saints of God of all ages, resurrected and glorified with bodies like Jesus' incorruptible resurrection body, immortal and eternal. **3. And I heard a great voice out of heaven, saying, Behold the tabernacle of God is with men** — the Greek word is *skene,* meaning a tent, a booth, dwelling place, here referring back to the tabernacle in the wilderness, where God dwelt in the midst of His people, Israel (See 11:19; 15:5; also 13:6 for its continuing use related to the heavenly tabernacle, Hebrews 9:23,24). Although replaced by the temple as a structure, the same word, *skene,* was often used for it. This same word in verb form is found in John 1:14; "The Word ... dwelt *(eskenosen)* among us." **...and he will dwell with them, and they shall be his people, and God Himself shall be with them, and be their God.** — Centering His omnipresence in the Holy City, God will dwell in the midst of His redeemed and glorified saints and in the midst of "nations of them that are saved" (vs. 24). No rival diety, no angelic rebellion, no evil shall spoil this new Creation. **4. And God shall wipe away all tears from their eyes** *(Kai eksaleipsei pan dakruon ek ton ophalmon auton)* — lit. every tear, the individual tears, elicited by each forever past sorrow, now all gone, wiped away. Some have suggested that even the glorified saints might weep at the Great White Throne Judgment as lost ones they knew are consigned to the lake of fire, that this wiping of tears would end whatever regrets might linger ... **And there shall be no more death** *(thanatos)* — this is not the millennium since isolated deaths may then occur (Isaiah 65:20; 1 Corinthians 15:26,54), but this "last enemy" to be destroyed is eliminated after the Great White Throne Judgment ... **neither sorrow** *(oute penthos)* — mourning as in 18:7 ... **nor crying** *(krauge)* — continual crying ... **neither shall there be any more pain** *(ponos)* — distress (see 16:10,11), both mental and physical ... **for the former things are passed away** or "departed" (Greek — *aplethon),* gone forever, the ultimate outcome of 2 Corinthians 5:17. **5. And he that sat upon the throne said** — evidently the Father, who is sitting on the throne ... **Behold I make all things new** *(Idou kaina poio panta)* — a glorious prospect all true believers can anticipate of which regeneration is the earnest ... **And he said unto**

me, **Write: for these words are true** (*alethinoi*) **and faithful** (*pistoi*) — i.e. accurate, incorruptible, and trustworthy, genuine. **6. And he said unto me, It is done** (*gegonen*) — all is as sure as if it had already, actually been fulfilled. See 16:17 ... **I am Alpha and Omega** — the first and last letters of the Greek alphabet as in 1:8,11; 22:13 ... "A and Z" ... **the beginning** (*arche*) **and the end** (*telos*), the origin and the completion of all things that have existance (Hebrews 1:10–12) ... **I will give to him that is athirst of the fountain of the water of life freely** — in our present state we drink of the streams, then of the fountain ... out of the free flowing fountain of spiritual water and refreshment shall come the thirst quenching and purifying, cleansing, satisfying liquid for the saved soul and the glorified body. **7. He that overcometh shall inherit all things** — the eighth and final promise to the overcomers (Revelation 2:7,11,17,26; 3:5,12,21 and compare to 1 John 5:4,5) ... as Paul indicates in 1 Corinthians 3:21–23 and Romans 8:16, 17, 32 ... what an inheritance, the universe! **and I will be his God and he shall be my son** — a son (or daughter for this is generic) inherits what is the Father's through gift and reward, not death in any sense. This is very emphatic in expression. **8. But the fearful** (*delois*) — those who are cowards, ignoble and contemptible, cravenly lacking in true courage, refusing to embrace salvation for fear of losing something ... **and unbelieving** (*apistois*) — rejectors of salvation, agnostics, atheists, refusers of truth and the gospel ... **and the abominable** (*ebdelugmenois*) — polluted, morally unclean, degraded in body, mind and soul, and impure ... **murderers** (*phoneusin*) — violent, death–dealing and malicious persons ... and **whoremongers** (*pornois*) — sexually addicted practicers of all kinds of immorality, sex libertines with unrestrained lusts ... **and sorcerers** (*pharkamois*) — dealers in illicit drugs (as in pharmacy), who enslave others with chemical addiction and are themselves enslaved ... also using chemistry and Satanic power for evil ... **and idolators** (*eidololatrais*) — worshippers of idols ... who give supreme allegiance to anything but the true God ... **and all liars** (*pseudesin*) — false lying ones, who never repented and received the Truth ... **shall have their part in the lake of fire, which burneth with fire and brimstone: which is the second death** — these terrible sins seem especially characteristic of the last days.

New Jerusalem (9–21)

9. And there came unto me one of the seven angels which had the seven vials full of the seven last plagues, and talked with me, **saying** — evidently the same angel who showed John the judgment on Babylon (17:1) now shows him the glory of the New Jerusalem, an appropriate contrast of the two cities ... one of the results of divine judgment on the church's foes is the blessedness that shall come to God's people ... **"Come hither"** (*deuro*) (4:1; 11:12; 17:1) ... **I will show thee the bride, the Lamb's wife** (*numphen ... ten gunaika tou arniou ...* **the wife of the Lamb)** — dwelling place of the redeemed, especially New Testament saints, constituting the bride in eternity. **10. And he carried me away in the spirit** (1:10; 4:2; 17:3) — indicating a spiritual vision, which will ultimately be a reality ... **to a great and high mountain** — in contrast to the wilderness (17:3) where John saw the Harlot Babylon but now sees the bride, New Jerusalem and its inhabitants, also the wife of the Lamb ... **and showed me that great city, Holy Jerusalem, descending out of heaven from God** — some commentators think the city hovers above the New Earth, while others suppose this is a millennial scene, but this writer thinks it comes down to the New Earth, after the millenium and after the Great White Throne Judgment. **11. Having the glory of God** (*echousan ten doksan tou theou*) — shining forth from this hallowed and consecrated city is the splendor and radiance of God who is Light, where dwell the children of light (See Philippians 2:15) ... **and her light** (*ho phoster autes*) — radiance, luminary, phosphorescence ... **was like unto a stone most precious**, (as a glittering diamond with a yellow hue) ... **even like a jasper stone** (*hos litho easpidi*) — similar to a jasper, which is wavy with various rainbow like colors, but on earth opaque, but here **clear as crystal**, transparent and luminous. **12. And had a wall great and high** — built of jasper, but not for protection against evil but as a glowing ornament of beauty and splendor ... **and had twelve gates** — the number of divine government, as in twelve tribes, twelve apostles, etc., **and at the gates twelve angels** — special messengers, protectors, sentinels and servants (Hebrews 1:14), who are posted as spiritual ministers ... **and names written thereon, which are the names of the twelve tribes of the children of Israel** — compare the earthly millennial Jerusalem (Ezekiel 48:30–35), where on the north side are the gates of Rueben, Judah and Levi; on the east side, are the gates of Joseph, Benjamin and Dan; on the south side are the gates of Simeon, Issachar and Zebulon; and on the west side are the gates of Gad, Asher and Naphtali. Whether these same arrangements will continue in the vastly larger New Jerusalem or not is unclear. In Numbers 2 there is a different arrangment and in Revelation 7 the list is slightly different with both Joseph (Ephraim?) and Mannasseh mentioned and Dan omitted. Obviously, the redeemed Israelites of the Tribulation, both the 144,000 and the survivors of the Final Holocaust along with the believing Israelis of the Millennial era will all have either residency or access to the Holy Jerusalem. In Christ during this age there is neither Jew nor Gentile, but in Eternity the special character of the children of Israel for all of God's earthly chosen people will be preserved in some way. **13. And on the east three gates; on the north three gates; on the south three gates; and on the west three gates** — to reduce this vivid description, as some do, to mere figures of speech, rather than a literal city with real gates, is a misuse and misinterpretation of language. **14. And the wall of the city had twelve foundations** — see Ephesians 2:20,21 for the present spiritual reality ... **and in them the names of the twelve apostles of the Lamb** — both Old and New Testament sets of twelve are incorporated in the eternal city with these special names inscribed most magnificently in the gates and in the foundations. The twelve apostles: Peter, James, John, Andrew, Phillip, Thomas, Bartholomew, Matthew, James the Less (short, possibly the Lord's brother), Simon the Zealot, Jude and Matthias (?) or, as some think, Paul, Apostle to the Gentiles ... **15. And he that talked with me had a golden reed to measure the city, and the gates thereof and the walls thereof**—compare the millennial Jerusalem for its much smaller dimensions in Ezekiel 48:35. John measured the Tribulation Temple in 11:1,2. **16. And the city lieth foursquare, and the length is as large as the breadth: and he measured the city with the reed, twelve thousand furlongs** — a furlong is 582 feet, or, if taken quite literally, a total of 1,600 miles in each direction. **The length and the breadth and the height of it are equal** — whether the shining golden city is like a cube or a pyramid is a matter of conjecture. **17. And he measured the wall thereof, an hundred and forty and four cubits, according to the measure of a man, that is of the angel** — the wall is twelve times twelve or 144 cubits high ... a cubit may be either eighteen inches or about twenty-two inches. **18. And the building of the wall of it was jasper** (iaspis) — a gem used in the High Priest's breastplate (Exodus 28:20; 39:13) ... **and the city was pure gold, like unto clear glass** — reflectant and transparent, surrounded by an aura of golden iridescence, emanating from the glory of God. **19. And the foundations of the**

wall of the city were garnished with all manner of precious stones** — they are ornamented, encrusted, adorned, decorated with these stones, or possibly, each foundation appears as though it were all of the listed precious stones ... **The first foundation was jasper** (iaspis), yellowish with rainbow colors; **the second, sapphire** (sapphiros), probably deep, pure blue and transparent; **the third, a chalcedony** (chalkedon), sky blue or in transparent layers of white and grey; **the fourth, an emerald** (smaragdos), rich and deep green (See 4:3). **20. the fifth, sardonyx** (sardonuks) — with the redness of cornelian and the whiteness of an onyx, mixed; **the sixth, sardius,** (Sardion) blood red, translucscent; **the seventh crysolyte** (chrusolithos) transparent with a golden brightness like a topaz; **the eighth, a beryl** (berullos), a sea-green color; **the ninth, a topaz** (topazion) — transparent green mixed with white to yellow, glow stone; **the tenth, a chrysoprasus** (chrusoprasos), purplish, like an amethyst with apple-green hues; **the eleventh, a jacinth** (huakinthos), a bluish, violet-red stone; **the twelfth, an amethyst** (amethustos), clear violet with a purple glow (Compare Exodus 28:15–20). **21. And the twelve gates were twelve pearls** (margaritai); **every several gate was of one pearl** — when the oyster encloses an impurity, the pearl forms around it, suggesting that our sins are enclosed and removed by Jesus, the Door to Heaven, who also regards us as the "pearl of great price" (45,46) ... the pearl symbolizes suffering to bring forth beauty.

The City's Worship and Service (22-23)

22. And I saw no temple therein: for the Lord God Almighty and the Lamb are the Temple of it — no need for a structure ever again. **23. No need of the sun, neither the moon** — the light of His presence illuminates all. **No night there** — both literally and figuratively. **24. And the nations of them which were saved** — the godly nations transported from the millennial earth into the New Earth. Some form of nationhood continues. **25. Lamb's Book of life** — only the godly of all dispensations admitted; all the wicked forever exiled in the lake of fire.

RAINBOWS FROM REVELATION
The Revelation of Jesus Christ

A chapter by chapter, verse by verse study

"There was a rainbow round about the throne like unto an emerald" (4:3)

CHAPTER TWENTY-TWO: Come, Lord Jesus!

References

Ps. 46:4
Ezek. 47:1
Zech. 14:8

Gen. 2:9
Rev. 21:24

Zech. 14:11
Rev. 3:21; 4:2

Mat. 5:8
Rev. 14:1

Rev. 7:15
Rev. 21:23
Ps. 36:9

Heb. 1:1; 10:37
Rev. 1:1

Rev. 3:11

Rev. 19:10

John 4:24

Dan. 8:26; 12:4

Ezek. 3:27
2 Tim. 3:13

1. AND he showed me a pure river of water of life, clear as crystal, proceeding out of the throne of God and of the Lamb.

2. In the midst of the street of it, and on either side of the river was there the tree of life, which bare twelve manner of fruits, and yielded her fruit every month: and the leaves of the tree were for the healing of the nations.

3. And there shall be no more curse: but the throne of God and of the Lamb shall be in it; and his servants shall serve him:

4. And they shall see his face; and his name shall be in their foreheads.

5. And there shall be no night there; and they need no candle, neither light of the sun; for the Lord God giveth them light: and they shall reign for ever and ever.

6. And he said unto me, These sayings are faithful and true: and the Lord God of the holy prophets sent his angel to show unto his servants the things which must shortly be done.

7. Behold, I come quickly: blessed is he that keepeth the sayings of this book.

8. And I John saw these things, and heard them. And when I had heard and seen, I fell down to worship before the feet of the angel which showed me these things.

9. Then saith he unto me, See thou do it not: for I am thy fellow servant, and of thy brethren the prophets, and of them which keep the sayings of this book: worship God.

10. And he saith unto me, Seal not the sayings of the prophecy of this book: for the time is at hand.

11. He that is unjust, let him be unjust still: and he which is filthy, let him be filthy still: and he that is righteous, let him be righteous still: and he that is holy, let him be holy still.

12. And, behold, I come quickly; and my reward is with me, to give every man according as his work shall be.

13. I am Alpha and Omega, the beginning and the end, the first and the last.

14. Blessed are they that do his commandments, that they may have right to the tree of life, and may enter in through the gates into the city.

15. For without are dogs, and sorcerers, and whoremongers, and murderers, and idolaters, and whosoever loveth and maketh a lie.

16. I Jesus have sent mine angel to testify unto you these things in the churches. I am the root and the offspring of David, and the bright and morning star.

17. And the Spirit and the bride say, Come. And let him that heareth say, Come. And let him that is athirst come. And whosoever will, let him take the water of life freely.

18. For I testify unto every man that heareth the words of the prophecy of this book, If any man shall add unto these things, God shall add unto him the plagues that are written in this book:

19. And if any man shall take away from the words of the book of this prophecy, God shall take away his part out of the book of life, and out of the holy city, and from the things which are written in the book.

20. He which testifieth these things saith, Surely I come quickly. Amen. Even so, come, Lord Jesus.

21. The grace of our Lord Jesus Christ be with you all. Amen.

References

Matt. 5:48
Heb. 12:14

Isa. 40:10
2 Cor. 5:10

Isa. 41:4; 44:6
Rev. 1:8,11

Dan. 12:12

1 Cor. 6:9
Phil 3:2

Rev. 5:5
Isa. 11:1
Jer. 23:5,6

Isa. 55:1
Jn. 4:14
Jn. 7:37
Jn. 3:16

Deut. 4:2
Prov. 30:6

Ex. 32:33

Heb. 9:28;
10:37

1 Thes. 5:18, 28

Scriptures for Comparison

John 14:1-3

Let not your heart be troubled: ye believe in God, believe also in me. In my Father's house are many mansions: if it were not so, I would have told you. I go to prepare a place for you. And if I go and prepare a place for you, I will come again, and receive you unto myself; that where I am, there ye may be also.

Titus 2:13

Looking for that blessed hope, and the glorious appearing of the great God and our Saviour Jesus Christ.

Summary of Chapter Twenty-two

The Bible's Final Messages

This 1,189th chapter in the Bible, this end of the written Word, this OMEGA portion of God's revelation, not only in this final book but of all the Word of God, is a logical conclusion indeed. Without these words the canon of Scripture might have been supposed to be yet open. It is not. Nothing more is to be added.

I. Final Heavenly Scene (1-5)

In the first five verses the scene of heaven is majestic and satisfying. John beholds the crystalline stream, the water of life, flowing from the very imperial throne of the Eternal God. Its sparkling waters flow through the midst of the broad golden avenue of glory. The tree of life, a heavenly kind of tree, is depicted as growing, blossoming and bearing fruit for the healing or health of the nations.

No more curse, no night there in the heavenly Jerusalem!

All of the redeemed of the Old and New Testament eras shall be the servants of God forever, seeing His face and reigning with Him.

II. Final Words of Scripture (6-21)

From verse 6 through the end of the chapter John records his closing words, the last words of Christ, and the words of the revealing angel.

So overwhelmed again is the great Apostle at the very words of Christ and the glory of all that he has beheld, that he falls again before the angel, as he did in 19:10. Again the command is sure, "Worship God."

Unlike the writing of Daniel 650 years earlier, these sayings are not to be sealed, but open for all to consider.

Even in these last paragraphs three warnings are evident.

First (11), the contrast between the unjust and the righteous is again drawn. No hint of a second chance appears at all.

Second, in verse 15 is the sad reminder that outside the city, outside of the cosmic realms, cleansed of sin there yet remains a place for "dogs" and sorcerers (evil magicians and drug addicts), whoremongers (the immoral), murderers (the violent), idolaters (worshippers of false gods), and lovers of lies. Those who never find forgiveness, who never wash their robes and make them white in the blood of the Lamb, shall remain in a shadowy burning lake of fire on the fringe of creation.

Replete with repeated promises to return, the closing verses form a grand finale to the entire Word of God.

Blessedness and bliss shall be the inheritance of all who do His commandments, supremely obedient to that Johannine instructive command, "And this is his commandment, That we should believe on the name of His Son Jesus Christ, and love one another, as he gave us commandment" (1 John 3:23). This completes the cycle introduced in 1:3, "Blessed is he that readeth and they that hear the words of this prophecy, and keep those things which are therein, for the time is at hand."

A warm and loving invitation from the Holy Spirit and the bride of Christ is issued, "Come" (vs. 17). Open to all is the opportunity of drinking "the water of life," the true message of the gospel, which alone can quench the deepest thirst of the human soul. "Whosoever will, let him take the water of life freely."

Third, a final caution is advanced to anyone bold and foolish enough to add to the Word of God or subtract from it. This rules out all other books, subsequently written as "inspired writings."

The chapter concludes with the last promise of Christ, the last prayer in the Bible and the last benediction.

While the Old Testament closes with the words, "lest I come and smite the earth with a curse," (Malachi 4:6), the New Testament ends with "the grace of our Lord Jesus Christ."

In conclusion, may it be understood that no good result can arise from setting arbitrary dates for the Rapture or the Glorious Appearing. No one can declare resolutely and absolutely that the twentieth or twenty-first century is the final end time. Throughout the New Testament, God's people are urged to watch and wait. So should we do in all ages.

Alert to the times, eager for the Return, but incessantly busy in the Master's Vineyard, though it might be the eleventh hour, we as believers are to live and walk in the Spirit, witness for Christ, study the Word, fellowship with each other in love, "not forsaking the assembling of ourselves together as the manner of some is; but exhorting one another: and so much the more, as we see the day approaching" (Hebrews 10:25).

Outline of Chapter Twenty-two

The Omega Message

OBJECTIVE: To bring the Book of Revelation and the canon of Scripture to a grand conclusion with final words from Christ.

OUTLINE:
I. The Last Things John Saw (1-6)
A. The Water of Life (1)

B. The Throne of God and the Lamb (1)

C. The Street in New Jerusalem (2)

D. The Tree of Life (2)

E. The Fruit of the Tree (2)

F. The Servants of God (3-5)
   1. They serve Him (3)

   2. They see His face (4)

   3. They bear His name (4)

   4. They need no natural light (5)

   5. They enjoy God's light (5)

   6. They reign forever (5)

II. The Last Things John Heard (6-11 and the 7 Affirmations of Christ)

A. The Angel's Admonitions (6-11)
   1. These sayings are true (6)

   2. The Lord only is to be worshipped (8, 9)

   3. This book is not to be sealed (10)

   4. The destinies are eternal (11)
      a. The unjust continue
      b. The righteous continue

B. The Savior's Admonitions (7, etc.)
   1. He affirms His coming (7)

   2. He declares the blessedness of the obedient (7)

   3. He promises rewards (12)

4. He proclaims His eternality (13)

5. He authorizes His messages to the churches (16)

6. He acknowledges His root and destiny (16)

7. He leaves a last promise (20)

III. The Last Things John Said (14, 15 and 18-21)

A. Blessedness of the Saved Affirmed (14)

B. Doom of the Last Declared (15)

C. Warning of Tampering with the Word (18, 19)
   1. Judgment on Those Who Add (18)

   2. Judgment on Those Who Take Away (19)

D. Prayer for Christ's Coming (20)

E. Benediction and Conclusion (21)

Another Way to View This Book

Four times the phase "in the Spirit" occurs in Revelation, each introducing a section of the book, as follows:

Prologue
Christ Communicating (1:1-8)

Vision One
Christ in the Churches (1:9 - 3:22)

Vision Two
Christ in the Cosmos (4:1 - 16:21)

Vision Three
Christ in Conquest (17:1 - 21:8)

Vision Four
Christ in Consummation (21:9 - 22:5)

Epilogue
Christ Challenging (22:6-21)
                                    – Merrill Tenney

Observations:
Spiritual lessons and applications from each verse
Chapter Twenty-Two

1. Those who partake of the living water of salvation on earth can partake of the heavenly living water in heaven, flowing from God's throne.

2. This city, the abode of the bride, is a real place with tangible streets, the growing tree of life and actual fruit.

3. To serve God and glorify Him forever in all of the Cosmos is the final end and purpose of redeemed peoples.

4. To see God's face is the pinnacle of relationships, for we shall see the invisible God, immortal and eternal, and enjoy Him forever.

5. Reigning forever with Christ is the prospect of the redeemed; how that contrasts with the doom of the lost is reiterated in this chapter.

6. Not only is Christ "faithful and true" (19:11) but so also is the spoken and written Word.

7. Christ reemphasizes the thought of 1:3, promising blessings for the keepers of these truths.

8. Sometimes God's riches are so overwhelming that we are compelled to worship.

9. Worship must never be directed toward angels or saints gone to glory, but only to God.

10. Throughout history God's people have always been taught to look for Christ, knowing the time could be at hand.

11. God will not relent at the last moment and allow the lost to escape the lake of fire and dwell with Him. No universalism is taught in the Bible.

12. Every believer needs to be laying up treasures in heaven.

13. Christ, the first and last, has all things under His control.

14. To enter the gates of the city will be the privilege of all the saved of every age.

15. Lying is classified as an evil sin and should be avoided by believers.

16. Christ is still speaking to His churches in the book of Revelation.

17. Observe the three "COMES," voiced by the Holy Spirit, the bride of Christ, and by the hearers. Anyone who thirsts for inner and eternal satisfaction is welcome to COME.

18. If the Bible is this important or the book of Revelation this significant, we dare not neglect it.

19. Taking away from the Word of God results in God taking away opportunities to have the blessings of being recorded in the Book of Life, or enjoying the City of God forever. A most serious warning!

20. A promise of His coming and a prayer for His coming is the closing major truth of the Revelation.

21. This apostolic benediction may be echoed in our times: "The grace of our Lord Jesus Christ be with you all. Amen."

Compare Chapters 2 and 3 with Chapters 19-22

Promises to 7 churches	Concept	Perfected Consummation
2:7	The Tree of Life	22:2
2:11	The Second Death	21:8
2:17	The White Stone	
2:27	The Rod of Iron	19:15
3:5	The Book of Life	20:15
3:12	The Temple of God	21:3,22
3:21	The Throne of Christ	22:3

Quotations
From Other Expositors
Chapter Twenty-two

Water of Life/Tree of Life (1-6)

"The first five verses of our chapter contain six challenging descriptions of the heavenlike earth. As you bear in mind the heavenly city and the new earth described in chapter twenty–one, we turn now to additional details to make this utopian state even more ideal.

"'And he showed me a pure river of water of life, clear as crystal, proceeding out of the throne of God and of the Lamb' (22:1). Man cannot live without water in this life or seemingly in the life to come. A study of history shows that man has always looked for water. The ideal fortress cities of the world have been located on high points of ground which had an adequate water supply. Many have died and nations have had to change their homeland because there was no adequate water supply. In the eternal paradise God has planned for man, an abundance of water will proceed out of the throne of God Himself, indicating that God will be the source of that life–giving substenance.

"'… the tree of life, which bore twelve kinds of fruits, and yielded her fruit every month' (22:2). When Adam and Eve sinned, God forbade them to eat of the Tree of Life. Genesis 3:22–24 states,

And the Lord God said, Behold, the man is become as one of us, to know good and evil; and now, lest he put forth his hand, and take also of the tree of life, and eat, and live forever; therefore the Lord God sent him forth from the garden of Eden, to till the ground from where he was taken. So he drove out the man; and he placed at the east of the garden of Eden cherubim, and a flaming sword which turned every way, to guard the way of the tree of life.

"This text clarifies that the eating of the Tree of Life makes man live forever. Man was forbidden to eat of that tree because he had first taken of the Tree of the Knowledge of Good and Evil, but in the eternal future he will be able to eat of it; this testifies of the eternity of man's blessed future state."

– Tim LaHaye

"The 'leaves of the tree were for the healing of the nations,' that is, the preservation of the nations which would bring their homage to the King of the City. There will be no need of 'healing', (as we know

it), for there will be no pain or disease, or sickness. Eternal health is indicated.

"'And there shall be no more curse,' which immediately takes us back to Genesis 3:14–19 and the curse of sorrow, labor pains, thorns and thistles, sweat of physical work, and death. All of this will be gone in this new earth!"

– Bill Lawrence

"And there shall be 'no more cruse.' When our Lord died on Calvary, He wore upon His brow the very symbol of the curse — a crown of thorns. He bore in His own body on the tree the curse of sin, as it is written, 'Cursed is everyone that hangeth on a tree,' (Galatians 3:13).

–Louis T. Talbot

"'They shall reign to the ages of ages.' The millennium and the eternal ages are here embraced. The saints on high shall never cease to reign. So long as Christ is on the throne, so long as He wears the crown, that determines the duration of the reign of the saints, for we 'shall reign in life by One, Jesus Christ,' (Romans 5:17). This character of reign is necessarily eternal, and is quite independent of economic or other change. The kingdom given up to God (1 Corinthians 15:24), is set up on the earth for a specified time, and to manifest the accomplistment of the counsels of God. The thousand years' reign comes in between the history of the world as it now exists and the eternal state. It is the kingdom of that period which the Lord delivers up, but His reign over all creatures never ceases; so long as there are angels and men — creatures of God — so long is government necessarily required. The throne is eternal, and the thrones and crowns of the saints too, are eternal. We understand therefore the expression, 'they shall reign to the ages of ages,' to signify the eternal reign of the heavenly saints. Both our service and reigning are forever and ever, or eternal.

"What a glorious and triumphant close to this section of the book! How full and magnificent are the declarations, and how true! They will soon be resolved into fact in our happy experience.

"May God grant grace to walk worthy of Him,

and of these prophetic truths and glories so soon to be realised."

–*Walter Scott*

Jesus Closing Words (7-19)

"These things are for the Christian; they are the message of the Lord Jesus 'for the churches.' 'I Jesus have sent my angel to testify unto you these things for the churches.' 'I am the Root and Offspring fo David, the Bright, the Morning Star' (v. 16). He is the Sun of Righteousness to Israel, but to the Church He is the Bright and Morning Star, rising long before the Sun, to herald the dawn of the approaching day.

"And yet there is room! Is any sinner out of Christ reading these words? To such, 'the Spirit and the bride say, 'Come!' That 'Come!' is from the very heart of God and it has been sounding out for thousands of years. 'And he that heareth, let him say, 'Come!' Pass along the word, 'Come!' 'And he that is athirst, 'Come!' O, how He wants you! He cannot give you up, and His longsuffering leadeth you to repentance; His longsuffering is salvation. And yet again: 'He that will — whosoever will — let him take of the water of life freely.'

"Now comes a warning. Men must not meddle with God's book. If any man alters it in any way, his doom is irretrievably sealed, for God shall pass the plagues to him and take away his part from the Tree of Life and the Holy City."

–*William L. Pettingill*

The Last Word (22:20–21)

"The last word is a word about glory. John writes, 'He which testifieth these things saith, Surely I come quickly: Amen. Even so, come, Lord Jesus.' Three times in this closing chapter, the Lord breaks in to remind us that He is coming quickly. This is His last word. It seems like a long time to us since this promise was given, as we trace the history of the past two thousand years. It is only two days to Him (2 Peter 3:8). At any moment now, He might cleave the sky and take His saints home to glory. No wonder the church responds: 'Even so, come, Lord Jesus.'

"The very last word is a word about grace. John writes, 'The grace of our Lord Jesus Christ be with you all. Amen.' How like God to close His Book with a final reference to His grace! Well might we borrow the splendid lines of John Newton and celebrate that grace:

" '*Amazing grace! how sweet the sound!*
That saved a wretch like me;
I once was lost, but now am found;
Was blind, but now I see.' " –*John Phillips*

The Last Frontier

"Heaven is the last frontier. Like other frontiers in human history, it will challenge us with new opportunities, possibilities and experiences. Unlike the previous frontiers on earth, Heaven will be unlimited in time and space. It will inspire us to join as participants in the dynamic, creative plans of Jesus Christ as we embark on a greater adventure than any we have ever dreamed of. The eternal quest of our human spirit yearns for a heaven in which we can explore the infinite possibilities of an unlimited universe. Our future blessings in heaven will begin with the ending of all evil, suffering and adversity. But it will also provide the fulfillment and enhancement of all the real joys and happiness of human life. The language in the Bible describes our rest after satisfying labor and the elimination of toil and grief. These passages do not suggest a life of inactivity or boredom. The promises are of an active, purposeful and joyful life in a creation filled with beauty, fairness and justice.

"In our present earthly life, it is difficult to reconcile the goodness and power of God with the apparent triumph of evil and death. However, in the New Heaven and New Earth we will see the final reconciliation of the accounts of life in which evil will be judged and good will triumph forever. The spiritual warfare which exists in the heart of men between our good and evil natures will finally end. Believers will enjoy their newly resurrected bodies with their heart, mind and spirit cleansed from the taint of sin.

"Eternity is not the absence of time; it is an infinity of time. The tragic consequence on this boring view of Heaven is that many people have lost all desire to go there. It is my desire to awaken in Christians an active interest and discussion of our future in a real life in the New Earth and the New Heaven. When we begin to study the passages on Heaven in the Bible, we will find that all the best things of life here will find a dynamic fulfillment in our eternal home in Heaven.

"How can I know that I will go to Heaven?

"The choices we make in time will determine our destiny in eternity. God has not left us in doubt regarding the citizens of the heavenly city. The Bible declares that God is holy and that His home in Heaven cannot contain sin or rebellion. It also confirms what each of us knows by observation, that 'all have sinned and come short of the glory of God' (Romans 3:23).

"The invitation is still open to all who are willing to accept Jesus Christ as their Savior."

– *Grant R. Jeffrey*

The Seven Last Sayings of Jesus Christ
An Expository Sermon

Chapter Twenty-Two

Introduction

We come now to the last chapter of this wonderful book. The grand panorama of an ending and renewing world has reached the point where everything enters upon the Eternal State. We have seen the churches and pondered the Lord's message to each one and applied those truths to churches of this whole Dispensation. With judgment beginning at the house of God and with the translation of believers strongly symbolized by the rapture of John the Revelator in 4:1, we have rolled along through the future judgments.

Seals have been opened.

Trumpets have sounded.

Vials of wrath have been poured out.

The 144,000 sealed witnesses have fulfilled their role.

The two witnesses especially sent from God, have continued for 1,260 days and then been martyred, yet rose again.

We have seen the Antichrist rising up from the sea, yea, from the abyss, running his course of unparalleled blasphemy.

We have seen the final deeds of Satan, both in heaven and on earth, then his arrest, his imprisonment for a thousand years, his release and final consignment with all of his followers to the lake of fire.

We have seen the shaking of the old earth and the passing away of the world as we have known it.

We have beheld the crowned princes of the First Resurrection, wedded to the ruling Lamb of God, King of Kings, Lord of Lords.

We have observed the supreme execution of divine justice, dispensed from the Great White Throne upon all those whose names are not written in the Lamb's Book of Life.

We have seen the New Jerusalem coming down from God out of heaven, blessed eternal home of the saints of all ages.

It now remains for us to listen to the last words of our Savior and to resolve to obey Him now and always.

I have adapted some of the foregoing thoughts from the words of Joseph Seiss.

Familiar we are with the Seven Last Words from the Cross, but also of urgent importance are the Seven Last Sayings of Christ in the entire Bible, here in the last chapter of the last book, the Revelation.

Seven is the number of divine completion and perfection, so evident in this great account of the close of time and the beginnings of a new age and era, lasting forever.

Remember Christ's words from the Cross:

1. "Father, forgive them; for they know not what they do" (Luke 23:34).

2. "Behold thy Son; behold thy mother" (John 19:26, 27).

3. "Verily I say unto thee, Today thou shalt be with me in paradise" (Luke 23:43).

4. "My God, My God! Why hast thou forsaken me?" (Matthew 27:46).

5. "I thirst!" (John 19:28).

6. "It is finished!" (John 19:30).

7. "Father, into thy hands, I commend my spirit" (Luke 23:46).

All of those wondrous sayings carry a powerful, meaningful significance.

But let us ponder these final sayings from the ascended and glorified Savior, spoken in heaven, recorded by John and set forth before us now.

I. First Saying
"Behold I come quickly!" (22:7).

The coming of Christ is the great hope of the church. Seven times He speaks of His coming in Revelation.

1. In 2:5, he warns the Ephesians, "I will come quickly unto thee and remove the candlestick out of his place, except thou repent." In this instance the coming may be in chastisement, spiritually, rather than His *parousia* at the close of the age. Nevertheless, many will be caught in a backslidden state and forfeit rewards.

2. In 2:16, the Pergamos church is told, "Repent, or else I will come unto thee quickly and will fight against them with the sword of my mouth," again suggesting a spiritual coming in judgment.

3. In 3:11, the Head of the Church says, "Behold, I come quickly; hold that fast which thou hast, that no man take thy crown." Even in these three warnings the hint of Christ's imminent and possible personal return is obvious.

4. In 16:15, our Lord says, "Behold, I come as a thief. Blessed is he that watcheth, and keepeth his garments, lest he walk naked, and they see his shame," an admonition always applicable, but especially to the future tribulation saints and martyrs.

5. In this last chapter of Revelation Christ three times affirms His personal second coming, beginning in verse 7, "Behold, I come quickly; blessed is he that keepth the sayings of the prophecy of this book."

6. In 22:12, He further urges His believers of all ages, saying, "And behold I come quickly; and my reward is with me, to give every man according as his work shall be."

7. Finally in 22:10, He repeats this promise for the last time. "Surely I come quickly."

Yes, He is coming again. "If I go away," He told His disciples in the Upper Room, "I will come again and receive you unto myself, that where I am there ye may be also" (John 14:3).

"Quickly" means suddenly, surprisingly, without warning, an imminent, any moment, event, whether in the near or far future.

Paul declares that we should be "looking for that blessed hope and the glorious appearing of the great God and our Savior Jesus Christ" (Titus 3:13).

THEREFORE, LOOK FOR THE RAPTURE!

II. Second Saying

"Blessed is he that keepth the sayings of the prophecy of this book" (22:7).

All this is in addition to the seven times repeated admonition, "He that hath an ear, let him hear what the Spirit saith unto the churches."

We have noted that there are seven of the "Blesseds" or beatitudes in Revelation.

1. **"Blessed** is he that readeth, and they that hear the words of this prophecy, and keep those things which are written therein, for the time is at hand" (1:3).

2. **"Blessed** are the dead who die in the Lord from henceforth: yea, saith the Spirit, that they may rest from their labors and their works do follow them" (14:13).

3. **"Blessed** is he that watcheth, and keepeth his garments, lest he walk naked, and they see his shame" (16:15).

4. **"Blessed** are they that are called to the marriage supper of the Lamb" (19:9).

5. **"Blessed** and holy is he that hath part in the first resurrection; on these the second death hath no power; but they shall be priests of God and of Christ and shall reign with him a thousand years" (20:6).

6. **"Blessed** is he that keepeth the words of the prophecy of this book" (22:7).

7. **"Blessed** are they that do his commandments, that they may have the right to the tree of life, and may enter in by the gates into the city" (22:14).

This sixth beatitude we are now considering simply challenges us to keep, obey, respond and put into practice the commands, principles, truths and teachings of Revelation in our own lives and times.

THEREFORE, LET US OBEY HIS WORDS, FOLLOWING THE SCRIPTURES.

III. Third Saying

"And behold I come quickly and my reward is with me, to give every man according as his work shall be" (22:12).

"We shall all stand before the judgment (Bema) seat of Christ," teaches Paul in Romans 14:10, adding, "So then every one of us shall give account of himself to God" (14:12).

"For we must all appear before the judgment seat of Christ; that every one of us may receive the things done in the body, according to that he hath done, whether it be good or bad," the same apostle instructed the Corinthian believers.

Reward time is coming, before the Glorious Appearing and after the Rapture of living believers and the dead in Christ (1 Cor. 15:51, 22).

While salvation is totally by grace through faith and "not of works, lest any man should boast," rewards both during the millennial era and in the future Eternal City will be based on how we have lived, what we have done, how well we have discharged our duties as stewards of God's mysteries, blessings and opportunities for service. His dealings will be just, loving and fair.

It well behooves every true believer to "lay up treasures in heaven, where neither moth nor rust doth corrupt and where thieves do not break through or steal."

As the familiar couplet suggests:

"Only one life; twill soon be past ... Only what's done for Christ will last."

THEREFORE, LET US SERVE GOD, WORSHIP GOD, PLEASE GOD IN ALL PHASES OF OUR LIVES, FOR HE WILL REWARD HIS OWN.

IV. Fourth Saying

"I am Alpha and Omega, the beginning and the end, the first and the last" (22:13).

In the Greek manuscripts the letter Alpha appears and the letter Omega, equivalent in a sense to A and Z, the first and last letters of the alphabet.

The Eternal Word has thus spoken to John earlier in 1:11, as He introduces the seven messages to the seven churches, while the Father assumes the same designation in 1:8, "I am Alpha and Omega, the beginning and the ending, saith the Lord, which is and which was, and which is to come, the Almighty."

"In the beginning God created the heavens and the earth ..." (Gen. 1:1).

"In the beginning was the Word and the Word was with God and the Word was God" (John 1:1).

The All-powerful Lamb, in His deity, always has been, always will be ... the Originator of the Universe and the Consummator of All Things. He is All and in all, upholding all things by the Word of His power.

THEREFORE YOU CAN TRUST HIM WITH YOUR PRESENT AND YOUR FUTURE.

V. Fifth Saying

"I, Jesus, have sent mine angel to testify unto you these things in the churches" (22:16).

Christ's grand institution on earth consists of His local churches. Not only were those first century believers to heed these words, but all people of all the churches of this Dispensation do well to heed His sayings. This is the only occasion in the Bible, when Christ personally addresses letters to His churches (chapters 2 and 3).

"He that hath an ear, let him hear what the Spirit saith unto the churches ..."

VI. Sixth Saying

"I am the root and offspring of David, and the bright and morning star" (22:16).

In this "I AM" statement, reminiscent of the seven "I AM" pronouncements in the Gospel of John, Jesus reminds us all of **His humanity**; His heritage as the Son of David and the Messiah of Israel, yet destined to fulfill the prophecies of His sitting upon the throne of His Father (ancestor, humanly speaking) David (Luke 1:32, 33).

Seven hundred years before Christ's birth Isaiah prophesied, "And there shall come forth a rod out of Jesse [David's father], and a Branch shall grow out of his roots," a clear prediction of Jesus' birth, life and ultimate destiny.

Both Joseph and Mary were descendants of King David and in the royal line, Jesus being the rightful heir through Joseph of the royal rights of dominion over Israel, as Matthew 1 so lists.

Yet, looking forward, He is also the "Star out of Jacob" (Numbers 24:17), who will come for His people before the dawn of the thousand year millennium, taking His believers to heaven, then shining as the "Sun of Righteousness" in splendor at His return (Malachi 4:2).

VII. Seventh Saying

"Surely I come quickly" (22:20).

The last promise in the Bible is an assurance of His return. The world supposes this is an impossible dream, that He will never come.

Some theologians say, "Dismiss His coming as a mere figure of speech for death or for the destruction of Jerusalem, or even for salvation itself."

But scoffers have always said, "Where is the promise of His coming?" (2 Peter 3:4).

If plain language means anything at all, if God is not intending to deceive — an inconceivable concept — then surely **He Will Come.**

Yes, He shall come ... in the soft quiet hours before dawn for some ... He will come in the brightness of noonday for others. In an hour when people think not, the Son of Man will come.

Will He find you ready?

Watching?

Waiting?

Looking?

Loving?

Serving?

"What I say unto you," Jesus exhorted in another place, "I say unto all, Watch!"

A Commentary on the Revelation
Expository, Exegetical, Devotional and Practical
Greek words from the Textus Receptus

Chapter Twenty-two

The River Of Life And Tree Of Life (1–7)

1. And he showed me a pure river of water of life *(kai edeiken moi potamon hudatos zoes)* — flowing in the New Jerusalem is a fresh and clear crystaline stream, unpolluted and life sustaining, superior to both the literal and figurative streams of Ezekiel 47:1, Zechariah 14:8 or even John 7:37,38. This continuous flow is real, but also signifies that eternal refreshing and ongoing life in heaven, life in fullness of joy and in perpetual vitality and strength ... **clear as crystal** *(lampron hos krustallon)*, lamp–bright and brilliant like pure crystal, free from every flaw (See 4:6, the "sea of glass like unto crystal" before the throne) ... **proceeding out of the throne of God** *(thronou tou theou)* **and of the Lamb** — clear and fresh fountain, constant and gentle flow, the river proceeds from God and the Lamb, who also are the temple (21:22). Symmetrically designed, the Bible begins with the rivers of Eden in an earthly Paradise (Genesis 2:10–14) and closes with "one grand river of sparkling waters, clear waters, pure waters of eternal life–giving nature" (Albert Garner). **2. And in the midst of the street of it** *(that is, the New Jerusalem)* — **and on either side of the river** — evidently, the broad and glorious street, the main boulevard of the New Jerusalem, is divided by the sparkling river, separating with park–like beauty the golden avenues on either side ... **was there the tree of life** — not a single tree but a kind of wonderful tree, perhaps there by the millions, a special kind of tree, declared to be "in the midst of the paradise of God" (2:7) ... **which bare twelve manner of fruits** — different kinds of fruit in a heavenly time–cycle ... **and yielded her fruit every month** — no seasonal fruit, as we know on this earth, but a continuous bearing of different kinds of fruit. Some sort of time demarcations not totally different from our months here will continue in the Paradise of God ... **and the leaves of the tree were for the healing of the nations** — these nations are, in my judgment, the peoples of the Millennium, not the glorified saints, not the resurrected Israelites in heaven, but rather those

who are conveyed from the old earth to the New Earth, when Satan is defeated and consigned to the Lake of Fire; they are a class by themselves, who shall live on the New Earth, because they believed in Christ during the Millennium and did not follow Satan's final revolution. They bring their glory and honor into the city, but do not live therein as does the bride of Christ. In some manner yet to be understood, the leaves of the tree of life are a health–giving preventive, securing the peoples of those nations from any slackening of perfect health. It is possible that the peoples of these nations will fulfill God's eternal plan for a human race, unfallen, as Adam and Eve were before their sin, eating of the tree of life and living forever (See Genesis 3:22–24). **3. And there shall be no more curse** *(kai pan katathema ouk estai eti)* — no curse as in Genesis 3:14–19, since the results of the Fall of man are fully reversed. This begins partially in the Millennium (Zechariah 14:11) ... **but the throne of God and of the Lamb shall be in it** — surely this is the grand Capital of the Universe, governed in righteousness by the Father and the Lamb ... **and his servants shall serve him** — rendering worshipful service (7:15), praising, honoring, enjoying Him forever. **4. And they shall see his face** *(kai opsontai to prosopon autou)* — beholding in some manner, yet mysterious and unknown to us now, the shining countenance of the invisible God, both spiritually and intuitively (See Matthew 5:8; I John 3:2; Psalm 42:2). The essence of God is immortal and invisible, but He manifests Himself especially in His Son ... **and his name shall be in their foreheads** — a symbol of ownership and identity (7:3; 14:1), for the saints are forever His own and His inheritance. **5. And there shall be no night there** — both literal and spiritual darkness are forever vanquished ... **and they shall need no candle** — no artifical light or natural beams ... **neither light of the sun for the Lord God giveth them light** — both real and spiritual, for "God is light and in Him is no darkness at all" (1 John 1:5) ... **and they shall reign** *(kai basileusousin)* — reign as kings with the King of

Kings (Hebrews 12:28) ... **forever and ever** *(eis aionas ton aionon)*, unto the eternities of the eternities, the ages of the ages, everlastingly without cessation or duration! What a destiny! This is the ultimate flowering and eternal outcome of having, through faith in Jesus Christ, "everlasting life." **6. And he said unto me, These things are faithful and true** — this is that angel of 21:9, who earlier had dispensed one of the vials of wrath, now affirming the authentic factuality and trust–worthy certainty of all that John saw and heard (See 19:11, where Christ is Faithful and True, the living Word, 19:13) ... **and the Lord God of the holy prophets sent his angel to show unto his servants the things which must shortly be done** — the word sent is *apostello* indicating an authoritative commission. This special informing angel, possibly Gabriel, was dispatched to convey all of this information to John, as in 1:1–3. All of this relates to things which must shortly or quickly or suddenly transpire, when once the process begins in the end times. **7. Behold I come quickly** *(kai idou erchamai tacher)* — suddenly of His own accord and in His own plan. This is the first word of Jesus since 16:15, the only personally spoken word of the Lord between 3:22 and here ... **blessed is he that keepeth the sayings** *(makarios ho teron tous logous)* — observes, preserves, guards and lays to heart the truths in this concluding book and apocalypse ... **of the prophecy of this book** *(tes propheteias tou bibliou toutou)*, specifically the unsealed scroll, which Christ unfurled, but also the entire content of the Revelation; also in a larger sense the sayings of the entire Bible.

Last Messages Of The Bible (8–19)

8. And I John saw these things, and heard them — these are not matters of imagination, fiction, delusion or mere dreams, but rather heavenly and eternal realities ... **And when I had heard and seen, I fell down to worship before the feet of the angel which showed me these things** — overwhelmed by the magnificence and majesty of what he had experienced, John again (as in 19:10) falls down almost worshipping the angel, but again the strong admonition will ensue, "Worship God." **9. Then saith he unto me, See thou do it not, for I am thy fellowservant** — a colleague in service and worship before the living and true God, "a ministering spirit, sent forth to minister to them who are to be the heirs of salvation" (Hebrews 1:14) ... **and of thy brethren, the prophets** — meaning that the angel, like John, was a servant and that John was of his brethren, the Old Testament prophets and New Testament

prophets who spoke truth in their times ... **and of them which keep the sayings of this book** — and of those who keep and sacredly guard the words of the unsealed scroll and the truth in the whole Revelation. The angel is a colleague — helper or fellow of those who guard, keep, respect, follow and obey the teachings of this book ... **worship God** — Only God Himself is the worthy and supreme Object of worship, as in John 4:24. **10. Seal not the sayings of the prophecy of this book** — *(me spragises tous logous test propheteias tou bibliou toutou)* — unlike Daniel in 12:9, this great revelation is not to be concealed, held back or made secret, but is to be read, obeyed, taught ... **for the time is at hand** (1:3) — the era or period when these things come to the crisis point and will take place is imminently near. Although much remains unfulfilled, the teaching and truths have applications for every age, beginning in the second century. **11. He that is unjust** *(adikon)* — unrighteous, wicked, never right with God, not justified by faith in Christ ... **let him be unjust still** — no final second chance here, but only eternal damnation ... **and he that is filthy** *(hruparos)*, vile, impure, the filthy one ... **let him continue to be filthy** — in the lake of fire those who did wrong will keep on doing wrong, eternally lost, as well the filthy, the morally defiled, which can include unrepentant adulterers, fornicators and perverts. Part of their punishment is the everlasting continuation of these evil things, but with torment ... **and he that is righteous** *(dikaios)* — just, right with God, upright ... **let him be righteous still** — justified and right with God forever ... **and he that is holy** *(hagios)* — eternally set apart for God, sanctified, untainted ever again by sin ... **let him be holy still. 12. And, behold I come quickly** — ever before us in all ages and at all times is the possibility of the imminent, the immediate coming of Christ (2:5,16; 3:11; 11:14; 22:7,12,20) ... **and my reward is with me** — to repay and render to all due pay, to recompense those who have served Him ... **to give every man according as his work shall be** — God will reward all of His children, small and great, rich and poor, according to their labors, according to their opportunities to serve (See Matthew 10:42; Colossians 2:18; 2 John 8; Romans 2:6; 14:12; 2 Corinthians 5:10). **13. I am Alpha and Omega** *(Ego A kai Z)*, **the beginning** *(arche)* **and the end** *(telos)* — originator and completer ... **the first and the last** *(ho protos kai ho eschatos)* — suggesting His eternality, priority, superiority, sufficiency, control and divine design throughout all of time and into eternity. **14. Blessed are they that do** his commandments *(thentolas autou)* — obeying His great commandment to believe on the Son (1 John 3:23), and then love one another and obey Him, remembering that we are continually being cleansed, our spiritual garments made white by His blood, as some Greek manuscripts also suggest ... **that they may have the right** *(hina estai he eksousia auton)* — exercising their authority of access to the city of God, based on believing on the Son and receiving His cleansing, effectual forever ... **to the tree of life** — approaching and enjoying it ... **and may enter in through the gates into the city** — eternal home of the redeemed, both Old Testament and New Testament saints (Hebrews 11:10; 12:22). **15. For without** — on the outside, in the lake of fire ... **are dogs** *(kunes)* — unregenerate, false teachers, as in Philippians 3:2; Isaiah 56:10–12 ... **and sorcerers** *(pharmakoi)* — those deceived and deluded by drugs and narcotics, witchcraft and demons ... **and whoremongers** *(pornoi)* — lovers of pornography, immorality, fornication, wicked lust, perversions ... **and murderers** *(phoneis)* — premeditating killers with malice; aforethought, violent life–takers ... **and idolators** *(eidolatrai)* — worshippers of idols and false gods (See 1 Samuel 15:23; 1 Corinthians 10:7; Ephesians 5:5) ... **and whosever loveth and maketh a lie** *(pseudos)* — those who deal in falsehoods, deception, untruths, error and cheating as a way of life, rejecting Jesus the Truth, who can forgive, cleanse and save. **16. I Jesus have sent mine angel to testify unto you of these things in the churches** *(ekklesiais)* — initially the seven churches of Asia (1:11), but then for all churches at all times. Notice the word "church" does not appear from 3:22 to this point, indicating that the church is not on earth during the time of tribulation ... **I am the root** *(hriza)* **and offspring** *(genos)* **of David** — looking back to His earthly humanity in the royal Davidic line, important to all Jews (See Isaiah 11:1,10; Matthew 22:42–45) ... **and the bright and morning star** — looking forward to His return and reign on earth (See Numbers 24:17–19; Matthew 2:2; Revelation 2:28). He will bring light and hope. **17. And the Spirit and the bride say come** *(kai ho pneuma kai he numphe legousin, erchou)* — both the Holy Spirit through the Word, conviction and power ... and the bride, the church, join in issuing the grand invitation to come to Christ for salvation now and throughout this age ... **and let him that heareth say come** — everyone who is listening, heeding and responding should echo the invitation after receiving Christ and seek to bring others to Jesus ... **and let him that is athirst come** — every

thirsty, dry, empty soul, desirous of real inner peace and joy and satisfaction, is invited to come to the only Satisfier, even Jesus who gives life, a figure here for the sustaining, life–giving power of God's truth and gospel, taken into the soul ... **and whosoever will** — the one who will from his soul and makes a volitional choice to come to Christ (See John 7:37–39) ... **let him take of the water of life freely** — receiving Jesus into the heart through the convicting and regenerating power of the Holy Spirit, who then indwells the believer and desires to use us to spread His spiritual truth, giving the water of life to others. **18. For I testify unto every man that heareth the words of the prophecy of this book** — comes now a solemn warning about tampering with either this Book of Revelation, or in a larger sense, the entire Word of God ... **if any man shall add unto these things God shall add unto him the plagues that are written in this book** — no other books must be added to the completed canon of Scripture, no other "bibles" or "inspired books." **19. And if any man shall take away from the words of this prophecy, God shall take away his part out of the book of life and out of the holy city and from the things which are written in this book** — to reject the Word of God, to subtract or add to it, brings judgment, since no such person can be truly right with God, thus forfeiting the opportunity for salvation and all that accompanies it. **20. He that testifieth these things saith, Surely, I come quickly** *(nai erchomai tachu)* — coming suddenly, abruptly, suprisingly, thus indicating we are to be in a constant state of readiness, serving the Lord. Here is Christ's last promise ... **Amen** — evidently the heart–felt response of the Apostle John, who now prepares to lay down His pen. From John until the last believer saved before the Rapture there has been the possibility of His imminent and sudden coming, but in this generation, His coming seems close indeed ... **Even so, come Lord Jesus** — the last prayer in the Bible. **21. The grace of our Lord Jesus Christ be with you all. Amen.**

Selected Bibliography

Barclay, William. *Letters to the Seven Churches.* New York: Abingdon Press, 1958.

Beale, David O. *The Eschatology of the Ante–Nicene Fathers.* Greenville, S.C.: Unpublished Dissertation, 1980.

Criswell, Wallie Amos. *Expository Sermons on Revelation.* Grand Rapids: Zondervan Publishing House, 1967.

Cooper, David L. *Messiah, His Glorious Appearance Imminent.* Los Angeles: Biblical Research Society, 1961.

DeHaan, Martin Ralph. *Revelation.* Grand Rapids: Zondervan Publishing House, 1967.

Fruchtenbaum, Arnold G. *The Footsteps of the Messiah.* Tustin, CA: Ariel Press, 1982.

Gaebelein, Arno C. *The Revelation: An Analysis and Exposition of the Last Book of the Bible.* New York: Louizeaux Brothers, 1961 reprint.

Gosey, C.C. *Riches in Revelation Simplified.* Norforlk, VA: Clear Vision, 1973.

Hendrickson, William. *More Than Conquerors.* Grand Rapids: Baker Book House, 1939.

Ironside, H.A. *Lectures on the Book of Revelation.* New York: Louizeaux Brothers, 1955.

Jeffrey, Grant R. *Apocalypse: The Coming Judgment of Nations.* Toronto, Ontario: Frontier Publications, 1992.

Kelly, William. *Lectures on the Book of Revelaiton.* London: G. Morrish, n.d.

LaHaye, Tim. *Revelation, Illustrated and Made Plain.* Grand Rapids: Zondervan Publishing House, 1973.

Larkin, Clarence. *The Book of Revelation.* Philadelphia: Clarence Larkin Estate, 1930.

Lawrence, Bill. *The Grand Revelation.* Buena Park, CA: World Mission Outreach Press, 1980.

Newell, William R. *The Book of Revelation.* Chicago: Moody Press, 1935.

Pettingill, William L. *The Unveiling of Jesus Christ.* Findley, OH: Fundamental Truth Publishers, 1939.

Phillips, John. *Exploring Revelation.* Chicago: Moody Press, 1974.

Ramsey, William M. *Letters to the Seven Churches of Asia.* Grand Rapids: Baker Book House, 1963 reprint.

Ryrie, Charles C. *Revelation.* Chicago: Moody Press, 1968.

Scott, Walter. *Exposition of the Book of Revelation.* London: Pickering and Inglis, n.d.

Scroggie, W.G. *The Great Unveiling.* Edinburgh, England: The Author, 1920.

Seiss, Joseph A. *The Apoclypse.* New York: Charles C. Cook, 1907.

Strauss, Lehman. *The Book of Revelation.* Neptune, NJ: Louizeaux Brothers, 1965.

Swete, H.B. *The Apocalypse of St. John.* Grand Rapids: William B. Eerdmans Publishing Co., 1965.

Talbot, Louis T. *The Revelation of Jesus Christ.* Grand Rapids: William B. Eerdmans Publishing Co., 1957.

Tenney, Merril C. *Interpreting Revelation.* Grand Rapids: William B. Eerdmans Publishing Co., 1958.

Trench, R.C. *Commentary on the Epistles to the Seven Churches in Asia.* London: Kegan, Paul, Trench, Truber and Co., 1897.

Walvoord, John F. *The Revelation of Jesus Christ.* Chicago: Moody Press, 1966.

Wilcock, Michael. *I Saw Heaven Opened.* Downers Grove, IL: InterVarsity Press, 1975.

Allusions to the Old Testament in the Book of Revelation

While there are no specific, cited references to the Old Testament in the Apocalypse, some Greek scholars have noted that as many as 278 verses out of 404 contain allusions from 27 out of 39 Old Testament books.

An allusion is a reference to something without indicating its source. It may be a quotation or a short phrase with identical or comparative wording. It may take the form of an apparent paraphrase; it may be drawn from the Greek translation of the Old Testament (The Septuagint LXX; Theodotian's version or other ancient Greek translations from Hebrew). It is fully recognizable in the original Greek, but also detectable in English or other translations.

In the Greek text there are 913 separate distinct words, or 871 omitting persons and places; 108 are not used elsewhere in the New Testament and 98 words are only used once elsewhere.

Incorporating well over 260 Old Testament passages or phrases, the Apocalypse is a literary and poetic masterpiece with a logical sequential flow of ideas, reaching to a grand conclusion. Consequently, the writing style and vocabulary differ from John's other writings.

No other New Testament writer makes larger use of Old Testament expressions. Thus both Testaments converge and climax in the Apocalypse, completing the Sacred Scriptures.

The following table, listing 269 out of 404 verses with parallel Old Testament allusions, while not exhaustive, well demonstrates an encyclopedic knowledge of the Old Testament Greek translations from the Hebrew. The keen spiritual and mental skill to utilize Old Testament words and phrases, thus creating this incomparable Apocalypse, doubtless came from Jesus Christ, who gave it and the all-knowing Holy Spirit who inspired it.

Chapter 1

1:1	Dan 2:28, 29
1:4	Isa 11:2; Ex 3:14
1:5	Gen 49:11; Ps 40:2; 89:27
1:6	Ex 19:6; Isa 61:6
1:7	Dan 7:13; Zech 12:10-14
1:8	Isa 41:4; Amos 4:13
1:12	Ex 25:37; 37:23
1:13	Dan 7:13; 10:5, 16; Ezek 1:26; 8:2
1:14	Dan 7:9; 10:6
1:15	Ezek 1:7, 24; 43:2;Dan 10:6
1:16	Judges 5:31; Isa 49:2
1:17	Isa 41:4; 44:6; 48:12;
	Dan 8:17-18 ;10:9, 10, 12, 15, 19
1:18	Job 3:17; Hos 13:14
1:19	Isa 48:6
1:20	Dan 2:29

Chapter 2

2:4	Jer 2:2
2:7	Gen 2:9; 3:22-24; Prov 11:30; 13:12; Ezek 31:8 (LXX)
2:10	Dan 11:14
2:12	Isa 49:2
2:14	Num 25:1-3
2:17	Ex 16:33-34; Ps 77:24; Isa 62:2; 65:15
2:18	Dan 10:6
2:20	1 Kings 16:31-32; 2 Kings 9:7, 22
2:23	Ps 7:9; 26:2; 28:4; 61:13; Jer 11:20; 17:10; 20:12
2:27	Ps 2:7-9; Isa 30:14; Jer 19:11

Chapter 3

3:1	Isa 4:1
3:4	Eccles 9:8
3:5	Ex 32:32-33; Isa 4:3; Mal 3:16; Dan 12:1
3:7	Isa 22:22
3:9	Isa 43:4; 45:14; 48:4; 49:23; 60:14
3:12	Isa 62:2; Ezek 48:35
3:14	Gen 49:3; Deut 21:17; Prov 8:22
3:17	Hos 12:8
3:18	Isa 55:1
3:19	Prov 3:12
3:20	Song of Sol 5:2

Chapter 4

4:1	Ex 19:16; Isa 26:20; Ezek 1:1
4:2	I Kings 22:19; Isa 6:1; Ezek 1:26-28; Dan 7:9
4:3	Ezek 1:26, 28; 10:1
4:4	1 Chron 24:5
4:5	Ex 19:16; 25:37; Isa 11:2; Ezek 1:13
4:6	Ezek 1:5, 18, 22, 26; 10:1, 12
4:7	Ezek 1:10; 10:14
4:8	Isa 6:2-3; Ezek 1:18; 10:12, 14
4:9	Deut 32:40; Dan 4:34; 6:26; 12:7
4:10	Dan 4:31
4:11	Gen 1:1

Chapter 5

5:1	Isa 29:11; Ezek 2:9-10; Dan 12:4, 9; Zech 5:1-4
5:2	Lev 25:23-25
5:5	Gen 49:9-10; Isa 11:1, 10; Hos 5:14
5:6	Isa 11:2; Zech 3:8-9; 4:10
5:8	Ps 111:2
5:9	Ps 40:3; 98:1;144:9; 149:1;Isa 42:10; Dan 5:19
5:10	Ex 19:6; Isa 61:6
5:11	Dan 7:10

Chapter 6

6:2	Zech 1:8; 6:3
6:4	Jer 25:29; Zech 1:8; 6:2
6:5	Jer 14:1, 2; Zech 6:2
6:6	Lev 26:25-33; Ezek 4:10, 11
6:8	Jer 14:12; 15:2-3; 24:10; 29:17; Ezek 14:21; Hos 13:14; Zech 6:3
6:10	Deut 32:43; Hos 4:1; Zech 1:12
6:12	Isa 50:3; Joel 2:10
6:13	Isa 34:4
6:14	Isa 34;4; Nah 1:5
6:15	Josh 10:16; Ps 2:21; 48:4-6; Isa 2:10-12,19; 24:21; 34:12
6:16	Hos 10:8
6:17	Ps 76:7; Jer 30:7; Joel 2:11; Nah 1:6; Zeph 1:14-18; Mal 3:2

Chapter 7

7:1	Isa 11:2; Jer 49:36; Ezek 7:2; 37:9; Dan 7:2; Zech 6:5
7:3	Ezek 9:4-6
7:4	Gen 49:1-28
7:9	Lev 23:40
7:10	Ps 3:8
7:14	Gen 49:11; Dan 12:1
7:15	Lev 26:11
7:16	Ps 121:5-6; Isa 49:10
7:17	Ps 23:1-2; Isa 25:8; Ezek 34:23

Chapter 8

8:1	Josh 6:10
8:2	Josh 6:4
8:3	Ps 141:2
8:4	Lev 16:12; Ps 141:2
8:5	Ezek 8:5, 6; 10:2; Ex 19:16
8:6	Ex 19:16
8:7	Ex 9:23-24; Josh 10:11; Ps 18:13; Isa 28:2; Ezek 38:22; Joel 2:30
8:8	Ex 7:17-19; 8:10; Isa 14:12
8:10	Isa 14:12
8:11	Jer 9:15; 23:15
8:12	Josh 10:12; Isa 13:10

Chapter 9

9:1	Isa 14:12-14
9:2	Gen 19:28; Ex 19:8
9:3	Ex 10:12-15
9:4	Ezek 9:4
9:6	Job 3:21
9:8	Joel 1:6
9:9	Joel 2:5
9:11	Job 26:6; 28:22; 31:12; Ps 88:11; Prov 15:11; 30:27; Amos 7:11 (LXX)
9:14	Gen 15:18; Deut 1:7; 32:17; Josh 1:4
9:20	Ps 113:13; Isa 17:8; Dan 5:23

Chapter 10

10:1	Ezek 1:26-28
10:2	Deut 11:24
10:3	Hos 11:10; Joel 3:16
10:4	Dan 8:26; 12:4-9
10:5	Gen 14:22; Deut 32:40; Dan 12:7
10:6	Gen 1:1; Deut 32:40; Neh 9:6; Dan 12:17
10:7	Amos 3:7
10:9	Jer 15:16; Ezek 2:8-33
10:10	Ezek 3:1-3
10:11	Jer 1:10; Ezek 37:4, 9

Chapter 11

11:1	Ezek 40:3-4; Zech 2:1-2
11:2	Ezek 40:17-20; Zech 12:3
11:4	Zech 4:1-2, 11-14
11:5	Num 16:35; 2 Sam 22:9; 1 Kings 18:37; 2 Kings 1:10-12
11:6	Ex 7:19-25; 8:12; 1 Kings 17:1
11:7	Dan 7:3, 7, 8, 21
11:8	Isa 1:9-10; 3:9; Jer 23:14; Ezek 16:49; 23:3, 8, 19, 27
11:9	Ps 79:2-3
11:10	Ps 105:38
11:11	Ezek 37:9-10
11:12	2 Kings 2:11
11:13	Dan 2:44
11:15	Ex 15:18; Ps 2:2; Dan 2:44-45; 7:13-14, 27
11:17	Ps 98:1
11:18	Ps 2:1-3; 46:6; 113:21; 115:13
11:19	Jer 3:16

Chapter 12

12:1	Gen 37:9-11
12:2	Isa 26:17; 66:7; Micah 4:9-10
12:3	Isa 27:1; Dan 7:7, 20, 24
12:4	Dan 8:10
12:5	Ps 2:8-9; Isa 66:7
12:7	Dan 10:13, 21; 12:1
12:9	Gen 3:1, 13; Job 1:6; 2:1; Zech 3:1
12:10	Job 1:9-11; 2:4-5; Zech 3:1
12:12	Isa 44:23
12:14	Ex 19:4; Deut 32:11; Isa 40:31; Dan 7:25; 12:7; Hos 2:14-15
12:15	Hos 5:10
12:17	Gen 3:15

Chapter 13

13:1	Dan 7:3, 7, 8
13:2	Dan 7:4-6, 8
13:3	Dan 7:8
13:4	Dan 8:24
13:5	Dan 7:8, 11, 20, 25; 11:36
13:7	Dan 7:21
13:8	Dan 12:1
13:10	Jer 15:2; 43:11
13:11	Dan 8:3
13:13	1 Kings 1:9-12
13:15	Dan 3:6

Chapter 14

14:1	Ps 2:6; Ezek 9:4
14:2	Ezek 1:24; 43:2
14:3	Ps 144:9
14:5	Isa 53:9; Zeph 3:13
14:7	Ex 20:11
14:8	Isa 21:9; Jer 51:7-8
14:10	Gen 19:24; Ps 75:8;Isa 51:17
14:11	Isa 34:10; 66:24
14:14	Dan 7:13
14:18	Joel 3:13
14:19	Isa 63:1-6
14:20	Joel 3:13

Chapter 15

15:1	Lev 26:21
15:3	Ex 15:1-18; Deut 31:30; 32:44; Josh 14:7; Ps 92:5; 111:2; 139:14
15:4	Ps 86:9; Isa 66:23; Jer 10:7
15:5	Ex 38:21
15:6	Lev 26:21
15:7	Jer 25:15
15:8	Ex 40:34-35; Lev 26:21;1 Kings 8:10-11; 2 Chron. 5:13-14; Isa 6:1-4

Chapter 16

16:1	Ps 79:6; Jer 10:25; Ezek 22:31
16:2	Ex 9:9-11; Deut 28:35
16:3	Ex 7:17-25
16:4	Ex 7:17-21; Ps 78:44
16:5	Ps 145:17
16:6	Isa 49:26
16:7	Ps 19:9; 119:37; 145:17
16:10	Ex 10:21-23
16:12	Isa 11:15-16; 41:2, 25; 44:27; 46:11; Jer 51:36
16:13	Ex 8:6
16:14	1 Kings 22:21-23
16:16	Judges 5:19; 2 Kings 23:29-30; 2 Chron 35:22; Zech 12:11
16:18	Dan 12:1
16:19	Jer 25:15; 6:21; Ex 9:18-25

Chapter 17

17:1	Jer 51:13; Nah 3:4
17:2	Isa 23:17
17:3	Dan 7:7
17:4	Jer 51:7; Ezek 28:13
17:8	Ex 32:32-33; Dan 12:1
17:12	Dan 7:24-25
17:14	Deut 10:17; Dan 2:47
17:16	Lev 21:9

Chapter 18

18:1	Ezek 43:2
18:2	Isa 13:20-22; 21:9; 34:13-15; Jer 21:9; 50:30; 51:8, 37
18:3	Jer 51:7
18:4	Isa 52:11; Jer 50:8; 51:6, 45
18:5	Jer 41:9
18:6	Ps 137:8; Jer 50:15, 29
18:7	Isa 47:7-8; Zeph 2:15
18:8	Isa 47:9; Jer 50:31-32
18:9-19	Ezek 26:16-18; 27:26-31
18:9	Jer 50:46
18:10	Isa 13:1
18:12	Ezek 27:12-25
18:20	Jer 51:48
18:21	Jer 51:63-64
18:22	Isa 24:8; Jer 25:10; Ezek 26:13
18:23	Isa 28:8; Jer 7:34; 16:9; 25:10; Nah 3:4

Chapter 19

19:1	Ps 105:1-5; 150:1, 6
19:2	Deut 32:43; Ps 119:137; Jer 51:48
19:3	Isa 34:9-10; Jer 51:48
19:5	Ps 22:23; 134:1; 135:1
19:6	Ps 93:1; 97:1; Ezek 1:24; 43:2; Dan 10:6
19:11	Ps 18:10; 45:3-4; Isa 11:4-5; Ezek 1:1
19:13	Isa 63:3
19:15	Ps 2:8-9; Isa 11:4; 63:3-6
19:16	Deut 10:17
19:17	Isa 34:6-7; Ezek 39:17
19:18	Isa 34:6-7; Ezek 39:18
19:19	Ps 2:2; Joel 3:9-11
19:20	Isa 30:33; Dan 7:11
19:21	Ezek 39:19-20

Chapter 20

20:2	Gen 3:1, 13-14; Isa 24:21-22
20:4	Dan 7:9, 22, 27; 12:2
20:5	Isa 26:14
20:6	Ex 19:6; Isa 26:19
20:8	Ezek 38:2; 39:1, 6
20:9	Deut 23:14; 2 Kings 1:9-12; Ezek 38:22; 39:6; Hab 1:6
20:11	Dan 2:35
20:12	Ex 32:32-33; Ps 62:12; 69:28; Dan 7:10
20:15	Ex 32:32-33; Dan 12:1

Chapter 21

21:1	Isa 65:17; 66:22
21:2	Isa 52:1
21:3	Lev 26:11-12; Ezek 37:27
21:4	Isa 25:8; 35:10; 51:11; 65:19
21:5	Isa 43:19
21:6	Isa 45:1
21:7	2 Sam 7:14
21:9	Lev 26:21
21:10	Ezek 40:2
21:11	Isa 60:1-2; Ezek 43:2
21:12-13	Ezek 48:31-34
21:15	Ezek 40:3, 5
21:18	Isa 54:12
21:19-20	Ex 28:17, 20; Isa 54:11-12
21:23	Isa 60:19-20
21:24	Isa 60:3-5, 16
21:25	Isa 60:11; Zech 14:7
21:26	Isa 60:5, 16
21:27	Isa 52:1; Ezek 44:9; Zech 14:21

Chapter 22

22:1	Ps 46:4; Ezek 47:1; Zech 14:8
22:2	Gen 2:9; 3:22-24; Ezek 47:12
22:3	Gen 3:17-19; Zech 14:11
22:4	Ps 17:15; Ezek 9:4
22:5	Isa 60:19; Dan 7:18, 22, 27; Zech 14:7
22:10	Dan 8:26; 12:4, 9
22:11	Ezek 3:27; Dan 12:10
22:12	Ps 62:12; Isa 40:10; 62:11
22:13	Isa 44:6
22:14	Gen 2:9; 3:22-24; Prov 11:30
22:15	Deut 23:18
22:18-19	Deut 4:2; 12:32
22:19	Deut 29:19-20